Rough Crossings

ALSO BY SIMON SCHAMA

Patriots and Liberators:
Revolution in the Netherlands 1780–1813

Two Rothschilds and the Land of Israel

The Embarrassment of Riches:
An Interpretation of Dutch Culture in the Golden Age

Citizens: A Chronicle of the French Revolution

Dead Certainties: Unwarranted Speculations

Landscape and Memory

Rembrandt's Eyes

A History of Britain, Volume I:
At the Edge of the World, 3500 B.C.–1603 A.D.

A History of Britain, Volume II:
The Wars of the British, 1603–1776

A History of Britain, Volume III:
The Fate of the Empire, 1776–2000

Hang Ups: Essays on Painting [mostly]

SIMON SCHAMA

ROUGH
CROSSINGS

Britain, the Slaves and the
American Revolution

HarperCollins books may be purchased
for educational, business, or sales promotional use.
For information, please write: Special Markets Department,
HarperCollins Publishers, 10 East 53rd Street,
New York, NY 10022.

First published in Great Britain
in a different format in 2005 by BBC Books,
BBC Worldwide Ltd.

An extension of this copyright page appears on page 477.

FIRST U.S. EDITION PUBLISHED 2006

Designed by Kate Nichols

Printed on acid-free paper

Library of Congress Cataloging-in-Publication Data
Schama, Simon.
Rough crossings : Britain, the slaves and the American Revolution / Simon Schama.—
1st ed.
p.   cm.
Includes bibliographical references and index.
ISBN-10: 0-06-053916-X
ISBN-13: 978-0-06-053916-0
1. United States—History—Revolution, 1775–1783—African Americans. 2. United
States—History—Revolution, 1775–1783—Social aspects. 3. Slavery—United States—
History—18th century. 4. Blacks—England—History—18th century. I. Title.
E269.N3S33 2006
326.0973'09033—dc22   2005049504

06   07   08   09   10   BVG /RRD   10   9   8   7   6   5   4   3   2   1

*Pages iv–v: Details of sketches of the black fleet sailing from
Nova Scotia to Freetown, Sierra Leone, by Lieutenant John Clarkson,
in his manuscript journal* Mission to America, *1791–2.*

for LISA JARDINE,

my idea of an historian

Contents

Dramatis Personae | xi

British Freedom's Promise | 1

PART ONE: Greeny | 19

PART TWO: John | 257

Endings, Beginnings | 399

Notes and References | 423

Further Reading | 449

Acknowledgements | 453

Index | 457

Dramatis Personae

Henry Washington, escaped slave of George Washinton, freed by British, later settler in Nova Scotia and Sierra Leone

Granville Sharp, leading British abolitionist and instigator of first black settlement in Sierra Leone

William Sharp, brother of Granville, surgeon to King George III and to London poor

William Murray, Lord Chief Justice Mansfield, responsible for seminal rulings on legal status of slaves in Great Britain

Jonathan Strong, Thomas Lewis, James Somerset: escaped slaves in London, victims of abduction and subjects of court cases brought by Granville Sharp

Henry Laurens, South Carolina Patriot, merchant, delegate to and president of the Continental Congress

John Laurens (son of Henry), aide-de-camp to George Washington, abolitionist officer in Continental army

Anthony Benezet, Quaker American in Philadelphia, correspondent with Granville Sharp

Thomas Jeremiah, free African-American in Charleston, hanged for alleged conspiracy to raise slave insurrection

John Murray, Lord Dunmore, last British governor of Virginia, responsible for 1775 proclamation offering freedom to slaves of Patriots in return for military service with the Royal Army

Lord William Campbell, last British governor of South Carolina

Thomas Peters, sergeant in the British Black Pioneers, settler in Nova Scotia and Sierra Leone

Moses Wilkinson, blind Methodist preacher in Birchtown, Nova Scotia

Mary Perth, escaped slave from Virginia, freed by British, settler in Sierra Leone

John Kizell, son of Sherbro chief, escaped slave, loyalist soldier in American volunteers, North Carolina, settler in Sierra Leone

James Moncrief, British officer in siege of Savannah commanding black loyalist soliders and sappers

General Sir Henry Clinton, British commander-in-chief in America, patron and protector of British Black Pioneers

David George, African-American Baptist minister, escaped slave, free settler with his wife Phyllis, in Novia Scotia and Sierra Leone

General Lord Charles Cornwallis, British military commander in America

Boston King, and his wife Violet, escaped slaves, loyalist settlers in Nova Scotia and Sierra Leone

Colonel Tye, former slave in Monmouth County New Jersy, loyalist partisan leader

Stephen Blucke, free African-American, settler in Nova Scotia

Murphy Steele, sergeant in the Black Pioneers, friend of Thomas Peters

Olaudah Equiano aka Gustavus Vassa, London abolitionist, author of *The Interesting Narrative of Olaudah Equiano the African* (1789)

Sir Charles Middleton, MP, abolitionist and Comptroller of the Royal Navy

James Ramsay, British naval surgeon turned clergyman and abolitionist

Thomas Clarkson, leading British abolitionist

Sir Guy Carleton, last commander-in-chief of British force in America, later Governor of Canada

Brigadier Samuel Birch, commandant of British garrison in New York, signatory of passport, certificate confirming freedom of black loyalists

Benjamin Whitecuffe, Long Island black farmer, loyalist spy for the British

William Wilberforce, member of Parliament for Hull and parliamentary leader of campaign to abolish the slave trade

Jonas Hanway, British reformer and philanthropist

Henry Smeathman, British scientist and eccentric, original proposer of Sierra Leone as site for black settlement

Thomas Boulden Thompson, commander of fleet carrying first settlers to Sierra Leone

Alexander Falconbridge, former slave-ship surgeon, agent in Africa for St George's Bay (later the Sierra Leone) Company

Anna Maria Falconbridge, Alexander's wife, author of *A Narrative of Two Voyages to the River Sierra Leone in the years 1791–3*

King Tom, Temne chief in Sierra Leone

The Naimbana, paramount chief in Robana, Sierra Leone

King Jimmy, Temne chief in Sierra Leone, destroyer of Granville Town

Sir John Parr, governor of Nova Scotia

Lieutenant John Clarkson, British naval officer, subsequently abolitionist and governor of second black settlement in Sierra Leone

Michael Wallace, entrepenuer, landowner and council member in Halifax, Nova Scotia

Benjamin Marston, Harvard-educated ex-merchant, surveyor in Shelburne, Nova Scotia

Henry Thornton, evangelical banker and abolitionist, first chairman of the Sierra Leone Company

Lawrence Hartshorne, Quaker merchant, Clarkson's friend in Nova Scotia

Dr. Charles Taylor, surgeon appointed by the Sierra Leone Company to accompany the black fleet to Africa

Cato Perkins, black Methodist preacher, settler in Nova Scotia and Sierra Leone

Stephen Skinner, New Jersey loyalist and Shelburne settler

Captain Jonathan Coffin, master of the *Lucretia*, John Clarkson's flagship

Isaac Dubois, American loyalist, Carolinan cotton planter, settler in Sierra Leone, friend of Clarkson

Isaac Anderson, free black carpenter from Charleston, settler in Sierra Leone, militant campaigner for black rights

Nathaniel Wansey, leader, with Isaac Anderson, of revolt against government of Sierra Leone

William Dawes, acting governor of Sierra Leone after John Clarkson

Zachary Macaulay, governor of Sierra Leone, father of the historian Thomas Babington Macaulay

Thomas Ludlam, fourth governor of Sierra Leone

Paul Cuffe, free black, landowner, trader with Sierra Leone, Quaker and abolitionist

Frederick Douglass, escaped slave-turned-abolitionist orator

The Hutchinson Family singers: Jesse, Abby, Judson and Asa, white religious and folk singers, abolitionist fellow passengers with Douglass on SS *Cambria*

Captain Charles Judkins, ex-slaver turned abolitionist, master of Cunarder SS *Cambria*

British Freedom's Promise

[CHAINED SLAVE, HULTON ARCHIVE/GETTY IMAGES]

TEN YEARS after the surrender of George III's army to General Washington at Yorktown, British Freedom was hanging on in North America. Along with a few hundred other souls—Scipio Yearman, Phoebe Barrett, Jeremiah Piggie and Smart Feller among them—he was scratching a living from the stingy soil around Preston, a few miles northeast of Halifax, Nova Scotia.[1]

Like most of the Preston people, British Freedom was black and had come from a warmer place. Now he was a hardscrabbler stuck in a wind-whipped corner of the world between the blue spruce forest and the sea. But he was luckier than most. British Freedom had title to forty acres, and another one and a half of what the lawyers' clerks in Halifax were pleased to call a "town lot."[2] It didn't look like much of a town, though, just a dirt clearing with rough cabins at the centre and a few chickens strutting around and maybe a mud-caked hog or two. Some of the people who had managed to get a team of oxen to clear the land of bald grey rocks grew patches of beans and corn and cabbages, which they carted to market in Halifax along with building lumber. But even those who prospered—by Preston standards—took themselves off every so often into the wilderness to shoot some birch partridge, or tried their luck on the saltwater ponds south of the village.[3]

What were they doing there? Not just surviving. British Freedom and the rest of the villagers were clinging to more than a scrap of Nova Scotia; they were clinging to a promise. Some of them even had that promise *printed* and signed by officers of the British army on behalf of the king himself, that the bearer so-and-so was at liberty to go wherever he or she pleased and take up whatever occupation he or she chose. That meant something for people who had been slaves. And the king's word was surely a bond. In return for their loyal service in the late American war, the Black Pioneers and the rest of them were to be granted two gifts of unimaginably precious worth: their freedom and their acres. It was, they told themselves, no more than their due. They had done perilous, dirty, exhausting work. They had been spies amidst the Americans; guides through the Georgia swamps; pilots taking ships over treacherous sandbars; sappers on the ramparts of Charleston as French cannonballs took off the limbs of the men beside them. They had dug trenches; buried bodies blistered with the pox; powdered the officers' wigs; and, marching smartly, drummed the regiments in and out of disaster. The women had cooked and laundered and nursed the sick; dabbed at the holes on soldiers' bodies; and tried to keep their children from harm. Some of them had fought. There had been black dragoons in South Carolina; waterborne gangs of black partisans for the king on the Hudson River; bands of black guerrillas who would descend on Patriot farms in New Jersey and take whatever they could, even (if the Lord was smiling on their venture) white American prisoners.

So they were owed. They had been given their liberty, and some of them even got land. But the soil was thin and strewn with boulders, and the blacks had no way, most of them, to clear and work it unless they hired themselves or their families out to the white loyalists. That meant more cooking and laundering; more waiting on table and shaving pink chins; more hammering rocks for roads and bridges. And still they were in debt, so grievously that some complained their liberty was no true liberty at all but just another kind of slavery in all but name.

But names counted. British Freedom's name said something important: that he was no longer negotiable property. For all its bleak hardships, Preston was not a Georgia plantation. Other Prestonians—Decimus Murphy, Caesar Smith—had evidently kept their slave names as they had made the passage to liberty. But British Freedom must have been born, or bought, as someone else. He may have shaken off that name, like his leg irons, on one of the eighty-one sailings out of New York in 1783, which had taken thirty thousand loyalists, black and white, to

Nova Scotia, for no one called British Freedom is listed in the "Book of Negroes," which recorded those who, as free men and women, were at liberty to go where they wished. There were certainly others who changed their names to reflect their new status: James Lagree, for instance, the former property of Thomas Lagree of Charleston, became, in Nova Scotia, Liberty Lagree. It is also possible that British Freedom could have found his way to Nova Scotia in one of the earlier loyalist evacuations—from Boston in 1776 or from Charleston in 1782. In the frightening months between the end of the war and the departure of the British fleets, as American planters were attempting to locate the whereabouts of escaped slaves, many of them changed their names to avoid identification. British Freedom may just have gone one step further in giving himself an alias that was also a patriotic boast. Whichever route he had taken, and whatever the trials he was presently enduring, British Freedom's choice of name proclaims something startling: a belief that it was the British monarchy rather than the new American republic that was more likely to deliver Africans from slavery. Although Thomas Jefferson, in the Declaration of Independence, had blamed "the *Christian* King" George III for the institution of slavery in America, blacks like British Freedom did not see the king that way at all. On the contrary, he was their enemy's enemy and thus their friend, emancipator and guardian.

Looking to the King of England as a benefactor had a long tradition. When plans for a slave uprising in Raritan County, New Jersey, were discovered in 1730, one of the black informers told a Dr Reynolds that the cause was "the pack of villains" who had defied "a positive order from King George, sent to the G-[overnor] of New York to set them free."[4] A generation later, blacks conspicuously excluded from the blessings of American liberty derided "what they *call* Free in this Cuntry [*sic*]" in the words of Towers Bell, a "true Brittam" as he signed himself. Bell wrote to the British military authorities at the end of the war that he had been taken from Britain against his will to Baltimore, and "sold for Four Years as a Slave which I suffered with the Greatest Barbarity in this Rebellious Cuntry." Now, with the hostilities over, he wanted nothing better than to return "home to Old England."[5]

Tens of thousands of African-Americans clung to the sentimental notion of a British freedom even when they knew that the English were far from being saints in respect to slavery. Until 1800, when its courts decisively ruled the institution illegal, there were slaves, as well as free blacks, in Nova Scotia, and there were hundreds of thousands more in the British Caribbean. Nonetheless, in 1829 one of the first militant African-American emancipationists, David Walker, wrote from Boston in his *Appeal to the Colored Citizens of the World* that the "English" were "the best friends the coloured people have upon earth. Though they have oppressed us a little and have colonies now in the West Indies which oppress us *sorely*—Yet notwithstanding they [the English] have done one hundred times more for the melioration of our condition, than all the other nations of the earth put together." White Americans, on the other hand, with their posturing religiosity and their hollow cant of freedom, he consigned to the lowest reaches of hypocritical infamy.[6] Parliamentary abolition of slavery in 1834 did nothing to change this generous assessment of British benevolence towards Africans, nor the Royal Navy's pursuit of slavers (some of them American) on the West African coast. In 1845–47, touring Britain as he lectured on the iniquity of American slavery, the black orator Frederick Douglass echoed Walker's fulsome view of the "English" as the emancipators. In 1852 he would ask in an Independence Day oration, "What to the Slave is the Fourth of July?" and would answer that "your high independence only reveals the immeasurable distance between us . . . you may rejoice, I must mourn."[7]

Whether the British deserved this reputation as the most racially broadminded among nations and empires is, to say the least, debatable. During the American Civil War of 1861–65, both policy and people leaned if anything towards the slaveowning Confederacy rather than the Union, not least because it would check the threatening expansiveness of the American republic. But during the Revolutionary War there is no question that tens of thousands of Africans, enslaved in the American South, did look to Britain as their deliverer, to the point where they were ready to risk life and limb to reach the lines of the royal army. To give this astounding fact its due means being obliged to tell the story of Anglo-American conflict, both during the revolution and after, in a freshly complicated way.

To be sure, there were also many blacks who gave the Patriots the benefit of the doubt when they listened and read of their war as a war for liberty. If there was a British Freedom, there was also a Dick Freedom—and a Jeffery Liberty—fighting in a Connecticut regiment on the American side.[8] Blacks fought and died for the American cause at Concord, Bunker Hill, Rhode Island and finally at Yorktown (where they were put in the front line—whether as a tribute to their courage or as expendable sacrifices is not clear). At the battle of Monmouth in New Jersey black troops on both sides fought each other. But until the British aggressively recruited slaves in 1775 and 1776, state assemblies, even in the North, as well as the multi-state Continental Congress, flinched from their enlistment. New Hampshire was typical in excluding lunatics, idiots and negroes from its militia. By the autumn of 1775 blacks who had already served in the Patriot militia were ordered to be discharged. George Washington, despite the voiced hostility of fellow officers and civilian delegates to his camp at Cambridge, was reluctant to let black volunteers go, so he put the question to Congress. There, the horror expressed by Southern representatives such as Edward Rutledge at the idea of arming slaves predictably overcame the lukewarm gratitude for black service. Even armed free negroes were a worry. Could they be trusted not to spread the seeds of insurrection among the unfree? In February 1776 Congress instructed Washington that, whilst free negroes might be retained, no more should be enlisted. Slaves, of course, were altogether excluded from the Continental army set up by Congress.[9]

By contrast, the proclamation of John Murray, Lord Dunmore, the last colonial governor of Virginia, from HMS *William* on the 7th of November 1775 unequivocally promised outright liberty to all slaves escaping from rebel plantations, reaching British lines and serving in some capacity with the army. The promise was made from military rather than humanitarian motives, and for every British Freedom who lived to see it kept, there were many more who would be unconscionably betrayed. Yet from opportunist tactics, some good might still arise. Dunmore's words, sanctioned by the British government and reiterated by Generals Howe and Clinton (who extended the definition of those entitled to liberty to black women and children), took wing in the world of the slaves, and they themselves took off, in their tens of thousands, shortly after. Seeing the Revolutionary War through the eyes of enslaved blacks turns its meaning upside down. In Georgia, the Carolinas and much of Virginia the vaunted war for liberty was, from the spring of 1775 to the late summer of 1776, a war for the perpetuation of servitude. The contortions of logic were so perverse, yet so habitual, that George Washington could describe Dunmore as "that arch traitor to the rights of humanity" for promising to free slaves and indentured servants, whilst those who kept them in bondage were heroes of liberty.

For blacks, the news that the British Were Coming was a reason for hope, celebration and action. Henry Melchior Muhlenberg, a Pennsylvania Lutheran pastor, knew what he was talking about when he wrote that the black population "secretly wished the British army might win for then all Negro slaves will gain their freedom. It is said that this sentiment is universal among all the Negroes in America."[10] And every so often truth broke through the armour of Patriot casuistry. In December 1775, Lund Washington wrote to his cousin George of both blacks and indentured servants, who were departing from the Washington properties at speed, that "there is not a man of them but would leave us if they believ'd they could make there [sic] escape . . . Liberty is sweet."[11]

The Founding Fathers were themselves candid about the extent of the disappearance of their slaves, not least because so many of them experienced serious personal losses. During the few weeks in the spring of 1781, when Lord Cornwallis's troops were not far from his home, Monticello, Thomas Jefferson, who had seen his own attempt to incorporate a paragraph attacking slavery in the Declaration of Independence stricken out by Congress, lost thirty of his own. He believed—and the judgement of most modern historians, such as Benjamin Quarles, Gary Nash, Sylvia Frey, Ellen Gibson Wilson and James Walker concurs—that at least thirty thousand had escaped from Virginia plantations in attempts to reach the British lines.[12] The same went for the rest of the South. As early as 1858 the historian David Ramsey estimated that two-thirds of the slaves in South Carolina had run away; many, though certainly not all, defecting to the British. In all, between eighty thousand and one hundred thousand slaves left the plantations during the war.[13] The more sententious the noises coming from the Patriot leaders about American enslavement to the odious Hanoverian tyrant, the more their own slaves voted with their feet. Ralph Henry, for example, evidently took his master Patrick Henry's theatrical announcement of "Give me Liberty or give me death" very much to heart, but not quite

in the way its author intended, since he ran away at the earliest opportunity to the British lines.[14] (Ironically, that same slogan would be invoked as a rallying cry by black abolitionists in the nineteenth century
and black liberators such as Malcom X in the twentieth!) Others among
the signatories of the document which asserted that "all men are born
free and equal" and who lost slaves were James Madison and Benjamin
Harrison (father of the ninth president, William Henry Harrison), who
lost twenty, including Anna and Pompey Cheese, who were destined to
make it all the way to New York, Nova Scotia and Sierra Leone. The
South Carolinan signatory Arthur Middleton lost fifty; Governor John
Rutledge's Pompey and Flora went over to the British; and Edward
Rutledge, the youngest signer of the Declaration and the ardent opponent of black enrolment in the American army, also lost slaves. General
Francis Marion, the "swamp fox" of South Carolina, whose slaves are
depicted in Mel Gibson's movie fantasy *The Patriot* as eager to follow
their master into the fight for freedom, had at least one, Abraham Marrian, who defected to the British. He may have been among the small
company of mounted Black Dragoons mobilized in the summer of 1782
who fought (more plausibly) *against* Marion, not alongside him, at Wadboo Plantation, South Carolina.[15] And, not least, while George Washington was encamped in early 1776 on Cambridge Common, wrestling
with arguments, pro and con, about the desirability of recruiting blacks,
his own slave, Henry Washington, born in West Africa, was finding his
way to the king's lines. In exile with other black loyalists in Birchtown,
Nova Scotia, Washington would describe himself, movingly, as a
"farmer," but it was the Union Jack that protected his forty acres and his
freedom.[16]

The story of this mass flight, aptly characterized by Gary Nash as
the Revolutionary War's "dirty little secret," is shocking in the best
sense, in that it forces an honest and overdue rethinking of the war
as involving, at its core, a third party.[17] This third party of African-
Americans, moreover, accounted for 20 percent of the entire population
of 2.5 million colonists, rising in Virginia to as much as 40 percent. When
it came to the blacks caught up in their struggle, neither side, British nor
American, behaved very well. But in the end, as British Freedom and
multitudes like him appreciated (even when they happened to be free
blacks already), it was the royal, rather than the republican, road that

seemed to offer a surer chance of liberty. Although the history that un-folded from the entanglement between black desperation and British paternalism would often prove to be bitterly tragic, it was, nonetheless, a formative moment in the history of African-American freedom. In Sergeant Thomas Peters, it produced the first identifiable African-American political leader.[18]

Born an Egbe prince, Peters was enslaved by the French, taken to Louisiana, flogged and branded for repeated attempts at flight, then sold to a plantation owner in Wilmington, North Carolina, from where he escaped to the British. Sworn into the Pioneers by Captain George Martin, he was twice wounded in combat and promoted to sergeant. Subsequently he settled, first on the north shore of Nova Scotia and then in New Brunswick, becoming a petitioner to the Crown in London on behalf of his fellow blacks. Peters was an authentic captain of his people: tenacious, brave and, though illiterate, evidently articulate, from the indirect evidence of a succession of whites, all offended by his presump-tion. That he is (with a few honourable exceptions) conspicuously miss-ing from the pantheon of African-American heroes, a name utterly foreign to high school history texts in the United States, is a scandal explained entirely by the inconvenient fact that Peters happened to fight for the Wrong Side. The same is true for blacks in Boston who chose the British rather than the American cause. Crispus Attucks has been canon-ized as one of the fallen in the Boston Massacre, when British troops shot down rioters in 1770. But the story of Newton Prince, the black barber who testified on behalf of the redcoats is, unsurprisingly, much less well known. For his temerity, Prince was tarred and feathered by infuriated Patriots, so naturally in 1776 he opted for General Howe and was evacuated with the British. Likewise Black London, another barber, who in 1776 told the commissioners for loyalist claims after the war that he had been compelled by his employer to join the Patriot militia, de-serted as soon as he could and served for four years with Sir Henry Clinton and then aboard two warships.[19]

However awkward for the orthodox history of the Founding Fa-thers and their revolution, the genesis of African-American liberty is, then, inseparable from the British connection during and after the war. If free black politics were born from the fires of that conflict, so were many of the distinctive forms of their Christian gathering. It was among the loyalist Africans that some of the earliest free Baptist and Methodist churches were created in and near Shelburne, Nova Scotia; there too that the first *whites* to be converted by a black preacher were baptized in those red rivers by the charismatic minister David George. The first schools expressly for free black children were opened in the loyalist diaspora of Nova Scotia, where they were taught by black teachers like Catherine Abernathy in Preston and Stephen Blucke in Birchtown. In Sierra Leone, where more than a thousand of the "Nova Scotians" ended up after journeying back across the Atlantic, this time as persons not property, the American blacks experienced for the first time (and all too ephemerally) a meaningful degree of local law and self-government. It was another first when an elected black constable, the ex-slave Simon Proof, administered a flogging to a white sailor found guilty of dereliction of duty.

The history of black loyalism, however, is much more than a catalogue of "firsts." The story also gives the lie to the stereotype of the Africans as passive, credulous pawns of American or British strategy. Whether they opted for the Patriot or for the loyalist side, many of the blacks, illiterate or not, knew exactly what they were doing, even if they could never have anticipated the magnitude of the perils, misfortunes and deceits that would result from their decision. Often, their choice was determined by a judgement of whether, sooner or later, a free America would be forced to honour the Declaration of Independence's principle that the birthright of *all* men was liberty and equality; or whether (in the South especially), with the spectacle of runaways being hunted down and sent to labour in lead mines or saltpetre works, finesounding promises were likely to be indefinitely deferred. It was not a good sign of things to come when enlistment incentives offered to white recruits in Georgia and South Carolina included a bounty of a free slave at the end of the war.

To their credit, there were a few Patriot leaders who, long before the revolution, had recognized the embarrassing discrepancy between the rhetoric of liberty and the reality of slavery. The "enslavement" of Americans by British governments was a commonplace of the most grandiloquent Patriot broadsides (especially in Boston) against the Stamp Tax in 1766 and dutied tea in 1773. A typical pamphlet of the Tea Party era thundered that the "baneful chests [of tea] contain in them . . . something worse than death—the seeds of SLAVERY."[20] James Otis, the fiercest of the Boston firebrand lawyers, was no exception in railing against the wicked insidiousness of such schemes of enslavement; but he was alone among Massachusetts Patriots in extending the logic of his argument to blacks, maintaining, outlandishly, that freedom was not racially divisible. "The colonists are by law of nature freeborn as indeed all men are, white or black. Does it follow that 'tis right to enslave a man because he is black?" Otis wrote in his incendiary *The Rights of the British Colonists Asserted and Proved*. "Can any logical inference in favor of slavery be drawn from a flat nose, a long or a short face? Nothing better can be said in favor of a trade that is the most shocking violation of the law of nature, has a direct tendency to diminish the idea of the inestimable value of liberty . . ."[21] And he warned that "those who every day barter away other men's liberty will soon care very little for their own."[22] But Otis's forthrightness only confirmed to less adventurous spirits his reputation for rashness, or even mental instability. John Adams, a younger but much cooler head (and evidently no egalitarian), commented later, "I shuddered at the doctrine he taught and I have all my life shuddered and still shudder at the consequences that may be drawn from such premises."[23]

Other American Patriots, too intelligent not to notice the contradiction and too honest to side-step it entirely, tried to disarm accusations of hypocrisy by confronting them head on, while always laying blame for the original sin of slavery on the British themselves and in particular His Majesty's Royal African Company, which had been chartered back in 1662 to trade in slaves, precious metals and timber. The "Well, you started it" school playground plea of mitigation was most aggressively converted into an indictment in Jefferson's Declaration of Independence. But long before his tour de force of disingenuousness, others had become adept at turning defensiveness into sanctimonious indignation at being so shockingly misunderstood. No one did this better than Benjamin Franklin, who had let it be known to friends of the slaves, such as the Quaker Anthony Benezet in Philadelphia and Granville Sharp in London, that he himself frowned on the iniquitous trade in humans and wanted nothing better than to hasten its end.[24]

In 1770, during his last year in London lobbying on behalf of his fellow independence-minded Americans, Franklin, apparently stung by

Granville Sharp's attacks on American hypocrisy, published "A Conversation between an Englishman, a Scotchman and an American on the Subject of Slavery" in the *Public Advertiser*. "You Americans make a great Clamour upon every little imaginary Infringement of what you take to be your Liberties and yet there are no People upon Earth such Enemies to Liberty, such absolute Tyrants," Franklin has his Englishman say, directing the affronted American to read Sharp's treatise. The indictment was, of course, overstated, allowing the American to respond that Sharp was making the gross and insulting error of lumping all his countrymen together, even though there were many, indeed at least as many, in the colonies as in Britain who wholeheartedly detested the iniquitous traffic in humans and were working for its destruction. That the accusation of double standards frequently found its mark, though, was betrayed by the hurt tone of the American's wounded complaint that it was "particularly *injurious* to us at this Time to endeavour to render us odious and to encourage those who would oppress us, by representing us as unworthy of the Liberty we are now contending for."[25] The transparent uneasiness of the defence was not improved when the "American" went on the counter-attack by accusing the English of inflicting a kind of servitude on their "working poor," who if they were "not absolutely Slaves there seems something a little like Slavery, where the Laws oblige them to work for their Masters so many Hours at such a Rate and leave them no Liberty to demand or bargain for more but imprison them in a Workhouse if they refuse to work on such terms." When the Englishman raised the inhumanity of the slave laws and in particular their prescribed punishments, the American responded that in colonies such as Virginia, where whites were so outnumbered by blacks, there was no alternative: "Perhaps you may imagine the Negroes to be a mild tempered, tractable Kind of People . . . some of them are indeed so. But the Majority are of a plotting Disposition, dark, sullen, malicious, revengeful and cruel in the highest Degree." Even odder, to the "Scotchman's" criticisms the American replied that in Scotland there were *also* slaves, who worked in coal mines and who were "bought and sold with the Colliery and have no more Liberty to leave it than our Negroes have to leave their Master's Plantation. If having black Faces indeed, subjected Men to the Condition of Slavery, you might have some small pretence for keeping the poor Colliers in that Condition: But remember that, under the Smut their skin *is white.*"[26]

It seems astonishing that Franklin should have thought a double-dose of colour prejudice should actually have strengthened his case. But double-thinking was a staple, even of those who cheerfully owned up to it, none more bare-faced than the Virginian Patrick Henry. Writing to Anthony Benezet from Hanover, Virginia, in January 1773, Henry worked up an impressive lather of indignation against the atrocity of slavery, especially since it was enduring "at a time when the Rights of Humanity are defined and understood with precision, in a Country, above all fond of Liberty." But having unburdened himself of amazement that such an evil should persist in an Enlightened age, Henry goes on with disarming candour: "Would anyone believe that I am master of Slave(s) of my own purchase?" As his reason for violating his own professed principles, however, Henry could manage nothing more than the lame, if honest, excuse that "I am drawn along by the general Inconveniency of living without them. I will not, I cannot justify it; however culpable my conduct I will so far pay my duty as to own the Excellency and rectitude of her [Natural] precepts and to lament my want of conformity to them." Henry prayed that there might come a time when this would all change, but, pending such great reformation, he hoped at least to treat his slaves "with lenity." No wonder, then, floundering in the morass of his own bad faith, all he could do by way of ending his letter to Benezet was to write, with unconvincing theatricality, "I know not where to stop, I could say many things on this Subject, a serious review of which give a gloomy perspective to future times; excuse the scrawl and believe me, with esteem etc . . ."[27]

Predictably, the exacting consciences of John and Abigail Adams would not allow themselves the same kind of careless breeziness as Patrick Henry when it came to the sin of the Great Contradiction. Reporting to her husband one of the many stories circulating in 1773 and 1774 of a black insurrection nipped in the bud, and anxious not to pour fuel on what was obviously a dangerous tinderbox, Abigail confessed to her husband that she wished "most sincerely there was not a slave in the province [of Massachusetts]" since "it always appeared to me to be a most iniquitous scheme . . . to fight ourselves for what we are daily robbing and plundering from those who have as good a right to freedom as we have."[28]

Abigail Adams's nervousness that American blacks might pounce on the glaring discrepancy between Patriot professions of liberty for all, and their unwillingness to extend it to slaves was well founded; 1773 and 1774 saw no fewer than five "humble" petitions written by blacks to the last colonial governors of Massachusetts, Thomas Hutchinson and General Thomas Gage. A number of articles in newspapers all demanded, with varying degrees of urgency and indignation, that something be done about the treatment of Africans as chattels. In an impassioned essay printed in the *Essex Journal and Merrimac Packet* in August 1774, Caesar Sarter, a freed man who "bore the galling yoke of bondage for more than twenty years," insisted that slavery was "the greatest, and consequently most to be dreaded, of all temporal calamities," whilst "its opposite, Liberty, the greatest temporal good with which you can be blest." Deprived of dropping a tear over the separation of dear friends "who were clinging to you, you must be plied with that conclusive argument, the cat o" nine tails to reduce you to what your inhuman masters would call reason." "Now," Caesar Sarter addressed his Patriot readers, "are you willing all this should befall you? If you can lay your hand on your breast and solemnly affirm that you should, why then go on and Prosper! For your treatment of the Africans is an exact compliance with the above mentioned rule."

The petitions were often anguished. One, addressed to Governor Hutchinson in January 1773 and signed, perhaps sardonically, "Felix," on behalf of "many Slaves living in the town of Boston" and other towns of Massachusetts, lamented the "intollerable condition" of people who "have no Property! We have no Wives! No Children! We have no City! No Country! . . . Not even *Life itself*, but in a Manner as the *Beasts that perish*." In April of the same year a second petition signed by four slaves, Sambo Freeman, Peter Bestes, Chester Joie and Felix Holbrook, expected "great things from men who have made such a noble stand against the designs of their *fellow-men* to enslave them": the members of the House of Representatives ought to allow them to work at least one day a week for a wage, from which money might be saved that could send the Africans home to their native country. Two months later yet another petition appeared on behalf of "all those . . . who are held in a state of slavery within the bowels of a free Country," insisting "in common with other men [on] a Natural Right to be free and without molestation to injoy such property as they may acquire by their industry."[29] A year later, a similar document declared that "we are a freeborn pepel and have never forfeited that natural liberty."

These appeals, whether to consistency or conscience, of course went largely unheeded by both the last British governors and by the Patriot politicians of the Massachusetts General Court. However, in colonies from Virginia to Massachusetts petitions were drafted and circulated by Benezet, Benjamin Rush and their fellow campaigners to halt further importation of slaves or at the very least to impose duties of twenty pounds on each new slave, a tariff heavy enough to act as a disincentive to buy and sell. (Rhode Island, with its major investment in the slave trade, was an exception to the non-importation movement.) In each case the royal governors, acting on instructions from Britain, refused consent. How unfair, it was said by way of explanation, for West Indian planters coming to America to repair their ravaged health to have to pay special import duties when bringing their body servants with them to their place of convalescence! The refusal of official assent allowed Jefferson and Southern Patriots to bounce the accusation of hypocrisy back to the royal government, which, it insisted, was cravenly beholden to the West Indian sugar lobby.

The charge was fair enough. But what the likes of Jefferson forbore from admitting was that this sudden attack of high-mindedness in the South was owed less to any kind of conversion on the part of the plantocracy to the inhumanity of slaveholding, than to a panic, after 1772, about the imminence of a slave insurrection in regions where blacks already outnumbered whites. This was not idle speculation. Three ferocious and bloody rebellions were under way, in Surinam, St Vincent and Jamaica, and all were widely and apocalyptically reported in the North American press. In Surinam, on the mainland of South America, a small force of European soldiers had been overwhelmed by a black and Amerindian army, perhaps numbering tens of thousands of heavily armed desperadoes. The marauders, it was said, had taken possession of estates and even towns, burned them down, and committed countless acts of robbery and murder against the largely defenceless Dutch colonists.

In St Vincent and Jamaica, regiments of British troops withdrawn from North America were tied down just attempting to contain a wildfire uprising that numbered Maroons (free blacks and mulattos living in the interior) along with liberated slaves in its legions.

So before there was a white American revolution, there were already black and brown ones sweeping through South America and the Caribbean. Although space is seldom given to the Surinam or the St Vincent rebellions in histories of the American Revolution, the connection was critical to the timing of Patriot mobilization in the South. The sudden urgency of armed white American resistance was driven not, of course, by any solidarity with captive people elsewhere in the hemisphere, but by precisely the opposite—by the terror that the insurrectionary contagion might spread north. The most feverish nightmare involved the British actually fomenting black rebellion as a way of intimidating the Patriots.

These suspicions were not altogether paranoid. By early 1775, many months before Dunmore's proclamation from the *William,* there had indeed been suggestions both from royal officials in America and within Lord North's own government that playing the "negro" card against the presumptions of the colonists might have to be considered, even though North himself (protesting a little too much) professed to be horrified by the idea. When the mounting evidence of an insurrectionary spirit sweeping through the world of the slaves was put together with the independent black voices heard in the Massachusetts petitions, it robbed nervous Patriots of their sleep. Abigail Adams's comments to her husband in the summer of 1774 about the selectiveness of Patriot rhetoric on liberty were made in the context of news of a "conspiracy of Negroes" who had had the temerity to ask the governor for arms so that they could fight for the king in exchange for their liberty!

Escapes were now imagined to be the prelude to a concerted rising. From New York to Georgia the tempo of reported runaways gathered ominous momentum throughout 1773 and 1774. In New York concern about illicit "assemblies" of negroes was so serious that instructions were issued to apprehend any blacks appearing in any sort of numbers after dark. To the jumpier Americans it did not bear contemplating what might happen should the slaves, especially in the Southern plantation colonies, take it into their heads that the vaunted liberties of Old England somehow applied to *them*, and that, as reported in 1730, they had a royal licence to disobey. Sambo Freeman in Boston had already alluded, in one of the petitions, to "those sublime ideas of Freedom that Englishmen have," contrasting the aspirations of blacks to those of their unfortunate counterparts in Spanish colonies who could expect nothing but despotism. If affected slaveholders are to be believed, these intoxicated delusions about British freedom had spread deep into the South. Educated flight had begun. In the *Virginia Gazette*, one of many advertisements offering rewards for the recapture of runaways mentioned a Gabriel Jones and his wife, said to be on their way to the coast to board ship for England "where they imagine they will be free (a Notion now prevalent among the Negroes greatly to the vexation and prejudice of their Masters)."[30] Now where could slaves get such absurd ideas from? Another advertisement supplies the answer. One Bacchus, it seems, in Augusta County, Georgia, ran away, leading his master to believe that he too might head for a port, there "to board a vessel for Great Britain from the knowledge he has of the late determination of the Somerset case."[31]

What was this? Did slaves read law reports? How could it be that a judgement rendered in June 1772 by Lord Chief Justice Mansfield in the court of the King's Bench in the case of a runaway African, James Somerset, recaptured by his master, could light a fire in the plantations? Mansfield had set Somerset free, but had taken pains *not* to make a general ruling on the legality of slavery in England. However, the "Negro frolicks" in London celebrating the court decision had swept legal niceties aside. Across the Atlantic word spread, and spread quickly, that slavery had been outlawed in Britain. In 1774 a pamphlet written by "Freeman," published in Philadelphia, told American slaves that they could have liberty merely by "setting foot on that happy Territory where slavery is forbidden to perch." Before the Patriots knew it, the birds had already begun to fly the coop.[32]

Part One

GREENY

I

MINCING LANE in the Ward of Cheap in 1765 was neither the worst nor the best address in the City of London. The Sisters of St Helen, known as "Minchen," who had given the street its name, were long gone, and piety had, unsurprisingly, been replaced by profit. Solid mercantile chambers and warehouses, many of them connected to the colonial trade, lined the street. At regular intervals in the morning, carts bearing chests of sugar and tea, coming from the East and West India wharves, would rumble up the lane from Great Tower Street, carve a path through the throngs of pie vendors, ale wagons, flower girls, beggars and balladmongers, pass through broad gates and unload in the cobbled inner courtyards. In short, there was not much to detain the curious tourist other than the Clothworkers' Hall, set back from the street and boasting a ceremonious row of Corinthian pilasters along its interior façade. It was all very middling. What was not middling, however, was the line of the woeful that trailed down the lane from a doorway at the northern, Fenchurch Street, end of the lane. These were the sickly poor: the bloodied and the bent; emaciated women and grimy, hacking drunks; small children on whom the first blisters of the pox had already erupted; and their places of domicile were assuredly not Mincing Lane. They came to the door on the lane from the empire of squalor that stretched beyond the Tower, through the Ald Gate and the Bishop's Gate, into the rookeries of St George in the East, Shadwell and Wapping, where refuse, human and animal, brimmed in the reeking alleys, and twopenny whores lifted their skirts to sailors observed by cutpurses and yowling cats.

The door opened and out stepped an angular man looking older than his thirty years. His tall but meagre frame, hollow cheeks, lantern jaw and short curled wig gave him the air of either an underpaid clerk or an unworldly cleric; the truth is that Granville Sharp was something of both. He had taken his customary late afternoon walk to his brother William's surgery from his own place of work at the Ordnance Office in the Tower, where he managed to fill five or six hours managing the supply of saltpetre and the conduct of unruly gentlemen cadets. Sharp's mind, however, was usually on much more important matters: for instance, his severe differences with Dr Kennicott on the catalogue the doctor had presumed to publish, listing the Temple vessels restored to the Jews by King Cyrus in the time of the prophet Nehemiah.[1]

Most evenings the Sharp brothers and sisters gathered at William's house for rehearsals of their Sunday concerts. Their origins were plain and provincial: the children of an archdeacon of Northumberland. But since coming to London in 1750, two of Granville's older brothers, James and William, had prospered. Deprived by their father's limited means of the Cambridge education given to two older sons destined for the Church, James had had to make his way as an ironmonger, whilst William had applied himself to medicine. For the most part, this meant setting broken bones, trepanning skulls and dispensing remedies to the poxed, but William had flourished in his art. Now risen all the way to being one of the surgeons to the king, he flattered himself that he had not forgotten the humble, and his way of showing it was to minister, gratis, to London's poor.

William Sharp, then, had something of a name, for how many organ-playing, horn-blowing surgeons were there, let alone physicians of such exemplary Christian benevolence, within the square mile of the City of London? On concert Sundays his rooms in Mincing Lane filled with pretty much everyone who mattered: David Garrick, James Boswell and Sir Joshua Reynolds. The attraction was the exemplary harmony exhibited by the family: James played the jointed serpent, often with parts he had transcribed from the violoncello; sister Judith played the lute and the theorbo; Eliza (before she had to go and marry Mr Prowse of Wicken Park, Northamptonshire) was mistress of the harpsichord; and Frances sang as sweetly as a trilling lark. Granville, who sometimes signed (or sealed) himself G# and was working on *A Short Introduction to Musick for the use of such Children as have a Musical Ear and are Willing to be Instructed in the Great Duty of Singing Psalms*, played the flute, his long, nimble fingers flying over the stops. Sometimes "to the delight and conviction of many doubters who had conceived such an accomplishment to have been impracticable," as William Shield, the Master of His Majesty's Band of Musicians, commented, Granville would play two flutes simultaneously.[2] Proud of their performances, the Sharps rehearsed together every evening with any additional musicians and singers they had recruited. But these meetings were also domestic, convivial affairs, with tea, dainties, gossip from the City and family news from Durham. In return, members of the clan living beyond the City would receive news of the doings in London from a circulated Common Letter, which took it as a point of honour to list, comprehensively, the dishes consumed at dinner as well as the items played in concert. The Sharps stayed close, always. "Whatever other engagements took place," Eliza recalled, "it was all our party."

So when Granville emerged from William's surgery and pulled up short at a figure whose dreadful condition horrified even someone inured to looking at the unfortunate, his impulse, once he had heard the poor black man's story, was to turn on his heel and straight away bring his brother out to help. It was not unusual to see blacks on London streets. There were at least five thousand and perhaps as many as seven thousand scattered over the metropolis, some living in fine town houses where, suitably got up in embroidered coats, powdered wigs and silk breeches, they served, ornamentally, as footmen or body servants to the quality.[3] Some, like Dr Johnson's Francis Barber, were minor celebrities, sketched and painted as charming "sable" curiosities. The less fortunate made a living as musicians or waiters in the taverns and brothels of Covent Garden, and went home to a bare, verminous room in neighbouring St Giles, where they were called "blackbirds." Far more congregated in the dockland parish of St George in the East, in the filthy streets that led from Nicholas Hawksmoor's eccentric church. Many of them were sailors, bargemen, haulers, carters and stevedores; and some for a few pence boxed bareknuckle or played on drums and fifes to crowds in the streets and piazzas. The "blackbirds," then, were mostly poor, and were known for flitting in and out of trouble. There would have been nothing out of the ordinary in seeing one in the queue for William Sharp's surgery that evening in 1765. But this particular black had very little left of his face.

His name, as the Sharp brothers learned, was Jonathan Strong, and once perhaps he had been. But his master, David Lisle, a lawyer from Barbados, had been so much in the habit of thrashing him senseless on the slightest pretext that Jonathan Strong had become crippled. London was full of the spectacle of pain. Sluggish cart horses were mercilessly flogged until they dropped; vagrant beggars were whipped until their backs had become beefsteaks; felons were stoned in the public pillory and sometimes died as they sat there; servants, both male and female, were cuffed and smacked in public; schoolboys were thrashed for insolence or troublesome high spirits; men caught by the press gangs were beaten with sticks as they were hauled off to the waiting ships. But what Lisle had done to Jonathan Strong seemed savage even by the rough standards of the day. The negro's face was reduced to crimson gore, the result of a pistol whipping so savage that after repeated, relentless blows the mouth of the gun had separated from the handle. Strong had been blinded with blood and when, finally, his master saw that there was nothing left to maim he had been thrown into the street to die. The negro had staggered to William Sharp's surgery, where he patiently waited his turn in the line of sickness and pain that gathered along Mincing Lane. Some time later, Strong himself remembered that

> I could hardly walk or see my way where I was going. When I came
> to him [William] and he saw me in that condition, the gentleman
> take charity of me and gave me some stoff to wash my eyes with
> and some money to get myself a little necessaries till next day. The
> day after I come to the gentleman and he sent me into the hospital
> and I was in there four months and a half. All the while I was in
> the hospital the gentleman find me in clothes, shoes and stockings
> and when I come out he paid for my lodging and a money to find
> myself some necessaries till he get me into a place.[4]

When Strong emerged from Bart's Hospital William Sharp found him work with the apothecary Brown, who supplied his surgery with most of its drugs, splints and bandages. Strong was still lame from his beatings and never fully recovered his sight, yet was well enough to run errands for the apothecary, picking up and delivering medical supplies to the City surgeons and hospitals. There were times too when he served as body or household servant for the Browns. On one of those days in September 1767, two years after the Sharps had found him, he was standing footman behind Mrs Brown's carriage when he had the misfortune to be seen by his old tormentor, David Lisle.

And what Lisle noticed was not the ruin of a creature that he had discarded in the gutter, but a disconcertingly trim and inexplicably repaired Jonathan Strong. Anger—with himself for throwing away an investment; with Strong for surviving; with whomever it was who had robbed him (for so he already thought of the matter) of his property— welled up in him, competing with an equally sudden surge of cupidity. Perhaps something could be done to redeem his loss. It was, after all, 1767. Four years before, peace had been signed with France, and the Caribbean was the engine of fortune. The market for slaves to work the West Indian sugar plantations, especially on the boom island of Jamaica, had never been hungrier, even for the likes of broken-down Strong. Among the city's black population were many who had originally been brought to London by American or West Indian masters—most of whom, if they were rich enough, kept up seasonal establishments in the capital of the empire—and who, as body servants, footmen or musicians, lived in a state of relative liberty. Some, such as Dr Johnson's Francis Barber or Lord Montagu's Ignatius Sancho, were given freedom after years of loyal service. Others had taken it by escaping into Cheapside or Wapping, where they could work for wages that would protect them against an enforced return to America or the West Indies. The pursuit of these runaways was the work of slavecatchers who prowled the coffee-houses and inns, eager to collect the many rewards posted in London and American newspapers. Once caught, such blacks were imprisoned, resold (for there were regular sales and auctions in London) and bundled off to waiting ships at Gravesend, destined for Jamaica, Havana, Santa Cruz or Charleston.

This is what Lisle planned for Jonathan Strong. Even before he caught up with Strong, Lisle had already traded him to a Jamaican planter, James Kerr. In a fit of uncharacteristic candour, Lisle may have admitted that Strong was perhaps not in prime condition, and accepted £30 for him in a seller's market in which "stout Negroes" fetched, on average, at least £50. Or perhaps Lisle was himself needy for funds, since he also accepted Kerr's condition that the money would not be handed over before the black in question was safely aboard a ship.

It remained, of course, for Lisle to secure his property. Keeping out of sight, he had followed Strong to a public house. Two days after first seeing him in the street attending on Mrs Brown, Lisle hired two Lord Mayor's officers to accost him in the pub, informing him only that a certain gentleman wished to speak with him. Either over-complaisant from his two years of liberty, or perhaps easily intimidated, Jonathan Strong went with the men, only to be startled by the appearance of his old persecutor. All pretence at politeness dropped, Strong was man-handled to the prison of Poultry Compter in Giltspur Street in Cheap, where, among felons and vagrants picked up by the sheriff's men, he could be detained before being conveyed as a recovered chattel to the ship. But this was not the end of the story. Two years of being treated like a human being had given Jonathan Strong a modest degree of fighting self-respect and, more decisively, a modest degree of education. The fate of blacks in Britain—and America—hung on this one puny but improbable fact: that lame, half-blind Jonathan Strong could read and write. He sent out a series of notes, first to Brown, the apothecary, signalling his predicament. Brown promptly dispatched a servant who, however, was refused admission or any kind of communication with Jonathan Strong.

When Brown himself arrived at Poultry Compter he was so browbeaten by Lisle, ranting that he had been robbed of his goods and waving a bill of sale, that the apothecary retreated lest he be arrested himself for theft as Lisle threatened. In extremis, Jonathan Strong sent a second note, this one to his old saviour, Granville Sharp. But Sharp's head was full of more pressing matters—a scheme to introduce the Anglican Church into the kingdom of Prussia, for example; the preparation of his *Short Introduction to Musick* . . . ; a second brief treatise called "On the Pronunciation of the English Tongue"—and the significance of the name Strong momentarily escaped him. It was not long, though, before it came back with guilty urgency. It was Sharp's turn now to send a messenger to the prison, and when no reply was received by return he went to see Strong for himself. There, in the ante-rooms and bare cells of Poultry Compter, with the creak of bare wood and iron performing sporadically gloomy music, he recalled everything. For the first time in his life, in matters that were not ecclesiastical nor military nor musical, Granville Sharp acted, insisting more from instinct than authority, that since the black had committed no offence he could not possibly be legally detained. He had enough of the air of a learned gentleman to persuade the officers that, should they make the mistake of releasing Strong to a third party before his case had been heard by the Lord Mayor, they would risk their own incrimination.

Against the odds, Jonathan Strong got his hearing. Sir Robert Kite, like most lord mayors of the 1760s and 1770s, could not possibly have held that office without the favour of the patrician merchants of the sugar interest. Yet whilst he would have not recognized himself in any way as a particular friend to blacks, the mayor was bound by an ingrained respect for due process. And the City of London was still a small enough community for the mayor to know all about the brothers Sharp. James, after all, sat in the City's assembly, the Common Council. So when Granville came to see Sir Robert and recited the facts of the case he received a fair and even sympathetic reception. A hearing was ordered, which was convened on the 18th of September at the Mansion House and attended by the Sharps, Laird, the captain of the ship in which Strong was to be conveyed, and Macbean, the lawyer for the new owner, James Kerr. As the arguments between Sharp and Macbean turned furious, Strong, who was not at all convinced of a happy outcome, became distraught, weeping and shaking with fear. After listening to both sides Sir Robert Kite made up his mind, saying, as Sharp reported in his casebook, that "the lad had not stolen anything and was not guilty of any offence and was therefore at liberty to go away."[5] Evidently Captain Laird was not listening, since after the mayor had withdrawn he grabbed Strong, claiming him physically as the property of Mr Kerr. The action was so brutally sudden and so disconcerting that for a moment it threatened to succeed—even Granville Sharp was dumbfounded into inaction. But the City coroner, Thomas Beech, still present in the room, stepped quickly towards Sharp and whispered urgently to him, "Charge him!" Novice at the law though he was, Sharp responded: "Sir!" he shouted at Captain Laird in the clear voice that was to characterize the new Granville Sharp. "I charge you with assault."[6]

For the moment it was enough. The slaver captain paused and Strong, still weeping, shook off Laird's grip. A few days later later Lisle, by no means reconciled to the decision, issued a writ against Granville Sharp and his older brother James for theft of his slave. But the law seemed less friendly to Lisle's interest than he had assumed. On an afternoon when he knew the Sharps to be at Mincing Lane he arrived at the house, was announced and admitted, whereupon he issued a personal challenge to Granville for "Gentlemanlike satisfaction because I had procured the liberty of his slave Jonathan Strong. I told him that as he had studied law so many years he should want no satisfaction that the *law* should give him."[7]

The words hit their mark. Strong's body may have still carried the marks of his beatings by Lisle, but, more crushingly, Lisle the lawyer had been beaten by the law. However, Greeny Sharp, as he was known to his brothers and sisters, was no longer so green in the ways of the courts as to dispense with the services of lawyers in case Lisle and Kerr should press their suit. Through the connections of his older brothers he retained the City recorder, Sir James Eyre, to advise him. Granville's boldness in rescuing Jonathan Strong from the clutches of Lisle had been coloured by the instinctive certainty that neither Christian propriety nor the majesty of English Common Law could possibly countenance the reduction of a person to a property. Imagine his shock and despondency, then, when Sir James brought him the opinion of the former Lord Chancellor Yorke and Solicitor-General Talbot in 1729, which judged otherwise: that persons brought to England from places where they had been slaves remained in that state of bondage, notwithstanding their baptism. When Yorke confirmed the opinion in 1749, it became the guiding rule by which owners seeking the recovery of their human property were usually upheld in their claims. Although there was now a new Lord Chancellor, the Chief Justice of the King's Bench, Lord Mansfield, before whom most of these cases were heard, was known to accept Yorke-Talbot. Sharp was advised that his fancy that Common Law could not accommodate slaveholding in England was merely sentimental.

This was the view not just of Sharp's lawyer, but of many others whose opinion he sought in 1767 and 1768, virtually all of whom wrote off his chances of successfully defending himself against the impending lawsuit for theft. But for all the weight of their authority, Sharp remained unconvinced. Neither God nor English antiquity (which for him amounted to much the same) could possibly permit such abomination in His Chosen Land. So he resolved to make himself his own authority on the legal history of slaves in Britain: "Thus forsaken by my professional defenders I was compelled through the want of a regular legal assistance to make a hopeless attempt at self-defence, though I was totally un-acquainted either with the practice of the law or the foundations of it, having never opened a law book (except the Bible) in my life until this time."[8] A page was turned, and for the lives of blacks in Britain and across the broad ocean nothing would be the same.

There had not been much to suggest that of the fourteen children of Archdeacon Thomas Sharp it would be Granville who would become famous as the apostle of freedom. True, he had been remarkable for his prodigious powers of concentration. As a child, he had sat in an apple tree to read the entirety of Shakespeare. But financial assistance from the family came in direct proportion to one's seniority in it. Even had Granville been brilliant (which he wasn't), the fact of his being born twelfth precluded much in the way of archdecanal help. After acquiring rudimentary learning at Durham Grammar School and a little more from a tutor, he had been apprenticed, at the age of fifteen, to a Quaker linen draper in London; then, after the Quaker's passing, to a Presbyterian and finally to a Roman Catholic, all in the same line of trade. This parade of sects passing before the young and insatiably curious Greeny gave him a compressed but valuable course in comparative theology, which he turned to good use when a Jewish fellow apprentice, seeing that Sharp had no Hebrew, was bold enough to ridicule his pretensions to biblical exegesis. Stung, Granville immediately set about mastering the ancient language, succeeding so well that he not only confounded his Jewish disputant but scored a knock-out by publishing, at sixteen, a (presumably short) essay demolishing the opinion of Rabbi Elias on the derivation and usage of the Hebrew consonant "Vav."

As his familiarity with the Talmud waxed, Sharp's interest in cambric and calico waned. After the death of his father in 1757, when Granville was twenty-two, his older brothers judged that the time had come to see if he had the makings of a merchant-manufacturer. A few months of unhappy incompetence gave them their answer: Granville was not destined to do for textiles what James was doing for ironwares. So the studded doors of the Ordnance Department in the Tower were opened to him, where, for six hours a day, during a time when Britain was fighting a war against the French on three continents, he could compile inventories and write and dispatch letters to junior officers regarding boot blacking and wig powder, even as his mind drifted to the doings of Hezekiah and the sayings of Habakkuk. In the evenings there were, as always, the family assemblies at Mincing Lane.

The Sharp establishment in Mincing Lane was a little academy, populated by music-lovers who happened also to be men and women of substance, learning and budding renown. So for all Granville's inexperience in the law, guidance on where to begin his researches would not have been missing. He was, himself, a natural antiquarian, in thrall not just to the chronicles of Omri and Bashan but, like many of his generation in Hanoverian England, to the Anglo-Saxon antiquarianism that was in romantic vogue. "Rule Britannia" had originally been written for *The Masque of Alfred*, performed in front of the Prince of Wales, and the cult of King Alfred as the fount of everything imperial and yet free had reached its eighteenth-century apogee. Granville Sharp believed that among other blessings brought to ancient England was the institution of Frankpledge, which, to his dying day he believed to be the most perfect, popular yet responsible form of government ever devised. Frankpledge was built on the primary unit of ten households, the "tithing," which then combined in a multiple of ten into a "hundred." Each tithing elected a tithingman, and ten tithingmen together chose a hundredor. That Sharp also believed Frankpledge to have been the form of government practised by the biblical Israelites (on the recommendation of Jethro, the father-in-law of Moses) and thus sanctioned directly by the Almighty did not, of course, do anything to compromise its appeal.

It was well known that Frankpledge and Anglo-Saxon liberty had been brutally damaged by the Norman Conquest, which had introduced alien forms of despotism and servitude into old free England. Yet its spirit, Sharp thought, had not been altogether extinguished; had lived on, indeed, in the immemorial revulsion against true slavery in the island kingdom. Villeinage—bonded labour in the fields—with the villeins denied the freedom to depart from the manor or even marry without the lord's consent, there had certainly been; although it was long extinct, as Sharp found. But even villeins had never been, so far as he could see from his plunge into the legal histories, negotiable chattels, transferable through sale. In 1547, in the reign of Edward VI, a law had been passed for the curbing of vagabondage, and this did provide for the enslavement of repeat offenders; but such was its alien character that it had been repealed two years later. In the reign of Elizabeth (in which, after all, the African slave trade had been promoted and aggressively practised by sea captains such as John Hawkins), Sharp nonetheless found what he wanted. In 1569, according to Rushworth's *Historical Collections*, a certain Captain Cartwright had brought a Russian serf-slave to England and, when he had "scourged" the slave without cause and been brought to book for it, had been told by the justice ruling on the case "that England was too pure an air for Slaves to breathe." The precedent conformed exactly to Sharp's own convictions about British freedom: that all subjects in the land, irrespective of rank, were equally subject to the king's laws and equally entitled to his protection.

What was more, notwithstanding Yorke-Talbot (which, Sharp discovered, had not been a ruling given on a court case at all, but merely an informal opinion voiced after dinner at Lincoln's Inn when the gentlemen were at their ease with pipes and wine), there was evidently an alternative legal history that did seem to assert the irreconcilability of slavery with the custom and practice of English Common Law. In 1679, during the reign of Charles II, for example, a law enacted for "the better securing of the Liberty of the Subject" had plainly stated that property in a black could only be upheld if proprietors could prove that the slave "is neither man, woman nor child." The reduction of a man to a beast, it was further said, was "unnatural and unjust." Faithful to that tradition, in 1706 Lord Chief Justice Holt had ruled that "as soon as a Negro comes into England he becomes free," and as recently as 1762 the Lord Chancellor Henley, had invoked (in Shanley versus Harvey) the Cartwright case in dismissing a claim to a negro as an item of property in a contested inheritance. As if to clinch matters, the most authoritative word on English Common Law, the *Commentaries* of William Blackstone, the Vinerian Professor at Oxford, published in 1765, stated quite cate-

gorically that "the spirit of liberty is so deeply implicated in our constitution and rooted even in our very soil that a slave or negro, the moment
he lands in England, falls under the protection of the laws and in regard
to all natural rights becomes *eo instanti* [from that moment] a freeman."

Sharp, then, had every reason to assume that Blackstone, both in
print and in person, could be recruited to what he was already calling
the Great Cause and wrote a personal letter seeking his support. To his
dismay, Blackstone was anything but supportive, deferring to Yorke-
Talbot's opinion. Granville Sharp, alas, had bought the first edition of
Blackstone's *Commentaries*, failing to notice that the second and third
editions altogether omitted anything that could be construed as jeopar-
dizing the rights of masters who happened to bring their slaves to England. In an elaborately courteous reply in 1769 Blackstone was careful
to insist (as he had in the later editions of his published work) that he
was not judging the propriety or even legitimacy of a master's right to
enslave; only that, if that right had been exercised in some other place,
it could not be set aside by the mere fact of both master and slave arriving in England. The long-term submission of the unfree, he said, was in
no qualitative sense different from the submission apprentices owed to
their masters and that was of course binding wherever their place of
residence.

This change of mind was especially discouraging to Sharp given the
fact that Blackstone was the protégé of the man who, as Chief Justice of
the King's Bench, represented the highest jurisdiction of Common Law:
William Murray, 1st Earl of Mansfield. Mansfield had been decisive in
procuring for Blackstone the Vinerian Chair at Oxford when it seemed
that the younger man would advance no further in the profession. Murray, born in Perthshire, but educated in the entirely English institutions
of Westminster School and Christ Church, Oxford, was the living embodiment of Scottish pragmatism. Harassed by the Scotophobic press as
a secret Jacobite sympathizer, he decided to prosecute its supporters
(including members of his own clan) with such unimpeachable ardour
that he was elevated, while a sitting Member of Parliament, first to
Solicitor-General, then, in short order, to Attorney-General. A dependable client of the parliamentary connection of the Duke of Newcastle,
"Silver-Tongue Murray," with his nimble wits and easy-going eloquence,

the close friend of Pope, Reynolds, Dr Johnson and his fellow Scot, James Boswell, was, in every sense that the word could convey, judicious. In the 1760s, which had begun with a fresh outbreak of Scotophobia when George III had made his favourite and tutor, the Marquis of Bute, first minister, Mansfield survived by an adroit combination of political pragmatism, social geniality and judicial intelligence. In court, typical of his affected nonchalance, Mansfield would interrupt laboured arguments with his own pithy summation of the essential issue at dispute and, having delivered the insight, continue to preside over the proceedings with his nose stuck in a gazette. Yet these antics aroused admiration rather than outrage. The full measure of his success was that it seemed to most people uncontroversial that it was a Scot who, as Lord Chief Justice of the King's Bench, was the high guardian of English Common Law.

The silver tongue was, then, at all times governed by a sensible wit. So what sense could it possibly make to alienate the rich and powerful sugar interest by determining, at the bidding of some well-meaning crank and double-flute virtuoso—no more than a clerk really—that the countless black body servants, footmen, porters, musicians and so forth were as other men and women in the kingdom? Did not Mansfield himself own a property in Virginia, where, doubtless, the negroes were treated with more tenderness than if left to their own devices in the brutish wilds of Africa? Why, the distress and ruin of acting upon sentiment was not to be thought of. There were, Mansfield had been told, as many as fifteen thousand bonded blacks in England alone, which would put the economic damage, should they be emancipated all at once, at some £700,000 to £800,000. And it was with these concerns weighing on his mind that Mansfield, in all likelihood, had prevailed upon William Blackstone to excise the embarrassing passages concerning the illegitimacy of slaveholding under Common Law from the later editions of his *Commentaries*.

And yet, as the Sharps would also have known, there was another Mansfield, father-protector to Dido Elizabeth Belle Lindsay, a black girl who lived as a member of his family in his elegant Robert Adam villa, Kenwood House, up on Hampstead Heath. Dido was the daughter of Mansfield's nephew, Captain John Lindsay. Her mother—whereabouts now unknown—had been taken by the captain, as was often the cus-

tom, as part of a Spanish prize. And while the captain was off somewhere building an empire for the Lords of the Admiralty, the Lord Chief
Justice and his wife, without children of their own, cared for Dido as
their own and made her companion to another of their nieces, Lady
Elizabeth Murray, whose father was ambassador to the emperor in Vi-
enna. The two girls, dark as coffee and blonde as wheat, grew up together at Kenwood amidst the Gainsboroughs and Dutch cabinet
pictures (for Silver Tongue had a shrewd and happy eye) as fast friends:
tending the dairy; gathering harebells in the meadow; picnicking by the
lake that Humphry Repton, famous for his Red Books, had built the
Chief Justice; and, sweetly bonneted and aproned, scattering grain for
his prize laying hens. The fashionable Johan Zoffany—who else?—was
commissioned to paint Dido and Elizabeth as a double portrait: the
dewy rosebud in pink watered silk, the dusky princess turbaned and
gowned in white satin with a rope of creamy pearls at her throat. A
muslin scarf gently winds them together, Elizabeth touching the thigh
and elbow of her black cousin who smiles and points a teasing little
finger at her own chin. Visitors, including the austere colonial governor
of Massachusetts, Thomas Hutchinson, were shocked to see the girls
arm in arm.

Was it possible, then, that such a benefactor should rule that a black
subject of the king was no person at all, but mere property, and so be
shut out for ever from his protection? That was what Granville Sharp
wondered to the point of consuming obsession, and was impatient to
test.

II

HARK! Ahoy there! Granville sings of the Thames and, by God, upon it!

> *Delightful Stream—that Life might pass*
> *Reflected from the Summer Glass*
> *Scenes of Innocence and Love.*
> *While sooth'd alike by many a Song*
> *Thy kindred Streams should glide along.*

The musical Sharps were afloat on their barge, the suitably named *Apollo*, capacious enough for a commodious cabin. On spring and summer nights, when the barge was moored at Fulham, James might spend the night there bobbing on the innocuous and scummy tide. Much exercised by the state of the water, Granville expended more of His Majesty's time in his office in the Tower penning some "Remarks on the Encroachments on the River Thames near Durham Yard."[1]

Zoffany painted the Sharp family concert and was criticized for being too fanciful with the number of people and instruments on the boat.[2] But the artist had been commissioned to paint an allegory of high-spirited family harmony, so he could be liberal about including members like an elder brother, Dr John Sharp, whose pastoral cares kept him in Northumbria. In most other respects, Zoffany got the crowded jubilation of the Sharps just right. One of Granville's preparatory memoranda includes the following to be taken on board: violins, kettle drums, horns, serpents for James, oboes for Granville, clarinets and a harpsi-chord, plus ample provisions of tea, bread, butter and honey, greatcoats for the inevitable showers, gear for the two big horses (all fringed hooves and heavy cruppers) who towed the *Apollo*, and, one supposes, a bone for Roma the dog, who seldom barked before Handel was done. The boat might even have accommodated William's small organ, known in the family from the time that their brother acquired her as "Miss Morgan."

Waterborne, the Sharps became still more celebrated—and more fashionable—than they had been for the concerts in Mincing Lane. After her husband died in 1767 Eliza, the harpsichordist, returned to London, and her diary records the Prince of Wales, along with his three brothers and their courtiers, standing for half an hour at the river's edge, listen-ing to the concert, requesting particular songs (and getting them played), and bowing graciously to the musicians at the concert's end. An appreciation for the Sharp chorale and ensemble may have been the only taste that the prince had in common with his father, since a few weeks later the family played for the king while he sat beneath an an-cient oak in the garden at Kew. The programme was based on the usual favourites, including Handel, a Concerto in G (of course) played by Granville on his double-flute with James oomping away on the serpent beside him. This was the kind of merriment to which George III easily warmed. In the midst of a song performed by "Signor Giordanio," the dark skies (for this was an English summer) opened, threatening to drench the monarch. In a trice the brothers and the bargeman pulled down the movable canvas awning that protected them from the ele-ments, jumped ashore and set it over the king's leafy but now inade-quate shelter. Decently, at the end of the music, before the Sharps could bow, their sovereign waved his own hat in salutation.

But there could be trouble in paradise. A few weeks later, in July 1770—while her son, the naturalist Joseph Banks, was in Queensland with Captain Cook, supping off giant clams and loin of kangaroo—Mrs William Banks of Turret House, Paradise Row, Chelsea, was woken by a frightful scream. Then there was cursing, slapping, the sounds of a brawl from the sloping, grassy embankment that led to the river's edge. She heard her own name called in heavily accented, frantic despair: "Mrs Banks, come help me for God's sake, they are going to trepan me and take me on board ship."[3] Concerned (but prudent), she sent her servants out to investigate: it was, as she had thought, the negro Thomas Lewis, whom three men were dragging on his back to the water's edge, two of them hauling the fellow by his legs.

Confronted, one of the three men waved a scrap of newspaper that they said advertised for the capture of the runaway, and swore they had the Lord Mayor's warrant for his detention. The servants had best clear off, they shouted, lest they fall foul of the law themselves. Intimidated, the servants shrank back but continued to watch as Lewis, struggling, was pushed down into the water and his hands and legs bound. Exhausted and half drowned, Lewis was finally thrown into the skiff, moaning piteously. So the men took some sticks and thrust them into the black's mouth and down his throat to gag him. They pushed off and rowed downstream into the darkness of the river, and when the boat passed Chelsea College and the Physic Garden nothing more was heard except the light dip and splash of the oars.

Given the details of the kidnapping, Mrs Banks lost no time in going to see Granville Sharp. By 1770 Sharp's reputation had gone far beyond the virtuosity of his double-fluting. In the three years since the Jonathan Strong case he had been transformed from an obscure clerk in the Ordnance Office to an eccentric but famously resolute warrior on behalf of slaves in England. In 1768, alerted by Strong to another case, he had helped bring a suit against the owners of a female slave who had shipped her back to the West Indies notwithstanding that she had married a free black. Invoking the unlawfulness of coercive transportation, Sharp and his lawyer managed to secure a judgment demanding the return, costs paid, of the woman.

The following year Sharp published the fruit of his exhaustive research into the status of slaves in England, *A Representation of the Injustice and dangerous Tendency of tolerating Slavery or even Admitting the Least Claim of private Property in the Persons of Men in England*. Even before the tract was printed, Sharp sent twenty manuscript copies to the great and mighty, including Blackstone and the Archbishop of Canterbury for their consideration, since he hoped to incorporate any criticisms they might have into the printed version. Whatever its effect on his correspondents, the circulation of the tract and the noise it made in London society caused the lawyers for Kerr and Lisle (still suing the Sharps for theft of their property) serious second thoughts about the wisdom of pressing their case. They procrastinated and then let the suit go. It added to the satisfaction of Strong's liberators that, by failing to bring the suit to trial, Lisle and Kerr incurred a penalty of triple costs.

By 1769 Sharp was driven by a burning sense of the vileness of the commerce in humans, calling it, as if it were too loathsome to be frankly uttered, the "Accursed Thing." In his letter to the Archbishop of Canterbury, Sharp urged him to campaign for the repeal of the brutal Plantation Laws, since they stained Britain and the British government with "the blackest guilt." (As the author of a study on divine retribution in the scriptures Sharp was convinced that, left untouched, something so abhorrent as the slave trade would some day bring down the full weight of God's wrath on the heads of the sinful British.) But his "little tract," as he called it with unconvincing modesty, was designed to avoid sweeping moral hyperbole and to appeal instead to the legal and historical fastidiousness of its intended readers, and to the unarguable record of case law. Yorke-Talbot, he insisted, had been superseded by Holt, and Justice Holt's determination that only a non-person could be deprived of the protection of the king's laws in England was itself rooted in immemorial custom. Repugnance for true slavery in England had swept away the draconian law of Edward VI; hence the Elizabethan dictum of air too pure for slaves had persisted. The notion that slaves could be held to have entered into a contract comparable to that applied to apprentices Sharp discounted as absurd. His message spoke, above all, of a kind of juridical patriotism, which Sharp did not have to affect an order to voice: he believed it with all his heart. English Common Law was the most precious of the nation's gifts. It was the rock of British freedom on which the "Accursed Thing" would surely be smashed.

Granville Sharp had become a tireless public nuisance. Nothing escaped his virtuous opportunism. When an advertisement offering a reward for news or recapture of a runaway "Poor wretched Negro boy" was posted in the *Daily Advertiser* by one "Mr Beckford in Pall Mall" he alerted William Beckford, the richest and most powerful of the City's aldermen and a power among the West Indian lobby, but also a figure much given to mouthing off radical views on the sanctity of liberty. "On a supposition that Mr Beckford in Pall Mall may be a relation of yours," Sharp informed William Beckford of this shameful notice, since "I believe you to be a sincere well-wisher to the true interests, constitution and liberties of this kingdom." He made so bold as to include his "little tract" in the hope that Beckford might now be prompted to "consider the subject" of slavery and the trade "more seriously than you have hitherto done."[4] He seemed to believe he could embarrass the powerful into goodness—a truly English strategy. To the Lord Chancellor, Lord Camden, he sent another advertisement, posted in the *Public Advertiser*: "To be sold, a Black Girl, the property of J.B—eleven years of age who is extremely handy, works at her needle, tolerably and speaks English perfectly well, is of an excellent temper and willing disposition—Inquire of Mr Owen at the Angel Inn, behind St Clement's Church, in the Strand."[5] Since the "frequency of such publications must tend very much to extinguish those benevolent and humane principles which ought to adorn a Christian nation . . . I am thoroughly persuaded that your Lordship will take such notice of this notorious breach of the laws of nature, humanity and equity, and also of the established law, custom and constitution of England as will be most consistent with that strict and unshaken regard for all these which has always been a distinguished part of your Lordship's character." Letters from a "Gentleman in Maryland" who saw plantation masters "flea" the backs of slaves "with Cow Hides or other Instruments of Barbarity" were copied and circulated to those on Sharp's growing list. His Maryland correspondent asserted that "they pour on Hot Rum superinduced with Brine or Pickle, rub'd in with a Corn Husk in the scorching heat of the sun," adding with the patriotic flourish that would become a commonplace in the British attack on American hypocrisy, "If I had a child I would rather see him the humblest scavenger in the Streets of London than the loftiest Tyrant in America with a thousand slaves at his Back." America and Americans were now classed as the tyrants.

So Mrs Banks evidently knew just what she was doing when, on the morning after the kidnapping of Thomas Lewis, she called on Granville Sharp at his lodgings in the City. As soon as he had heard her out, the two went together to Justice Welsh to obtain a warrant for Lewis's release. At Gravesend, where the mayor endorsed the warrant, Mrs Banks's servant attempted to serve it on the master of the ship carrying Lewis to Jamaica, the *Snow*, but he brusquely shook it off and got under way. Refusing to admit defeat, Sharp then did the rounds of magistrates and pestered the Lord Mayor until he got what could not be denied: a writ of Habeas Corpus. Since the *Snow* had been delayed at The Downs by contrary winds, the writ was taken to Spithead by Mrs Banks's servant Peter, riding hell for leather to the south coast. Rowed to the *Snow* from Spithead, Peter found Thomas Lewis "chained to the mainmast, bathed in tears and casting a last mournful look on the land of freedom which was fast receding from sight."[6] The writ was duly served on the captain, who "on receiving it became outrageous" and let fly some ripe nautical curses, "but knowing the serious consequences of resisting the law of the land, gave up the prisoner whom the officer carried, safe, but now crying for joy, to the shore."[7]

Back in London, Lewis related his history to Sharp. He had been born a free man on the Gold Coast in West Africa; had lived with his uncle after his father's death, before being approached by an English officer, who asked him if he would like to travel to learn the English language. Thomas had gone with the officer—only to discover that he was being shipped off to Santa Cruz, where English was definitely not the lingua franca. He then worked for a succession of masters, including Robert Stapylton, who took him to Boston and New York. But throughout his journeyings, whether working as body servant, waiter or hairdresser's assistant, Lewis received wages, and that fact alone argued for his never having been a chattel slave. Shipwrecked, Lewis was captured by a Spanish captain, who took him to Havana where by chance he saw Robert Stapylton again and appealed to him for rescue. Claiming Lewis as his property, Stapylton took him to Philadelphia and New York and eventually to England. But it was now clear that the price of that rescue in Havana was permanent bondage to Stapylton. Although Stapylton offered as evidence of his benevolence to Lewis the fact that he had got him admitted to St George's Hospital, a surgeon testified that he had been asked about Lewis's prospects so that, once recovered, he could be "taken away." Understanding the precariousness of his situation, and fearful of being sold and shipped to the Caribbean, Lewis escaped twice and was twice hunted down.

That second kidnapping had taken place on the night of the 2nd of July. Stapylton, who evidently knew just where to look for Lewis, had approached him, protesting he truly meant no harm. Since his master was by now old and blind, Lewis may have believed him. But it was precisely Stapylton's increasing infirmity that may have made the need for the money to be got from Lewis's sale all the more urgent. At any rate, the strategy for taking Lewis was elaborately planned. Claiming to be anxious about chests of tea and gin that he had stored at Chelsea College wharf so as not to attract the attention of customs officers, Stapylton asked Lewis to fetch them back—presumably with a consideration for himself. For the sake of discretion, he told Lewis, Richard Coleman, his waterman, would be taking him to the wharf by a circuitous route. (Coleman later testified that he had been approached by Stapylton to "carry the Black down.") Somewhere in a side alley between the Physic Garden and Paradise Row two other watermen, Aaron Armstrong and John Malony, had jumped Lewis, and the tell-tale scream carried to Turret House, Paradise Row.

Five days later, Lewis, Granville Sharp and Mrs Banks told their story to a Grand Jury in a private prosecution for assault against Stapylton, Armstrong and Malony. Sharp was worried that a Grand Jury would never return an indictment on behalf of an assault made on a black. But Thomas Lewis's chance for liberty had been the work of many *white* men and women: Mrs Banks; the servants who made sure that she knew exactly what had happened; Peter who rode first for Gravesend and then on to Spithead, following the *Snow*; and, not least of course, the self-appointed band for the negro cause, the Sharp family. Indeed, Mrs Banks and Granville Sharp continued to take a vigilant interest in the welfare of Thomas Lewis during the seven months between the indictment and the trial, an interest motivated as much by the necessity of hanging on to their prime witness as by concern for the safety of his person. When John Thomas, the black servant at whose house Mrs Banks had thought to lodge Lewis in safety, himself departed with his master to the colonies, she expressed to Sharp her fears that this might leave Lewis unprotected as well as unemployed. Evidently, they also fretted about how well Lewis and his case would stand up at trial, especially since he was apparently playing truant from the schoolmaster who had been assigned to his instruction and had become agitated at the prospect of appearing before the court. Their concerns became so serious that Mrs Banks and Sharp approached Stapylton, offering to drop the prosecution if he would make a public apology for the kidnapping and sign a solemn, notarized pledge for Lewis's safety and liberty.

But sensing his adversaries' pessimism about the outcome of the case, Stapylton not only declined the compromise, but insisted through his lawyers on going to trial before the King's Bench, where he must have calculated his best chance of acquittal lay.

So, on the 21st of February 1771, the case against Stapylton and the two watermen came before Lord Chief Justice Mansfield and, unusually for a judge who customarily chose to do without one, a jury. Perhaps it was the presence of a jury that had made the old captain suddenly more pessimistic about the outcome, since the day before the trial opened he tried to pre-empt it by leading a press-gang to seize Thomas Lewis as he was sitting in a nearby coffee-house, waiting to be summoned. This was not a well thought out scheme. Lewis's lawyer was close by, interrupted the seizure and threatened drastic consequences for all those involved.

Committed as he certainly was to the fate of Thomas Lewis, Sharp thought of the trial as the long-awaited judicial test of his "little tract." Its cardinal principle was that, under the Common Law of England, there could be no property in persons; and that all men, women and children, of whatever colour, were subject to the equal protection of the king's laws. The lawyer appearing for the prosecution, John Dunning, was exceptionally faithful to this brief, holding up Sharp's *Representation* in court while keeping his place in the book with a finger and quoting, over and over again, its central arguments.

Mansfield, however, refused to be drawn. The issue, he instructed the jury, was not, as Dunning had insisted, whether or not there could *ever* be property in persons in England, but merely whether Lewis, *in particular* could be proved, at the time of his abduction, to have been Stapylton's possession. The fact that the prosecution counsel chose to recite details of Lewis's own biography—his birth as a free man on the Gold Coast; his residence with his uncle after the death of his father; his signing up around 1762 as a servant with Stapylton, then a sea captain himself, and his travels with him in America—all reinforced the impression that the case was *ad hominem*, not philosophical, and that, whatever the outcome, it would not determine the more general issue of whether or not British freedom was ever compatible with the presence of slavery. "Perhaps," opined Mansfield, who had wanted the whole grievance to be settled by Mrs Banks buying Lewis his liberty and was now adopting the sententious manner of a schoolmaster adjudicating a fight between unruly boys, "it is much better it should never be finally discussed or settled . . . for I would have all masters think them [their slaves] free and all Negroes think they were slaves because then they would both behave better."

The jury found that Lewis could not be transported against his will, but they did so, at least according to the Lord Chief Justice, because no adequate bill of sale had been produced, not because they accepted Sharp's premise that slaves imported into England became, at once, free under the Common Law. But Stapylton and the watermen were found guilty and this, Mansfield assumed, should have been enough to satisfy Mrs Banks, Granville Sharp and Lewis himself. So he held back from prescribing any kind of penalty for the convicted men. But Sharp was convinced that the jury had meant to vindicate his treatise rather than simply find on a technicality, so he and Mrs Banks asked the court for a final judgment; instead, they received a rap on the knuckles for their temerity. The Lord Chief Justice confessed himself much surprised at being so pressed for a judgment; and for good measure let it be known that, on reflection, he rather regretted the jury's verdict, seeing that he now had second thoughts about some of the evidence presented by the prosecution. In so many words he told Mrs Banks that she had her free black man and should now desist before she wore out the goodwill of the magistracy.

For his part, Granville Sharp was as exasperated as Mansfield by the outcome of the Lewis case and in no mood to let the Lord Chief Justice off the hook. In his private notebook he commented, with much indignant underlining, that "the refusal of a proper judgment in this case is so far from being a proper precedent that it ought to be esteemed an open contempt of the legislature and a notorious breach and perversion of the laws." Setting Mansfield squarely in his sights for the next round of the dispute, Sharp wrote, "I am the more solicitous to protest against this precedent because I had the mortification to hear the same judge upon the same trial quote some precedents of his own making which are equally contradictory to the Spirit and meaning of the English Laws."[8] Did Mansfield still think Sharp a presumptuous nonentity who would be amusing were it not for his irritating parade of self-righteousness? Well, the Lord Chief Justice was not so impregnable in his power and authority as to be invulnerable to instruction when so truly in the wrong!

Thus it became personal, a judicial duel between the two men; absurdly unequal, Lord Mansfield must have thought, which is what made the outcome so surprising. At stake for Sharp was not just the fate of slaves, but that of English liberty. The word "liberty" was the battleground in the 1770s on both sides of the Atlantic, bandied around by Bostonians and Virginians asserting that their free-born English liberty had been put in chains by the ministerial tyranny reigning in London; by London radicals such as John Wilkes, prevented from taking his seat in Parliament by a conspiracy of oligarchs; and by Yorkshire radicals such as Christopher Wyvill berating "Old Corruption" and demanding reform. But for Sharp the matter was still bigger. He was acutely conscious that, as the descendant of an archbishop and before that of a dynasty of Yorkshire Puritans, he had inherited a religious obligation to defend English freedom as a legacy intended for all humanity. Scripture and history came together in this momentous self-appointment. Like one of the Old Testament prophets whose utterances he had worried over during the drowsy afternoons at the Ordnance Office, Sharp made himself the oracle of a new British Empire—one upright in word and deed, cleansed of the taint of the "Accursed Thing." Only thus reborn could such an empire escape the retribution that God had visited on all previous empires, from the Medes and the Persians to the Spanish and the Portuguese.

On the look-out for a case that would bring Lord Mansfield to the test, Sharp had very little time to wait before the perfect opportunity presented itself. On the 26th of November 1771, less than six months after Mansfield's irritable parade of "second thoughts" in the Lewis case, James Somerset, erstwhile slave of Charles Stewart, was kidnapped near Covent Garden, bundled off to the *Ann and Mary* bound for Jamaica and clapped in irons below deck.[9] He had been at liberty for less than two months and, unlike the situation with Thomas Lewis, there was no dispute over prior ownership and thus no pretext for the Lord Chief Justice to claim that such a case turned on *ad hominem* matters and not on the general principle. James Somerset had been bought by Stewart, then a customs officer, on arrival in Virginia as long ago as

1749, and had been in his service ever since. When Stewart had been moved north to Massachusetts as a paymaster Somerset had gone with him, and had been his body servant for twenty years when the two men arrived in London in 1769, just as Granville Sharp's *Representation* was being published. Ironically, Stewart went to live in Cheapside, a stone's throw from the Sharp brothers and, indeed, from many of the haunts of the London blacks among whom the news of the Strong and Lewis cases had freely circulated. Knowing that his master's stay in England was going to be only temporary, and that he might be sold, Somerset had evidently decided that escape was his only chance to avoid being shipped back to the Caribbean. If he were ever to be free, it was now or never. One day in September 1771 he disappeared.

Slavecatching in London was so common that kidnappers seldom bothered to conceal themselves from witnesses. Three people observed the taking of James Somerset, and one of them, Elizabeth Cade, seems to have taken the initiative (much as Mrs Banks had done with Lewis) in securing a writ of Habeas Corpus, which ended in the "body" of Somerset being produced for the magistrate on the 9th of December. But the person on whom it had been served had the right of "return to the writ," and Stewart, along with Captain Knowles of the *Ann and Mary*, took full advantage of his right to complain about the larceny of their property. By running away, James Somerset had robbed *them*. Mansfield's demeanour must have encouraged Knowles, who had to defend himself against the charge of illegal detention, and Stewart. For it was Somerset, not the captain and the slaveowner, who was strictly bound over, on pain of draconian penalties, should he abscond. Those who had organized the kidnapping, on the other hand, were not required to appear in person to answer the case and could indeed free themselves from prosecution at any time simply by relinquishing the claim to Somerset.

On hearing that Somerset, rather than Stewart and Knowles, had been made to feel the guilty party, Sharp became furious at the conduct of his antagonist, the smooth and smiling Mansfield. When Somerset was brought to see Sharp in his lodgings in Old Jewry on the 13th of January 1772, Sharp plunged into the affair, certain that this time, whatever Mansfield's sophistries, the matter of slavery's legality in England would finally come to the test in the court of the King's Bench. His first move was to lay out the six guineas needed to retain two counsel for James Somerset. That something tremendous was impending struck not only Granville Sharp and his family, but a much wider circle of the incensed, who had either followed the Lewis case in the press or heard about it on the winding grapevine that extended from Mrs Banks at Chelsea to her friends and fellow slavery-haters Dr Johnson, Reynolds and Garrick. For the first time in British history the individually indignant were coming together in a concerted campaign against the slave trade.

One of those freshly recruited to the negro cause was a young lawyer, Francis Hargrave, scarcely out of his student years at Lincoln's Inn, who on the 25th of January wrote to Sharp volunteering his services. He had, he said, already sent Mr Sharp some of his opinions on the matter of negro slavery during the Lewis affair and had not heard back from him, but since those opinions were less well considered than he should have wished, that was perhaps just as well. Should Mr Sharp still have them in his possession, he begged, he would be exceedingly obliged if he would now suppress them. Since that premature expression of his views he had undertaken careful research (for Hargrave's father was an antiquarian), and the abundance of evidence had made left him in no doubt whatsoever that slavery was indeed incompatible with the Common Law of England. He would be happy to air those opinions either informally or as counsel, although he was painfully aware that "never having argued anything publicly I distrust my abilities to acquit myself as such a cause requires." The next day Sharp replied warmly, accepting Hargrave's offer to assist Serjeant Davy, who had already been retained as principal counsel, and letting him know that in so doing he would be performing "a great act of private charity as well as public good." What cause could possibly be more important, since "I apprehend that the honour or degradation of human nature depends upon the present question."

Although Sharp had sent him a retainer, Hargrave declined any fee for his services—as did Somerset's other four lawyers. Appearing beneath Richard II's hammerbeam ceiling at Westminster Hall before Lord Mansfield and his three associate justices, and beside the two Serjeants-at-Law, William "Bull" Davy and John Glynn, was recompense enough, for such opportunities for instant glory seldom came the way of a novice lawyer who had yet to plead a case. Both the coiffed Serjeants (for the mark of their office was a peculiar and ancient headgear) were extravagant personalities, favourites with the press for their shameless play-acting in court. Bull Davy had failed as a druggist in Exeter before taking up the law, and had won lasting fame in 1754 as the (unsuccessful) defender of a gang of particularly ruthless highwaymen. John Glynn was the more conspicuously political of the two, an ostentatiously advanced radical; prominent member of the Society of the Bill of Rights; defender of John Wilkes and elected, along with his client and hero, to a seat in Parliament for Middlesex. Glynn was also such a hostile opponent of the government's policies in America that he was accused of virtually fomenting rebellion in the colonies. This formidable team was completed by another young unknown, John Alleyne, who proved every bit as impassioned a legal orator as Davy and Hargrave, and James Mansfield (later Sir James), another adviser to the maverick John Wilkes. He had been born James Manfield, but during his undergraduate years at King's College, Cambridge, had inserted the additional "s" in his name, whether in the hope of being confused with the august Lord Chief Justice or to do him mischief remains obscure.

As if all this were not already good enough for the newspapers, which, from the beginning of the hearings in February, if not before, exhibited a hungry relish for what promised to be a prime performance of judicial theatre, the principal counsel for Stewart and Knowles turned out to be none other than John Dunning, who had so adamantly insisted on the illegality of slavery just a year before in the Lewis case! Dismayed by Dunning's betrayal, Sharp took it as further evidence of the "abominable and insufferable practice in Lawyers to undertake causes diametrically opposite to their own declared opinions of law and common justice."[10] Although, mystifyingly, Sharp attended none of the sessions in person, the balefulness of his displeasure at Dunning's treachery seemed to cast a shadow on the normally quick-witted and assertive young lawyer, whose pleading for the violated property rights of Charles Stewart was at best half-hearted. "I hope I shall not suffer in the opinion of those whose honest passions are fired at the name of slavery," he pleaded, over-optimistically, towards the end of the case. Facing a public audience in Westminster Hall in which friends to the negro were so obviously in the majority, Dunning seemed constantly on the defensive as if cowering from brickbats. "It is my misfortune," he lamented rather pathetically, "to address an audience much the greater part of which, I apprehend, wish to find me in the wrong." Deeply disappointed with his lawyer's transparent lack of conviction, Stewart wrote to a friend in Boston noting that, while the other side "flourished away on the side of liberty" and "gained much honour," his own counsel was "dull and languid" and, he thought (correctly), would have far preferred to have been appearing for the other side.

None of this play of personalities escaped the press, or for that matter coffee-house gossip, both in London and in provincial cities such as Liverpool and Bristol, where the West Indian sugar interest and the slave trade were strongly established. The newspapers usually refrained from direct commentary while a case was *sub judice*, but none of the most important papers—not the *London Chronicle*, the *General Evening Post*, the *Gazetteer*, nor polemical weeklies like the *Craftsman*—were willing to miss this golden opportunity.[11] From the first session in early February to Mansfield's final judgment on the 22nd of June, their pages were open not just to reports of the speeches made in court but also to letters and articles commenting on the state of slavery in both England and the Americas, and on the evils or necessities of the slave trade. Letters on the bestial treatment of field slaves in America were published from correspondents there, as were impassioned denunciations of any prejudices that might treat British subjects differently according to the colour of their skin, and strenuous attempts to defend slavery on the grounds that, compared to the brutal world of the African forest warrior, the plantations of the Caribbean and the American South were an idyll. These were the opening salvoes in what was to be a debate that would continue in Britain at least until the abolition of the entire institution of slavery some fifty years later.

Although not in court himself, no one worked harder than Granville Sharp to stoke the fires of abhorrence. Such was his newly won fame, both as crusader and as musical virtuoso, that he exploited the connections made through his music to lecture the great on behalf of his cause. The prime minister, Lord North, for example, who used the *Apollo* for musical entertainments, was the recipient in mid-February 1772, of a startlingly prosecutorial letter threatening him with celestial retribution should he fail in his duties to do something about the iniquitous trade: "*To be in power* and to neglect (as life is very uncertain) even a day in endeavouring to put a stop to such monstrous injustice and abandoned wickedness, must necessarily endanger a man's *eternal* welfare, be he ever so great in *temporal* dignity or office." To hammer the point home Sharp took the liberty of enclosing his own book, with "two or three pages" to which he especially wished to draw Lord North's attention conveniently indicated with paper flags "because I cannot suppose your Lordship will be able to find leisure for the whole." However busy Lord North might have been attempting to forestall the separation of the American colonies from British allegiance, Sharp still thought that if he marked the passages in red ink the statesman must be horrified by the laws of Barbados that prescribed a fine of fifteen shillings as the penalty for a master who "wantonly or bloody-mindedly" killed his own slave. This surely, he added somewhat gratuitously "was the most consummate form of wickedness of which a legislature was ever guilty."[12]

Sharp was equally tireless in supplying Somerset's lawyers with all that they could possibly need for the trial. To Serjeant Davy he sent not only the massive results of his own researches into medieval villeinage, and Common Law's case history on slavery, but also (probably acquired through his brother James, since the item came directly from the ironmonger who made them for the colonies) an example of the iron bit used to prevent slaves from eating cane when labouring in the fields, and another contraption designed for the opposite effect—to force open the jaws of slaves who refused to take food. Heated, the monstrosities could be used to scald the gums and mouth as a punishment; and sometimes, Sharp said, they were used to prevent the most despondent or "sulky" slaves from committing suicide by pathetically cramming their mouths with dirt.

From the outset of the proceedings, however, it seemed that Serjeant Davy needed none of these kinds of incentives to ensure that the case would turn on the plain matter of slavery's lawfulness in England, rather than the niceties by which Mansfield was constantly trying to duck the main issue. (True to form, Mansfield had suggested to Elizabeth Cade, one of the witnesses to Somerset's kidnapping, that all the unpleasantness might be resolved by her purchasing his liberty. To her credit, the widow sent the Lord Chief Justice away with a flea in his ear, saying that to do so "would be an acknowledgement that the plaintiff had a right to assault and imprison a poor innocent man in this kingdom and that she would never be guilty of setting so bad an example.") Before he embarked on a lengthy and learned trail through the history of villeinage and case law regarding slavery, Davy made it abundantly clear that counsel for Somerset would maintain that "no man can be a slave, being once in England, the very air he breathed made him a free man [and] that he has a right to be governed by the laws of the land" on exactly the same basis as any other man. When the case of the Russian slave was judged in Queen Elizabeth's time, "it was resolved that England was too pure an air for Slaves to breathe in." And then Davy added, perhaps with an ear to all the radical complaints levelled at "Old Corruption" with whom Mansfield was altogether too friendly, "I hope, My Lord, the Air does not blow worse since." Now what of it, if slavery may be acknowledged in lands unluckier than England? What, indeed, if slavery was legitimate under the laws of Barbados or the colonies of America where "a New Species of Tyranny" had been created "entirely by Colony government"? (This was the first of many jabs suggesting that if critics were looking for a despotism to attack, they had better look for it on the western side of the Atlantic rather than the eastern.) Why should such laws, made by bodies other than Parliament, have any more "influence, power or authority in *this* country than the laws of Japan"?[13]

Three hours later (fellow-Serjeant Glynn, a notorious sufferer from gout, was mercifully briefer), Mansfield allowed himself a heavily judicial sigh and observed that since "this thing seems, by the arguments probable to go to a great length . . . let it stand over to the next [legal] term." But if Mansfield imagined that in the three intervening months passions might subside, he was mistaken. On the 7th of May his alter ego, James Mansfield, gave possibly the most shamelessly theatrical speech in the entire trial, in which he adopted the persona of James Somerset himself: "It is true. I was a slave, kept as a slave in Africa. I was first put in chains on board a British ship and carried from Africa to America . . . never from the first moment of my life to the present time, have I been in a country where I had a power to assert the common rights of mankind. I am now in a country where the laws of liberty are known and regarded and can you tell me the reason why I am not to be protected by those laws, but to be carried away again to be sold?" No one could. The negro Somerset was a man, was he not? Well, then, it was impossible that he could ever be a slave in England unless through the introduction of some sort of new property law yet unknown to the national constitution.

A week later it was the turn of the junior team, Francis Hargrave and John Alleyne, and they too showed no embarrassment about beating the patriotic drum. Whilst less histrionic than James Mansfield, Hargrave was shrewd enough to play to public patriotic sentiment about the singularity of English Common Law as the bedrock of liberty. Whatever villeinage might or might not have been, it had little in common with modern slavery, which demanded perpetual, unconditional and coerced labour, a bond dissolvable only at the owner's will; which carried with it absolute power of arbitrary punishment, which was unbreakably hereditary and which made a human a negotiable thing. Warming to his lecture, Hargrave added a little sermon about the damage done to masters by the practice of slavery: the corruption of their morals; their endangerment from a state of permanent hatred on the part of the slaves; and the insidiousness by which slavery made an entire society degenerate, dispensed as it was from the nourishing incentives of industry and ingenious enterprise. Slavery was, in short, alien to everything that England and Britain was. Allowing foreign laws, whether Virginian, Turk, Polish or Russian, to be enforceable in England was tantamount to introducing a new species of "domestic slavery" in the very bosom of the land of liberty. Whatever was the case in ancient empires, absolute monarchies or, indeed, American colonies to this day, "it is contrary to the genius of the English law to allow any enforcement of agreements or contracts by any other compulsion than that of our courts of justice." "The laws of England," Hargrave declared, making his (successful, as it turned out) bid for the acclaim of his profession, "confers the gift of liberty entire and unencumbered; not in name-only but really and substantially."

In a breathtaking reversal of rhetorical expectations, Alleyne added that the task now was to preserve the English law from foreign, that is to say American, contamination. "Ought we not . . . to guard and reserve that liberty by which we are distinguished by all the earth! . . . The horrid cruelties, scarce credible in recital perpetuated in America, might by allowance of slaves amongst us, be introduced here." Unless Britain in effect declared in this year, 1772, judicial independence from America, it would all be over and Middlesex would turn into barbaric, tyrannical Virginia! "Could your Lordship . . . endure in the fields bordering on this city, to see a wretch bound for some trivial offence to a tree, torn and agonizing beneath the scourge . . . ?" No wonder Benjamin Franklin, who saw the proceedings from the throng in Westminster Hall, was first bemused, then unamused, then scandalized.

As if helping a lame defence over a stile, Lord Mansfield at this juncture began to wonder out loud about the social and economic consequences were every enslaved black in Britain to suppose he had got his freedom along with Somerset. Dunning gratefully took this line of anxiety even further by painting an alarmist picture of chaos in the colonies, in which, drawn by the prospect of British freedom, "they will flock over in vast numbers [and] overrun this country and desolate the plantations." Dunning's motive in sounding an alarm bell was entirely tactical. How could he know that just three years later, in the midst of the American war, his prophecy would prove at least partially accurate?

Concluding for Somerset, Davy was at his most bullish. Drawing a devastating line through case histories that (unlike Yorke-Talbot) had found slavery inadmissible in Common Law, Lord Mansfield interrupted, commenting: "If what you say is true then I had better burn all my law books." "My Lord," Davy coolly replied, "had better read them first."[14]

YET ANOTHER MONTH WENT BY. A sullen pause for the moment prevailed in America, during which Patriots in Boston, such as Sam Adams, denounced the insidious dumping of cheap East India tea, while attempting to collect a paltry excise, as: SLAVERY!

In his chambers Lord Mansfield, hard pressed to come to judgement at last on what his personal picador, Granville Sharp, called the Cause, shifted and fidgeted for ways to avoid it, more fearful of the damage he might inflict than of the justice he might mete out. He tried again to persuade various parties to buy Somerset's liberty. Failing, he grasped at the straw that young Hargrave had given him (so very apt, these

novices, and yet so charmingly passionate; he had been bound to commend them). Hargrave had said that even were slavery to be upheld as
some sort of fact in England, it would still be wholly inconsistent with
the right usages and custom of the law for any such person, be he slave
or no when he came into the country, to be plainly forced against his
will out of it to some other place, and out of the land of liberty. So might
he, the Lord Chief Justice, then rule against such a particular transportation without presuming to judge the matter at large?

On Monday the 22nd of June 1772, at 11 o'clock in the morning, all
of London and beyond seemed to have come to Westminster Hall, spilling from the coffee-houses and taverns, the law courts and mercantile
establishments, the shops and exhibition rooms, coming by carriage and
sedan chair and horse and foot, from the trim new squares to the west
and the clattering City streets to the east. Since 1740, the interior of the
ancient Gothic chamber had been divided by an elaborate wooden
screen. On one side were the two courtrooms of the King's Bench and
Chancery; on the other, a vast public space, a field of stone where people
stood, sat, perused the shops at the walls and, when judgement was to
be given, halted and listened. Among that crowd this day were black
faces who greeted Mansfield and Justices Ashton, Willes and Ashurst as
the four long wigs passed through the screen and into King's Bench,
carefully ascending the low steps where once the judges of Charles I had
hectored the deposed king, and took their high-backed seats. Silver-
Tongue appeared, for the moment, tongue-tied, uncharacteristically
leaden, his habitual affability oppressed by the burdensome expectations of history. More than ever the hall seemed not merely a court of
law, his court of law, but as it had been centuries before, the true *curia
regis*, the court of the king and the kingdom. England glowered in a
summer chill, and for once the Lord Chief Justice wore his famous
learning moodily.[15]

But, in the dim and stony silence he proceeded, his Perthshire lilt
lost to many as it floated through the wooden screen and out into the
dusty vastness, where at first it competed with the hubbub of people
browsing the pen and wig stalls that lined the hall's perimeter. But then
it became understood that judgement was to be given and there was a
hush. Mansfield resumed. It was not, he said, as some, indeed many,
might suppose, some great and general issue that was to be judged, but

merely whether or not there was sufficient cause for the "return"—Captain Knowles's reply to the writ of Habeas Corpus charging that he and Mr Stewart, not the negro, had been the victims of an unlawful act. If there were cause, then, the negro must be detained; if not, not; it was as plain as that. Unease rippled through the hall. For some time the Lord Chief Justice made his way through not just this case but others concerning similar escapes and detentions, and became warm when affirming, somewhat improbably given all that had been said against it, that Yorke and Talbot had stated that neither the fact of a slave coming into England, much less his or her baptism, could be held to set the rights of masters at naught. And yet (the public heard this shift), while slavery had been and was many things in "different ages and states . . . the exercise of the power of a master over his slave must be supported by the Laws of particular Countries; but no foreigner can in England claim such a right over a man; such a claim is not known to the laws of England . . . the power claimed never was in use here or acknowledged by the Law . . . no Master ever was allowed here to take a Slave by force to be sold abroad because he had deserted from his service or for any other Reason whatever, we cannot say the Cause set forth by this Return is allowed or approved of by the Laws of this Kingdom; therefore"—the Lord Chief Justice made sure not to pause—"the Man must be discharged."[16]

He rose, and so did Justices Ashton, Willes and Ashurst. But, before they disappeared through the low door at the side of the hall opening on to the robing room, something happened that stirred even the jaded sentiments of the port-and-pipe hacks there in force from the *Gazette*s, *Chronicle*s and *Post*s (*Morning* and *Evening*) and the *Daily Advertiser*. As Mansfield and his colleagues emerged through the screen, the group of blacks in the public space "bowed with profound respect to the Judges." Then they shook hands vigorously with each other, congratulating themselves "upon their recovery of the rights of human nature, and their happy lot that permitted them to breathe the free air of England." "No sight upon earth," wrote the reporter for the *Morning Chronicle*, "could be more pleasingly affecting to the feeling mind than the joy which shone at that instant in these poor men's sable countenances."[17]

It was a scene that, perversely, Granville Sharp himself missed. But later that morning there was a knock at his door in Old Jewry, where his new life had so abruptly begun seven years earlier. "James Somerset came to tell me," he wrote, almost laconically, in his journal, "that judgment was to-day given in his favour," and then, as if writing the history of some quite other notable person, "Thus ended G. Sharp's long contest with Lord Mansfield, on the 22nd June, 1772."[18]

Perhaps Sharp ought to have been present in person at Westminster Hall, for then he might not have declared victory prematurely. For although it is quite true that, in the interests of a clear-cut moral and legal drama, the press and public opinion in London had all taken the freeing of Somerset to vindicate Serjeant Davy's axiom that "as soon as any slave sets his foot on English ground he becomes free," that was not, in fact, what Mansfield had said; indeed, he had inflicted contortions on himself to avoid saying it. What he had said was that the power of a master to *transport* his slave against his will, out of England and to a place where he might be sold, had never been known or recognized under Common Law. And that, indeed, was the ground on which Somerset had been liberated.

But aside from the exceptionally attentive, neither party—neither the West Indian sugar interest, which now launched a furious lobby for legislation to recognize their property rights when in England, nor the elated crusaders for negro freedom—took the measure of Mansfield's fastidiousness. Both sides did, in fact, think he *had* made slavery illegal in England. Many owners continued, nonetheless, to act as if the Somerset judgment had never happened. Auctions and sales were advertised and held, not just in London but in the provincial centres of colonial trade. Runaways were still hunted down. In May 1773 a newspaper reported the case of "a black, servant to Capt. Ordington, who a few days ago ran away from his master and got himself christened with the intent to marry his fellow-servant, a white woman; being taken and sent on board the captain's ship in the Thames, took an opportunity of shooting himself in the head." The twenty-four-year-old Thomas Day, future moralizing novelist and utopian educator, currently (and ephemerally) a law student, saw the story, grieved and, together with his friend John Bicknell, was moved to write a poem entitled "The Dying Negro," in effect a long suicide note in verse:

> Arm'd with thy sad last gift—the pow'r to die,
> Thy shafts, stern fortune, now I can defy . . .

Better in th'untimely grave to rot
The world and all its cruelties forgot
Than, dragg'd once more beyond the Western main,
To groan beneath some dastard planter's chain.

What Day and Bicknell undoubtedly lacked in poetic talent they more than made up for with a flair for high-strung sentimental melodrama of the kind that struck directly at the post-Somerset generation's hearts. "The Dying Negro" tracked the African back to the place of his original abduction, then to the horrors endured by plantation slaves who "Rouz'd by the lash, go forth their chearless way." Borrowing heavily from *Othello*, Day then has the negro woo and win the love of the white servant girl ("Still, as I told the story of my woes / With heaving sighs thy lovely bosom rose") only to move the story to its tragic denouement. Deceived in his hope that baptism would save him, the negro angrily confronts the God who abandoned him while seemingly preserving his captors, and before killing himself curses the slave-ship, prays for its wreck and asks that "while they spread their sinking arms to thee / then let their fainting hearts remember me!"

Published in 1773, Bicknell and Day's poem was an immediate popular sensation. Its second edition, printed in 1774, added an essay that harangued American hypocrisy—notwithstanding the fact that Day thought of himself, as did Sharp, as the friend of America against the coercion of Lord North's government. "Such is the inconsistency of mankind," Day exclaimed, that "the men whose clamours for liberty and independence are heard across the Atlantic Ocean" yet insist on owning slaves. There was at least one young American on whom the message was not lost: John Laurens, the son of a South Carolina businessman, rice planter and future president of the Continental Congress, Henry Laurens. Sent to London to study law at the Middle Temple, John had been placed in the Chancery Lane chambers of Charles Bicknell, younger brother of the co-author of "The Dying Negro." Charles the lawyer may have been "the merest machine, the most barren in Conversation and the least calculated to improve of any Man I was connected with," but John Bicknell was another story.[19] The story young Laurens heard was that of Granville Sharp's crusade. It changed his life, and five years later it almost changed America.

Few Americans were so receptive to being sermonized, even (or especially) when they were declared friends to the negro. Benjamin Franklin, for one, in London during the Somerset trial, thought the British, not the Americans, were the hypocrites for indulging themselves so heavily in an orgy of self-congratulation on their "virtue, love of liberty and equity in setting free a single negro"[20] while remaining deaf to the pleas of colonies such as Pennsylvania that were petitioning the government for an end to the importation of slaves. And the Quaker Anthony Benezet, whose letter congratulating Granville Sharp on his efforts arrived on the very morning of the Somerset judgment, hoped rather for a union of British and American friends of the negro, rather than a common cause soured by mutual recrimination. In fact Sharp would become so agonized by the British decision to wage war in America that he would resign his post at the Ordnance Office.

But beyond the finger-pointing, beyond the mutual accusations of greater or lesser hypocrisy, beyond Lord Mansfield's obstinately tortured efforts to duck the great issue, the liberation of James Somerset had done something startling to the society of the free and the enslaved that stretched across the Atlantic. It had made the idea of British freedom a germ of hope. On the evening of the 22nd of June 1772, blacks in London had no doubt at all that there was reason to celebrate, and they did so at a "frolick" for some two hundred people at a London tavern. And Charles Stewart, Somerset's erstwhile owner, received confirmation—if he needed it—of the effect of Mansfield's ruling when he heard from one of his remaining slaves that "he had rec'd a letter from his Uncle Sommerset acquainting him that Lord Mansfield had given them their freedom & he was determined to leave me as soon as I had returned from London which he did without even speaking to me. I don't find he has gone off with anything of mine. Only carried off all his own cloths which I don't know that he had any right so to do. I believe that I shall not give myself any trouble to look after the ungrateful villain."[21]

There would be a lot of ungrateful departures in the years ahead.

III

I.T STOPPED RAINING in Charleston just long enough for the freshly hanged black man to be properly burned.[1] It was the 18th of August 1775, and Thomas Jeremiah, fisherman, pilot, man of property, had been tried just a week earlier, accused of being the very worst thing imaginable in South Carolina: a fomenter of negro rebellion. Still more diabolical, Patriots believed, he had planned this infamy with the British. For there was nothing to which the royal government would not stoop—not even the liberation of slaves—to prevent revolution in the South.

Desperate to shore up the crumbling power of the Crown and Parliament, but with precious few soldiers to do it (for General Gage in beleaguered Boston could spare none), the royal governors of the Southern colonies had resolved, so it was said in places such as Charleston's Corner Club, to play the savage card. Secret caches of arms were to be off-loaded from British ships and delivered to Indians and blacks. Once the slaves had slaughtered their masters and burned their houses, they would be rewarded with their liberty. This nightmare is what Thomas Jefferson meant in the Declaration of Independence when referring, otherwise cryptically, to the king having "excited domestic insurrections." In the world of the slaveholders, nothing demonstrated so well the transformation of royal paternalism into brute despotism as this plot to arm the slaves; there could be no more self-evident cause for revolutionary separation.

SOUTH CAROLINA, CHARLES TOWN DISTRICT.

Before Me, Mr John Coram, One of His Majesty's Justices of the Peace, for the said District, Personally came and appeared Jemmy, a Negro Man Slave the property of Mr Peter Croft, who upon His Solemn Declaration saith, that about ten weeks since being in Charlestown at Mr Preolias Wharf, one Thomas Jeremiah, a Free Negro who declared That He had something to give Dewar, a run away Slave belonging to Mr Tweed and wished to see them and asked Jemmy to take a few guns to the said Dewar, to be placed in Negroes hands to fight against the inhabitants of this Province, and that He, Jeremiah was to have the Chief Command of the said Negroes; that He Jeremiah said He believed He had Powder enough already, but that He wanted more Arms which he would try to get as many as He could

Declared before me on this

16 June 1775, JOHN CORAM[2]

And this was not all.

Sambo says that about 2 or 3 months ago being at Simmons Wharf, Jerry [Thomas Jeremiah] says to Him Sambo do you hear any thing of the War that is coming, Sambo answered No, Jerry's reply's yes there is a great War coming soon—Sambo replies what shall we poor Negroes do in Schooner—Jerry says set the schooner on fire, jump on Shore and Join the Soldiers—that the War was come to help the Poor Negroes.[3]

Not everyone was convinced that "Jerry" was guilty; certainly not the last royal governor of South Carolina, Lord William Campbell, himself the target of every kind of insinuation, but helpless to exercise authority or to resist unfounded rumours. Arriving at Charleston in June 1775 aboard HM sloop *Scorpion*, Lord William found that he had been preceded by a letter sent by Arthur Lee, the American agent in London, to Henry Laurens (about to preside over the Provincial Congress in South Carolina) insisting that the British government had decided to raise the Indians and slaves against the Patriots. Aboard the *Scorpion*, Lee maintained, were fourteen thousand stands of arms for that nefarious purpose. Although the fourteen thousand guns were a myth, Lee's letter provoked wrath in Charleston. "Words," wrote Campbell to the Secretary of State for the Colonies, the 2nd Earl of Dartmouth, "cannot express the flame that this occasion'd amongst all ranks and degrees; the cruelty and savage barbarity of the scheme was the conversation of all companies & no-one dared venture to contradict intelligence conveyed from such respectable authority."[4]

Mere suspicions, Campbell believed, would never be enough to "impress the minds of the people with the worst opinion of His Majesty's Ministers," namely that the said ministers had become a foe so pitiless as to have no scruple about unleashing African murder on them. Evidence of a plot was needed to demonize British power, and so it was that the unfortunate Thomas Jeremiah had become a victim of "the accursed politicks of this Country." By the time the governor moved into his residence at 34 Meeting Street on the 18th of June for what would be an exceptionally brief and unhappy tenure, Jeremiah was already incarcerated in the city workhouse while his prosecutors were busying themselves finding evidence against him.

Lord William, a scion of the Argyll Campbell clan, which had ruled the western Highlands and Islands of Scotland in the Protestant interest for generations, was convinced there was no truth to the allegations against Jeremiah. He was no stranger to the rice plantation country along the Ashley and Cooper rivers. During the Seven Years' War of 1756–63, Charleston had been his home port while commanding HMS *Nightingale* against the French. And he had got on well enough with the slaveowning planters to marry one of their daughters, Sarah Izard, at the end of the war in 1763; they had gone back together to Britain, where Campbell had served, like innumerable Campbells before him, as Member of Parliament for Argyll. From old Scotia he had gone to Nova Scotia as its governor, where he prided himself on his honourable disinterest. But his Scottish pedigree—like that of John Murray, 4th Earl of Dunmore, the last royal governor of Virginia—only helped confirm Anglo-American Scotophobes such as Jefferson in their conviction that Caledonians were just another species of mercenary. (In December 1775 Jefferson referred to the presence of the "Scotch" along with other "foreign mercenaries" in one of his lists of crimes committed by the Crown and its ministers.) Sarah Campbell, however, had found Halifax too wintry, and it was on her account that her husband, with unfortunate timing, manoeuvred to return to South Carolina.

Although the crisis in America was hardly a secret in England, Campbell, like so many other Britons, might have imagined that it was, essentially, a New England affair. He reckoned he knew the Carolinans, and they were staunch. But of course he did not. By the time he arrived in Charleston, executive power in the city and the province had fallen into the hands of a thirteen-member Council of Safety, dominated by militant Patriots such as William Henry Drayton. Like its counterpart in Virginia, the Council and the Provincial Congress interpreted the bloodshed with which hostilities had commenced at Lexington and Concord in April 1775 to mean that the Crown meant to resolve its differences with the American colonies by military coercion (as indeed it did), and that a quasi-war was already under way. So the Congress and Council authorized the levying of taxes to pay for the raising of a militia before troops could arrive and make unholy alliance with blacks and Indians. Like all the Southern governors in the spring and summer of 1775, Lord William Campbell felt himself in an unenviable and ultimately untenable position. With virtually no troops available to enforce the will of the Crown, he was forced to depend on His Majesty's ships, such as the sloop of war *Tamar* anchored beyond Charleston harbour and unable for the moment to sail over the bar.

Which is why the case of Thomas Jeremiah had caused such agitation. For "Jerry" was a pilot, perhaps the best and certainly the most independent, in Charleston. Jerry was also a free black—indeed, one who owned seven slaves himself, not to mention property worth close to £1000; a king's ransom, one might say. Henry Laurens, by no means the most rabid negrophobe in the town, disliked him intensely and described him to his son John, then in London, as "puffed up by prosperity, ruined by Luxury and debauchery and grown to an amazing pitch of vanity and ambition; a silly coxcomb withal."[5] To Governor Campbell it seemed as though Thomas Jeremiah's real crime was social temerity. When he had got into a fight with a white captain he had been put in the stocks, a serious ordeal in a place like Charleston, where delivering salutory correction to an uppity nigger would qualify as civic duty. In the circumstances Jerry was just a disaster in the offing. He had been conspicuous in helping to put out Charleston's many fires; why then should he not, when time and occasion presented itself, set them? And since it was known that he had expressed willingness to pilot the *Tamar* over the bar (in fact the royal authorities had made it plain that pilots had no choice in the matter), Jerry was evidently a mortal threat to the Congress and the Council of Safety and everything they represented.

That Jeremiah's accusers had no real case against him, Campbell believed, was plain from their haste to try him under the terms of the Negro Act, introduced in the reign of George II, by which slaves accused of inciting or participating in rebellion were tried by a bench of three to five freeholders as well as three judges, rather than by royal justices alone. As a free black, Jeremiah should have been tried as such, and, as someone accused of speech rather than deed, should have been liable to lesser penalties. This important procedural difference had been ignored because, as one of the judges who heard the case admitted, "it might be of the most fatal consequence to the lives and properties of the white inhabitants if these fellows once got it into their heads that free Negroes were not punishable under this [Negro] Act for such an enormous crime."[6]

Nor was the governor at all convinced by the witnesses against Jeremiah. They too had been victims of a terror, generated when black house servants had heard their masters speak at table of insurrectionary plots by slaves. Out of fear of being incriminated themselves, they had been over-ready to point the finger at others. The slave Jemmy was just one such poor fellow who had been indicted as co-conspirator and, so Campbell thought, been made to believe that his only chance of escaping the noose was to incriminate Jeremiah, which he had duly done. But he had later recanted his testimony, insisting after all that Jeremiah was innocent. Then there was the account given to the governor by a Reverend Smith of a prison meeting with Jeremiah. Expecting a confession, the clergyman (as did another man of the cloth) said that he had heard the opposite; that the prisoner continued to protest his innocence, and that "his behaviour was modest, his conversation sensible to a degree that astonish'd them and that at the same time he was perfectly resigned to his unhappy, his undeserved fate. He declared he wished not for life, he was in a happy frame of mind and prepared for death."

As the day of execution approached, the governor became daily more distraught about Jeremiah's fate and his own powerlessness to save him from the gallows. Rather pathetically, he made a last-minute appeal to Laurens to intervene. "Surely, Sir, I may appeal to your feelings for me as the Representative of Majesty in this unhappy Province, Think, Sir of the weight of Blood, I am told I cannot attempt to save this Man without bringing greater Guilt on this Country than I can bear even to think of."[7] To Lord Dartmouth he confessed even greater distress: "I leave your Lordship to conceive the poignancy of my agony . . . I was almost distracted and wished to have been able to fly to the remotest corner of the earth from a set of Barbarians [the gentlemen of the Council of Safety] who are worse than the most cruel Savages any history has described."[8]

But alas, there was nothing to be done. Street gangs in Charleston were busy intimidating anyone whom they suspected of lukewarm feeling, let alone outright opposition, to the Patriots. A gunner from Fort Johnston overheard abusing the American cause was swiftly tarred and feathered and dragged to the governor's door. Should he dare to issue a pardon to Jeremiah, "that Monster the Mob which now governs Charles Town," wrote the Attorney-General, would "erect a Gallows by his Lordship's Door and oblige him to hang the Man himself." To conclude this heartrending story, Campbell wrote, "the man was murder'd, I can call it nothing else, he asserted his innocence to the last, behav'd with the greatest intrepidity as well as decency and told his implacable Persecutors God's Judgement would one day over take them for shedding his innocent blood."

In the letter to Dartmouth Campbell predicted "that things are hastening to that extremity which will in all probability oblige me to withdraw from Charles Town, to avoid fresh indignities." It was the Thomas Jeremiah case that had made him most painfully aware of his vulnerability, and bitterly incredulous that the government at home seemed unwilling to send troops to make its authority felt in South Carolina. A month after Jeremiah's execution the Council of Safety had taken control of Fort Johnston, where the British had neglected to spike the guns. Perhaps getting wind of the militant Patriot William Henry Drayton's proposal to take the governor hostage, since it was thought that he might rally the South Carolina backcountry loyalists, Campbell made a break for it and took refuge along with his wife and infant son on the

Tamar. It was still raining: sultry downpours peppered the green harbour water like grapeshot.

Henry Laurens gave Campbell credit for the sincerity of his doubts about Jeremiah's guilt. But he had none himself. The second slave, "Sambo," had not withdrawn his testimony, and it was odd that Jeremiah should profess not to have known his accuser, Jemmy, when the man turned out to be his brother-in-law. Guilty or not, there is no doubt that Lord William was too quick, or too naive, to dismiss any possibility that the British government would countenance anything so incendiary as an armed slave rebellion. In fact, for several months the governors of Virginia and North Carolina, Lord Dunmore and Josiah Martin, along with General Thomas Gage in Massachusetts, and in full consultation with Lord North's government in London, had been considering exactly such a strategy. For all concerned, except the blacks, it was a desperate response to desperate circumstances. In a shockingly brief period, during the spring and summer of 1775, British military confidence had turned into startled pessimism.

The Massachusetts fights at Lexington and Concord in April had triggered mass recruitment to the provincial militias and transformed debates within the provincial assemblies and congresses. The second Continental Congress meeting in Philadelphia, which began in May, remained torn between outright independence and using resistance to effect dignified reconciliation. In an effort to forestall a radical Patriot victory, a last good-faith effort at compromise was made by Lord North's government graciously "forbearing" to tax the colonies on condition that they agreed to share the costs of common defence. But, aside from raising hackles by simultaneously forbidding the colonists to engage in any trade outside the British Empire, the "conciliatory" measure failed to grant what the assemblies most wanted: an acknowledgement of their exclusive *right* to levy their own taxes and duties. And the government refused to yield on that point because a majority in Parliament—including some of the staunchest friends of America, such as the Earl of Chatham—still insisted that the right to tax, along with the power to regulate imperial trade, belonged in the end with themselves.

Inevitably, then, the more radical wing in Congress prevailed to the extent that a Continental army was mustered, and in June 1775 George

Washington was appointed to its command in Cambridge, Massachusetts. Some eleven thousand British and Hessian regulars were now effectively besieged in Boston by twenty thousand American troops. In July, any thought that the rebel soldiers would be no match for the redcoats disappeared in the slog and carnage of Bunker Hill. With the bulk of its army pinned down on Massachusetts Bay, and more troops needed to defend Quebec and Lower Canada against incursions, how was Britain to contain or deter rebellion in the South? In Richmond, Virginia (if his first biographer is to be believed), Patrick Henry had delivered the famous speech in which he insisted that, whatever his less aggressively minded compatriots might imagine, a war had, in fact, already begun. In the circumstances, British generals, such as Gage, and governors, such as Dunmore in Virginia, Josiah Martin in North Carolina and Sir James Wright in Georgia, were bound to exploit whatever small advantage might be gained from raising a black army.

Even so, it was not the British, as the Patriots assumed, who had put ideas of insurrection into the heads of the slaves of the American South; they were there already. "Uncle Sommerset" and his British freedom were, as the runaway advertisements appearing in the *Virginia Gazette* made clear, well known through the tidewater country from Maryland to the Carolinas and in the interior too. News so electrifying spread fast, widely and irreversibly. John Adams, writing in his diary while staying in South Carolina later that year, learned that "the negroes have a wonderful art of communicating intelligence among themselves; it will run several hundreds of miles in a week or fortnight."[9] There seemed no question but that the slaves, more of whom were escaping from plantations with every month that passed, were in a state of heightened expectation. In late 1774 James Madison had reported that, in anticipation of the liberty that would be brought by the British, some negroes had secretly met and chosen a captain who would lead them to the safety of the king's army and to freedom.[10] In Charleston, according to William Henry Drayton, the slaves "entertained ideas that the present contest was for obliging us to give them liberty" and the rumoured arrival of arms with Lord William Campbell had "occasioned impertinent behaviour in many of them."[11]

In late April 1775 the governor of Virginia, Lord Dunmore, had barrels of gunpowder taken from the Williamsburg "Powder Horn" to the safety of HMS *Fowey* off Yorktown lest they should fall into the hands of forces ill disposed to maintaining the British connection. As a result, a group of blacks came to his house and asked for arms with which they would fight for the Crown in return for their liberty. For the moment Dunmore, who owned slaves himself, affected horror and aversion at the very idea, ordered the blacks to "go about their business" and warned them of "his severest resentment should they presume to renew their application."[12] But news of Lexington and Concord changed Dunmore's mind fast. His own position at Williamsburg was not much better than Campbell's in Charleston, protected as he was by a mere handful of troops. He would, he wrote to Dartmouth, in early May, arm all his own negroes "and receive others that will come to me whom I shall declare free."[13] At the very least, he calculated, the threat to liberate slaves would give the rebels pause in their headlong rush to arms, and at the worst, if they could not or would not be stopped, it would supply him with a black army that might hold the fort until regulars arrived.

The strategy backfired, as it did throughout the South. Instead of being cowed by the threat of a British armed liberation of the blacks, the slaveholding population mobilized to resist. Innumerable whites, especially in the habitually loyal backcountry of Virginia, had been hitherto sceptical of following the more hot-headed of their Patriot leaders. But the news that British troops would liberate their blacks, then give them weapons and their blessing to use them on their masters, persuaded many into thinking that perhaps the militant Patriots were right and that the British government, in tearing up the "bonds" of civil society (as Washington had put it), might be capable of any iniquity. It is not too much, then, to say that in the summer and autumn of 1775 the revolution in the South crystallized around this one immense, terrifying issue. However intoxicating the heady rhetoric of "rights" and "liberty" emanating from Patriot orators and journalists, for the majority of farmers, merchants and townsmen in Virginia, the Carolinas and Georgia (the vast majority of whom owned between one and five negroes), all-out war and separation now turned from an ideological flourish to a social necessity. Theirs was a revolution, first and foremost, mobilized to protect slavery. Edward Rutledge, one of the leading South Carolina Patriots, was right when he described the British strategy of arming freed slaves as tending "more effectually to work an eternal separation between Great Britain and the colonies than any other expedient which could possibly have been thought of ."[14]

By the summer and early autumn of 1775 a full-scale panic about the imminence of a black rising, armed and sustained by the British, was under way from tidewater Virginia to Georgia. In July, Cape Fear in North Carolina lived up to its name. Sixty percent of the population on the Cape and up the Cape Fear River were slaves, but since many worked in the marine trades as sawyers, millwrights, tar-burners, carters and stevedores they enjoyed more freedom than field hands, congregated on the docks and sometimes even lodged in Wilmington. The local Committee of Safety, panicking at the rate of "elopements" from plantations, ordered street patrols to disarm and arrest any blacks found with weapons, or any who met in suspicious gatherings. After the British commander at Fort Johnston at the mouth of the Cape Fear River had started not only to encourage runaways but to promise protection to them, the rate of flight into the woods became nearly uncontrollable. Worse, word spread among the terrified whites of Wilmington and Cape Fear that "every Negro that would murder his Master and family . . . should [by British fiat] have his Master's plantation."[15]

One of those Wilmington blacks who was on the verge of taking the British up on what he thought was the chance of freedom was Thomas Peters, a millwright and slave belonging to another Scottish William Campbell—this time, however, very much a Patriot and a member of the local branch of the radical Sons of Liberty. Like Patrick Henry's slave Ralph and George Washington's Henry, Peters could hardly have missed his own master's opinionated table thumping and might just have taken offence at the presumption that airing such views could have no possible effect on dumb human chattels. But Peters was not dumb; very far from it. Like many who would shake off their chains and go to the British, he had a family: a wife, Sally (not that his master recognized the legality of slave marriage), and a daughter, Clairy. Even if he was not fully literate, Peters certainly understood the ambiguities of the principles that the white revolutionaries supposed him incapable of comprehending. And he would, when the time was right, act on them.

But that time was not quite come. In the first week of July a plot was uncovered in which, on the 8th of the month, slaves were "to fall on and destroy the family where they had lived, then to proceed from House to

House (burning as they went) until they arrived at the Back Country where they were to be received with open arms by a Number of Persons there appointed and armed by Government for their Protection and as a further reward they were to be settled in a free government of their own."[16] Forty blacks implicated in the aborted rising were arrested, one killed and the rest subjected to brutal floggings and ear croppings before crowds in Wilmington. Peters, and many like him, decided to wait.

But no sooner had one rising been stamped on than another was discovered. Later that same month another conspiracy to "take the country by killing the whites" was said to have been hatched in St Bartholomew's parish, near Charleston, More startling was the fact that this rebellion seemed to have been encouraged and blessed by black preachers, two of whom were women. Ecstatic secret religious assemblies had gathered in the woods, where devotees were told of a mysterious book, given to "the Old King" who was commanded to "Alter the World." The old king had disregarded the book and had paid the price by descending straight to hell. But now there was a new young king, George III, who had hearkened to the Gospel "and was about to alter the World and set the Negroes Free."[17] More unnerving was the fact that the leaders of this ordained exodus were almost all slaves belonging to conspicuous Patriots, such as Francis Smith. It was Smith's slave, George, who was hanged as the prime suspect.

Up and down the Atlantic tidewater, from Chesapeake Bay to the estuaries of the Potomac and the Rappahannock and down to the sea islands of Georgia, word had spread that a godly deliverance was about to be brought by the soldiers of the king. Gleanings of those rumours, together with a sudden but unmistakable acceleration in the rate of runaways, was enough to put fury and trepidation in equal measure into the hearts of the masters. Patrols were mounted on roads and waterways. Slave cabins were searched without notice, and gatherings of more than four negroes outside of work hours deemed a criminal conspiracy. On the 24th of September 1775 John Adams met two rattled planters from Georgia who "gave a melancholy account of the State of Georgia and South Carolina. They say if one thousand regular troops should land in Georgia, and their commander be provided with arms and clothes enough and proclaim freedom to all the negroes who would join his camp, twenty thousand negroes would join it from the two Provinces in a fortnight."[18] Later in the year Washington, who had already heard from Virginia friends and neighbours of their evaporating labour force, was just as apprehensive about the potential threat posed by a combined force of liberated blacks and redcoats. "If that man is not crushed before spring," he wrote of Dunmore, "he will become the most formidable enemy America has; his strength will increase as a snowball by rolling; and faster, if some expedient cannot be hit upon, to convince the slaves and servants [for white indentured servants had gone missing from Washington's own estate at Mount Vernon as well] of the impotency of his designs."[19]

This was the most richly undeserved backhanded compliment that John Murray, 4th Earl Dunmore, ever received. For although he was vilified, almost apocalyptically, in the Patriot press and in Congress as "our devil Dunmore," a Machiavel in wig and plaid, he was in reality no more than the standard issue Scots-Hanoverian imperialist, handicapped by a rigid sense of duty, a political tin ear and, as events would show, a fatally imperfect grasp of military tactics. And whilst Dunmore was ready to exploit Southern white nightmares of being engulfed by the much greater numbers of blacks, he was certainly no social revolutionary. Whatever damage would be done to the property of wicked rebels would be repaired and restored after the war, Dunmore supposed, along with their right allegiance. There was never any question in his mind, after all, of freeing the slaves of *loyalists*.

Dunmore was in his late thirties when he took up residence in the Governor's House at Williamsburg in 1772: just another Scottish minor aristocrat, anxious (like William Murray, Lord Mansfield) to dispel the faint suspicion of Jacobitism that still vaguely tainted the family name, notwithstanding the fact that there were as many ferociously Hanoverian Murrays as there were obstinate followers of the Stuarts. Dunmore was, then, even in the tam-o'-shanter and clan plaid in which he chose to be painted, the personification of British union, the most loyal servant imaginable of George III and his ministers. But he had arrived in America at an intemperate time. By 1774 the punishment meted out to Boston in the wake of the Tea Party, especially the closing of its port, was regarded, even by those who deplored the destruction of property, as so vindictive that it inspired, especially in Virginia, an outpouring of sympathy and a determination to link the colonies in common cause. The proposal to establish a Committee of Correspondence to co-ordinate protests against the "Intolerable Acts" inflicted on Boston provoked Dunmore into dissolving the Virginia assembly, the House of Burgesses. He repeated this dissolution when the House voted for a day of fasting and prayer on the 7th of June 1774 in solidarity with Boston. Shut out of their assembly, the delegates merely repaired to the Raleigh Tavern, where they proceeded to beat the drums of fraternal indignation and plan the colony's participation in a boycott of British goods.

Two hitherto fairly distinct political and social cultures—the patrician clans of the tidewater tobacco plantations, the Carters, Byrds and Lees, and the more independently minded and politically assertive farmer-gentry of the Piedmont hills, such as Jefferson, Patrick Henry, George Mason and James Madison—were coming together in resistance to the clumsy intimidation of the British Crown. The Piedmonters had been particularly displeased by what they took to be Dunmore's feeble prosecution and abrupt termination of a backcountry war against the Shawnee tribe; another egregious instance, they supposed of the Crown's suffocating determination to confine their territorial expansion.

On the 20th of April 1775, just two days after Lexington and Concord, Dunmore succeeded where General Gage in Boston had failed. But the coup achieved by his pre-emptive seizure of munitions at Williamsburg was short-lived, triggering a furious counter-reaction not just there but throughout Virginia. Much of the rage that Dunmore's action provoked was coloured by anxieties about the kind of people—not to mention their race—likely to get their hands on the powder. Nor did that fear go away when Dunmore agreed to pay some £350 for the gunpowder, thus providing the Virginians with money for its replacement while saving some face.

On the 8th of June, acutely conscious that he could call on just three hundred or so loyalist volunteers, soldiers and sailors, Dunmore followed his powder kegs to the safety of HMS *Fowey* and proceeded to stall any business sent to him by the House of Burgesses unless it was presented in person on the ship. In response, the House declared His Lordship to have abdicated executive authority; this was reinvested (as in Charleston) in a Committee of Safety, which then proceeded to levy taxes and arm a militia. It was, indeed—as Patrick Henry, ever the self-fulfilling, as well as the self-appointed, prophet, pronounced it—already a war.

Dunmore lost no time before waging it. From his floating head-quarters aboard the *Fowey* he sent out raiding parties in tenders and cutters, small vessels normally used to ferry provisions to the warships. Along the Rappahannock, Piankatank and Elizabeth rivers, and on the eastern shore farms owned by Patriots, especially those absent and serving in the militia, were burned and their livestock and slaves seized. But the tenders also picked up scores of blacks who, it is clear from the increasingly distressed letters sent by planters and from runaway advertisements in the *Virginia Gazette*, were already making their way, in a small but steady and growing stream, to wherever they thought the Union Jack or the White Ensign might fly.

Over the next year, and despite all the setbacks suffered by the British cause in Virginia, the slaves of the Chesapeake and tidewater Virginia came in droves. Sometimes they came from much further off: Cato Winslow, for instance, made it all the way from New York to join Dunmore's regiment.[20] Sometimes they came en masse: eighty-seven alone arrived from John Willoughby's plantation in Norfolk County, comprising its entire labour force. The escapees included Abby Brown (then twenty-three), William Patrick, Zilpah Cevils, just eight, and her sister Hannah, three. The long odyssey of Mary Perth, then thirty-six, who would reach New York and certified freedom, who would survive the snows and poverty of Nova Scotia and end up as the dowager queen of river trade in Sierra Leone, began with her flight in late 1775 from Willoughby's plantation to the waiting ships of the Earl of Dunmore.[21] Most often the escaped slaves travelled by night in small groups of four or eight—family or friends, mothers and children—lying in the flat-bottomed, two-masted boats known as *piragua* or, in the corrupt tidewater English, as "pettiaugers" or "pettingers," which were used to navigate the tidal creeks and rushy inlets. Lying low in the water, they were perfect for concealment, and the slaves of the southern Chesapeake and Potomac, who for years had fished there and carried provisions to and from the plantations, knew exactly how to navigate them through the tributary basin. It was particularly painful for plantation owners who had entrusted these kinds of men—not only river pilots and ferrymen, but the most skilled of their hands, sawyers and coopers, carters and smiths—with a degree of generous freedom only to be "re-paid" with their stealing off with the boats. Colonel Landon Carter of Sabine Hall was especially indignant that no fewer than eleven of his best slaves—his son's personal slave, Moses, as well as Postillion, "Mul-latto," Panticove, Joe, Billy, John, Peter, Tom, Manuel and Lancaster Sam—had all run off to Lord Dunmore, taking his son's gun, bullets and powder in the newly trimmed pettiauger. To add insult to injury, they had also taken silver buckles, shorts, waistcoats and breeches.[22] Others, such as James Jackson, who escaped from Robert Tucker's plantation in Norfolk, may not have taken boats, but used their knowledge of the riv-ers to find a way to Dunmore's ships, and readily served the British as pilots on raids and expeditions through the waterways.[23]

Not all the Virginian escapees of 1775 and 1776 were adult males and "stout negroes," of course. Hannah Jackson was thirty-two when she left the plantation of Thomas Newton with her little boy, Bob, then just five. Chloe Walker, property of James MacKay Walker, was twenty-three when she departed together with her six-year-old son Samuel and a bundled-up baby, Lydia. Sukey Smith and Hannah Blair were both only eighteen when they left, respectively, Major Smith at Gloucester and Jacob Hancock on the East Shore. Patty Mosely was a mere girl of eleven when she too disappeared from Edward Mosely's plantation in Princess Ann County. Brothers and sisters sometimes made their escape together: Samuel and Mary Tomkin, for instance, left Richard Tomkin at Little York. And some, too, managed the journey to British safety de-spite literally crippling handicaps. Moses Wilkinson, who would be preacher and prophet to the flock of black loyalists in three countries, was twenty-nine when he ceased, through his own hobbling exodus, to be the property of Miles Wilkinson of Nansemond—despite the fact that he was both blind and lame.

At least eight hundred male slaves of serving age reached Dunmore in the second half of 1775 and early 1776. But even that conservative figure takes no account of the many women and children who went with their men, so the total figure of escapees to the British is likely to be at least two or three times that number. The historian Allan Kulikoff gives an estimate of three thousand to five thousand *adult* blacks for the entire period of the war, a figure that again needs multiplying for a hypothetical total.[24] If, as seems to be the case, Jefferson's figure of thirty thousand Virginian escaped slaves is dependable for the duration of the war, the number finding their way to the British is best seen as a resolute but extremely significant minority. Tens of thousands of the remainder must simply have taken advantage of the chaos and low-intensity warfare to disappear into the swampland.

So, without exactly seeking the part, John Murray, this pink-cheeked time-server who had never thought himself much of a soldier, and who alternately fumbled and blustered his way through a sorry, unwinnable predicament, had become the patriarch of a great black exodus. He was now and for ever "Lord Dunmore," no longer just an obliging and forgettable nonentity on the benches of the upper house of Parliament, but, depending on your skin colour and your politics, either the Belial of the foulest and most iniquitous scheme ever unleashed on defenceless Americans, or the revered saviour of the suffering and the enslaved. Wags and hacks in Charleston and Williamsburg, themselves wandering between derision and paranoia, composed satirical verses vilifying him and the "speckled regiment" whose general he had stooped to be. Politicians in Philadelphia, pontificating about the dawning of an American future, fixed on him as the epitome of swaggering despotism and tigerish cruelty who would get his come-uppance from the battalions of the free. A man who would unleash the Africk hordes on so many decent Patriots could only be a perverted, inhuman monster! And all the while blacks in the tidewater, or on the rice rivers of South Carolina, or in the upland Piedmont of Virginia, when they knew a belly was swelling with the future thought they might (and in some cases did) name the child "Dunmore."

But Dunmore was not the man they imagined. He was, sad to report, a bit of a trembler:

LORD DUNMORE TO THE EARL OF DARTMOUTH,
6TH DECEMBER 1775

I have often prayed to be instructed . . . for many months past, but not one line have I had the honour of receiving from your lordship since yours of the 30th of May. God only knows what I have suffered since my first embarking from my anxiety of mind, not knowing how to act in innumerable instances that occur every day, being one moment diffident of my own judgement (and not having one living soul to advise with) and then on the other hand fearing, if I remained a tame spectator and permitted the rebels to proceed without interruption, that they would by persuasion, threats and every other art in their power, delude many of His Majesty's well-disposed subjects to their party.[25]

To be fair, there was much to tremble about. Even with his new black recruits (for whom clothes and weapons had to be found), and 134 soldiers shipped in from St Augustine in eastern Florida, Dunmore's force was only in the hundreds, whereas, the Virginia "shirtmen" militia numbered, by October 1775, between two thousand and three thousand. The British fleet had itself grown with the addition of two more sloops, the *Otter* and the *Mercury*, and a ship, the *William*, to which Dunmore transferred his command. But the raiding tenders regularly put out in the Hampton Roads were coming under increasing fire when they got anywhere near villages and towns. On the 27th of October a raid on Hampton had badly misfired when shirtmen militia, emerging from their sniping positions in houses facing the creek, had rushed a pilot boat, killed two sailors from the *Otter* and taken seven prisoner—losses the British could ill afford.

Watching the odds against him mount, still hearing nothing from London and with scant hope of any further reinforcements, Dunmore arrived at a moment of truth. From the deck of the *William* on the 7th of November he issued, in the name of the king, and "to defeat such treasonable purposes and that all such Traitors and their Abettors might be brought to justice and that the Peace and Good Order of this Colony may again be restored, which the ordinary Course of the Civil Law is unable to effect," a famous proclamation. It was, for good or ill, the deed for which he has ever since been remembered:

By His Excellency the Right Honourable
JOHN EARL OF DUNMORE,
His Majesty's Lieutenant and Governor General of the Colony and Dominion of virginia and Vice Admiral of the same
A PROCLAMATION

Martial law was declared. And for the swift restoration of good order

> I do require every Person capable of bearing Arms to resort to His Majesty's standard or be looked upon as Traitors to his Majesty's Crown and Government and therefore be liable to the Penalty the Law inflicts upon such offences, such as forfeiture of life, confiscation of lands &c &c. And I do hereby further declare all indented Servants, Negroes or others (appertaining to Rebels) free that are able and willing to bear Arms, they joining His Majesty's Troops as soon as may be, for the more speedily reducing this Colony to a proper sense of their Duty to His Majesty's Crown and Dignity.[26]

There was the word, there in black and white, for black and white: "free" was now proclaimed, published, indelible. This was the word that no American in any authority or office had ever dared print. Never mind the exigency of the occasion; never mind the unworthiness of the utterer or the transparent opportunism of his motives; no free or slave Patriot militiamen (currently being weeded out from the Continental army) could match what Dunmore had done. And the shock it gave the American side can be measured in the sudden furious venting of their hatred: Dunmore was anathematized as "arch traitor to humanity." For the blacks, though, the prophecy of the sacred book was true. The young king did indeed mean to alter the world.

Hundreds now, not scores, made their way towards the British ships. A thirty-foot boat, captured near Surry, came down the James River packed with blacks. Seven broke out of jail in Northampton and took a pettiauger off towards the fleet. "Numbers of Negroes and Cowardly Scoundrels flock to his Standard," wrote John Page, a rattled member of the Virginia Committee of Safety, to Jefferson.[27] In anticipation of ships and troops arriving up and down the coast, slaves began disappearing from plantations in the Carolinas and Georgia, even in Maryland and New York. This was the moment when the leaders of the revolution, in Charleston, Williamsburg, Wilmington and Philadelphia, saw their own blacks take off from the plantations of the Rutledges, the Middletons and the Harrisons, the moment when Henry Washington deserted General George for King George. A Pennsylvania forge-owner from Berkshire County, Mark Bird, who advertised for the capture of his runaway slave Cuffe Dix ("a most excellent hammerman"), put in his notice what was general knowledge: "As Negroes in general think that Lord Dunmore is contending for their liberty it is not improbable that said Negroe is on his march to join his Lordship's own black regiment, but it is to be hoped he will be prevented by some honest Whig from effecting it."[28]

Put on the defensive, fearful that their world might go the way of Dutch Surinam where a slave army was still unvanquished, painfully conscious of the drainage of manpower to the militias, the plantocracy of the South did everything in its power to counteract the Dunmore effect. Stories appeared in the press (to be read to servants) that Dunmore's offer of freedom was a ruse to entrap slaves who would then be sold in the West Indies for his personal benefit. It was pointed out that the vaunted liberty was, in any case, only for adult males who could bear arms, the implication (untrue) being that families would be divided, with women and children left behind in servitude, perhaps to bear the brunt of the wrath of masters. How could Lord Dunmore pose as the Emancipator, when all the world knew he had slaves himself (true) and that they were treated most cruelly (untrue)? The tobacco planter Robert Carter assembled his slaves at Nomini Hall to read them a list of these solemn warnings, and for the moment they heeded his advice. But in 1781, when the British returned in force, no fewer than thirty-two of those slaves ran off.[29]

In case, despite all these intelligences, poor black wretches who knew no better were still tempted to succumb to the earl's blandishments, the Virginia Convention solemnly warned them against taking up arms. There would be a grace period of ten days for runaways to lay down their weapons and return to their masters. Should they persist, they should know that the penalty for rebellion was death without benefit of clergy. Those who were caught escaping (but as yet not in arms) were to be treated differently, depending on whether they belonged to Patriots or loyalists. The former would be imprisoned and then returned for their masters to do with them what they wished; Tory slaves, on the other hand, would be sent to forced labour in lead mines in Fincastle County in the interior or in the saltpetre works in Montgomery County.

Many were caught. A group of nine slaves, including two women, were taken from an open boat out at sea, by a Virginian maritime patrol. Another pair of escapees celebrated prematurely on sighting what they thought was a British ship before realizing it was American, and paid with their lives on the yard-arm for their mistake. But others did everything they could to outrun the patrols that had now been placed on virtually every major river and creek around the British base of operations. In Northampton County, thirteen escaped slaves lay in wait and took a schooner, and sailed it into the bay before being overtaken by a Patriot whaleboat.

Whatever the deterrents, however many were taken in the attempt, blacks continued to go to Dunmore, as both the newspapers and private correspondents bitterly complained. Indeed, they arrived much faster than Dunmore and the captains of the *Otter* (Matthew Squire, with runaway slave pilot Joseph Harris) and the *Mercury* could accommodate them, much less clothe, feed and arm them. But, together with the regulars from Florida, there were enough for Dunmore, in the weeks after his proclamation, to flirt with a small-scale offensive near Norfolk. When he learned that militiamen from North Carolina were on their way to join the Virginians, time not being on his side, Dunmore felt that he needed to act swiftly. The reinforcements could be stopped at Great Bridge, about twenty miles south of Norfolk, where the long bridge itself spanned the southern arm of the Elizabeth River. On either side of the bridge were fetid swamps buzzing with mosquitoes and biting flies. At each end of the bridge drier ground—in effect islets—connected to the land proper by narrow causeways.

Some ten miles south of the bridge, at a place known as Kemp's Landing, a camp of about 300 Virginian shirtmen had been established with the intention of marching on Tory Norfolk. On a night in November, a company of 109 British troops—soldiers from the 14th Light Foot, loyalist volunteers from Norfolk and, not least, around two companies of freshly armed and drilled black soldiers (almost half the entire force)—attacked Kemp's Landing. For a while it seemed to be going the usual way, the Lexington and Concord way, with the British infantrymen advancing in parade ground formation and stepping over their casualties while being shot at laterally from the woods. But the volunteer loyalists, both black and white, had been sent to outflank the snipers from the rear, and once they had opened fire, the Virginia militia broke and fled into the forest. Five of them were killed and eighteen taken prisoner. Two of these prisoners were officers, and they were taken, probably with extreme satisfaction, by black loyalist soldiers. It was a first.[30] But in this campaign it would also turn out to be a last.

For the moment Dunmore, if not exactly elated, was restored to confidence, especially as the strongly loyalist population of Norfolk had been encouraged by the show of force at Kemp's Landing to declare itself. Three thousand of its inhabitants swore to uphold their allegiance to the king and forswear the rebels. The governor-commander and vice-admiral now thought of forming a Queen's Own Loyal Virginia Regiment from its volunteers. And there was, of course, another group for whom the successful skirmish at Kemp's Landing meant everything. The armed blacks, now numbering more than three hundred, were formed into what (with a touch of exoticism) their chief called Lord Dunmore's Ethiopian Regiment. On their coats was emblazoned the simple but, to their enemy, devilish device: "liberty to slaves." The emotions of those who sported the badge can only be imagined. Apart from the Ethiopians, many more blacks in Dunmore's little force acted as foragers, guides and pilots, spies, diggers and carters. Hundreds of them worked on throwing up, at the northern end of the bridge, in front of Norfolk, "Fort Murray," an improvised structure built from planks, logs and dirt; known to the Patriots as "the hog pen," and defensible only against musket shot, it was still a bastion for the badly outnumbered British army. For a few weeks at least, Fort Murray flew the flag and ex-slaves manned the stockade. Whatever the strength or opportunism of Dunmore's convictions, and however this had come about, a bond had been forged between the British and the liberated blacks.

The triumph of the slaves over the masters was cruelly brief. On the 9th of December, an action that was supposed to consolidate Dunmore's position in Virginia and preclude the colony being supplied with either provisions or reinforcements from North Carolina went horribly awry. At the outset Fort Murray still stood, but precariously. At least eight hundred fresh American troops of the 2nd Virginia Regiment and the Culpeper militia were besieging it. Raft attacks were launched daily. Inside his headquarters at Norfolk, Dunmore brooded unhappily over the imminent and inevitable arrival of American artillery that would either flatten the fort or force a passage over the bridge, cutting the fort off from supply by either land or sea. His only defence, he thought (against the advice of his senior officer, Captain Samuel Leslie), was a pre-emptive attack. The Virginians and Carolinans had established themselves at the end of the southern causeway behind daunting breastworks. Dunmore's strategy was to send two companies of black troops around its flank along the edge of the islet, drawing the American riflemen from the breastworks so that when regular troops, including Grenadiers, attacked from the front its defences would be fatally compromised. Dunmore also believed the intelligence of a spy masquerading as a loyalist, who informed him that the Patriot stronghold was manned by a mere three hundred men.

Everything that could go wrong did. The black companies sent as decoy were mysteriously dispatched, not to the perimeter flank of the Patriot position, but to an altogether different area that had been probed by an American patrol the previous night. None of the American defenders (a much larger force than Dunmore supposed) had moved from their positions, although many were held in the rear. So it was with recklessly misplaced confidence that Captain Leslie ordered an advance south across the bridge early on the morning of the 9th of December. There were hardly more than 100 grenadiers and other regulars of the 14th Light Foot, together with around 60 white loyalist volunteers, which meant that at least 250 members of this attacking force, carrying the standard of George III, were Ethiopians: an army of free blacks on the march against America and slavery.

Black and white were slaughtered together beneath that flag in the dim sanguine dawn, as the sun rose from the swamps. The American commander, Colonel Woodford, cool when he needed to be, held fire until the British infantrymen, advancing again in parade step to the beat of two drums, only six abreast for that was all the narrow causeway could take, got within fifty paces. A tearing volley of fire began. In about ten minutes, Great Bridge turned into one of the more spectacularly suicidal epics of British imperial history: pipes, screams, falling scarlet coats. The calamity even featured a gentleman-martyr with a perfect name, Captain Charles Fordyce, the fuzz barely scraped from his cheek—"very genteel," "a completer Officer never lived," wrote his American foes awed at his lunatic, futile bravery. Fordyce led his grenadiers relentlessly on, taking a shot in the kneecap, rising as though it had been a mere mosquito bite, waving his hat merrily in the air to lag-gards behind him and shouting optimistically, "The day is our own!" Fourteen bullets later Fordyce lay dead, twelve slaughtered grenadiers at his back fifteen feet in front of the American breastworks. Behind him, taking the ferocity of massed rifle fire, was the rank and file of Dunmore's army. Tories from Norfolk, infantrymen and hundreds of black soldiers, seeing the carnage in front of them, paused. The cause-way grew choked with soldiers dragging the wounded back towards the bridge, for they had been told by Dunmore that the Americans were partial to scalping. After a one-hundred-strong detachment of Culpeper militia made it, in a rush, to a battery on the eastern side of the penin-sula the British took fire from two sides and broke under the attack, as black troops on the bridge were picked off with the ease of a duck shoot. Leslie ordered a retreat north across the bridge to the fort. Two officers, as well as Fordyce, had been mortally hit: Lieutenant Napier, of the fam-ily that would give and give to the British Empire in glory and disaster, and Leslie's own nephew Peter, who sank, bled and died in his uncle's arms. The two young officers, wrote Dunmore as he struggled to ex-plain the appalling debacle, were "both very deserving young men . . . really a loss to their corps."

It had taken no more than half an hour; but a lot of damage can be done in that short time. In this case Virginia, and perhaps the whole South, was lost to Britain. And the vision of a formidable little army of freed slaves—two thousand strong at least, Dunmore had thought—with perhaps as many again of white loyalists, disappeared into the bloody mire. The word "skirmish" ought never to be used for Great Bridge. It was, wrote Captain Meade, "a vast effusion of blood, so dreadful it beggars description, a scene when the dead and wounded were bro't off that was too much; I then saw the horrors of war in perfec-tion; worse than can be imagin'd ten and twelve bullets thro many; limbs broke in two or three places; brains turning out. Good God, what a sight!"[31]

Dunmore reported a mere seventeen dead and forty-nine gravely wounded, but these were among the regular British troops alone. An-other eighty-five, overwhelmingly black, soldiers died or suffered seri-ous wounds. Casualties on the American side were one man with a wounded hand. Shattered by the defeat, Dunmore's army fell back first to the fort, which, after the two four-pounder cannon had been spiked with nails, was abandoned as the demoralized force withdrew into Norfolk. A week later an American force of two thousand converged on the town. Panic swept the loyalist community, as it became increasingly obvious that Dunmore would re-embark on his fleet, ending the brief dream of a black and white loyalist insurgency in Virginia. Mournful Tories embarked along with the remnant of British troops and the Ethiopians. Dunmore reported to Lord Dartmouth: "I do assure your lordship it is a most melancholy sight to see the numbers of gentlemen of very large property with their ladies and whole families obliged to betake themselves on board of ships at this season of the year, hardly with the common necessities of life and great numbers of poor people, without even these, who must have perished had I not been able to supply them with some flour."

Five days later Dunmore's flotilla, lying off Norfolk, was reinforced by two more ships and he became more aggressive. With the town now in the hands of the Americans, he had no compunction about cannonading the docks and sending boats to fire the warehouses. What followed was a conflagration that reduced the town to cinders. But whilst that is not in dispute, who was responsible for Norfolk's destruction is not at all clear. Most American narratives assume that Dunmore, his Tory citadel fallen to the Whigs, petulantly decided to destroy the place. But his dispatches to Dartmouth, in all other details entirely truthful, tell a different story: that the American troops, perhaps as a response to the mass loyalist oath of allegiance, began to burn houses on both sides of the river. "From every transaction they appear to me to have nothing more at heart than the utter destruction of this once most flourishing country."

On board his ship, staring gloomily at the ashy remains of royal Virginia, Dunmore penned his lament to the new Secretary of State, Lord George Germain: "I wish to God it had been possible to have spared some troops for this colony" since he was "morally certain" that, had he had just five hundred six weeks before, nothing could have opposed his march through Virginia. As it was, though, it was to be expected that by the spring of 1776 there could well be ten thousand rebels under arms. The last straw was learning, belatedly, from London that Sir Henry Clinton's army was to be sent not to Virginia but to North

Carolina, "a most insignificant province when this, which is the first colony on the continent, both for its riches and power, is totally neglected . . . To see my government totally neglected, I own is a mortification I was not prepared to meet with after being imprisoned aboard a ship between eight or nine months, and now left without a hope of relief either to myself or the many unhappy friends of government that are now afloat suffering with me; but I have done."[32]

For neither the British nor the Americans believed that the threat posed by black insurrection had been disposed of by Dunmore's eviction from the mainland. The Ethiopian Regiment, now aboard Dunmore's "floating town" of more than one hundred vessels, had been badly mauled but not destroyed. In the satires against a black army that issued from the Virginia presses there was more than a hint of anxiety as well as contempt. The author of "The Blackbird March," a parody for the Ethiopians, sneeringly declared it suitable for "their *native* warlike genius," scored as it was for "the sprightly, and enlivening barrafoo, an instrument peculiarly adapted to the martial tune "Hungry Niger."[33] "Hail! Doughty Ethiopian Chief," chuckled the *New York Journal,* "Though ignominious Negro thief / The black shall prop thy sinking name / And damn thee to perpetual fame."[34] And Richard Henry Lee, like many Virginian Patriots, snorted when he referred to Dunmore as the "African Hero." The trouble, however, was that Lee, Washington and the rest knew that, even after Great Bridge, he was. When, in the early spring a trio of slaves were taken by an American patrol boat that they had mistakenly thought was a British tender, before they were disabused they declared their "resolution to spend the last drop of their blood in Lord Dunmore's service."[35] In Cambridge and Philadelphia, the response to this continuing alarm was to ban all blacks, free and slave, from military service with the Continental army. That decision would be reversed only in the dire military predicament facing Washington after he had been chased from New York and New Jersey.

While Washington in Congress was making it impossible for blacks to serve in the Continental army, escaped slaves such as Thomas Peters were taking the king's shilling. In February 1776 the sloop *Cruizer* had appeared off Cape Fear; Wilmington was hastily evacuated, and Peters, like thousands of blacks in the area, was left without a master. For two months Sir Henry Clinton's fleet of twenty ships controlled the North

Carolina coast and sailed up the Cape Fear River raiding plantations. At some point Peters came on board, and when he had reached New York in November was sworn into Clinton's newly formed Black Pioneers and Guides by its commanding officer, Captain George Martin.[36] For the very first time in their lives slaves got to use the words "freely and voluntarily" in a little ceremony that effectively changed them back from thing to human: "I Thomas Peters do swear that I enter freely and voluntarily into His Majesty's Service and I do enlist myself without the least compulsion or persuasion into the Negro Company commanded by Capt. Martin and that I will demean myself orderly & faithfully and will chearfully [sic] obey all such directions as I may receive from my said Captain . . . So help me God."[37]

Kitted out in greatcoats, sailor jackets, white shirts and hats, the Pioneers were to have white officers and black NCOs—the latter, along with privates, to be paid at the same rates as their white counterparts. Clinton himself was surprisingly and consistently solicitous for their welfare, writing to Martin that "it is my direction that they are to be regularly supplied with Provisions and to be decently clothed and that they are also to receive such pay as may hereafter be determined . . . and further that, at the expiration of the present Rebellion [they] shall be intitled (as far depends on me) to their freedom—And from my knowledge of you I shall rely on you and desire that it may be particularly recommended to the rest of the Officers to treat these people with tenderness and humanity."[38]

It was the continuing dread of men such as Peters going to the British and stirring up armed insurrection on top of mass flight that prompted extraordinary, brutal pre-emptive action from the Americans. The string of long, low islands off the coast of Virginia, South Carolina and Georgia had become sanctuaries for thousands of escaped slaves, who had somehow made it off the mainland in little boats and were camped between the dunes and the salt marshes, hoping against hope to be picked up by the British fleet. When the ship *Scarborough* appeared off Cockspur Island, for example, some two hundred to three hundred escaped slaves told Governor Wright of Georgia (who, like his Virginian and Carolinan colleagues, had now made his base on board) that "they were come for the King."[39] By the same token, it became an urgent priority for the troops of the Southern colonies to attack those unarmed camps before the escaped blacks had a chance to become recruits. On the 19th of December, a company of South Carolina Rangers attacked an encampment on Sullivan's Island just beyond Charleston harbour, where, according to the captain of the British ship *Scorpion,* he could have taken on five hundred blacks who were eager to fight the Americans. Tipped off about the raid, most of the blacks had been taken off in boats sent from the British ship *Cherokee,* but eleven were captured and four killed, a punishment that, the Charleston Council predicted, "would serve to humble our Negroes in general."[40]

In view of this very partial success against an elusive quarry, a more draconian solution was proposed in the spring of 1776 when it was learned that at least two hundred escaped slaves were sheltering on Tybee Island off the Georgia coast. To Henry Laurens, who, decent as always, flinched at the idea, Colonel Stephen Bull said forthrightly that "it is far better for the public and the owners if the deserted Negroes . . . be shot if they cannot be taken." Perhaps in guilty recognition that for white soldiers a massacre in cold blood might be a little much, even if their victims were runaway slaves, Bull recommended that the wholesale killing be done by Creek Indians. "If Indians are the most proper hands let them be employed on this Service," Laurens replied to Bull as he agreed, Pilatically, to the expedition, "but we would advise that Some discreet white men be encorporated with or joined to lead them." Whether the slaughter was then carried out is not known; but, given the state of hysteria prevailing throughout the South in the spring and summer of 1776, there is no reason to rule it out. (Since Tybee Island now enjoys a happy reputation as a prime spring and summer resort, complete with Beach Bum Festival and birding amidst the woodstorks and herons, it seems safe to assume that no one is going to go poking round the dunes looking for the remains of African-Americans.)

By the late spring and summer of 1776, both sides were making grand promises of liberty while both were delivering death. On the 13th of May a three-man committee—John Adams, Richard Henry Lee and Edward Rutledge—presented to Congress Adams's draft preface to a resolution that was an irreversible act of separation and stated that "humble petitions . . . for the redress of grievances" having gone unanswered, "it is necessary that the exercise of every kind of authority under the said crown [of Great Britain] should be totally suppressed."[41]

Some weeks later Jefferson's long passage on slavery, pinning the blame on the "Christian King" and heralding its abolition in the new republic, was entirely stricken in the editing process, "in complaisance," Jefferson's notes record, "to the delegates from Georgia and South Carolina." The delegates included Arthur Middleton and Edward Rutledge, whose slaves—John and Lucy Banbury, and Pompey and Flora Rutledge— were at that moment enjoying the protection of Lord Dunmore and the British fleet.

The enjoyment must have been limited. For all around them, whether on board or on land, was disease and distress. Dunmore's fleet of over one hundred vessels, big and small—and there were twenty-nine more under the command of Sir Henry Clinton attempting, and failing, to take Fort Sullivan at the mouth of Charleston harbour— looked, on the face of it, formidable. But there was something defective about the authority of an armada that, running low on supplies, tacked along the coast from island to island, looking for havens that were close enough to allow tenders to go out and forage, and mount raids on plantations, while steering clear of American shore batteries that could do a surprising amount of damage. Even worse was the unmistakable fact that what Dunmore had hoped to be his great advantage—the recruitment of escaped slaves—was now turning into a liability. For although, as he reported to Lord George Germain, six to eight blacks came to him every day, their number was immediately wiped out by deaths from smallpox and an unidentifiable "fleet" fever, probably typhus.

Overcrowded conditions on the ships and on the island encampments, initially at Tucker's Point near Portsmouth in Virginia, all but guaranteed an epidemic.[42] Smallpox struck the blacks with disproportionate ferocity. The fleet surgeons recommended inoculation, but while this procedure, which involved creating an infection through deliberately contaminating an incision, had a high chance of reducing the fatality rate, it also meant that those who had been inoculated would be incapable of labour or military duties during the active cycle of the disease, a matter of months rather than weeks. Since Dunmore felt he could not afford to do without either his white or black soldiers and labourers, in late May a ruthless decision was taken to cut his losses by leaving the hopelessly ill behind and sailing north to another harbour: Gwynn's Island, at the mouth of the Piankatank River. But things went no better there. Although the Ethiopians had been inoculated, they were placed in a separate camp from the white soldiers and sailors, where, languishing for want of decent food and adequate clothing, they sickened and died in hundreds of the "rotten fever" that was eating alive the strength of Dunmore's rapidly depleting troop. By early July, wrote the captain of the *Roebuck,* Andrew Snape Hamond, the little regiment was "too weak to resist any considerable force."

On the 9th of July, before an assault could be mounted, Dunmore abandoned Gwynn's Island, along with the most incurably sick, overwhelmingly black population. Some of the smaller boats and many of the infected cabins were burned, together with the bodies inside them. Then Dunmore set sail to the mouth of the Potomac, where he made a base for a few weeks on St George's Island and raided some of the tidewater plantations and houses, but found once more that he could seldom get close enough to do serious damage before presenting a target to the American guns. Finally, on the 6th of August, he admitted (probably prematurely) the hopelessness of his task. Of the 103 remaining vessels, 63 were burned, and the remaining 40 split into three squadrons. One sailed north to New York to continue the fight, another south to St Augustine in eastern Florida, whilst the third returned to England.

When the Virginia shirtmen landed on Gwynn's Island they were greeted by an appalling spectacle. "We found the enemy had evacuated the place with the greatest precipitation and were struck with horrour at the number of dead bodies in a state of putrefaction strewed all the way from their battery to Cherry Point, about 2 miles in length without a shovelful of earth upon them." Some of the sufferers were still alive, but barely "gasping for life . . . some had crawled to the water's edge who could only make known their distress by beckoning to us."[43] Captain Thomas Posey found bodies, not all of them dead, "strew'd about, many of them torn to pieces by wild beasts."[44] The American soldiers also discovered the remains of those who had burned in the final conflagration. It was hard to count the bodies, half-rotted and charred as they were, but there were at least five hundred. Perhaps some, before catastrophe overtook them, had felt for a moment at least that the world had indeed been altered; but there was no way to tell from the piles of corpses strewn among the scuttling crabs.

TWO MONTHS EARLIER Lord William Campbell, that most reluctant warrior, had done his duty. A fleet of 29 British ships commanded by Commodore Peter Parker had appeared at the mouth of Charleston harbour. Carrying 270 guns and nearly 2,000 soldiers and marines, it seemed highly likely that they were capable of taking the fort on Sullivan's Island, after which they could, in effect, blockade the port. Campbell quartered himself aboard the flagship *Bristol*. But the task was much harder than it seemed on paper. In an ill wind two ships, including one of the most recently commissioned, the *Actaeon,* ran aground while attempting to sail close enough to put shore guns in range of the ship's cannon. A raid on the fort and then on an island close by were botched. The closer the flotilla came, the more furious the fire. Lord William himself manned one of the *Bristol*'s guns and while he was at it, took a large splinter of decking in his thigh. The wound never healed, and the last royal governor of South Carolina died two years later, his planter wife by his side.

IV

I T WAS NO GOOD. Granville Sharp could not go on as before. The undeniable fact was that he had no stomach for the fight. It had been all very well issuing instructions from the Ordnance Office for the dispatch of so many powder horns, so many flintlocks, to Trichinopoly or Trincomalee. But to think that it had been his hand that had supplied the bayonets puncturing American breasts at Bunker Hill, or that had delivered the grenades that had put the houses of Charles Town to the torch—why, his conscience revolted at it. The dead might be friends of his Philadelphian correspondents Anthony Benezet, Dr Rush or Benjamin Franklin—Quakers, men of peace, haters of slavery. It would be as if he had signed his letters in blood. So when, on the 28th of July 1775, he read in the *Gazette* of the battle near Boston and received urgent demands from the beleaguered General Howe for munitions of all kinds, Sharp wrote at once to his superior, Mr Boddington, declaring his "objections to being concerned in any way with that unnatural business."[1] The gentlemen of the board might well have asked him in which office did he suppose he served? Remarkably, they did not. Such was the esteem, even the affection, for their cranky subordinate with his nose in the Pentateuch and his heart on his sleeve that they dealt mildly with him, recommending he ask for two months' leave, a consideration that would be taken "more kindly" than an abrupt resignation in the midst of a war.

The leave granted, Granville travelled north to see his older brother,

Dr John Sharp, now an archdeacon. He found him in the craggy red ruin of Bamburgh Castle, where Dr Sharp gathered the infirm and destitute, nursed their bodies and schooled their minds (to the general astonishment of the country thereabouts), and sent out riders to scan the stormy shore for signs of wrecks or the odd survivor washed on to the rocks. As his leave expired, Granville wrote once more to Boddington, distressed by the failure of efforts at reconciliation between Britain and the colonists. He still found himself unable, he confessed, to "return to my ordnance duty whilst a bloody war is carried on unjustly, as I conceive, against my fellow subjects."[2] At once the brothers rallied round to allow Greeny to exercise his conscience as he thought fit. James, the serpent-playing ironmonger, wrote that perhaps there would be a change in the direction of public opinion, but if not,

> and you should think it proper to give up your employment—I will now speak for my brother William as well as for myself—we are both ready and willing, and God be thanked at present, *able*, to take care that the loss shall be none to you; and all that we ask in return is that you would continue to live amongst us as you hitherto have done without imagining that you will, in such a situation, be burthensome to us, and also without supposing that it will be your duty to seek employment in some other way of life; for if we have the needful amongst us it matters not to whom it belongs.[3]

Sharp's superiors were still reluctant to let him go. Were his worries not the admirably affecting mark of a Christian sensibility? Doubtless they would abate as his natural patriotism and sense of duty returned. Three months' additional leave was granted.

But his pessimism only deepened. On the 26th of October 1775 the king opened Parliament. The speech from the throne—written, of course, by his ministers—was adamant.[4] Under the guise of a protest against grievances, imagined or real, a conspiracy of rebellion had been prepared and had now been consummated. Its design, now and always, had been for an independency: the outright severance of the American colonies from their proper allegiance to Crown and Parliament. Before anything positive could be attempted in the way of answering grievances, that rebellion had to be put down. Critics of the government, in both the Lords and the Commons, dismissed the premise of the argument. Their American friends were not, they insisted (somewhat behind the news), committed to independence; they had merely been put in a posture of so seeming by the blundering brutality of the government and its dependence on odious military force. Knowing his Philadelphians to have been loath to embrace outright separation, Sharp was of a similar opinion.

And he worried about the effect that a war would have on Benezet's endeavours to make his fellow Americans aware of the abomination of slavery. Sharp himself had never shrunk from pointing out to them the inconsistency of their claims to liberty while denying the same to their black brethren. In his 1774 *Declaration of the People's Natural Right to Share in Legislature,* a broadside that he meant to be applied as much to the overtaxed and unrepresented English as to the Americans, he had spoken frankly: "Let them put away the accursed thing before they presume to implore the interposition of divine providence!"[5] The great work of persuasion had indeed been started, thanks to Benezet. Two hundred and fifty copies of the *Declaration* had been sent to Franklin after he had returned to Philadelphia in the hope that he would circulate them to those who mattered. Sharp had every hope that America would recoil from appearing before the world as "the land of the brave and the land of the slave,"[6] and his hopes seemed to be rewarded. In April 1775 the very first American anti-slavery society had been established in Philadelphia. Five days later British soldiers and Patriot Minutemen exchanged shots on Lexington Green. Not a lot would be heard from the Philadelphia Society for years to come.

There was no way, of course, for Sharp to know that the arrival of British troops in America, far from setting back the cause of liberty for slaves, had accelerated it. When Sir William Howe's armada of 260 sail en route to Philadelphia passed tantalizingly close to the New Jersey shore blacks flocked to it, whilst "scarce a white person was to be seen." In a single day the ships picked up 300 escaped slaves. But they were the more fortunate ones, who had managed to reach the fleet in small boats or canoes. Others, when vessels came close to the shoreline, tried to reach them by swimming and as often as not were drowned in the attempt.[7]

In England, the notion of arming liberated slaves was intensely controversial. During the debate on the speech from the throne in October 1775, William Lyttelton, who had been governor of South Carolina during the French and Indian War of 1756–60, had said forthrightly that, as far as he was concerned, should a "few regiments" be sent to America "the negroes would rise and embrue their hands in the blood of their masters," making pretty smart work of rebellion.[8] The proposal struck the liberal-minded opposition to the government as unconscionably barbaric—"too black and horrid to be adopted," said John Wilkes.[9] A coalition of the appalled rapidly made its voice heard. The sugar and slave interest in Bristol and Liverpool, already alarmed by risings in Jamaica, attacked the tactic as a monstrosity. Friends of America, even when, like Burke, they identified themselves as enemies of the slave trade, dismissed the idea of armed negroes (which might also involve arming Indians) as tantamount to licensed murder.

There is no sign in Granville Sharp's correspondence of his views on the strategy of arming negroes, but since he stood by a policy of peaceful persuasion in America, he is unlikely to have been an enthusiast. Although he finally resigned from the Ordnance Office in April 1777, when the patience of his superiors was exhausted, and although many of his friends had finally accepted that the Declaration of Independence seemed to mean what it said, Sharp himself had still not abandoned hope of bringing America back to the imperial fold as a free dominion under the Crown. It remained his conviction that if only Americans could be represented—either directly at Westminster or in legislatures that would have the exclusive right to tax—then the sources of discontent would go away. Since, by early 1778, British arms had occupied both New York and Philadelphia, was not this the moment for prudent magnanimity?

Sharp went to see the Secretary of State and impressed on him the need to grant the colonies "as fair and equal rights as those enjoyed by the counties of England." How was it that the most senior men in North's administration were prepared to give an ex-clerk of the Ordnance the time of day? Because Granville Sharp was also piping for peace. After his brother William had fitted out a fine new yacht, the *Union*, even more comfortable and capacious than the *Apollo*, the waterborne concerts were in greater demand than ever before. In early September 1777, while the armies of Howe and Washington were

manoeuvring for position in Pennsylvania and preparing for the carnage at Brandywine, the Sharps "played a variety of music, songs and
glees" for the king and queen. "We then took our leave by giving three
cheers and playing *The Retreat*." A year later, in the autumn of 1778,
General "Johnny" Burgoyne was marching confidently towards disaster
at Saratoga as swallows circled above the plump and cheerful face of
Lord North while he enjoyed a little Handel on the *Union* between Ted-
dington and Kew.[10]

A S USUAL, it was blacks who made the difference. On Christmas
Eve 1778 a naval squadron carrying three thousand troops—
Highlanders, Hessians and New York loyalist Volunteers—anchored off
Tybee Island at the mouth of the Savannah River, where, two years before, hundreds of runaway slaves had sheltered. A black pilot called
Samson got the fleet over the bar and would guide raiding expeditions
off the Georgia and Carolina coast during the next year. His capture or
death became urgent for the American and French troops struggling to
keep control of the South against the fresh onslaught of the British
army.

Savannah's best defence against the oncoming troops was its topography: the town was perched on a bluff on the west bank of the Savannah River with the Yamacraw swamp to its north, leaving just one
exposed road to secure, east of the city, manned by Georgia and Carolina troops who had taken the precaution of destroying an access bridge.
The wooded swamp was watered by the creeks of the St Augustine and
Tybee rivers, but there was one firm track through the treacherous mud,
and on the 29th of December 1778 Quamino Dolly, an elderly slave,
showed Lieutenant Colonel Archie Campbell exactly where it was. The
Highlanders (minus their packs) and the New York Volunteers got to
the rear of the Georgia and Carolina militia, who now faced an infantry
attack from one side and an artillery barrage from the other.[11] The
American position broke. Four hundred and fifty prisoners were taken,
including thirty-eight officers along with forty-eight cannon. Nearly
one hundred of the Georgians and Carolinans were counted dead or
seriously wounded, and another thirty died floundering in the morass
through which they had tried to escape. British losses were three dead

and ten wounded. What was left of General Robert Howe's army disintegrated. The British occupied not only Savannah but outlying small towns such as Ebenezer, where the Hessians were able to speak German with the Salzburger Lutherans who had settled there. "Many respectable inhabitants," Campbell wrote to Lord George Germain in January 1779, "joined the [British] army . . . with their rifles and horses who are formed into a corps of rifle dragoons for the purposes of patrolling the country . . . I have now the honour to acquaint your lordship that the inhabitants from all parts of the province flock with their arms to the standard."[12]

Not all of them were white.

THE MASTER HAD GONE. His carts and his people had rolled off north, leaving them all behind. It was time, now, to go to the British soldiers; time to be born again, to be free. So the preacher David George gathered together his wife, Phyllis, and their children and all the slaves, fifty or more, along with their sticks and their bundles, and they all started to walk in the opposite direction from the plantation, their backs to Augusta, making for the fort at New Ebenezer, between the Ogoochee and Savannah rivers, where they had been told the soldiers of the king were.[13]

So many journeys. The first had been that of his mother and father, taken from Africa and brought to Virginia, to the Nottoway River in Essex County on the western bank of the Rappahannock River. They were called John and Judith. John slaved in the tobacco and cotton fields for Mr Chapel, while Judith cooked, and the two of them produced for their master eight children besides David, all set to work while they were still small fetching water for the hands and carding the cotton. But the children grew up restive, seeing bad things, having bad things done to them, wanting to be gone.

> My oldest sister was called Patty; I have seen her several times so whipped that her back was all corruption, as though it would rot. My brother Dick ran away, but they caught him and brought him home and as they were going to tie him up he broke away again and they hunted him with horses and dogs, till they took him; then

they hung him up to a cherry tree in the yard, by his two hands, quite naked except his breeches with his feet about half a yard from the ground. They tied his legs close together and put a pole between them at one end of which one of the owner's sons sat, to keep him down and another son at the other. And after he received 500 lashes or more, they washed down his back with salt water and whipped it in as well as rubbed it in with a rag and then directly sent him to work in pulling off the suckers of tobacco.

David, too, had been flogged over and again. His back's pink lacing told his story, line by line. But the worst of the pain had been to see his mother, her clothes torn off, on her knees sobbing and begging for mercy, her body cut by the whip anyway. She was so ill used by this treatment that she died of it, and it was when she lay on that death bed, her eyes rolling up, that David, maybe twenty or twenty-one, sickened of weeping, ran off and made his first journey.

Men said the Church saved, so he ran to the English church at Nottoway even though he drank, had no thought of heaven and no belief in hell, for whatever demons there were could surely be no worse than Mr Chapel. There were many rivers to cross on his way south: first the Roanoke, and then the Pee Dee in North Carolina, where he found white people who took him aboard their boats and would not give him up even though there was a reward of thirty guineas for his capture. But when the slavehunters were coming the men on the Pee Dee River told him to go south, all the way to the Savannah River, and he did. Still the hunters came for him, so he fled again up the Okemulgee deep into the wooded hills of backcountry Georgia, and there the Creek Indians took him and knew him by his tracks for a black man because, while there was a hollow in the underside of their feet, his own lay flat on the red dirt as he ran. The king there was called Blue Salt and David became his prize, digging holes for the corn rows, eating bear and turkey, and looked after kindly until Mr Chapel's son came all the way into the Creek Nation, tracking him with hounds like a deer. And Blue Salt would surely not have given up his black prize, but Mr Chapel's son offered rum and linen and a gun, so he was tempted, and before it could happen off went David again, westwards, to King Jack of the Natchez people. And there was a man called John Miller, who came to the Natchez for deer pelts and sold them to the great Indian agent George Galphin, who lived in Silver Bluffs, South Carolina, and this man Miller and King Jack and Mr Chapel's son (who was tired now of all this following and ready to be paid off) agreed between them on a price. So King Jack sold David to John Miller, and for two years David sewed skins and tended the horses and made sure they didn't stray. Every year he took the skins downstream, piled high in a leather canoe, to Mr Galphin at Silver Bluffs. And there must have been something of a fatherly way about the man, for David asked if he might live with him and he said yes. David stayed with the Indian trader four years.

Later, "a mass of sin," he was ashamed of how he had lived at that time, but God helped him find a wife, his part-Indian, part-black Phyllis, and their first child was born. But he still lived so badly that when Cyrus, a black man from Charleston, told him if he carried on so he would never live to see the face of God in glory, he began to pray. But when he was not praying he was sinning, and so he went on praying and sinning and sinning and praying all the time with Mr Galphin at Silver Bluffs, until one day his saviour on this earth came and he was called George Leile and David was born again and became in his honour David George. Now the wonder of it was that David had known this Leile in Virginia when they were boys together, but since then he had seen God and was much altered. And when he preached, "Come unto me all ye that labour and are heavy laden and I will give you rest" David told him how it was with him. Together they went to a church some distance from Silver Bluff, where Brother Palmer preached in a big old mill of Mr Galphin's. Brother Palmer then came to Silver Bluffs and spoke directly to some of Mr Galphin's men, and baptized eight, David and Phyllis among the flock, in the rushing mill stream amidst the rocks and flashing trout. A church was built at Silver Bluffs, and David and the rest took the Lord's Supper and sang the hymns of blessed Isaac Watts, and as the spirit crept on him, so others saw it and asked him to preach. Ashamed because he was a stammerer and unlettered, he turned away from the task until Brother Palmer told him not to be a Jonah lest he offend the Lord, and so it was that he became Brother David and an Elder and began to speak to the people at Silver Bluffs and have them turn their faces to the shining countenance of the all-forgiving God.

When the war came to the low country of rice and swamp, the masters stopped ministers such as Brother Palmer from coming to the blacks in case they got ideas. So there was nothing for it now except for David to minister to his flock of more than thirty souls, and as he had the care of them, he thought he had better learn to read. But this too was forbidden, so David went to the white children and practised his abc with them until he could make out words and then pages of the Bible. The little children gave him his lessons, and David would go away and recite them in his head and then go back to the children and ask if it was right and repeat it until it was so. And now he could preach and teach and read and write and the whole glory of Scripture was his—and his church, did he but know it, was the first black church in all of America.

Now it was Christmas 1778 and they were told that they were in peril. There were said to be British ships off the islands, and soldiers, thousands of them, were coming. At dinner they heard talk about how the British would raise the Indians, and suddenly there was a lot of yelling and running around and carts loaded with people and dogs and a few fine things like mirrors, and off they went, the children looking back at the house with sorry faces. Mr Galphin, being warm for America and knowing the Indians as he did, was one who left in a real hurry, so now David and his flock were quite alone with nothing and no one to keep them, but also not much in the way of food in the hard, grey winter.

A T LEAST FIVE THOUSAND of Georgia's slaves, one-third of the total, went from their plantations, knowing that the British had offered freedom and protection in return for service to the king. This was what had made up David George's mind and put him and his flock (now numbering fifty) on the Augusta-Savannah road. Twenty miles from the city they reached Ebenezer, where Hessians and Highlanders had already occupied the fort. But the British general was deluged with incoming blacks and sent them away again, over the Ogeechee to a place called Savage's Plantation. It was full of white loyalists who, seeing David leading his flock, accused him of marching them away from Savannah and towards the Patriots. Despite his protests that this was the opposite of what he was doing, he was thrown in prison and stayed there for a month until one of the British officers, Captain Brown, came and fetched him out.

At Yamacraw by the marshy woods David George was reunited with George Leile and his family, and the two of them preached the word of God together until in the summer of 1779 an allied force of more than five thousand American and French troops, bent on retaking Savannah, closed in fast; so the Georges, fearing capture by the Americans, moved into the town. Once there, they found more than six hundred blacks, including fifty-nine Pioneers, digging deep ditches, building up the palisaded ramparts, cutting and sharpening the abatis breastworks that were designed to impede and impale oncoming attackers, and manning the redoubts. James Moncrief, the Scots captain commanding the Engineers, looked after them, making sure they were properly fed, clothed and (to the consternation of Tory planters who were slaveowners themselves) armed. By early October 1779, when the French and Americans were finally ready to advance, Savannah was girdled by formidable defences that covered its entire western flank, from the broad river basin to the creek-run swamps.

But the British ability to defend Savannah from an allied attack owed itself to black help in another, decisive respect. On the 16th of September the allies issued an ultimatum to the British general Augustine Prevost to surrender the city in twenty-four hours. But Prevost knew, or at any rate hoped, that help was on its way, a detachment of troops under Colonel James Maitland coming from Beaufort. Black guides speaking Gullah, the dialect of the sea islands where slaves had first been landed after the wretched crossing from Africa, had shown Maitland a way round the blocking French army, through otherwise impassable bogs and under a shroud of dense Georgia fog in a country known only to "bears, wolves and runaway Negroes."[14] Tipped off that these reinforcements were fast approaching, Prevost used his twenty-four hours to stall; and sure enough Maitland's troops arrived, enough of them to make the British confident that they had a decent chance of surviving whatever the French and Americans threw at them. Then the city waited; 250 armed blacks stood in the centre of the defenders on the ramparts, some of them manning the guns—slaves waiting to kill their masters.

A week later, on the 23rd of September, the bombardment opened up, with eight- and ten-inch mortars and more than fifty cannon firing from both batteries and from frigates moored in the river.[15] From the 3rd to the 8th of October the artillery fire was incessant, shot and shell raining relentlessly down on Savannah. Scarcely a house in the neat grid of streets was spared and a choking mantle of smoke hung over the town. But most of the artillery missed the fortifications completely, as though terror were the main point. Despite collapsing buildings and burning debris, few were hurt, and before long black children ran through the streets looking for spent cannon balls to play with. Not everyone thought the French were playing games, however. When a shell came straight through the roof of the stable where the Georges were living, David and Phyllis, anxious about their children, Jesse, David and Ginny, thought better of staying and went back to Yamacraw, where, for a time, they hid beneath the floor of an abandoned house and survived as best they could.

Once d'Estaing, the French commander, thought the city sufficiently softened up, an attack was ordered for dawn on the 9th of October. Belatedly, for it was already light, his grenadiers climbed Spring Hill at the north end of the defences, emerging from a dense fog just in time for their brilliant white coats to supply a perfect target: as they plodded grimly upwards they fell under fierce musket fire. An American cavalry company led by a Pole rode at the defences, got tangled in the abatis and was shot up. Their commanding officer, Pulaski, died snarled up in the sharpened poles, his body riddled with shot. Carolinans, commanded by John Laurens, followed and made it to the ramparts just long enough to plant a flag before being fired on from two sides. British grenadiers and marines now charged over the palisades with bayonets, and for an hour a brutal hand-to-hand fight ensued; soldiers of five white nations—American, English, Scots, German, and French—blazed and stabbed, clawed and bludgeoned at the top of a greasy bluff over a smoke-dark river. And in the middle of them all were blacks, cutting and firing, as they must have thought, for their freedom. (There were free blacks from St Domingue on the Franco-American side too, but they were held in reserve so that a tragic scenario of black fighting black—which happened elsewhere in the Southern theatre of war—did not materialize on the heights at Savannah.)

When the firing ceased, the ditches were full of French bodies, white coats dappled with blood. Two hundred and three more bodies were picked off the breastworks, between the carcasses of impaled horses, and buried. Others had galloped downhill headlong into the swamp, where their riders had drowned. In the debacle the allies lost nearly eight hundred dead and wounded, although Prevost claimed more than one thousand; the British just eighteen dead and thirty-nine wounded. It was a Bunker Hill in reverse. Nine days later the Americans gave up the siege, and three days after that d'Estaing set sail. Prevost, who was not in the habit of handing out compliments, wrote of the blacks (as if he were slightly surprised) that "they certainly did wonders in the working way and in the fighting they really shewed no bad countenance." This new courage showed itself—alarmingly to the Patriots—beyond the ramparts of Savannah. After the siege was lifted, out at McGillivray's Plantation a company of black troops, probably those under Captain John McKenzie of the British Legion, fought a pitched battle with Patriot soldiers and drove them from their positions, retreating (with one dead and three wounded) only after their ammunition had run out.[16]

But then, the blacks had something serious to fight for. On the 30th of June 1779 at Philipsburgh, before leaving New York for a campaign in South Carolina with Charleston as the intended prize, Sir Henry Clinton had issued a third proclamation warning that negroes taken in arms fighting for the rebels would be bought for public works. "But I do most strictly forbid any Person to sell or claim right over any Negroe, the property of a rebel, who may take refuge with any Part of this Army; And I do promise to every negroe Who shall desert the Rebel Standard, full security to follow within these lines any Occupation which he shall think proper."[17]

For one American officer who had been at Savannah the lesson could not have been clearer or more urgent, both strategically and morally. In February 1780, from inside Charleston, his home town, the twenty-five-year-old Colonel John Laurens urged the general in charge of the city's defences, Benjamin Lincoln, to use blacks both in armed battalions and on artillery crews.[18] His stay in London from 1774 to 1776 had defined the rest of Laurens's life. The agony of distance from the accelerating crisis in America had made a passionate Patriot and republican of him, and his friendship with John Bicknell and Thomas Day had made an emancipator of him. Put together, the two causes spelled out the indispensability of black soldiery, without which he thought the American cause would be both morally compromised and militarily handicapped.

By the time that Laurens became aide-de-camp to Washington in 1777, the commander-in-chief had obliged the Southern states by prohibiting slaves from service in the Continental army. But as the Americans became harder pressed, the exclusionary policy gave a little. In that same year, Vermont became the first and only state to abolish slavery. And when it was difficult, in Rhode Island and Connecticut, to fill the quotas for the Continental army, the deficiencies were made good by blacks, principally within white regiments. But since many, if not most, of those soldiers served as substitutes for white masters, what their presence says about the relative enthusiasm of either of them for the American cause is open to debate. The exception may have been Colonel Christopher Greene's 1st Rhode Island Regiment, expressly organized after the decimating winter of 1777–78 at the Valley Forge camp as a black fighting force—albeit, as on the British side, with white officers. It initially consisted of about 120 men, of whom two-thirds were slaves—not hard to find, since Newport was still the home port of the African-American slave trade—and who saw action at the battle of Rhode Island in August 1778.[19]

John Laurens, all of twenty-three, had been with George Washington when the general wrote to the governor of Rhode Island recommending quota shortfalls be filled with blacks. It was enough to stir his always restive conscience to action. He wrote to his father asking him to free his slaves "instead of leaving me a Fortune."[20] But what he really wanted was to mobilize, equip and lead a full black regiment. Military service, he thought, was the perfect way to fit such men, accustomed only to servitude, for liberty. Henry Laurens, who owned three hundred slaves, unsurprisingly thought differently. Why should blacks, he asked his son, want to leave "circumstances not only tolerable but comfortable from habit for an intolerable. Taken from their Wives and Children & their little Plantations to the Field of Battle where Loss of Life and Limb must be expected by every one every day."[21] The son, however, in keeping with what he had learned from Sharp, Day and Bicknell, rejected his father's assumption that blacks were passive creatures. They were, he insisted, quite human enough to share the ardour for liberty that sanctified the present struggle.

With the fall of Savannah, and the alarming news in the late spring of 1779 that Sir Henry Clinton would be sailing south with an army of eight thousand men, the argument about arming blacks suddenly became less philosophical and more strategic. Only "the adoption of my black project," Laurens wrote to his father, now president of Congress in Philadelphia, could save South Carolina. Perhaps "impending calamity" would finally persuade his countrymen where mere argument and appeals to morality and reason had proved weak. In a page straight from the novels of sentiment and sensibility, the burning idealist son appealed to his father's hitherto dormant nobility as well (for John was no fool) as to the old man's vanity. Leading the charge in Congress and in his state, "you will have the glory of triumphing over deep-rooted national prejudices in favour of your Country and humanity at large."[22]

Sure enough, Henry's scepticism—although soon to return with a vengeance—gave way to an improbable surge of idealism. But the elder Laurens also knew that his fellow planters in the South Carolina low country were in a bind. The state was having trouble filling its militia ranks precisely because adult whites were needed on the plantations to guard against the likelihood of slave insurrections and mass flight. Ironically, then, young Laurens's proposal could be promoted as a way of actually controlling black violence by harnessing it against the enemy, rather than risking it being turned on the masters. Even so, with a number of his own slaves gone to the British or taken by them, Washington was worried about the possibility of an escalating armed-slave race, each side outbidding the other. In the end the slaveholders of the South had the most to lose. Alexander Hamilton, protégé of Washington and mentor to John Laurens, supported his young friend's scheme. But whether his argument for doing so—that slaves were either sufficiently abject to wear military discipline well, or else sufficiently savage to fight like demons—gave the general much reassurance seems questionable.

Yet on the 29th of March Congress authorized the raising of three thousand able-bodied blacks in Georgia and South Carolina, to be commanded by white officers. Owners would receive $1,000 compensation per slave, since each black who served satisfactorily was to have his

freedom and $50 after the war. This would have been a revolution in-
deed, and at a stroke would have disposed of British accusations of
hypocrisy. But it was precisely because a New Hampshire delegate to
Congress, William Whipple, believed that "such a measure will produce
the Emancipation of a number of those wretches and lay a foundation
for the Abolition of Slavery" a huge loophole was included. In view of
the "inconveniences" that the measure would cause the two Southern
states, they would reserve the ultimate power to judge its practicality.
The bitter conflict between North and South that would poison the new
republic was there from the very start.

The outcome was predictable. When the black regiment was debated in the South Carolina House of Representatives at the end of
August 1779 it managed to secure just twelve votes out of seventy-two,
even with the British virtually at the gates. "It was received with horror
by the planters," wrote Dr David Ramsay, a Pennsylvanian transplanted
to Charleston and an early historian of the Revolution, "who figured to
themselves terrible consequences."[23] And just as suddenly as he had
been a convert, Henry Laurens was now a sardonic obituarist for the
grand design. "I learn your black Air Castle is blown up with contemptuous huzzas," he wrote to his furious, bitter son, adding, with a note of
unsympathetic sarcasm as if he had had no part in it, "A Man of your
reading & of your Philosophy will require no consolatory reasonings for
reconciling him to Disappointment."[24]

John Laurens, however, had not entirely given up on his plan. Early
in 1780, with the British armada on its way, Congress reminded the
South Carolinans of its proposal, and Laurens, thirsty for action as always, was in Charleston to press it on his countrymen. He managed to
persuade General Lincoln, to request one thousand slaves from Governor Rutledge. But no one who mattered would hear of it. Five thousand
slaves from low country plantations had, in fact, been impressed to
work on Charleston's fortifications; but, unlike the blacks who had done
the same for the British in Savannah, they did so without any promise
of freedom. None of them, of course, was armed; and none was used,
even without arms, on gunnery crews. Laurens's measure, the House of
Representatives judged, was still "premature" and should be adopted
"only in the last extremity."

The last extremity duly arrived. Black pilots found British frigates a way over the sandbank guarding Charleston harbour just as Quamino Dolly had got them through the Yamacraw swamp. In April black and white sappers dug the lines of trenches that advanced slowly and inexorably down the peninsula between the Ashley and Cooper rivers until they were in range to bombard the city. Caught between British ships in the harbour and British guns behind them, not to mention slaves disappearing en masse from plantations throughout the low country, Governor Rutledge—to John Laurens's horror—made an offer of South Carolina's neutrality for the duration of the war in return for the preservation of the social order, meaning the slaveholding society. In May the American garrison surrendered, delivering to the British more than five thousand prisoners, including John Laurens. It was, he wrote to Washington, "the greatest and most humiliating misfortune of my life," and he remained convinced that a black army could have saved the city and the state.[25] But the Southern states wanted a white army and used slave bounties as incentives to recruit white volunteers. In October 1780 the legislature of Virginia voted to give every recruit who pledged to serve until the end of the war three hundred acres, plus a choice of either "a healthy Negro" between thirty and sixty years old or else £60 in gold. In South Carolina, in April 1781, General Thomas Sumter instituted the practice of giving captured loyalist slaves as bounties to white recruits, and Georgia followed suit by offering to give a slave outright to every soldier who could prove he had fought in a campaign. When money was tight, slaves were sometimes given to soldiers in lieu of pay.[26]

In May 1780 a band played "God Save the King" as Sir Henry Clinton rode through Charleston in triumph. Among the musicians was likely to have been John Marrant, literate, black, a Methodist convert and master of both the fiddle and the French horn. Born in New York, Marrant had had an eventful past: brought to South Carolina; converted by the Methodist missionary preacher George Whitefield; captured by the Cherokee; saved at the last minute from being burned alive by the intercession of the chief; minister to a small flock while still wearing buckskins and braids and bearing a tomahawk; and impressed (for his music) on HMS sloop *Scorpion*, which had seen a lot of action, from Dunmore's raids in 1776 through to the taking of Charleston four years later. Marrant certainly knew of Clinton's Philipsburgh proclamation, but it was the Indian riding with him down Broad Street who caught his attention, for it was his old friend, benefactor and convert, the "king" of the Cherokees. When he saw Marrant he "alighted off his horse and came to me; said he was glad to see me; that his daughter [whom the black had also converted] was very happy."[27]

But if, after the fall of Savannah and Charleston, the blacks of the low country expected South Carolina and Georgia to turn from hell to heaven, or at least from bitter servitude to heady liberation, many of them were destined for cruel disappointment. Twenty-five thousand blacks—a quarter of South Carolina's slave population, and a third of Georgia's—left the plantations in what was by far the greatest exodus from bondage in African-American history until the Civil War and Emancipation.[28] But it was precisely those huge numbers of escaped blacks pouring out of the farms and plantations and towards the British that created a massive logistical crisis. Where Dunmore's original proclamation had been impelled by a manpower shortage, now Clinton, and his successor, Cornwallis, were faced with too many bodies and not enough food, clothing or arms. And many of those bodies were, predictably as in Virginia in 1775 and 1776, seriously ill, either from smallpox or from typhus; these conditions were not helped by extreme want, as the plantation system collapsed in late 1779 and 1780.

The response of most British commanders, as might be expected, was dictated more by the cold-blooded needs of military self-preservation than by the warmth of humanity. This was certainly true of Howe and Cornwallis, the former of whom shared Alexander Innes's distaste for using black soldiers in the Northern theatre. On the other hand Sir Henry Clinton, arguably the most important of the three throughout the war, was a much more complicated case. He was certainly no abolitionist, and like most of the senior officers had no interest in alienating the loyal or neutral planters by convincing them that he was out to destroy their world. When a slave rebellion broke out at the plantation of Ralph Izard (the late Governor Campbell's brother-in-law) Clinton promptly sent troops to crush it.[29] When slaves were taken *in situ* from rebel plantations, rather than received as runaways under the terms of the Philipsburgh proclamation, they often remained slaves and were impressed on public works or even given as rewards to loyalists. But any commander-in-chief who used the word "tenderness" in his instructions to junior officers concerning the treatment of the Black Pioneers was evidently not a conventional general. In fact Clinton never ceased to be as concerned about the Pioneers, whom he regarded as his personal project, as of the engineers and artificers working with Moncrief. Nor was he always indifferent to the fate of the thousands of civilian "Followers of Army and Flag." On the 3rd of June, before leaving Charleston (where there were at least five hundred blacks working on the fortifications) for New York, Clinton wrote a memorandum for his successor as commander in the Southern theatre, Cornwallis, much of which concerned the treatment of blacks.[30] Slaves who had run away from *loyalist* plantations, he directed, should be returned to their masters *only* after those masters had given a formal undertaking "in the presence of the Negro, not to punish runaways for "past offences." Should loyalist slaveowners be proved to have inflicted punishment notwithstanding this order, "he or she shall consent to forfeit their claim to the Negro." Negroes belonging to rebels, Clinton thought right to emphasize yet again to Cornwallis in case he did not share his view, which indeed he may not have done, after faithfully serving "are entitled to their freedom." They were to have "adequate pay provision and clothing" and be "under the care and protection of some humane person with a proper salary." Even more surprising, the same letter to Cornwallis proposed what would not be done, if done at all, until Reconstruction after the Civil War some eighty years later: "Why not settle the Negroes on forfeited land after the war?"

In a logistical pinch, even Clinton was capable of returning slaves to masters as a way of discouraging a tide of fugitives if their numbers threatened to overwhelm short supplies. If they were disabled by sickness, they were even more of a nuisance. Blacks who were already ill and half starved were strictly isolated, often with little or no sustenance or shelter, to prevent infection from spreading to the troops. (The Continental army practised much the same policies of prophylactic isolation.)

Boston King was one of those countless blacks who suffered from the conventions of military self-preservation. King had been born on a plantation twenty-eight miles from Charleston, and had served a racehorse trainer, who beat him unmercifully for other people's transgressions, for example, when nails went missing.[31] Evacuated with his master after the British had taken Charleston, King borrowed a horse to visit his parents, twelve miles away. Impetuously, he lent the horse to another servant, who promptly disappeared with it for days. Terrified by the certainty of brutal punishment, King took the step that thousands of blacks like him had already made. "To escape his cruelty, I determined to go to Charles-Town and throw myself into the hands of the English. They received me readily and I began to feel the happiness of liberty of which I knew nothing before altho' I was much grieved at first to be obliged to leave my friends and reside with strangers." The happiness, however, was fleeting.

> In this situation I was seized with the smallpox and suffered great hardships; for all the Blacks affected with that disease, were ordered to be carried a mile from the camp, lest the soldiers should be infected and disabled from marching. This was a grievous circumstance to me and many others. We lay sometimes a whole day without any thing to eat or drink: but Providence sent a man who belonged to the York volunteers whom I was acquainted with, to my relief. He brought me such things as I stood in need of; and by the blessing of the Lord I began to recover.
>
> By this time, the English left the place; but as I was unable to march with the army, I expected to be taken by the enemy. However when they came and understood that we were ill of the smallpox, they precipitately left us for fear of the infection. Two days after, the wagons were sent to convey us to the English army and we were put in a little cottage (being 25 in number) about a quarter of a mile from the Hospital.[32]

The British record towards their black charges, then, was neither one of exceptional compassion, nor one of unalloyed callousness and inhumanity. For every General Prevost who had no compunction (like Dunmore before him) about dumping the sick on places such as Otter Island, where hundreds died uncared for, there were individual British officers, for instance Boston King's benefactor, who tried to do something about their plight. David George, who also succumbed to smallpox in his cabin outside Savannah, survived because his wife, Phyllis, earned something by working as laundress for the British army and for a while for General Clinton himself. As David's condition deteriorated Phyllis finally agreed, in anguish, to his demand that she abandon him so as to "take care of herself and of the children, and let me die there." Although David was on the verge of perishing when the cornmeal his wife left him was eaten by a dog, he somehow came through the crisis. He was by no means friendless. One white loyalist, Joseph Wright, let him have the use of his vegetable garden and field near the Ogeechee River, and posted a notice in Savannah that "any person Molesting or disturbing [this] good subject of King George [and] Free Negro . . . in the possession of the premises will be prosecuted to the utmost rigor of the law."[33] With the help of another sympathetic white, "Lawyer Gibbons," he got back into Savannah, where he was reunited with his family and ran a butcher's stall for two years. David's half-Indian brother-in-law supplied him with fresh meat; and even after he was robbed of it by British cavalry, the Savannah blacks rallied round and lent him money to buy the hogs that he took to Charleston, along with his family. Staying in Charleston for two years until the evacuation following Yorktown, David adds that "Major P"—Major-General James Paterson—"was very kind to me."[34]

In the experience of both David George and Boston King (the best sources we have for the experience of blacks in the Revolutionary War), the British could appear as both benefactors and thieves, hard-hearted and kind-hearted; yet there was never any question about the ultimate allegiance of these two. And overall the royal army, for all its rigours and even cruelties, was, for many of those hoping to make their escape from servitude permanent, an asylum and a source of hope rather than of despair. Despite all the physical and material ordeals, brutal disappointments and betrayals endured by the blacks, the stark fact that the British were their enemies' enemies made them keep coming to the royal standard. The majority of slaves wanted nothing to do with the new American republic of bondage.

That was the view, at any rate, of the Methodist Boston King, who certainly experienced his fair share of suffering at the hands of both sides.[35] After a battle with Americans, Captain Grey, the British officer who had tended him when he was sick with the smallpox, was brought wounded to the field hospital, allowing King "to return him the kindness he had shewed me." Once the bond was tied—not as slave and master, but as officer and servant, which was altogether different—Boston King stayed loyal. Left alone with a white officer who had decided to desert to the Americans, who had stolen fifty horses, and who threatened King with being put in irons and "a dozen stripes every morning" if he did not follow him, King remained steadfast. Managing to escape from the officer, he walked for days to reach the British position and tip them off about the defection. "Three weeks after," he recorded laconically, "our Light horse went to the island, and burnt his house; they likewise brought back forty of the horses, but he escaped." On another occasion at Nelson's Ferry, where the British were faced with a much larger American force, King walked and ran nearly thirty miles to bring reinforcements for its relief. The British army was full of such blacks who rowed, rode, hacked tracks through the woods and carried messages at extreme peril to themselves, all to give the British troops an edge.

There were, of course, moments of doubt. Like many Southern blacks caught in an increasingly ferocious war—for the taking of Savannah and Charleston merely launched a new and brutal phase of the conflict in which competitive marauding was the only rule—Boston King made for what he imagined was the more secure loyalist haven of New York. Working as a pilot, he was captured by an American whaleboat and taken to New Brunswick in New Jersey. He was, he says, "used well" by his captors, but "my mind was sorely distressed at the thought of being again reduced to slavery and separated from my wife and family." Escape seemed difficult or impossible, given the breadth of the rivers he needed to cross to reach either New York or Staten Island. Sorrowing, King prepared to reconcile himself to servitude. But then he went to see a "lad" whom he had known in New York, who had attempted escape and been caught, and the excruciating agony of slavery rose again within him as he recalled the misery of bondage and the terror of flight.

He had been taken prisoner and attempted to make his escape, but was caught twelve miles off. They tied him to the tail of a horse and in this manner brought him back to Brunswick. When I saw him, his feet were fastened in the stocks and at night both his hands. This was a terrifying sight to me as I expected to meet with the same kind of treatment if taken in the act of attempting to regain my liberty. I was thankful that I was not confined in a jail, and my master used me as well as I could expect; and indeed the slaves about Baltimore, Philadelphia and New York have as good victuals as many of the English for they have meat once a day and milk for breakfast and supper and what is better than all many of the masters send their slaves to school at night, that they may learn to read the Scriptures . . . But alas all these enjoyments could not satisfy me without liberty! Sometimes, I thought, if it was the will of God that I should be a slave, I was ready to resign myself to his will; but at other times I could not find the least desire to content myself in slavery.[36]

As so often, and against steep odds, the burning thirst for freedom overcame the fear of capture and the understandable need for a settled life. Boston King stepped gingerly into the river near Perth Amboy at low tide around one o'clock in the morning, and then carried on wading deep into the cold black water even when he heard a sentry say, "I am sure I saw a man cross the river." Later he wondered whether they were reluctant to fire at him for fear they would be punished for letting him get that far. But there were no shots. King reached the far bank and "when I got a little distance from the shore, I fell down upon my knees and thanked God for this deliverance." He walked on through the night until dawn, then hid again until it got dark. Even so, he carefully followed the course of the road north through reedbeds and marshes, rather than walk directly on it in case he might be discovered. Opposite Staten Island he took another chance by cutting the rope of a moored whaleboat and paddling it over to the island. The narrative of the escape concludes with a statement so matter-of-fact that it belies what in the lives of slaves such as Boston King was a revolutionary alteration of their world: "the commanding officer, when informed of my case, gave me a passport and I proceeded to New York."

For escaped slaves, British New York was a haven. From newspaper advertisements for escaped slaves, at least 519 are known to have made their way there; but if, as was the case in South Carolina, one in four masters actually published runaway notices, the number rises steeply and credibly to more than 2,000.[37] As in Virginia, the Carolinas and

Georgia, the closer New York and New Jersey came to war, the greater the number of runaways, so that by 1775 patrols were being mounted and pre-emptive arrests made of any parties of blacks seen before sunrise and after dusk. As deterrents against revolt, the usual brutal punishments—flogging, hanging in chains, the display of heads after execution—were resorted to with more frequency. But the black population of the region, 18,000 by 1771, had been difficult to control, precisely because it was either already partly urbanized or else dispersed in relatively small farms from Long Island to the lower Hudson valley. That dispersion might also have made it harder for blacks to organize their resistance, except for the fact that they represented, compared to the South, a better educated and often highly skilled workforce, undoubtedly alert to the shifting fortunes of the embattled armies and the implications of the war for their own destinies. Blacks around New York undoubtedly knew of Dunmore's Proclamation, and even those who did not would certainly have been aware of General Howe's formal reissue of freedom for service for those slaves who deserted rebels, made in 1778 and printed in the loyalist press over many months. William Fortune, a twenty-nine-year-old slave belonging to John Morgan of Harrington New Jersey, got to know of the Proclamation and departed.[38] Two years earlier, a slave from Colt's Neck in Monmouth County, New Jersey, known as Titus, shortly to be reborn as "Colonel Tye," escaped from his Quaker master (for not all Quakers were averse to slaveowning) and made it all the way to Dunmore's Ethiopian Regiment. As one of a hundred black soldiers who survived the epidemics in Virginia and the Chesapeake, Titus came back to New Jersey with a vengeance and fought in the campaign of 1777. At the critical battle of Monmouth, where John Laurens fought on the other side, Tye took prisoner Elisha Shepherd, a soldier in the Monmouth County Militia, who could not have been happy about being marched off by Tye and incarcerated in the Sugar House in New York.[39]

There were certainly blacks, especially from southern New Jersey, Rhode Island and Connecticut, who fought on the Patriot side, but with little prospect of liberation if they were not already free. In 1777 the American governor of New Jersey, William Livingston, wanted to include in the state constitution a clause allowing for abolition of slavery, but "the house thought of us in too critical a situation to enter in on the consideration of it." When an abolitionist minister, Jacob Green, had the courage to preach from the pulpit, "I cannot but think that our Practicing Negro Slavery is the most crying sin in our land," his church was destroyed by a hostile mob and the minister forced to keep quiet.[40]

To see the embryo of the first authentically free African-American society one has to look to the Union Jack.[41] At the end of 1776, when the American army evacuated New York, an incoming British soldier saw "black children of the slaves hugging and kissing each other" with joy and relief.[42] Life during the years that followed would fall short of euphoria. Not long after the British took possession of New York a violent fire, possibly begun by rebel arsonists, destroyed a quarter of the city's property, very little of which was rebuilt during the war. Many of the incoming and escaped blacks lived in "Canvas Town" tents in fields west of Broadway, and, during the terrible winter of 1779–80, when snow lay three feet deep, must have suffered cruelly from exposure to the cold. Others lived in overcrowded dormitory "Negro Barracks" in lower Manhattan on Broadway, Church Street, Great St George Street and Skinner Street, and in Brooklyn near the navy yard, where many of them worked as pilots and carpenters. Conditions, as usual, were perfect for typhus and smallpox.

And yet, for all the hardship, this *was* a new life for African-Americans. They could worship at the Anglican Trinity Church, where they could also be legally married, something impossible under slavery. Their children could be baptized, and parents were encouraged to do so by Anglican ministers who also undertook dangerous baptizing missions into the neutral zone of eastern New Jersey, one alone performing six ceremonies a week. Blacks could go to the theatre—to see *Othello* if they liked, since Shakespeare underwent a sudden revival during the British occupation. There was horse-racing (so that Boston King could see racehorses without being beaten by the trainer) and boxing matches at which pugilists, such as Bill Richmond (the first great black boxer on either side of the Atlantic), fought under the patronage of the army in bare-knuckle contests, usually against white, especially Irish, opponents. Blacks could frequent taverns, where they could listen to their own banjo, drum and fiddle music, and go to the "Ethiopian Balls" where spectacularly dressed black women acted as hostesses and where, as in Charleston, blacks and whites danced freely together. This was, in its way, another small milestone: the first time that the two races had come together in any sort of social festivity. Predictably, the Patriot press thought the very idea of mixed-race dancing—the Sambos and the gentry having a ball—repellent and ridiculous: "At the entertainment lately given by the officers of the Royal African Regiment, his Excellency opened the ball with Colonel Quaco's Lady and danced very gracefully to the music of a full orchestra of banjoes and hurdy-gurdies."[43] Never mind, the soldiers of the king marched to African-American music, or at least African-American musicians, for there was not a regiment that did not have its black (usually ex-slave) drummers, fifers and trumpeters. General Benedict Arnold had two trumpeters he particularly liked and who would leave with the loyalist diaspora for Nova Scotia when Arnold went back to England. And the Hessians, who also recruited blacks for their own regiment, had no fewer than eighty black drummers on their regimental books. For the Patriots, this music served as further proof of the beastliness of the foe: decadents entertained by primitives.

Still, they knew from experience that, given a chance, the blacks would fight, if not enthusiastically for the British, then certainly *against* Patriots and sometimes with a fierceness that belied all the platitudes about feeble, comical Sambo. There may have been as many as eight hundred blacks, including the remnant of Dunmore's Ethiopians, fighting for control of Brooklyn Heights at the battle of Long Island in 1776. In February 1777 deserters from the British army reported that there was a company of one hundred black soldiers stationed at Newport, Rhode Island. Although, in the interest of purging the army of what he presumed to be undesirable elements, Alexander Innes, inspector-general of the provincial corps in 1777, had ordered the discharge of blacks and mulattos (thus following the American precedent), hundreds of blacks who had escaped from owners in Essex, Monmouth, Somerset and Middlesex counties found work as cartmen and foragers in General Howe's army as it pursued Washington's retreat through New Jersey. As in the Southern theatre, they also served as woodcutters, labourers, batmen, boatmen, musicians, couriers and spies.

It was along the ragged borderline between the two Americas, loyalist and Patriot—through the "neutral" zone of eastern and northern New Jersey; especially Monmouth and Bergen counties, and on the other side of the Hudson in southern Westchester—that the violence was most brutal and blacks were, as in the Carolinas, most enthusiastic in committing it themselves or in helping white loyalists to do so. It was here that old scores were settled; that slave and free black miniature armies used the war to make their points in cattle, property and blood. This is not to say that many of them were not also genuine enthusiasts for King George; undoubtedly many were, since they believed him to be their sponsor, protector and even liberator. What was so striking about the guerrilla war on the lower Hudson is that black and white loyalists acted together; and that some of the most implacable actions were taken against Patriot irregulars or militia identified as having acted brutally or summarily against Tories.

It was, somehow, personal; or at any rate it certainly was for "Colonel" Tye, the rank given as an honorific by the British as they often did to soldiers not formally attached to the provincial corps but who, as in Tye's case, merited some recognition. Tye's "Black Brigade" does seem to have been connected, in the first instance, with a regiment of the Queen's Rangers under the command of the famously pitiless Banastre Tarleton. For the most part, though, his companies operated as near-autonomous units targeting Patriot militia officers in northern New Jersey, or Patriot irregulars who themselves were conducting raids on British camps on Staten Island or Long Island.[44] From Tye's base at Sandy Hook detachments—often supported by the white loyalist Refugee Cowboys who operated alongside the Black Brigade—would sally out, usually at night, to hit isolated farms or houses, especially if they were known to have caches of arms or even cannon. Cattle were taken for the British army; guns spiked or seized; houses burned; prisoners taken back to New York and some of them, if thought guilty of violence against Tories, sometimes killed on the spot. Memories were long and mercy was in short supply. It was no accident that one of Tye's first recorded raids in the summer of 1779 was at Shrewsbury in Monmouth County, where he had been a slave. Eighty head of cattle were taken, twenty horses and, doubtless satisfying for him, two prisoners.

In the bleak winter of 1779–80 organized and sometimes armed units of blacks became important in supplying the army and the loyalist militia with fuel and cattle, while denying the supplies to the American side. At Fort Lee and especially at Bull's Ferry, loyalist partisans (for that is really what they were) combined business and guerrilla war by establishing armed bases from which black woodcutters and foragers would go forth and take timber in Bergen County for both the army and civilian New York. Blockhouses were built (as at Kingsbridge on the southwest tip of what is now the Bronx, from which logs were floated to Manhattan) that were half warehouse, half fort, manned by 150 blacks and whites known as the Loyal Refugee Volunteers. When Patriot troops or militia, exasperated by the removal of valuable resources, attempted to wipe them out with a display of superior force they not infrequently ended up with a bloody nose.

Often, the battles took the form of vendettas between rival bands of irregulars. At the end of March 1780 Tye took out John Russell, a Patriot marauder on Staten Island, burned his house and badly wounded his son. For a while in the spring and summer of 1780 Tye's guerrilla army seemed so unstoppable that Governor Livingston of New Jersey declared martial law. It had no effect at all on Tye's operations. In June, over the course of just two weeks, he killed one of the most conspicuous executioners of loyalists in Monmouth County at his house; then took twelve prisoners after an all-out battle at the house of one of the leaders of the Monmouth County Patriots (and a famous racehorse entrepreneur), Barnes Smock; and, finally, leading a force of nearly one hundred men, black and white, sacked the houses of Monmouth militia officers, taking to Refugeetown at Sandy Hook eight prisoners, including a captain and the second major of the militia. Tye's Black Brigade took no casualties at all.

All this was a prelude, however, to getting to Tye's main mark: a determined and courageous Patriot called Joshua Huddy, a captain in the Monmouth County militia. Huddy was someone out of the ordinary. He had married a Jewish widow from the little community known, alas, as "Jewstown" and had taken over her first husband's tavern, which became a headquarters for the local Patriot militia in which Huddy served as captain. He had many raids on British-held Staten Island to his credit, so Tye's attack on Huddy's house at Colt's Neck on the 1st of September 1780 was a showdown. For the black colonel, however, it went fatally wrong. Although massively outnumbered, Huddy and a woman friend, Lucretia Emmons, held off Tye and his men for two hours, fighting from room to room of the house at Tom's River, New

Jersey. Eventually the house was torched, smoking Huddy out (he later escaped by jumping off the whaleboat taking him to New York), but during the fighting Tye had been shot in the wrist, a wound that developed into the lockjaw that killed him not long afterwards.[45]

Tye's death did not end the raiding wars around New York. He was succeeded as leader of the brigade by Colonel Stephen Blucke, a literate free black from Barbados and an officer in the Black Pioneers and Guides. Even as the war was ostensibly winding down after Cornwallis's capitulation at Yorktown in October 1781, there were still some determined acts of resistance. When General Anthony Wayne attacked the 120 defenders of the Bull's Ferry blockhouse with 1,000 troops, he failed to storm it and sustained 60 casualties. William Luce's armed whaleboats, almost always in the hands of black boatmen and known as the Armed Boat Company, continued to hit Patriot posts, and in January 1782 there was a water battle between rebel and loyalist whaleboats off Long Island. On the 23rd of March that year the Armed Boat Company, together with forty Associated Loyalists, attacked a Patriot blockhouse at Tom's River, killing and wounding several and taking prisoner most of the garrison. Among those most unhappy to be captured and transferred to a prison ship was Tye's old nemesis, Captain Joshua Huddy.

The struggle was bitter to the end because so much was at stake. Simsa Herring, William Dunk and Thomas Smith had all left masters at Tappan; Lydia Tomkins had left her master, Elnathan Hart, at Philipse Manor on the Westchester side of the Hudson; Anna had left Edmund Warde in East Chester; Gabriel Johnson had left James Petsworth in Quibbletown, New Jersey; Cathern van Sayl had left John VanderVeer in Monmouth County; Anthony Loyal, of Monmouth County, was free but his wife, Hagar, was not; Thomas Browne had left Ahasuerus Merselis at Hackensack—these and thousands like them around New York were desperate to hang on to their liberty, while they were dimly, terrifyingly aware that their eventual fate was being decided far, far away in the South.[46]

RIDING THE THERMALS in the damp Virginian heat, a keen-eyed turkey vulture (and there were plenty of them in the dog days of summer in 1781) would have picked out below, curls of smoke from newly burned houses and fields, a puff here, a puff there; and along the roads beside those charred fields, the gold and green turned to brown and black, a long defile of soldiers, cannon, carts and wagons pulled by patiently plodding horses, the "everlasters," as they were called in the South,[47] their heads breaking the rhythm of the walk to shake away the flies; in some of the open carts heaps of groaning men in dirty bandages; then sleeker mounts, with or without riders, walking not even at much of a trot; an inexplicably sudden charge of light cavalry exploding out of the line three abreast, tearing off somewhere as if they knew where they were going, kicking up red dust and disappearing into the woods or beyond a knoll; and behind the men and the carts and the guns, cattle, driven along and lowing as they went; and behind them, with the baggage train, more men and women and children, most of them black, dressed, when they were dressed at all, in a brilliant motley, as if returning home from a carnival a long way away. There would have been men in silk breeches and nothing else; others in perruques and silk waistcoats, their arms protruding; women in corsets and laced bodices; others in flashy, long-trailing house peignoirs; everything taken from the wardrobes of masters and mistresses who, if they were sensible, had long since high-tailed it out of the theatre of action.[48]

Behind the curling train of the army there were: geese, hogs, even cattle butchered but, in the haste to move on, left unconsumed beside smouldering fires or piled up in open wagons.[49] But then something still more pungent: the bodies of black men, women and children, near naked, covered with the blisters and running sores of smallpox. "Within these days past," wrote a Connecticut soldier, almost certainly inoculated, as were the vast majority of the Continental army, "I have marched past 18 or 20 Negroes that lay dead by the way-side, putrifying with the small pox . . . these poor creatures having no care taken of them, many crawled into the bushes about & died where they lie, infecting the air around with intolerable stench & great danger." Most of these unfortunates were simply jettisoned, much as had been the case with Dunmore's forces in 1776. But one letter from General Alexander Leslie in July 1781 suggests a much more sinister intent. Announcing that he would "distribute" seven hundred smallpox-infected Negroes "about the rebel plantations," the general was obviously attempting to spread the disease among the American army, much as the British had done with infected blankets in the Indian wars, as it closed in on the increasingly defensive British manoeuvres.[50] This was the last military use that the British generals had for the blacks who had followed them with dogged faithfulness.

And that is what Cornwallis's army was capable of as it accomplished the remarkable feat of defeating itself, rather like Laocoön thrashing in the tightening coils of serpents and thus ensuring strangulation. That the North Carolina and Virginia marches were its endgame no one could have predicted. After the crushing defeat of the Americans under General Horatio Gates at the battle of Camden in August 1780 the cause of the Crown looked anything but done for. Despite a brutal war of competitive marauding in South Carolina, each side outbidding the other in violence to civilians as well as to soldiers, the South, and Virginia in particular, seemed open for a final and definitive conquest. Or so, at any rate, it seemed to Cornwallis, who in late April 1781 decided to take his troops from North Carolina into Virginia for what he thought would be the knock-out blow, north towards the tobacco country by the shore. Now you would think, even with the promise (so Cornwallis would later claim) of reinforcements from Clinton's army in the North, that redcoats and loyalists, black and white, would have seen quite enough of the Chesapeake, of the broken shore with its sandy islands and inlets, marshes and pines. After Benedict Arnold had torched and pillaged Richmond (with Governor Jefferson *in situ*) he had returned to the scene of Dunmore's brief triumph and eventual disaster, Kemp's Landing and Great Bridge, in a second attempt to create a fortified position blocking the route to and from North Carolina. This time, in March 1781, it was black labourers and Pioneers who built the fort and demolished the long access bridge. The outcome was not much better than it had been for Dunmore. Lafayette's army and Destouches' fleet converged on Great Bridge; the blackflies and gnats of spring began to bite; and black soldiers and labourers started to go down with fevers, the speciality of the Virginia lowlands.[51] Only the news of a squadron sent from New York and the arrival of another two thousand men under General William Phillips got them off the Great Bridge more or less intact. The raiding started again up the James River: a flotilla taken at Portsmouth and tobacco chests burned.

For all the chaos and brutality; for all the untended sickness and the abandoned sick; for all the slaves forced on to public works, some of them even sent back to masters; for all the chronic uncertainty about their eventual fate; for all the rumours (mostly untrue) that they would be sent to the Caribbean and sold; wherever the British army went, in big battalions or small, in North Carolina and then in Virginia, slaves still continued to pour into their camps by the score, then in hundreds and finally thousands.[52] Many of these were slaves who had initially decided to sit out the war on their plantations, fearful of being caught by American patrols, especially after it had been made clear to local American commanders that "severe examples must be made of all negroes who carry provisions of any kind, aid or assist or carry any intelligence to . . . the enemy . . . all such negroes shall suffer death."[53] But staying put could also seem like a death sentence since it made them targets for the brutal raids carried out by both sides. Crops were cut even while they were green, and animals slaughtered. In June 1781 John Cruden, the loyalist Commissioner for Sequestered Estates in Charleston reported that many plantations were "totally destitute of that most indispensable necessity"—the harvest. "The slaves in general were almost, if not altogether naked, very scanty supplies of cloathing having been attainable for many years."[54]

So, the ongoing social catastrophe accelerated the flow of slaves to the British army, with the black refugees hoping desperately for some source of sustenance, even when the choice seemed to be between dying of hunger or dying of smallpox, since yet another wave of the disease, along with "camp fever," had hit the British camps. This was the time when the Middletons in South Carolina and the Lees, the Carters, Jefferson, George Mason and Madison in Virginia all lost substantial numbers of slaves to the British. William Lee had all sixty-five of his go; and his brother Richard Henry reported that neighbours of his had "lost every slave they had in the world . . . this has been the general case of all those who were near the enemy." Of the seven hundred slaves belonging to Thomas Nelson, the Secretary of the Virginia Council, only eighty to a hundred remained.[55] And while they exchanged laments for their losses, the planters were forced to concede that they had never seen or heard the British coercing the blacks to join them; in which case the phenomenon could be explained only by "fraud."

Cornwallis had decidedly mixed feelings about this immense, unstoppable migration. Paradoxically, the closer the British came to a conquest of the South; the more reluctant he became to engineer, even inadvertently, the wholesale destruction of its slaveholding social system. Loyalists, after all, had been guaranteed in the possession of their negroes. Some of the British commanders, notably Tarleton, came from dynasties of slave traders; and all of them were anxious not to alienate "neutrals" in the South, whose allegiance might well make the difference between victory and defeat. Whatever else he was, Cornwallis was emphatically no abolitionist. In South Carolina he had already been sufficiently anxious about the effect of so many black camp followers on the army's resources that he ordered those without a proper "Mark," indicating to which regiment or military department they were attached, to be driven, or if necessary, flogged out of camp. But it was like Canute resisting the tide. Later in the campaign as he slogged from one end of North Carolina to the other, he dealt with the inflow of yet more slaves by assigning as many as six, male and female, as servants, maids, cooks, laundresses and batmen to each of his officers and one to each of the NCOs. By the time the campaign turned north to Virginia the army was like an immense swarm of red soldier ants, marking a swathe of voracious destruction and consumption through the plantation South, grabbing what it could before its enemies got there first.

Whatever Cornwallis thought of the blacks, they still thought of him as benefactor and protector, right to the bitter end when he would do something as predictable as it was monstrous. But in August 1781, en route to that ultimate calamity, he was to Sergeant Murphy Steele of the Black Pioneers the man appointed by God to lay low the new Pharaoh: George Washington. *Go down*, Moses-Murphy, the vision had said to him, *go down* down and tell them *thus* it must be!

AUGUST 16TH, 1781. OFFICE OF THE ADJUTANT-GENERAL

Murphy Stiel [*sic*] of the Black Pioneers Says, That about a fortnight ago at Noon, when he was in the Barracks of The Company in Water Street he heard a Voice like a Man's (but saw no body) which called him by name and desired him to go and tell the Commander in Chief, Sir Henry Clinton to send word to Genl Washington That he must Surrender himself and his Troops to the King's Army and that if he did not the wrath of God would fall upon them.

That if General Washington did not Surrender, the Comm. In Chief was then to tell him that he would raise all the Blacks in America to fight against him. The Voice also said that King George must be acquainted with the above.

That the same Voice repeated the aforesaid Message to him several times afterwards and three days ago in Queen Street insisted that he should tell it to Sir Henry Clinton upon which he answered that he was afraid to do it as he did not see the Person that spoke. That the Voice then said that he must tell it, that he was not to see him for that he was the Lord and that he must acquaint Sir Henry Clinton that it was the Lord that spoke this; and to tell Sir Henry also, that he and Lord Cornwallis was to put an end to this Rebellion, for that the Lord would be on their Side.[56]

God must have been joking, for he let Cornwallis march or stagger into the trap carefully laid by Washington and Rochambeau, whilst Clinton let him stay there. The two British commanders had not seen eye to eye over Cornwallis's obstinate decision to take the campaign north into Virginia, the tardy timing of which determined its eventual fate. But if Clinton had not been deceived into thinking that an attack on New York was imminent and decided therefore to stay put, he might have put obstacles in the way of Washington's move south and perhaps have prevented the union of French and American forces closed in on Cornwallis's dug-in position on the York peninsula.

The siege began on the 23rd of September and would end almost a month later with the capitulation. British America, then, ended where it had begun more than 150 years earlier in the reign of King James I: on the Chesapeake. The French fleet under de Grasse prevented an escape into the bay, and French and American troops sealed off exit routes by land. Bombardment began and was returned. By the second week of October, ammunition and food had run disastrously low. A desperate British sortie was attempted on the night of the 15th of October, but was pushed back. After that, the outcome was just a matter of time. Cornwallis took to sulking in his tent.

On both sides of the redoubts, embrasures and trenches at York-town were thousands of blacks. A German observer wrote that as many as one in four of the Continental soldiers were black; which means that in addition to the one hundred or so of the 1st Rhode Island Regiment, and many hundreds of slaves and free blacks from St Domingue (who were not far from their own revolution), an extraordinary percentage of the Southern troops must have been black substitutes. But the notion, much aired, that this represented an "integrated" army ought to be qualified by one of the few illustrations made of a black Continental soldier: the very image of a grinning Sambo, complete with grotesquely enlarged goggling eyes, thick lips and exotically plumed hat.

At least, however, the black American soldiers were decently fed, dressed and, most important of all, inoculated. On the British side, the terrible distress that hit the black "Followers of Army and Flag," as well as the Pioneers, only got worse as the siege tightened. In mid-October Cornwallis, who had already cast off the sickest to fend for themselves in the woods, and who had ordered the slaughter of horses to pre-empt their death by starvation, now took the brutal decision to expel the blacks from the camp. "We drove back to the enemy all of our black friends," wrote the Hessian Johann Ewald, "whom we had taken along to despoil the countryside. We had used them to good advantage and set them free and now, with fear and trembling they had to face the re-ward of their cruel masters." Some of the British senior officers were deeply troubled by what they had to do. General Charles O'Hara, who would undertake the formal capitulation a week later (since Cornwallis declared himself "indisposed"), wrote that "it ought not to be done," knowing that the expulsion was a death sentence for those who were ill, and a sentence of re-enslavement for those who were not. Although he turned away four hundred blacks in his own charge, he attempted to leave them in the care of relatively sympathetic local Virginians whom he asked to be humane to the terrified and suffering blacks.[57]

Black drummers beat the muffled slow march out of Yorktown, just as they had beat the triumph at Charleston eighteen months earlier. John Laurens (at liberty after a prisoner exchange), whom Washington had appointed commissioner in charge of the surrender formalities, re-fused to grant the British the dignity of a march out with colours, bit-terly remembering Clinton's refusal of the same courtesy to the defeated

Americans in South Carolina. The ignominious capitulation was not just the best possible news for the American cause; it was also the beginning of the end of the great American slave uprising. White Virginians lost no time at all in rounding up as many errant slaves as they could, and if humanity was piously invoked as the reason, so was property. Governor Benjamin Harrison—who had lost slaves himself—made it an immediate high priority to track down as many fugitives as could be found and have them returned to their masters. On the day of the surrender General George Weedon posted sentinels along the shoreline of the York peninsula to prevent any blacks from escaping to British ships. (Despite everything they had suffered, multitudes still made desperate efforts to do just that.) Apprehensive blacks in Savannah (where a corps of 150 armed ex-slaves served in an infantry regiment under Colonel Thomas Brown) and in Charleston could have been under no illusions about what lay ahead for them should they too be discarded by, or taken from, their British protectors. In April 1782, 46 loyalists were taken from the British ship *Alert*; 11 of them were black and were promptly auctioned at a tavern in Trenton, New Jersey.

When the British prime minister, Lord North, heard the news of the surrender at Yorktown he famously cried, "Oh God, then it is all over!" It was indeed with him and his government. But it was far from self-evident that, from a purely military standpoint, the war had been irreversibly lost. Among those who refused to throw in the towel was Lord Dunmore, who returned to Charleston in December 1781 after the British position to the north had collapsed. There was an air of defiant unreality in the South Carolinan city, evidently mingled with some apprehension. There were still thousands of blacks there in both military and civilian work. Lavish "Ethiopian Balls" were held, such as the one given at 99 Meeting Street by Hagar Roussell, Izabella Pinckney and Mary Fraser, three black women who had usurped their former mistresses' names in a neat reversal of the conventions of slaveholding nomenclature, and that so disgusted Daniel Stevens, an American officer with General Greene, that he held it as a mark of the "shame and perfidy [that] the officers of that once great Nation [Britain] has arriv'd too [sic]."[58]

Restive for action, Dunmore listened attentively to the Commissioner for Forfeited Estates, John Cruden, who insisted that all was not lost; that no fewer than ten thousand black troops "inured to fatigue" could be mobilized and equipped and "when these men are raised, there can be no doubt that with the force here [in Charleston] they will be able to drive the enemy from the province and open a large door for our friends from North Carolina to join us, till such time as it may be policy, and we have a sufficient command of the sea to enter Virginia."[59] The blacks were to be drawn from the "estates of our enemy" as well as from loyal masters who would be compensated. Endorsing the plan in a letter to Clinton in February, Dunmore added that he would give his black soldiers not just a guarantee of their freedom at the end of the war, but a guinea each "and that they may be fully satisfied that this promise will be held inviolate, it must be given by the officer appointed to command them."[60]

The caution that Dunmore had shown in Virginia seven years earlier was now being thrown to the wind. What he and Cruden, and a number of fight-to-the-end generals, such as Alexander Leslie, had in mind was nothing less than an all-out revolution against the revolution; a huge insurrection, which, together with the stronghhold at Charleston, would make South Carolina (notwithstanding the fact that its countryside was over-run with Patriot partisans) the last-ditch centre of bitter resistance. Daniel Stevens, the South Carolina Patriot who had been scandalized by the "Ethiopian Ball," was even more outraged when he discovered that "the British tyrants, lost to all sense of honour, have arm'd our slaves against us."[61] At the end of March 1782 (when violent actions were still being carried out by the black and white loyalist irregulars in New York as well), Leslie carried out some hard-riding British cavalry actions in an attempt to save blacks on loyalist plantations from being taken by the Americans and to take others from rebel properties. In July he created a regiment of mounted black dragoons, which included ex-slave captain March Kingston, two lieutenants, one of whom was Mingo Leslie, three sergeants and twenty-three mounted black troopers, who fought a skirmish with Francis Marion's soldiers at Wadboo River. The regiment stayed in being for a least three more months.[62] Although Leslie made clear to Lord George Germain that he himself had no desire to command the new black brigade, the man whom most of the officers believed was right for the commission was

James Moncrief, who had been in charge of the defences at Charleston and had proved himself a considerate officer of black troops.

But Moncrief was himself a realist. In March 1782 he was more concerned that the blacks who had worked tirelessly for him "and who look up to me for their protection in this part of the country" should not be betrayed, like so many others, and that promises made to them should be honoured. Writing directly to Clinton, Moncrief reminded him of "the many advantages which his Majesty's service has derived from their labour in carrying on the different works in this and the province of Georgia. I would therefore request that your Excellency would be pleased to direct upon what footing they are to be freed before I take my departure." And he warned that "if the want of proper care and that degree of attention which is necessary to be given them should prove the means of making them lay [a]side the confidence which they always placed in us, it will be very difficult to keep them together, and should any future service be going forward which may require the labour of men carrying on works, I would beg leave to mention as my opinion that great advantage may be gained by [employing] a Brigade of the Negroes of this country."[63] But Clinton was in no position to authorize anything any more. Humiliated, embittered and embroiled in undignified rows with Cornwallis over who bore greater culpability for the fiasco in Virginia, the commander-in-chief had resigned before he could be recalled.

That same month, March 1782, North's ministry in London was replaced by a government led by the Marquis of Rockingham, a long-time critic of the American war and strongly in favour of entering peace negotiations, the basic premise of which would be the granting of independence. But a handful, at least, of the king's black soldiers were not ready, and would never be ready, to sue for peace with their former masters. In 1786, three years after the Treaty of Paris had been signed, a band of some three hundred former slaves, trained in arms by the British during the war, were still operating as freebooting partisans (or, depending on your point of view, outlaws) on both sides of the Savannah River. At a camp on Bear Creek in Effingham County on the border of Georgia and South Carolina, the blacks had created a fortified village, one mile long and four hundred feet wide, within which twenty-one houses had been built for shelter. The citadel was protected by palings, and a barrier just over four feet high of piled logs and sharpened breast-works. Crops were raised to feed what was, in effect, a free black settle-ment in the middle of the Savannah River marshes—the same swamps through which Quamino Dolly had guided Archie Campbell's troops seven years earlier to the gates of the city itself. The blacks were so suc-cessful and so famous among the field hands thereabouts that, accord-ing to Samuel Elbert, one of the officers of the Georgia militia assigned the job of tackling them, "fears were entertained of a servile insurrec-tion."

In May 1786 Governor John Mathews, who had served with Na-thanael Greene, ordered a descent on the camp at Bear Creek. In a four-day operation, using South Carolinan as well as Georgian troops and Catawba Indians, the fort was penetrated and taken. The houses were burned and the crops destroyed, although, according to Elbert, "num-bers escaped who, concealing themselves in tangled brakes, continued, as opportunity occurred, their work of theft and violence."

To the affronted slaveholders, the blacks of Bear Creek were just a criminal gang. But to the blacks of the South they were something more. They were exactly what they had decided to call themselves: "The King of England's Soldiers."[64]

V

THE FIFTH OF MAY 1783: a hostile day on the Hudson; the sky low, the wind easterly and the dull surface of the river torn by waves slapping angrily against the hulls of two British frigates as they beat ponderously upstream. In this weather the *Greyhound* lagged and the *Perseverance* (thirty-six guns, master Captain Lutwyche) persevered, as did its principal passenger, Sir Guy Carleton, His Majesty's last commander-in-chief of British forces in the thirteen revolted provinces of America.[1] He was sailing to an appointment with George Washington, although against the advice of his friend the loyalist Chief Justice, William Smith, who had told Carleton he should not do such a thing until British prisoners had been satisfactorily exchanged and the Americans had agreed to restore confiscated loyalist property or to recompense its owners for the loss. In any case, Smith suspected that Washington would "fish" for intelligence and that the "ceremonial civilities" of such occasions would cause the loyalists of New York acute pain. But Carleton was determined, and Smith accepted the invitation to accompany him, to ensure that no more careless damage would be done to the loyalist cause.[2]

Sir Guy Carleton had been in America for exactly a year and had yet to meet Washington. For months he had been seeking just such a conversation, but now that had been arranged—at Washington's invitation, not his—Carleton was feeling surprisingly out of sorts. It was not just the inconvenient touch of ague that made him wheeze and sweat, but rather a spreading sourness within. Generally, Sir Guy was not a bilious fellow. He had always sought to do his best by the Empire, which meant taking as well as giving knocks. But since returning to America the previous spring following the calamitous surrender at Yorktown, and at the express request of the king himself, he had been undercut and undercut until he had no idea of the ground on which he stood, or, indeed, where there was any left on which to stand. When he disembarked in New York his ambition had been noble, his resolve firm. He would bring rebellious America back to where it truly belonged: within the benevolence of a magnanimous, chastened (yes, he would admit as much) but more pliable British Empire. Veteran soldier though he was, Carleton knew that such a reunion could never be accomplished by force of arms alone. It would need altered dispositions and wise reforms on both sides of the ocean.

Beneath the impeccable coat and heavy frogging of the Irish military man, then, was an incurable romantic on the subject of British America. His large, dark eyes would mist at the thought of it. For how could Sir Guy not be keenly sensible to its splendour when he had been at Quebec with his friend James Wolfe and seen him die a hero's death so that British America might live? He had inherited the legacy; defended Quebec against the rebel invasion of Canada; turned back Benedict Arnold's forces on Lake George, resisted the siege that followed and stoically forbore when he was blamed for failing to take the frontier fort of Ticonderoga, and, worse, the ensuing disaster that was, in truth, the fault of his military colleagues Johnny Burgoyne and William Howe. But Canada had not become the fourteenth state of the rebel republic, so there was still a British America. Like many of his old friends and companions in arms, Carleton persisted in believing that the rebellion had been the work of a few headstrong and malevolent individuals, who time and again had mischievously frustrated efforts to abate the fury. What had been the result of their success? The wreck of the country; havoc and misery; orphans and widows. The same malcontents had purported to establish an independency that he knew could not possibly be the wish of most Americans who, given proper assurances that taxation would be entirely their own business, would like nothing better than to return to their former allegiance. The trouble, Carleton believed, had been the damnable revolutionary assemblies, too easily taken and held in thrall by vicious demagogues. Once Britain's aristo-cratic constitution—a system admirably contrived to ensure that the weight of interest prevailed over the heat of faction—was transplanted to America, moderation and temperance, the source of political felicity, would assuredly return and British America would be possessed once more of its brilliant, commanding future.

Or so Carleton understood his mission to be on his arrival on the 5th of May 1782.[3] His official appointment, shared along with Admiral Robert Digby, was, after all, "Commissioner for restoring peace and granting pardon to the Revolted Provinces." Sir Henry Clinton, the butt of rebel derision and loyalist obloquy, was about to depart for England—and good riddance too. On the 22nd of February, on the motion of General Conway, an old friend of America, the House of Commons had passed a motion to cease offensive operations, much to the displeasure of loyalists crowded in New York. In March Lord North's government had fallen, to be replaced by a ministry led by the Marquis of Rockingham and Lord Shelburne, both of whom had thought the war, from its beginning, imprudent and unjust. None of which meant that Shelburne in particular was in favour of independence, for up until now, at least, he had been emphatically against it. So even at this moment Carleton did not think all was lost—not even, should it come to it, the war. There remained eighteen thousand British, Hessian and loyalist troops in and around New York and he had been dependably informed that, with rebel militia going home in multitudes, Washington would have difficulty in getting together much of an army for a further spring campaign. Carleton had ordered two thousand German troops, ostensibly going to Nova Scotia, to decamp to New York instead. And Vermont, to which many New England loyalists had gone, was said to be crowded with friends of Britain and on the brink of repudiating Congress. As for the Royal Navy, his confidence that it would get the upper hand over the French, breaking any blockade, had been triumphantly vindicated by Admiral Rodney's destruction of de Grasse's fleet in the Caribbean in April—a retribution for the French admiral's part in the humiliation in Virginia. So, for a few months in the spring of 1782, everything seemed, to Carleton, in abeyance, and an independent America far from a foregone conclusion. He had been besieged by fervent loyalists imploring him, should Congress prove unyielding, to march.

But then, in July, as the rebels were celebrating the sixth anniversary of their Declaration, had come the deadly blow. A long-awaited letter of instruction from the new government had arrived in which Lord Shelburne, freshly designated Secretary for Colonial and Home Affairs (an office he seemed to have invented), condescended to inform the commander-in-chief that there was, in effect, nothing more to command. Unbeknownst to Carleton, the government had decided to accept Congress's adamant position: any negotiations must presuppose the fact of national independence. All at once Carleton's lofty vision of a repaired, restored and reunited British-American empire vanished like a castle in the air. He was told that his primary concern was now the detachment of America from its unfortunate dalliance with France, and to that end he should busy himself with "captivating hearts." But Carleton was a general; in his own mind a statesman too, not much concerned with exercises in captivation. Instead of being the proconsul of a regenerated British America, he was now reduced to being merely an "inspector of embarcations." His task, apparently, was simply to manage the removal of all British troops, and as many loyalists as wished to depart, in as orderly and a timely fashion as was possible. (Even this, he realized as he was pressed by the Americans to do the same, would be a Herculean task given the shortage of vessels.) Worst of all, it appeared that the discussions concerning a peace treaty taking place in Paris between British and American emissaries had already conceded independence. Not content with what Carleton let it be known he thought "a capital error," these negotiations were now proceeding without any reference whatsoever to His Majesty's commander-in-chief in America itself.

How was he to deliver these stony truths to the loyalists who had looked to Carleton as their champion and protector? They had cheered him on his arrival, and admired his fortitude in dealing with Washington over matters such as the exchange of prisoners and the securing of their confiscated property. Should it come to it, they expected him to be their general, a match even for Washington and a welcome change from the dismal procession of vainglorious incompetents who had preceded him. All this accumulated esteem, however, evaporated on the 2nd of August, when Carleton, much pained at having to be the agent of an act of monstrous bad faith, informed leading loyalists of what the government in London truly had in mind for them. William Smith, Chief Justice in New York and one of Carleton's earliest and best friends in America, was aghast. He too had been imagining a new kind of British America: one with an American Parliament invested with full fiscal authority, thus removing the great source of rancour without the trauma of imperial separation. Now he was being told that, since the British government had already conceded independence, all such speculation was futile. In response he told Carleton that so unprincipled and cowardly an act of betrayal would not only cause consternation in loyal America but must certainly "light up civil war in Great Britain." Government ministers would not be safe from assassination on the streets of London for their infamy. The abandonment was so iniquitous, Smith informed Carleton, that in their rage good loyalists were capable of throwing themselves into the arms of the Most Catholic King of France.

When the news got out to a wider circle later that month, horrified loyalists urged Carleton to fight. If he would lead an army of whites and blacks, they would follow, for death was preferable to living in republican America. When the general declined the role of leading a last-ditch resistance his standing with the loyalists plummeted, no matter how much he protested (mostly in private) that he too felt deeply the ignominy of so craven an accommodation. A week later a group of leading New York loyalists petitioned the king himself to reconsider the views of his government—but the sovereign, alas, seemed bafflingly deaf to their entreaties.

Overnight an entire community of three-quarters of a million souls, 100,000 in New York alone, had been written off in the greatest loss-cutting exercise in British history. "Our fate seems now decreed," one of them wrote bitterly, "and we are left to mourn our days in wretchedness [with] no other resource but to submit to the tyranny of exulting enemeys or settle a new country."[4] Loyalists would have the choice of exile or of believing Carleton when he told them that Congress would "recommend" the restitution of confiscated property for those opting to stay in the new republic. (The "recommendation" was never included in the published form of the treaty, which was as well since it was mostly ignored.) Carleton, shamed by the dishonour of it, wanted to resign; but he decided for the moment to stay, if only as the conscientious steward of the uprooted loyalists. On his own initiative, and knowing from first-hand experience the trials of Canadian settlement, he promised them free transportation, substantial grants of land and free supplies for a year, provisions that the home government subsequently endorsed. It was the least, thought Carleton, the guilty could do for the betrayed.

Predictably, the peremptory liquidation of British America generated rage and panic amongst the beleaguered loyalists holed up in Savannah, Charleston and New York, islands of British allegiance in a tidal surge of American patriotic euphoria and recrimination. If the situation looked forbidding, none had better cause for apprehension than the tens of thousands of black slaves who, one way or another, had served the British cause, and who (if they had them), clung to their "certificates of service" as a lifeline to freedom. Those certificates were, to be sure, just pieces of paper, albeit printed with words that had never before seen the light of day in America: an IOU liberty, the entitlement to go where the bearers pleased and to work at whatever they wished. And although such entitlement may have been contemptuously brushed aside by loyalists hustling their own slaves on to ships bound for the West Indies, or by army officers grown accustomed to having their own servile orderlies, or by the unscrupulous, who, in the economic *sauve-qui-peut* that accompanied the evacuations, thought to profit from the sale of blacks in the Bahamas or Jamaica, for all that, there were plenty of cases where the scrap of paper was honoured. One such certificate, held by Phillis Thomas, a free black in Charleston, licensed her to "go to the island of Jamaica or elsewhere *at her own option*."[5]

By the end of the war at least fifteen thousand and perhaps as many as twenty thousand blacks were living in the three British enclaves. There were many who had a stake in their fate, and few who could be counted as disinterested guardians. Southern planters, needless to say, demanded immediate and unconditional restoration of their property, and petitioned Congress for it. Some went so far as to demand that there should be no exchange or release of British prisoners, nor any finalization of the peace, until their full complement of surviving slaves had been restored. When the commandant of Charleston, General Alexander Leslie, asked Governor Mathews of South Carolina and General Greene for permission to buy rice from plantations in the countryside around the city, it was denied, since, as Greene brutally reasoned, the hungrier they were, the quicker the British would be to depart and "the fewer Negroes they will have with them."[6] Mathews also threatened Leslie with the repudiation of debts owed to British merchants or other private citizens, unless the issue was resolved to the satisfaction of slaveowners.

Conversely, white loyalists who had been given slaves taken from confiscated rebel estates were determined to resist demands for their restitution. But they had no interest in liberating the blacks in their charge. Instead, the blacks were to be taken, still enslaved, to wherever the loyalists ended up—in East Florida, Bermuda, the Bahamas, the Caribbean or Nova Scotia. Although, in this respect, there was not much to choose between returning American owners and new British masters, all the evidence suggests that the blacks themselves, still clinging to the promises of Dunmore and Clinton and fearful of punishment on the American plantations, opted in overwhelmingly greater numbers for the British. In early August 1782 General Leslie directed all those who wished to leave to register with the army; 4,230 whites and 7,163 blacks *immediately* did so.[7] When, in July, ships left Savannah in what was the first mass loyalist evacuation, their complements included some 4,000 blacks, including the 150 black infantrymen of the garrison. Notoriously, when vessels departed from Charleston in December 1782 blacks who had not been authorized to sail were so desperate to leave that they clung to the small boats taking refugees out of the harbour.

Many of those black emigrants were tragically misled. There is no doubt that the terrors of the slaves about what might be in store for them, should they return to their American owners, were cynically exploited by profiteers, who packed them on ships and resold them in the West Indies. But the complicity of the British authorities in this tragedy—assumed by Americans both at the time and in much historical writing since—is another question. When John Cruden, the South Carolina loyalist who had been in charge of "sequestered" rebel estates during the British occupation, discovered that slaves had been taken by "a Mr Gray" and resold in Jamaica, Tortola and East Florida, he was indignant enough to write to the respective governors and, shocked as much by the larceny as by the inhumanity, ask for them to be returned. In the spring of 1783 Cruden even went looking for them himself. From Tortola in March he wrote to George Nibbs that the infamous Gray "under pretence of bringing Negroes from Carolina to prevent them from being punished by their owners, has either sold or resold them for sale on this island . . . [and that] nothing can be more shocking to humanity than the deceit this man is said to be guilty of and . . . in express contradiction to the orders of the Commander-in-Chief . . . [having] brought away Negroes that are in his possession."[8] Gray and others, including one Gillespie, had apparently been trading in these shipments from other garrisons, such as Savannah and St Augustine in East Florida, and Cruden now set himself the task of preventing "unprincipled Individuals from making a property of those poor wretches" as well as bringing the criminal traders to justice. Cruden had been told the sad tale by the blacks themselves, some of whom believed they qualified under the proclamation. So while Cruden's business (seldom fulfilled) was with getting blacks back to their American owners, he was also concerned to identify those who had genuinely earned their freedom.[9]

The accelerated timetable of the Southern evacuations and General Leslie's sense of being overwhelmed by the challenge played into the hands of ruthless businessmen who were only too happy to expedite sailings. There were so many blacks to deal with—either slaves whom the loyalists said were their own, or those claiming to have won their liberty through service—that a "monstrous expence" was bound to be incurred, even if room could be found for all those wanting to leave. Directed by Carleton, a compromise solution was reached, although not wholly satisfactory to former American owners: all slaves would be returned to their American masters except those who, for whatever reason, had "rendered themselves obnoxious" to their owners, or those who had been granted their freedom by the Crown for wartime service. But this was a huge loophole. Almost any runaway from the plantations could claim, by virtue of that fact, to have become "obnoxious" and be fearful enough of what awaited them to resist being returned. Nonetheless, a joint British-American commission was to be established in Charleston to distinguish those who would be taken back to the plantations from those having a legitimate claim to be free. In the latter case, masters would be compensated by the British government for their losses.

Unsurprisingly, the arrangement quickly broke down. Thousands of blacks, their names changed to avoid identification, claimed to come under the terms of the Philipsburgh Proclamation and, as one Hessian adjutant-general noted, "insist on their rights . . . and General Carleton protects these slaves."[10] On the 12th of November Carleton had indeed restated his intention of honouring the promise to grant freedom for service, and had ordered the army not to take such persons away against their will. The fact that so many of those wanting to make good on the promise of British freedom now had what the officers called "sweethearts," as well as small children who could not have worked or fought their way to liberty, created another moral headache (and potential expense) for the commissioners. In the heyday of the property calculus, slavers would have had no compunction about dividing families, for they were treated as mere breeding units. Now, however, even hardened military men were sufficiently affected by the currently fashionable cult of sensibility to be averse to tearing apart mothers and children, husbands and wives.

Of course, white loyalists could use the pretext of keeping families united to justify removing the lot of them when they themselves departed. As the transport ships arrived in Charleston and began to load, suspicions became aggravated. Arguments and even fights broke out at the docks on the eve of sailings when American inspectors claimed peremptory rights of search and seizure. In one such incident three British soldiers were taken prisoner and the system broke down altogether. When 136 slaves claimed by Americans were discovered hidden on a British ship that was already under way, Governor Mathews threw a tantrum, declared the joint commission a fraud, and ordered the American inspectors to have nothing more to do with it. Since this meant that, before the last sailings in December 1782, between 6,000 and 10,000 blacks left Charleston on ships whose passenger lists were uninspected, this was tantamount to Mathews cutting off his nose to spite his face. The historian Sylvia Frey calculates that, along with those who had escaped during the war and gone elsewhere than Charleston, and those who had perished, at least 25,000 slaves disappeared from the South Carolina plantations: an entire world of bonded labour gone.

O N THE OTHER SIDE of the Atlantic, in Paris, British and American negotiators charged with drawing up a provisional treaty of peace believed, by late November 1782, that they had completed a mutually acceptable draft. John Jay, Benjamin Franklin and John Adams had good reason to be satisfied. The frontiers of the new state would be expansive, access to Newfoundland fisheries granted, restitution for war damages accepted. In return, not a great deal had been achieved for Britain other than the de facto end of the Franco-American alliance. The Americans would only, after all, pay debts incurred to British and loyalist creditors, but it would be *recommended* to the states that they should either return confiscated loyalist property or else reimburse owners for their losses.

But it was done and, with the draft ready for signing and sealing, all concerned were on the brink of celebrating with a dinner at Benjamin Franklin's house at Passy when, on the 30th of November, they were belatedly joined by Henry Laurens. At this eleventh hour, still evidently preoccupied by "the plunders in Carolina of negroes," Laurens insisted on inserting an additional article, specifying that the British withdrawal was to be effected "without the destruction or carrying away of American property, Negroes &c."

Securing slaves evidently mattered a great deal, then, to Laurens, even though his son had been the author of the only serious American effort made during the Revolutionary War to liberate them through military service. But Colonel John Laurens was dead, killed the previous August in a gratuitous attempt to prevent the British from foraging for the rice General Greene had denied to the Charleston garrison. The British expedition on the Combahee River, near the plantation of the Laurenses' friend Arthur Middleton, had naturally been armed. (Carleton, too, led an armed foraging expedition into Westchester on the 15th of September and took three thousand troops with him to ward off trouble.) Suddenly aware that his force of fifty men was outnumbered three to one, and faced with the choice of waiting for reinforcements or taking action, John Laurens did what he always did: he charged the guns. "Poor Laurens is fallen in a paltry skirmish," reported General Greene, who in some sense had caused it.[11] Friends who were deeply fond of John Laurens, including both Washington and Hamilton, mourned his loss, as indeed did the British themselves, who knew a gallant fool when they saw one; but no one was much astonished. His father got the heartbreaking news in mid-November in the same letter from John Adams that requested his presence at the peace negotiations in Paris. For

Henry Laurens, then, the summons of duty would master the anguish of loss—the kind of dependable Calvinist wisdom that Adams himself leaned on in adversity.

But Henry Laurens was not well. After being taken from a ship bound for France by Captain (afterwards Admiral) Keppel in HMS *Vestal* in September 1780, he had spent fifteen months in the Tower of London until Lord Mansfield granted him bail pending a prisoner exchange for Cornwallis.[12] There, in a cell about twelve feet square plus bedchamber, for which he paid rent, Laurens was subjected to periodic victimization by the petty martinet who was his warder—serenaded with pointedly satirical renditions of "Yankee Doodle Dandy" by the Yeomen of the Guard, and stingily rationed in his walks and his writing paper. He was, after a little while, allowed to have his black slave boy, George, with him, but only when others were in his cell. Although he occupied himself by annotating Gibbon's *Decline and Fall* for analogies with the British Empire, Laurens's gout became a torment and he suffered from a touch of "Thames lung." When he eventually arrived in Paris, Adams and other old friends were shocked at his shrunken appearance and doddery gait.

None of his infirmities, however, explains quite why Henry Laurens should have wanted to include, in a treaty he had little business in drafting, an article so decidedly uncharacteristic of his dead son. Perhaps the old planter, who had built his own fortune on slave labour, had reverted to type? Perhaps the act was shadowed by bitterness towards the idealism that had driven John so very often to foolhardiness—the griever aggrieved? But then Laurens may have been influenced by one of his most frequent visitors in the Tower: the Scottish businessman and African imperial venturer Richard Oswald. In his time Oswald had been many things—merchant and munitions contractor, as well as radical in many of his views, and a decided friend to America; certainly this was why he had been appointed by the Rockingham-Shelburne government to negotiate the peace treaty with Franklin and Adams. Before leaving for Paris, Oswald had confided as much to Laurens; and it had been Oswald who, with a word in the ear of the powerful, had expedited Laurens's release at the end of 1781, even when Washington had seemed in no hurry to exchange him for the Earl of Cornwallis (on parole in England!). Oswald certainly had a hand in suggesting to Adams and

Franklin that Laurens—whose son, after all, had already been a diplomat in France securing a loan for the war (what had John Laurens not done in his short life?)—should join them in Paris. But Richard Oswald also had another life—that of a slave trader who had made a cool fortune from his domination of the slaving entrepôt of Bance Island at the mouth of the Sierra Leone River, where he bought captives from the Temne people. And when those human cargoes had docked at Charleston en route to being auctioned for the low country plantations of South Carolina, it was none other than Henry Laurens who took a nice 10 percent on the transactions.

Interest, as usual, overcame piety. For although Article VII forbade "the carrying off of property," what other property could be carried off on those ships, and was more obviously valuable, than slaves? By inserting his article into the draft treaty Laurens was obliging not only his fellow Carolinans but the entire slaveholding class of the South who had made the revolution: the victors and inheritors who, with the single exception of John Adams, would dominate politics and the presidency for an entire generation.[13] There was, after all, hardly one of them who had not lost slaves as runaways to the British, and many of them, especially Virginians, approached George Washington and Congress, determined to recover their human property or, at the very least, make good financially on their losses.

SAILING UP THE HUDSON on the 5th of May 1783 against adverse winds and tides for his meeting with Washington, Carleton could have been under no illusion that restoration of negroes would not be a matter for discussion and was perhaps the most pressing reason for the general's sudden interest in a personal interview after so many months of chilly distance. This business was going to be difficult. On other matters—the speedy evacuation of British troops from Westchester, where de Lancey's loyalist Refugee Cowboys had continued their rampages undeterred by the deliberations of a few men in Paris—he could be obliging. But as regards the blacks who had been promised their liberty, he never doubted that he was bound to honour the pledge. In April that year he had sent directives to all those under his command to execute the terms of the treaty with the utmost scrupulousness. This meant doing what had been proposed at Charleston: restoring all slaves taken from rebel estates *other* than those to whom the Crown had an obligation. Of the three-thousand-plus blacks in New York, the latter would constitute the vast majority. So the machinery to examine their claims to freedom had already been set in place. A Book of Negroes had been opened, recording the names and ages of all those blacks wanting to leave with the British evacuation from New York; their physical characteristics ("stout boy," "likely wench"); and, most important, the date on which they had come to the British lines. Only those who had arrived before the end of hostilities (although that could be deemed to have occurred as late as the autumn of 1782) could take advantage of the Philipsburgh Proclamation. Those judged entitled to freedom would be issued certificates by the commandant of New York, General Samuel Birch; those judged not at liberty would be restored to their owners. All these arrangements, Carleton would patiently explain to Washington, were demonstrably in the best interests of the slaveowners themselves, since at least they would have a document of losses and thus an entitlement to compensation.

Waited on by his own black servant, Pomp (who himself had a certificate of freedom although Sir Guy dearly wished him not to leave his service), Carleton rehearsed these vexing issues as the *Perseverance* lay to at Dobb's Ferry late in the afternoon. His own Major Beckwith, who had made better time in his whaleboat, and a Major Humphreys from Washington's staff came aboard with an invitation from the American commander to dine with him on the morrow at Tappan on the west bank of the river. Carleton accepted, but must have wondered how he would be received by Washington, especially since it was known that he was now only the commander *pro tem*, until his replacement, Sir Charles Gray, could arrive? Would this undermine his authority? Could there be a true meeting of minds, an understanding between two officers and gentlemen? It had become a commonplace to remark how alike the two men were, with their taciturn sobriety, and solid, often impassive, bearing that seemed to set them above the general run of human pettiness. But even as he thought that matters could be properly settled between the two of them, Carleton knew that the history of the past, difficult year gave as many grounds for apprehension as for reassurance.

Relations between the two men through the summer and autumn of

1782 had been, at best, frosty. This, Carleton firmly believed, had been none of his doing. He had arrived in a region where civil war still raged with unsparing violence long after the guns had been silenced in Virginia. His object—especially once it had become clear that there would be no more campaigning—was to try to minimize any further misery. He had hoped, for example, for a swift exchange of prisoners (especially since he had some five hundred, whilst the Americans held more than six thousand). But Congress, outraged at the atrocious conditions to which American prisoners had been subjected on board the notorious British hulks in New York and Brooklyn, had insisted that Britain pay arrears of charges for their keeping of its own captured soldiers before any such exchange could be finalized. It even threatened to reduce prisoners' rations unless the matter was promptly settled. Predictably, Shelburne, who had become Prime Minister in July after Rockingham's death, balked at being presented with a bill. Distressed about the privations endured by British prisoners, many of whom were in rags or half-naked, Carleton proposed that at least army surgeons and chaplains might be immediately released; but he had no success. He then asked for a personal meeting with Washington to try to reconcile differences, but met with no warmer response. A conference of commissioners from both sides at Tappan, New York, in September 1782 merely ended up sharpening the acrimony. Passes were applied for to take rudimentary supplies of food and clothing to British prisoners, but were denied. Why, Carleton wondered, with the kind of genteel innocence that was his hallmark, was Congress so determined to "bring the war to the last extremities of rage"?

Washington's implacable severity dismayed him. In the matter of Captain Charles Asgill, he thought, it bordered on the inhuman. Asgill had become a pawn in the brutal vendetta between Patriot and loyalist irregulars in New York and New Jersey. At the eye of the storm was the Patriot partisan Captain Joshua Huddy. By fatally wounding Colonel Tye, Huddy had earned the hatred of black loyalists. By summarily executing a loyalist militiaman, Steven Edwards, he was detested by their white counterparts. So when the Associated Loyalists marched the captured Huddy to the Dover Cliffs, and instead of exchanging him for a British prisoner, hanged him, it may have been a crime, but it was no surprise. Nonetheless, when Washington got news of Huddy's death, he was apopleptic, demanding that Sir Henry Clinton immediately hand over the loyalist responsible, one Lippincott, to American justice. But Clinton had replied cooly that the matter was under investigation and that Lippincott might be tried by British court martial.

Inheriting the dispute, Carleton had written a politely conciliatory letter to Washington regretting the "passions of private and unauthorised persons" and daring to hope that the cycle of retaliations might be over. As a gesture of good faith, he released the son of Governor Livingston of New Jersey. But this cut no ice. Strongly implying that, if acts of barbarism had been committed in the late war, it was the British who had been responsible for the most atrocious of them, Washington replied to Carleton that the "unnatural war" had been disfigured by "inhuman excesses which in too many instances . . . marked its progress." He declared that in the circumstances he would have no option but to choose, by lot, from among the British prisoners a surrogate for Lippincott who, if the matter was not properly settled, would be executed in his stead.

The lot fell on the nineteen-year-old Charles Asgill, the heir to a baronetcy and a captain in the 1st Guards, who was among the thousands of prisoners taken at Yorktown. Although the terms of the capitulation expressly forbade any of those prisoners being used as hostages, on Washington's orders, Asgill was taken from Lancaster, Pennsylvania, to Morristown, New Jersey, put under close confinement and made aware of his fate should the British position not change. Shocked by the cold-blooded application of the *lex talionis,* an eye for an eye, along with Washington's grim resolve to see it through, and aware that the British garrison in New York, enraged by Asgill's misfortune, would much rather see Lippincott punished than Asgill (the loyalists, of course, felt the opposite), Carleton thrashed around for a judicious solution. He promised Washington that the court martial of Lippincott—postponed first so that the defendant could have time to prepare his case, then a second time while the legality of a court martial on an irregular soldier was adjudicated—would be hastened. And so it was; but its verdict— acquittal on the grounds that Lippincott had acted merely on orders from others in the Associated Loyalists—was unlikely to help Asgill very much.[14] Nor did Carleton's insistence that he would find those really responsible for the hanging.

What saved the young guards officer was the inflation of the Asgill matter into *"L'Affaire Asgill,"* the talk of the European salons and gazettes in the autumn of 1782. It had all the elements of the sentimental romance, much in vogue in this, the same year as the appearance of Rousseau's *Confessions*: a stricken mother; a father on his death bed; a sister distraught and in "delirium"; one sternly unbending general, and his opposite number desperate for a solution that would be both humane and just. Given the news about her son, the anguished Theresa Asgill had written to Carleton to implore his personal intercession. Instead of shrugging his shoulders Carleton had a stroke of genius, suggesting that the mother write instead to the French Foreign Minister, Count Vergennes, in the knowledge that the fashionable cult of sensibility had a strong grip on the French aristocracy. Theresa Asgill, as it turned out, knew just what to do and how to do it.

> Figure yourself, Sir, the situation of a family in these circumstances. Surrounded as I am with objects of distress, bowed down by fear and grief, words are wanting to express what I feel and to paint such a scene of misery: my husband given over by his physicians some hours before the arrival of this news is not in a condition to be informed of it; my daughter attacked by a fever accompanied with delirium; speaking of her brother in tones of wildness and without an interval of reason . . . let your sensibility, sir paint to you my profound, my inexpressible misery and plead in my favour, a word, a word from you like a voice from Heaven would liberate us from desolation, from the last degree of misfortune. I know how General Washington reveres your character. Tell him only that you wish my son restored to liberty, and he will restore him to his desponding family; he will restore him to happiness . . . I feel the whole weight of liberty taken in presenting this request but I feel confident, whether granted or not, that you will pity the distress by which it was suggested; your humanity will drop a tear on my fault and blot it out for ever
>
> May that Heaven which I implore grant that you may never

need the consolation which you have it in your power to be-
stow on

THERESA ASGILL

Once he had stopped sobbing, Vergennes passed the letter on to Louis
XVI and Marie Antoinette who—mother to mother—melted in sympathetic sorrow. The *philosophe* Diderot's correspondent, Grimm, began to
embroider the scene, claiming that a gallows was being built directly
outside Charles Asgill's cell and that he had been taken thrice to the
gibbet only for the agonized Washington to find himself incapable of
giving the order for his execution. The journals and gazettes reported
that passengers disembarking from ships coming from America were
immediately asked, "What news of Asgill?"

Representations were made from Versailles to Philadelphia and
New York. Informed that Lippincott would indeed be brought to trial,
Washington was beginning to be plagued by a troubled conscience. He
wrote uncharacteristically guilty letters to Asgill himself, expressing his
earnest wish that the matter, properly resolved would result in the
young man's release. And in August he told Asgill that his fate and the
whole issue was to be laid before Congress. A combination of sentiment
and prudence eventually did the trick. A stormy three-day debate took
place in early November, with a majority of the Congress still bent on
the execution. On the third day of the debate a letter from Washington,
known to be on the side of clemency, was read out along with those
from Louis XVI and Marie Antoinette as well as Theresa Asgill's personal appeal to the queen that "on the whole," Boudinot reported, "was
enough to move the heart of a savage." The substance was a request
from Washington to spare the life of young Asgill, which operated like
an electric shock—each member looking at his neighbour in surprise as
if saying, "Here is unfair play." The most hardened members, suspecting some sort of fraud, demanded to see Washington's letter and examined his signature for authenticity. Since it seemed to be in order, it was
unanimously resolved that Asgill's life should be preserved as a "compliment to the King of France."

Delivered from her agony, Theresa Asgill wrote again to Vergennes
with no apparent loss of poetic passion: "May this tribute bear testi-

mony, to my gratitude long after the hand that expresses it, with the heart which at this moment only vibrates with the vivacity of grateful sentiments, shall be reduced to dust." A hugely relieved Washington ordered Charles Asgill's release, and at the same time sent him a letter begging, in effect, to be absolved from blame; he asked Asgill to appreciate that the order for his detention and execution had been signed not from any "sanguinary" motive but merely from a right sense of duty, and that no one other than the young man himself could possibly have greeted the news of liberty with more complete happiness than the general. Needless to say, hack playwrights in Paris immediately started to write Asgill plays, which, in one case at least, were a huge hit. Asgill himself went on to a long career in the British army fighting the French, thus biting the hand that had liberated him.

It was uncertain which Washington would confront Sir Guy Carleton: the stone-faced defender à l'outrance of American interests, or the humane, philosophical statesman?

O N THE MORNING of the 6th of May, two barges took the British party across the river. In Carleton's barge were his secretary, Maurice Morgann; the British lieutenant-governor of New York, Andrew Elliot; and Chief Justice Smith. Captain Lutwyche and a party of naval and military officers followed to show the flag for the king. At Tappan Sloot beneath the cliffs of the Palisades, where the boat docked, there was a smart military band and a full American guard of honour for Sir Guy in his scarlet dress coat to inspect. There, too, was George Washington, come from Newburgh and awarding the first medals of the freshly created order of the Purple Heart. Both generals were suffering afflictions: Carleton a heavy cold and Washington toothache. But history beckoned them to a show of cordiality. There was an exchange of courtesies, a shaking of hands, before Carleton climbed into a coach and four with Washington for the short drive to the Amos de Wint house where the meeting was to take place. Others took the horses they were offered, while William Smith and Andrew Elliot chose, rather Britishly, to walk.

The de Wint house was, did Carleton but know it, an inauspicious place for Anglo-American reconciliation. It looked innocent enough: a standard Hudson valley Dutch farmhouse, parlour and kitchen on the ground floor, two bedchambers above, with flaring gables overhanging whitewashed brick and stone walls on which, in the Dutch fashion, the date of its construction, 1700, had been set. There was a fenced grassy yard; the dogwood had uncurled its papery buds, and on a weedy pond ducks paddled about, indifferent to great men and moments.[15] But the de Wint house had a grim history. In 1780 it had been Washington's headquarters, and there Major André, the British spy who had orchestrated Benedict Arnold's defection and the failed attempt to surrender West Point, had been tried and sentenced to death. On the 6th of May, however, its doorway was the scene of an hour of meaningless pleasantries, after which business was convened in the larger of the two rooms that took up the ground floor. There were Delft tiles on the wall, oak beams in the ceiling, and precious little light admitted through the leaded windows. The mood was weighty. Around the table sat Washington's secretary, Jonathan Trumbull, the attorney-general of New York Egbert Benson, the American governor of New York, George Clinton (who, William Smith acidly noted, had once been his legal clerk) and John Morin Scott, New York's Secretary of State. For all the courteous preliminaries, neither Clinton nor Scott was prepared to tolerate temporizing from the British. They should go, go soon and without the negroes. Opening the proceedings, Washington got to the heart of the matter right away, bringing Carleton's attention to Article VII before asking for a definite timetable for the remaining evacuation from Westchester, New York and Long Island. He spoke, as he generally did, in a low, even tone: the voice of gravitas, of history. But the famous mask of dispassion broke when he heard Carleton's response.

Before they had ever met, there was something about Sir Guy Carleton that had irritated Washington. It was the British general's habit to lecture him, in their correspondence, on the general subject of humanity and what he presumed was their common duty towards it. Dear General Washington, on the subject of the piteous plight of the prisoners. . . . Your Excellency, knowing full well your concern to relieve the unfortunate young Captain Asgill . . . General Washington, would not it be possible to grant some leave for clothes to be delivered to the neediest . . . ? And now, it seemed, the man was concerned with the fate of negroes, *our* negroes, *my* negroes! When Carleton began his reply there had been no cause for concern, except that the general seemed determined to address the concerns in the opposite order from the one in which Washington had set them out. On the changing of the guard in Westchester? To be done and done swiftly; already orders had been given to withhold supplies from de Lancey's Refugee Cowboys. Long Island? Not so fast, for want of both ships and some security to protect loyalists during the departure. But it would happen; all in good time, as soon as the vessels were come—they would be gone before the year was out.

Indeed, Carleton was doing all he could to expedite the embarkations. There had already been two previous sailings, one as early as October 1782, in which 56 blacks are recorded among the 501 passengers sailing for Halifax, followed by a much bigger departure at the end of April 1783 when 6,000 had left for Nova Scotia.[16] The ships had been, and would be, inspected for any irregular carrying off of negroes; a book had been begun to record them so that owners might be compensated.

What? Washington reddened and interrupted. "Already imbark'd!" Carleton stared back, his voice still even, his demeanour cool, his manner maddeningly superior. Now the general must know, of course, that whatever the draft treaty might or might not say, "no Interpretation could be put on the Articles inconsistent with *prior Engagements binding the National Honour which must be kept with all colours* ."[17]

All colours. It was Carleton's moment of truth and, he supposed, the vindication of his woeful, defeated kingdom, which, as long as he had anything to do with it, would at least rescue from the sordid debacle a shred of decency and honour. And it was his revenge over the Paris negotiators, British and American both, and their easy, blithe abandonment of the promises made to unfortunate blacks—promises that should and would be kept.

Incredulous, Washington kept his peace and remained stonily silent. But uproar broke out in the room as John Morin Scott became heated, accusing the British of violating articles already agreed on in Paris whilst the Americans had fully honoured their side. The British hit back by charging that the recent Trespass Act, which allowed owners of property to sue for damages those who had occupied it during the war, was irreconcilable with all known conventions of war. It got worse when (with Vermont still reputed to be against independence) Governor

Clinton was asked by the British side whether, in the event of states disagreeing with Congress, they could be allowed to go their own way. Not at all, shouted Clinton. Voices rose, tempers flared. Carleton attempted to douse the sparks, expressing a *liberal* desire to look at any propositions made. An awkward, angry pause followed, broken by Washington and Carleton returning politely to the expediting of the evacuation. They were going round in circles, with the huge, unresolved, irreconcilable matter, in the middle of it all. There was nothing more to be done. Washington pulled out his watch, "and observing it was dinner time, offered Wine and Bitters. We all rose with Sir Guy."[18]

A tent had been set up on the grass beside the de Wint house. Within was the very best that Samuel Fraunces, who kept a tavern in Manhattan and whom Washington would bring back as chef in his New York, Germantown and Philadelphia houses, could lay on for the princely sum of £500: oysters, cutlets, pies, roasts and the enormous puddings for which he was deservedly famous. Would that he could have eavesdropped on the earlier proceedings, for Fraunces was Black Sam, a free negro whose entire life had been a stirring Anglo-American adventure. His first New York tavern had been named the Queen's Head in honour of Queen Charlotte, George III's consort, but had then become a favourite meeting place for radical Patriots. His daughter Phoebe was credited with undoing a plot to poison Washington's peas, which, thrown out of the window, promptly killed some chickens pecking below. But he had also entertained the British during the occupation before making his way to the American side in New Jersey. Now Black Sam, in the glory of his immaculate coat and white wig moved among the gentlemen and the puddings, ensuring that copiousness, if not harmony, prevailed.

There was supposed to have been reciprocity, Captain Lutwyche and General Carleton inviting Washington and his side to dine on the *Perseverance* the following day. They did indeed come, and for the first time Americans were accorded the honours of high officers of army and state: a seventeen-gun salute, repeated on their departure that evening. Absent from the lengthy dinner was Carleton himself, confined to bed by an aggravation in his condition—although the possibility that his indisposition might have been at least partly diplomatic could not have escaped the Americans. When it was time for the Americans to leave in their boats Carleton got up and bade them farewell, late enough to ensure that nothing of importance on the issue of the blacks could be said.

In any case, Carleton's mind was made up. Washington followed up the meeting at Tappan with a testy letter and Carleton duly replied, repeating his position that, whilst every effort would be made to record most faithfully all negroes wanting to leave, and whilst American officials had already joined the inspection of outgoing ships, he would do nothing to impair the liberty of "Negroes who had been declared free previous to my arrival; as I had no right to deprive them of that liberty I found them possessed of." By acting correctly, Carleton insisted he was doing the slaveowners a favour since, should the blacks have been denied the right to embark, they would "in spite of every means to prevent it, have found various means of quitting this place so that the former owners would no longer have been able to trace them and of course would have lost in every way all chance of compensation." But then Carleton could not resist the opportunity of once again putting Washington in his place. "I must confess," he added, "that the mere supposition that the King's minister could deliberately stipulate in a treaty an engagement to be guilty of a notorious breach of the public faith towards the people of any complexion, seems to denote a less friendly disposition than I could wish and I think less friendly than we might expect."[19]

Nothing could be more perfectly calculated to make Washington livid. But he was also a realist and understood, for all the rage boiling over in the South and in Congress, that he had limited options through which to enforce Article VII. It would be many years before the democratic American republic would give up attempting to restore slaves to their old owners and claims for compensation were still being argued after the War of 1812, when yet another wave of blacks sought protection and freedom in the British lines. What could he do in 1783? Should he go along with those who advised the repudiation of British debts? That would be taken as an abrogation of the treaty and even though the most infuriated, such as James Madison, argued that by their stand on the negroes the British had already made it a dead letter, Washington was not about to restart the war—not with the Royal Navy dominant once more in the western Atlantic. So Washington—who was, in any case, conflicted about the morality of his own slaveowning—became fatalistic about the loss of the blacks. When the agent hunting for escaped slaves, including two Black Pioneers from the plantation of Benjamin Harrison, was briskly told by Carleton that there was no question of their returning without their own consent, Harrison appealed directly to Washington. But the meeting at Tappan had convinced Washington, for he wrote that same day to Harrison that "the Slaves which have absconded from their Masters will never be restored to them." He understood perfectly Harrison's chagrin and added that indeed "several of my own are with the Enemy but I scarce ever bestowed a thought on them; they have so many doors through which they can escape from New York [so Carleton had been right about that!] that scarce any thing but an inclination to return . . . will restore many."[20]

Not every slaveowner was quite so stoical. Thirteen Virginian owners who among them had lost three hundred slaves made a combined effort to recapture them and petitioned Congress to intervene.[21] Theodorick Bland hired a special agent, Jacob Morris, to track down his own slaves, but with little luck. One whom he did find told him that the blacks in New York knew very well that many of those who had returned "have been treated with very great severity by their former masters"—usually a flogging—and that it was unlikely, therefore, that many would either let themselves be caught or come of their own accord. The expense of tracking down the slaves over weeks or even months when so many of them had, in any case, changed their names could be even more ruinous than the loss of the blacks themselves. To have any chance of locating the runaways the agents needed help from New Yorkers, but that in turn risked the draconian punishments that Carleton imposed on anyone caught colluding in illegal returns. Thomas Willis, a policeman found guilty of taking a bribe to force a black called Caesar on to a ship that took him to Elizabeth, New Jersey, and who had been shameless enough to beat the man through the streets with his hands tied, was fined the huge sum of fifty guineas and deported. Another slave, recaptured by his owner, Jacob Duryea, and tied to a boat, was liberated on the Hudson River by a black partisan named Colonel Cuffe and a party of Hessians, who themselves had many blacks in their regiment.[22]

None of this managed to assuage the fears felt by the black community in New York, knowing that their old persecutors were free to come to the city and track them down. For them, the end of the war meant the renewal of terror. Boston King, who had taken so many pains to escape "the Americans" and who now had a wife, Violet, and children, captured perfectly the dread that swept through the black community of New York.

> About this time, peace was restored between America and Great Britain which diffused universal joy among all parties except us, who had escaped slavery and taken refuge in the English army; for a report prevailed at New-York that all the slaves, in number two thousand, were to be delivered up to their masters, altho' some of them had been three or four years among the English. This dreadful rumour filled us with inexpressible anguish and terror, especially when we saw our old masters coming from Virginia, North-Carolina and other parts and seizing upon slaves in the streets of New-York, or even dragging them out of their beds. Many of the slaves had very cruel masters, so that the thought of returning home with them embittered life to us. For some days we lost our appetite for food, and sleep departed from our eyes. The English had compassion upon us in the day of our distress, and issued out a Proclamation importing "That all slaves should be free who had taken refuge in the British lines and claimed the sanction and privileges of the Proclamations respecting the security and protection of Negroes." In consequence of this, each of us received a certificate from the commanding officer at New-York, which dispelled our fears and filled us with joy and gratitude.[23]

Those certificates, signed by Brigadier General Samuel Birch, represent a revolutionary moment in the lives of African-Americans. They affirm that the bearer, having "resorted to British Lines . . . has hereby his Excellency Sir Guy Carleton's Permission to go to Nova Scotia, or wherever else He/She may think proper." Only one of the Birch certificates survives, made out in the name of Cato Ramsey, formerly slave to a Dr John Ramsey of Norfolk, Virginia, from whom he escaped in 1776.[24] Ramsey, according to the Book of Negroes "45, slim fellow," was a fugitive who had somehow reached Lord Dunmore's ships; survived everything the war could throw at him—smallpox, typhus, privation and wandering; and had still made it to New York and liberty. Now he was on the brink of a new life that could begin with a farewell to America.

There were thousands like Cato Ramsey, men, women and children, anxiously awaiting their fate. And the evidence suggests that, unlike the brutal and chaotic exodus from Charleston, on this occasion Carleton and his officers took pains to try to make the ordeal less harrowing. A document headed "Precis relative to Negroes in America," probably drafted by Carleton himself in the latter part of 1783, took an even more liberal view of black eligibility for departure than Boston King suggested. The cut-off date for qualifying entry to the British lines was set as late as "the day the Treaty came Forward"—November 1782 at the earliest. The same document makes clear that the Board of Inquiry appointed to adjudicate claims made by American masters on their former slaves, considered as free even those blacks who as yet had "no regular protections or certificates." This presupposes yet another milestone in the history of black liberation in America: that in the British, they had finally found white authorities who would believe what they said when they related their life histories, irrespective of any written documentation. Of the 3,000 certificates granted in New York, 813 were honest enough to make no pretence of having answered the Proclamations, but pleaded none the less that they had escaped from rebel masters and gone to the British during the war. And this was good enough.

Even more surprising is the fact that, as the "Precis" makes irrefutably clear, by 1783 there was a "Somerset effect" (the benign misreading of the Mansfield judgement) operating on the decisions made by Carleton and his principal officers. For, in contrast to Dunmore's purely military opportunism, the "Precis" adds that the negroes who came into the British lines were considered free, "the British Constitution not allowing of slavery but holding out freedom and protection to all who came within." The certificates given to the departing blacks were, according to the writer of the "Precis," unequivocally and "universally deemed equal to Emancipation."[25]

Once again, Black Sam Fraunces was at the scene of the drama. For it was at his tavern that the Board of Inquiry deliberated disputed claims every Wednesday noon from April to November, when the last sailing left New York. Americans sat with their British counterparts hearing cases, even after Washington had been instructed in mid-July that they should cease participating in what Congress clearly decided was a mockery. To American displeasure, only a handful of blacks were ever returned to their masters as a result of these proceedings, sometimes even when loyalists were the claimants. Judith Jackson had fled her master near Norfolk, Virginia, as early as 1773 along with her baby daughter, and had stayed in the loyalist town until the arrival of Dunmore two years later when she got work as a laundress for the regiment, following the army first to South Carolina and finally to New York. Her case for a certificate (already given to her) seemed foolproof. But in 1783 a second party, a Mr Eilbeck, to whom she had been consigned after her owner left for England, showed up before the board in New York and insisted that, as a loyalist, he had the right to Jackson and her children. Stumped, the board forwarded the case to Carleton himself, who had no difficulty in deciding. Judith Jackson and her children went free.[26]

Anxieties did not end in the Fraunces tavern. Down on the dock a group of four inspectors, including Americans, went through a final, on-deck examination, first of the passenger list and then of the black passengers themselves, to ensure that persons matched names, and that no one was aboard who had not been recorded in the Book of Negroes. Masters had to swear on pain of "severe penalties" that nothing or no one illicit was being carried off. In theory blacks could be removed at the very last minute, but in practice this last excruciating denial seems to have happened only very rarely. Doubtless it was an ordeal, but it was the last inspection that more than two thousand blacks would ever undergo.

On the waterfront in the rank, grimy sweat of high summer, on the days before embarkation, a passer-by would have observed a heaped mass of rope and canvas; a logjam of wagons and horses; the creak of masts, the crack of whips; cursing drivers, opportunist gulls, hogs and dogs; ship's cows lowing as they were herded on board; skinny ship's cats already prowling the decks; barrels and tuns of salt tack and biscuit, tar and rum, blocking the wharf, drunks from the grogshop lurching between them; chests piled high as a house on the decks before being lowered into the hold; the usual swarm of sailors and stevedores, and buyers and vendors, thieves and whores; much pissing and kissing; a capering fiddler; a thunderer handing out tracts to save all souls lest the deep take them. But also, amidst the mêlée, an observer would have seen the passengers, men with their hats on and their coats off, bonneted women and scatters of children, some dozing, some scampering, some slouching towards their frightening future; hundreds, on some days thousands of them, many of whom had seen better days, and some of whom had seen much, much worse.

Two different worlds were going with the *Lady's Adventure*, the *Grand Duchess of Russia*, the *Peggy*, the *Mars*, the *Hesperus*, the *Fishburn*, the *Kingston*, the *Stafford*, the *Clinton* and *L'Abondance*. Between April and November, 27,000 loyalists embarked, uprooted, disconsolate, demoralized, stripped of power, wealth and property, or even simple farms and cottages; many of them roiling with bitterness at their betrayers in London—the fat politicians counting their gold from East India opium, salt and tea (*that* tea!), and the generals who got to retire to a country estate in the shires, while decent loyalists had to make shift hundreds of miles to the north, beginning again in the piny desert amidst ravening beasts, bears and wolves, or on the cobbled byways of an alien town. And these dispossessed loyalists were less than delighted to be cheek by jowl with that other class of people, dressed who knows how, scarcely more than beggars or low tavern musicians, their babies sucking at the tit; a class of people who might teach their own slaves insolent manners. Worse, the blacks had the gall to sing while they were lost in sorrow. *Sing*! What was there to sing about?

Everything. Rebirth. British freedom. God's loving kindness; His all-encompassing mercy; the honest goodness of the king; the word of Sir Guy Carleton; the promises of food for a year; a piece of land for the rest of their lives. Born again. Born again, dear Lord. The wide sea-water lay before them, out beyond the harbour, trembling in the July haze, the tips of the wavelets transformed into melting bars of light. There had been so many boats, so many passages in the night, so many experiences on the water over which they were about to be conveyed to a new life. There were the pettiaugers they had taken while they lay low in the reeds of Carolina; the tenders that had taken them out to the big ships; the ins and outs of the islands and marshes of the Chesapeake; their folk dying on the sands from fever; the whaleboats that had hunted them and the whaleboats in which they themselves had hunted; the mud they had walked, hard or enveloping; the rivers they had swum across. And wherever they found themselves they had been looking always for Jordan, for Milk and Honey.

The gangway was thrown down. On to *L'Abondance* (master, Lieutenant Philips) in the last three days of July 1783 came every age and condition of African-American: Judith Wallis, two weeks old, at her mother Margaret's breast; Elizabeth Thomson, carrying Betty, four months old; the septuagenarian Jane Thompson from Norfolk, Virginia, described in the Book of Negroes, understandably, as "worn out," who came with her eleven-year-old grandchild.[27] The Americans had said that the British would take only stout (meaning healthy) adult negroes, leaving the sickly and decrepit behind. But there were more than 20 "worn out" blacks among the 335 on *L'Abondance,* including the sixty-seven-year-old John Sharp and the prematurely worn out forty-year-old Juno Thomas from Savannah. Henry Walker, on the other hand, although sixty, was optimistically classified as a "stout man of his age."

There were nearly as many females as males among the departing blacks: *L'Abondance* took on board 137 women and 29 girls, as well as 35 infants. This was remarkable since, before the war, 80 percent of all runaways had been men. But these women—Hannah Whitten, who had left William Smith in Virginia in 1778 with three children (now she had five); plain Margaret, who had got up and gone when she was sixty and who now (with his parents presumably dead) had charge of her fifteen-year-old grandson, Thomas; Nancy Moody, who had left Henry Moody of Williamsburg when she was only nine; Lydia Newton, who had been eight when she had walked off; Charlotte Hammond, "small wench," who had left John Hammond on the Ashley River in South Carolina when she was fifteen in 1776; or her near neighbour, Venus Lagree, who had gone with her one-year-old son from Mallaby Rivers; or Judy Weedon, fourteen, "fine girl," who seemed all alone but "free as per bill of sale"—all these women and girls were, in their several ways, heroic survivors of the worst the war could throw at them: disease, starvation, terror and siege.

Some women, such as Cathern Van Sayl from Monmouth, New Jersey, who had come to the ship with her husband, Cornelius, and their two daughters, travelled as a family. Some, such as Violet and Boston King (he in his early twenties, she in her middle thirties) came together but childless. Many had come from different places, finding each other along the way in some army camp or in the black quarter of Savannah or Charles Town or in Negro Town in New York itself. Daniel Moore had left Wilmington, North Carolina, and met Tina from Portsmouth, Virginia, who in 1777 had given birth to their daughter Elizabeth, "a fine child . . . and born within the British lines." Not all were so lucky with the health of their babies. Duskey York, from Charles Town, who had escaped in the British advance into the South in 1779, and Betsey, from the Eastern Shore of Virginia, had with them Sally, now eighteen months, and classified, ominously as "sickly." Many more, for instance, Jane Milligan and her nine-month-old Maria, or Abby Brown and her three-year-old Dinah, another sickly child, were single mothers, just doing what they needed to keep their children safe and sound.

Though the odds were long, the mothers and fathers had something precious to take with them, something that no slave children had had before them: a piece of paper certifying that they were "Born [or Born Free] Behind British Lines"; sometimes it was a mere abbreviation, "BB"—and yet it was a birthright of liberty. Sometimes the BB babies were New Yorkers—Keziah Ford, two; Simon Roberts, six months; Mary Snowball, three months; and Violet Collett, just three weeks old. Others had got their birthright on the campaign trail—Grace Thomson, two; Betsey Lawrence, three; and four of Hannah Whitten's five children (eight, seven, six, five and one!). But all of them were, in some fashion, the godchildren of King George and Sir Guy: a generation whose life, at least in the summer of 1783, promised something other than treatment as merchandise.

To L'Abondance, to the ark on the dock, they came from all over slave America, from Charleston and Norfolk, Savannah and Paramus, Hackensack and Princeton—even from relatively enlightened Boston and Philadelphia; from Swansea, Massachusetts, from Poughkeepsie, New York, and Jamaica, Long Island; from Portsmouth, Rhode Island, and Portsmouth, Virginia. There were those destined to be makers and leaders of a new world for blacks, such as Thomas Peters, the sergeant in the British Pioneers, now with his wife, Salley, and their daughter, Clara, and his fellow sergeant, Murphy Steele, who had had the headless vision in Virginia; Stephen Blucke, the commander of the Black Brigade after Colonel Tye's death, with his wife, Margaret, and his rather grand airs; and the blind, crippled preacher Moses Wilkinson, doubtless carried on board praising, as was his wont, the wonders of the Lord's doing.

But where were they going? Somewhere called Port Roseway, a harbour in Nova Scotia; a new Scotland, so perhaps carpeted in heather and running with deer? They would have land; they would have liberty; they would have dignity; they would have churches; they would have each other. It was, probably, cold. But they had been warm and had been slaves. And whatever it might be, this second Scotland, it could not possibly be worse than where they had come from.

Could it?

VI

I T WAS NOT as easy as you might think, throwing slaves overboard—not live ones, anyway. Of course, it was done all the time
with dead negroes. The wastage rate on most passages from Africa
to the Caribbean and America was 15 percent. For all the searching in-
spections at the forts and factories on the slave coast, all the yanking of
jaws and pinching of gams, the surgeons still could not say, not for sure,
who was truly a "stout negro." What with the bloody flux and the white
flux, the retchings and the fever sweats, the blacks became dehydrated
and, before you knew it, were too weak to eat their horsebean pulp or
to sip from the pannekin at the tub. Their eyes would turn yellow and
glassy and they would tremble in a feverish shiver. Or else (and this was
a worse sign) they would lie quite still in a waking swoon, their lips
caked and white. White was the African colour of death. After a few
days they either got well or were gone.

When the surgeon had finished his morning tour, the dead were
brought up. Sometimes they were still shackled to the living. Since it
was easier to get the pair of them on deck before loosing the irons, the
live black was regrettably obliged to witness the disposal of his dead
companion as the battenboards at the waist of the ship were lowered
and the body cast overboard.[1] No one was happy about this, other than
the schools of sharks that had learned to follow the ships. Such a loss of
investment—thirty guineas written off for each adult negro! And since
Liverpool and Bristol underwriters had been careful to exempt them-

selves from making good any losses from "natural wastage," an especially heavy toll of blacks could eliminate the profit from a voyage altogether.

There was, however, a loophole, and Captain Luke Collingwood, the master of the *Zong* trading from the Slave Coast of Africa to Jamaica on the account of Messrs Gregson (John, James and William), Cave, Wilson and Aspinal, believed he had found it. If circumstances should arise when a *parcel* of a cargo had, perforce, to be jettisoned in order to save the remainder, the insurers were liable for the full value of the abandoned goods. In November 1781, bound for Jamaica and with negroes dying at an alarming rate, Collingwood, who apparently had once been a doctor himself, believed that such circumstances had in fact arisen.[2] He had begun the voyage at São Tomé island off the coast of Gabon on the 6th of September with a full complement of 440 slaves. The traders' euphemism for these goods was "live cargo." But by November, death had eaten away the inventory: 60 slaves had already perished from a foul fever that had also carried off 7 of the 14 white passengers. To make matters worse, the voyage of the *Zong* had been prolonged by a navigational error so gross that it would have been hard to credit had this not been Collingwood's first command. Jamaica had been in sight; but for some reason Collingwood supposed the shore to be that of Santo Domingo/St Domingue, the island divided between the French and Spanish, both of whom, in 1781, remained at war with Britain. Denied the prospect of safe harbour and worried about privateers, Collingwood had ordered a course hard to the lee, which had extended his sailing by a wholly unnecessary week.

Down in the hold, amidst the slop of mucus, blood, shit, piss and black vomit, slaves continued to sicken.[3] From the beginning, the *Zong* had been a mistake. When she was taken as a prize from the Dutch, someone had misread the "r" of the name painted on its side as an "n." So the *Zorg,* the "Care," had become in name a sunny, sing-zongy vessel of old Africk, destined for fair winds and prosperous trade. But, truly, *Zorg* it stayed, a shipload of worry.

On the 29th of November Collingwood summoned his officers and suggested a course of action that he represented as a mercy killing. With so many blacks grievously sick, it would be, he asserted, "less cruel to throw wretches into the sea than to offer them to linger out a few days under the disorder with which they were affected."[4] Moreover, he said, their unexpectedly protracted journey had depleted the water supply, without which not only the slaves but the crew and passengers would suffer and perhaps perish. To conserve what water there was for the healthy meant, regrettably, the sacrifice of the ill. This particular problem evidently came as a surprise to the first officer, James Kensal. There remained on board three butts which, when inspected, proved to be some seven to eight inches short of full, but at a consumption rate of just over four pints a day for adults, it was enough, Kensal supposed, to get the ship to Jamaica, Tobago or St Lucia, whichever was closest for resupply. And this was not to count the water stored in "spirit casks," which, although disagreeable to the palate, could be resorted to for the preservation of life.[5] So Kensal, who was accustomed to seeing sorry things and to doing them himself, nonetheless spoke up against the "horrid brutality" of Collingwood's proposal.[6] The captain then made his instruction an order.

All the same, it had been no easy thing. Collingwood had taken on himself the work of selecting. He had gone below, swinging a lamp into the fetid rankness, to decide who would live and who would not. There had been some nonsense spoken about lots being cast so that the blacks would know in advance who was to be sacrificed, but to what end except to create inconvenient terror and make a hard task harder? So, ignorant of their imminent end, 132 shackled Africans in varying states of sickness and distress were brought up on deck and sat down amidships. There was nothing untoward in this. To preserve the "live cargo," weather permitting, blacks were set on deck each day, fastened by a long chain that passed through their leg irons and locked at a ring-bolt fastened to the deck. Should any trouble threaten, the swivel-guns, mounted at the gunwales, barrels pointing inwards, would make a menacing sweep.[7] It was the fact that the chains were not fastened to the ring-bolt on this occasion that must have triggered unease. And before they knew it the officer had shouted something, the crew had laid hands on them and the first had been cast over. With the children it could not have been much labour, made light and soft from their sickness as they were. But with the adult men and women two crewmen were needed, sometimes even a third, before the blacks could be turned on their backs and thrown into the waves, their bodies briefly arcing in the light before the plunge.

As the remainder suddenly comprehended what was to be done to them, the screaming and flailing against the shackles started, and then, from those already in the water, there was some further impotent thrashing until the waves closed over them. Scenting a meal from the wounds opened by the chafing of the irons, sharks slid economically towards their prey. The crew were too busy to be bothered. After the first dozen or so had been thrown into the sea, even the squeamish Kensal did Captain Collingwood's bidding without a grumble. And when there was a reckoning, it was found that fifty-four had been cast over. Next day, the 30th of November, another "parcel" of forty-two met the same fate. One of the passengers, Robert Stubbs, erstwhile governor of Annabona Island, the slave depot, and thus much inured to witnessing indelicacies, later testified that he had indeed seen bodies thrown over the side but, if it please Your Honour, had been below betimes and so was not able to recollect just who had done the work. Mr Stubbs did, however, credit the captain's argument that, had not the thing been done, "they all apprehended they should have died from want of water."[8]

Then, as if in confirmation that it had been right to cast so many black Jonahs overboard, there came a heavy squall, which delivered so much rain that the ship's butts, casks and puncheons brimmed with ample water for all, crew and slaves, sound and sick alike. So there was now no cause, even if the captain's account was to be believed, for any further doing away with negroes. But Collingwood's mind was now a very abacus of gain and loss, and was this not a most commercial age? With Jamaica almost (again) in sight, the last parcel of thirty-six were prepared. But while some were being set in chains and fetters so that they might sink with merciful promptness, another ten leapt into the sea of their own accord, their unshackled arms freed to swim, achieving a last moment of liberty in their inevitable end. One man, however, managed to swim unseen to the stern of the *Zong*, clutched a hanging rope and, after an interval when the watch had retired, clambered back on board. Discovered, he was graciously granted his life. As for those who had jumped, this was a matter of complete indifference to Luke Collingwood. They had saved his exhausted crew the trouble, and the result was the same. But could he in all conscience claim the value of those last ten from the insurers as jetsam if they had not actually been jettisoned?

The sun warmed the air, damp breezes blew, terns skimmed the waves, dipping here and there. The Caribbean water lapped green and pale against the reef, flecked with rills of foam where the coral broke the surface. It was as though nothing untoward had happened—nothing, really, to be exercised about.

UNLESS, that is, you were Granville Sharp. On the 19th of March 1783, some fifteen months after the killing of the *Zong* slaves, Sharp was called on by a Mr Gustavus Vassa. Vassa, whose African name was Olaudah Equiano, was one of the best known of the educated, free Christian blacks in London, an impassioned enemy of the slave trade and writer of indignant letters to the newspapers on behalf of his oppressed brethren. In 1789 his autobiography would be the first bestseller published by a black writer, and Vassa/Equiano would become a paragon for all those who defended Africans against the slavers' truism that they were an inferior species of humanity, more brute than man. The story that Equiano told (and he must certainly have told it long before it was published) was a prodigious odyssey from enslavement to hard-won emancipation, from unlettered anguish to articulate rage and from spiritual desolation to a state of grace. It was, in other words, a story that an age of tender sensibility could not resist. And it was, besides, an adventure to compare with the most dashing of romances and the most epic of travel yarns. And some of the tale, according to Vincent Carretta, may be too good to be true.[9]

Equiano's *Narrative* says he was the son of a well-to-do Igbo chief who owned slaves himself, as a young boy was then kidnapped by slavers, taken across the Atlantic and sold in Virginia to a naval lieutenant who, like many fellow officers, also traded in the merchant marine. But a baptismal certificate and a naval document discovered by Carretta record his birthplace as South Carolina. According to the *Narrative*, it was Lieutenant Michael Pascal who, on board the *Industrious Bee,* had told Equiano that henceforth he was to be Gustavus Vassa. Just why he should wish his personal slave to take the name of the Swedish kings rather than the usual Scipio, Pompey or Caesar, remains a mystery, unless perhaps Pascal had served on a vessel of that name to which he still had some sort of sentimental attachment. He would rather be called Jacob, Equiano told his master, a presumption for which he was liberally cuffed for as long and as often as it took to have him answer, like an obedient puppy, to his designated pet name.

Pascal repaid Equiano's loyalty with doubtful currency, giving him a close-up view of what it meant to fight an imperial war against the French. Everywhere the action was hot, there were the lieutenant and his black. And as the British Empire acquired fresh territories and military glory, Equiano acquired an accelerated education in the ways of a world at war. At Louisbourg on Cape Breton Island off Nova Scotia, as marines were being landed, Equiano saw an order of the supervising officer halted as a musket ball passed through the officer's open mouth and out again through a cheek. Later that day a cheerful Highlander put into Equiano's hand the freshly cut scalp of an Indian chief. In 1759, serving in Admiral Boscawen's war fleet, fetching powder and cartridges in the thick of the night battle against the French and Spanish, his ship's rigging shredded, main and mizzen masts broken like a child's rickety limbs, Equiano escaped splinter and shot while "many of my companions . . . in the twinkling of an eye, were dashed to pieces and launched into eternity." Equiano's own "annus mirabilis" was consummated with the baptism that, he understood over-optimistically, would not only bring him to the saving light of the Gospel but would also guarantee his emancipation. How could his liberty be denied, seeing that he had been baptized at the very crib of Empire—St Margaret's Chapel, Westminster—situated as it was between Parliament and the Abbey?

Agonizingly close, British freedom was snatched from Equiano when his master, Pascal, to whom the slave had faithfully and tenderly ministered even as he lay wounded, and who had seemed so extremely solicitous to his man, nonetheless unceremoniously sold him at the end of the war. Well, he was short of funds. This was the way of the world. To make matters worse, the master had taken Equiano's best coat and his Bible before trading his man. Terrified now that he would end his days as a field slave on some West Indian plantation, Equiano fortunately now became the property of a (relatively) benign Philadelphia

Quaker, Robert King. Although in the America of the 1760s virtually all the tiny band of abolitionists were Quakers, the reverse was by no means invariably true. Robert King was just one such slaveholding Friend, owning plantations in Montserrat and trading in the islands and on the mainland from a small fleet of sloops. Much taken with Equiano's learning and abilities, King employed him as mercantile clerk, courier, island trader (handler, amongst other things, of "live cargo") and even as inspector of estates, where Equiano reconciled himself to the dirty work by believing he could do something to mitigate its extreme cruelty.

But there was such wickedness done beneath the Almighty's sun! Equiano learned of black girls, not ten years old, who had been raped and the white perpetrator untouched, whilst a negro caught with a white prostitute was "staked to the ground and cut most shockingly and then his ears cut off bit by bit." In palmy Montserrat, beneath the growly, puffing volcano, Equiano was a favoured man, a trusty man, a knowledgeable man, and so listened in silence as a trader bragged airily of selling forty thousand negroes and of cutting off the leg of one who had tried to run away. He saw fathers torn from their children, mothers muzzled with iron bits and masks, scalding sealing wax dropped on the backs of discovered stowaways; lightweight blacks sat on merchants' scales to be sold, like groceries, by the pound. In South Carolina, which may have been his birthplace, he saw celebrations for the repeal of the hated Stamp Tax while slaves were whipped, and in Georgia he was beaten himself. His craving for freedom became urgent.

He could have had worse masters than Robert King, he knew. But then he would rather have had no masters at all. In his growing agitation to get away, Equiano made the mistake of taking lessons in navigation from a bosun on one of King's sloops. On learning of this iniquitous betrayal, the master flew into a rage, accused his man of ingratitude and told him he would have no recourse now but to sell him, however invaluable he had proved. But King was pre-empted, literally, by one of his captains, who had taken such a shine to Equiano as to pay him sufficient wages, over the years, to cover the price of his redemption. Although King was much displeased to be so presumptuously put to the test of his liberal opinions, and of his casual promise to manumit Equiano some day, the captain shamed him into it. "Come, Robert," he said, jovially clapping the merchant on the back, "I think you must let him have his freedom. You have laid your money out very well; you have received good interest for it all this time and here now is the principal at last. I know GUSTAVUS has earned you more than a hundred a year and he [as a free man] will still save you money as he will not leave you."

However grudging, Friend King did what he had pledged. Equiano could hardly believe it:

> These words of my master were like a voice from heaven to me: in an instant all my trepidation was turned into unutterable bliss . . . My imagination was all rapture as I flew to the Register Office [to have the manumission document drawn up]. "Heavens! Who could do justice to my feelings at this moment? Not conquering heroes themselves in the midst of a triumph—Not the tender mother who has just regained her long-lost infant and presses it to her heart—Not the weary hungry mariner at the sight of the desired friendly port—Not the lover when he once more embraces his beloved mistress after she has been ravished from his arms . . . The fair as well as the black people [in Savannah] immediately styled me by a new appellation—to me the most desirable in the world—which was "Freeman."

Needless to say, Equiano's manumission was no warranty against the unscrupulous, who, in the years that followed, often threatened him with re-enslavement. Sometimes these constant dangers moved him to despair. But the articulate fashion in which he defended himself made potential captors nervous, especially when he mentioned the names of influential gentlemen with whom he appeared acquainted or even connected (tangling with the expensive pest Granville Sharp was to be sedulously avoided). One of the gentlemen, and Equiano's employer, was Dr Charles Irving, the Great Desalinator, who busied himself making saltwater sweet. Equiano acted as Irving's general factotum, and in that capacity, both with and without him, embarked on travels as extensive as any Grand Tour. In Naples he saw Vesuvius erupt. In Turkish Izmir he was offered two wives and ate locusts, which he thought remarkably like French beans, only longer. In the Arctic Ocean, with Dr Irving still furiously desalinating as long as the closing ice floes permitted, the black man saw Horatio Nelson try to kill a white bear and "vast quantities of sea-horses"—which may have been walruses, since he describes them neighing "exactly like any other horses." Back in the Caribbean, Equiano was shipwrecked and survived in a small boat with the help of Miskito Indians, whose potent liquor fermented from roasted pineapples he greedily drank from gourds. Squatting on leaves in the forest village, he ate dried turtle and saw vertical alligators, suspended live from trees before being slaughtered for a feast—a delicacy Equiano could not quite bring himself to share, though he regretted the discourtesy.

Back in London dressing hair, playing the French horn, telling stories, writing to the gazettes, allowing himself to be noticed, periodically taking merchant voyages again, Equiano was fretful for the state of his soul. Encyclopedically, as the sceptical philosophers counselled, he sampled what the Quakers, the Catholics, and even the Jews had to offer, although his stays in perfumed Izmir had made him think so well of the Turks that for a while Islam seemed much the most promising road to grace and mercy. Then one day he stepped into a plain Methodist chapel where the room rang with Hallelujahs. Born aloft to the crest of the ecstasy, something evidently distant, and yet very close, spoke to Equiano more strongly of God's love than anything he had ever before experienced. He trembled with the sweetness of recognition. "This kind of Christian fellowship I had never seen, nor ever thought of seeing on earth. It fully reminded me of what I had read in the holy Scriptures, of the primitive Christians who loved each other and broke bread, in partaking of it from house to house."

And all this while he kept his political eyes open. In the legal skirmishings between Granville Sharp and Lord Mansfield, Equiano understood that he was witnessing a moment when history might actually alter the lives of slaves in the British Empire. Of Sharp's own honesty, acumen and Christian zeal, Equiano had no doubt. In the unprepossessing, hollow-cheeked flautist he had found a hero, and in 1774 he needed Sharp's help. Travelling back to Izmir as a steward, Equiano had recommended a black acquaintance, John Annis, as cook for the Turkey trader *Anglicania*. But like Jonathan Strong and Thomas Lewis, Annis had a covetous master from the Caribbean, one Kirkpatrick, who regretted the agreement permitting Annis to depart from his service and whose mind dwelled on the money to be secured from his resale. Annis was already aboard the *Anglicania* cooking for the crew while waiting to sail, and this gave Kirkpatrick his opportunity. The cook was followed, abducted and packed on to another vessel bound for St Kitts. To Equiano's disgust, neither the captain nor the mate whom Annis had served, unpaid, for two months would lift a finger to deliver him: "I proved the only friend he had who attempted to regain him his liberty, if possible, having known the want of liberty myself." And Equiano knew what to do to mobilize British freedom: he secured a writ of Habeas Corpus for Annis. Whitening his face in some semblance of disguise, he went with a tipstaff to Kirkpatrick's house in St Paul's Churchyard. There they confronted the master, but he claimed no longer to have the body in question.

It was then that Equiano sought out Granville Sharp, the veteran of such struggles. Still basking in the Somerset triumph, and expecting its provisions against the abduction and transportation of black subjects of the king to be enforced, Sharp had been optimistic. He gave Equiano advice on what to expect from the law. But the advice did not, alas, include caveats about unscrupulous lawyers. Equiano was duly robbed of his money, whilst those who took it did nothing for the plight of John Annis. "When the poor man arrived at St Kitt's he was, according to custom, staked to the ground with four pins, through a cord, two on his wrist and two on his ankles; was cut and flogged most unmercifully, and afterwards loaded cruelly with irons about his neck." Letters arrived for Equiano from Annis, which were "very moving." In desperation he tried to pursue the case but, after the fact, nothing was to be done, and there, in servitude, Annis remained "till kind death released him out of the hands of his tyrants."

Equiano and Sharp do not seem to have had much contact between the case of John Annis and that of the drowned slaves of the *Zong*. There had been a great and momentous war; they had each been busy. Almost to the end of hostilities Sharp had hoped against all reason that America might yet be reconciled to a chastened, reformed Britain in which liberty and humanity were once more enthroned. And once that hope had evaporated, he set about restoring the connections he most valued: with Anthony Benezet, Benjamin Franklin and a new correspondent, John Adams, all of whom he hoped would be steadfast in the coming crusade against the Accursed Thing. Swept up by his new-found zeal, Equiano had gone all the way back to his own origins and the source of the evil, West Africa, where he served as an unordained chaplain and preacher to Governor Matthias Macnamara at Cape Coast Castle. And he applied to the Bishop of London for ordination so that he might return to Africa as a missionary, thus, as he supposed, simultaneously saving the bodies and the souls of his fellow Africans.

Equiano, then, knew slavery about as well as anyone could, within or without the institution. He had seen enough to believe that nothing could shock him further, until, on the morning of the 18th of March 1783, he read an anonymous letter in the *Morning Chronicle and London Advertiser* reporting the fate of the slaves on the *Zong*. Monstrous though it was, the story might never have come to light had not the insurers, faced with a bill from the owners for £3960 (£30 per African), decided to contest the purported "necessity" dictating the drowning of the blacks. The case had come before the court of King's Bench in Westminster Hall and, although its macabre details were, according to the *Chronicle*'s reporter, "enough to make every one present shudder," the jury had returned a verdict for the owners without even leaving the chamber for deliberation.

As a devotee of Common Law, Sharp felt the ignominy acutely. As if slaving were not itself bad enough, should the verdict be upheld, the jettisoning of "human cargo" would be deemed lawful and others would certainly hasten to profit from this precedent. The seas would bob with wantonly murdered Africans. For their part the insurers, Messrs Gilbert and Others, were not about to concede the point, and brought a motion before the Bench (to be heard, of course by Lord Mansfield) for a retrial. And, however painful and repugnant it was to be for both Sharp and Equiano to argue the responsibility for a massacre entirely in terms of commercial liability, they recognized that the insurers' questioning of the purported water shortage put them in the position, however reluctantly, of accusing the captain and owners of the *Zong* of having committed murder for gain. Sharp was determined to do everything in his power to support that position in the hope that by so doing he would be able to initiate the criminal prosecution the infamy assuredly warranted.

After Equiano's visit Sharp contacted an Oxford law don, Dr Bever, and when the case came before Mansfield on the 22nd of May made sure that he himself was present in Westminster Hall together with a clerk he had hired to take shorthand notes of the proceedings. This busy scribbling attracted the attention of the counsel for the owners, Sir John ("Honest Jack") Lee, currently Solicitor-General and shortly to be Attorney-General, a Yorkshireman with a well-earned reputation for blunt, if not profane, speech voiced in a broad accent and for the bullying manners of a waggoner in a hurry. There was a "person in Court," he boomed at Mansfield and his fellow justices, pausing to glare operatically at Sharp, a person who had made known his intention to bring "a criminal prosecution for murder against the parties concerned." But, Lee blustered on as if lecturing a particularly dull room of schoolboys, "if any man of them was allowed to be tried at the Old Bailey for murder, I cannot help thinking if that charge of murder was attempted to be sustained it would be folly and rashness to a degree of madness; and so far from the charge of murder lying against these people, there is not the least imputation. Of cruelty, I will not say, but—of impropriety: not in the least!" No one, Lee insisted, should pay heed to the "pretended appeals" of counsel for the underwriters to "the feelings of humanity," for the master had a perfect right to do as he thought fit with his "chattels or goods." The issue was not whether making property of men was or was not deplorable: "whether right or wrong we have nothing to do with it." For it was unarguable that "for the purpose in insurance, they are goods and property." Thus the only issue to decide was whether the preservation of the remainder did indeed depend on their being disposed of.[10]

But Pigot, Davenport and Heywood, lawyers for the insurers, were not browbeaten. They argued, unapologetically, that the matter of whether a human might ever be a cargo was most certainly material; that this was therefore "a new cause." Indeed Heywood, like Dunning in the Lewis case and young Alleyne in the Somerset case, rose to the occasion and was not averse to setting the niceties of commercial law aside for the larger truth. "We are not now merely defending the underwiters from the damages obtained against them," he asserted. "I cannot help thinking that my friends who came before me [a nod to Sharp and his trials] and myself on this occasion appear as counsel for millions of mankind and the cause of humanity in general." It was grandiloquent, but if there was ever a time when grandiloquence was pardonable, this was it.

It had been eleven years since Somerset. Which Lord Mansfield would preside over the ghosts of the *Zong*—the cautious legal conservative, embarrassed by the popular misunderstanding of his ruling that it had made slavery illegal in England, or Dido Lindsey's Uncle James of Kenwood House? Mansfield could, of course, see Sir John Lee's point, and respected the stringent narrowness of the issue on which the jury had been asked to decide. For the earlier jury, "though it shocks one very much, the case of the slaves was the same as if horses had been thrown overboard." He could see that it had to be so and yet, Mansfield said again, "It is a very shocking case." A new trial was granted.

This was all Sharp needed to set him off. Pamphlets and newspaper articles were circulated to those who mattered in lay and ecclesiastical circles; they accused, among others, the Solicitor-General, whose "argument was so lamentably unworthy of his dignity and public character and so banefully immoral in its tendency to encourage the superlative degree of all oppression, *Wilful Murder*."[11] It was, Sharp thundered in his letters to the Duke of Portland, to sundry bishops and archbishops and to the Lords Commissioners of the Admiralty, a "*necessity*, incumbent upon the whole kingdom to vindicate our national justice" by the prosecution and punishment of the murderers, and, once that was done, to put "an entire stop to the Slave Trade," short of which (warming to his favourite refrain) nothing would stay the "avenging hand of God who has promised *to destroy the destroyers of the earth.*"

Predictably, the Lords Commissioners of the Admiralty, whose responsibility it would be to bring a prosecution before the Grand Jury, failed to act on Sharp's appeals to their humanity, much less on their own sense of elementary justice. In fact they failed to act at all. So was it entirely quixotic for Sharp to have imagined they might?

Not quite, for there was at least one senior figure in the brutally pragmatic world of the Royal Navy who at the very least had mixed feelings about the slaving empire he was called on to protect and preserve. As Comptroller of the Navy, and thus responsible for its finances, Sir Charles Middleton had custody of one of the biggest and juiciest bowls of plums in the gift of government. And yet there was no sign that Middleton had been much tempted by sins venal (or any other sort). After living the life of a naval commander he had, as expected, settled into the life of a country gentleman. Once captain of HMS *Arundel*, he was now master of Teston Hall in Kent. This did not mean, however, that Middleton had settled for a life of reclusive provincial mediocrity padded by a naval sinecure. He was also Member of Parliament for Rochester, on the river Medway, and thus at the heart of the omnipotent beast that was the Hanoverian Royal Navy. Dockyards, seamen, chandlers and sawmills all laboured under the eye of the Comptroller. Complementing the assiduous Sir Charles was Lady Middleton, who, in the way of those times, was passionately drawn to good Christian works.

And there were few causes dearer to Lady Middleton's heart, or indeed to her husband's, than the vicar of St Peter's and St Paul's, Teston. The Reverend James Ramsay, with his soft Aberdeen lilt, was not the kind of parson you would expect to fetch up on the Medway—to say nothing of his wife, born Rebecca Akers, a creole lady whose complexion could not quite be described as Kentish. In fact, the Medway was just right for James Ramsay seeing that he had begun life as a naval surgeon, serving under Middleton on HMS *Arundel*. In 1759, the same year that Vassa was blooded in combat, Ramsay saw a different kind of action in the Caribbean.[12] A slave ship, vulnerable to being taken by the French, joined Middleton's fleet for protection. But it was flying the yellow flag of contagion. A hundred, both black slaves and white crew, had already died and the master asked Middleton for the care of a surgeon. None except Ramsay would go. Returning to the *Arundel* from his rounds, Ramsay stumbled getting on deck and fell awkwardly, fracturing his thigh-bone. He would be lame for the rest of his life, and Middleton never forgot this painful reward for his surgeon's selflessness.

Determined on being Luke, both doctor and priest, Ramsay abandoned the navy and took holy orders, but returned to the Caribbean to minister, as he supposed, to black and white alike. On St Kitts, where he had three livings, he became notorious as the parson who invited blacks to his vicarage to be schooled and converted—and, even worse, tried to insert into the bidding a prayer for the conversion of the slaves. A Christian field hand, to be sure, would still be a field hand, but there was something damnably uncomfortable about subjecting Christians to the kind of lashing that from time to time must needs be applied to recalcitrant beasts of burden. Further, not content with interfering where he had no business, Mr Ramsay would not be quiet as he went about his parson's business, presuming to admonish overseers and even the gentlemen of the plantations, from Christ Church to Basseterre to Nicholastown, on what he judged to be their un-Christian behaviour towards the blacks. Unconscionably he even permitted, actually encouraged, blacks and whites to worship together in his church. Clearly this could not be. For his presumption and meddling, Ramsay was reproved, first quietly, then more noisily in the island newspapers. When he seemed to heed none of this, more drastic gestures were made. Notes were pinned to the church door wishing ill to him and his creole wife. Should he persist, "merciless revenge" would be exacted. At some point the apostle, like most apostles, felt he had had enough.

So in 1777 James Ramsay came back to England. Spoken highly of by Sir Charles Middleton, he became chaplain to the fleet under, successively, Admirals Barrington and the notoriously testy, gout-racked Rodney. More mutilated bodies came Ramsay's way: splints and intercessions amidst the smoke and juddering din. He published *Sea Sermons* and prayed that Rodney would not deal quite so harshly with the Jews of St Eustatius for running guns and rum to the Americans. Indeed, it was not the Americans whom James Ramsay wished to fight but the satanic deeds he had seen in the islands. In 1779 he went back to St Kitts, where again, he made himself unwelcome, a burr in the breeches. Two years later, he was chased once more from the plantations. This time, advised gently but soundly by Sir Charles, he settled for the livings at Teston and Nettlestead. Yet between writing sermons and tending to the parish Ramsay was all the while ordering his memories and his moral sentiments. If he could not fight the Accursed Thing from the pulpit he would do so from the printed page. The revulsion stirred by the monetarization of evil embodied in the *Zong* case seemed to give the Kentish parson his opportunity. In the summer of 1784 his *Essay on the Treatment and Conversion of Slaves in the British Sugar Colonies* was published.

If James Ramsay was expecting a hornets' nest, he certainly got it. His tour through the barbarities he had witnessed during nineteen years in St Kitts—the cart whip that "cuts out flakes of skin and flesh at every strike"—was greeted with a storm of derision and abuse, not least from the "island agents" who remembered him well. They accused him of being a hypocrite. Had the sainted abolitionist not owned slaves himself? Yes he had, but only house slaves whom he freed on departure. The lameness? On the island it was said that he had fallen while administering a kick to the breeches to one of his blacks, and now the man had the gall to pretend to have broken his thigh in the navy, the better to pad his pension! It was an outrageous slander, and Ramsay felt it keenly as the abuse rained down. He understood nothing of the world, the indignant advocates of the Society of West India Planters and Merchants charged, neither the way it had always been, nor the way it must be if the British Empire was to be sustained, especially after the grievous blow it had suffered in America. Did the reverend gentleman know history? Apparently not, for even a cursory reading of antiquity would enlighten him to the knowledge that since the records of humanity commenced there had never been a society without slaves, any more than there had been a world without the wars that habitually produced captives and bondsmen. Did the reverend gentleman know anything of Africa? Evidently not, or he would be aware that the poor natives there were subject to cruelties and atrocities beside which the worst that a plantation overseer might commit would resemble the very milk of Christian charity and benevolence. Did he know the economy? Obviously not, for he would otherwise appreciate the general ruin that would be brought upon countless deserving Britons from the wreckage of the sugar trade he so carelessly and piously proposed. And for that matter did the Kentish parson know England? Surely not, for if he did he would have to concede that the condition of the plantation negro, however unfree, well fed and sheltered as he must needs be if the plantation was to prosper, was far preferable to that of the rustic labourer evicted from his strip by enclosures and doomed to roam the hedgerows for a pittance, or that of the city beggar trapped in filth and degradation.

Rattled, but sheltered by the Middletons, Ramsay stood his ground. On one point he remained especially adamant. Blacks were not, as the Jamaican Edward Long had averred, closer to the orang-utan than to man. They were in every quality and faculty fully our humanity. "That there is any essential difference between the European and African mental powers, as far as my experience has gone, I positively deny."[13] With this one empirically acquired conviction, James Ramsay was already the moral superior of David Hume and Thomas Jefferson.

In the sultry summer of 1784, buzzing with swarms of wasps and gnats, heavy with daily thunder, the battle was joined. Defenders of slavery—who were beginning to mobilize their own advocacy—liked to depict the dispute as one argued between the worldly and the un-worldly, men of business against men of the cloth. But this was not at all true. The leaders of the Quaker campaign—an informal committee of six who met every two weeks to concert their publicity in the London and provincial press—were all businessmen and, they liked to think, hard of head if tender of heart. They included a young banker, Samuel Hoare, and a tobacco merchant, John Lloyd, who had been repelled by what he'd seen of slavery on business trips to Virginia.[14] Adam Smith's attack on the slave trade was republished, arguing against it principally on the grounds of its economic inexpediency. For most of the Quakers, though, a trade in humans was no proper trade at all. "No right ex-ists . . . to alienate from another his liberty," wrote Joseph Woods, a wool merchant, sounding a deliberately transatlantic note, "and therefore every purchase of a slave is in contradiction to the original rights of mankind."[15]

The horror of the *Zong* drownings and the stir created by Ramsay's and Woods's tracts even woke up the politically drowsy academic world. That same summer of 1784, in Cambridge, the vice-chancellor, Dr Peter Peckard, another conscience-stricken divine who had begun as a chaplain in the Grenadier Guards, chose as the subject of the Latin es-say for senior bachelors *Anne liceat invitos in servitutem dare?* Can men be lawfully made slaves against their own will? It was won by a twenty-four-year-old ordained deacon studying for his MA in divinity, Thomas Clarkson, evidently no fool, since he had graduated as a mathematician and had already won one of the university's Latin prizes. The cleverness of Clarkson, the son of a Wisbech schoolmaster who had died when Thomas was just a small boy, was never in doubt. But until he began to apply himself to Dr Peckard's question, Thomas Clarkson had paid scant attention to the evils of slavery.[16] All this changed as he laboured on his Latin essay. An academic exercise turned into a mission. He had supposed, Clarkson later wrote, that, as was his habit, he would derive pure intellectual "pleasure from the invention of the arguments, from the arrangement of them." But unaccountably, in the manner of roman-tic moral panic, he found himself slipping over the edge of an abyss. "It was but one gloomy subject from morning to night. In the daytime I was uneasy. In the night I had little rest. I sometimes never closed my eyelids for grief. It became now not so much a trial for academical reputation as for the production of a work which might be useful to injured Africa."[17] The subject had already possessed the man.

In June 1785 Thomas Clarkson was summoned to read his prize essay in the University Senate House before a convocation of dons. He left with their acclaim ringing in his ears. And that might have been that. Known to the right people, Clarkson might well have climbed the ladder for which he had been destined, rung by rung all the way to a bishop's seat. But riding along the old Ermine Street in Hertfordshire near the village of Wadesmill, just north of Ware, Clarkson had a roadside epiphany. Tormented by the sense that he had begun something he had no idea how to finish—something that ought never to be boxed within the confines of an academic exercise, however gravely wrought— he got off his horse. He walked a little way, leading his mount by the reins; then hiked himself up again on the stirrups, rode a little further and dismounted again. Finally, "I sat down disconsolate on the turf by the roadside and held my horse . . . If the contents of the Essay were true, it was time some person should see these calamities to the end." It would be him. He had become, as one of his admirers would put it, "the slave of the slaves."

Impending saints were starting to see the light. Five months after Clarkson sat down on the Hertfordshire grass and faced the truth another twenty-five-year-old Cambridge graduate, William Wilberforce, a small, trim, clever man known for his witty banter, his smart social connections, his sure hand at cards, his graceful dancing and the tenor voice that had earned him, now that he was MP for Hull, a reputation as the "nightingale of the Commons," confided to his diary: "True Lord, I am wretched and miserable and blind and naked. What infinite love that Christ should die to save such a sinner." If those sentiments sound suspiciously like lines from "Amazing Grace," it is because they were. Twelve days after writing them Wilberforce went to see the author of the hymn, the erstwhile slave trader John Newton, now vicar of St Mary Woolnoth in London, at his house in Hoxton. He had already met Ramsay at the Middletons' in 1783 and heard from him at first hand of the cart whips and the brandings. But Wilberforce left Newton's house in

Charles Square a different man. "I found my mind in a calm, more tranquil state, more humbled and looking up more devoutly to God." Newton too was emboldened by the new fraternity. He and his friend the poet William Cowper, co-author of the *Olney Hymns,* were beginning to sound a music of indignation.

The Dover road must have seen a lot of hard spiritual riding, for much travelling was done between London and Kent as the marshals began to mobilize their godly army. In the capital, preparing an extended English translation of his essay, Clarkson was introduced to James Phillips who in June 1786 published on his behalf the *Essay on the Slavery and Commerce of the Human Species.*[18] Clarkson's grand survey of slavery in antiquity was retained, but the essay now included a footnote on the *Zong* and other decidedly un-donnish anecdotes such as that of the unsold slave who, returning to ship but at a walking pace not smart enough for the accompanying ship's officer, was beaten to death on the spot with a rattan stick for dragging his chains so sluggishly. The body had then been slung into the harbour where it was promptly eaten by sharks.[19] Lost in admiration at what he read, James Ramsay came up from Kent to congratulate Clarkson in person.

Back at Teston, Ramsay could scarcely wait to spread the word to the Middletons about what he had discovered in Clarkson: intelligence, toughness, eloquence, virtue without humbug. In July 1786 the pieces of the campaign fell into place. Clarkson was brought down to Teston, and at the Hall found that the Middletons had brought together the veterans of the campaign: Granville Sharp and Beilby Porteus, the Bishop of Chester and London, who had long been preaching the conversion and redemption of slaves. At Middleton's dinner table, his own moral fire stoked by the flattering enthusiasm of his elders, Clarkson made an unembarrassed declaration that his life would henceforth belong to the cause. He later wrote that he had no choice. "I was *literally*"—he meant virtually—*"forced into it* . . . All the tragical scenes . . . passed on horrible review before me and my compassion for their suffering was *at that moment* so great, so intense, so overwhelming, as to have overpowered me and compelled me to form the resolution which I dared not resist . . . of attempting their deliverance."

In the vision of Ramsay, Sharp and the Middletons, Clarkson and Wilberforce were to be complementary generals of the campaign. With his entrée into the world of the quality, even the court, his parliamentary standing, and his easy relationship with William Pitt, the prime minister, also a serious young man in his twenties, Wilberforce was to take the cause to the decision-makers. Clarkson, his reputation made by the *Essay*, would be both the organizational leader, its commanding intelligence and the face of the battle to the troops out-of-doors. And Sir Charles Middleton offered immediate—and rather astonishing—official assistance. The records of the Royal Navy on the slave trade would be made available to him, as would his many influential London friends and associates. With the additional encouragement of Sharp and the Quaker London Committee, Clarkson now set about systematic research. His brother John, now a lieutenant on half-pay, was turned from an indifferent witness of the world of slavery into one of Thomas's best sources of its practices. The older brother roamed the docks, snooping into the holds of Triangular Trade ships bound for Africa or coming from the Indies; peering through the gratings at the darkness where he knew slaves had been packed in suffocating closeness; talking to seamen who had been on the slavers and discovering, to his amazement, that the fatality rate amongst the crews was even greater than that of the slaves themselves! One black sailor aboard a slaver, a man named John Dean, had, he learned, committed some trivial misdemeanour and then had hot pitch poured on his back, after which incisions were made with tongs in order to rub it in. Another black steward, Peter Green, had died aboard the *Alfred,* and Clarkson felt sure it was from mistreatment.[20]

Yet there was one interested party whom Thomas Clarkson, it seems, never thought to sound out: the thousands of black Londoners who had themselves once been slaves. But most of them were not, like Olaudah Equiano or his friend Ottobah Cugoano, articulate celebrities who could be summoned to fashionable parlours to inspire the troops. Nor were they the powdered and liveried body servants of the quality. They were, instead, the importunate black beggars who swept the crossings before the feet of the well-to-do in the bitter winter of 1785–86. They were not heroes; they were just an unsightliness on the streets.

GETTING HIMSELF HANGED was just the start of Benjamin White-cuffe's problems. Once, he had had serious prospects. His father, a free-born mulatto, like many blacks around New York, had made a living from coastal trading around the Sound—a good living, too, since he owned a sloop. But the Jeffersonian dream visited Pa Whitecuffe and he had traded the boat for a farm at Hempstead, King's County in Long Island—and not a mere scrap of waste either, but over sixty acres of prime, lush pasture, a two-acre orchard and some land in the village besides. And there was a team of good plough oxen to work it. So he had evidently been very much his own man: the model of a sturdy, independent smallholder on which the new republic was supposed to be based. His son Benjamin learned the trade of saddler, a handy enough occupation in the Whitecuffes' rural world.

Come the revolution, this little felicity disappeared. Whitecuffe senior had heeded the patriotic call, joined the Continental army and risen to the rank of sergeant. He had also taken Benjamin's brother along with him in the American cause. But Benjamin himself was stubborn, and had taken the opposite view, thinking to do better by the king than by the revolution. The divided family, no doubt with a heavy heart but also with a prudent eye to the future, decided that, should the British come to Hempstead, Benjamin should claim it as his own.

Whether Benjamin's allegiance was determined by principle or opportunism is impossible to gauge. But his loyalism went well beyond prudent self-interset. As a free black, he had no need of Sir Henry Clinton's incentive to join the army but did so anyway—and, what was more, in the dangerous office of spy. During the erratic pursuit of Washington's army across New Jersey he delivered intelligence to Sir William Ayscough about American troop movements and was credited with saving a force of two thousand from marching into an engagement against overwhelmingly superior odds. But during his two years' spying, Benjamin took one chance too many and was captured by the Americans near their lines. Only one fate was deemed proper for a spy, and Benjamin was duly strung up near Cranbury, New Jersey. There he swung for three minutes while the noose failed, as they sometimes did, to break his neck. He was still hanging and still alive (though barely) when a troop of the 5th Light Horse arrived and cut him down from the gibbet. His father and brother had not been so fortunate. The one was killed during the skirmish at Chestnut Hill, the other done for at the battle of Germantown.

So Benjamin was now the outright owner of the Hempstead farm and the yoke of plough oxen. But he was not about to sit out the war and hope for the best. Undeterred by his brush with the hereafter, he boarded a ship at Staten Island bound for Virginia to offer his services again in the Southern theatre. But the ship was intercepted and taken to the Grenadines islands, where, now notorious, he was once again sentenced to be hanged. En route to Boston, where the execution would be carried out, the ship on which Whitecuffe was held prisoner was attacked and taken as a prize by a Liverpool privateer, the *St Phillips Castle*. Whitecuffe was happy to stay aboard when the ship sailed east, since he must have felt that in England he might receive fair consideration for all he had suffered. And still that service was not done since, like most of the blacks who had come from America, he found himself in the middle of the naval war, seeing fierce battle at Port Mahon and Gibraltar. In 1783, when the war was finally over, he arrived back in London but with neither land nor the Royal Navy to give him a living.

Benjamin, however, had no choice in the matter. His family was either dead or had moved away from the farm at Hempstead. With his career well known in New York, there was no possibility of his returning to Long Island, much less regaining his land. And now he had a white English wife, Sarah. So in June 1784 he told his story and, with the help of a lawyer (for he was illiterate), had it written down for the five commissioners appointed by Parliament to hear loyalist claims and, if merited, to offer compensation for losses. Benjamin must have been optimistic. Since his father had traded his sloop, worth perhaps £300, for the land, the farm must have been worth, conservatively, £120. And he managed to find a sailor, one Thomas Stiff, who could swear that indeed the Whitecuffes had owned fifty or even sixty good acres in King's County. Then there were the oxen and the cart, worth another £11. Whitecuffe hoped and prayed that "yr Memorialist may be enabled under your report to receive such aid or relief as his losses and services may be found to deserve."[21]

What Whitecuffe eventually got was scant reward for everything he had gone through for His Majesty: £10. But since many of his comrades received nothing at all, this award still made him one of the more fortunate of the forty-seven blacks petitioning the commissioners for help and redress. By adding his £10 to Sarah's modest dowry he could set up

GRANVILLE SHARP.

Granville Sharp, by George Dance, 1794.

[PENCIL; NATIONAL PORTRAIT GALLERY, LONDON]

The Sharp Family, by Johan Zoffany,
1779–81. The Sharp brothers
(FROM LEFT TO RIGHT): James *(playing
the serpent)*, Granville *(leaning on the
piano)*, William *(in Windsor uniform
with hat raised)*, and John
(dressed in black).

[OIL ON CANVAS; ON LOAN TO THE NATIONAL
PORTRAIT GALLERY, LONDON]

ABOVE: *Dido and Lady Elizabeth Murray*,
by Johan Zoffany, 1779–81.

[OIL ON CANVAS; COLLECTION OF THE EARL OF
MANSFIELD, SCONE PALACE, SCOTLAND]

LEFT: *General Sir Guy Carleton,
Lord Dorchester*, copy by
Mabel B. Messer, 1923.

[ORIGINAL DESTROYED; OIL ON CANVAS;
LIBRARY AND ARCHIVES CANADA]

FACING PAGE: *John Murray,
4th Earl of Dunmore*,
by Sir Joshua Reynolds, 1765.

[DETAIL; OIL ON CANVAS; SCOTTISH NATIONAL
PORTRAIT GALLERY, EDINBURGH]

Thomas Clarkson,
by Carl Frederik von Breda, 1789.

[OIL ON CANVAS; NATIONAL PORTRAIT GALLERY, LONDON]

James Ramsay,
by Carl Frederik von Breda, 1789.

[OIL ON CANVAS; NATIONAL PORTRAIT GALLERY, LONDON]

William Wilberforce, by Sir Thomas Lawrence, 1828.

[OIL ON CANVAS; NATIONAL PORTRAIT GALLERY, LONDON]

Abolitionist medallion, by Josiah Wedgwood, inscribed with the slogan
"Am I Not a Man and a Brother," 1790s.

[JASPER; WILBERFORCE HOUSE MUSEUM, HULL CITY MUSEUMS AND ART GALLERIES, HUMBERSIDE]

John Eardley-Wilmot, by Benjamin West, 1812. In the background,
a painted allegory shows the black loyalists, led by William Franklin,
being received by Britannia in 1783.

[OIL ON CANVAS; YALE CENTER FOR BRITISH ART, NEW HAVEN, PAUL MELLON COLLECTION]

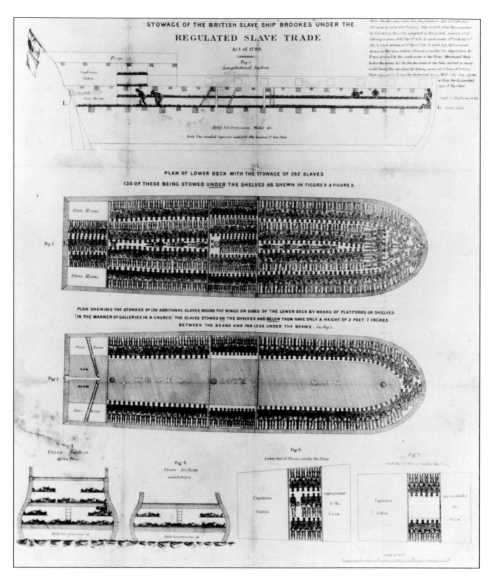

Stowage of the British Slave Ship 'Brookes' under the Regulated Slave Trade Act of 1788.

[AMERICAN SCHOOL; ENGRAVING; LIBRARY OF CONGRESS, WASHINGTON, DC]

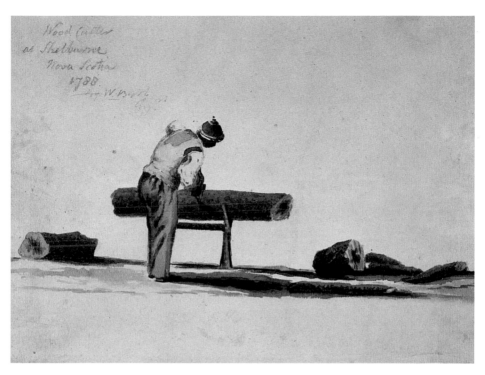

A Black Wood Cutter at Shelburne, Nova Scotia, by William Booth, 1788.

[WATERCOLOUR; LIBRARY AND ARCHIVES CANADA]

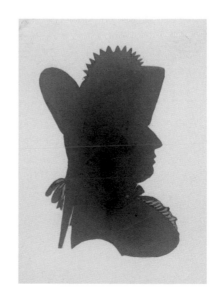

John Parr, Governor of Nova Scotia,
artist unknown, circa 1780s.

[SILHOUETTE; NOVA SCOTIA ARCHIVES AND
RECORDS MANAGEMENT]

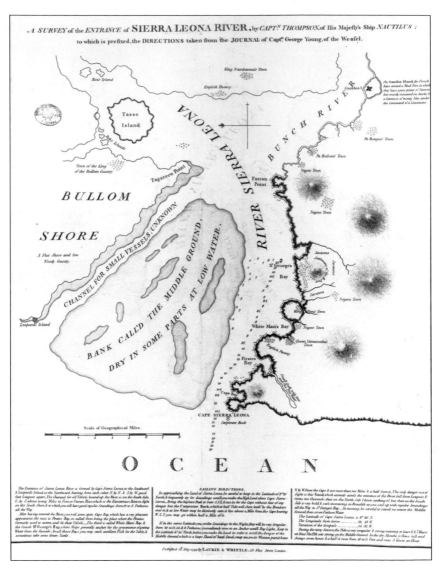

A Survey of the Entrance of Sierra Leona River . . ., drawn in 1787 by Captain Thompson of HMS *Nautilus,* which escorted three ships carrying blacks from England. A black settlement, labeled "Settlement of the B. Poor," appears by St George's Bay (*center*).

A View of the Province of Freedom, showing the free-black settlement at St George's Hill, from *Voyage à la Rivière de Sierra-Leone sur la côte d'Afrique . . .*, published in 1797, Paris, by Captain John Matthews, RN.

Lieutenant John Clarkson, RN, artist unknown, circa 1790s.
[MINIATURE; PRIVATE COLLECTION]

FOLLOWING PAGE:
The black fleet from Nova Scotia, en route to Freetown, Sierra Leone, sketched by Lieutenant John Clarkson in his manuscript journal *Mission to America*, 1791–2. The brig *Lucretia*, Clarkson's flagship, appears at top right.
[COLLECTION OF THE NEW-YORK HISTORICAL SOCIETY]

336

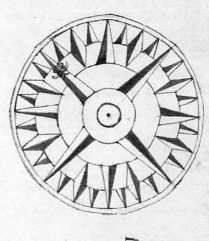

The black fleet moored on the Sierra Leone River,
watercolour painted by John Beckett, 1792.

The silver dollar piece, obverse and reverse, issued in 1791
by the Sierra Leone Company.

Negresses of Sierra Leone, by Francis B. Spilsbury, 1803; sketch published in his
Account of a Voyage to the Western Coast of Africa: Performed by His Majesty's Sloop
Favourite, *in the year 1805 . . . ,* published in 1807, London.

Frederick Douglass, daguerreotype, circa 1840–50.

again as a saddler and chair-caner.[22] A few others received more sizeable pensions, one of the most generous being (eventually) awarded to Shadrack Furman from Acamac County, Virginia, who, after his house had been burned down by the Continental army in January 1781, had joined Cornwallis's campaign as a spy and guide. Caught by the Americans, Furman was tortured (there is no other proper term) to extract intelligence: he was given five hundred lashes and left, tied up in a field, so badly beaten about the head that he was virtually blinded, then cut with an axe on his right leg, just enough not to sever it but to cripple it permanently. "His health is so much impaired from the wounds in his head," Furman's petition to the commissioners stated, "that he is sometimes bereft of reason."[23] Mutilated and sight-impaired though he was, Furman had continued to serve the British, first on a privateer, then with the Pioneers around Portsmouth, unmasking American double agents. In Nova Scotia, after the war, he had been too sick to attend the board hearing loyalist claims. Improving a little, he had shipped to London to put his claim directly, invoking General Leslie's promise to him "that if [he] were not cured he should be maintained out of the royal Bounty." But, alas, he and his wife had since fallen into "the lowest poverty and distress." All that came between Shadrack and an anonymous end in the rookeries was his fiddle, for he could still "scrape the gut" for a few pennies. Yet the commissioners failed to be moved by his story, at least initially. It was only in 1788, after enduring hard winters on the London streets, that he was certified loyal by both a sergeant in the 76th Regiment and a serjeant of police in New York. Shadrack Furman was now judged to have "suffered great cruelties in America on account of his Attachment to Great Britain" and was finally awarded the relatively liberal pension of £8 a year.[24]

Scipio Handley of Charleston must also have had good testimonials to confirm that he had taken a musket ball in the right leg while carrying grapeshot to the defences in the siege of Savannah, a wound that escaped amputation but that had never properly healed, since he was awarded the princely sum of £20 compensation for loss of his property.[25] Many of the petitioners, most of whom were in London rather than Nova Scotia because they had ended up serving on British warships and had returned with the fleet, got much less. The upper limit was £20, whatever their story and however serious their wounds, whilst even the poorest of the white loyalists received at least £25 and usually much more.

The commissioners, sitting in their panelled chamber overlooking Lincoln's Inn Fields, were sensible of the hardship, but what, pray, could they do? They must, as one of their number, Sir John Eardley Wilmot, Chief Justice of the Court of Common Pleas, declared, be stringently faithful to the law. And the law demanded proof before they could justly act—proof of the same kind as if the petitioner had been a supplicant or a plaintiff from the shires. Had the petitioners been slaves until they joined the army? Well, then, it followed that they could not possibly have had any property for which to be compensated! Indeed, it should be enough for them that they had received their liberty, been permitted to come to Old England where the air was "too pure for slaves to breathe," and been delivered from the American state where they would be vulnerable to re-enslavement! Their proper attitude ought surely to be one of un-alloyed gratitude and devotion. A man named Jackson, who had been a last-maker in New York and had lost his tools and stock-in-trade, had been taken prisoner by the Americans, but had escaped to serve on HMS *Shrewsbury* under Admiral Keppel, was nonetheless rejected since he belonged to that category of blacks who "instead of being sufferers of the wars, most of them have gained their liberty and therefore come with a very ill-grace to ask for the bounty of government."[26]

By the lights of the commissioners, then, only those blacks who said (and could prove) that they were free-born were likely to receive serious consideration. And the fact that petitioners were given only one month from their initial submission to come up with supporting testimony, sometimes from officers who were far away in Nova Scotia, only increased their dependence (especially since many were illiterate) on any white Londoners who offered help. Two of these—written off by the commissioners as petty confidence tricksters—were Jonathan Williams and Thomas Watkins, lodging house keepers who offered their services for a consideration and with whom six of the petitioning blacks—Moses Stephens, George Miller, Henry Browne, Prince William, Anthony Smithers and John Baptist—were residing.

Certainly, the claims for property compensation filed on behalf of these petitioners were pitched, the commissioners thought, suspiciously high: nearly 90 acres, 15 cows, 3 horses and a 120 head of poultry for Moses Stephens, for instance, and 100 acres for George Miller. The commissioners decided that Williams and Watkins "have an interest in representing a falsity to us as many of the blacks lodge with them and if they should obtain any money from the treasury, probably these men are to have a considerable share in it."[27] But whilst Jonathan Williams demanded a share for his services from the blacks, it is not true, as the commissioners claimed, that the formulaic way in which the petitions were drafted necessarily meant that they were mostly fabricated. The commissioners implied that such claims betrayed their fraud by being virtually identical, but patient reading reveals that they were not. Anthony Smithers claimed to have lost his father's fourteen acres in Gloucester County, New Jersey, when he joined the British army in Philadelphia as a sixteen-year-old, whilst John Baptist, from the same area, claimed only three acres, a house, and some livestock and poultry. That two blacks should hail from the same area and have both joined the British in Philadelphia did not necessarily indicate fraud but was, rather, a commonplace of their social history.

To secure any kind of serious consideration, then, presupposed a rock-solid testimonial from a white officer or loyalist, or a well-known reputation. Colonel David Fanning, a North Carolina Tory who lived in New Brunswick, was able to write on behalf of six of his men, including Samuel Burke, who had been servant to Brigadier General Mountford Browne (who also wrote to support his claim) but had seen active combat, too, was badly wounded at Danbury and then even more seriously at Hanging Rock in South Carolina, where he claimed to have killed ten rebel soldiers. As a result of these firm testimonials, Burke received £20 and went on to work at "an artificial flower garden."[28]

Those who were less lucky—left out in the cold to fend for themselves after choosing to come to what they must have imagined as the fountainhead of freedom rather than take their chances in the Bahamas or Nova Scotia—must have felt cruelly betrayed. So the picture painted by the loyalist Benjamin West for Sir John Wilmot, featuring a group of his fellow loyalists gathered to the bosom of a welcoming Britannia, commits what, even by the romantic standards of the late eighteenth century, is an outrageously self-serving fiction. For in the midst of the grateful throng is a "sturdy black," his chains struck, his posture upright, his countenance noble, holding out his arms to his British benefactor. The truth of the matter was rather different. The truth was Peter Anderson, a sawyer who had been working for John Griffin in the Virginia tidewater before being pressed to join Dunmore's Ethiopians. Anderson had been among the blacks captured at the climactic, bloody battle of Great Bridge. But even after the defeat, Anderson had made his choice, and it was not America. Escaping from his American captors, he had returned to Dunmore's regiment, with "Freedom to Slaves" emblazoned on their coats and stayed with it, losing "all that I had in the World: four chests of cloaths, twenty hogs, four feather beds and furniture." He had then survived the hell of the smallpox- and typhus-ridden ships and island camps, the nightmare of the siege of Yorktown and the even greater nightmare of the surrender. Finally he had made it all the way to London, where, from his sad note to the Commission, it seemed he would perish of hunger. "I endeavoured to get Work," he told the gentlemen of Lincoln's Inn, "but cannot get Any I am Thirty Nine Years of Age & am ready & willing to serve His Britinack Majesty While I am Able But I am realy starvin about the Streets Having Nobody to give me a morsel of bread & dare not go home to my Own Country again." Dunmore himself intervened to vouch for Anderson and got him his £10.[29]

Two very different kinds of blacks, then, impressed themselves on the sensibilities of the British in the winter of 1785–86. For the high-minded philanthropists, there were the "Poor Blacks" who needed delivering from the wicked trade. In their imagination the crusaders saw noble, tortured Africans being herded on to the ships or mercilessly beaten on the plantations, but in any case suffering far away on a burning shore. But then there was another population altogether, the "Black Poor" who were uncomfortably close at hand, in the East End and Rotherhithe: tattered bundles of human misery, huddled in doorways, shoeless, sometimes shirtless even in the bitter cold, or else covered with filthy rags, consumptive or attacking their sores and scabs and sticking out bony hands for help. One lot needed help from pamphlets and parliamentary motions; the other needed help, rather more urgently, from bread, broth and physicians. And their plight was all the more serious because the Poor Law then in operation required indigents to return to their parish of origin to qualify for relief. But the "parish" of the Americans who had been slaves and sailors, powder monkeys and army drummers, carters and cooks was on the high seas or back in the plantations of the American South. Baptism, of course, could change that by linking them with the parish where the deed was done; and at least one humane clergyman, the Reverend Herbert Mayo, rector of St George in the East at the Wapping end of Stepney, where its campaniles and turrets looked down on the rope-walks and tar-boilers, did what he could to bring the destitute and distressed blacks into the fold.[30] Mayo gave them first instruction, then water from the font, and at last soup.

In January 1786, when the winter was at its harshest, someone other than the amiable rector felt something ought to be done. After all, Jonas Hanway had done something for just about everyone else in London who needed it: the small climbing boys who died of asthma or cancer of the scrotum contracted through working in soot-caked chimneys; the sexually diseased for whom he founded the Misericordia Hospital, many of whom were prostitutes who could then be sheltered and reformed in his Magdelen Society House for the Reception of the Penitent—eleven ounces of meat, three ounces of cheese, four pounds of bread and one and a half gallons of beer every day to help them stagger their way to a cleansed life; and foundling boys who might be taken into his Marine Society schools for the better supply of seamen to crew the Empire.[31] After this tireless life in philanthropy, not to mention penning countless would-be helpful manuals—*Advice to a Farmer's Daughter; Moral and Religious Instructions Intended for Apprentices; The Sentiments and Advice of Thomas Trueman, A Virtuous and Understanding Footman; The Seaman's Christian Friend*, and many more that all said more or less the same thing: abhor vice, pray, get up early—Hanway had come to represent a certain kind of busy, charitable Englishman. This was partly so because he had strong views about two items that, to foreigners, defined Englishness: tea and umbrellas. The first he thought so pernicious that he ran a public campaign against it (the definition of an uphill battle); the second he introduced into middling society, being the first man to carry his own umbrella, made of green silk, about the streets. In January 1786 this industrious man was elderly, exhausted and sick. But he was not prepared to depart until he had done what he could for the suffering black poor.

Hanway made sure that he was not alone. As a young man he had been a venturer in the Russian trade, and now he called in some of his long-standing business connections to launch a charitable subscription designed to tide blacks and "lascars" (poor Indians and half-caste Asians, usually unemployed seamen) over the worst of the season. Early in that month a Committee for the Relief of the Black Poor was established, and met, first in Bond Street and then at Batson's coffee-house in the City, opposite the Royal Exchange, a place better located to pull in the businesslike and charitably minded. Joining Hanway on the committee were, among others, George Peters, governor of the Bank of England; John Julius Angerstein, born in St Petersburg, rumoured to be a bastard of Catherine the Great (but then, who wasn't?) and now one of the major Lloyds' underwriters, a good friend of the prime minister, William Pitt, and a voracious art collector of spectacularly good taste; and, less flashily, the Quaker banker Samuel Hoare. Angerstein owned slaves in Grenada, whereas Hoare was an avowed abolitionist, but they both saw the relief of the black poor as a humane emergency.[32]

The committee men who sat at Batson's were, in their turn, able to mobilize the great and the good as subscribers to the relief fund. Duchesses (Devonshire), countesses (Essex and Salisbury) and marchionesses (Buckingham) were eager to demonstrate their love of suffering humanity with their famously bounteous purses. The prime minister, the Reverend Mayo and, of course, Granville Sharp all gave, and Samuel Hoare made sure that the Friends, his co-religionists, were the biggest collective donor of all, subscribing £67. But the charity, as intended, struck a chord with much humbler givers, one of whom sent a bowl and spoon and another her "Widow's Mite" of five shillings.[33] It was not just the spectacle of destitution that set off this surge of giving. No one was proposing to do the same for white beggars. It was, rather, the history of these particular blacks, the Americans who had stayed true to Britain but had been rewarded with poverty and suffering. They were truly on the national conscience. "They . . . have served Britain," one correspondent to a newspaper complained, "have fought under her colours and after having quitted their American masters, depending on promises of protection held out to them by British Governors and Commanders, are now left to perish by famine and cold in the sight of that people for whom they have hazarded their lives and even (many of them) spilt their blood."[34]

The £800 collected by the committee was used for food, medical care and clothes: shirts, shoes, stockings and trousers. From the third week of January, those who applied to Brown's the bakers in Wigmore Street would be given a quarter-pound twopenny loaf twice a week, and at the Yorkshire Stingo tavern in Lisson Green in Marylebone and the White Raven in Mile End the needy got bowls of broth and a piece of meat as well as bread. An infirmary in Warren Street cared for blacks suffering from "very bad ulcerated legs," abscesses or a condition identified, imprecisely but graphically, as "foul disease," and some of the worst cases were admitted to St Bartholomew's Hospital on the committee's account.

But as winter softened into spring, the queues outside the White Raven and the Yorkshire Stingo, contrary to the committee's expectations, got longer, not shorter. The hoped-for work failed to materialize, and by May some four hundred were regularly receiving food and their tiny allowance of sixpence. The committee had never intended the relief campaign to become permanent, and since Hanway was a great enthusiast for colonial settlement, it was no surprise that as early as March he had already mooted the idea that perhaps the blacks might be better off somewhere else, where they would be more likely to get work.

Once this thought had been entertained, the spectacle of blacks shivering on the streets of Stepney led naturally to a second thought: that they might be happier and do better in some place where the climate suited them. But were they Africans or were they Americans? If the latter, then perhaps they should (as some had already suggested themselves) join their fellow black loyalists in Nova Scotia, or in the adjoining new province of New Brunswick. If that were too chilly, then perhaps a Bahamian island such as Great Anagua? If, however, they were truly African, then surely the best solution would be a return to their native country, not as slaves but as free men, a colony of liberated black Britons who, by their honest toil and enterprise, would create an exemplary alternative to the degraded world of the slave economy.

This was certainly what another friend of Hanway's was telling him. To his friends, and to some who were not, Henry Smeathman was "Mr Termite." No one knew more about ants, red and white: how they constructed their mounds and pinnacles; the hierarchy of their formidable social organization (with both a king and a queen at its head, Smeathman made clear to a shocked readership); even how they tasted:

"most delicious and delicate eating. One gentleman compared them to sugared marrow, another to sugared cream and a paste of sweet almonds."[35] But then the epicurean possibilities of the Grain Coast of West Africa were, according to Smeathman, just the start of its countless delights and prospects. In fact, his knowledge of the climate, flora and fauna and soil fertility of Sierra Leone, the territory he was recommending to the committee as the ideal place for settling the blacks, was far from exhaustive. In 1771 he had been sent by the scientist and future president of the Royal Society, Joseph Banks, to the offshore Banana Islands to collect botanical specimens for Banks's collection at Kew. He had stayed there for three years, turning himself from botanist to entomologist, convincing himself that the Grain Coast was not just a wonder of natural history, but that its climate and soil made it ideal for the cultivation of the cash crops currently in such heavy demand in Europe and the Americas: rice, dyewood, cotton and sugar. With the right investment, these staples might be produced by free labour and (in harmony with Adam Smith's and David Hume's economic and philosophical arguments), since the steep rise in the price of slaves was notorious, more cheaply than by slave labour.

On his return from Africa, however, Smeathman had failed to interest any kind of serious investment. In the 1780s he had pottered along giving his insect lectures, a harmless but slightly marginal figure in all three communities where he reckoned himself a figure: scientific, commercial and philanthropic. But then, in 1786, the cause of the black poor gave him a sudden, belated opportunity, and Smeathman set before the committee and, by extension, the Lords of the Treasury who would have to foot the bill his "Plan of Settlement" for the creation of a thriving free black colony in "one of the most pleasant and feasible countries in the known world." It was, he assured them, a place fanned by balmy zephyrs and with a soil so rich that the merest prod of a hoe would guarantee a bumper crop. Given such natural blessings, each settler should "by common consent" be allowed to "possess as much land as he or she could cultivate." Surely the blacks would see that "an opportunity so advantageous may perhaps never be offer'd again for they and their posterity may enjoy perfect freedom settled in a country congenial to their constitution" and one where they "will find a certain and secure retreat from former suffering." And all this could be done for a mere £14 per capita. He, Smeathman, would see to it, upon his word.

But the word of Smeathman, whether on the toothsome eating of white termites or the benign climate of Sierra Leone, was to be taken with a grain of salt. Just the previous year, in 1785, appearing before a parliamentary committee inquiring into suitable locations for penal colonies, Smeathman had expressly advised against the Gambia, a little further north on the West African coast, because of the deadliness of the climate. Without a physician and drugs, he warned, "not one in a hundred would be alive in Six Months." True, he had thought principally of its effects on white Europeans. His own assistant, the Swede Anders Berlin, had died of fever only a few months after arrival, and every so often his own body would weaken and shake from the residual effects of putrid fever contracted there, although he maintained that the high European mortality rate was the result of poor diet and indulgence in strong spirits. But between his fly-catching and termite-gathering, Smeathman must also have had ample opportunity to see just how deadly a toll malarial fevers could exact on blacks as well as whites. Like most of his contemporaries, and despite being an entomologist, Smeathman assumed that malaria was caused by the miasmal vapours rising from rotting vegetation and stagnant water. But then again, the torrential rainstorms, which began in May and continued through until September, all but guaranteed a six-month rot.

There was another glaring discrepancy between Smeathman's ebullient salesmanship and the truth. The "Land of Freedom," as Sierra Leone was to be called, also happened to be the province of slavery. The Royal Navy, which was to escort and possibly protect the infant colony of the free, was at the same time assigned to protect the busy British slave-trading depot on Bance Island, a little way up-river from the estuary. Smeathman's view, whether sincerely held or not, was that somehow the two systems could and would co-exist, until such time as the evident superiority of free agriculture over slaving would, by the pure force of economic logic, secure its own happy future. That neither the slavers of Bance Island nor the Temne people who supplied them with captives would have viewed the irruption into their world with equanimity must have occurred to Smeathman. But, urgently needing a go-ahead from the committee and the government for his plan, he had no interest in dwelling unduly on this difficulty. Since he himself was to go with the expedition and would directly face the issue, impatience and myopia rather than outright deceit seem to have been his most glaring faults.

There were some, including Hanway, who continued to wonder whether Nova Scotia, with no slave trade threatening a settlement of free blacks, might not, after all, be a more suitable place for the great experiment. But the advocates of the warm but worrying option prevailed over those of the cold but free. First the committee, and then, in mid-May, the government signed on to the scheme. At a cost of £14 per person, the Treasury would bear the expense not just of free transport to Africa but also of provisions, clothes and tools for four months.

To many historians, this entire operation has seemed more like social convenience than utopian idealism. If Smeathman's own motives for promoting the settlement are now seen as something short of altruism, the reasons impelling official support have been judged by its severest historical critics as even more scandalous: a poisonous combination of hypocrisy and bigotry.[36] In this view, what both the committee and the administration wanted was just to be rid of the blacks as irksome beggars, petty criminals and (since inter-racial sexual liaisons were becoming commonplace and noticed) a threat to the purity of white womanhood. As Stephen Braidwood, who argues for a more mixed assessment of the motives, concedes, this ugly vein of race prejudice was indeed among the reasons given by some of its supporters, including some of the most vitriolic defenders of slavery, such as Edward Long. But Long and others among the hired pens of the West India Association would also have favoured the scheme as a way to rid themselves and Britain of some of the most likely foot soldier recruits to the gathering abolitionist crusade.

The involvement of slaveowners such as Angerstein and Thomas Boddington in the Sierra Leone plan, and the approval of Long, who may indeed have thought of it as an experiment in social hygiene, does not, however, make it the conspiratorial racist deportation of recent historical writing. For every Long, there were ten dedicated abolitionists. Some, for instance Thomas Steele, one of the two Treasury men assigned to administer the expedition, were gradualists, in favour of doing away with the trade but not the institution of slavery. Others, such as his Treasury colleague overseeing the plan, George Rose, were heartfelt, militant abolitionists, committed to closing down the whole sinful institution. Nothing, moreover, could have happened without the wholehearted collaboration of the Comptroller of the Navy, who had to approve the arrangements for the naval escort and the outfitting of the ships; and he, of course, was Sir Charles Middleton, the patron of James Ramsay, Thomas Clarkson and William Wilberforce.

Then, as always, there was Granville Sharp, who was in no doubt at all, provided slaveholding of any kind was strictly forbidden, that Sierra Leone could indeed be made into "The Province of Freedom." Frank-pledge in the tropics was in the offing! In letters to his American friends Benjamin Franklin and John Jay he excitedly urged those appointed with the work of drawing up a constitution to consider it seriously as the most perfect institution of God-pleasing liberty. Sharp knew that Franklin was now president of the Pennsylvania Society for Promoting the Abolition of Slavery, and had heard to his inexpressible pleasure that the Commonwealth of Massachusetts had outlawed slavery in its own constitution and that a vigorous campaign was under way for stopping the trade. From the Reverend Samuel Hopkins in Rhode Island, once the very harbour of iniquity, he learned that some of the recently freed blacks in New England had already expressed a desire to re-establish themselves in liberty in their native Africa,[37] and wished that Britain, its honour and dignity already wounded by the misguided war, would redeem itself with an act of comparable public virtue. Had not the American disaster taught his country that henceforth the only rock on which an enduring British Empire could possibly be built was that of Christian liberty? Properly established, Sierra Leone might indeed be the foundation stone of this new, virtuously reborn empire. How auspicious it would be, moreover, for black Britons, many of them liberated slaves, to reinstitute the purest form of British liberty: the unique marriage of Saxon Frankpledge and Israelitish commonwealth that would define self-government for free Christians.

As early as 1783, in the midst of the agitation about the *Zong* atrocity, Sharp had envisioned such a place in Africa: an idyllic liberty village amidst the banyans and acacias, where a church, school and hospital would rise on the greensward, and rows of tidy white cottages would have their own modest allotments on which to grow fruit and vegetables. Domestic animals would safely graze. Taxation would be in units of public labour—uncontentious because citizens committed to the common weal would abide religiously by their ward and watch duties, uncomplainingly taking their shifts, when the village bell tolled, to work on the construction and maintenance of canals, bridges, forts, roads and, of course, sewers. At four in the afternoon, after eight hours of work, there would be a refreshing siesta. The courts would be punctilious, regular and humane. Conscientiously voting for their tithing-men and hundredors, their assemblies empowered to enact any legislation consistent with the Common Law of England, blacks would teach complacent and corrupted whites what responsible, free government truly was. Now, three years after sketching his great design, Sharp saw a chance for this vision to be realized.[38]

God seemed to be sending him opportunities to demonstrate the importance of the project. For in July 1786 Sharp was tipped off about another black abduction, of one Harry de Mane; his informant was Ottobah Cugoano, a Ghanaian Fante now known by his baptized name of "John Stewart" and a close friend of Olaudah Equiano. When the captain, at the helm of the ship bearing de Mane off and on the verge of sailing, was confronted with a writ of Habeas Corpus the man was released. Brought to London to see his benefactor, he told Sharp that, barring some miracle, he would have jumped into the sea "choosing rather to die than to be carried into slavery."[39] The Province of Freedom was, for Sharp, exactly the place where the likes of Harry de Mane could make a new life. Buoyant with optimism about its prospects, Sharp donated twenty-five guineas for the "Present" to be given to the King of the Temne in exchange for land, and spent £800 of his own, redeeming pawned goods for the blacks, paying off arrears of debt to get them out of jail and otherwise helping lame cases to get to the docks.

So Granville Sharp was persuaded, the committee was persuaded and the government was persuaded. But, as Jonas Hanway found out in early June, the London blacks themselves were not universally enchanted by the idea of a return to Africa. Henry Smeathman, the salesman-in-chief of the idea, was mysteriously ailing—perhaps another visitation from the putrid fever—and unable to do much to silence their worries. So it was left to Hanway, who himself was far from well, to go to the Yorkshire Stingo during a hand-out of the allowance and talk up the project among the blacks. Inside the tavern, surrounded by rows of pipes and pewter tankards filled with the strong, red, muddy beer that gave the place its name, he listened to their anxieties. They all amounted to one serious apprehension: could they really hang on to their freedom in a part of Africa so dominated by slavers, both black and white? This was the place, after all, where many of them or their parents had been seized as small children and herded to the coastal forts. Some said that, all things considered, if they had to leave Old England they would rather go to Nova Scotia; others preferred the West Indies or even, in a few cases, America. On being given to understand that continuing to receive their allowance was conditional on agreeing to be resettled, at least thirty refused further largesse.

Hanway heard them out. Then, in the manner of his most earnest advice to footmen and seamen, treated the blacks to an uplifting address that was half rebuke, half exhortation. After being liberated by His Majesty's grace and goodness, how could they possibly doubt the "pure and benevolent Intentions of Government" or the "Charity and Benevolence of the good People of Britain" who had given freely that they might be fed and clothed? As for himself, he was merely "an old man on the Confines of Eternity, who had no worldly interest to serve," so if he was colluding in this ensnarement that they feared, "he must be the worst of all the wicked on Earth to deceive them." No, as far as he could see, the Grain Coast was much the better prospect for them than bleak and barren Nova Scotia.[40]

Hanway's eloquence—reprised at the White Raven down the Mile End Road later in the month—seems to have briefly calmed the blacks' fears. By the third week of October, with a deadline looming after which the allowances would be discontinued, over six hundred had signed an "Agreement" indicating their willingness to be "happily settled on the . . . Grain Coast of Africa" in a place "to be called the Land of Freedom under the protection of and by the encouragement and support of the British Government." In return for continued support, they promised to embark promptly when required, and to "assist in navigating and doing such work as we are severally capable of doing." They would have provisions and clothing not just for the voyage but enough to last for four months after their arrival.

Even for the six-hundred-odd who had signed the "Agreement," there was some understandable nervousness about what exactly the "protection" was to which they were submitting. Was it actually instituted for their defence or for their confinement? The rumour that there was to be some sort of fort in Sierra Leone and the preparations under way for the "first fleet" of ships transporting convicts to Botany Bay in Australia only fed this anxiety. Perhaps remembering their insecurity after they had left their American masters, and the importance they knew the British attached to official pieces of paper, they could not think of emigrating, they said, without an "Instrument of Liberty." This would be a document bearing the stamp of a high official of government, guaranteeing that they could not be re-enslaved and that they might invoke should they need the government's help against slavers. The "Instrument" would be their covenant on the tropical shore.

The London blacks may have been "poor," but they were neither naive nor mute. In order to organize the emigration better, Hanway had divided the blacks receiving assistance into companies of twelve to twenty-four, appointing a "corporal" or "chief" for each, often someone who could read if not write. Surprisingly quickly, men like the free-born Philadelphian Richard Weaver, whose claim for compensation had been denied by the commission, John Cambridge, a net-maker and domestic servant from New Jersey, and John Lemmon, a Bengali "lascar" hairdresser, became spokesmen for the whole community. As de facto delegates, the corporals went to meetings of the committee and, when they felt strongly, let the chairman and his colleagues know in no uncertain terms the mood of their people. When, after the death of Henry Smeathman on the 1st of July 1786, the committee had belated second thoughts about the whole business of slave-ridden Africa, and revived the alternative destinations of the Bahamas and New Brunswick, the corporals let it be known that the minds of the blacks were resolved on Sierra Leone! Someone from that country living in London had told them that the native people of the river region were exceptionally "fond of the English and would [therefore] receive them joyfully."[41]

Remarkably, and unhelpfully, the parties involved in the project had, then, completely reversed positions. As long as "Mr Termite" had been alive, no one on the committee, not even Hanway, could bring himself to contradict Smeathman's sunny optimism about the Sierra

Leone plan. After his death, Hanway, who had pushed the plan in the taverns (and who was himself to die in early September), launched a vitriolic attack on Smeathman, accusing him not just of incompetence but of corrupt self-interest. Gloomy predictions were made about the likely belligerence of the slave traders, black and white, in Africa. But it was too late. The earlier pro-African Hanway had done his job all too well. Although sixty-seven of the potential emigrants thought New Brunswick, apparently rich in timber, fish and game, might indeed be an alternative, they were overruled by the majority. In a petition to the committee, fifteen of the corporals spoke glowingly of "Mr Smeath-man's humane plan" and insisted on having Smeathman's clerk, Joseph Irwin, appointed in his place as superintendent, since Irwin had "conducted this business from the beginning with humanity and justice."[42]

Whatever its misgivings, the committee gave in. The Province of Freedom would be where Smeathman had mapped it. But now there were other things the blacks wanted: mobile forges, constables' truncheons, tea, sugar, "portable soup" for the sick, stationery and, most importantly, the document that would certify their freedom, printed on parchment and signed and stamped by an official of the Admiralty. (In the event this was George Marsh, the Clerk of the Acts.) Imagining the trials they might have to go through, the blacks even specified the container that was to house the precious document of their liberty: "a small Tin Box, value about Two Pence." Then they demanded something that whites were not accustomed to giving blacks: weapons. They would need them for hunting, they said, and they would need them to defend themselves. The Commissioners of the Navy blinked, balked, but did not turn the request down, sending it on to the Treasury, which sent it on to the committee, saying that they should have the last word. The committee, those Quaker men of peace, plus a few harder heads, assented: 250 muskets and 250 cutlasses were to be provided, along with enough flint, powder and ball for 400 "stands" of arms.

Then something even more remarkable happened. The expedition was to be led by three officers: the senior naval officer, who would escort the little fleet during the voyage and see it safely landed; Joseph Irwin, the superintendent who had been chosen by the blacks themselves; and a "commissary" responsible for supplies and stores, both on board and on land, and accountable for them to the Treasury. Equiano was appointed as the commissary, the first black to hold any kind of office from the British government, although not, alas, for very long. Later, after things had gone seriously awry, Equiano wrote that he had had misgivings all along about attempting to plant a settlement of free blacks amidst slavers. But, because he believed the design was "humane and politick," and because he was pressed so warmly to accept, he swallowed his doubts and took the post.

The emigrants were all supposed to have embarked on the two ships lying at Blackwall, the *Atlantic* and the *Belisarius,* by the end of October. It was important, if the fledgling settlement was to have a chance, that it should arrive on the Grain Coast before the onset of the rainy season in the spring. But the delays were endless. In late October Irwin reported that more than 600 had signed the Agreement, and he expected 750 in all, making a third ship essential. If they were all to sail together, they should wait until that vessel, the *Vernon,* was equipped and loaded. But no sooner had this decision been acted on than the numbers began to shrink. By late November, of that 600-plus, no more than 259 had actually come aboard the two ships. And they were, evidently, freezing cold, cramped, dangerously sickly and generally unhappy. Some reported being treated by the white officers no better than if they had been "in the West Indies." Going aboard, Equiano was shocked at the lack of proper clothing and medication for treating the sick, and began to wonder whether the sums supplied by government were in fact being spent as authorized or misappropriated, possibly by Irwin himself.[43] Irwin, for his part, complained of the blacks' "want of discipline." It was said that they burned candles and fires all through the night (hardly surprising, in view of the bitter cold that descended on the Thames), and that they wasted water. Granville Sharp was, however, shocked to hear that they had been drinking rum and even giving it to their children, a habit for which he blamed the high rate of illness aboard ship. As many as 60 may have died before the ships ever left England, most of them on the *Belisarius,* where a "malignant fever" was taking a deadly toll, especially of the children.

Of those remaining on board, not all had signed the Agreement; and of the signatories only a fraction had gone on board. Blacks were seen still begging in the streets and, in an attempt to get more to embark, the committee asked even the most charitably minded citizens not to give them alms. Rumours appeared in the press that after a certain date blacks found begging would be arrested as vagrants, something that the committee never, in fact, contemplated.

But the evaporation of the people of the Province of Freedom continued apace. More false stories circulated in the press—that since both the Australia-bound convict fleet and the Sierra Leone fleet were going to rendezvous at the "Motherbank" (Spithead, near Portsmouth) their fate and purpose were likely to be the same. Some of the blacks even went ashore to visit the notorious Lord George Gordon, the demagogue who had fomented violent anti-Catholic riots in 1780 and still a hero of the London poor, to ask his advice about their intended form of government. One eccentric judging another, the ebullient, mad Gordon scanned Sharp's lengthy document (called, naturally, "A Short Sketch of Government") with its fifty pages devoted to forms of daily prayer, its Israelito-Saxon elections and its severe penalties for most of the seven deadly sins, and advised against it. Still more blacks departed.

Whites, however, got on. By February, when the three ships were finally ready to sail from Spithead along with their escort, the *Nautilus*, commanded by Captain Thomas Boulden Thompson, they did so with a full cabin-load of white artisans and professionals—a gesture that might have struck the blacks as either sensibly precautionary or gratuitously patronizing. There may have been good reason to sign on William Ricketts, a nurseryman and seedsman, to give the first rice planting the best chance of success. Doubtless it was a good idea to include two physicians, Dr Hackney and Dr Young, an engineer, Mr Gesau, and a surveyor, Richard Duncombe. Possibly the tanner, the bricklayer, the brushmaker and even Hugh Smith, the "flax dresser," were needed to pass on their skills to the settlers. But why, given the fact that at least half of the emigrants were African-Americans and that the escaped blacks were almost always skilled in some practical craft or other, even (or especially) if they had been at sea, it seems over-pessimistic to have recruited tailors, carpenters, gardeners, two people described as "husbandmen" (meaning rural labourers), and even perhaps Mr Schenkel the baker, along with his wife and children. Free or slave, the blacks had been cooks; and some must certainly have been "husbandmen."

They were not the only whites on board the fleet bound for Freedom. By sailing time in late February there were also more than sixty white women, Margaret Allen, Elizabeth Ramsey, Amelia Homan, Martha James, Mary Jacob and Mary Tomlinson among them. Who were they, and what were they doing on board the *Belisarius*, the *Atlantic* and the *Vernon*? The passenger lists describe them as "White Women Married to Black Men"—and the names of Ann Holder, presumably married to Thomas Holder (with Thomas Holder junior as their son); Rebecca Griffith, married to Abraham Elliott Griffith (Welsh-African-American, educated at Sharp's expense); Sarah Whitecuffe, Benjamin's widow; Sarah Cambridge, married to Corporal John Cambridge, the New Jersey net-maker; Elizabeth Lemmon, married to the Bengali hairdresser Corporal John Lemmon; and Elizabeth Demain, married to Harry de Mane, whom Sharp had rescued from the ship about to carry him away to slavery, all bear this out.[44] Until recently the white women were thought to be, as a Swedish botanist who went to Sierra Leone in 1794 described them, "chiefly strumpets."[45] But he was merely following the account given by Anna Maria Falconbridge, wife of an ex-slaver surgeon-turned-abolitionist, Alexander Falconbridge, who was in Sierra Leone in 1791. There, Anna encountered seven white women "decrepid with disease and . . . disguised with filth and dirt" who, she asserted, told her that they had been lured aboard the ships at Wapping, a haunt of dockland whores, by tankards of drink and rich promises. The next day they were woken, so the Falconbridge account went, and informed to whom they would be "married."

The story was just the kind of thing the late eighteenth-century public liked to hear: fallen women pounced on by the unscrupulous agents of a crackpot enterprise; compelled to service the animal needs of black men in a revolting pretence of bogus domesticity; ending up covered in sores and flies somewhere up-river in the steaming forest, with parrots and apes hooting a chorus of derision. Such is what happens to the naive and the dissolute, the wise reader could add, nodding vigorously. Beware well-intentioned cranks. Beware the likes of Granville Sharp!

A pity, then, that Anna Falconbridge's story is so improbable. The fleet never was at Wapping, although the women could conceivably have been made senseless with drink and taken down-river to Blackwall. More seriously, why would Granville Sharp who went to such pains to make sure there was both a chaplain on board to preside over the church of freedom, and a sexton, and who kept an eagle eye on the passenger list, have countenanced for a moment the presence of sixty women of the streets, bagnios and taverns? The entire story tells us more about the chroniclers than the chronicled, as well as the contemporary taste for sensation. Weeping over the plight of the poor slaves did not preclude a frisson of horror and aversion at the thought of them sharing the beds of white women. The liaison between the Duchess of Queensberry and her black fencing master, Soubise, was the stuff of exactly this kind of scandalous excitement. For a whole troop of white women to surrender themselves to blacks so completely as to sail away with them could only be explained by their being the grossest and most vicious of their sex.

The truth was otherwise and actually more remarkable. Women such as Anne Provey, who was married to John Provey—once slave to a North Carolina attorney, later enrolled in the Black Pioneers—and mother of Ann-Louisa, were in all likelihood of very humble background. Given that many of the black poor were living in the parish of St George in the East, it is also entirely possible that some of the women may have met their black husbands in surroundings not typical of the rituals of courtship in Jane Austen's novels. Some of them may indeed have been tavern girls, laundresses, seamstresses or something of all three—anything to keep the wolf from the door. But the concept of white women who worked is not necessarily synonymous with "working girls." The passenger lists point to a domestic connection rather than a hasty sexual one: the mere fact that many of the white women in these mixed-race marriages had small children with them (described as "black") presupposes something more than a spurious marriage cobbled together with gin and false promises in the rookeries of dockland.

Nothing quite like these emigrants had been seen before: 411 of them, at least half from America, slave or free, some 61 families among them, were going resolutely back to the country in which their suffering had begun. Some were black and white, with mixed-race children, such as the Holders; others black and black, such as James and Mary Hadwick and their small child; and yet others white families, such as Schenkel the baker, his wife, Ann, and their children, Richard and Rosina. There was the occasional widower, like James Yarrow, for instance, with his three small ones, Israel, John and Mary; a few white women, such as

Milly Shimmings and Mary Allen, were described as "wanting to be married"; and there were many young black men, among them Thomas Truman, Mishick Wright, Edward Honeycot, Christian Friday and James Neptune. Most of these voyagers were, no doubt, facing their future with the usual mixture of relief, hope and fear.

Fear may have got the upper hand much too quickly, for the ships were barely under way when they found themselves in trouble. The naval escort *Nautilus* ran on to a sandbank, although with the help of high winds and tides managed to get itself off again. Those winds went from fresh to dangerous in a matter of hours as the fleet found itself in the teeth of the worst kind of gale the Channel can whip up: churning billows, huge swells and vicious, swiping gusts. The *Vernon*'s fore top-mast came down; the ships lost sight of, and contact with, each other; and the unlucky *Nautilus*, labouring "very hard . . . the waist full of water," limped to Torbay. The next day Captain Thompson attempted to sail to Plymouth in the wake of the *Atlantic* and *Belisarius*, but was beaten back to Torbay by the foul weather. Not until the 18th of March did the fleet manage to reunite at Plymouth. It had been almost four months since the embarkations had begun on the Thames. Men and women had died, babies had been born, blacks and whites had got off the ship and others had got on—and the Province of Freedom seemed further away than ever.

Nor were the venture's troubles over. The two non-naval leaders of the expedition, Irwin and Equiano, were at loggerheads with each other. Equiano's suspicions that Irwin was pocketing Treasury money intended for purchases of food, clothing and medical supplies were, as far as he was concerned, confirmed at Plymouth. Wanting to make good on supplies already exhausted during the long delays Equiano checked what had, and had not, been bought. Purchases earmarked by funds already received by Irwin seemed not to have been made. When the matter was reported to Steele and Rose at the Treasury, Irwin responded that Equiano was inciting the blacks to "make trouble." Since Equiano also objected to both the numbers of "unauthorized" whites aboard (by which he did not mean the white wives but "passengers" such as Thomas Mewbourn, and sundry others) and the way in which they treated the blacks, Irwin may have been right that he was encouraging protest. Equally there may well have been something to protest about.

Whatever the rights and wrongs, the festering dispute got worse when, not knowing how long they would be stalled in Plymouth, blacks were allowed to disembark and go into the town. The spectacle of hundreds of them walking the cobbled streets, possibly (since they had suffered from cabinfever—literally) without the kind of attention to politeness expected in Devon, so distressed many of the good townspeople that a hue and cry was raised and the offending blacks ushered back to confinement on board. In these aggravated circumstances, Equiano, who thought he was only discharging his responsibilities as the on-board representative of government as conscientiously as possible, appealed to Captain Thompson as arbiter.

Thompson blamed both of them. But for the sake of the peace of the expedition, already compromised by tempests and sickness, he told the Treasury men that one of them had to go. No doubt Irwin was no angel but Equiano, Thompson wrote, "had taken every means to actuate the minds of the Blacks to discord" and unless the "spirit of sedition" was quelled the damage done to the whole venture might be fatal. Although Sir Charles Middleton argued for him in the dispute, it was Equiano, predictably, who was discharged, and thirteen others identified as "troublemakers" were barred from resuming the voyage. Fourteen whites, including Irwin's son and two daughters, the sexton and six white women were also removed. In addition, some of the white artisans, including a weaver, surgeon and brickmaker, decided against continuing the journey.

Back in London, furious at his shabby treatment, Equiano turned violently against the entire project. Far from inciting trouble, he was the "greatest peacemaker there ever was," he wrote in a letter to Ottobah Cugoano that was published in the *Public Advertiser* on the 4th of April 1787. Not only Irwin but the chaplain, Dr Fraser, and one of the surgeons were "villains." The whole enterprise, he said, had been, in its haste and criminal inefficiency, little more than a veiled attempt to "hurry out" blacks from where they were not wanted. "I do not know how this undertaking will end . . . I wish I had never been involved in it."[46] In his own diatribe published two days later, Cugoano was even more hostile, declaring that blacks had been virtually press-ganged into getting back on board at Plymouth and that any of them who cared for their lives ought to jump overboard and swim back to England rather than entrust themselves to so disastrous and brutal an enterprise.

It was entirely natural that Equiano should feel bitter. He had done precisely what the government had required of him by exercising scrupulous oversight of stores and supplies, and his reward had been humiliation and dismissal. But when he had taken the post he had eagerly endorsed the expedition to create the Province of Freedom, which was, after all, his friend Sharp's pet project. And two years later, when he published his autobiography, he still judged the venture "humane and politick." Whatever its failings, they ought not be laid at the door of the government since "every thing [promised] was done on their part." It was the "mismanagement" of the way the plan was carried out that had doomed it. The committee, the Treasury men and Sir Charles Middleton, all distressed to some degree or other, agreed that Vassa should be paid £50 for his services, a sum handsome enough to suggest their shared guilty conscience. A year later he was being courted again for the abolitionist crusade. During the debates over the Dolben Bill, introduced to regulate the conditions under which slaves were transported, James Ramsay suggested that Members of Parliament should be greeted at the doors of the House by a black man—Equiano—who would hand each of them a damning tract against the trade.

Back in Plymouth, on the 9th of April the little fleet sailed away, dirty weather left behind with the British coast. The usual mix of fortunes attended its progress. Cooped up, husbands and wives argued and sometimes came to blows. As the ships wallowed in the swell, there was puking and drinking, and thus more puking. As usual, fevers mounted; bodies, fourteen of them, were slid overboard—far too many according to Sharp's protégé, Abraham Elliott Griffith, aboard the *Belisarius*, for the surgeons were most neglectful of their duties. But at Tenerife in the Atlantic spring the ships took on cattle and fresh food and water, and the knell of mortality seemed to have abated. Patrick Fraser, the chaplain recommended by Sharp, described the expedition in a letter to the *Public Advertiser* as a happy ark, enjoying "the sweets of peace, lenity and almost uninterrupted harmony." Better yet "the odious distinction of colours is no longer remembered."[47] Black and white worshipped together. Jerusalem lay just over the horizon. Praise be to God.

VII

WOULD IT HAVE MADE any difference if they had known the Temne name, *Romarong*—the place of the wailers, the place where men and women wept in the storms? All that Captain Thomas Boulden Thompson knew, as he spied the site from the deck of the anchored *Nautilus* on the 10th of May 1787, was that it had been called "Frenchman's Bay" and he had it in mind to rename it St George's Bay. The wooded hill rising gently from its southern shore had been called who knows what by the natives? Well, now it would be St George's Hill. For the captain, patriotic overstatement conceded nothing to topographical imagination. St George and England, along with some 380 free black Britons, had arrived at the mouth of the Sierra Leone River.

It had been noticed. The next day, wasting no time, the local Koya Temne chief, King Tom, appeared, big and affable, a glory in blue silk and ruffled shirt, the flap of his hat thick with gold lace. His wives, standing at a proper distance, were still bigger and even more affable in brilliant taffeta and turbans wound high. Punctiliously naval, Thompson made sure the *Nautilus* greeted them with a thirteen-gun salute. On deck there was an exchange of pleasantries and a preliminary offering of presents from the naval captain to the king (more hats—they always went down well). Thompson announced his intention to buy from the king a territory of some four hundred square miles, stretching from the harbour and the hill south, east and inland perhaps twenty miles;

the land that would be the Province of Freedom. King Tom raised no objections. But then, why should he? He was no *ingénu* when it came to dealing with Europeans. A pidgin English, much coloured with pidgin Portuguese, had been a lingua franca on the coast for at least a century since the slavers had first leased Bance Island. It was understood by the Temne and their neighbours the Bullom as the language of the "rogues"; and they were prepared, if not actually eager, to compete with them in roguery.[1] They also were at pains to make sure that the Europeans properly appreciated the order of things on the coast and up the river. Although Messrs Anderson, the holders of the slaving concession, and their agents Mr James Bowie and Mr John Tilley formally paid their tribute rent to the Bullom chief on the north shore, they knew they were there on the sufferance of King Tom on the south shore, just as King Tom accepted that his own authority was ultimately subject to the greater chief, the Naimbana, further inland at Robana. And even the Naimbana was regent rather than the "king" that the Europeans styled him. Whether the Europeans wished to slave or, as this captain seemed to be saying, settle free black men was all the same to King Tom; just so long as they understood that what they were "buying" was not ownership of land (for no one truly owned it) but permission to stay.

Which is, of course, exactly what did not get understood, especially not on the 15th of May when Captain Thompson went through the customary ritual of an act of imperial possession: the planting of a flag. Beaching their skiffs on the curving stretch of creamy sand, a party of blacks and whites walked beneath the grove of palms fringing the shore, hacked a way through the razor-sharp grass, the ten-foot-high tangle of thorny scrub, and the grove of cotton-silk and camwood trees, and made their way up the slope that Sir George Young, a fellow naval captain, had assured Thompson would be best suited for the foundation of the Province of Freedom. It would be cooler there, he had said, more salubrious than the mangrove-strangled swampy lowland to the north. Running down its sides were brooks rushing with sweet, pure water. Once the party had arrived on the brow, Captain Thompson ordered a small tree to be felled and its trunk trimmed and set deep in the red earth in a clearing. Then the Union Jack was run up. Let Granville Town arise![2]

From the crest of the "eminence," the prospect may not have been quite the terrestrial paradise Granville Sharp described to his brother James ("the hills are not steeper than Shooter's Hill [in Kent] . . . the woods and groves are beautiful beyond description").[3] But on that day in May the view may still have looked auspicious. Below the flag party, down a gentle gradient, stretched the broad mouth of the Sierra Leone river, a harbour so naturally inviting that it had attracted ships since 1462, when the Portuguese mariner Pedro da Cintra, imagining he saw the shape of a leonine head in the mountainous peninsula, called it Serra Lyoa. And since this was the only natural harbour in all of West Africa without a barrier of high surf, there was not a day when the bay did not see brigs, sloops and schooners at anchor, and canoes busily shuttling between ships and shore, loading supplies, chests and slaves. True, much of the coast, especially north of the river mouth, was sunk low in muddy mangrove swamp, interlaced with creeks where basking sharks shared the shallows with crocodiles. Twice a year, in spring and autumn, the sea carried the coffee-coloured ooze over the low plain, making the estuary good for nothing except the extraction of salt. Once the sun had hardened the mud into a solid crust, the people of the northern shore would walk out on to the cracked desolation and cut slabs of it to carry away. The tangy brown muck would then be dissolved again in big terracotta pots and finally boiled down in brass pans, leaving the salt behind. It was, many travellers observed, a particularly fine salt.[4]

But free men could not live on salt alone. And as far as they could see, there was damned little else to sustain life on the north shore, although a few saturated fields swayed with meagre yellow stalks of rice. The promised land had to be behind them as they stood on Captain Thompson's eminence, in the hills of the peninsula that stretched south all the way to the cape facing the Banana Islands, where Henry Smeathman had attended to his ants, looked at the mantled mountains and pronounced them fair. The high, conical peaks were, to be sure, forbidding (if very beautiful in the picturesque way of things); but in the foothills there were camwood, ebony and copal gum trees, indigo (said to be the best in the world), cotton and perhaps coffee. There, on upland pasture, flocks and herds could graze.

In due course the Naimbana came downstream, saw the tents of Granville Town perched on their hill and went on board the *Nautilus*.

But, as with the dealings with King Tom, each of the two parties understood the negotiation quite differently. Thompson believed himself to be buying land outright and unencumbered, as a permanent possession. For the Naimbana, on the other hand, this was a direct and personal agreement with the captain, and any acceptance of the right of these black men and women to live in and around his bay was conditional on their acknowledgement of his concession along with the implied right to withdraw it as he saw fit. There could be no freehold for the Province of Freedom. In the world of the Temne (as in that of other tribes of the region, the Mende, the Bullom, the Sherbro and the Fula) the permanent alienation of land was strictly inconceivable. Land was held, not owned, and it was invariably held from someone else.

The Naimbana, tall, thin and stately, with his grizzled beard, white satin waistcoat and embroidered coat, seemed gracious enough and was politely responsive to the overtures.[5] Bowie and the other slavers had warned him that these free blacks and the white officers were in Sierra Leone to make big trouble for him and his chiefs. For all the presents, the newcomers would ruin the business that had made them all prosper and, worse, would try to make his people worship the Christian god and then push him off his ceremonial stool, take his kingdom and force him back into the uplands. But looking at Captain Thompson, taking his measure, the Naimbana shrugged off such prophecies as self-serving. Perhaps Mr Bowie and the Andersons might have something to fear, but not he. And yet, as Thompson noticed, the Naimbana did not actually say "yes," not in Temne, Bullom or Mende; still less did he sign anything set before him on the deck of the *Nautilus*.

But if the Naimbana was not ready, King Tom was. On the 11th of June he and two other local chiefs, the Bullom queen Yamacouba and another Temne, Pa Bongee, set their marks alongside Tom's on the parchment prepared by Thompson. The captain declared this a "treaty," and 8 muskets, 3 dozen "hangers and scabbards," 24 laced hats, 4 cotton towels, 34 pounds of tobacco, 117 "bunches of beads," 10 yards of scarlet cloth, 25 iron bars and 120 gallons of rum, altogether amounting to £59 and a few shillings, were duly handed over to the chiefs. In return, it seemed that they had promised to cede to "the free community . . . their Heirs and Successors forever" the four hundred square miles of the Province of Freedom, stretching inland and upstream from Granville

Town, albeit imprecisely, to Gambia Island in one direction and perhaps as far as the Sherbro River to the south. More improbably, the chiefs of the province had sworn "true allegiance to His Gracious Majesty King George the Third" and had promised, rather like a Lord Lieutenant of the counties or an imperial governor, "to protect the said free settlers his subjects to the utmost of my power against the insurrections and attacks of all Nations and people whatsoever."[6]

Two weeks later came the deluge. And these were not the rains of Shooter's Hill. They were not even the kind of heavy downpour against which Jonas Hanway's green silk device had offered protection. They were, rather, an attack. In June the storms threatened in the early hours as innocent, chubby bunches of vapour, but as the day went on and they sponged the saturated estuarine air, the towers of cloud rose and darkened, so that the light turned a deep bottle-green and it seemed like midnight at noon. When at last the storm broke, the bolts of lightning that flared over the high forests were so intense that the forks imprinted themselves on the eyeball, even with lids shut fast against their violence. The thunder that went with them was a two-note musket crack followed by a cannon boom, a rending of the firmament. Water fell on the Sierra Leone peninsula as if it were made of stone, hammering the earth, making frothing lagoons and gulches of tawny mud. When the torrent thinned into mere heavy rain, the relief was greeted by the jubilant song of thousands of river frogs and the rasping percussion of millions of cicadas. Every so often there would be another phantom bolt, as if the storm were irritated by its own recession.

As the season deepened in mid-year, it got worse. The sky disappeared into a muffling grey void, the drowning pausing only with the sudden arrival of tornadoes for which the capes were notorious—sucking gales that lifted and tore apart anything that had the bad luck to be in their path. Then the temperature would suddenly drop so that those exposed to the brutality of the elements shivered as they were drenched in the tempest. Thus it was that the sounds of *Romarong* came to Captain Thompson's emerald hill.

By July, when the storms were at their most ferocious, the Union Jack on that green eminence drooped in soggy desolation. To the beleaguered, demoralized settlers it seemed madness to be planted on such an exposed outcrop. Some of them gingerly descended, camping instead at its base, where nature seemed to give a little more shelter—even if the mosquitoes, the snakes, mambas and kraits, especially the little pale green *synyak-amusong*, the spitting cobra, whose venom would instantly blind you, and the *bugabug* white and red ants, which seemed to survive both flood and fire, were also looking to share a home.[7] Against this onslaught, elemental, zoological and epidemic (for fevers were taking their toll, too), what did the London blacks and the remaining six whites have? The navy surplus canvas supplied for their tenting proved useless against the ripping winds. With the soil flooded there was no hope of planting the seeds brought out from England, and any rice seedlings set in wet fields were directly washed away by the contemptuous storms. All that could be done with the 161 shovels, 386 axes and 150 hoes was to try to prevent them from rusting. Self-sufficiency was out of the question. Survival depended on the stores that had been brought on the ships, and those were rapidly mouldering; in their desperation the settlers consumed them anyway. When these provisions were gone, the settlers began to trade their tools and, before long, their clothes in exchange for food from the only dependable source—the slavers on Bance Island and on the Bullom shore.

Before the Province of Freedom ever had a chance to establish itself, its people began to disappear. In mid-July Joseph Irwin died. By the third week of that month, 24 whites and 30 blacks were dead and half the remainder gravely ill. By the 16th of September, when Thompson boarded the *Nautilus* for the voyage home, having ostensibly seen the settlement through its teething pains, 122 of those who had landed in May had perished. Among them were Benjamin Whitecuffe's white widow, Sarah, and the wives of both John Cambridge and Abraham Elliott Griffith, Sharp's protégé. Many of the whites—all of the baker Schenkel's family save one daughter, the nurseryman, the sexton, the flax dresser, the carpenter, the tailor, the surveyor and a surgeon named Currie, whom Equiano had called a "villain"—died early in the tempestuous equatorial winter. Most were victims of fevers of one kind or another, malaria being probably the most common, despite the cinchona bark, the raw material of quinine, which had been brought on the ships and could be infused in wine.

The 268 survivors were then further thinned as deserters decamped to where shelter, food and wages were offered—the slave depots. Patrick Fraser, the man of God personally selected by Sharp, was among those to make this pact with the devil. But then he must have felt that God was not on his side. No one could be found to build his promised chapel amidst the torrents, so he had had no choice but to hold services beneath a spreading tree, probably a banyan. Increasingly sick and tubercular, he finally accepted the offer of more solid lodging on Bance Island, preaching to the white slavers and artisans and to bemused slaves who understood nothing of his prayers and sermons. Periodically he would go down-river to see to his abandoned flock, but would come back to the island, coughing and choking on blood. The surgeons of Granville Town followed him, leaving the stricken settlers without medical help when they most needed it. But whites were not the only ones to go over to the enemy, just as Jonas Hanway and, eventually, Equiano had feared. Blacks, too, took paying jobs up-river on Bance Island with Bowie, some of them turning from slaves to slavers. One of those who chose to take slaves on the Bullom shore was Harry de Mane, whom Granville Sharp had rescued just the previous year from a ship carrying him in chains to the West Indies.

O N HEARING THE NEWS of this betrayal, Granville Sharp felt as though he had taken a sword-thrust. His life's work had been made fools' play. "I could not have conceived that men who were well aware of the wickedness of slave-dealing and had themselves been sufferers . . . under the galling yoke of bondage . . . should have been so basely depraved," he wrote to the settlers at Granville Town in September 1788, "as to yield themselves instruments to promote and extend the same detestable oppression over their brethren."[8] It was an unspeakable betrayal, and "Mr Henry Demane (whom I am informed is now a great man on the Bulam shore)" the greatest of all the traitors, he thundered. None of those who had defiled the purity of the cause would ever be forgiven by its promoters, nor could they ever expect to be reconciled and readmitted to the Province of Freedom (sadly, a vain threat since none of the defectors ever showed the least sign of wanting to). "Warn them, from me," the distressed and aggrieved Sharp wrote again in 1789,

. . . of the horrors and remorse which must one day seize those authors and abettors of oppression who do not save themselves by a timely repentance. Remind Mr Henry Demane of *his own feelings* under the *horrors of slavery* when he turned his face to the mast of the ship into which he was trepanned by his wicked master and formed a resolution, as he afterwards confessed, to jump over-board that very night rather than submit to a *temporary slavery* for life but he is now in danger of *eternal slavery*! Remind him also of the joy he felt when he saw two men, sent with a writ of Habeas Corpus so exactly in time (most providentially) to rescue him, that a single minute later (as the anchor was up and the ship under weigh from her last station, the Downs) must have rendered his recovery impossible! Tell him I have ample reason to be convinced that his escape was by a real interposition of God's Providence . . . tell him . . . that the species of *slave-dealing and slave-holding* are inimical to the *whole species of man* by subverting charity, equity and every social and virtuous principle on which the peace and happi-ness of mankind depend, that they may fairly be deemed *unnatural crimes* and ought to be ranked with the horrible unnatural deprav-ity of man devouring man.[9]

As far as Granville Sharp was concerned, then, free blacks turned slavers were no better than cannibals. And his rage and chagrin were stoked by the frustration of being so far away from his wards and therefore unable to harangue them back to virtue as indeed he would have attempted, even with that base ingrate Harry de Mane. If anything, his vexation was aggravated by the reflection that the two years since the Province of Freedom had been founded had been a time of unparalleled promise for the campaign against the Accursed Thing. On the 22nd of May 1787 the formation of a Committee for the Abolition of the Slave Trade was an-nounced, with the Quaker crusaders Joseph Woods, Samuel Hoare and the Phillipses at its core, along with Clarkson and Wilberforce. Its presi-dent—the human emblem of its zeal, its will to prevail—could, of course, be none other than Granville Sharp. A campaign of mass petitioning against the trade was mobilized, and Thomas Clarkson travelled around the country to drum up enthusiasm and collect signatures. A seal for the committee showing a kneeling negro and bearing the inscription "Am I

Not a Man and a Brother?" was fired in Etruria in the Potteries by an ardent convert to the campaign, Josiah Wedgwood, and manufactured in thousands as a jasper medallion. Ladies wore it about their necks or on their dresses as a pin.[10] The essays of Ramsay, Clarkson, John Newton and Alexander Falconbridge, the penitent slave-ship surgeon, were all reprinted in editions of up to fifteen thousand.

In December 1788, for the first time, a print was published showing a view from above of the opened hold of a slave ship; it was modelled on a Liverpool slaver, the *Brookes*. Now a public that had read much about the traffic in "live cargo" could actually see it. Originally engraved for the Plymouth Committee for Abolition in a run of fifteen hundred, the print was modified a little by the London Committee, which added longitudinal sections and ran off an edition of eight thousand. The blacks were shown head to toe and side by side with no arm room, stacked like so many logs. At the bow, where the curve of the ship allowed a little more space, it was crammed with yet more bodies. However much had been read on the subject, it was this image that brought the campaign out from its secure base among Quakers and Evangelicals to a much larger public. Framed copies were seen as far apart as Scotland, the cities of the industrial north, especially Manchester where the cause was strong, and the southwest of England. Samuel Hoare's daughter remembered her family's obligation to display "horrible engravings of the interior of a slave ship . . . pinned against the walls of our dining room."[11]

Sharp was in the thick of all this, far more than just an honorary patriarch of the good fight. Through his correspondence with Benjamin Franklin, John Jay and Samuel Hopkins of Rhode Island he put together what was becoming a genuinely transatlantic campaign. News of the abolition of the trade in six American states was publicized in Britain, whilst news of the petitioning movement, the passage through both Houses of Parliament of Sir William Dolben's bill regulating the physical conditions of transportation, and Pitt's momentous creation on the 11th of February 1788 of a Privy Council committee to examine the state of the trade was circulated in the United States. While all this was happening, Sharp was very much aware that the ratification of the Constitution was being debated in Philadelphia, but also that, for the sake of an expedient unity, the delegates to the convention had agreed to defer for some years the consideration of proposals to outlaw the slave trade. There was no question of slavery itself being abolished throughout the entire United States. This was the same convention, after all, that decreed a slave to be, for the purposes of apportioning representation, three-fifths of a human. Thus the same economical gesture that affirmed the partial humanity (only) of blacks, ensured, through demographic finagling, that the Southern states would be protected from any federal attempts to undermine their "peculiar institution."[12]

Granville Sharp too, so he thought, was a Founding Father, busy at precisely the same moment as his friends Franklin, Jay and Adams with the foundation of a free society. Unlike the American republic, his would be one that would not only encode in the law its abhorrence of racial distinctions, but in its practices have blacks set the standard for active citizenship. Sharp believed in this idea strongly enough to spend time urging on his distinguished American correspondents the particular virtues of what he had always felt was the purest form of liberal democracy: Israelito-Saxon Frankpledge. Watch and ward, public labour as a unit of currency, universal suffrage, voting by households, tithings and hundredors—all this, he felt sure, was right for, say, the backlands of the Appalachians.[13]

The stake that Sharp had in the success of his experiment only made his anxiety over its fate more acute, and he lamented the dearth of information concerning what he called, rather unhappily, "my poor little, ill-thriven, swarthy daughter, the unfortunate colony of Sierra Leone."[14] For a very long time—especially considering that Sierra Leone was but a month's sail—there was no news, and then intermittently there was, but mostly bad news. Abraham Elliott Griffith, the manservant and protégé whose education he had provided for, had written to him at the end of July in the throes of the rains and had not spared him at all.

Honoured Sir,

I am sorry, and very sorry indeed, to inform you, dear Sir, that this country does not agree with us at all and without a very sudden change, I do not think there will be one of us left at the end of twelve month. Neither can the people be brought to any rule or regulation, they are so very obstinate in their tempers. It was really a very great pity ever we came to this country after the death of

Mr Smeathman; for we are settled upon the very worst part. There is not a thing put into the ground, will grow more than a foot out of it . . . quite a plague seems to reign here among us. I have been dangerously ill myself but it pleased the Almighty to restore me to health again and the first opportunity I have I shall embark for the West Indies.[15]

This, too, was deeply shocking; that Griffith would rather hazard his liberty and his life in the Caribbean than try to endure in Granville Town. In the event, Griffith did not take ship but, asked by the Naimbana to open a school at Robana, became a personal secretary, interpreter, emissary and, when he married Princess Clara, son-in-law to the old king. His story in Africa was not yet ended.

Was there any hope at all to be salvaged from the wreckage of Sharp's utopia? Frankpledge, all too obviously, was not functioning in the floods of West Africa; nor had church, courthouse, school or prison been built. But, desperate for encouragement, Sharp doubtless noticed that the letter he received from the Philadelphia black loyalist Richard Weaver, who had been one of the corporals of the London black poor, referred to "the body of the people" calling "a meeting to choose their officers whereby they choosed me to be their chief in command." Other letters referred to a "senit" (senate).[16] Some sort of elections, then, had taken place, and the people of Granville Town had a black "governor." Detecting at least the germ of the free polity he had hoped to inaugurate, Sharp continued for some time to refer in his letters to Sierra Leone to the settlers' "Common Council," as if they had established a deliberative assembly with the capacity to make laws as provided for in his "Short Sketch of Government." However, another letter written six months later, in September 1788, by one James Reid, announced that he was now "Governor," a change that Sharp might have taken as evidence of active politics had not Reid and Weaver engaged in mutual recrimination over the theft of some sixty muskets from the settlement store.[17] Reid, who had been elected while Weaver was seriously incapacitated for three months, complained that he had been unjustly accused:

Mr Weaver and Mr Johnson . . . told them [the assembled people] that I made away with them myself and got them under arms and they rised against me and seized my house and took it from me and all what little I had in the world and sold it to pay for those things that was lost . . . After they broke me they thought to have God's blessing as they said. The first thing [misfortune] was a young lad found shot in the woods but never found who was the person who did it. The second was that they got into a little trouble with King Tom and he catched two of them and sold them on board a Frenchman bound for the West Indies. The third was, five of them went up to Bance Island and broke open a factory belonging to one Captain Boys [Bowie] and stole a number of things but they were detected and Captain Boys sold the whole five of them.[18]

This succession of disasters seemed to bear out only too well the returned Captain Thompson's report that there was nothing good to be expected from the settlers since they were, for the most part, a drunken, vicious, scoundrelly lot, who either lived in anarchy or had sold out to the slavers. But of course Thompson would hardly take kindly to the conspicuous and, as he saw it, unseemly lack of deference on the part of the blacks. Sharp, the incurable optimist, was not going to give up on Granville Town. He noted from Reid's correspondence that huts had at last been built to protect the settlers from the worst weather, and that although the English seeds had failed, they had had better luck with native crops. And since the mortality rate seemed also to have ebbed somewhat (even though the colony was down to fewer than half the original emigrants), Sharp put the early disasters down to moral turpitude—especially demon rum, which he felt had weakened their resistance to "distempers"—rather than to the contagion-friendly nature of the local climate. Doses of wine infused with cinchona bark had kept death away from the sailors who had stayed up-river aboard the *Nautilus* in 1787, and, advised perhaps by his doctor brother William, he saw no reason why it should not act with similar benevolence for those on land.

Far from abandoning Granville Town, Sharp resolved, almost certainly with the help of his charitably minded brothers, to come to its rescue. In the summer of 1788 he spent £900 outfitting a two-mast brig, the *Myro*, intended to bring relief supplies and fifty new settlers, black and white, amongst them two replacement surgeons, as well as fresh livestock, including draft oxen, which were to be bought by Captain

Taylor en route at the Cape Verde Islands. With the *Myro* Sharp sent letters for the settlers, yet another version of his advice and instruction on their good government, "six stout watch coats for the night watch," a box of leather caps "with capes to secure the necks of the wearer from the cold and the wet" and a batch of presents to the value of £89, to renew the agreement for Granville Town with King Tom's successor, King Jimmy.[19] To his surprise and pleasure, Pitt's government, now a friend to the anti-slave trade cause, chipped in with another £200, and the *Myro* sailed for Sierra Leone in September. A day after it had weighed anchor at Blackwall Sharp sent a cutter to catch it with twelve hogshead of porter, courtesy of his new friend and supporter the brewer Samuel Whitbread—a healthier alternative, he thought, to rum.

As with every voyage in this venture, the expedition of the *Myro* was not trouble-free. Only thirty-nine prospective settlers were aboard rather than the hoped-for fifty, and for some reason Captain Taylor failed to buy cattle and pigs at Cape Verde, instead delivering to the settlers monies to the value of the animals—not at all what Sharp had intended. Predictably, the surgeons defected to the slavers on Bance Island as quickly as possible. Yet the surviving remnant at Granville Town was overjoyed to get the relief, if only as an affirmation that, in the midst of their hardships and adversities, they had not been forgotten and abandoned. Twelve of them signed a letter to Sharp and "the rest of our honourable and most humane friends" thanking them "for the manifold cares and gracious providences which they have been pleased to extend to us." Although they had endured many miseries "which is clearly evident from the very crowded appearance of our burials . . . we have the pleasure to inform you, great Sir, that we have made good progress in clearing our land, all except our water lots which remain as yet in a state of anorky through our weakness in number of people but we hope to have some tolerable good crops this season."[20] The twelve signatories—including James Frazer, Thomas Carlisle, Jorge Dent and Thomas Cooper—ended their note with the kind of peroration, a mixture of pride and painful contrition, that might have been calculated to fortify Sharp's perseverance:

> We need not use many words. We are those who were considered as slaves, even in England itself till your aid and exertions set us

free. We are those whose minds and bodies are bartered from hand to hand on the coast of Africa and in the West Indies as the ordinary commodities of trade. But it is said that we are the factors of our own slavery and sell one another at a market price. No doubt but in our uncivilized state we commit much evil, but surely the trader cannot believe that the strong on the coast of Africa are entitled to deprive the weak of every right of humanity and to devote to the most cruel slavery them and their posterity or that it belongs to him . . . to execute so horrid a doom.

But yet, Sir you may allow us to believe that the name of GRAN-VILLE SHARP our constant and generous friend, will be drawn forth by our more enlightened posterity and distinguishingly marked in future times for gratitude and praise.[21]

And could he, by the way, send six or eight cannon so that a proper fort could be built on St George's Hill? (He could not.)

All was not yet lost with Granville Town; not yet. Sharp-haters (a growing number in Britain as he and his fellow crusaders became not just a nuisance but a threat) had pounced on stories of anarchy said to characterize the settlement at Sierra Leone; the comedy, as they saw it, of black men playing democratic farmers. This just shows what happens when negroes are so ill-advisedly thrust into liberty, they wrote. What would you expect? But one report from Granville Town by "Leo Africa-nus" (albeit based on Sharp's own information), published in *The Diary or Woodfall's Register* in November 1789, painted an altogether different picture: of "snug" cottages "formed of mangrove frames, wattled, plaistered, whitewashed and neatly covered with rushes with a piece of land adjoining, inclosed and well planted with bananas, yams, sweet potatoes, cassada [cassava] &c."[22] And what would an Anglo-African village be without a whitewashed church, freshly built, also of wattle, mud and rushes? An English bell had been sent for.

It was precisely the possibility that the little enclave (numbering, now, only around a hundred) might actually survive that, so Sharp believed, provoked its enemies, the slavers of Bance Island, to nip it in the bud. And despite the fresh batch of presents and the new "treaty," King Jimmy was becoming a lot more restive than his predecessor about the presence of the settlers. When James Bowie and John Tilley warned

Jimmy that unless the settlement were checked it might be the end of their lucrative trade, he listened. Every so often, as Sharp's correspondents had informed him, settlers would be abducted and sold as slaves, ostensibly in reprisal for a theft or some other misdemeanour committed by one of the Granville Town men.

Infuriated though he was by this treatment, in the interests of the settlement's survival Sharp was forced to modify his original uncompromising principles. He still clung to his stubborn belief that in time his colony of free Africans, built on the foundation of Frankpledge, would be the germ of a great and general emancipation as it grew to maturity. But for now, with the Province of Freedom under immediate and dire threat of obliteration, he was persuaded into pragmatism. Within the Province slavery would never be tolerated, but beyond its bounds, it was only prudent, he wrote to the settlers, to avoid provoking the traders or the native chiefs with whom they did business. They would be well advised to "be courteous and kind to all strangers that come to the settlement even though you know them to be slave dealers or slave holders provided they do not offend your laws during their stay."

Easier said than done. But in 1789 Sharp must have felt that, if only his Province could somehow hang on, the success that the campaign against the trade was enjoying in Britain itself would sooner or later enlist the powerful to its protection. In a stroke of brutal irony, it was precisely that power, in the imposing shape of His Majesty's Ship *Pomona*, that brought about the ruin of Granville Town.

No one could have foreseen it. The enactment of Sir William Dolben's bill regulating the physical conditions of the trade meant that, for the first time in modern history, state power was being used to intervene in the traffic of "live cargo." And the *Pomona*, with Captain Henry Savage commanding, had been ordered to sail to the African coast, distribute copies of the Dolben regulations amongst the slave factories and the agents of the Liverpool and Bristol concerns, and see that its provisions were complied with. After anchoring in St George's Bay in late November 1789 Savage did his duty, but was instantly beset by complaints from representatives of the free settlers and the slavers, both of whom looked to the captain to uphold their grievances. Abraham Ashmore, the current governor of Granville Town, complained bitterly about his settlers being abducted and sold. James Bowie and John Tilley, on behalf of Messrs Anderson, counter-groused that the settlers were thieves and lawless rogues who had threatened their own establishment. And although Savage had come armed with the paper of parliamentary righteousness, he was, after all, a naval officer and an English gentleman and therefore credited what the white traders, not the blacks, told him.

On one issue, however, Ashmore and Bowie made common cause. King Jimmy had become a menace, violating the agreements he had made with both parties, attacking the settlement, and taking and selling slaves that were not his to sell. He needed to be brought to book and reminded of his solemn undertakings, and the captain of the *Pomona* should see to it. Savage obliged. On the 20th of November a gun was fired and a flag of truce hoisted to signal that the king might safely come aboard for a parley. No Jimmy appeared. That same afternoon a party of men, including armed marines, four settlers and Bowie himself, was sent to find him. Savage watched from the deck as the boats were beached and Lieutenant Wood and his companions disappeared into the trees. Quiet. Then the crack of musket fire, a sudden plume of flame behind the shoreline and smoke rising over the palms. Someone, probably a young midshipman, had got jumpy as boys do, thought he had heard something, fired into a village, Jimmy's village, and set a thatched roof on fire. It was the dry season, and it took only minutes for the entire compound to be reduced to charred sticks.

This was just the start of what was to turn into a very bad day for the brand-new British Empire of freedom. From the deck of the *Pomona* sailors and marines were seen running back in hasty confusion to the shore. Alarmed, Savage sent a second boat to pick them up. As some of the men were swinging their legs over the gunwales, a volley of fire broke from the line of trees fringing the beach. A marine sergeant, the lieutenant of the relief boat and a black settler were all killed, their blood staining the white sand. Now that the skirmish had gone colonial Savage trained the guns of his ship on the shore, "clearing" the bush. Over the next few days he repeated the exercise. In response, Jimmy's men shot at anyone attempting to land for water. Only the well-disposed Naimbana could arbitrate, and one of the settlers was sent to Robana to call for his intervention. When he came back with the message, as he stepped out of his boat he too was felled by a shot.

A week later, on the 27th of November 1789, the Naimbana's deputies came to order Jimmy to desist, and for the moment he did so, albeit
grudgingly and biding his time. Savage agreed to sail away with the
Pomona, but only after a general palaver had been arranged, which was
supposed to settle grievances peacefully. However, once the warship
had set sail on the 3rd of December, King Jimmy was free to impose his
notion of what a just settlement should be, and issued an ultimatum to
the settlers to leave Granville Town within three days. Then he burned
the village down to the ground.[23]

Although now homeless, the people of Granville Town were not
entirely helpless. A small group of them accepted shelter at Robana with
the Naimbana, but a larger group of about seventy, kept together by
Abraham Ashmore, went up-river to Bob's Island in the territory of
another local chief, Pa Boson—much to the displeasure of the Bance Island agents, who still thought them close enough to be a nuisance. They
were no longer in the Province of Freedom. But nor had they been reduced to slaves. Sharp did not hear of the destruction of Granville Town
until four months later, in April 1790. His immediate reaction, beyond
anguish, was to try to send yet another relief ship, this time a modest
forty-ton sloop, the *Lapwing*—but under whose auspices? Even with the
government top-up, the *Myro* had been expensive, and there was a limit
to his and even the Sharp family purse. But there was another possibility: that the newly founded St George's Bay Company might finance the
voyage of the *Lapwing*.

This commercial enterprise had come into existence as a result of
Sharp's second thoughts about the self-sufficiency of his experiment.
The relentless rain of misfortune that had fallen on the settlement had
obliged him to recognize that although one day his vision of British
freedom might be realized on African soil, that day had not yet come.
Perhaps when the trade had been abolished, as he hoped, through legislation the attempt could be renewed. But in the meantime the frail
colony desperately needed resources other than the yams, rice and bananas it might grow in a merciful season. In a letter to Sharp sent in
September 1788, James Reid had written, "Dear Friend . . . there is one
thing that would be very helpful to us; if we had an agent or two out
here with us, to carry on some sort of business in regard to trade; so that
we could rely a little sometimes on them for a small assistance, until our

crops were fit to dispose of and then pay them. It would be of infinite service to all the poor settlers as provisions are scarce to be got—not one mouthful sometimes."[24] Now Granville Sharp had nothing against trade at all. Was not his brother James an iron-monger? Were not so many of his good colleagues and friends, staunch for the cause, whether bankers or brewers? And wise men such as Adam Smith had projected an African trade in which the products of free labour would find a market far beyond that of the traffic in men.

Provided, then, that it never lost sight of the lodestar of liberty, there could be no harm in establishing a commercial company that might well be in a position to help the settlers with advances against their crops, and that would allow them to trade up-river and inland with the natives. Indeed, replacing the slave-tainted Royal African Company with a St George's Bay Company would be to purify the spirit of commerce. A charter from Parliament would not only encourage investors by limiting personal liability, it would also give the company the protecting power, legal and if need be military, to stave off the inevitable assaults from the slave interest.

The idea was no sooner floated than it took off. The good rallied with their subscriptions: Thomas Clarkson; William Wilberforce; the Evangelical MP brothers Thornton, Samuel and the banker, Henry, the brewer Samuel Whitbread. But, to Sharp's dismay, what was not forthcoming in the summer of 1790 was support from the government. Repeated letters to William Pitt went bafflingly, and then woundingly, unanswered. All the time, the hounds of the West India and Africa lobbies were baying loudly, protesting that the abolitionists sought a monopoly and were about to destroy the profit and power of the Empire. Worse still, the government, formerly thought to be sympathetic to abolition, now seemed at best tepid and at worst sceptical. The Attorney-General actually voiced his outright opposition to the project.

Undaunted, Sharp and his friends resolved to outfit and dispatch the *Lapwing* even before a charter of incorporation had been enacted. The sloop, commissioned for what was to become the Sierra Leone Company, sailed at the end of 1790 loaded with hardware: yet more hoes, forks and shovels, blacksmiths' tools, quantities of nails and, for some reason, a quantity of children's knives (Sharp's enemies said this was to oblige his iron-monger brother). Alexander Falconbridge, the Bristol ex-slaver surgeon who had become well known as the author of the most widely read and graphic account of the physical cruelties of the trade, had been appointed to oversee the resurrection of the Province of Freedom and negotiate a more lasting settlement with King Jimmy. But he had literally missed the boat, and together with his wife, Anna Maria, and his brother, William, had to be sent on in the *Duke of Buccleuch*.[25]

During these months, Granville Sharp was plagued with harrowing anxieties. Did the avowedly commercial character of the St George's Bay Company mean sacrificing his Frankpledge utopia? Would its directors in London and the agents they might appoint for Africa now rule the blacks to whom he had solemnly promised self-rule? Was the great work of building freedom to be surrendered to the lesser work of making money? Then there was another foreboding that gnawed at him. What of the *people* with whom he had tried to make his place of liberty? How many of the trusty ones had survived? How many, like the unspeakable Harry de Mane, had betrayed him? How could a new world be made from just seventy or eighty souls? He had no appetite to trawl the streets of Wapping and Stepney again for recruits. Perhaps he was not looking in the right place? The Reverend Samuel Hopkins, evidently a good man, had written that in Rhode Island and other places such as Massachusetts where the trade and even the institution had been outlawed there were free blacks who had heard of his enterprise in Sierra Leone and wished to emigrate there—to go from an uncertain American future to British freedom. How he wished he could oblige them!

And Granville Sharp was still wishing and fretting when the good Lord provided. There was a black man, he was told, who had come to London from Nova Scotia and had heard of his project. This man had apparently been a sergeant in the British army during the late American war, serving in the Guides and Pioneers. Before that he had been a slave—a millwright who, along with multitudes like him, had escaped his master in North Carolina and joined the forces of the king, understanding that his loyalty would be repaid with freedom and enough land to make a decent living. Sharp had heard such stories before, of course, from those among the London poor who had been with the British. But they had been a sorry few and there was nothing hangdog about this sturdy sergeant, greying at the temples—this quiet, angry, illiterate but eloquent Thomas Peters.

Peters had travelled on his own account from Nova Scotia, commissioned by fellow blacks who said they had been grievously wronged, carrying a "Memorial" that he had himself drafted. Addressed to the Secretary of State William Grenville, it asserted that the wishes of the king had been set aside; that land promised had not been delivered. With no friends, Peters had sought out those who could commend him: the captain, George Martin, who had sworn him sergeant in the Black Pioneers; and Sir Henry Clinton, who remembered him, had introduced him to Wilberforce and even, through a letter, to Grenville. This Peters spoke of things dear to Granville Sharp's heart: of the English air too pure for slaves to breathe; of the British constitution that could never tolerate the ignominy and indecency of servitude; of Common Law, the equity of which had never been surpassed in the history of the world. He was a man, by God, this Peters, and he was also, if ever there was such a thing, a true Briton. If there were more like him in Nova Scotia, then the Province of Freedom would, Lord willing, find its citizenry. He would make sure Thomas Peters had a hearing. London would listen to his story.

VIII

THE TWO MIDDLE-AGED MEN sat together in a room in Old Jewry. Sharp was even more gaunt as he had aged, the eyes still keen above the sunken cheeks; Thomas Peters, also in his fifties, was by turns expansive and taciturn. As Sharp listened, he began to grasp something repellent. The burden of Peters's accusations—the hurt the Pioneers and their families had suffered in Nova Scotia—began to oppress him. It was not just that they had been denied the land they had been promised and so robbed of their little self-sufficiency. It was much worse than that. Into the country that ought to have been the birthplace of a new, free British-American empire, as spotless of corruption as a fall of fresh snow, the old stain had obscenely seeped. There was, it seemed, slavery in Nova Scotia. Loathsome though it was, Sharp understood that white loyalist planters and merchants coming to their northern refuge would not permit their "servants" to be uncoupled from their bondage. But as for the black men who had faithfully followed the king's flag: that they and their families should have been reduced to servitude again, even if it were not called by that name, Sharp found inconceivably abhorrent.

But this seemed to be what Thomas Peters was saying. That through being made landless and hungry, free blacks had been forced into indentures so punitive that they might as well be in chains. Some had even been made off with and sold in the West Indies, breaking families apart. His people around Annapolis and in New Brunswick, Peters said, "have been already reduced to Slavery without being able to obtain any Redress from the King's Courts." Peters spoke feelingly of monstrous things: of a free man he knew, reduced to slavery, who "did actually lose his life by the Beating and Ill Treatment of his Master and another who fled from the like Cruelty was inhumanly shot and maimed by a Stranger allured thereto by the public advertisement of a Reward." Sharp, as was his wont, had someone write all this down, and was so distressed by it that, as he helped Peters draft a second version of his petition to government, he made sure that the document spoke not just of the deprivation of land but of the deprivation of liberty. As far as Sharp was concerned, Lord Mansfield's ruling in the Somerset case ought to have changed everything: what held in England should hold in Nova Scotia. A free black in Halifax ought to be as protected from forced transportation as any subject of the king in Britain.

At the heart of the petition drafted by Peters with Sharp's help was an appeal to the indivisibility of British freedom. That was what, in both their views, distinguished Britain from the United States where, even though slavery had been abolished in four states (Massachusetts, Vermont, Rhode Island and Pennsylvania), it had been preserved in many more. On the other hand, could it possibly be the case, they wrote, that

> ... the happy influence of his Majesty's free Government was incapable of being extended so far as America to maintain Justice and Right in affording the Protection of the Laws of the Constitution of England? [Nor since] the oppressive Cruelty and Brutality of their Bondage ... in general Shocking to human nature but more particularly shocking, irritating and obnoxious to their Brethren of the same kindred, the free people of Colour [could they] conceive that it is really the Intention of the British Government to favour Injustice or tolerate Slavery.[1]

Then Peters related his odyssey. The difficulties had begun early, on the ship that brought them out of New York, the *Joseph*. Peters, Murphy Steele, their wives Sally and Mary, and a fellowship of Black Pioneers— most of them from Virginia, the Carolinas and Georgia, men who had dug and shovelled for the king, and cleaned out their officers' necessar-

ies, together with women who had cooked and laundered for the colonels—had not got aboard at Staten Island until very late in the embarkation season.[2] The army had been the last to leave New York. That was
hard, little John "Born within the British Lines" being only eighteen
months old, and all of them cooped up in the hold until the ship finally
sailed in the second week of November, just a few weeks before the
king's flag finally came down in New York. In fair weather the voyage
to Nova Scotia usually took a week, or at most two. The *Joseph* had delayed so long that the dirty weather had started in earnest, and a gale, a
bad one, had caught the brig, blown it sharply off course and done so
much damage that there was nothing for it, so they were told a little
suspiciously, but to put into Bermuda and sit out the winter. So there
they were, stuck aboard, looking at the breezy island with its skirt of
pink sand. When they did get on shore what did they see but gentlemen
and ladies with slaves waiting on them by their carriages in the lanes
outside the white churches, just as they had in Carolina?

It was not until May 1784 that the *Joseph* set sail again for Nova
Scotia, where, so they had been led to believe, the Pioneers would finally get their due. Peters carried with him a special passport, signed by
Colonel Allen Stewart, intended for "all commanders" and testifying
that he had served "faithfully and honestly," that he was "a good and
faithful subject of Great Britain" and that he had earned "the good
wishes of officers and his comrades."[3]

The place where the others who had come before them had been set
down, Shelburne, and the black village beside it, Birchtown, were so
crowded that their ship had been directed instead to make for Annapolis Royal on the north side of the peninsula. When they disembarked
they would have seen naval vessels anchored in the neat little harbour;
a walled bastion with guns facing the sea; and a few lanes of white
houses, inns and trim yards lined up parallel to the water. But from Annapolis the blacks were sent off across the river to another place called
Digby, just a straggling row of mean cottages, shingles peeling in the
salty damp, with grog shops lurking in muddy corners beside the jetty.
Those who had come to Digby were making do in smoky little cabins.
But even this was not thought right for blacks, so they were set down
still farther off at Little Joggin, some sixty families, with tents, or huts

covered in bark and sod, for shelter. And when they had asked again, they had been told yes, they would get land, which after all they knew was their right.

But in the meantime, how were they to sustain themselves and their children in the wilderness, with precious few axes to go round? Such as could be carpenters and sawyers and the like might make a boat and tar it well, for there was plenty of lumber and pitch from the forest; and such as could sail might make their way around the coves and out into the sea now that the spring had come. Some cast their nets for mackerel and herring from boats at Little Joggin; others, lacking the wherewithal to see their families through the winter, would have to leave them behind and sign up for months aboard the ships fishing for cod or salmon.[4]

Peters was one of those who had been continually moved on. He had seen promises set aside so that the free people of colour were having to sell what little they had, even themselves and their children for service, if they wanted to eat. If he was bold in voicing his complaints, it was only because he had been given trust by the local government of the province and so thought he could address it as a free man. The Pioneers ought not to be so slighted for they happened to be skilled in just the work the country needed: the building of roads through the trackless forest, bridges over the salt marshes, the making of havens. Among the thirty thousand loyalists there were few who could, or would, do that!

So at Brindley Town, which is what their black village near Digby was called, Sergeant Peters, with his resolute manner, became the fixed point, the man on whom government depended. It was to him that the supplies for the blacks were to be delivered: 12,096 pounds of flour and 9,352 pounds of pork, precisely. While the loyalists were getting themselves established, government had pledged to give them free provisions for the first year, two-thirds free for the second and one-third for the third. After that they could rub along on their own. But this pork and flour, as much as it seemed, sufficed for just 80 days for 160 adults and 25 children, a ration that would barely see them through to the end of the summer, much less the winter. Yet as one of the white officers flatly announced, "It is all they are to git."[5] Even this meagre supply, however, did not come to Peters for distribution but was diverted to the

Reverend Brudenell at Digby, who stored it in his church until it could be taken to one Richard Hill, who in turn locked the food in his cellar, making himself the judge of just who got what and when. It soon became clear that pork and flour would be doled out only to those who agreed to work on the road from Digby to Annapolis, and this at the fair time of year when they should be clearing their own lots. What had been promised was food for three years; what they got, if they laboured, was food for three months.

So they were to be a work gang again, were they? To swing a pick and sweat their blood for a little something to stay alive? Was this what they had been promised? It was not, for Peters knew that the government in London had made a point of declaring that they should not have to become wage labourers and so be at the beck and call of others. Sir Guy Carleton, who had thought it a good idea that the Pioneers be kept together for public works, had also insisted that any such labour be strictly voluntary.[6] But this was more like the slavery they had thrown off when they had gone and sworn themselves to the king. And perhaps it was what the white loyalists wanted, for from the time they had all gone on the ships the whites had made it absolutely clear that they took it unkindly to have so many blacks giving themselves airs and forever canting their rights. It came back to the land, always, for without it, and their flour and bacon gone, what choice did they have but to indenture themselves and their wives and children for years at a time? Their families were broken apart, their precious freedom an empty word.

What made it even harder was that *white* loyalists seemed to have little trouble in getting settled on their plots. No one had ever said, neither in London nor in Halifax, that there was to be a difference in the property received by blacks and by whites, only in the portions given to officers (one thousand acres) and to privates (one hundred acres). As for "ordinary refugees"—those who had not served in the army—they were to be allotted the same one hundred acres, plus fifty more for each family member. Surely there was enough land to go around for all forty thousand of them, those who had sailed from Boston and Charleston, Savannah and New York? Half of Nova Scotia's 26 million acres had been set aside for the loyalists, although the government had reserved what it deemed it might need for naval timber. (Spruce and fir made strong yet flexible masts.) But the government had also determined that land would be apportioned according to what had been lost in America. Those suffering the greater losses would receive the greater share, and get it, moreover, before those judged to have lost little. First in line, then, were loyalists who had themselves owned farms, plantations—and slaves; then the townsmen, merchants and lawyers; then the ordinary soldiers—not just English, Scots and Irish, but many Hessians and other Germans who had got on the ships. At the very back of the line, of course, came the blacks, judged to have lost nothing at all but their chains.

So the same reproof that had been given to the poor blacks in London when they had come seeking their due—that they should be mighty grateful to His Majesty for their freedom and be content with the leavings after his other loyal subjects had been served—was now heard in Halifax, Shelburne and Annapolis. Instead of the one hundred farm acres, they would be fortunate to have between twenty and thirty, plus, if they were lucky, a small plot of "town land" on which to build a cabin. Usually, those meagre acres would be on land too stony or too densely forested to be of much use to whites. Fewer than half of the 3,500 blacks—10 percent of the loyalist population of Nova Scotia—ended up with any land at all.

In response to Peters's complaints about how tardy the grants were, it was said that it was indeed regrettable, but he should understand that there was a deplorable want of men to do the surveying and that first the survey had to go to the governor's office in Halifax and then back to the Surveyor of the King's Woods, all of which, he must appreciate, took time. But in fact by August 1784 the theodolites had been busy in the woods and on the shore, and twenty thousand white loyalists had somehow managed to be settled on their acres, whilst hardly any of the blacks—nor, for that matter, the demobilized white soldiers—had been accommodated.[7] It was at this moment, frustrated by the delays, many of which he suspected were deliberately engineered so that the whites at Digby and Annapolis could exploit the blacks as cheap labour, that Peters and Steele had written directly to Governor John Parr in Halifax. In the name of their fellow Black Pioneers, they asked that the promises made by General Clinton be fulfilled. For "when the war was over we was to be at our own Liberty to do and provide for ourselves which since we came to this place . . . we have not received . . . we would be verrey much obliged to Your Excellency if you would be so good as to grant the Articles allowed by Government to us the same as the rest of the Disbanded Soldiers of His Majesty's Army."[8] As for the provisions due to them, these had been stopped (by the likes of the Reverend Brudenell) and "wee . . . would be ever bound to pray for Your Excellency if you would be so good as to Order what we was allowed by Government the same as the rest." Parr, to whom the very existence of black loyalists came as a surprise since Lord North had neglected to inform him, was not, in fact, unsympathetic. He wrote to the surveyor at Digby and Annapolis, Major Thomas Millidge, that the black petitioners should be put "in the most advantageous Situation" and that he should "comply with their wishes as far as lies in your power."

Nothing in Nova Scotia was that simple, however. By March 1785 Millidge, who was also concerned about the blacks, had surveyed and assigned house lots of an acre in Brindley Town, as well as the little twenty-acre farm plots approved by Parr. Pending final approval, the blacks had been living at Little Joggin, and after much work had got themselves vegetable gardens on which they grew some corn, turnips and potatoes. "The Negroes have been in a very unsettled state at this place until last summer [1784]," Millidge reported, until "at some expense . . . several of these people have built themselves comfortable huts in which they are now in prospect . . . with industry to make themselves a comfortable living."[9] But in July that year, not long before they were finally supposed to get their farms, Millidge was told by Charles Morris, the Surveyor of the King's Woods in Halifax, that, regrettable though it was, he seemed to have given the blacks land that had already been reserved for the Society of the Propagation of the Gospel. There was nothing for it but to move the people on. Defending the blacks, Millidge insisted that "as the Negroes are now in the county, the principles of humanity dictating that I make them usefull to themselves as well as to society, is to give them a good chance to live and not to disturb them."[10] His appeal fell on deaf ears. No land was given. The blacks must fend as best they could.

Thomas Peters thanked Millidge for his solicitude. But he had had enough of Nova Scotia: its martinets, its bitter, hostile, white disbanded soldiery, its sanctimonous churchmen, its procrastinating clerks and its partial magistrates. In the autumn of 1785 he crossed the Bay of Fundy to the newly created province of New Brunswick, where Sir Guy Carleton's brother Thomas had been made governor. There, perhaps, he would get better treatment, both for himself and for his people.

I N AND OUT of Halifax, "Cock Robin" Parr had his share of enemies—to begin with, those who had given him his nickname, he being a short, peppery fellow with something of a martial strut to his gait, though of late the gout had hobbled it. Parr could be a little testy but, then, being governor of Nova Scotia in 1783 was an unrewarding post. He was yet another of the Anglo-Irish lieutenant colonels on whom the English had laid the most thankless burdens of empire, such as cleaning up after the American debacle. Serving the Empire had been his whole life: he had been secretary to James Wolfe (through whom he must have met Lord Dunmore), and had been wounded many times in the line of the 20th Foot. It was not, then, in John Parr's character to shrink from his duty. Besides, for someone who had, as yet, governed only the Tower of London (the office that had made him Henry Laurens's despised jailer), Nova Scotia was a decided promotion. Lord North had made the appointment in 1782 before the war had officially ended, and had sent Parr to the province to determine its suitability for the reception of the expected tens of thousands of loyalist refugees.

For those in London who took the decision to make Nova Scotia the main asylum for displaced and dispossessed loyalists, its principal recommendations were proximity to New York and New England and its emptiness. In 1782, on the eve of the loyalist immigration, there were just ten thousand inhabitants of the province. But some saw the rocky, densely forested Atlantic peninsula as much more. Nova Scotia would be the place from which a new British America would be resurrected. Unlike Quebec, there was no large French population obstinately devoted to the Catholic Church to complicate matters. Given the vast area of unoccupied land, half of which would be made available to the incomers, both North and Parr hoped that each loyalist might have, should he so wish, at least five hundred acres with which to start afresh. As for the two commodities without which an American empire could never prosper—timber and codfish—Nova Scotia was abundantly supplied. There was game in the shape of moose and white-tailed deer, and there was a fortune running around on the furry backs of marten and muskrat. The climate, to be sure, was challenging—deep snow in the winter, blackfly in the summer. But, with much of its shoreline washed by the benevolently tepid Gulf Stream, Nova Scotia was less inhospitable than many supposed. So, at any rate, ran the early reports.

They were not all wrong. Although the population was scattered thinly over the long, meandering coastline and the low-backed islands, leaving the forest interior to the native Mi'kmaqs and the wolves, Halifax was the sleeping princess waiting for the kiss of Empire. It was the perfect combination of port and fort, lying on a huge natural harbour, a yawning open mouth of a haven, three miles wide. The engineers of the port in the mid-eighteenth century must have been ambitious for its future, since they created a harbour capable of holding a thousand ships at anchor, and then enclosed it with a thick granite wall. From the western end of the harbour a steep hill rose, and on its flank rows of gravelled streets, some of them fifty-five feet wide, were already filled with stores—chandlers, hatters, haberdashers—as well as tall, narrow, timber-frame houses climbing the slope, and painted white or buttercup yellow in cheerful contrast to the slate grey of the sea. On Saturdays, farmers from Dartmouth, Preston and other outlying villages carted in their cabbages and turnips; the streets milled with all sorts, and the Halifax breweries did brisk trade. The accents heard in the dim taverns were, as usual, lowland Scots and Irish, but also the drawl of Maine and the clipped Massachusetts voices of the New Englanders who had brought their seamanship and their keen nose for opportunity north in the 1750s and 1760s. There were other, thicker styles of speech too: the clogged gutturals of German Lutherans and the dipthonged French patois of the Acadians, the fortunate ones who had managed to escape from Maine across the Bay of Fundy in the early 1750s before the British, in a moment of strategic ethnic cleansing, deported the rest all the way south to Louisiana.

The hill overlooking both Halifax town and harbour was crowned by a formidably armed and walled citadel, with heavy cannon pointing out to sea to deter any thought of a presumptuous French (or, now, American) attack. Directly beneath the fort was a clock tower, and around the Anglican diocesan church of St Paul's (in which blacks were banished to the gallery) a little piazza had shaped itself. In the gentler summer months the quality of the town walked about in the milky evening light, doffing hats, twirling parasols and inclining bonnets, while their children bowled hoops as if, for all the world, they were taking the air in Bath or Lyme Regis. There were coffee-houses, ropeyards, courthouses, warehouses, gambling houses, musical evenings, theatricals, gazettes, quacks and harlots. There was the North British Club, where the Scots could rub their chins, exchange gloomy intelligence about the shocking state of trade and shake their heads at the follies of the world. There was the Salt Fish Club, where the Anglo-Irish could speak their piece about the Scots and pass the decanter. There were prayers and blusters, wagers and seductions. It was like most other eighteenth-century commercial towns in the British Atlantic empire: greedy, gossipy and parochial, with eyes much bigger than its stomach.

But Halifax was nicely scaled for the restive ambitions of someone like Michael Wallace, the Scots-born merchant who shipped in manufactures from Glasgow, and with them bought James River tobacco and Havana muscovado sugar, which he sold in Nova Scotia, along with Cape Breton coal and Irish linen. Wallace was king of the Halifax hill: president of the North British Society; the canniest head on the governor's Executive Council (without which the said governor could not so much as order the clearing of stray cats); provincial treasurer; Commissioner for Roads (a nice fortune to be made there); and a magistrate in the Court of Common Pleas, judge of the Court of Admiralty. With an eye to rents, Wallace was also a substantial owner of land near Dartmouth across Halifax harbour, all the way east to Preston. But he was not all business. Like his ilk in both Auld Scotland and New Scotland, Wallace was a charitable man. His coin rang heavily in the collection dish on Sundays, and there was nothing he would not do to see that the unfortunate orphans had a Christian upbringing to make them into upstanding Britons for the new American empire—perhaps mariners or even merchants. But within limits, of course; everything orderly needed limits.[11]

To Michael Wallace's tidily managed, humming little Halifax with its American trade connections (many of them with the slave-laboured sugar and tobacco states) came, in the spring, summer and autumn of 1783, tens of thousands of the embittered, the distressed and the fearful. These British Americans had lost much, but most of all their confidence that to be British was the most fortunate destiny possible since it meant a share of imperial omnipotence. Is there anything in the world more pitiable and yet more unappealing than obstinate arrogance confounded by defeat? Every day those people salted their soup with rancour. What made their bitterness worse was the fact that they were, for the most part, not really the well-to-do. Those with substantial fortunes had gone back to Britain to try to forget that they had ever been American; or to the West Indies to remake their fortunes with sugar and the slaves they had taken from Georgia, Carolina and East Florida. The majority of the Nova Scotian refugees were middling sorts who had backed the wrong horse—farmers, small merchants, the odd advocate; people accustomed to a decent fashion of life, which usually included black house servants to wait upon them, and hands to help with the cows, the carts or the cooking. Abraham Cunard from Philadelphia was a typical example: he had run a small shipping business down on the Chesapeake, had stayed fiercely loyal and had left with the British army. He hoped, if only with his skills—carpentry, boatbuilding—and with the labour of his children and a government grant, to start a life again. All they needed was a little advance to tide them over.

For some of these middling people, places and land could be found in and around Halifax and Annapolis. But very soon Halifax began to burst at the seams. Parr wrote to Guy Carleton that "there is not any Houses or Cover to put them [the loyalists] under Shelter . . . And when I add the Scarcity and difficulty of providing fuel and lumber for building which is still greater, the many inconveniences and great distress these people must suffer if any come into this Province this Winter will sufficiently appear.[12]

It would be even worse for those who were not middling, so another surveyor, the Harvard-educated ex-Massachusetts merchant Benjamin Marston, thought. What he saw coming off the ships was just "a collection of characters very unfit for the business they have undertaken, Barbers, Taylors, Shoemakers and all kinds of mechanics bred and used to live in great towns . . . inured to habits very unfit for undertakings which require hardiness, resolution, industry and patience."[13] Marston's territory, and the place where almost half the loyalists, some twelve thousand both black and white, would end up by 1785, was called Port Roseway, and lay 130 miles south and west of Halifax, all the way round the heavily indented coastline. There were no roads to speak of, so the only way to travel was to follow the dangerous shore and, braving the unpredictable winds, put in at the few safe anchorages— Liverpool, Yarmouth or Lunenburg. Here the traveller would be greeted by a few fishing boats and the odd schooner, or even a two-masted brig lying moored in the little harbour; a raucous chorus of herring gulls and cormorants; the simplest of rough-planked docks; a small inn with a sign bearing the face of a king, duke, general or admiral; a huddle of whitewashed cottages; and, invariably, a shingled church or chapel (or both, for the confessional enthusiasms of the fishermen and shipbuilders were most particular). In some places where the congregation and their vicar believed they had the special dispensation of Providence the church boasted a belltower or steeple, its frame sometimes picked out in black in what became the peninsula vernacular.

So it was to be in Port Roseway, the original name of which was something of a mystery to the thousands of incomers. Like so much in Canada, where a thin British veneer had been laid over an older, stronger, deeper presence, the apparently English name concealed a French past. The Acadian mariners, descendants of Breton fisherfolk, had named the two obliquely angled arms of a natural harbour cutting through the sandbars Port-Rasoir for their resemblance to the razor clams that lay all around the beaches and coves. New England fishermen who had supplanted the expelled Acadians had already corrupted "Rasoir" into "Roseway." But for the port that would swell, in just five years, to become the most populous town in British America (indeed, at twelve thousand inhabitants the fourth biggest town in all of North America) a more emphatically British name was needed. So the decision was taken to call the place after the First Lord of the Treasury and Prime Minister. On the 20th of July Governor Parr, on an official tour of the loyalist settlements, came to the bay; swore in five Justices of the Peace, including Benjamin Marston, a notary and a coroner; made sure to mark out five hundred acres for his own summer residence; and then, from the porch of one of the grander houses in town, declared officially that the town was henceforth to be known as Shelburne.[14]

It was not a good start. Lord Shelburne was, after all, the minister whom the loyalists held most responsible for their betrayal, so hasty had he been to evacuate British troops that might yet have exerted pressure for the restitution of confiscated property. But Shelburne it became, and Shelburne it stayed: in the beginning a cramped, unkempt little place that struggled to be ceremonious (the Freemasons were much in evidence) and was, in fact, pretty rough. With ships arriving every week to disgorge their unhappy, insecure and fearful load of exiles, the wharves and streets leading from them were clogged with dumped chests and rows of tents to shelter the newcomers. Others stayed in the berthed ships, on which, at night, fires were lit and rowdiness carried over the water. And in the midst of all this were about a thousand unhappy, impoverished, demobilized soldiers, the hub of the uproar.[15] There was a choice of more than twenty taverns in which they might drink themselves senseless: McGragh's or Mrs Lowrie's dens of cursing, retching and brawling. Bare-knuckle pugilism became a favourite spectacle since the army was a famous nursery of boxers; these were bitter, slugging fights, and only exhaustion and a face reduced to what boxing scriveners, such as Pierce Egan, called a "claret mash" would end the matter so that wagers could be settled. Soon places of ill repute opened for business, where the soldiers could discharge their passions and expose themselves to the usual larceny and infection. Whenever they could, the loyalists of Shelburne danced, though they had precious little to dance about. They danced in the taverns and they danced in the streets between the tree stumps, their evening jigs lit by bonfires. For the moment, then, Shelburne was a Wapping by the sea in which the improvised chapels of the righteous stood cheek by jowl with the grimy resorts of the vicious.[16]

In this fractious, jostling tent city, muddy when it rained, dusty when it didn't, it took very little to make for ugliness. There was lumber everywhere, so fires often broke out, flames suddenly leaping from the piles of dry goods stacked in the streets while incoming ships were unloading. Some believed they were set deliberately by the resentful and the covetous.[17] The desperate wish of those responsible for governing Shelburne was that its population might be satisfied, as quickly as possible, with the one thing that never failed to calm bad tempers: property.

Benjamin Marston was supposed to get it to them. Although he had no prior experience at surveying, Marston, a loyalist merchant from Massachusetts, worked as quickly as he could to get people "settled" on their lots, aware that lengthy delays would only deepen the (well-founded) suspicions that a small group of loyalist well-to-do were somehow in league with men sent from Halifax, such as himself, to pre-empt the best land. The snobbish Marston grumbled constantly about men with no civility, learning or scruples having been appointed "captains" of loyalist companies in New York ("gentlemen and of course their wives and daughters, ladies whom neither nature or education intended for that rank") and who were now parading in a most high and mighty manner. Worse, the captains of these "companies" into which the loyalists had been divided—for administrative rather than military purposes—were a touchy lot, much given to shouting challenges and fighting duels. Everything made Marston jumpy. On the 4th of June 1783, in a show of truculent defiance exactly one month before the Americans would be celebrating their independence, Shelburne's loyalists insisted on marking the king's birthday, and doing it, moreover, in traditional British-American style, with flags, anthems and the usual show of fireworks. With so much to do, Marston sulked at the idle effrontery of it. But the Nova Scotia weather helped him to be the wet blanket: "Towards evening," he reported, gloating, "some fine showers which have come very opportunely to prevent the ill effects of a nonsensical feu de joie which was performed just at dark and would have fired the streets in a hundred places but for the rain. A Ball tonight—all our Tent over to it but myself and I am very happy to be absent."[18] The next day, everyone but Marston was sleeping off the effects. "These poor people are like sheep without a shepherd," he observed with his usual loftiness.

It was as though Marston, running lines in the woods in his waistcoat and shirtsleeves while being mercilessly punctured by blackfly, had been made to relive his worst days in Boston before the revolution. There, before he had fled in 1776, Marston had seen a commonwealth pulled apart by ill will between plebs and patricians, with government getting the blame. Here too in Shelburne the "republican spirit" of which he grumbled was aggravated by the selfishness of the few who somehow managed to acquire the best of the fifty-acre lots. Quite how this happened, given that there was supposed to be random drawing of lots, he was unsure, but he was suspicious. And Marston tried to keep on his guard against Halifax speculators and adventurers purporting to be distressed, or even apparently innocent people who curried favour, such as a Captain Maclean who sent him a large green turtle, a great delicacy. "I am obliged to him. He is to have a house lot, but this must not blind my eyes. He must run the same chance as his neighbours who have no turtle to send." It was not as if Marston did not have a grander vision of the Shelburne that might be; an elegant town of grace and civility, with wide, tree-lined streets built on a classical grid pattern. But with such unpromising human material to populate this ideal city, he brooded on how this vision would ever reach fruition.

There was one section of the population, however, that Marston thought merited special attention and would, if decently treated, repay it with loyalty and perseverance: the free blacks. Around 15 percent of the incoming loyalists to Nova Scotia were black—perhaps five thousand in all—although only half to two-thirds came as free Britons, emancipated through their war service (some others among the euphemistically designated "servants" were given their freedom on arrival). Parr and the council in Halifax had decided to scatter them about the province, the largest number going to the Shelburne area, where blacks made up almost half of the population. But groups of between fifty and a hundred families, including that of British Freedom, were settled at Preston (mostly on Wallace land), in the Digby area across the Annapolis River, where Peters had tried to settle, a few more in what was about to become New Brunswick, and, most remote of all, out on the rugged Atlantic shore about a hundred miles east of Halifax in ocean-blown Guysborough County.

Five hundred blacks went to Shelburne in the first wave of immigrants in the summer of 1783. Many of them immediately got work, since it was a good time to be a carpenter or sawyer, and camped in town. But white loyalists had mixed feelings about so many unpoliced blacks in their very midst. On the one hand, they depended on their low-paid labour. On the other hand, they fumed over the insolence spread by free blacks among their own slaves and house servants. As for the shockingly indecent "Negro frolicks"—drumming, jumping, dancing and singing—such exuberant entertainments were frowned on and eventually forbidden in Shelburne. Noisy or licentious violations could then result in a spell in the House of Correction. There were also complaints about fighting among the blacks, even between their women.

One "Negro Sally" was sent to the House of Correction for fighting with "Diana a Negro woman" whom Sally and her friend Jemimah claimed had struck her with both a stick and a bayonet! Diana, Sally and Jemimah all got spells in the workhouse, and Jemimah ten stripes on her back into the bargain.[19] So when another 409 new free black immigrants—including Henry Washington, Boston and Violet King, Cathern Van Sayl and her baby daughter Peter "Born within the British Lines"—arrived in Shelburne in August aboard *L'Abondance* it was decided that these problems could only be dealt with by creating a separate township, six miles distant from Shelburne proper.

On the 28th of August Marston went to inspect the site out on the northwestern arm of the bay. With him were a number of the free black captains who had been appointed over "companies" on board, among them Nathaniel Snowball, who had belonged to Mrs Shrewsbury in Princess Anne County, Virginia; Caesar Perth, once the property of Hardy Waller at Norfolk; and John Cuthbert from Savannah. But the man on whom Marston most relied was Colonel Stephen Blucke—a colonel only by virtue of the fact that he had succeeded the deceased guerrilla chief of the New York Black Brigade, "Colonel Tye." But Blucke was cut from a different, fancier cloth than Tye or, for that matter, Snowball and Perth. A free mulatto from Barbados, he was well enough educated to be hired to run a school for the Society for the Propagation of the Gospel, as well as a fishing smack. As a white officer put it, failing to conceal his astonishment, Blucke carried himself "as a man of surprising address, being perfectly polite," while his wife, Margaret, also a free mulatto, behaved and dressed similarly and gave herself very much the same airs.[20] Whites were vastly amused to discover a black man who took it as a point of self-respect to wear a good coat, a ruffled shirt, cocked hat, wig and hose, an effect of quality completed by his cane. Why, he had even been seen to partake, every so often, of a pinch of snuff![21] That Blucke had ambitions to be thought of as the squire, magistrate and patriarch of the new black town was signalled by his later acquiring, with the help of his New Jersey loyalist patron, Stephen Skinner, a lot of some two hundred acres on which he laid out the lines of a house as grand as anything on Shelburne's King Street.[22]

Twenty years earlier, a land speculator called Alexander McNutt had tried to establish a fishing and farming settlement populated by

Irish immigrants on the western arm of Port Roseway. With the usual booster's optimism, he had called it New Jerusalem, although it had in fact lasted only a few years.[23] And the site set aside for the blacks—who were certainly looking for their Jerusalem—seemed, at best, a challenge. Those who crossed by boat would see the makings of a fair fishing harbour, the water gently shelving to a flat, marshy landing site covered with bright reeds. The odd pair of slender silver birches stood close to the water, almost as if rising from the shallows. Grey herons perched on tall, smooth granite rocks, waiting for opportunities. Two streams, both stained a strange, transparent amber-red from rocks containing iron oxide—yet full of small, lively fish—ran over pebbly beds into the shallows. But at the back of the reedmarsh loomed the usual forbidding curtain of blue spruce, mixed with some stands of oak and maple. In the few places where natural clearings had opened after the fall of old hardwood trees there were granite boulders, elephantine in both colour and size, but fringed with yellow and red lichen. It was a daunting place to think of farming—although not, at first sight, heartbreakingly hopeless. The woods promised moose and caribou, and the blacks were excellent, practised hunters. Most important of all, this would, at last, be a town of free black Britons, the first such free black town in all of America. In honour of the officer who had given them their certificate of liberty it was called Birchtown. And whether or not its founders thought of Birchtown as a haven for runaway slaves inside Nova Scotia, it soon became one. Marston reported that, having inspected the land, Blucke and the captains pronounced themselves "well satisfied with it."[24]

But once the site of Birchtown was seen to have potential, it immediately attracted the attention of the more powerful white captains who, much to Marston's disgust, insisted they had already claimed the choice lots. They had sent their own surveyor, "a Mr Sperling," to the western end of the harbour with a line to mark out fifty-acre properties, and had included the Birchtown site. Sperling had been paid $2 a head to make the claims without "even a shadow of a license." To the detriment of his already shrinking popularity with the white loyalists, Marston literally stood his ground on behalf of the blacks of Birchtown. He would pay a price for this stand of principle.

The title, though, was but a nominal thing. As families began to move on to the site—the Andersons (Daniel, aged thirty-one; his wife,

Deborah; Daniel Jr., aged two; and the baby, Barbara); the Dixons (Charles, pater-familias, forty-eight, his wife, Dolly; Miles, aged seventeen; Luke, fourteen; Richard, thirteen; Sophia, Sally, six; and Polly, just one and a half); Mingo Leslie, who had fought as a Black Dragoon, with his wife, Diana, and their baby, Mary; the entirely female Quacks family (Elizabeth, the grandmother, her daughters, Jenny and Sally, and granddaughters, Katy and Polly)—it became quickly apparent that, to have any chance of a good start, Birchtown was going to need active help from Shelburne, the place least likely to offer it. Daniel Anderson listed his trade as "farmer," and Charles Dixon said he was a carpenter, and both came with axes, but neither could do much without supplies of saws and teams of horses and oxen to clear the boulders and stumps before the heavy snows made labour impossible and before the vestigial trees could produce spring sports. All this effort would inevitably take money, but the only way to get the money was by labouring for the town, which, in turn, would rob the Birchtowners of the time they needed to transform their wilderness into a garden and a farm. Even supposing that could get under way, they would still need provisions from the government in order to get them over the first winter.

Few of these hopes were realized. By the summer of 1784, Shelburne, now some nine thousand strong, did indeed offer the blacks an incentive to get on with building their own township—but it was not the kind they had been hoping for. On the 26th of July Marston recorded "Great Riot today," the work of the still unpaid and largely unsettled veterans of the king's army. Reduced to poverty and humiliation, they had come to see the blacks as robbing them of work by accepting wages far lower than anything whites were prepared to settle for. In fact most of the blacks worked for nothing at all except food and sometimes shelter, for their wages went unpaid for months or even years at a time. The white soldiers blamed the victims, the "blackies." They came as a gang, waving clubs, roaring that they would drive them from the town. Twenty houses belonging to blacks were torn down, their few possessions looted, the blacks themselves, women as well as men, forced to run for it. Benjamin Marston, accused of showing favour to the "blackies," was a particular target. Needless to say, none of the leaders of the white loyalists in Shelburne, whom he had antagonized by interfering in their land claims, lifted a finger in his defence. Alone, scared and fearing the worst, Marston fled to the local barracks and ventured out next day only to take the first ship back to Halifax. His hasty exit, he soon discovered, had been prudent. When friends came to see him a week later they told him that, had he not left so speedily, he might not have survived. "I find I have been hunted down to Point Carleton and had I been found should have had a bad time amongst a set of villainous scoundrels. I find I should have been fairly hung."[25] The mayhem went on for ten days, and sporadic episodes of violence and intimidation were reported for at least a month. The situation was serious enough for the govenor himself to come to Shelburne where, having listened to local complaints and exercising his talent for expediency, Parr decided to blame Marston, rather than the offices of the surveyor in Halifax, for the delays in distributing land to the soldiers.

Among those who had lost his house in the riot was the Baptist pastor David George, described by a local merchant, Simeon Perkins, as "Very Loud," and who had persisted in preaching to his flock in the Shelburne meeting house, even while the mob surrounded it with flaming torches, threatening to burn it to the ground.[26] But then David George was not one to abandon his faith, for while the Lord was with him, he feared no evil.

THE WORK WOULD ENDURE; but what tribulations had been sent his way! In Charleston, in October 1782, David George, his wife, Phyllis, and their four children had been swallowed up in the panic that marked the end of British rule in the Carolinas and for a while he had been parted from his family. Ships such as the *Free Briton* were hastily loading with free blacks, most of whom had got their liberty through serving the king. Now they were free but hated. The white loyalists who scarcely gave them room to board on the gangplank detested them for sowing wicked and ridiculous notions of freedom among their own servants and slaves. The white Americans whose property they had been looked at them as though they would hunt and kill them if they could. And the blacks still in bondage, who boarded with their masters, envied them their freedom.

It was a twenty-two-day sail to Halifax, and David George wrote that he was "used very ill on board."[27] Perhaps wanting so badly to preach and convert made matters worse. In the hilly Nova Scotian port David managed to find his old benefactor, General James Paterson, and was at last reunited with Phyllis and the children. But in that city those of his colour were not permitted to preach to the blacks, much less to baptize (indeed, they were not even allowed to pray in St Paul's alongside whites). So when General Paterson went to Shelburne David accompanied him, for the moment leaving the family in Halifax. In the tented town he discovered "numbers of my own colour," but once more met with suspicion and resentment from the white people. This hostility fed his calling and made David George more convinced than ever of what he must do. He shone with its necessity.

> I began to sing the first night, in the woods at a camp, for there were no houses built . . . The Black people came [from] far and near, and it was so new to them: I kept on so every night in the week and appointed a meeting for the first Lord's day in a valley between two hills, close by the river: and a great number of White and Black people came, and I was so overjoyed with having an opportunity once more of preaching the word of God that after I had given out the hymn, I could not speak for tears. In the afternoon we met again in the same place and I had great liberty from the Lord.[28]

Liberty from the Lord. It was all he craved. Let his unfailing goodness be sung. Every evening now there were meetings, and the many who were still ignorant of the gospel came to David. Voices were raised on high. There was exultation and witness. But the Shelburne "White people, the justices and all, were in an uproar and said I might go out into the woods for I should not stay there."[29] And he would have been driven out altogether but for one good white man (there was always one good white man), and this one had known him in Savannah and now gave him his own lot on which to stay and build a house. "I then cut down poles, stripped bark and made a smart hut and the people came flocking to the preaching every evening for a month as though they had come for their supper." When Governor John Parr went to Shelburne he brought Phyllis and the six children, along with six months' worth of provisions for the Georges, and made it known that he should have a quarter acre on which to grow food. There was running water through his plot, "convenient for baptizing at any time," and when snow fell David and his helpers built a platform for the flock to stand on, for their feet were often bare—although there was still nothing to cover their heads.

Brothers and sisters came and chanted their experiences before David and Phyllis as before the Great Judge and Father, and there was more praying and preaching and singing, and then, just before Christmas, the first baptism in their little Jordan creek; and the chapel walls rose and there were more baptisms every month even as the water froze. By the next summer there were fifty black Baptists in his flock and the meeting house was roofed and floored, although as yet there were still neither chairs nor pulpit. The Georges were now desperately hard up, having used their coppers to buy nails for the meeting house. They were saved only by the intervention of the Taylors, husband and wife Baptist missionaries from London, who gave them seed potatoes. David's voice was so strong now and his work for God so famous that whites from well beyond Shelburne began to approach him, first from curiosity, then from yearning; and this was both a gift and a trouble. A certain William Holmes, who lived at Jones Harbour, converted to the light but not yet cleansed, came in his schooner to Shelburne, sought David out and asked him to come and preach along the coast at Liverpool, which he did, and, although it was a mixed communion, when David preached the "Christians were alive and we had a little heaven together."[30] So William and Deborah Holmes went back with David to Shelburne, testified in the church and were to be baptized on the Lord's Day.

Their relations were very angry; raised a mob and endeavoured to hinder their being baptized. Mrs Holmes's sister especially laid hold of her hair to keep her from going down into the water, but the justices commanded peace and said she should be baptized as she herself desired it. Then they were all quiet. Soon after this the persecution increased and became so great that I thought I must leave Shelburn. Several of the Black people had houses upon my lot; but forty or fifty disbanded soldiers were employed who came with the tackle of ships and turned my dwelling house and every one of their houses quite over and the Meeting house they would

have burned down had not the ring-leader of the mob himself prevented it. But I continued preaching in it till they came one night
and stood before the pulpit and swore how they would treat me if I
preached again. But I stayed a preacher and the next day they came
and beat me with sticks and drove me into a swamp. I returned in
the evening and took my wife and children over the river to Birch
Town where the black people were settled and there seemed a
greater prospect of doing good than Shelburn.[31]

David George's sense of asylum in Birchtown lasted only a few months,
for the Methodists had been busy there. William Black, a Methodist missionary, had arrived in 1784 and found two hundred worshippers listening to the sermons of Blind Moses Wilkinson. Black and Daddy Moses
were jealous of their flock, and neither took very kindly to what they
thought might be the taking of apostates. When they made this known
in no uncertain terms David decided to go back to Shelburne, so made
his way across the bay again, cutting through the frozen water with a
whipsaw, only to find that his meeting house had been turned into a
tavern. "The Old Negro wanted to make a heaven of this place," the
tavern keeper had boasted in David's absence, "but I'll make a hell of
it." There were still enough friends in town, however, to see to its restoration, and by the next year, 1785, the revival was under way.

Through the years that followed "Black David" turned itinerant
missionary, tramping from one end of Nova Scotia to the other, creating
seven "New Light" Baptist churches and appointing deacons when he
moved on. Then he travelled north, across the Bay of Fundy to New
Brunswick, where he was already so famous for his hosannas, his tear-
stained exclamations and his mass baptisms that when he landed at St
John "some of the people who intended to be baptized were so full of
joy that they ran out from waiting table on their masters with the knives
and forks in their hands, to meet me at the waterside." There was a great
baptism of blacks and whites all together in the river, men and women,
their clothes unseemly wet, which caused such a scandal that the governor of New Brunswick, Thomas Carleton, announced that henceforth
David was licensed to minister only to blacks in the province.[32]

Yet more waters to cross, some of them cruel even to the true servants of God. After ministering and baptizing at Preston, where British

Freedom and his fellow settlers were gathered, David made his way back, first to Halifax and then to Shelburne, on one of the small ships that followed the coast south and west. But there was an ill wind and the vessel, with thirty passengers on board, was blown far out to sea, utterly losing its course. Fog settled and the temperature fell. Without a blanket to warm him, David froze, the frostbite creeping up his feet, ankles and calves all the way to his knees. When they finally docked at Shelburne he tried to walk, but collapsed and lay on the ground until someone from the church was sent for and he could be carried home. "Afterwards, when I could walk a little, I wanted to speak of the Lord's goodness, and the brethren made a wooden sledge and drew me to Meeting." In the spring he felt a little better and could totter about here and there, although mostly he still slid to the chapel. The strength had been taken from him—but not the spark, never that.

D AVID GEORGE'S FLOCK needed the comfort of God because too often it was all they had. The winter of 1785–86 was harsh at Birchtown, a taste of what was to come. Some of the settlers had, nominally, received their twenty-acre lots. But without ox teams, most of the lots stayed uncultivable. Dwellings scarcely deserved the name. Even as huts, most were shockingly rudimentary, a pit dug some six feet deep, the lean-to entry serving as the only source of light; the dirt floor was lined with crude planks or sometimes just with leaves, and the pitched roof made of logs and sometimes covered again with sod or bark or both. More like animals' lairs underground than cabins, for the first few years these dwellings offered shelter to those who slept in them from the worst that the Nova Scotian winter could do—snowfalls three to four feet deep, and drifts at least twice as high.[33] Even so, the Birchtowners were often on the edge of famine. Unless there were further food handouts from the government, one report to Halifax succinctly judged, "they must perish."[34] So cornmeal and molasses, occasionally supplemented with a little dried codfish, went on well beyond the first year.

But it was never enough to make liberty something more than a notion. In Shelburne, those blacks who went back to the town after the riots found work as carpenters, sawyers, boatbuilders, fishermen, sailors and general labourers, whilst their wives and daughters were cooks and laundresses. But their plight became worse when the embryonic whaling industry, crippled by tariffs the British government imposed on oil and bone, went under. The once-promising cod fishery also contracted, throwing many more on to the labour market and reducing their bargaining power. Shelburne became the gloomy wreck of John Parr's failed dream. Thousands of white loyalists, especially the poorer ones, went back to Halifax or returned to the United States. Those with a little more capital either stayed put in their houses on Water Street and King Street or emigrated with their slaves and servants to the West Indies or the Bahamas. The downward slide of the loyalist economy took the occupants of the coastal villages and harbours with it: the boatbuilders and fishermen of Lunenburg and Liverpool and the little satellite hamlets such as Port l'Hébert and Lockeport. Further off, on the shores of the Bay of Fundy the choice for the free blacks and their families was between hiring themselves out on punitive terms of indenture or starvation.

Socially, the mass indenturing of the free blacks may have looked like re-enslavement, and their representative Thomas Peters characterized it thus when he was in London drumming up support from Granville Sharp and like-minded souls. But the distressed and impoverished blacks who signed indentures with white masters and mistresses were adamant that they were not so utterly defeated, nor so forgetful of their status and what had been promised them, as to surrender once more to bondage. The indentures (which bound not just blacks but also many poor whites through the years of Nova Scotian hardship) were drawn up for a specific term. Although board and lodging were to be supplied, they were not in lieu of wages, but in addition to them. The mere fact of those wages, however pitiful, was itself an indicator in law, as many of the recipients pointed out, that they were not enslaved. And this, as much as the pure hardship incurred by their habitual non-receipt, was why, when the blacks complained to the county courts of General Sessions of their treatment (demonstrating awareness of their freedom and rights under the law), or when they defended themselves against being confused with blacks who had come to Nova Scotia as house slaves, they made sure to stress that, whilst they might have lived in with employers, they were in fact owed arrears of wages.

Court records document a fierce struggle between two worlds. On the one hand the white loyalist caste, many of them from the American South and accustomed to owning slaves, assumed that the institution would be upheld by the Nova Scotian courts. They were right in that in the 1780s slavery was de facto legal in the province; notices of sales and auctions could be read in Halifax. But the climate of opinion, moral and legal, was changing, just as it was in England and in the United States north of the Potomac. Halifax was becoming more like post-Mansfield London. Indeed, Mansfield's ruling that blacks could not be coercively transported out of the province was taken as valid for Nova Scotia by at least some justices. Others, like Chief Justice Thomas Strange and Attorney-General Sampson Blowers, were beginning an active campaign to outlaw slavery from the province altogether. So the white slaveholding loyalists and those who wanted to convert the impoverished free black labour force into slaves ran into impressively fierce resistance. However grim their circumstances, however excluded from the vote or refused common places of worship with whites, blacks were still strikingly conscious of their rights—whether they had gained that understanding from the transatlantic awareness of the Mansfield cases, through knowledge of the Dunmore and Clinton proclamations, or whether they had learned it while on active service. This first generation of free British African-Americans put up a fight against re-enslavement and especially against their families being divided.

The more unscrupulous white loyalists made a deliberate habit of blurring the critical distinction between free and unfree, and were accustomed to treat indentured blacks as a negotiable commodity, receiving money from prospective hirers when "their" blacks were transferred. Equally, though, there were many others in the white loyalist community, often in official positions, who clearly acknowledged the difference between hired labour and slave. When, for example, William Shaw, the provost marshal of Nova Scotia, was making muster lists around the province in the spring of 1784, he made a particular point of the fact that out on the rugged eastern shore of the peninsula, at Country Harbour, he had discovered (and he italicized his comment for emphasis) that *"many of them* [the blacks] *are not the property of the Persons they live with."*[35] Nonetheless, it often came as a shock to the whites, who themselves used the courts to press claims of ownership, that "their" blacks had the gumption as well as the knowledge to do the same. Some of the blacks, indeed, were showing signs of being their own Granville Sharp.

When Captain Thomas Hamilton and Daniel MacNeill abducted four blacks—Moses Reed, Jameson Davis, Phoebe Martin and Molly Sinclair—from Halifax with the intention of taking them in MacNeill's sloop, the *Adventure*, and selling them in the Bahamas, they could not have imagined they would be thwarted by the courts.[36] The two men, Reed and Davis, had run away to the British at Charleston from their master in Bute County, North Carolina, and had served with Lord Francis Rawdon's loyalist Volunteers of Ireland. Following the 1782 evacuation, they had served in the Royal North Carolina Regiment in East Florida, one of them probably as servant to its senior officer, Lieutenant Colonel John Hamilton. Like many of the free blacks, they had been re-employed in Nova Scotia by a relative, in this case Captain Thomas Hamilton of Country Harbour. At Hamilton's house Reed and Davis met Phoebe Martin and Molly Sinclair, both originally from South Carolina, also servants, also working without wages. Yet at no time, as Phoebe Martin would tell the court, did she or any of the others think of themselves as Hamilton's slaves.

Suspecting Hamilton's design for them, the four decided to escape and made their way to Halifax in the spring or early summer of 1786. But they were tracked down by a gang of five, including MacNeill and Hamilton himself. Jameson Davis was ferociously beaten; once subdued, he and the rest were chained and thrown into the hold of a ship in the harbour. But this vessel sailed only as far as Shelburne, where the blacks were to be transferred to another ship that would take them south to enslavement. This proved to be a mistake. Somehow MacNeill and his ship were known to the black community in Shelburne and Birchtown, and what they knew they feared and hated. Word was got out to the magistrates that the four blacks were being taken without a hearing, and in the spirit of the post-Mansfield ruling against coercive transportation one was granted. Surprised to be arraigned, MacNeill argued that he had been authorized to take the blacks by none other than Michael Wallace in his capacity as Atlantic trader, and indeed that it was Wallace who had arranged the trans-shipment from Shelburne and the sale. But by five to two the magistrates of the Shelburne General Sessions chose to believe the stories given by the blacks rather than the authority of one of the most powerful men in Halifax, and ordered their liberation. British freedom had not yet perished, then, in Nova Scotia.

Strikingly, many of the successful black plaintiffs were women. Taking a leaf from Granville Sharp's book, Susannah Connor went to court to prevent John Harris from taking her son, Robert Gemmel, who was indentured to Harris but not enslaved, out of the country "contrary to the laws of the province." Mary Westcoat and her husband likewise sued James Cox for the release of a "Negro Boy named Stephen," and succeeded in gaining his liberation when Cox was unable to produce a bill of sale or even articles of indenture.[37]

Not all cases ended as happily. Joseph Robbins told the court at Shelburne that he had owned two blacks, Pero and Tom, who now lived "under the pretence of being Free Negroes." In reply Pero said he had in fact been the property of a rebel, not a loyalist; that he had run away, so earning his liberty; that he had agreed to go with Robbins to St Augustine, but as a free man, not a slave; and that he had never been sold. Tom too told a story of escaping from a rebel master to British Charleston. But both men were delivered by the court to Robbins as his property.[38]

Much more tragic was the case of Mary Postell, who was taken by Jesse Gray for sale and was summoned to the Shelburne court to give evidence to support her statement that she was in fact free. She had been, she told the court, the property of an American rebel officer, Elisha Postell, but had escaped and taken refuge "within the British lines" at Charleston, where she worked on the forts and public works along with other blacks. Since she and her husband, William, were impoverished, he had persuaded her that it would be safe to enter the service of Jesse Gray as a house servant, and even to go with him to East Florida on the evacuation of Charleston. There she had worked for his brother Samuel, and when that territory had been ceded to Spain she had gone to Nova Scotia with Jesse Gray. However, as soon as she had discovered that he meant to sell her, she had "quitted his Familly, taking with her two children, Flora and Nell, and went to live in a house which she hired for that purpose in the north division of the Town." In April 1786, by some ruse or force, Gray had seized her and her children and taken them to Argyle, where he had sold her to a Mr Mingham for 113 bushels of potatoes. Mary further claimed that Gray had taken her children away from her and sold them elsewhere. With no choice in the matter, she had stayed with Mingham for three years until she had escaped to come to Shelburne and put the whole matter before the justice of the court.

Then it was Gray's turn to interrogate Mary in court: an unequal battle, one might suppose. But Mary held her own; she spoke what she knew. Was it not true, Gray demanded of the black woman, that in East Florida she had asked "some persons" to *buy* her daughter Flora back from his brother Samuel—the implication being she understood Nell to be enslaved? No, said Mary, it was not true; she had never said such a thing. Brushing aside the denial, Gray stormed on: and was it not also true that he himself had bought *her* from one Joseph Rea in St Augustine? No, it was not, repeated Mary; she had never belonged to any such person. Pressed harder—and this may have been fatal to her case—Mary said yes, she did not mind being sold to Mr Mingham for those potatoes, for she would do anything to get away from Jesse Gray since, she said pointedly, "*he* used her so ill."

Witnesses were called for both sides. Against Gray's people, Mary called Scipio Wearing and his wife, Diana. Wearing, who had himself left an American master, had known Mary in Charleston, and as a Pioneer had worked on the defences of Charleston under Colonel James Moncrief. He had lost contact with her when he had gone to New York and she had left for East Florida, but Scipio was in no doubt at all that she had escaped a rebel master and so was, like him, entitled to her full liberty. His testimony was of no avail. Gray, acquitted of illegal abduction, took Mary from her children and, returning to America with her, sold her again to his brother Samuel. Her daughter Nell was delivered into the custody of the court and, with her infant brother John, doubtless ended up in the hands of the Poor Commissioners.

But Scipio Wearing was punished much more painfully for his temerity in casting doubt on the word of such men as Jesse Gray. When he got back from court he found his house in flames and along with it the "whole of his Furniture . . . Apparel and other property was consumed." There was worse. One of Scipio and Diana's children had been in the house and had burned to death. Scipio went back to the court, this time praying "for such relief as this Court may be pleased to grant him." He was told to apply to the Overseers for the Poor, where he may have received charity along with Nell and John Postell.[39] It was an open secret, of course, that the firing of the house and the resultant murder of the child had been an act of vindictive retribution. But nothing could be proved; no one in Shelburne came forward, and no one was charged.

Would Mary Postell and Scipio Wearing and their families have been saved this suffering had they been in Birchtown? Possibly, although the village was not altogether safe from slavecatchers.[40] At least two of its male inhabitants had been seized while on a purported errand beyond the town limits, imprisoned in the kind of ships owned by Daniel MacNeill and sold in the West Indies.[41] But although not watertight against wickedness, Birchtown was nonetheless, by 1787, a true community, around two hundred families strong. By this time the primitive shelters had been replaced by modest cabins, probably similar to the huts the former slaves had known either in Africa or on the plantation: a single chamber barely more than ten feet square, but with a loft and an excavated cellar to store winter provisions, plus a hearth and chimney, and the whole topped with a gabled log roof. Birchtown was still something of a makeshift camp, squeezed between the wooded wilderness, Beaver Lake and the sea. But it was still, as the Methodist patriarch John Wesley noted across the Atlantic, "the only town of negroes that has been built in [the continent of] America." Recent site excavations have turned up fragments of glass together with ceramic bowls and dishes like English creamware, some decorated with flower patterning, that suggest a milieu more domestic than just a crude encampment of hunters and diggers.[42] Birchtown was hardly a Home Counties village, but nor was it a place where, as subsequent myth had it, the settlers were forced to live in "caves." Although most of the population were still artisans and fishermen, there were at least thirty who described themselves as farmers and took goods to market in Shelburne, much as the Prestonians did in Halifax.[43] Blucke and his wife, Margaret, ran their school to ensure that the next generation would be literate, and there was also, of course, the church, the heartbeat of Birchtown, shared contentiously among the Methodists, who dominated worship; Anglican "New Lights" of the Connexion of the Countess of Huntingdon; and, despite David George's initial frosty reception, eventually (and unstoppably) a group of enthusiastic Baptists. So there was a lot of noise on Sundays, and the fact that the warring sects sometimes shut their doors on each other and to visiting missionaries of the wrong denomination only emphasizes the way in which Birchtown was becoming an independent free black community.

None of this was enough to impress a companion of Prince William Henry (later King William IV), who was then stationed with the Royal Navy in Nova Scotia. Staying at Shelburne barracks, Captain Dyott and some friends (although not the prince) decided to take a look at Birchtown, where they were entertained to dinner by Colonel Blucke and his wife. The visitors were glad to leave what Dyott described as a "place beyond description wretched . . . their huts miserable to guard against the inclemency of the Nova Scotian winter and their existence almost dependent on what they could lay up in summer. I think I never saw such wretchedness and poverty so strongly perceptible in the garb and countenance of the human species as in these miserable outcasts."[44]

But then Dyott came to Birchtown in 1788, at one of the lowest points in its admittedly rocky fortunes. The previous year there had been another wave of the smallpox epidemic, which had never quite relinquished its grip on the escaping blacks and had travelled with them from Virginia and the Carolinas, Boston and New York. The collapse of the Shelburne trading economy after 1786 meant that there was less casual labour required, which had previously enabled them to supplement their meagre subsistence; and the proposed solution of the Shelburne authorities—to make the town into a free port, open to business with the United States—filled the blacks with terror again lest their haven be opened to slavecatchers who, they knew, were still relentless in their quest to recover human "property." Many of the Birchtown blacks had still not received their land allotments, and those who had were required to offer days of "statute labour" (usually on roads) as a condition of receiving assistance or in discharge of the "quit rents" they were shocked to discover they were supposed to pay. (Quit rents were a fiscally expedient anachronism, a single annual sum to be offered to the government in lieu of ancient demands of goods and services, and a source of bitter provocation to the Americans before the revolution.) Sir Guy Carleton, the new governor of Canada, had promised that the loyalists would not be burdened with quit rents, but the London government obtusely granted only a temporary suspension. To cap the misfortunes, the winters of 1787–88 and 1788–89 were so ferocious, and the springs and summers so cold and wet, that such arable crops as there were, especially of corn and potatoes, failed and famine dug its talons into Birchtown. Boston King, the South Carolinan escaped slave who had already survived smallpox and capture by the Americans, had been converted to Methodism in Birchtown. King who took walks in the snow-covered woods to interrogate himself about his sins, remembered these years as a time of the wolf: "Many of the poor people were compelled to sell their best gowns for five pounds of flour in order to support life. When they had parted with all their clothes, even to their blankets, several of them fell down dead thro' hunger. Some killed and eat [sic] their dogs and cats and poverty and distress prevailed on every side."[45] There was nothing for it, he concluded, but "to my great grief" to leave Birchtown and find work where he could.

It was not only the winter that was cruel. On the verge of begging, the threadbare Boston King walked the streets hawking his skills as a carpenter, and eventually found a captain who ordered a chest from him. Back he went to Birchtown, worked day and night, and then carried the chest through snow three feet deep to the captain. He was paid with the coin of contempt. "To my great disappointment he rejected it. However he gave me directions to make another. On my way home, being pinched with hunger and cold I fell down several times, thro weakness and expected to die on the spot. But even in this situation I found my mind resigned to the divine will and rejoiced in the midst of tribulation; for the Lord delivered me from all murmuring and discontent altho I had but one pint of Indian meal left for the support of myself and wife." Dragging the new chest through the drifts, and fearful that the captain would once more find it unacceptable, King took with him a saw, first to destroy it and spare himself the agony of hauling it back. But this time the captain took the piece and, what was more, paid for it in cornmeal. King then sold the original chest for another half crown and his saw for three shillings and ninepence. The tool had cost him a guinea, five times what he was offered for it now, but he was in no position to haggle.

His luck began to turn. At some point soon King would have needed his saw back, for he was commissioned by two Shelburnians to build three flat-bottomed boats for the next season's salmon fishing. Paid £1 for each, and supplied with more corn, as well as the tar and nails he needed, King and his wife, Violet, were saved from having to follow many of their Birchtown friends and neighbours into long-term indentures. The next winter he built some more craft, and was evidently a skilled enough carpenter to be asked by a merchant to build a house at Chedabucto Bay. Once he got there after the thaw, the merchant told him he had changed his mind and that he could easily buy a new house for what it would cost to have one built. But he still had work for him. He was short of men for his salmon fleet and would rather King served him that way. It was May. In all likelihood King would not get back to Violet and the children until the autumn. And he worried about having to forsake his calling as Methodist missionary and lay preacher. But he need not have worried on that score for, having accepted the work, he discovered that the fishing people of Chedabucto were shockingly profane and steeped in sin: "I endeavoured to exhort them to flee from the wrath to come and to turn to the Lord Jesus."

They chuckled, and sure enough, in the Gulf of St Lawrence, the fleet ran into a monstrous tempest and the sailors "expected every moment would be our last." When the storm abated they found themselves on the Grand Banks in a deep, impenetrable fog in which the supply ship carrying all their provisions for the season disappeared. King redoubled his prayers to the God of forgiveness and was heard. Two weeks later the missing ship reappeared, and four days after that so did the glittering salmon. Despite this abundant blessing, King still feared that the enterprise had been put in jeopardy by the filthy blasphemies of his employer, who was much given not only to flying into rages, but also to taking the name of the Lord in vain when he did so. Ever since he could remember, as long ago as the age of six when he was put to mind his master's cattle in South Carolina and been taught the merry joys of a good oath by his comrades, King had suffered from guilt at this particular sin. As a cowherd dozing beneath the shade of a great tree, he had dreamt that the world was on fire. God was descending on a "great white throne," Judgement was nigh—and he was numbered among the tribe of the cursers! Now, years later, he was trapped in a boat with a man whose terrible language was putting them all at risk while they were drifting on the deep. Summoning up his courage, King reminded the arch-curser that "all profane swearers shall have their portion in the lake that burneth with fire and brimstone." For a brief while the captain was sobered into quietness, but the next morning he was at it again, verbal demons flying from his mouth. Unable to close his ears to the unholy torrent, Boston King, with some temerity, now banned the captain from his own boat, asking for daily orders in advance and at more than arm's length "for if he persisted in his horrible language I should not able to discharge my duty. From that time on he troubled me no more and I found myself very comfortable having no one to disturb me."

There were more challenges. Hardly returned to Chedabucto, the fleet set off again, this time for the herring run, and ran into yet another North Atlantic storm. But after King had finally been paid off in late October he was able to go back to Violet and to his lay preaching richer by some £15 and two barrels of fish. With this little fortune, Boston King was able to escape the worst that had befallen other members of his community. "I was enabled to clothe my wife and myself, and my Winter's store consisted of one barrel of flour, three bushels of corn, nine gallons of treacle, twenty bushels of potatoes which my wife had set in my absence and the two barrels of fish so that this was the best Winter I ever saw in Birchtown."

I T WAS JUST POSSIBLE, then, fighting against steep odds and deep prejudice, to make it in British America and stay a free black. But Thomas Peters, now in New Brunswick, evidently did not think so. He had fared no better in Fredericton and St John than he had in Digby and Brindley Town, and Governor Thomas Carleton had been no more responsive to his complaints and petitions than had Governor John Parr. Land had still not been given as asked. Or when it had it had, as at St John, it was at an outrageous distance—nearly eighteen miles—from the town lots where the settlers kept their homes. Some of the grander white people in New Brunswick, such as Stair Agnew, Beverley Robinson and the Reverend Jonathan O'dell, had come from exactly the kind of planter country he had fled, Virginia and Maryland, along with their full complement of slaves.[46] So it was hardly surprising that whilst black people were denied a voice and fair dealing in the courts, they were still made to pay taxes and to labour on the roads. To stay alive they had been forced to hire themselves out for a pittance, and even that had not been paid—and for more years than had ever been set down in the indentures. When, driven near to starving and utterly in despair, they took a loaf, the lash was laid across their backs, women as well as men, so that the blood poured from their torn flesh, or worse, they were hanged. Was this not slavery?

Unlike David George and Boston King, Thomas Peters could not see all these troubles as having been sent by God as part of his mysterious plan for the people. But he still had faith in the king, in the gift of his British freedom. But he had no trust in the men whom the government had set up over them in New Brunswick and Nova Scotia. So the illiterate but redoubtable Peters turned politician—the very first acknowledged leader of African-Americans. Petitions regularly went from "Thomas Peters, a Black Man Serjt of the Late Black Prs who Servd His Majesty 7 years" to Governor Thomas Carleton (who sometimes even responded).[47] Peters wrote on everything affecting the blacks: their land assignments or lack thereof; the charity schools; relief, during times of distress, from labour service and taxes. Why, after all, should the blacks, themselves so impoverished, be charged with paying the poor tax rather than receiving it? Gradually his energy and determination made him recognized in the province as the "One Person nominated and Appointed to Act for and in behalf of the whole of us; in all matters both Civil and Religious."[48]

Yet, for the most part, in New Brunswick Peters encountered the same barriers of hostility and procrastination that he had found in Nova Scotia. Nothing would change, he decided, unless he could somehow get the ear of government—in London, rather than in Halifax and St John. Some time in 1790 he drafted his "Memorial" to William Wyndham Grenville, the Secretary of State, setting out the services the blacks had rendered in the war, reminding the government of what had been promised, and cataloguing the failure of those promises to materialize. Then he took the petition in person back and forth across the Bay of Fundy, managing in the end to get the marks of 202 free black families in the two provinces and to appoint him their duly commissioned delegate to seek redress for their afflictions. Peters then took his commission, his petition and the precious passport signed by Captain Stewart with him to Halifax, there to find a ship bound for London. Doing so, of course, put him in great peril, for Nova Scotian blacks were constantly being seized for sale, whatever scraps of paper they imagined would defend them. But Thomas Peters was not short of courage and he was burning with determination. He may even have worked his passage across the ocean.

Once in London he was probably in touch with Equiano and Cugoano, both now hugely celebrated as authors and witnesses to the tragedy of slavery. Peters certainly sought out his old officers from the Pioneers, and with their help wove his way through the network of the great and the good. Although he was not lionized like other exotic visitors, such as the Tahitian prince Omai, or the Creek Indians currently in town to petition for trade to the West Indies, the arrival of Thomas Peters out of the blue turned him into a courier from an epic tragedy, the bearer, as General Clinton wrote to Secretary of State Grenville, of "a melancholy tale." But quite independently, and early in the stay, Peters would naturally have sought out Granville Sharp. And after he had finished reciting the grievances of his people, and Sharp had done reassuring him that they would be addressed in the highest quarters, the two wearied fighters considered each other and Sharp asked Peters if, by any chance, he had heard of this place in Africa, the Province of Freedom. And yes, as it happened, Peters had.

It had been at a dinner, somewhere in Nova Scotia or New Brunswick. The blacks, as always, waited on table; stood against the wall, treated as though they were deaf, dumb and invisible. As the decanters moved smoothly over the mahogany, there was talk of Sierra Leone and of the man whose most peculiar fancy it was to take the negroes back to Africa: Granville Sharp. Suddenly, behind the chairs, ears opened and eyes widened. There was hardly a black, free or slave, in North America who did not know those two words: Granville Sharp. Word was got to the people and then to the man who had become their champion and delegate, Thomas Peters.[49] His first business had always been to right the wrongs there in British America, but this story of Sierra Leone set him wondering. Was he to understand, if you please, that there was to be a going home?

Part Two

JOHN

[*LIEUTENANT JOHN CLARKSON, RN*, ARTIST UNKNOWN, C. 1790s,
MINIATURE / PRIVATE COLLECTION]

IX

NEW PALACE YARD, Westminster, the 26th of April 1791: a sombre conclave assembled in a room above the Parliament Coffee-House. The gathering of soberly dressed men, thirteen of them, was doing its best not to be utterly downcast, but not altogether succeeding. How close they all were to Parliament, yet how far from making it do its duty before the bar of God and of British history!

The Committee for Effecting the Abolition of the Slave Trade was meeting one week after William Wilberforce's motion to arrest the importation of slaves to the West Indies had been denied, at three thirty in the morning on the 19th of April, and by the dispiriting tally of 163 votes to 88. William Pitt, Charles James Fox and Edmund Burke had all spoken in favour of Wilberforce's motion. William Smith's speech to the House had been so eloquent that Fox had burst into tears and had had to hide himself behind the Speaker's chair until he had regained his composure.[1] They were the giants of the House, as one of the motion's adversaries conceded, adding, however, that "the minor orators, the dwarfs, the pigmies . . . would [nonetheless] carry the day." Watching from the gallery, Thomas Clarkson gloomily agreed. How galling it was that the eloquence of Pitt and Fox (seldom in concord) had gone unheeded, whilst the crackpot ravings of the Lord Mayor of London who protested that an end to the slave trade would entirely ruin the market for rotten Newfoundland codfish (the diet, he supposed, of slaves) had been listened to with even a modicum of respect. The committee put a brave face on the disaster. It was a "retarding," they declared, rather than a defeat, and lest any apologists for the Accursed Thing delude themselves, they would "renew their firm protestation, that they will never desist from appealing to their Countrymen till the commercial intercourse with Africa shall cease to be polluted with the blood of its Inhabitants."[2]

But the truth was that, for Thomas Clarkson, William Wilberforce, Granville Sharp and the rest of the committee, the vote on the 19th of April was a crushing blow, for it had come after four years of the broadest mobilization of public opinion Britain had ever seen. Clarkson, relentless, had ridden the length and breadth of the country, crucified by piles, seldom getting more than four hours' sleep a night. He had brought out the righteous in their thousands, made converts, got mass petitions signed, distributed literature, exhibited his "specimens" of shackles, branding irons and the *speculum oris,* which forced the mouths of slaves open to push down food, and handed out boxloads of "Am I Not a Man and a Brother?" medallions. After the vote Clarkson suddenly felt the full measure of his exhaustion, and friends began to fret over his health. Yet he would not desist now, however hard the rejection of Parliament.

As the mouthpiece of the committee in Parliament, Wilberforce must have felt the rejection even more painfully. He had broken his health for the cause and for some weeks in 1788 had collapsed altogether, yet he had somehow rallied to deliver three-hour orations against the impolicy as well as the inhumanity of the trade. Alluding to the great stir in the country of which the evidence was, every day, more unmistakable (as well as to campaigns for parliamentary reform that attacked the Commons as a sink of corruption), Wilberforce had challenged the House: "Let not Parliament be the only body that is insensible to the principle of natural justice."[3] But that had been in May 1789, when the exhaustive Privy Council report had been set before the Commons for debate, and the committee was deluging MPs with prints of the conditions on the *Brookes* and narratives of slaving on the Guinea Coast. Notwithstanding this saturation, or possibly because of it, opponents of Wilberforce's "Propositions" to end the trade argued that with "insufficient" evidence the Commons still needed to commission its own inquiry. With Pitt's Cabinet deeply divided on the issue, making it impossible for the prime minister to adopt it as a measure of government, the forces of temporizing inevitably prevailed.

Procrastination, that most polished vice of British politics, worked its morphic spell. The lumbering machine of evidence-gathering lumbered again, brushing aside the committee's efforts to hurry, and staggering on until (as was, of course, the idea) that session of Parliament was over. A new Parliament would not assemble until November 1790. During the intervening election campaign in Liverpool, defenders of the trade, such as Banastre Tarleton, were so confident as to appear at the hustings with a banner featuring a negro in chains.[4]

In the meantime, the founding patriarch of abolitionism, James Ramsay, had died on the 20th of July, still the scourge of the "murdering Guinea captains" and "oppressing sugarplanters" who had accused him on his sick bed of "over-strained humanity" to the Africans. He died, probably of stomach cancer, in Sir Charles Middleton's house, Teston Hall, not knowing whether the parliamentary measure would succeed, but expressing, so Clarkson wrote, "great satisfaction at having been made an instrument in the hand of his merciful Creator in promoting his beneficent purposes towards an afflicted portion of his creatures."[5] Wilberforce put it more succinctly in his diary. "Heard that poor Ramsay died yesterday at ten o'clock. A smile on his face now."[6] Perhaps Ramsay was smiling at the recollection of being told by Hannah More, the formidable Evangelical, that Teston would be considered by future generations as the "Runnymede of the Negroes."

Something more serious happened in the long interval between Wilberforce's first great speech in the spring of 1789 and his second in April 1791: the collapse of the French monarchy. To the friends of humanity, among whom Clarkson and Sharp especially numbered themselves, this was a cause for great rejoicing, as a matter both of principle and of interest. A predictable objection of their opponents to the closing down of the British slave trade had always been that it would hand an immensely lucrative commerce over to the arch-enemy, whose empire would flourish as that of Albion shrivelled. Although the committee's public position was that sugar produced by free labour would undercut that produced by slaves and so capture the world market, in private they acknowledged the effect that this mercantilist argument against abolition had on those in power. Foregoing a British stake in the slave trade would merely be to concede the business to the old transatlantic enemy. So there was great interest, in both senses of the word, in reports of a budding *French* campaign against the slave trade in the years after 1787. In the winter of 1788–89, as the elections to the Estates General were taking place, Thomas Clarkson sent his younger brother John, who had served in the Caribbean with the navy, to Le Havre, the busiest of all the French slaving and sugar entrepôts, to gather more evidence on the cruelty of the trade to deliver as testimony to the Privy Council.

But Thomas Clarkson had another motive for his brother's Channel crossing: the cultivation of fraternal links with the Société des Amis des Noirs (Society of the Friends of Blacks), recently founded by the young lawyer Jacques-Pierre Brissot. The Frenchman had been in London in 1787 and had become a convert to Clarkson's way of thinking. Back in France he had recruited to the cause the grandest aristocratic names of enlightened reform: the Marquis de Lafayette, the Vicomte de Mirabeau and the Marquis de Condorcet. Should the French move towards abolishing the slave trade at the same time as the British, the argument of the planters, that the old enemy would profit from abolition, would be confounded.

Until the spring and summer of 1789, this view of cross-Channel abolitionist fraternity might have seemed unduly sunny—not least because French sugar merchants had never enjoyed such a boom in both production and profits as in the last years of the *ancien régime*. But the creation of a National Assembly at Versailles, and the fall of the Bastille changed everything. Thrilled by what he had heard and read, hoping to do what he could to persuade the National Assembly to take up the cause, Thomas Clarkson, who spoke very little French, decided to embark on a pilgrimage. He arrived in Paris in the second week of August 1789, at the moment when the city was in the full rhapsody of its revolutionary euphoria. The tricolor cockade had just been introduced by Lafayette's National Guard and was instantly put into political mass production: already there were tricolor sashes, ribbons, pins, badges and, finally, flags. The big, bull-like Englishman moved through this jubilant festival of liberty with his senses pleasurably shaken, wandering wantonly (for him) amidst fire-eaters and dancing bears as his ears rang with the music of hope. At the heart of those festivities was the great demolition. "Patriote" Palloy's work gangs, reinforced by crowds of excited volunteers, were beginning to pull down the Bastille stone by stone.[7] The site had already become the most frequented place of public celebration in Paris. Drinks were served to tourists, while new-minted citizens heaved stones into the redundant moat. Following the throngs into the murky, stifling cells, Clarkson found scratched into one wall a Latin inscription that read: "[An illegible name] wrote this Line in the anguish of his heart." Moved, he paid two of Palloy's workmen to dislodge the stone for him as a souvenir.[8]

Thomas Clarkson was an instant and wholehearted convert to the cult of universal possibility. On the 4th of August the nobility of France, transformed into citizens in the National Assembly, had ostentatiously surrendered their feudal prerogatives to the bonfire of history. No more seigneurs; why then should there still be slaves? Since Clarkson's closest allies in this cause happened to be the two most influential men in France at this moment—Lafayette and Mirabeau—he had reason to be sanguine. At Lafayette's generous table he encountered six "Deputies of Colour," mulattos from St Domingue in the French West Indies, proudly cockaded and wearing the Order of St Louis, who were in Paris to demand equal representation with whites.[9] When asked by Clarkson whether they too (for some were slaveowners) would favour abolition of the trade, they called it "the parent of all miseries" in their island and the cause of "hateful distinctions" between whites and people of colour. One of those deputies who came to visit Clarkson was Vincent Ogé, who, on returning to St Domingue and being outraged by the killing of fellow creoles for seeking the rights of citizens, armed his slaves and started a rebellion. Ogé was caught and broken on the wheel, inaugurating a long and bloody war that would end in the creation of Haiti.

A thousand copies of the famous slave-ship print, together with hand-coloured illustrations, had been imported for Clarkson, who distributed them freely to well-disposed members of the National Assembly. When given his own copy of the print of the *Brookes*, Mirabeau turned playful propagandist, commissioning a three-foot-long wooden model as a conversation piece for his dining table, complete with removable, tiny, black slaves crammed into the decks. But when the great Demosthenes of the revolution sounded out his colleagues in the National Assembly he found that only three hundred out of twelve hundred deputies supported abolition, and that pragmatism intervened just as decisively as it would at Westminster two years later—and for precisely the same reason. Put *fraternité* and the Indivisible Rights of Men and Citizens up against the national-imperial interest, and even the most grandiloquent friend to humanity would retreat into the shell of a hardened chauvinist. The first priority, Clarkson was told over and over, was to secure the revolution, and anything that might, however unjustly, be deemed to undermine it would be viewed with suspicion. Clarkson himself began to be targeted for attack by militants, and was even accused of being a British spy.[10] Lafayette waxed fulsome in writing to Clarkson, just before the latter returned to London in February 1790, that "He hoped the day was at hand when the two great nations, which had hitherto been distinguished only for their hostility, would unite in so sublime a measure [abolition] and that they would follow up their union by another still lovelier, for the preservation of eternal and universal peace."[11] In the mutual embrace of freedom the two nations, Lafayette suggested, might even become one! But it was precisely this fear that Lafayette was an aristocratic cosmopolitan that demonized him in the eyes of narrower revolutionary militants, especially in Paris. The hard fact was that, for all its professions of universal brotherhood among men, the revolution was always, fundamentally, about the remaking of France *toute seule*.

Back home, precisely the same doubts about allegiance now shadowed Clarkson, complicating his work, and it would only get worse after he rashly joined the London Bastille Day celebrations in 1791. Much had happened in France to tarnish, in some English eyes, the original lustre of the summer of 1789: lynchings from the *lanternes*; the scenes at Versailles when crowds of market women and other citizens had burst in on the king and queen in their private apartments, forcing them into a public embrace of the tricolor and an ignominious march back to Paris. Lurid and exaggerated reports of physical assaults on the person of Marie Antoinette and the massacre of the Swiss Guards were what had finally turned the romantically tempered Edmund Burke from a warm supporter into a permanently outraged enemy of the revolution, much to Clarkson's distress. Although Burke still gave his support to the Committee for Abolition, others were given pause by the sugar lobby's accusation that abolishing the slave trade was tantamount to encouraging "revolutionism." When a bloody rebellion broke out in St

Domingue, they claimed to be vindicated in their argument that any interference with the status quo would be bound to end in massacre and destruction. Clarkson pointed out that there had been rebellions in the West Indies long before the campaign for abolition had started, and that *not* to do something about it was to court catastrophe of precisely the kind unfolding in the French sugar islands. But the argument fell on deaf ears. Instead, perennial considerations of expressly British imperial welfare and security, menaced, so its guardians said, by misguided utopian interference, had their effect on the parliamentary vote of the 19th of April 1791. By this time, the French friends of abolition in France were in no position to do their bit for a common campaign. Lafayette was a beleaguered figure believed to have connived with the queen for the restoration of royal power. Mirabeau, who had fallen under the same suspicion, was dead, and so, for the moment, was the grand vision of a French imperial abolition that would be more than just rhetorical lip service. Why, then, the anti-abolitionists asked, give an even more dangerously bellicose and fanatical France the gift of a destroyed British sugar trade?

The argument did its damage; the vote was lost. But could anything be rescued from the "retarding"? To sustain the faith of the tens of thousands of Britons who had enrolled in the crusade against the slave trade over the past four years some sort of energetic action was needed. Responding, as he always did, to the crisis of the moment, Clarkson hit on an idea of spectacular creative simplicity: rejection of West Indian sugar. Proclaimed tainted by the blood of Africans, the confection was declared moral poison. Thousands heeded the call, replacing Caribbean by East Indian sugar, or substituting honey or maple sugar. The campaign went from London bakers to Scottish vicarages and, through its domestic appeal, made wives, mothers and cooks the guardians of Christian wholesomeness.[12]

There was also a project that, if supported by the government, might yet compensate for the failure of Wilberforce's motion. The presence of Thomas Peters in London, and his openness to the possibility that the free blacks of Nova Scotia might be willing to transplant themselves to Sierra Leone, suddenly made the prospects of reviving the Province of Freedom much brighter. Through the agency of the St George's Bay Company, which had sent out the *Lapwing* to pick up the survivors of King Jimmy's raid, Clarkson and his colleagues ambitiously imagined a beacon of commercial and moral energy radiating out into the African continent from Sierra Leone. In 1788 Clarkson had met the Swedish naturalist Carl Bernhard Wadstrom, who had been to West Africa, and helped publish the Swede's attack on the slave trade. Unlike Henry Smeathman, Wadstrom seemed to be all soundness and science; and his own relatively optimistic assessment of the potential of the region, indeed, his eagerness to return to help establish a free province there, infected both Thomas and John Clarkson with a fresh burst of enthusiasm. They told Sharp they would themselves be happy to go to Sierra Leone, and were so convincing that Sharp happily passed this news on to the settlers, asking them to set aside reserved lots for the incoming distinguished gentlemen from Cambridgeshire.

The business of the parliamentary campaign and the burning of the settlers' village had postponed this ambition. But Thomas Clarkson still clung to his cheerful vision. At the back of a reborn town, set in a busy harbour, would stretch hundreds of little farms, busily cultivated by their freeholders, growing melons and beans and rice for themselves and cotton, gum, pepper, dyewood, coffee and, of course, sugar for the market. In no time at all, Clarkson thought, free sugar would cut the world price in half and capture the global market. And since nowhere in all Africa rivalled Sierra Leone as a natural harbour, it would also be a receiving and exporting station for goods from the whole West African coast and even the caravan trade across the Sahara! Ivory and gold would come to St George's Bay, and for the first time it would not come on the backs of slaves. In no time at all Britons would be trading with 50 million Africans. The plan to replace the old, infamous Royal African Company, which had done virtually nothing but slave, with the new Sierra Leone Company, which would strictly forbid it, was taken to the government. It was warmly received by Henry Dundas, Pitt's Secretary for the Colonies—not least because it seemed a way to pre-empt the always opportunist French.

News from Alexander Falconbridge, the company's agent in Sierra Leone, further heartened the supporters of the project. Up-river, he had found sixty-four survivors of the Province of Freedom—a pitiful remnant, to be sure, of the four hundred who had sailed out on the *Atlantic* and the *Belisarius* four years before. But, Falconbridge reported, whatever their distress, they had no wish to end the story there. On the contrary, they had been overjoyed to realize that they had not been forgotten, and had told Falconbridge they should very much like to return to the site of their original village.

Falconbridge, the former slave-ship surgeon, now did what he could to resurrect the Province of Freedom. At Robana he and his wife were granted a palaver—even though Anna Maria had caught the Naimbana in a "state of dishabille . . . in a loose white frock and trowsers."[13] During their meeting, the Naimbana changed his splendid costume three times, from purple coat to black velvet to scarlet cape, smiled constantly while chuckling at the foreign "rogues" and expressed (through Griffith, his African-American son-in-law and interpreter) his warm friendship for his brother King George. After receiving fifteen hundred "bars" and £39 he agreed to renew the lease on the land that had been granted originally to Thompson and the settlers. Falconbridge sent his Greek deputy with the cutter up-river to the island of Pa Boson, the chief who had sheltered the fugitives. Meanwhile, Anna Maria walked around Robana in a state of agitated half-excitement, half-horror, through a landscape of fetishes (rusty cutlasses and animal remains) at the foot of poles. She looked a little too closely at the sheen of bodies heavily greased with palm oil, listened to the Temne drums, admired the brilliantly striped taffeta of the queens' robes, and gaped at the pendulousness of mature women's breasts, a fashion she was astounded to discover was, among the local people, universally desired.

Not far from Captain Thompson's hill was an abandoned Temne village of seventeen huts, which was declared suitable for the rebirth of the settlement. When the cutter arrived, bearing the bedraggled company of blacks with the seven white wives whom Anna Maria decided must have been prostitutes, she thought it one of the most depressing spectacles she had ever seen. But the misery was dispelled, at least for a moment, as Falconbridge distributed clothing brought in the *Lapwing*, and made a buck-up speech worthy of a small town alderman or a beleaguered brigadier, promising, should they show themselves willing, that they should have tools and weapons to protect themselves and all would be well. Finally, with a flourish "he named the place GRANVILLE

TOWN after their friend and benefactor GRANVILLE Sharp Esq., at whose instance they were provided with the relief now afforded them."[14] Huzzah. God bless.

So there was, after all, a saved remnant. Together with the Black Pioneers, whom Peters would bring over from Nova Scotia, they might yet make something of Granville Town. The only person unhappy about all this was Granville himself. He had been assured, not least by Clarkson, that the new Sierra Leone Company would be a dagger to the heart of the slave trade, but he could not quite believe it. His dream of a society built on black Frankpledge had perished, destroyed as much by white pusillanimity and cupidity as by the torches of King Jimmy. For this new place would be, he protested, barely bringing himself to write the word, a *colony*. He had not thought he would ever be in the business of establishing commercial colonies. The Province of Freedom had belonged to those who lived in it (never mind that it had actually belonged to the Temne and the Sherbro). Now it was to be the property of the Sierra Leone Company, and the settlers merely there by the company's grace. Certainly, when things had become difficult, he had been ready to transfer administration from himself to the St George's Bay Company, but only on condition that the essential political character of the Province of Freedom—self-rule, watch and ward, the freehold of the lots—remained sacrosanct. In the proposals for incorporation of the new company all this seemed to have been done away with, replaced by the distant government of a board of directors and, even worse, by their appointed (white, he assumed) councillors in Sierra Leone itself. What was left—just black juries and constables? Gone was the currency in units of public common labour; gone his experiment in direct black democracy in the assembled Common Council; gone the justice and "liberty" that had been the heart of his enterprise.

What was Sharp to do? He could not bring himself to write off the whole enterprise, as Equiano and Cugoano had done. He knew that the handful of survivors in Africa still placed their trust in him, and that he owed them whatever measure of benevolent vigilance he could still exercise. His name still meant something, surely. So, with deep misgivings, Granville Sharp accepted the new company and even a place among its directors. But he made sure to write to well-disposed Members of Parliament requesting the provision of certain safeguards for the settlers. He worried that, in a more purely commercial system, the settlers would be forced to sell produce cheaply to the company, which would then sell it dear at home. Should those prices not be satisfactory to them, the settlers ought to be able to ship it themselves at nominal cost. It should be understood that they held their land freely, not as lease-bound tenants, and that it should be automatically inherited by their children. Any land not used for cultivation ought to be set aside for commons, where settlers might graze cattle, hunt or fish. And, most important, there should be a single, race-blind system of justice.

Some of Sharp's provisions became articles of incorporation. But even as an exercise in capitalist colonialism the company still faced strident opposition from the slave and sugar lobby, especially in Liverpool. But Thomas Clarkson was optimistic. Many MPs, he thought, were nursing a guilty conscience over their vote against abolition of the slave trade and would vote for the company, or at least abstain from opposition, to feel a little more Christian. He was right: the proposal passed easily through both Houses of Parliament. The company came into being in July 1791 with Henry Thornton, a young Evangelical banker (and William Wilberforce's cousin), as its first chairman. Mobilizing the capital of the faithful, especially Quakers and Evangelicals, produced an initial fund of £42,000. Now as a director of the company, Thomas Clarkson took his new passion on the road, boasting of the millions of Africans who would shortly be trading with Britain. A one-man chamber of commerce, he developed the habit of keeping in his pockets samples of peppercorns and coffee beans, which he would invite guests to sample, having first roasted the latter in a shovel over an open fire.[15]

A new page was about to be turned in the epic history of the African-Americans who had opted for British freedom. But everyone concerned with the rebirth of the Sierra Leone venture recognized that its success depended on a transfusion of fresh blood from Nova Scotia. It became a commonplace, when lamenting the fate of the first settlement, to remark that perhaps it had not been made from the most promising human material; that *those* "poor blacks" had been, after all, dependent on charity for some years and were unaccustomed to the challenges of hard work. But the Nova Scotians, from what Peters had said, were the cream of the black loyalists and would need no homilies about perseverance in adversity. Just how many of them would emigrate, however, was uncertain. Henry Dundas, on behalf of the government, assumed no more than perhaps thirty families, which would nonetheless be a good start and perhaps all that the infant settlement could, for the moment, absorb. In conversations with Clarkson, Peters himself estimated no more than a hundred-odd souls. But however many might make the move, it would be done with the blessing and protection of His Majesty's government. On the 6th of August Dundas wrote to Governors Parr and Thomas Carleton in Canada, enclosing copies of Peters's petition and implying that they would have to address its grievances. An inquiry should be launched to see if land had been withheld, for, if Peters were right, his people would "have certainly strong grounds for complaint." Redress should be made, but for any blacks not wishing to stay the government was committed to providing free passage to Sierra Leone and resettlement on land there, or, should the alternative be more attractive, military service in free black regiments in the West Indies.[16] That two of Britain's colonial governors were being required by the Westminster government to pay serious attention to the complaints and concerns of an illiterate sergeant of the Black Pioneers, someone they had brushed aside as an inconsequential gadfly, was a breathtakingly improbable turn of events.

Peters was to return to Nova Scotia himself to spread the word among the black communities. In addition, agents on the spot, specially appointed by the company, were to interview and gather together any who wished to emigrate, whether to Africa or the Caribbean. But given what Peters had told them about the conduct of the white loyalists towards the blacks, not to mention their dependence on them as a source of cheap labour, Clarkson and Sharp worried whether their sergeant would be capable of ensuring that the wishes of government and the company were faithfully executed. Someone else, someone white, needed to go to Nova Scotia: someone of tenacious determination, irreproachable integrity and inexhaustible energy; someone capable, not just of canvassing the blacks, but of chartering a ship and organizing the voyage and seeing it safely to Sierra Leone, after which a "superintendent" appointed by the company would take over.

Heads were scratched, wondering who such a paragon might be. Thomas himself was far too busy to be spared. But then, with a sudden unexpected alternation of joy and sobriety, he thought of his brother.

H E HAD ALWAYS BEEN the "other" Clarkson—second born, perfectly affable, sweet-tempered Johnny, easy in his disposition, not
a great engine of thought and deed like Thomas and not, perhaps, destined for great things, but always willing to do his duty and do it without cavil. The two brothers were affectionate, perhaps because (aside
from the same prominent Clarkson nose) they were so dissimilar, and if
profession were decided by physique and temperament, they ought to
have changed places. Thomas, the clergyman, was big-boned and
square-jawed, with a great forehead, as burly as a carthorse and hopeless at small talk. John, the naval officer, was slender, tall, naturally so-
ciable, with somewhat delicate features and the quick animation and
tender sentiment that, beside the adamant Thomas, made him seem almost puppyish. The younger brother was as much in awe of the elder
as the rest of well-disposed Britain, which is to say, abjectly.

Yet young John Clarkson had certainly not been sheltered from the
world's pounding. He had been two years old when his father, the Wisbech schoolmaster, died, leaving the widow, Anne, not only bereft, but
a martyr to crippling rheumatism. Each year she would take the three
children (for there was a sister, also called Anne) to stay with their cous-
ins, the Gibbses of Horkesley Park in Essex. There, amidst the usual
re-landscaped pastoral of the times (ornamental sheep, tall sash windows on the west front), the young Clarksons encountered blue coats
and gold braid, for the Gibbses were married into the naval clan of the
Rowleys, and it was with Captain Joshua Rowley that the twelve-year-
old John Clarkson had his entry into the Royal Navy. So while Thomas
was parsing Latin poetry and steeping himself in Erasmus at St Paul's
School, John slung his hammock aboard HMS *Monarch*, a seventy-four-
gun man-of-war as a cadet. There he spliced rope, diligently got to grips
with his sextants and quadrants, climbed aloft to keep watch above the
rolling ship, and learned that it was his duty to stand by the guns during an action, pistol cocked, quite ready to shoot anyone attempting to
flee the deck.[17]

In five and a half years as cadet, midshipman and acting lieutenant
John Clarkson served on nine ships, from a third-rater man-of-war such
as the *Monarch* to a swift, predatory frigate named the *Proserpine*, ending

up on the trim little raiding sloop *Bloodhound*. His apprenticeship in the navy coincided almost exactly with the American conflict, so by the time he was commissioned lieutenant, in March 1783, he had experienced just about everything the wartime navy could throw at him. When barely more than a child he had watched as sailors had plunged headlong from the top mainmast, one to his death on the guns; had become inured to the grim ceremony of daily floggings (cracks, grunts, opened flesh sluiced with brine); had felt the sickening impotence of a great ship run aground in a violent gale, the stern wheeling madly about as the crew frantically dumped everything overboard except the guns; had cheered himself hoarse as the king was rowed through the fleet at the Spithead Review; had registered in his bones the juddering smash and splinter of a direct broadside, so violent that it felt as if the walls of the vessel would fall away; had watched helplessly as mainsails shredded by fire collapsed, shrouding the deck like a suddenly disarticulated fallen seabird; had skidded in the miry blood of the gundeck despite the sand strewn to prevent it; had seen an officer's arm taken clean off by a cannon ball in battle and he not so much as utter a cry; had agonized at the excruciating deliberateness of manoeuvre either getting into, or out of, lines of fire; and, worst thing of all, had stared, paralysed, at the brute carnage of an unequal boarding, his own shipmates whooping as they hacked and cleaved and shot their way through the pitifully determined crew of a small French sloop, the *Sphinx*, a massacre he could never afterwards quite put out of his mind.[18]

Amid so much action, there was no time nor place nor point for Midshipman Clarkson to develop a tender conscience. For much of the American Revolutionary War John had been stationed in the Caribbean, where Admiral Rodney had been ordered by the Admiralty to engage the French as much as he could so as to keep them from blockading British America or seizing British sugar islands. If he could, at the same time, perhaps snatch some of theirs or those of the Spanish, the Sea Lords would be most tremendously obliged. During those years, slavery was all around John Clarkson and he showed no signs of minding. Some of the gunners and powder men were slaves, some free. In harbour, in Barbados and St Lucia, slaves manned the cutters, piloted the ships to safe anchorage, bore hogsheads on their carts and bales on their backs; and as yet more shackled Africans were auctioned near the quay.

In languid Jamaica he heard the drums for Jump-Up and John Canoe; saw the creole women parade their satin in the sun; watched young planters, some his own age or less but sallow with fevers and debauchery, tumble groggily from the taverns—and never, ever, did he give a thought to the iniquity of that world.

That was before the *Zong* atrocity; before his brother Thomas's Hertfordshire epiphany by the roadside; before he had ever heard of Granville Sharp and James Ramsay. But John had barely slipped into his lieutenant's coat when the war against the Americans and the French ended. Like thousands of other young officers, he found his ship decommissioned and he himself put on half pay. Family connections and friends were importuned to see if someone could find John a ship, but no one could; and he managed to talk himself out of an interview with Lord Howe for the command of a small cutter off the East Anglian coast. At an uncharacteristic loose end, he drifted, rather than sailed, into the infectious aura of his older brother's non-stop zeal. He began to read, to talk, to breathe abolition, and then, with his own share of genuine emotional fervour, to act. He had, after all, practical assets to bring to Clarkson and Wilberforce's campaign: a first-hand knowledge of the West Indies and of matters nautical. He helped Thomas ferret around the dockyards for shy witnesses and reluctant testimony; examined bills of lading with a seafarer's eye; and wrote it all up for the committee whose meetings he punctiliously attended. Some of his old shipmates were not pleased by this conversion. One of them, John Matthews, had published an account of Sierra Leone, where he had travelled, in order to defend the slave trade. The Rowleys hurrumphed, and made noises about there always having been such things and leaving well alone. The Bishop of Bangor told John yes, well, but they have such disagreeable noses, do they not? To which the young man replied, in the slightly sanctimonious but morally impeccable manner that was to be the mark of the new John Clarkson, that he felt sure God would not make anything disagreeable.

He still wanted a commission. And briefly, in 1790, with a war scare—against Spain rather than France—one came up in the shape of Rodney's old flagship, HMS *Sandwich*, now reduced to acting as a receiving station for the unfortunates press-ganged into service. It was about as squalid a post as could be imagined, and one that both Jonas Hanway and Granville Sharp had spent much energy attacking. But for the last time John Clarkson put his career above his humane conscience. Although the brothers did not entirely sever relations over this ugly work, Thomas was aghast at John's defection and pointedly took to seeking out and caring for the wives and children of men seized by the gangs. One of them, distraught and with a babe in arms, told Thomas her husband was aboard the *Sandwich*. A boat took them out to the ship, where John gave his brother and the weeping woman the grievous news that the man had already sailed.[19]

The friction ended when the *Sandwich* was put out of commission altogether in May 1791, around the time that the Sierra Leone Company got its incorporation. John was once more available, and reconciled with his hectically busy brother. He was at a crossroads. There had been an auspicious engagement to Susannah Lee, the daughter of a City banker and East Anglian landowner. At twenty-seven years old, John could look forward to the inoffensive life of a philanthropically inclined, rather pious country gentleman—should he not be called back to the fleet. But those to whom he was most devoted—his brother Thomas and William Wilberforce—had entirely other ideas.

It seems likely, knowing that the company wanted someone to go to Nova Scotia to second Peters's efforts, that John volunteered rather than was pushed by Thomas. But he must have known how pleased his brother would be at this initiative; how the goodness of the one commission would erase the infamy of the other. From the company's and the committee's point of view they could not have had anyone better. John Clarkson was still young, just twenty-seven—but then the prime minister, Pitt, had first attained his high office at three years younger than that! And if there was to be some sort of sailing from Nova Scotia to Sierra Leone, who better to manage it than the lieutenant, seeing that he represented a marriage of naval experience and godly zeal?

Perhaps most compelling was the indisputable fact that William Wilberforce loved John Clarkson at least as much as did his own brother. John's impishness was a refreshing change from Thomas's uninterrupted solemnity and goodness. It was possible to be sly with John. Wilberforce, five years older, addressed him in letters and sometimes in speech as "dear Admiral" and gave the impression that there was winking and even horseplay between the two of them. Surrounded though they were by all this gravity, they were still boys. But the boys would do the work of men, and tough saints at that. That the "Mission," as it was already called, would be the making of the young lieutenant Wilberforce had no doubt. He personally saw to it that members of the government, such as Dundas and Evan Nepean, the under-secretary responsible for Canadian matters, would provide the necessary letters of instruction, authority and introduction that would ease John's way in Halifax. To Nepean, Wilberforce wrote that he had the utmost faith in John Clarkson, a "young Man of very great merit & a thousand good qualities both professional & personal amongst which, believe me, discretion is one . . . added to all this he is a person for whom I feel a very sincere Regard."[20] On the 5th of August John Clarkson requested and was granted a twelve-month leave from the navy.

His brother Thomas, of course, was not about to slow down. He was touring again, promoting what was now called the Anti-Saccharine Campaign and chasing up the Sierra Leone subscriptions. He walked for pleasure only at night. He wrote letters while he ate. When his Shropshire host, the Reverend Plymley, was a little later for dinner than arranged, Clarkson voiced his regret at the precious minutes wasted and got Katherine Plymley, the man's sister, to furnish him with pens, ink and desk forthwith. After he was obliged, Clarkson then suggested she might like to seal the letters as he polished them off, to avoid squandering further time. Always mindful of the good of the cause, Thomas instructed John to keep a journal of his mission, for he thought that such a document, properly edited and published (by him), could be of inestimable value to the anti-slavery crusade. Obedient as always, John promised to do this.[21] Then he went to see his fiancée, Susannah, to get her blessing for, or at least consent to, the postponement of their marriage. It was not, after all, as if he would be gone for years. His work was to see whether there were any takers in Nova Scotia for the Sierra Leone colony; and, if so, to get them there. That was all. The company in its wisdom would then appoint a governor or a superintendent. Within a year at the outside he would be home; satisfied, he trusted, with a high vocation properly fulfilled.

John boarded the *Ark* at Gravesend, twenty miles down-river from London. Then, suddenly, his older brother seems to have had an attack of apprehensiveness about the venture. "In the Rivers of Africa, take care of the Allegators [sic] and on the land, of the snakes,"[22] he wrote in a parting letter; but his fretfulness went deeper than this cautionary advice. He could not quite let go of John; he needed a more complete farewell. And the winds—adverse and blustery—were with him, if not with the *Ark*. Progress into the Atlantic was out of the question. Thomas, who seldom interrupted his carefully planned itinerary for anything so sentimental, now adjusted it to take in visits to Plymouth and Exeter and rode frantically southwest trying to discover just where the *Ark* had put in, finally catching up with John at Weymouth. There was a last serious encounter, a last embrace, and—for these were, after all, the Clarksons—doubtless a quiet, anxious prayer.

W AS IT halfway across the Atlantic, with an autumnal fog so dense that the *Ark* almost collided with a brig right under its lee, that John Clarkson first experienced an untimely sinking feeling? He kept recalling Wilberforce's strange advice before he had embarked. Do not be too close to Peters, Wilberforce had written him in early August, lest you share in any blame he might incur; cultivate the governors; be careful not to oversell the scheme.[23] It was not counsel designed to reinforce his equanimity, which now and again would suddenly darken like the colour of the waves when the sun was crossed by cloud.

> During the voyage, my mind has been constantly occupied with the importance of my mission. I see it in a different point of view to what I did when first I offered my services, for then I was influenced by the feelings of the moment in consequence of the affecting story I had heard Peters relate and the difficulty the Directors seemed to have finding a suitable person to conduct it; but when I got to sea and had time for reflection, the case was altered. I had then leisure to perceive the magnitude of the undertaking and although I felt an equal desire to assist these unfortunate people yet I almost shrank from the responsibility I had imposed upon myself, but having embarked in it I had no alternative but to go on.[24]

Was he to be, then, Jonah rather than Moses? Constant self-interrogation was a habit of the Evangelical cast of mind. But hitherto he had not been much beset by the kind of doubt that came flooding in along with an equally stern summons to duty. Suppose Peters, for all his obvious integrity and passion, was *not* right, and that the blacks were better off staying where they were? For Sierra Leone, to be sure, would have its own share of risks and perils. Why, then he would be most culpable of misleading them. True, he came armed with a document, in the form of a handbill published by the company in August 1791, that could be posted or be read to the blacks, and which promised precisely what they did not presently have: a guaranteed plot of land to cultivate (twenty acres per man, ten for his wife and five for each child), and a system of justice that would include black juries. The handbill also contained the first explicit anti-discrimination document in Western history, a strict instruction from the government that "the civil, military and commercial rights and duties of blacks and whites shall be the same and secured in the same manner."[25] And above all, as Sharp had insisted, there was to be no slavery tolerated in Granville Town, nor were any of the agents of the company, much less settlers, to engage in the traffic themselves. So it would be a new place for them, and surely an improvement over their experience in Nova Scotia. All the same, Clarkson thought, he owed it to them (and perhaps to himself), as Wilberforce had counselled, not to advertise this future with excessive enthusiasm so that only the most determined would go. He would simply state the policy of the company and His Majesty's government and then leave it to the good people "to make their own choice, for I considered them as men having the same feelings as myself and therefore I did not dare to sport with their destiny."

On the 7th of October the *Ark* dropped anchor in the broad harbour of Halifax. Standing on deck, Clarkson was charmed by the jumble of yellow and white houses climbing the hill. But he was already nervily impatient to set about his task. Lodgings were rented in the merchants' coffee-house by the harbour, where he was called on by Lawrence Hartshorne, the Quaker merchant who was the company's agent in the Halifax area and who struck Clarkson right away with the frankness and modesty of his character, qualities he would find in short supply among other white Nova Scotians. A group of Swedenborgians put in an appearance; they were especially well disposed to Clarkson's mission, since their Church professed the belief that in Africans were to be found the true uncorrupted spirit of Christianity. Thomas Peters, Clarkson learned, had preceded him and already left Halifax for Annapolis. That Peters had received a warm and cooperative welcome from Governor Parr he presumed unlikely.

That same afternoon John Clarkson presented himself and his instructions to Parr, who, even before Peters's arrival, knew about both men through the letter sent by Dundas on the 6th of August. What Clarkson did not know was that there had been a further communication from Evan Nepean, which, in a gesture of mysterious underhandedness, had already undercut his authority. The gist of Nepean's note was to counsel Parr not to hasten Clarkson's enterprise unduly. If, indeed, it could be somewhat retarded, that might be politic. Just why Nepean (and perhaps Dundas) should have wanted to express second thoughts so directly against the spirit and letter of their own official instructions is unclear, unless they concurred with Parr's own view that to promote the Sierra Leone expedition was to invite trouble from the white loyalists, perhaps even hasten a mass defection back to the United States. And Parr and Thomas Carleton, of course, were bound to take exception to the implication of Peters's complaints, since it reflected badly on their own stewardship.

The next day Parr gave a dinner for Clarkson, with the notables of Halifax in attendance. They included Michael Wallace, naturally, and Bishop Inglis, who had formerly been vicar of Trinity Church in New York and who was, at best, lukewarm in his sympathy to the blacks (his pews, after all, were closed to them except in the gallery). Also at the table was a Mr Hammond, a British diplomat to the United States, who had come to Halifax in the Falmouth packet. Suspiciously encouraged by the governor, Hammond said that on the boat he'd heard reports of the annihilation of the Sierra Leone settlement by local natives. His gloomy account led Parr to make sceptical noises about the wisdom of any mass departure of Nova Scotian blacks for so perilous a destination. Clarkson, of course, knew all about King Jimmy's attack of 1790, and supposed this latest report to be of a second, purported raid on the village re-established by Falconbridge. But, already alert to what might be a self-interested campaign of dissuasion, Clarkson dismissed the veracity of this latest "intelligence." But Parr wouldn't let it go, insisting he had heard many similar reports of the unhappy fate of the Sierra Leone settlers. Then, at Parr's table, against the backdrop of goblets and silver, the tall, nervous young man in his lieutenant's blue, with his face and bright eyes, discovered his own authority. Neither the directors nor His Majesty's government, he said smartly (and a little officiously), could possibly have countenanced his mission, nor authorized him to make the offer of transport to Sierra Leone, had they had any reason to believe such reports. There must have been some unfortunate misunderstanding on the part of these informants. At this point, so Clarkson wrote in his journal, "the conversation dropped by the Governor pushing about the bottle . . . I could plainly see that the Governor would rather I should not succeed in my business . . . probably from an idea that if the people were averse to leaving the province it would be a good argument to prove that they were content."

All the same, the news unsettled Clarkson after he had begun to spread word of the company's offer of resettlement in Halifax and neighbouring villages, such as Preston, and deepened his self-inflicted anxieties. Perhaps it would be prudent that "arms and ammunition . . . be sent out with a proper Armourer" to Sierra Leone? But then he could not prevent the romantic imagination from taking hold. Visions of "his" blacks set upon by hostile tribes on arrival in Africa preyed on him; worse, perhaps his masters in London had kept something from him and *knew* he was being sent on a wild goose chase. Why, then, of what account was *he*? And how would he ever forgive himself for leading the blacks into yet more suffering?

'I will tell you now," John wrote to an imaginary reader—himself, perhaps, or his brother—as he collapsed into the stream-of-consciousness broken syntax that betrayed his inner agitation,

> . . . what will certainly happen, should I meet with any determined resistance [in Africa] while the people are under my protection; I shall keep uppermost in my thoughts that I have several innocent men under me, many of whom were comfortably settled in peace and quietness and would have been well content, had it not been for the inclemency of the weather for some part of the year—that these people placed a confidence in me, to perform the promises made by the Company and assured by me that there was no immediate danger from the kings of the country, but that I thought it necessary that all good citizens should be on their guard—that

these poor unfortunate men have, ever since Europe called herself
Enlightened, experienced the greatest treachery, oppression, murder and everything base, that I cannot name an instance where a
body of them collected together have ever had the promises made
them performed in a conscientious way; and therefore, after considering what I have said in its fullest intent and particularly after
recollecting that these people were in peace and quietness before
they put their confidence in me, I shall be at a loss (supposing we
meet with resistance) to convince them of the Integrity and real
feeling of my heart towards them, and I do declare that you will
never see me more if any thing of the kind should happen, for I will
sacrifice my life in the defence of the meanest of them on board,
sooner than they should entertain a doubt of the sincerity of my
intentions . . .[26]

What exactly was John Clarkson threatening, should he, at journey's
end across the ocean, discover he had been wilfully misled and, worse,
had unknowingly misled the blacks? Armed resistance? Suicide? And
what had suddenly brought on this passionate, even violent, private
outburst?

First, he had been keeping company in Halifax with men who were
all too ready to confirm the reports of the systematic mistreatment of the
free blacks. The two principal legal officers of Nova Scotia, Chief Justice
Sampson Blowers and Attorney-General Thomas Strange, regularly
heard cases that grieved and outraged them and that had, in fact, made
them the advance guard of a small faction in Halifax that favoured the
complete outlawing of slavery in the province. Then Lawrence Hartshorne had introduced him to the Quaker loyalists, who, in common
with Friends in Britain and America, had always been of a similar
mind.

But it was almost certainly Clarkson's own exposure to the blacks
themselves, particularly at Preston, that had caused him so much per-
turbation. Another of the worries that came crowding in on him after he
had moved from the coffee-house to rented lodgings down by the harbour concerned the procedure by which prospective emigrants were to
be allowed to leave Nova Scotia and New Brunswick. The company had
insisted that all such people should be examined for their "industry,

honesty and sobriety." Only those men and women exhibiting all three qualities would be issued with the "certificates of approbation," which would, in effect, be their passport to depart for the place that the directors had decided should be called (no more references to the eccentric Mr Sharp) "Freetown." But Clarkson and Hartshorne deeply mistrusted the agents who had been entrusted to spread the word to the blacks and to issue those certificates of worthiness. The white loyalists were already bitter about the prospective departure of the fittest and ablest blacks. Why would they help them on their way with testimonials? So Clarkson determined that he would personally see as many of the free blacks throughout the peninsula as he possibly could, read them the company's offer, take the names of those expressing an interest in going, review their fitness and sign their certificates. "The white people now threaten to refuse certificates of character to force the blacks to remain in this province; but if I see a man's hut in decent order, his land cultivated as well as it can be and if he should be a man of moderate property such as several bushels of Potatoes . . . I shall not withhold any certificate from him if his general character be good."[27]

Hence the ride out to Preston, inland a little from the north, on the Dartmouth side of Halifax harbour, together with Hartshorne and James Putnam, the Halifax barrackmaster, who had a high opinion of the people there.[28] For what Clarkson had seen in the village there had evidently made his privately mixed feelings about the enterprise still more mixed.

The hamlet, one of the few to be shared by blacks and whites, was dirt poor, with the farmers struggling to eke something out of the thin, windswept soil. The visitors heard from the Prestonians dismal stories of children fraudulently held in indentures far beyond what had been understood to be their contract; threatened with sale; the usual horrors. And only about half the Prestonians had any land to speak of at all. Those who had little "have so completely worked the land up that it will not yield half crops."[29] But then there were others, such as British Freedom, who had indeed been settled on his forty acres in addition to the "town land" on which he had built a small cabin. Having survived the worst winters and the famine years of 1788–90, those who had endured had made something of their lots, taking potatoes, corn and chickens to the Halifax market, and were successful enough for Clarkson to contract with them to supply the African fleet with laying poultry.

Still more significantly, Clarkson could see that the hundred-odd families of Preston were gathered into what he recognized as a true village; which is to say that they had a school and a church, recently consecrated. The school, supported by a fund in England, was run by Catherine Abernathy, wife of one of the cultivators, Adam Abernathy; she taught some thirty children the rudiments of reading, writing, religion and arithmetic. Some time back there had been complaints about the peculiarity of Mrs Abernathy's spiritual leanings and the excessive enthusiasm with which she imparted them to her charges.[30] But evidently she had moderated somewhat, was abiding by the Anglican catechism, and her log-cabin schoolroom, built by the blacks, was now thought exemplary. The church was shared by the three principal denominations. David George, who had visited Preston before the misadventure that had frozen his legs, had ordained one of his deacons, Hector Peters (no relation to Thomas), to minister to the Baptists and to immerse new converts. There was also room for the considerable following of the Countess of Huntingdon's "New Lights" Connexion, a more stringently Calvinist form of Anglicanism that had been spread by the missionary John Marrant—the same Marrant who had served in the Royal Navy and been greeted by the loyalist Indian chief during General Clinton's triumphal entry into Charleston in 1780. And, not least, the Methodist pastor was Boston King, the peripatetic ex-slave, chestmaking carpenter and boatbuilder of Birchtown, salmon fisher and scourge of the blasphemers, who had been sent to Preston by his church. There, for a while, he struggled with the embarrassment of his lack of learning when whites came to hear his sermons and to keep his small black congregation of around thirty. When he preached from James 2:19 ('Thou believest that there is one God; thou doest well. The devils also believe and tremble.") "the divine presence seemed to descend upon the congregation. Some fell flat upon the ground as if they were dead; and others cried aloud for mercy." After the service a Miss F knocked on the door of the chapel and proclaimed that she had seen the light, after which "all the society were melted into tears of joy when they heard her declarations [and] from this time on the work of the Lord prospered among us in a wonderful manner."[31]

The bonds of community at Preston, then, were strong enough to move Clarkson deeply. He noticed how the blacks of the village were true neighbours in that they often cared for each other's children, even when not related, or brought them into their house when a parent had to go away to work. Idealizing Preston as he did (calling its villagers, on the eve of their departure, "the flower of the black people"), it was not surprising that his worry about uprooting them never quite went away. The fact that so many Prestonians, when they heard about the company's offer of moving to Sierra Leone, responded with such ardour— seventy-nine came to Halifax to sign up—only made his pangs of queasiness worse; especially as they wanted assurances from him that in Africa they would not be turned into "debt slaves" as in Nova Scotia. What reassured Clarkson that he was doing the right thing was the flow of harrowing stories of outrageous mistreatment that the settlers habitually endured at the hands of the whites—many of them had been reduced to sharecropping, labouring for white landowners for a paltry subsistence. All in all, he was certain he was doing right by them. And he would, after all, be with them every league of the perilous wide sea.

> If we should be able to accomplish our wishes in sailing together I shall be very happy as I feel myself so much interested in the welfare of these poor oppressed people; indeed I never viewed the business I have undertaken to perform with that degree of awe as I do at this moment . . . I have desired all those who say they wish to go with me, to reflect upon the danger they are about to make and if they should make up their mind to attend me for a certainty, that they must from that moment look up to me as their Guardian and Protector and that in return I shall expect their obedience and good behaviour.[32]

THE THIRTY-TON SCHOONER *Dolphin*, one of many small vessels plying the coastal waters south and west of Halifax, was making heavy weather of the sailing, for it was late October and stiff adverse winds were blowing in from the North Atlantic. On board were John Clarkson and the young surgeon appointed by the Sierra Leone Company, Dr Charles Taylor, who was to accompany the emigrants to Africa and perhaps stay and practise in Freetown. The two men got on well, and were at one in the importance of their appointment. But they recognized that a critical moment was about to be faced. Clarkson and Taylor were travelling to Shelburne and Birchtown, where more free blacks lived than anywhere else in the province. Already surprised by the enthusiasm with which his proposals had been received in Preston and Halifax, Clarkson wondered what Shelburne would have in store. He had received a letter from Colonel Stephen Blucke, schoolmaster and apparently some sort of magistrate at Birchtown, asking for more information. He would bring it in person.

As happened this time of year in Nova Scotia, a fair morning turned into a foul afternoon when, south of Liverpool, a squall came up from the northeast and pitched the *Dolphin* about. The swell turned nasty and the master decided to put in at an inlet to wait out the worst of the weather. The haven was no more than a cove where a broad river ran gently into the whipped-up sea. There was a primitive dock and a few fishing boats, most of them hardly bigger than rowing boats, straining against their moorings; a dull beach where tawny sand, strewn with pebbles and mussel shells picked clean by the gulls, disappeared into the usual marshy reedbed; and straggly, windblown trees protruding from behind tall, glabrous rocks. Somewhere flocks of geese were honking. On the eastern bank of the river were a few scattered huts of generally miserable aspect, much weathered and not looking firm against the blows of the oncoming winter. Yet this mournfully sparse hamlet had a grand name, Port l'Hébert, given to it by some intrepid Acadian imagining a harbour sitting on this broad river that one day would take salt cod to the French Indies and perhaps, along with pelts, even back to Brittany. Clarkson, already a connoisseur of rustic indigence, feared the worst, his picturesque response to the wildness of the scene ("an illimitable wood presenting itelf in every point of view") competing with his melancholy impression of the tenuousness of survival in Port l'Hébert. Beside the cabins "a few wretched inhabitants" had cleared woebegone patches of garden where bedraggled leaves suggested that had been a corn harvest. The odd sheep and cow wandered through the mud. How could winter possibly be endured in such a place, Clarkson wondered, picturing the inhabitants as they "traverse the woods with their dog and gun properly accoutred with snowshoes in search of wild fowl, moose, deer, caribooes."[33]

The wind had grown worse and was now accompanied by driving rain. Out of both curiosity and necessity, Clarkson and Taylor knocked on the door of one of the huts, a log cabin roofed with twigs and caulk, and to their astonishment met "with the most agreeable reception from a young [white] girl of about fifteen years of age, entrusted with the care of the house and two small children, her brothers, during the absence of her parents, who had for several days been gathering in their winter stock of potatoes on the contrary side of the river." Her name was Jenny Lavendar and she was indeed, to the imagination of John Clarkson, behind her unassuming appearance, sentimental fragrance itself. "Her behaviour and polite attention would have done credit to a person of the first rank and education . . . her manners so simple, mild and unaffected, her general deportment so modest and respectful, left me at a loss for language, to express the esteem I felt for this amiable little girl." With the rain beating down outside, Jenny offered the gentlemen what she had: potatoes, buttermilk and a "few salt fish." It was a feast. Afterwards Taylor and Clarkson struggled to their feet and left the cabin, but realized, in the pitch darkness that the little creek through which they had waded to the hut was now impassably high. With some difficulty they found their way back to Jenny's hut and were received by the "little hostess with her own peculiar grace"; she then, apologizing for the rudeness of the lodging, made worse, she said, by her parents locking so much up during their absence, offered the gentlemen the bed "which contained a small infant," one of her brothers. While the two men slept in relative comfort, Jenny sat up all night tending the fire "in order to render us less sensible of the inclemency of the weather. The wind and rain was beating in at every part of the house."

The next morning, the 2nd of October, the storm had hardly abated at all, but Clarkson and Taylor found their way back to the *Dolphin*, picked up some provisions and took them back to Jenny Lavendar as a token of their gratitude. With the schooner still stuck in harbour, they decided to try to reach the cabins of the black sharecroppers on the far, eastern side of the river, which meant tramping upstream and then turning inland. The way was so beset with swamps and tangled woods that only Mi'kmaq hunting trails offered any path. Finally they reached a sad clearing where they found two black families, evidently destitute: the Shepherds and the Martins, both escaped slaves from Norfolk, Virginia. Thomas Shepherd's wife was ill and he complained bitterly to Clarkson about the necessity of sharecropping—of being denied land for so long that he had no alternative but to sharecrop for a white. "It has reduced them to such a state of indigence," wrote Clarkson, "that in order to satisfy their landlord . . . they have been obliged to sell all their property, their clothing and even their very beds." He explained the proposals to them although, in his sixties and with a sickly wife, it was unlikely Shepherd would go to Africa. Clarkson resolved to have medicine sent to the woman once he reached Shelburne. The Martins, however, seemed more promising material for Freetown.

Back at the Lavendars' Clarkson met Jenny's mother and father, who begged the gentlemen to stay a further night and then disappeared into the woods again to gather fuel. Before they took their leave, Clarkson reflected on the sad circumstances that had "entombed" so "valuable a mind" as Jenny Lavendar in a wilderness "forever secluded from the social comforts of mankind in a state of society."[34] Resuming the interrupted journey aboard the *Dolphin,* Clarkson brooded on what the episode at Port l'Hébert had meant: the simple goodness of the poor, whether black or white, at the mercy of distant power and wealth, yet not quite robbed of dignity and generosity.

On the quayside at Shelburne Clarkson literally bumped into a black man of the cloth about to get on a ship bound for Halifax. It was the Baptist David George. He had heard of the Sierra Leone proposal and intended, on behalf of his congregation at Shelburne, to find out more. Now he would hear it from the horse's mouth. The two men, so utterly different, yet matched in candour and passion, warmed to each other right away. But George seemed nervous, and, once Clarkson was settled in rooms and able to receive him, explained why. Furious at the prospect of losing their source of cheap labour, especially now that the economy of the town was in the doldrums, the whites had launched a campaign of dissuasion. Stephen Skinner, who had been charged with organizing the inquiry and departure was doing precious little to stop it—rather the contrary.

Rumours had been spread that, once landed in Africa, the blacks would be sold as slaves; that hardly anyone who went to Sierra Leone lived out the year; and that they would be subject to an onerous quit rent for their land. (There was, in fact, more than a measure of truth in this last allegation, although Clarkson was as yet unaware of it.) On the other hand, the proposal to try to revive Shelburne by turning it into a free port, thus opening it to American trade, had terrified all the free blacks there and in Birchtown, who could see nothing but the return of their old masters and their slavehunters, and imagined themselves led back to Virginia and the Carolinas in chains. They were, then, George told Clarkson, fearful to stay yet apprehensive to go. Indeed, the Birch-town community was itself divided between a group of about fifty families, led by Stephen Blucke, who were more inclined to remain, and the rest who were eager to leave before it was too late. The mood in Shelburne was so ugly on the subject of the Sierra Leone venture that George (who had personally been victimized by it) felt that violence was in the air again. "He said that . . . if it were known in the town that he had conversed with us in private, his life would not be safe . . . he cautioned us from appearing in the town or country after it was dark for as some of the inhabitants were men of the vilest principles, our busi-ness in this port might probably induce them to do us an injury." Clark-son and Taylor had meant to travel, probably on foot, across the neck of the peninsula, north to Digby and Annapolis, a journey of some seventy-odd miles, but now they took George's friendly warnings seri-ously enough to change their plans, since "it appeared probable that we might be waylaid by some of these violent people."

The next day, the 26th of October, accompanied by Taylor, Clarkson crossed the bay to Birchtown, where he was to put the company and government proposals directly to the free blacks at a general meeting. So many were interested, George had warned, that it was assumed there would be an open-air assembly, but that morning a grim, drenching rain was falling and the meeting was held instead in Moses Wilkinson's Methodist chapel. Through the downpour, the blacks of Birchtown—among them Henry Washington, Caesar and Mary Perth, and Cato Perkins and their families—converged on the chapel. Daddy Moses ar-rived, borne high on his litter followed by his faithful, and then the New Lighters and the Baptists all trooped in until the chapel was overflowing with men, women and children; latecomers huddled in the porch outside, straining to hear against the downpour. Never in his whole life had John Clarkson faced such a moment; no battle at sea had flooded him with such "awful sensations." As he mounted the pulpit, he was simultaneously exhilarated, borne aloft by the indisputable nobility of his mission, and close to feeling crushed by the weight of his responsibility. He cleared his throat but, almost at a loss for words, took refuge in an official reading and extracted a well-thumbed document from his coat: "Considering that the future happiness, welfare and perhaps the life of these poor creatures depended in a great measure upon the discourse I was about to deliver," he wrote later, "and seeing the eyes and attention of every person fixed upon me, I thought it best to state to them the intentions of Government from Mr Dundas's letter to Governors Parr and Carleton."

Then he parsed the dry formulae for the upturned faces. "In consideration of their services" during the war, and seeing that some—many—of them had not received the land to which they were entitled, His Majesty's government had directed the governors to act swiftly in amends "and in a situation so advantageous that it might make some atonement for the delay." This was incredible coming from a white British gentleman. He went on. Should there be any (and as yet there were scant few) who wished to take up the offer to serve in the army in the West Indies, they should understand that they too would have their liberty guaranteed by His Majesty and on discharge be entitled to the same land grant. Should any of them prefer to go to Sierra Leone, the government would supply free transport for them, but once there, they would be in the charge of the company, which offered them land. Rumours notwithstanding, Clarkson assured the crowd, they would not be subject to a quit rent but would pay a general tax for the support of common defence and public institutions, such as the school and hospital. Should this last option attract them, he desired them most earnestly to "weigh it well in their minds and not to suffer themselves to be led away on the one hand by exaggerated accounts of the fertility of the soil or on the other by representations of the badness of the climate." If they wished to survive, to thrive, they must needs work and work hard, otherwise they would surely starve and "I hoped they would not blame me should it not turn out according to their expectations." Above all, they should not be too hasty in selling their land and possessions, burning their boats.

Clarkson, standing in Moses Wilkinson's pulpit, had done his duty. He had been as stern and cautious as he had promised himself he should. Yet every so often, as he said something about their land or about Africa, cries and shouts of joy and exultation had gone up as if he were a prophet. And at the end—he could not help himself—he had to offer himself indeed as their father-patriarch, their white Moses. As soon as they had all got themselves to Halifax, he said,

> . . . they must look up to me as their friend and protector; that I should at all times be happy to redress their grievances and ready to defend them with my life, in return for which I expected their good behaviour during their passage, that they would give me as little trouble as possible and lend a willing hand whenever their assistance might be required, giving them, however to understand that this last request would be entirely voluntary on their parts, for they must consider themselves in every respect as passengers [not slaves!], no compulsive methods would be adopted towards them, nor would a white sailor upon any account be suffered with impunity to lift up his hand against them.[35]

When they got to Africa, Clarkson solemnly promised, he would personally see that they each got their allotted land "and declared I would never leave them till each individual assured me he was perfectly satisfied."[36]

No white man had ever spoken to them like this. They had endured captivity, then degradation. They had been sold, flogged, made to labour like beasts. Then they had endured the terrors of flight; had seen smallpox-wasted bodies lying untended and unburied on the shore, and soldiers and Pioneers shot about; had frozen in the wastes of the Nova Scotian winter and had had their entitlements stolen from them; and somehow, through their ministers and men of God, they had still not entirely abandoned hope. And here was this pale young officer in his blue coat, thin as a swaying birch, saying these things that opened their ears, their eyes, their hearts. Clarkson was done now, and again there was a burst of great exultation from the congregation, with shouts of praise and affirmation. Coming down from the pulpit he was swamped by effusive, rowdy joy. "They assured me they were unanimous in their desire for embarking for Africa, telling me their labour was lost upon the land in this country and their utmost efforts would barely keep them . . . that being sunk to the lowest pitch of wretchedness, their condition could not otherwise be meliorated and as they had already made up their mind for quitting this country, they would not be diverted from their resolution though disease and even death were the consequence." Some of them who had been born there, said, alluding to the pepper trees they remembered from their childhood, that they would be going "to their dear Malagueta."[37]

One of them put it in his own fashion when he came to see Clarkson in his Shelburne lodgings in the morning hours (nine to one) he had allotted for interviewing prospective emigrants.

> Well, my friend I suppose you are thoroughly acquainted with the nature of the proposals offered to you by His Majesty . . .
>
> No Massa me no hear nor no mind, me work like slave, cannot do worse Massa in any part of the world therefore am determined to go with you Massa if you please . . .
>
> You must consider that this is a new settlement and should you keep your health you must expect to meet with many difficulties if you engage in it . . .
>
> Me will know that Massa, me can work much, me care not for climate, if one die had rather me die in me own Country than in this cold place.[38]

Not everyone in Birchtown wanted to leave. Stephen Blucke, in fact, had taken the whole business as something of an affront to his own leadership. Stephen Skinner and other Shelburne notables had urged him to do what he could to dissuade potential emigrants. An offer of sheep and a cow had been made to those wishing to stay. About fifty had taken it up, and Blucke had written down their names and sent the list to Governor Parr.

But the scene both inside and outside Clarkson's rooms in Shelburne, every morning between the 27th and the 30th of October was extraordinary: the rooms themselves were crowded with people and, as Stephen Skinner inscribed their names on a roll, the long line of people waiting patiently outside gradually took their places within. For all his doubts about the enterprise, Skinner, a tough loyalist, was moved by the spectacle, and at dinner with Clarkson after the first day's interviews made an uncharacteristic declaration of personal appreciation, saying that whatever should come their way and whatever should become of this venture, he, Skinner, would always defend Clarkson's conduct as just, equitable and above reproach. Indeed most, if not all, Shelburnians he had spoken to felt much the same. David George, still deeply fearful for both himself and Clarkson, took a less cheerful view since he was being personally and (as usual) violently threatened for taking his Baptists en masse.

Over the next few mornings Clarkson found it difficult to keep his composure. Many of the blacks who came to see him told him they must go, not for their own sakes but for that of their children who deserved better. And this unselfishness, expressed so naturally, was often painfully heroic. A black man by the name of John Coltress, still a slave, had decided to resign himself to parting from his wife and children, for they were free and entitled to go.

> With tears streaming down his cheeks he said that though this separation would be as death to himself, yet he had come to a resolution of resigning them up forever, convinced as he was that such a measure would ultimately tend to render their situation comfortable and happy—he said he was regardless of himself or of the cruelties he might hereafter experience, for although sunk to the most abject state of wretchedness, he could at all times cheer himself with the pleasing reflection that his wife and children were happy. Much more he said which is impossible to convey in language adequate to our feelings upon this occasion. The room as usual was crowded, hearing this pathetic address and every individual both Black and white were struck with the noble and elevated sentiments of this poor Slave, joining in paying a willing tribute of tears to such an unparalleled instance of heroism. I was so much affected with this

same that admiring the man and commiserating his condition told him I would purchase his freedom if I could do it and wrote to his master immediately upon the business.[39]

Skinner, however, informed Clarkson that the law's "intricacies" made this impossible, at least in the brief time he would be at Shelburne, since Coltress was part of a complicated property dispute in which the master, Greggs Farish, was embroiled. Reluctantly, Clarkson resigned himself to being unable, for the time being, to make Coltress free. Although he persisted in his case, the owner, remained obdurate. The Coltresses would stay together, but none of them would go to Sierra Leone.

Clarkson rapidly learned that the dilatoriness of the courts would not help the blacks, so on some occasions he was prepared to ignore them altogether. At Birchtown he had heard from a black whose son was indentured as apprentice to a Shelburne butcher, a man "of the most vile and abandoned character," who had decided to return to America and take up residence in Boston. The boy would come too, torn from his family and a future in Sierra Leone. Indignant, Clarkson applied to the Shelburne magistrates but was told that, under the terms of indenture, the butcher was indeed free to take him wherever he liked. Worse, Clarkson was convinced that, once in the United States, the butcher would sell the boy as a slave. The issue seemed simple—British freedom or American slavery? The ship was loading cargo and passengers in the harbour. There was no time to lose. So what was the counsel offered to the father by the representative of HM government and the Sierra Leone Company? Kidnap your own son. Hide him in the woods until the ship has sailed. Do it. We shall worry about a trial once the butcher has gone. And the father came in secret to John Clarkson one afternoon and said: it is done.[40]

It was the right thing. "Having obtained the best legal opinion in the business I secured the boy and came forward openly to justify the measure, but no-one appearing against him, he continued with his family and was enrolled for embarkation."

IT HAD BEGUN to snow. Aboard the *Deborah,* on his way back to Halifax, Clarkson felt the deep chill. On the 4th of November, two days before his departure, David George, whom he now called friend, had been to see him. George was more anxious than ever that some sort of physical force would be used to stop the Baptists from leaving. But it was too late for their intimidation. Despite Clarkson warning against precipitate action, he had sold his fifty acres, had told Phyllis and the six children that their future was in Africa, and was now impatient to be off. Clarkson brooded that he had been too successful at Shelburne and Birchtown; that some of the blacks, panicking at the return of American masters to the free port, had acted over-hastily and sold their land cheap to unscrupulous speculators happy to snap up bargains. It was all happening too impetuously. He and the company had imagined that two or three vessels would be adequate for any emigration. But 514 Birchtowners (150 men, 147 women and 217 children) had been inscribed on the rolls in just three days, so Clarkson now had to think of chartering and fitting out an entire fleet for his black exodus. In Halifax he would need all the help he could get.

Instead, he found hindrance on every side. A fierce attack on him and the Sierra Leone scheme had been published in the Halifax press under the name "Philanthropos." It declared the scheme at best misguided and at worst a malicious design to destroy the prospects of loyalist Nova Scotia. Should they be so foolish as to depart, the writer claimed, the blacks would face certain re-enslavement, sickness and speedy death. A delegation of blacks from Preston came to see Clarkson in his rooms expressly to warn him that whites were going about reading aloud to the blacks this and other articles designed to dissuade, and to reassure him that they held such men and their utterances in the greatest contempt. The *Weekly Chronicle* conceded that "a very considerable proportion of the sooty Brotherhood" seem determined to emigrate and begged the company to take applicants indiscriminately so that the province would not be left merely with "the maimed, the halt, the blind and the lazy."[41] More seriously, Clarkson discovered that Governor Parr had decreed the application rolls at Shelburne closed. On the 12th of November, when the two men dined together, Parr explained that he had done this in the blacks' own interests, so many of them being "infatuated with the notion of a change of situation which he thought would be the means of sending many of them to their graves."[42] Clarkson took umbrage at the notion that he had wilfully misled the blacks, although he said it was indeed his personal opinion—never expressed to any black man, either in private or in public—that, having seen what they had to endure in Nova Scotia, they could only be happier in Sierra Leone. Moreover, he went on, it was an affront to the blacks as well as to the company's policy to suppose the blacks were incapable of deciding their future for themselves. "The Governor replied I might think so but he was of a contrary opinion."

Two weeks later John Parr was dead, aged sixty-six, felled by a violent attack of gout. On the 29th of November there was an elaborate funeral that Clarkson uncharitably dismissed as extravagant considering Parr's "inferior abilities . . . in my opinion not calculated for the situation he filled."[43] Parr's duties were temporarily assumed by the president of the Governing Council, Richard Bulkeley; but the sudden death of the governor undoubtedly weakened the obstruction of Clarkson's enterprise precisely at the time when he most needed to assert his authority.

Emigrants were now beginning to arrive in Halifax in numbers that were transforming the entire character of the venture. The roll at Shelburne had risen to 560 (although Clarkson thought that not all of them would be allowed to leave). Virtually the whole of black Preston, at least another 250, was bent on going. He himself had travelled to Windsor, about forty miles northwest of Halifax, to announce the proposals to isolated blacks. Wading through the deep snow, Clarkson had briefly suspended his managerial anxieties by losing himself in the romantic sublimity of the scene: pyramids of densely packed spruce rising and falling over the hillsides, all wreathed in curtains of freezing mist.[44]

On the day of Parr's funeral Thomas Peters, whom Clarkson had not seen since they both left London, arrived in Halifax, bringing with him more than ninety people from the Annapolis area and from New Brunswick. He had endured much, not least defamatory rumour that he was guilty of entrapping blacks who would then be sold by the company; Peters would supposedly collect a commission for each one re-enslaved. Whilst he was assembling the people who remained impervious to the slander in Digby, Peters had been insulted and knocked down in the streets. For once, the law was unequivocally on his side, but knowing his assailant was drunk, Peters magnanimously decided, on returning to the town, not to proceed with a prosecution.[45]

Stories such as the attack on Peters confirmed Clarkson in his desire to accelerate the exodus. But every day the enterprise was becoming more ambitious. Even by the most conservative count he would have at least eight hundred and probably over a thousand souls under his protection. Winter was coming on fast, and even if he managed to sail, as he hoped, before the 20th of December he needed to find temporary shelter in Halifax for these people, many of them close to destitute and lacking warm clothes, while he chartered, provisioned and scrupulously inspected what would now have to be a substantial fleet. With the Shelburne people about to leave en masse, he frantically tried to get detailed instructions to David George and the other leaders as if he were Noah guarding the entrance to the ark. There would be a quota of one dog per six families (although, typically, he softened the rule for puppies). No pigs were allowed on board, although poultry were to be permitted; there could be small beds and bedding, but no tables or chairs for they took up too much room. Pots and pans had to be properly secured in sealed barrels so they did not go cannonading around the holds in rough seas, banging into passengers.[46] Clarkson was also beginning to give attention to the physical needs of his black passengers. Some of them, he knew, had begun their journeying as slaves taken from Africa, and almost certainly had never forgotten the horror of the passage. He was determined that those traumatic memories should never be reawakened by conditions aboard his ships. With the print of the slaver *Brookes* in mind, Clarkson specified that the space allotted to each passenger should be at least five feet wide and that on double-decked ships there should also be at least five feet of good clearance between decks. On vessels that lacked them, ventilation scuttles would have to be cut to enable foul air to be fanned out of the compartments. Diet should not be the usual hard tack and weevily biscuit, but include ample brined or cured beef, pork and fish.

All this would cost money, for which the directors may not have originally budgeted. (The expenses rose in the end to nearly £16,000, or three times the annual cost of the Nova Scotia civil government.) Clarkson's letters to Henry Thornton and Wilberforce took on a new and increasing urgency through November, not least because since his arrival he had received not a single communication from London. Now, in the light of reality, Wilberforce's teasing about him being the "Admiral" had lost its humour. "I am sure you will feel for me when I tell you that I am to have the command and direction of not less than eight vessels," Clarkson wrote, "all of which I hope will be ready to sail by December 20th." Had he had any inkling of the magnitude of this duty, he was not at all sure he would have accepted it, but as he was now committed, he would certainly persevere. He reassured the directors that the people he would be taking were, just as they had hoped, "the majority . . . better than any people in the labouring line of life in England. I should match them for strong sense, quick apprehension, clear reasoning, gratitude, affection for their wives and children and good will towards their neighbours." Yet it would be of the greatest help to him in his proceedings, not least with recalcitrant white Nova Scotians or dubious contractors, if the directors would furnish him with some further guidance before the sailing.

JOHN CLARKSON may not have heard from the directors (including his own brother), but they certainly knew all about him. News that there would be more like a thousand than a hundred black Nova Scotians making the journey to Sierra Leone electrified the company and did wonders for its funds. The original capital of £42,000 rose first to £100,000 and then to £235,000, all fully subscribed. In between promoting the Anti-Saccharine Campaign Thomas Clarkson went about the country with his peppercorns, singing the praises of a colony that would not only redeem commerce from the loathsomeness of slaving, but begin an inevitable transformation of the entire continent of Africa. Doubtless he glowed with quiet satisfaction at what his brother had already accomplished. Henry Thornton suspended his engagement in the banking business in order to devote his time and energies to the same cause. What had begun as a consolation for the loss of the anti-slave trade had now taken on a life of its own. Even Granville Sharp, still one of the directors, seemed to have reconciled himself to it in the cause of the greater good. There would, he was told, still be elected black tithingmen and hundredors in Freetown, even though they were to be merely local officers of the peace.

In some other respects, however, the additional instructions drafted by the company in November 1791, and that would be waiting for John

Clarkson when he arrived in Sierra Leone, were a drastic and shocking departure from the assumptions he had taken with him to Nova Scotia. The most serious alteration, and the one that would make for much future trouble, was the matter of taxation. In response to anxious enquiries, Clarkson had specifically reassured the blacks that there would be no quit rent, but the company had, in fact, decided to impose one—and at the onerous rate of a shilling a year for the first year, rising to a level of 4 percent after three years. In a letter waiting at Sierra Leone, Henry Thornton explained to Clarkson that the company preferred this means of recovering "all our huge expenses" to a customs duty on produce and added, "I trust the Blacks will not consider it a grievance." They would.

Nor would Freetown be governed by them, except in the matter of local policing. And this too would come as an unwelcome surprise and be a source of deep grievance. A white man, meeting up with a group of blacks on the road to Shelburne, asked them where they were going and was told they were bound for Sierra Leone where they would all be "majesties."[47] And most of them certainly thought that blacks as well as whites would be "magistrates" of their own community. But the company had ruled this out and replaced Granville Sharp's assembly of free men with a superintendent and a body of white councillors, more akin to the governance of British Madras or Bombay than the experimental polity originally designed for Sierra Leone. The councillors would be, for the most part, the professionals deemed to be needed as stewards of the foundation: a surveyor, an engineer of works, a physician, a gardener, a chaplain and so on, all, so the company thought, carefully screened for their integrity, their enthusiasm for the settlement and their scrupulousness in abiding by the directive to be strictly colour-blind when it came to matters of administration and justice. The first superintendent was to be a decommissioned army officer called Henry Hew Dalrymple, who had testified to the Privy Council on the horrors he had seen at the slave factories in Goree. It had affected him so powerfully that, on inheriting a plantation in Grenada, Dalrymple had freed his slaves and locked the place up.[48]

But somebody was unhappy about this last preferment; Alexander Falconbridge, the company's agent, who had returned to Britain from Sierra Leone in late September 1791, a few weeks after Clarkson had sailed. He and his wife, Anna Maria, had survived a nightmare journey home on the tiny thirty-four-ton *Lapwing*: almost sunk by tornadoes en route to the Cape Verde Islands, their livestock washed overboard; most of the nine crew and passengers violently sick and feverish; their fresh water leaked from casks riddled with marine worm-holes. Anna Maria survived on a daily teacup of flour made into a pap with salt and rainwater.[49] After a period of recuperation they sailed through the islands, only for the ship to run aground. It would have certainly been driven on to the rocks of São Tomé had not Anna Maria been walking the deck on a moonlit night, seen the imminent disaster and roused the crew in the nick of time. Fearing that the schooner might break up, the passengers got themselves into a small boat (Anna bringing "a few shiftings of clothes and our bedding"), only to find there was nowhere on the rocks that could offer any kind of safe landing. "Despondency was pictured in every face! What shall we do, or what is best to be done was the universal cry. Conscious of a woman's insignificance in such matters I was silent till then, when finding a general vacancy of opinion among the men, I ventured to say 'Let us return to the *Lapwing* and put our trust in Him who is all sufficient and whose dispensations are always just.' " Whether or not providence came to her aid, Anna's instinct turned out to be sound. The ship eventually got afloat—although only to run straight into another "tremendous storm" between Cape Verde and the Azores, which lasted five days, "augmenting the miseries . . . almost unbearable and past representation."

Once their man was safely home, the company seemed to have added insult to Falconbridge's injuries, since, although the remnant of settlers had hoped he would be made their governor, he was passed over for Dalrymple. Even after a number of arguments with Dalrymple, serious enough for the directors to dispense with the new governor's services, Falconbridge was not named in his place but appointed instead as "commercial agent"—although with a trebled salary of £250 per annum, and responsibility for managing the company's investment in Sierra Leone.

Learning of the scale of John Clarkson's planned emigration, and notwithstanding his regard for Thomas, Falconbridge thought the plan imprudent, or, as Anna Maria put it (possibly in retrospect), "a premature, hair-brained [sic] and ill-digested scheme."[50] Nevertheless, whatever reservations the Falconbridges may have had were swept aside by their delivery to the directors of one piece of evidence that promised great things for the future of Freetown. He was the "Black Prince." John Frederic, the twenty-nine-year-old son of the Naimbana of Robana, had been sent, probably under the influence of the king's son-in-law, Abraham Elliott Griffith, to be educated in England. (Hedging his bets like the pragmatic ruler he was, the Naimbana had sent another son to France.) The king's England-bound son was carrying a letter from his father to Granville Sharp, promising to protect the settlers and declaring that he remained "partial to the people of Great Britain, for which cause I have put up with a great deal of insults from them, more than I should have from any other country." He hoped that Sharp would take care of his son "and let him have his own way in nothing but what you think right yourself ."[51]

The "Black Prince," who had shared all the privations of the voyage of the *Lapwing,* was described by the not unprejudiced Anna Maria as having "a person rather below the ordinary, inclining to grossness, his skin nearly jet black, eyes keenly intelligent, nose flat, teeth unconnected and filed sharp after the custom of the country, his legs a little bandied and his deportment manly and confident."[52] But if, through his education and cultivation, he could be made into a friend and ally of Freetown, then, given that his succession to the old Naimbana could not be far off, the settlement would be secure against any repetition of the King Jimmy disaster.

Invited to stay at Henry Thornton's house in Kent, and supplied with a Reverend Gambier as tutor, the prince was baptized with Thornton and Sharp standing as godfathers. Before long Sharp was able to write to the Naimbana that his son showed a "natural good disposition, modesty . . . great diligence and application to learning." Indeed John Frederic, so his tutors reported, could hardly bear to stop reading and "would express regret if he had been let into any company where the time had passed away without improvement." Taken by Thomas Clarkson to see the Plymouth dockyards, the young African could not understand what he was doing there when he might be in London, deep in his reading. Yet if the "Black Prince" seemed an almost unbelievable paragon of studiousness, he never forgot that he was indeed black and an African. "He was quick in all his feelings and his temper was occasionally warm," it was said, especially when he suspected he was being drawn out on the subject of Sierra Leone only so that white men and women could parade their superiority. In fact the prince was a dab hand at irony, retorting to those who wanted to make invidious comparisons that a country so "unfavourably circumstanced" as Sierra Leone was not supposed to have been capable of any attainments that could possibly make it worthy of a British conversation. When someone passed a remark offensive or condescending about Africans "he broke out into violent and vindictive language, and when reminded of the Christian duty of forgiving enemies responded that 'if a man should rob me of my money I can forgive him; if a man should shoot at me or try to stab me I can forgive him; if a man should sell me and all my family to a slave ship so that we should pass all the rest of our days in slavery in the West Indies I can forgive him but', rising from his seat with much emotion, "if a man takes away the character of the people of my country I can never forgive him.' "[53]

Evidently, Sierra Leone was going to be the pet project not just of those who had declared themselves its benefactors.

D AY BY DAY, the lieutenant was turning into a messiah, a reluctant saviour racked by nagging doubts about his own worth and about the fate of his mission. Yet for the sake of his people too (and by now, in December, they were his people), John Clarkson kept his terrors and his trepidations to himself, not even confiding in the good Lawrence Hartshorne. Every day, since he had made it known that his rooms in Shelburne were open to the incoming blacks for the answering of questions and the hearing of grievances, he had been swamped by crowds of them. They stood two and three deep at the back, with others trailing from the open door, while one of their number recited whatever ills worried them or threatened to detain them: debts into which they had been fraudulently ensnared, terms of indenture falsified, kidnappings, verbal and physical intimidation. To his great amazement he even had white soldiers, British and Hessians, at the door, themselves desperate to leave, soliciting him "with tears in their eyes" for a passage to Sierra Leone; something he could not give, although he felt for them, too.[54]

Although Clarkson supposed there could be nothing left to shock him, some of the stories he heard still stirred him to bitter fury. One afternoon a slight woman called Lydia Jackson had come to see him, and the tale she told was appalling.[55] She and her husband had lived near Manchester, which he had left to find work. Finding her in "great distress," a local loyalist, Henry Hedley, had invited her to work in his house in return for board and lodging. Lydia moved in, but after eight days Hedley demanded rent for her accommodation. Knowing she was destitute, he offered her the alternative of a seven-year indenture. After she refused, Hedley offered her instead a one-year indenture and drew up the papers on which she put her mark—but not, as she thought, for a single year but for a term of thirty-nine years! Still ignorant of this misfortune, Lydia was told next day that she would serve out her year with a Dr John Bolman of Lunenburg and was put on a schooner bound for that port. Bolman, a Hessian surgeon who had served with the army, let her know right away that he had paid £20 for her, that she was his for thirty-nine years and that she had better resign herself to her fate. His methods of bringing about this resignation consisted of regular doses of physical assault. Lydia told Clarkson that she had been beaten with fire tongs, had had rope tied about her face that cut into the flesh, and that in the eighth month of her pregnancy Bolman had knocked her to the floor and stamped on her belly.

Like other free blacks, Lydia Jackson, although illiterate, believed she had recourse to the courts and found a lawyer in Lunenburg prepared to present her case. Once in court, however, she was intimidated into silence on the witness stand by the terrible Bolman; case dismissed. Back at his house he told her that he had done with such an ingrate, sent her to labour on his farm with instructions to his servants to beat her as they saw fit, and periodically threatened to sell her to a West Indian planter as a slave. Lydia endured three more years of this hell before escaping, running and walking through the forest all the way to Halifax, where she took her tale of woe to Chief Justice Blowers and Attorney-General Strange. When they did nothing, she came to John Clarkson's door. Moved, he took her case to a friendly lawyer, who warned that if she sued Bolman for back wages and fraud, the case would take so long that the Sierra Leone fleet would have gone without her. Gently, understanding Lydia Jackson's burning sense of unaddressed grievance, Clarkson advised her nonetheless not to proceed with legal action, which he doubted she could win. He will not dare to take you now that he knows you are under my protection, was the comfort of his counsel. Leave him to his gall; make a new, free life in Africa.

Increasingly, Clarkson tried to find ways to skirt the law or to soften its rigour, especially when it concerned terms of indenture. Especially distressing to him was the thought that the Sierra Leone sailing might end up dividing families, some members of whom could leave and others not, and on occasions he would personally intervene to try to persuade employers to let their servants go. Caesar Smith's young daughter had three years left on her indentures to a Mr and Mrs Hughes, after which, Clarkson gloomily reckoned, with her parents gone away "this child will be sold for a slave." Unable to persuade Hughes, Clarkson tried a sentimental approach to the wife:

> I saw Mrs Hughes and solicited her in the most affecting way to induce her to give up the child; I called upon her as a mother and described the distressed state of Smith's whole family at the thought of leaving the girl behind and brought to her recollection the circumstances which occasioned the child to be indented for five years which happened in consequence of Smith's family having lost all they had in the world by their house being burnt down . . . that the poor Mother was constantly in tears about the child and I therefore hoped she would feel the case as if it were her own and do as she would be done by.

Mrs Hughes was unmoved, Clarkson sorrowfully recording that he "could not make the least impression."[56]

Sometimes, between distress and despair, it was all too much. On the 12th of December, near collapse, Clarkson recorded: "Came home today at four o'clock extremely ill from anxiety and fatigue—It is impossible to describe my situation every day. There are not less than eight hundred souls of every description here under my particular care, who come to me for all their trifling wants in spite of the regulations I have made to prevent it and perplex me more giving answers to each than any other part of the business." But whenever he was close to prostration, some fresh instance of the blacks' wish to go being shamelessly frustrated by local magistrates, masters or officials would recharge

Clarkson's engine of outrage and he would go into action for them once more. Three days earlier a group of men from New Brunswick had shuffled through the door to see him—Richard Corankapone, William Taylor, Sampson Heywood and Nathaniel Ladd. Before they would allow the four to leave, officers at St John, as elsewhere in both provinces, had demanded to see original General Birch Certificates or other passports dating from the American war testifying to their loyal service. Often, the blacks had kept these yellowing pieces of paper safe; but, considering everything that had befallen them, there were some who could not produce them on demand. As Clarkson pointed out, for the black New Brunswickers to have had (as was conceded) their land assignments registered at St John they must some time earlier have produced those documents; but because they could not do so now, at the last minute they were prevented from boarding the ship taking the other New Brunswickers to Halifax for the grand "rendezvous."

This setback, however, did not deter them. "These people were determined to quit a Country at the peril of their lives, whose inhabitants treated them with so much barbarity." They had walked the long route around the Bay of Fundy—some 340 miles—in the depths of winter, "their passage, for a few days, lying through such parts as I am convinced were never before visited by man." There was a fifth companion, but he had become lame just forty miles away from Halifax and had persuaded them to go ahead lest they miss their ship, although he was "expected every hour." Stirred by their epic perserverance, Clarkson confessed to his journal that he wished he could have given the four men some sort of immediate reward, but since he had so many in his care suffering acutely, he had to beware of any gestures that could be misconstrued as favouritism. "Prudence [must] get the better of my feelings till I have a proper opportunity of indulging them."[57]

Still the blacks continued to arrive in Halifax from every part of the two maritime provinces: another eighty from Annapolis; and over five hundred from Shelburne and Birchtown, including fifty who had been born in Africa, such as John Kizell, the nephew of a Sherbro chief, who had been kidnapped when he was just twelve and was finally going home. And, like Kizell, the vast majority of the emigrants were going as families: husbands, wives, sometimes three or four children. And, from the pregnant mothers arriving in Halifax, Taylor expected at least seven or eight more to be born on the Atlantic crossing. Put together a collection of families, simple, honest, industrious and Christian, with an almost complete repertoire of artisanal skills—smiths, sawyers, fishermen, farmers, tanners, bakers, weavers—and you surely had the makings of an ideally constituted small market town. This new Freetown would correspond exactly to the late eighteenth-century romantic view of an ideal community: neither the hell of a factory, nor the appendage to some aristocratic estate. Stripped of both the vicious criminal and the useless landowner, this would be black Merrie England in the tropics.

For the moment, however, Clarkson had a serious problem of finding temporary accommodation, made urgent when he saw twenty-two vessels arrive in Halifax harbour with people from Shelburne. Given his tortuous negotiations with the ubiquitous entrepreneur Michael Wallace, who was handling the fleet contract, it was unclear just when the fifteen ships now needed for transportation would be ready to sail, even though time was of the essence if they were to reach Sierra Leone before the onset of the devastating rains. On the day that the Shelburnians arrived, Clarkson and Hartshorne raced around the harbour area searching for a warehouse that they could use for temporary shelter. Discovering that the Sugar House Barracks might do, they had it swept clean, installed stoves, and laths on which to place bedding, and somehow managed to get it ready by the same evening. It came not a moment too soon. Many of the blacks lacked adequate clothing for the winter cold, and Clarkson appealed to the acting governor, Bulkeley, for an immediate distribution of shifts, petticoats, shirts and jackets "for more than half the people from Shelburne are entirely naked."[58] Conditions soon became so crowded in the Sugar House that Clarkson, with good reason, became worried about the spread of contagion—especially smallpox—and moved two hundred out to another warehouse. At moments when he succumbed to an overwhelming sense of the sheer impossibility of the whole venture, Clarkson would take himself down to the warehouses at time of worship and sneak in by a back door, the sole white face among a sea of swaying, singing blacks, surrendering to the pure transport of the moment. The Methodists had the best sermons, and Blind Moses Wilkinson would soar on wings of exclaimed prayer: "During this man's discourse I felt frequently distressed for him, his feelings were so exquisite and he worked himself up to such a pitch that

I was fearful something would happen to him." But David George's Baptists, gathered at the top of the Sugar House, had the best voices: "I never remember to have heard the Psalms sung so charmingly before in my life; the generality of the blacks who attended seemed to feel more at singing than they did at prayers—I left sooner than I wished fearing that David George, if he had seen me might have been confused but I have too good an opinion of him to think that the presence of anyone would in the least deter him from offering up his praises to the Creator."[59]

Dealing with Michael Wallace brought Clarkson down to earth. With the horrors of the middle passage always in his mind, Clarkson had decided to err on the side of dietary generosity. Daily breakfast was to be eight ounces of cornmeal (as mush sweetened with molasses or brown sugar); dinner, either one pound of salt fish, two pounds of potatoes and one ounce of butter, or one pound of beef or pork and half a pint of pease pudding, or bacon with turnips; and supper, rice or cornmeal again. There would be tea, bread, ale, vinegar, and some wine for the poorly. This generosity meant, of course, a bonanza for the local purveyors in Halifax who, along with the ships' chandlers, timber merchants and clothiers, suddenly began to appreciate the value after all of the great black exodus from Nova Scotia. The fifteen vessels—some of them two-hundred-ton full ships, such as the *Eleanor* and the *Venus,* and a larger number of brigs that were hardly more than coastal schooners—were necessarily drawn from local fleets around the peninsula, as were their captains and crew. Clarkson could not afford to wait much longer and therefore had to trust Wallace to make a fair bargain for the cost of charters and provisions. He suspected he was being taken advantage of, and when, as sometimes happened, that trust broke down, he and the Scotsman would have blistering rows.

At the same time that he was trying to liberate his black emigrants from imprisoning indentures or crippling debt, Clarkson had to be a scrupulous commodore of the fleet, leaving nothing and no one uninspected, from barrels of brined beef and pork to the new interior decking, often made from green planking, which he required to be thoroughly dried with charcoal fires before being certified fit for loading. There were new storms, not all of them meteorological. A few days before Christmas, with some of the black passengers already on board, Clarkson recorded an abrupt and ominous argument with Thomas Peters, probably over the stringency of the discipline he was demanding that the blacks observe on board ship. "I could not possibly make him comprehend how necessary it was for the regularity and subordination . . . he still persisted in his obstinacy; he vexed me extremely and I went to bed much indisposed."[60]

A few days later he made a gesture of reconciliation. When Peters came to him asking for a full allowance of fresh beef for each of the blacks to celebrate their last Christmas in America, Clarkson readily and happily granted the request. He was increasingly consumed by problems of human management, unable to find a healthy balance between authority and benevolence, and every day there was a new challenge to irk him. In his rooms he was besieged by families demanding to be placed in the same ship as friends and neighbours; others requested the opposite. With winter gales still precluding an early sailing, some of the ships were nonetheless docked at the Halifax wharf. As the sleet and freezing rain steadily fell, the blacks were beginning to load chests and dogs and chickens and pots and pans and bedding, as well as the boxes of seeds they were prudently taking with them—squash and pumpkin, sage, thyme and purslane, cabbage and watermelon. In the midst of these preparations, the Halifax harbour-master-general suddenly ordered them to sail away again—the penalty, he said, for having neglected to ask his express permission to tie up. Exasperated beyond forbearance, Clarkson acidly wrote, "I am sorry to observe how little the interest of Government is attended to even by those whose conduct ought to be influenced by the highest feelings of Honour and Patriotism." The masters of the ships—especially Samuel Wickham, a friend of Hartshorne's and like, Clarkson, a lieutenant on half pay—he thought decent enough company, especially after a dinner a week before Christmas, when they had stood as a man, filled their bumpers and drunk "the commodore's health." This toast was followed by three rousing cheers, a gesture he duly appreciated, although he also wished it had not been followed by carousing that continued until one in the morning.

Nothing preyed on Clarkson's mind so much as his determination to avoid anything in the voyage that could possibly remind any of the blacks of a slave passage. Never had the word "sympathy," with its demand that the fortunate enter into the sentiment and even the physical sensibilities of the less fortunate, meant so much to a lieutenant of the Royal Navy. His list of printed rules, distributed to all the masters, was, in effect, a comprehensive reversal of everything that he and his brother Thomas had learned about slave ships such as the *Brookes*. First, the ships were to be impeccable. There were to be three daily sweeps of, and between, decks. After breakfast the bed place of each black was to be scrupulously cleaned, and the lower decks were to be swabbed three times a week in the mornings (to give time for drying) with vinegar scalded by a hot iron so that "steam may get into every crevice" for effective fumigation. Every day that the weather permitted, bedding was to be aired on deck, and two days a week were to be allowed for washing of clothes. When casks of salt beef and pork were opened, the exact amount should be declared to the black captains whom Clarkson would appoint, and if there were any measure short, it was to be entered in the log book. The chests belonging to the blacks should be secured on deck and be available for opening on a specified day every two weeks in case their owners needed any items from them. Clarkson even required ships' masters to make a daily inspection of the sanitary arrangements aboard.[61]

By eighteenth-century standards this was all very extraordinary—and must have been designed by Clarkson to benefit the white crews as well as the blacks, for the mortality of the former on slaveships had become a staple of abolitionist literature. Even more remarkable were the instructions that Clarkson issued to the captains concerning the way they should behave towards the blacks. "I was fearful," he wrote just before sailing, "that the Captains and sailors of the different vessels would not behave to their passengers with that kindness and attention they had promised (from the Black People being considered in this Province in no better light than beasts)." He insisted that the blacks be "considered as passengers who have paid the price demanded by the Owners for their accommodation" and that the captains ensure that the blacks were not subjected to "ill language and disrespect as is too often the case, but that you and your crew exercise patience towards those unfortunate people whom the King is indeavouring to render more happy by sending them to their native shore."[62]

This consideration Clarkson asked to be unstintingly reciprocated.

Assuming the mien and manner of a parson, the commodore required the blacks to exhibit

> . . . a modest and decent behaviour towards the officers of the ship considering the old proverb that "soft words turneth away wrath"; this we recommend to prevent broils, not to make free with the seamen lest they in turn should make free with you and by improper behaviour bring on disturbance, to live in friendly terms with each other, to mutually bear and forbear, considering that very little inconveniences or hardships which you may experience on the passage will be of short duration we farther recommend a particular attention to Divine worship in the best way you are capable of, constantly remembering with humble gratitude the goodness and power of God and that if you conduct yourself in such a manner as to have His approbation you must be happy.[63]

If this founding fleet of the Sierra Leone Company was in no danger of being confused with a slaving expedition, neither would it quite resemble any other kind of sailing—naval or mercantile. What John Clarkson had designed was an inter-racial, floating Christian republic: bound for freedom, glory and the merited blessings of God. The journey was not just about an escape from bondage, as all the others had been; it would be an experimental voyage of social transformation. Because no distinctions would be tolerated between blacks and whites, Clarkson wrote, "they [the blacks] are to become Men." What was more, he wished them, in their own land, to throw off all the old habits of servility, not just as slaves but even as servants. "I have . . . told the men that I shall form a very unfavourable opinion of those who may show an inclination to be servants when they have an opportunity of becoming their own masters and valuable members of society if they please and that . . . the character of the Black people for ever after will depend on the manner they conduct themselves and that the fate of millions of their complexion will partly be affected by it."[64] And now it was time for the blacks to begin to exercise their own authority. Clarkson appointed forty black captains, including Peters, Steele, another Pioneer originally from St Croix, Henry Beverhout, David George and Boston King, who were to be distributed among the ships. They were to have supervisory and even judicial powers on board. In cases of drunkenness or fights, the senior black captain would appoint a panel of five to hear the offence and sentence the culprit. Only in cases of theft, violence or improper conduct to women should the offence be reported to Clarkson himself.

So if Granville Sharp's vision of a self-governing black democracy had already been sacrificed to the demands of a commercial colony, at least Clarkson went to great lengths to give the blacks, on a voyage that was bound to be fraught with all sorts of anxieties, the sense that they held their destiny in their own hands. And in some ways Clarkson's passion for the African-Americans went well beyond anything Sharp could possibly have felt. The blacks in London had been, for Sharp, a cause, and his exposure to them had been limited to those whose cases he had championed, to the "Black Poor" whose fate had given him much heartache, and to articulate advocates such as Equiano and Cugoano. John Clarkson, on the other hand, who had spent years in the slaving Caribbean without ever being moved to anger or dismay by what he saw every day in Jamaica or Barbados, had had a truly Pauline conversion. Every day for almost three months he had been surrounded by the free blacks. Old men, young women and small children had crowded about him, had opened his doors and his suddenly enlarged sympathies to their agonies; and he had counselled them in their distress, understood the depths of their bitterness and desolation, and become enraged at the whites whom he held responsible for it all. He cared for each and every one personally; was saddened that Sarah, the wife of another Pioneer, Charles Wilkinson, had died of a miscarriage en route from Shelburne, and beside himself with fury that Thomas Miles had died aboard one of the ships in harbour, asphyxiated by fumes from the charcoal fires used to dry the green planking, an accident he was sure could have been prevented had his instructions on ventilation been properly followed. Clarkson made up his mind to sail, not in one of the larger ships, but in the brig he had designated for the fleet hospital, and which would have the largest share of the elderly and sick. He hoped that this would "convince the blacks of my ardent and disinterested zeal."[65] They had been through so many shabby betrayals. He would stand by them. He would be their British freedom or die in their defence.

On New Year's Eve there was an unexpected change in the skies.

The wintry gales, which had postponed the sailings and almost over-turned one of the lighter schooners in the harbour, disappeared and were replaced by "the most pleasant mild weather such as the oldest inhabitant never witnessed before." Clarkson drew the obvious lesson, that "it really appears as if Providence favours the plan." The next morning, New Year's Day 1792, there was another happy surprise. "A little before eight this morning thirty of the Black People going to Sierra Leone came to my door, each of them with a gun, to salute me and wish me happy returns of the day."[66] Delighted, but keeping his demeanour of correctness and propriety, Clarkson asked if they would be so good as to go to the wharf, where his personal pennant would be hoisted on the *Lucretia* and could be greeted with an appropriate salute. His mood skipped now, high and low. Aboard one of the ships twins had been born, mother and children doing very well; but then immediately after-wards Clarkson learned that a man on the *Somerset* had somehow suf-focated below deck—he felt sure it was through just the kind of negligence he had been at pains to warn the captains against. It was as well, he thought, that, together with those he most trusted, like David George, he would sail on the brig he had designated the hospital ship.

On the 7th of January Clarkson packed his clothes and was rowed with his chest of personal possessions to the *Lucretia*, where for the first time he dined aboard. The next night he slept on the ship. Everything was moving, at last, towards the waterborne exodus. There was a church service at St Paul's, and prayers were offered by Bishop Inglis and others for the safety of the voyage. Clarkson had hoped to hear a sermon preached on the exemplary behaviour of the blacks, "a pattern for others to imitate having had not less than twelve hundred people in the town for upwards of five weeks in the depth of winter and not so much as the least disorder from any one of them." But somehow that sermon did not get preached.

On the 9th the *Lucretia* hauled off from the wharf and joined the rest of the fleet in Halifax harbour, a spectacle to make the heart leap and one that deserves remembering in the annals of African-American his-tory: the *Betsey*, the *Beaver*, the *Mary*, the *Felicity*, the *Lucretia*, the *Cathe-rine*, the *Parr*, the *Somerset*, the *Eleanor*, the *Morning Star*, the *Prince William Henry*, the *Two Brothers*, the *Venus*, the *Prince Fleury* and the re-named *Sierra Leone*. It was a convoy of almost 2,000 tons, carrying 1,196 people, 383 of them young children. Behind them, the little towns and villages in which the emigrants had struggled to make a free life in British America were mere shells: Preston virtually emptied, Brindley Town reduced to a lingering vestige, and Birchtown suddenly a hopeless place with just a fifth of its population left in the care of Stephen Blucke. But Blucke's best days were past too. His grand manor house never got finished; his wife, Margaret, left him and went back to New York. He became increasingly unpopular, and his patron, Skinner, was unable to shield him from rumours and accusations that he had misappropriated funds. Three years after the sailing of the fleet, Blucke's torn body was found in the woods, mauled and partly devoured, it was said, by wild animals.

At the last minute, when the endless paperwork that so irritated Clarkson was finally concluded, there was yet another delay. The skies over Halifax were fair, but the winds were unhelpfully adverse. On the 10th of January, feeling exhausted and somewhat unwell, Clarkson attended ceremonies arranged by the acting governor, Bulkeley, and Attorney-General Strange, who made speeches praising his conduct, so that on parting Clarkson actually felt a twinge of affection for Halifax—or at least for the section of its society that had been hospitable and courageously sympathetic. Later that evening his old sparring partner Michael Wallace, who after many disputes had arrived at a healthy respect for the stamina and determination of the nervous lieutenant, helped him go through a muster of the full passenger list. Clarkson then had himself rowed through the entire fleet, stopping at each of the ships to read the regulations of conduct that both blacks and whites were to follow and to make a little speech of exhortation, congratulation and blessing. But the climax of the little ceremony was his reading of the roll of passengers and the presentation to each family of the certificate he had had specially printed in town, dated the 31st of December 1791 and indicating the plot of land "free of expence" they were to be given "upon arrival in Africa." It was the document each of them must have yearned for ever since the moment they had taken their lives in their hands and fled their American slavemasters.

This John Clarkson did fifteen times, from the *Beaver* to the *Felicity*, until well into the night, when the temperature in Halifax harbour abruptly dropped from "excessive heat to a keen frosty air." Just as suddenly the sweat beneath his boat coat changed to a shiver, and John Clarkson began to feel really "inconvenienced" by a sense of creeping malady. He went to bed at midnight, burning with fever.

And still the damned "baffling" wind, stronger now, blew against them. Desperate to be off, Clarkson filled the hours fretting over the number of blankets aboard and the rapidly depleting provisions; he wrote further farewells, but uttered them in person to his closest friends, such as Hartshorne. And it was surely during this last week that Clarkson took his pen and made graceful drawings in the journal of the pennants of his fleet, and then, most beautifully, filled a double page with the fleet itself, each schooner, brig and ship precisely drawn, sailing east-southeast across the vellum, their jibs, spinnakers and mainsails billowing with cheerful breezes onward to their destiny.

On the 14th of January there was some hope that the wind direction was changing. His indisposition masked by growing excitement, Clarkson shrugged it off with a vengeance, went on a night sleigh ride with Hartshorne and some lady friends and returned to Halifax for a late supper and an attempt at sleep. The next morning, at long last, "a light air sprang up" and Clarkson, aboard the *Lucretia*, signalled the fleet to weigh anchor at eleven o" clock. The *Felicity*, with Wickham commanding, would lead the fleet out and he would bring up the rear.

At noon the lieutenant-turned-commodore was piped aboard again, and as the *Lucretia* got under weigh made sure to salute the admiral of the Halifax fleet and the town by lowering his mainsail topgallant in respect. On the quay there was a surprising crowd, much waving of hats and handkerchiefs and even cheering—though doubtless some were happy to see Clarkson go. He went below, settled himself in the commodore's cabin at a modest desk, reached for the goose quill and wrote on this auspicious day, the 15th of January 1792, to Henry Thornton:

> Dear Sir, I am now under sail, with a fair wind and fine weather having on board 1192 souls in fifteen ships, all in good spirits, properly equipped and I hope destined to be happy.[67]

Well might he hope.

X

SOMETHING WAS AMISS with the commodore. Whatever it was that he had caught that chilly night in Halifax harbour, rowing around the fleet, would not loosen its grip. There were moments when he feared it might be the death of him. The peculiar mildness for mid-January with which the voyage had begun had vanished almost as soon as the last rocks of North America had disappeared over the horizon.[1] Now the full force of an Atlantic winter bore down on the fleet and seemed to break against Clarkson's slight body, engulfing it with sickness. By turns he trembled with fever, broke into dripping sweats and shuddered with cold. Violent pain throbbed within his skull as if pincers were tearing at his brain. All the while he struggled to keep command of the fleet, beset by violent gales, and of himself, likewise storm-racked. Four days out from Halifax sheets of rain crashed down on to the *Lucretia,* and then turned to hailstones which drummed against the deck and scoured the faces of the sailors as they struggled with the shrouds. Two days later a gusty snow squall descended on the fleet and ships he had managed to keep in sight even in the dirty weather now dissolved into the slanting veil of snow. Forcing himself to navigate, Clarkson signalled with guns, hoping they would sound through the shrieking wind that the fleet should alter course, and for a while the vessels managed to skirt the worst of it. Then, on the 20th of January, another gale blew up, one so savage that Clarkson ordered the fleet to heave to on a starboard tack and wait it out. Scanning the horizon with his telescope, he was unable to account for two of the ships. Worried sick, he reversed himself, ordering the ships to close a little.

Next day, come the light, three more ships had gone. Clarkson signalled for the speediest of the remaining vessels, the *Felicity*, to come within hail and then asked Samuel Wickham, her master, to haul in a quarter and search for the missing ones. Then he collapsed, feeling so ill that he had to leave the deck and go below. Wickham was given orders: at all costs to keep the fleet together and to signal the faster ships, the *Sierra Leone* and the *Mary*, that they should shorten sail. By four o'clock in the afternoon Wickham was able to tell Clarkson that all ships were now in their stations except the *Somerset*, which had disappeared at the height of the storm the night before and not been seen since. Swept in turn by relief and anxiety, but his head still pounding with pain, Clarkson asked his friend Charles Taylor, the physician, what he should do. Taylor's advice was that the burdens of command in such weather would not help his recovery, or indeed the welfare of the fleet. Turning over the day-to-day command to Samuel Wickham, Clarkson wrote, "I shall not interfere in the management of the fleet until I get better."

Thereafter, Clarkson's journal turns into a nautical log; but what it reports, however summarily, is the kind of oceanic thrashing that only the Atlantic at its most merciless can inflict. Two days after he relinquished control of the fleet, mere gales turned into a titanic storm. A series of elemental upheavals, each one with its own measure, now seemed to run into one another to form a chain of terrifying immensity. On one of the other beleaguered ships Boston King, who had sailed enough in his life through the worst he had thought the Atlantic could do, was shocked and frightened at this towering sea, the black and green walls of water veined with spume. "Some of the men who had been engaged in a seafaring life," he wrote, "declared that they never saw such a storm before."[2] In the teeth of the tempest King watched helplessly as one of the free blacks was taken by a vast wave and washed clean overboard, leaving a grieving wife and four children. His own wife, Violet, was sick, so seriously that he resigned himself to her dying, and hoped only that she would hang on for he had a terrible aversion to burial at sea. "In the simplicity of my heart I intreated the Lord to spare her at least till we reached the shore that I might give her a decent burial." He did better than that. "The Lord looked upon my sincerity and restored her to perfect health."

On the 22nd of January a tremendous bolt of lightning hit the mizzenmast of the *Lucretia*, not taking it down entirely, but shredding the top mainsail and forcing Captain Jonathan Coffin to reef the rest of the mizzenmast sails and heave to. Most of the blacks aboard were violently ill; one of them died on the 25th, the second burial at sea since leaving Halifax. Hardened though they were to rough swells, many of the crew were felled by this one; and others were sick from the same fever that ailed Clarkson, leaving Coffin with too few hands to put up the repaired sails once the winds allowed. The great storm had scattered the fleet beyond any hope of reassembly now—only five of the original fifteen were within sight of each other. They included some of the bigger ships, however, the *Felicity*, the *Venus* and the *Eleanor*, and when the winds had abated somewhat, boats were sent to collect able men from each to repair and hoist the *Lucretia*'s mainsail.

John Clarkson was oblivious to much of this ordeal, for he was, so Dr Charles Taylor thought, dying. Clarkson lay in his bunk trembling with fever, drifting in and out of consciousness, never coherent, often comatose. When Taylor looked in on him and saw the body convulsed with shivers beneath the blanket, he knew at least that there was some life left, although he was horrified one day to notice four blisters that had raised themselves, perhaps the sinister heralds of smallpox. But then, as the height of the sea fell back, so did Clarkson's vital signs. For a whole day and night, he was utterly motionless. Feeling no pulse, not a whisper of breath, Taylor declared him gone.[3] His body was brought to the deck and prepared for the rites of burial at sea: it was placed in a stitched canvas shroud and draped in the flag.

It must have been just before the open-ended coffin was raised by the two bearers and pointed down at the waves when someone noticed a faint movement under the canvas. Clarkson was not, after all, ready to be committed to the corruption of the deep. Still unconscious, he was carried below to his cabin at the stern of the ship and made warm.

This, it transpired, was not the best place for him to be. There had been a lull in the storm, which crews and passengers took to be a sign of its ending. They were brutally deceived, for the tumult would drive on mercilessly for more than two weeks, relaxing its grip just a little to give the seamen and passengers a moment of hope before pouncing again with even greater ferocity. On the 29th of January the next gale within the gale struck the *Lucretia* with sudden, horrifying swiftness. There was no thunder and lightning this time, but sharply building winds that screamed through the canvas and whipped up waves of dumbfounding height, so that the brig's timbers groaned as it climbed and reared before dropping into the depths of the trough. Churned iron-grey water washed over the decks as the *Lucretia* rolled at so steep an angle that the rising wall of water entirely blotted out the sky. Something had to give, and it was the deadlights at the stern, immediately in front of which lay Clarkson's cabin. In the deafening roar of the gale he had somehow raised himself and was stumbling about in the throes of delirium just as the ship was pooping, its bow pointing almost vertically to the sky, the stern plunging below the waterline. Windows and timbers at the deadlights splintered into flotsam and the ocean rushed in, taking Clarkson, unconscious once more, into the seething flood—but not, fortunately, out into the open ocean. Feeling the shock, the master of the *Lucretia* had raced below, screaming orders. If the damage was not made good and the deadlights secured right away the brig would surely sink. In Clarkson's cabin Coffin found the lieutenant on the floor, helplessly rolling from side to side, slammed between the walls, badly bruised, cut and "covered in blood and water."[4]

The *Lucretia* and Clarkson survived—barely—but Captain Coffin, their rescuer, would not. Once the worst of the storms had receded, in the second week of February, some accounting was made of what had endured and what had been lost. Still only five ships from the original convoy could be seen. Although her masts, astonishingly, had come through the ordeal intact, the *Lucretia*'s rigging and sails had been badly mauled and torn, and the crew was too short-handed to repair them. Only the mate and the master were well enough to fulfil their duties, the rest not just sick from the storm but also taken by whatever fever was now raging through the ship. Men were taken aboard from the *Venus*, the *Eleanor* and the *Felicity* to help, but they too soon fell ill. More than forty of the passengers and crew on the *Venus* were dangerously weak, and Wickham sent Charles Taylor to her to help with the stricken.

On the 15th of February, in much gentler breezes, the fever caught up with Jonathan Coffin, who was forced below—the second invalided master forced to relinquish control of his ship. Clarkson, on the other hand, was now awake most of the time and able to speak to the officers and passengers, although certainly not recovered to anything like his old self. His limbs were flaccid, he still shook as if he had the palsy, and, worst of all, his poor brain seemed either tortured by nail-boring pains or else oddly muffled, as if it had grown an extra cladding of membrane closing it off from the world (it was perhaps meningitis). Most distressing and humiliating for Clarkson was the loss of his short-term memory and some of his longer memory too, both of which reduced him on occasions to anguished panic. Given a piece of information, a few minutes later he would have absolutely no recollection of it. Trying to recover his grasp of navigational skills, he discovered with rising horror that he could recall nothing of what he had learned as a midshipman and put into practice on ten successive ships. In the circumstances, he asked the masters of the other vessels to come aboard so that he could frankly explain to them his predicament, and have them assume more responsibility for the welfare of their own ships and especially that of their black passengers. "My illness has made me so nervous and occasioned such debility of mind and body that I requested the Captains on board today to speak their minds freely to me upon every occasion as to the course we should steer, for I find that I cannot remember anything as yet as to the navigation of a vessel."[5]

To make matters worse, Clarkson was sunk, much of the time, in a stew of guilty melancholy. His black manservant Peter Peters, who had cared so conscientiously for him during the terrible depths of his delirium, died himself on the 18th of February and Clarkson inevitably felt culpable since Peters was "supposed to have caught the fever of [sic] me." But he himself was well enough at last to take some air, although not capable of walking or even staggering about. So Clarkson was carried on deck upon a mattress by Samuel Wickham and another seaman while his cabin was vigorously swabbed with scalded vinegar and fumigated with tar and gunpowder balls to purge it of sickness.

But the contagion merely slunk off elsewhere. On the 22nd, three weeks after he had saved Clarkson from certain drowning, Jonathan Coffin died. Now Clarkson was tormented by an even more merciless spasm of guilt, since, after the death of Peters, Captain Coffin had made a point of personally seeing him through his rocky convalescence, sitting with him and inevitably catching the fever. "He was a worthy, good man and his loss will be greatly felt by his owners," grieved Clarkson.[6] Almost committed to the deep himself, Clarkson now had to perform the same service for Coffin. He was again carried up on deck and "as the last mark of attention to his memory I endeavoured to read as well as I could the burial service over him although I was not able to stand or hold on to the book." The Bible fell from his hands. Coffin's body slid into the sea.

It was Charles Taylor, now, who saw that something had to be done to preserve Clarkson from being overwhelmed, and suggested it would be good both for him and for the morale of the fleet if he were to show himself to the ships. The salt air could do no harm; rather the reverse. "I was accordingly lifted into the boat and lowered into the water with her. Upon my going alongside each ship, the black passengers had collected themselves upon deck with their muskets and fired three vollies [*sic*] and afterwards gave three cheers, as they had entirely given up all hopes of my recovery, which was to them of the greatest consequence."

Later, Clarkson marked this moment as a turning point. Certainly the weather improved: the temperature climbed, the winds were merely fresh and the water turned from dull grey to the deep cobalt of the South Atlantic. The *Somerset,* one of the lost ships, now came in sight, and in the last week of February Clarkson felt well enough to summon all the captains aboard the *Lucretia* for dinner. He could still overdo things. Trying to read Sunday prayers and deliver a shipboard sermon, he was suddenly overtaken by a massive sense of exhaustion which felled him for some days. On the 28th he had recovered sufficiently for a tour of inspection of the vessels, hoisted aboard on his chair. On the *Eleanor* he dined with Captain Redman, who told him that one of the black passengers was particularly anxious to see him. She was an ancient blind woman of one hundred and four, who had been abducted by slavers as a child in Sierra Leone and had implored Clarkson (who had made it a special point in Nova Scotia to satisfy himself that the passengers were fit for an arduous Atlantic crossing) to take her with him so that she might "lay her bones in her native country." He had consented, and here she was on deck, overcome with joy, pumping his hand and congratulating him on his recovery.[7]

They were not far now. Whales sounded, fish flew, and in the bright calm the seas were gentle enough for the blacks to make visits in pinnaces to each others' ships. There were embraces, tears, cries. And for some, with Africa not far off, there were mingled memories of childhood happiness and terror. On the 4th of March, a few days out from Sierra Leone, another ship called the *Mary* sailed past; but this was the *Mary* of Bristol, bound for Annamabo to pick up its usual "live cargo." Clarkson thought this the right moment to summon all his strength to speak to the blacks on the *Lucretia,* expressing his pleasure at how well, through all the storms, they had conducted themselves since leaving America. The next day he repeated the avuncular performance on all the other ships in sight. "All seemed in high spirits and promised obedience and attention to all orders given upon their landing. I was much pleased with the happy and contented countenances of all of them; their expressions of respect and gratitude upon this occasion were most gratifying and affected me much—most ardently do I hope the change they are about to make will ultimately turn out to the advantage of them and posterity."[8]

Two days later he ordered the *Eleanor,* the fastest ship, to sail ahead and begin to make fathom soundings, signalling with her guns when she sounded eight deep. For all his enervation, Clarkson was beside himself with anticipation: "I could not be prevailed upon to quit the deck." At two in the morning on the 7th of March he heard the *Eleanor*'s guns, and before long the *Lucretia*'s own sounding hit seven fathoms. The waters were growing shallower and the coast could not be far off. Finally, Clarkson took to his bed but found it almost impossible to sleep, such was his intermingled agitation and anticipation. At seven he abandoned the attempt and rose under cloudy skies and dawn mists. Restlessly striding the deck, opening and shutting his glass, he was the first to catch sight of Cape Sierra Leone about five leagues off to the southeast. Hardly had he seen it than guns sounded from two other ships, followed by cheering from the whole squadron and volleys of fire that rang into the bay ahead.

But then, in the midst of all this jubilation, being John Clarkson, and having gone through everything he had gone through, he had a sudden strange feeling in the pit of his stomach. "It is not in my power to describe my sensations at this moment, for I knew not what the next hours might produce—the fatigue of being up the greatest part of the night added to great anxiety of mind quite exhausted me and filled me with gloomy ideas."[9] Suddenly the talk at John Parr's table on the second night of his stay in Halifax, and his own peremptory dismissal of the rumours of hostile natives, came back to him with brutal clarity. What if that Falmouth captain had been right? What if there had been another attack? Suppose—since he had still heard not a word from the directors since leaving England—they had received none of his letters either, and no proper provision had been made for the reception of the blacks? Suppose they still imagined a mere ship or two, with perhaps one hundred or fewer? "Particularly when I reflected upon the small quantity of provisions on board the Transport (not having more than sufficient with the most rigid economy for a month) with no probability of recruiting them should it be necessary, our ignorance of the coast and its inhabitants and my total inability to any exertion should it be required, I could not help giving way to those desponding reflections which, had I been in health, would probably have never occurred."

At noon they passed Leopard's Island and could plainly see now the forested peaks of the peninsula rising, it seemed, right out of the water. "The high mountain . . . appeared like a cloud to us," wrote David George.[10] Then, to Clarkson's "inexpressible joy," one of the leading ships of the fleet made the signal that indicated there were ships at anchor up-river. Clarkson took out his glass and saw a small squadron that, from the size of one of the vessels, he immediately took to be the supply fleet sent by the Sierra Leone Company. When its flag could be made out, he saw on its green face a lion and clasped hands, black and white—the device of the company. Relief flooded him. "The succours from England had arrived." At last, he thought, the journey was truly over, and Clarkson indulged himself in a "hope of speedy termination to my anxieties and fatigue."

XI

Awake! and sing the song, of Moses and the Lamb
Wake! Every heart and every tongue
To praise the Saviour's name! . . .
The Day of Jubilee is come
Return ye ransomed sinners home[1]

A THOUSAND BLACK VOICES raised in song beneath the white sailcloth flapping gently in the breeze. Jubilation pouring into the Sierra Leone morning, down to the bay where the exodus fleet lay moored; drifting out to the dark-horizoned humpback offshore islets; penetrating the compound of King Jimmy's village half a mile off; climbing into the forested slopes, where the chorus competed with the gibbering of monkeys; an irresistible euphony, the basses vibrating, soprano notes leaping and floating like the dance of angels, a sound such as Africa had not yet heard.

The singers were in the Canvas Room, a large tent quickly improvised as assembly place and church, and although the hymn was from Lady Huntingdon's book, they all sang it—Baptists and Methodists as well as her "New Lights"—because it sang of the marvel of their arrival. There were no hangers-back that first Sunday, the 11th of March. They had all come: Blind Daddy Moses, David George, Phyllis and the six children, the last named John after the "Honoured Sir" who had brought them safely through the tempest; Boston King, with his wife, Violet. Many among the congregation had truly returned home: Lucy Banbury, now forty-nine, born in West Africa, stolen away as an adolescent, then slave of Arthur Middleton until she ran to the British the year he signed the Declaration of Independence; John Kizell, the Sherbro chief's son, who had fought with Patrick Ferguson's American Volunteers at the battle of King's Mountain in North Carolina in 1780;[2] Frank Peters, twenty-nine years old, another child abductee from Sierra Leone, sold to Woodward Flowers at Monks Corner, South Carolina, and field slave there until he joined the British army in 1779, then a Birchtown wood-cutter until their exodus. Two weeks later an older woman would run to Peters and fold him in an embrace: it was his lost mother.[3]

There were also white men and women—119 of them sent out by the Sierra Leone Company on its supply ships *Amy* and *Harpy*, doubt-less singing a little more reedily than the blacks. The young Anglican minister, Nathaniel Gilbert, was the son of a rich Antigua planter, but he had Seen the Light and now preached from Psalm 127: "Except but the Lord build the house, the labour is but lost that built it."[4] To which John Clarkson, at the front of the congregation, would doubtless (had he but the strength) have cried *Amen!* Clarkson was a long way from being better: he was still suffering from chronic memory loss, severe head-aches, fits of shortness of breath and even unpredictable swooning spells from the pure physical effort of getting himself off the ship and on to the shore. His moods swung sharply between a modicum of satis-faction and self-punishing depressive panic. There were some things he could feel rightly proud of, not least the miraculous survival of all fif-teen ships of the fleet that had left Halifax seven weeks before. The last to limp into the bay had been the *Morning Star*, about which Clarkson had been particularly anxious, since he had fitted her specially to take pregnant women. To his happiness he discovered that there had been three births, mothers and babies all doing well. He also felt a rush of pleasure receiving the black captains of companies, "very neatly dressed," who "expressed the general joy of themselves and . . . my safe arrival . . . at the Land of Promise . . . The respect and gratitude ex-pressed in every look affected me very sensibly, their decent dress and their becoming behaviour . . . noticed by all who were present for the most perfect peace and harmony reigned aboard each Transport."[5] Just as satisfactory, the white ships' captains thanked Clarkson for the "regu-lar and orderly" conduct of the blacks towards themselves and their crews. None of the blacks, moreover, had any complaints of ill-treatment from the white sailors; Clarkson's hopes that the crossing from Halifax to Sierra Leone would be a reversal of slave-ship passages in more than just geographical direction seemed, astonishingly, to have been fulfilled.

But while he mingled with the captains, both black and white, Clarkson was also attacked by moments of deep unhappiness that two of the ships' masters—his personal saviour, Jonathan Coffin of the *Lucretia*, and Captain May of the *Betsey*—had died, along with his servant Peter Peters. As soon as he heard that the number of shipboard mortalities had been as many as sixty-five (mostly, as might be expected, from among the old, the sick and the very young), Clarkson was shaken by paroxysms of guilt. After chatting a while, he suddenly collapsed so completely that "I was obliged to be carried to bed where I was in violent hysterics for nearly two hours."[6]

This was not the kind of behaviour expected from the man who was now, apparently, the "superintendent" of Sierra Leone and the as yet unbuilt Freetown. This unsought appointment had only added to Clarkson's shock and distress. As the *Lucretia* had anchored in the bay on the morning of the 7th of March, Clarkson had ordered a special pennant to be run up (oddly, the Dutch flag reversed) as a prearranged signal to Henry Hew Dalrymple, whom, in the absence of recent news, he assumed had already been installed as governor. Not long afterwards, a pinnace was seen approaching Clarkson's ship, but instead of carrying Dalrymple, it appeared to be full of overdressed white gentlemen perspiring in their hats. Only one of them, Alexander Falconbridge, the commercial agent, was known to Clarkson; the others were introduced as Dr Bell, the surgeon sent by the company, whom Clarkson immediately suspected of being a devotee of the bottle; and Richard Pepys and James Cocks, respectively surveyor and engineer. Together with the Reverend Gilbert and a Mr Wakerell (accountant, yet to arrive), these gentlemen were, apparently, constituted as the "council" appointed by the company directors to govern Freetown along with Clarkson himself, who, he was now informed, was to be superintendent in place of the dismissed Dalrymple.

This was neither what he had expected nor what he wanted. Even had he not been feeling so unwell, Clarkson had assumed his work would have ended once the free blacks were safely ashore and the plots of land to which they were entitled had been surveyed and distributed. This, he supposed, would take only a few weeks, after which he would go back, marry his handsomely propertied fiancée, continue to assist his brother in the good cause and, on the strength of his achievement in Nova Scotia, renew his applications for a naval command. Now, as he read through the stack of letters handed to him, John Clarkson felt himself trapped by what his brother Thomas, William Wilberforce, Joseph Hardcastle and Henry Thornton were telling him was his duty, his unavoidable destiny. "The Eyes of England are upon you and this Infant Colony," Thomas wrote fulsomely: "No Establishment has made such a Noise as this in the Papers or [been] so generally admired . . . To your lot it falls to be Governor of the Noblest Institution ever set on foot."[7] Personally, of course, Thomas could wish for nothing better than to set eyes on his dear brother once more, but such personal wishes, he knew, must be set aside for the greater good. John, Thomas hoped, would consider staying for at least a year, adding unconvincingly at the end of the letter, "You are the best judge of your own Happiness: and therefore whether you stay or not, you will please me." The insistence grew louder with each message. Joseph Hardcastle, for instance, married Quaker prophetics to Enlightenment utopianism in a style perfectly calculated to make it impossible for Clarkson to resist: "You have brought from afar & planted in Africa a precious Seed which is perhaps destined to become a great tree, under whose shade many are to rejoice but your superintendence, your constant influence, like the Sun and the rain must cherish and fertilize it. You are filling the singularly interesting station of presiding over society in its rudimental State, you are to draw forth its latent energies and cherish the embrio Virtues of untutored man."[8]

Suffocating in the praise, and sure that, for the sake of his health, "I ought not to hesitate in doing justice to myself and connexions by returning to a northern climate," John nonetheless knew he was caught. He would stay for the sake of the blacks, not for the sake of the directors to whom, despite his shaky memory, he suddenly felt superior in practical wisdom. They seemed obsessed with their vision of pan-continental free African commerce blossoming out from Sierra Leone. Perhaps that was why they had sent so much sugar-boiling equipment. But John Clarkson was no longer much interested in that grand plan, if ever he had been. He was much closer now to Granville Sharp's vision of a free and virtuous black society, something new and thrilling in the world. He would do his utmost to make it happen.

But his brother and the rest of the directors had made that work incomparably harder with their "constitution" and their "council," which he could summon and over which he could preside with a casting vote, but never overrule, no matter how foolish its decisions! Ensnared in what he thought an unworkable system, Clarkson would later snap at his own brother for saddling him with "your ridiculous form of government." Not having been with him in Nova Scotia, not to mention on the perilous crossing, the councillors could not be expected to understand how important it was for the welfare and effectiveness of the settlement, and for the trust of the blacks, that they should look to him, above all, as a proper governor. The blacks needed to know that, whatever troubles they might have with the many whites, their chief would be a fair, impartial and sympathetic judge and protector. And trouble, Clarkson felt sure, there would certainly be. For he was horrified to see on arrival in Sierra Leone that, despite his requests to the company, nothing whatsoever had been done for even the temporary accommodation of the thousand-plus settlers, despite the fact that the transport ships had arrived two weeks earlier. The councillors had stayed on board their ships, devouring supplies, emptying the rum, feeling faint, bickering with each other and with the captains. Not a tree had been disturbed at the forest's edge, not a patch of grass scythed. It seemed to have been considered beneath the dignity of the whites to begin making clearings or erecting tents and the huts that were urgently needed for shelter before the harmattan got under way in April. Such things would, of course, be black men's work. With no time to lose, Clarkson mobilized his black captains, and within a few days of arrival, eighty acres had been cleared and a start made on huts, built quickly, after the local fashion, of poles, mud and grass thatch.

The white councillors and their many employees and hangers on—marines and sailors, storemen and artisans, and the councillors' ladies—were another story entirely. After a week of incredulity and disgust, Clarkson wrote that, as a group, they demonstrated "nothing but extravagance, idleness, quarrelling, waste, irregularity in accounts, insubordination and everything that is contrary to what is good and right." This was not merely a matter of administrative incompetence. With the exception of Falconbridge and the Reverend Gilbert, they behaved as if they were masters of some commercial or military colony, not people who were supposed to be helping the blacks as friends and protectors and setting them an example of a society founded on "good and virtuous principles." For Clarkson, the profoundly moving experience in Nova Scotia and on the crossing had been a supreme moral and spiritual course of instruction, almost akin to the experience of one of the Early Christian Fathers or apostles. He could not expect gentlemen sent from England to emulate that, but he did expect them to be guided by him, and the discovery of his impotence in that respect so "completely at variance with the advice I had given the Directors in my letters" galled him intensely. What he wanted were Plato's Guardians. What he had were vain, imperious, disputatious, dissolute popinjays and nonentities, many of whom spent the day drunk.

The worst of the lot was the surgeon, Dr Bell, appointed for his reputed expertise in tropical diseases. When Clarkson saw him on the man's return from seeing the slavers at Bance Island, probably to stock up on liquor, Dr Bell was invariably too inebriated to have the slightest idea who he was, a failure of deference to which the superintendent did not take kindly.[9] Dining aboard the *Harpy,* one evening he endured "the delirious ravings of Dr Bell" who, at half past nine, was taken to bed with a fever brought on, so Clarkson thought, by the bottle. Half an hour later he was discovered dead by a servant—the victim, so the other councillors generously decided, of an epileptic fit. Clarkson was not exactly distraught. "I determined, had he not died to send him [back] to England." Rather than welcome an act of providential relief, Clarkson was aghast to learn that the councillors planned a full military funeral complete with struck colours flying from the ships and thirteen-gun salutes. "I replied that had I not heard it from their own mouths I could not have believed it possible that any set of men situated as they were as the representatives of the Directors of the Sierra Leone Company, to form a colony on virtuous principles could have made so extraordinary [a] request, for the person to whose memory these honours were designed had been almost constantly drunk from the time he left England to the day of his death."[10] Clarkson would have liked to forbid this lavish funeral on the grounds that it would shock the blacks, who would not understand the honour shown to such a person. But he was out-voted by the council—who told him, moreover, that they expected his presence. Feeling weak, Clarkson was carried up the hill at the back of the settlement, where he saw the flags at half mast and heard the funer-ary guns. Later that afternoon he was told that, during the firing, a gun-ner named Thomas Thomas had had his arm accidentally blown off, and had subsequently died from the wound. "This completely over-came me and on arrival aboard the *Amy* [where he slept] I was seized with the most violent fainting fits and hysterics which closed the morti-fications of the day."[11]

How was he ever to get better? Only, as he wrote in the journal, by a "return to a northern climate without loss of time." And, whatever his brother and the directors thought, he was not honour-bound to stay in Africa beyond a short time. Yet to leave now, given the calibre of the men the company had sent, was to condemn Freetown to ruin before it had ever begun. He could not abandon the blacks in their hour of need; not now. With a flourish of the slightly self-aggrandizing desperation in which he was beginning to wrap himself, John Clarkson wrote, "I was compelled to sink all private considerations and agree to remain here, and although I may be disgraced by blending my services with those of others over whom I have no proper control, I have made my mind up to take the consequences and accept the Government under its present objectionable form and to remain with the poor Nova Scotians till the Colony is established or lost."[12]

On the 18th of March 1792 Clarkson crossed a line beyond which there was no going back. He ordered his commodore's pennant struck and the transport fleet discharged. The ships that had borne the blacks to Africa—the *Felicity, Morning Star, Sierra Leone, Betsey, Eleanor, Cathe-rine* and the rest—were free to return to Halifax. There they would dis-abuse the white loyalists, still nursing a deep sense of grievance over the mass emigration of "their" blacks, of stories circulating in the port city that Clarkson's fleet had met with utter destruction—that barely twelve people had survived from the twelve hundred who had left, and even they in such pitiable condition that they lamented ever leaving Nova Scotia.

THERE WOULD COME A DAY in Sierra Leone, not far off, when things had come to such a pass that John Clarkson felt he should ask the distressed and the disgruntled whether they did, in fact, wish to return to North America. And the question would be greeted with laughter.[13] But in the first weeks and months there was plenty to cry about. Another forty of the free blacks died, including Violet King, who had gone through so much with her husband since leaving Colonel Young's plantation in Wilmington, North Carolina: the terror of recapture in Charleston and New York; in wintry Birchtown physically thrown to the ground by the force of Moses Wilkinson's preaching and then raised up again so purely that her husband, Boston, the oath-hater, felt himself by comparison a terrible wicked sinner who must take himself off at night to the deep snowdrifts of the forest to ask forgiveness. They had come through the Atlantic tempest and her sickness only for Violet to catch the "putrid fever" at the end of March. "For several days she lost her senses and was as helpless as an infant," but then suddenly recovered her tongue, sure she would meet her Maker very soon. "On Sunday while several of our friends were with her, she lay still; but as soon as they began singing the hymn "Lo! He comes with clouds descending, Once for favoured sinners slain" she joined in with us till we came to the last verse when she began to rejoice aloud and expired in a rapture of love." Two months later, at the height of the rains, Boston caught the same fever but managed to survive. Many others did not. "People died so fast," he wrote, "that it was difficult to procure burial for them."[14]

Medical care and drugs—mostly cinchona bark to be used against malaria—were in desperately short supply. Dr Bell (for whatever good he might have been) was no more, and his replacement, Dr Thomas Winterbottom—much admired by Clarkson, and the author of the first serious account of African diseases—did not arrive until July. The timber intended for a hospital did not arrive until later in the year, by which time the worst of the fevers had abated. Rotting food, discarded from the stores, lay strewn around, attracting vermin and adding to the health hazards. Settlers, both black and white, were subsisting principally on "worm-eaten bread" and salt meats and fish, distributed at half allowance. Local villagers brought cassava and groundnuts, but the Nova Scotians had no idea what to do with them. When fresh fruit came—limes, papaya, pineapples, melon and bananas—it was a godsend.

It was the white population, with little or no immunity, that perished fastest and in the greatest numbers. Anna Maria Falconbridge lay gravely ill for three weeks, "stone-blind" for four days and "expecting every moment to be my last," and was forced to suffer her head being shaved, turning her into what she described as "a ghastly figure." She wrote of five, six or seven deaths a day at the height of the epidemic being commonplace, the victims buried "with as little ceremony as dogs or cats." The habitual greeting of a morning, she recorded, became "How many died last night?"[15] By the time the mortality rate ebbed in late July and August, barely 30 of the original 119 whites remained.

Along with the pestilence came other kinds of plagues and torments. Watching the ominous towers of clouds mass over the forested peaks towards the end of March, Luke Jordan, one of the black captains, anxiously wrote to Clarkson, "I would Not Write to You because I know You are not As well as Aught to be but It is because we are in a Strange Country and we are not well aquinted [sic] with the Rainey Season . . . but If it Should Come and we have know house what Should we do with Our Selvs?"[16] It was a good question. The colony was still a fragile huddle of tents and primitive huts. When, in the early hours of the 2nd of April, the first thunderstorm, with violent gusts of wind, unloaded its deluge, the black settlers discovered just how porous their thatched roofs and wattled walls could be. The rains brought out sudden infestations of ravening insects: swarms of cockroaches, colonies of a red and black striped beetle six inches long and half an inch thick, whose colouring Clarkson likened to Pontypool pottery, and, most terrifyingly, ferocious swarms of ants, black, white and, worst of all, red. Anna Maria wrote feelingly that it might seem strange "that such an insignificant insect is in England should be able, in another country, to storm the habitations of people and drive out the inhabitants," but she had seen twelve or fourteen families dislodged from their houses and forced to use either fire or scalding water to protect themselves. Sometimes houses caught fire in the attempt to halt the relentless march of the red ants, which would pick a way clean through anything in their path, living or dead, sometimes as big as a chicken or goat. Even some of the deadlier snakes would take avoiding action once the ants were on the march, dropping from hidden nesting places in the roof thatch on to the floor of the huts. The venomous mambas, cobras and kraits were bad enough, but there were also large constrictors (Anna Maria claimed to have seen a nine-foot "serpent") lying in wait for the domestic animals.

Pythons were not the only opportunists. Leopards sometimes padded into the village for goats, chickens and the settlers' dogs. After a big cat had been seen at the very doorway of a hut, Clarkson was terrified others might come for the small children, especially when he was told that not so long ago a leopard had taken a sleeping man by the neck and had dropped him only when the man had defended himself by punching the creature in the face! There were other stealthy creatures foiled at the last moment from kidnapping. On the 27th of March a large baboon, foraging at night, seized a twelve-year-old girl and attempted to drag her out of a tent. Her screams woke a man sleeping in the same tent, who caught hold of one of the girl's arms just as the baboon was leaving with her. "A trial of strength now took place," Clarkson wrote, "the baboon endeavouring all in its power to carry off the girl and the man equally determined to prevent him."[17] Only when their cries brought more help did the animal give up and run off into the forest.

Clarkson surveyed the desolation with increasing despondency, although not hopelessness. Just when he felt on the brink of despair and resignation, something wonderful would happen. One day at the end of March, between heavy storms, one of the local natives brought him a chameleon in return for rum. Clarkson took the reptile and watched it closely, feeding it sugar from a basket, marvelling at the flickering six-inch tongue, the protuberant eyes swivelling their orbits, the leathery skin going through its rainbow alterations from dark grey to deep blue, then to bottle green, then brighter leaf green, and golden yellow; it made him feel curious, and thus happy. He also knew that, as feeble as his body often felt, he could command his energies and his dignity enough to be respected by the local chiefs who had given the Granville Town settlers so much trouble. King Jimmy had refused invitations to come to Freetown but, dressed to the nines in his old naval uniform complete with cocked hat, had welcomed Clarkson to his village and had offered him wine and water, lifting the calabash to his own lips first to demonstrate its safety—a great gesture of brotherly friendship. Clarkson had sat in the shade beneath the rushes extending out from the circular roofs, surveyed the palms, plantains, papaya and citrus trees flourishing between the round houses, and imagined a kind of tropical plenty that his own people might yet enjoy.

A few days later the *Lapwing* brought the Naimbana down to King Jimmy's village for a palaver. He was older, greyer, thinner and sorely missing his London-domiciled son John Frederic. Slightly agog at the chief's appearance, Clarkson took in the sky blue silk jacket embroidered with silver lace, the striped trousers and green Morocco slippers and the gold-braided cocked hat. Presently the Naimbana removed this bizarre headgear to make way for an old-fashioned hanging judge's wig (rather past its prime), next to the tail of which swung a necklace carrying as pendant an incongruously Christian resurrection votive, the flag-bearing Lamb, the significance of which Clarkson doubted the Naimbana was fully aware. He was glad to have taken pains himself, dressed in full Windsor scarlet with a brilliant military order pinned to his breast, so that he could assure the Naimbana, on his polite enquiry (after the embrace), that yes, his good friend King George was very well. It worried Clarkson slightly that during this first encounter the Naimbana could not keep from smiling and laughing at him; finally he let it be known that he had never seen so young a king before (among the Temne, advanced age was a sine qua non of highest authority). In the evening they went ashore and Clarkson, now aware of the Naimbana's respect for the venerable, introduced him to the blind old woman who had congratulated him on his recovery, and who now insisted that she was entering her hundred and eighth year, having aged another four years in as many weeks.

The palaver was attended by the other local chiefs, the Bullom queen Yamacouba and the Afro-Portuguese chief "Signor Domingo," as well as the Naimbana's other, French-educated son, who seemed to want to pick a fight; it was a tricky moment. The old grievance of Captain Savage's raid, which had resulted in the burning down of King Jimmy's village and the "insulting" conduct of the Andersons' slave agents on Bance Island, were raised all over again. Clarkson protested that he had had nothing to do with either, and that "as our intentions were peaceable we would endeavour all in our power never to give them cause for offence and would be equally slow in feeling anger towards them . . . as they knew we had ample means to defend ourselves from any unjust attack, so they would find us resolute and determined in doing ourselves justice upon every occasion." (Every so often, Clarkson would order the firing of the howitzers to make his point.) Anticipating—correctly—that he would be asked to pay again for the use of the land whose lease had been negotiated by both Thompson and Falconbridge, Clarkson produced a record of what had already been paid and agreed, and asserted that any idea of him paying again was just "fool palaver."[18] As usual, nothing much was agreed, but the edge was taken off the tension—especially when, much against his conscience, Clarkson handed over the hard liquor all the chiefs were demanding. "It was in vain for me to moralize at such a time when the whole population at King Jimmy's town might be said to be in a state of intoxication." He was already becoming something of an African pragmatist. And he knew he had, in one important respect, dissembled the intentions of the company directors. For Thornton, Hardcastle and Thomas were full of grandiose plans to expand the colony up and down the coast and up-river, whilst John had been at pains to reassure the chiefs that he had no designs at all on more land. He could not shake out of his head the vision of a young African woman "of a very pleasing countenance" who had come to the settlement one afternoon and argued angrily that the whites meant to take her country and make the people their dependants. When Clarkson had again strenuously denied any such ambition, the handsome woman had pointed to a gun lying on the beach and said, "Those great guns . . . you white men bring here to take my poor country." Clarkson records no retort.[19]

He had known the rains would come. But John could not have expected the tornadoes to be quite so savage, crushing the flimsy huts, sending canvas whirling and flying. First, at sea, a storm the like of which no mariners could recall; now a rainy season that the natives said was the worst in memory. There were certainly days when he felt overcome with revulsion and impotent fury—the days when the torrid humidity built up unbearably and Clarkson would look despondently at unloaded crates, some of them left to wash in the surf, spilling their contents among the salty weed. Or he would consider how everything sharp and precise—scissors, knives, nails—turned rusty and dull in the film of damp that settled over everything. What time was it? How could he know except by the arc of the sun, since his watch and those of the rest of his company had also surrendered to the wetness. Sometimes, mistrusting everyone else, he would go over and over the inventory of dwindling supplies, sure that the councillors, marines, sailors and white workmen were helping themselves to anything that was not actually putrid with mould, especially rum and brandy. In the meantime, his blacks, so abused by the whites, laboured amidst the beasts of the forest, doing what they could to master their terror of the crashing storms and secure the huts before they were swept away in the flood.

If anything, Clarkson felt even more strongly about the free blacks here than he had in Nova Scotia and on the ocean odyssey. He had been proud to line them up in their companies before the old Naimbana, who had gone round shaking hands. "The Nova Scotians, if left to themselves, would fully come up to the Character I have invariably given them, but they have not had fair play." The wretched system he had been stuck with had given the whites the chance to lord it, unscrupulously, over the blacks, thus undoing all the trust for which Clarkson had laboured so hard through the Nova Scotian winter and that he had preserved on board the fleet. Now they were subjected to the worst of colonial contempt: whites who would abuse and insult them; sometimes be caught raising a hand to them, snigger at them when they complained of not having received, as promised, their plots of land and town lots. These were whites who had pushed the blacks out from waterfront properties; worse, who were so plainly un-Christian—drunken, promiscuous, syphilitic—and who never went near their assemblies of worship to ask forgiveness from the Almighty for all those sins. Clarkson, indeed, feared they were "atheist." In the meantime, he would get pathetic notes of heartbreaking poignancy from some of the most afflicted blacks:

> Sir, I your hum bel Servent begs the faver of your Excelence to See if you will Pleas to Let me hav Som Sope for I am in great want of Som I hav not had aney Since I hav bin to this plais I hav bin Sick and I want to git Som Sope verry much to wash my family Clos for we ar not fit to be Sean for dirt
>
>   your hum   Susana Smith
>   bel Servet[20]

Worst of all was the steady corrosion of trust this misconduct inflicted on the relationship between Clarkson himself and the free blacks, his "children," who for so long, whatever their questions and querulousness, had always been calmed and reassured by the transparent honesty and authority of the "Honoured Sir." Gradually he began to sense a welling of grievance and disaffection among people, who were beginning to feel (and perhaps speak their minds) that the promises made in the chapel at Birchtown—for self-government, self-judgement and tax-free land—had been betrayed. Since their stormy dispute before the departure from Halifax, Clarkson was acutely aware that the disaffected had someone of their own to turn to, someone he began to think might now be growing dangerous: Thomas Peters. On the 22nd of March any doubts on this score were removed.

> Thomas Peters called upon me this evening and made many complaints; he was extremely violent and indiscreet in his conversation and seemed as if he were desirous of alarming and disheartening the people; his conduct brings to my recollection a passage in a letter I received from my friend and co-adjutor, Mr Hartshorne, who put it into my hands when I took my leave of him, requesting me not to read it until I had been at sea some time; he says in a part of this letter "I would not have you to be too much mortified if Peters should prove a different man than you have a right to respect. I am much afraid that the great attention paid to him in England has raised his idea of his own importance to too great a pitch for either his good or your comfort." His behaviour this evening would fully impress any stranger with the truth of these observations and he has vexed me extremely.[21]

Even so, given the list of grievances that Peters had set before Clarkson in so shockingly discordant a manner, he felt duty bound to assemble the people at the "Canvas Room" (now multi-purpose, for dining, praying, palavering and, for the white officers, sleeping). After patiently going through the sources of their discontent, Clarkson thought he had "completely quieted their fears and satisfied them generally of the folly of his [Peters's] arguments." Nonetheless, the tension set off the terrible jangling within him once more. After his address in the tent Clarkson went back to his bed just as the crickets and bullfrogs began their chorus, making "the Town and Woods Ring," and then abandoned himself yet again to "violent hysterics for two or three hours."[22]

P ETERS observed all this with growing anger and disgust. As soon as he understood that nothing remotely resembling Granville Sharp's vision of a free black community, or even a colony which could at least police and judge its own people, was going to be realized, he felt that he and his fellow emigrants had been sold to a gang of idle, insolent, bigoted whites who were doing everything they could to rob the free blacks of their due. Was it to be the Nova Scotian story yet again under the tropical sun? Not if Peters was to have anything to do with it. It was, after all, supremely his responsibility, since it had been his appearance in London in November 1790 and his story, told to Sharp and Wilberforce and Thornton, that had led to the great exodus in the first place. And was he now to be implicated in the betrayal? Doubtless Mr Clarkson meant well enough, but he was a sick man with no strength to stand up to the villainy of the councillors and the haughtiness of the whites.

Even before he grasped the situation his people had been placed in, Peters acted as if he had at least a share of Clarkson's authority. On landing in Sierra Leone, he bypassed both Clarkson and the directors and wrote instead, directly and almost ambassadorially, to Henry Dundas, the Secretary of State for the Colonies. Thanking "Your Lordship" for the favours that had led to the emigration, Peters wrote that "we are intirely Satisfied with the Place and the Climate; and hope that our Fellow-sufferers [back in Nova Scotia] whose circumstances did not permit them to join us, may soon enjoy the same Blessing." Their treatment on the passage, he reported, had been "very good" even though the provisions were "ordinary": salt fish four days a week, half of it spoiled, as were most of the turnips. The Sierra Leone natives "are very agreeable with us and we have a Gratefull Sense of His Majesty's goodness in removing us. We shall always endeavour to form ourselves, according to His Religion and Law's and endeavour to instruct our Children in the Same." And Thomas Peters, the first African-American leader, ended with a ringing declaration of his true allegiance: "Long

May His Majesty and Royal Family live Blest with Peace and Prosperity here and Eternal Glory hereafter."[23] Peters's loyalty, then, was to George III and his ministers, to Britain and the promise of British freedom—not to those whom he increasingly thought had suborned it, among whom he was beginning to include Lieutenant Clarkson.

On Easter Sunday four children were baptized by David George, whom Clarkson still counted among his best friends. On leaving the Canvas Room, he was as usual besieged by black settlers who gave him letters and petitions to read. At dinner aboard the *Amy* later that day he read one from Tobias Humes, warning him of "divisions and fictions" [*sic*] determined to "elect Mr Peters as their Governor and to petition the Honourable Company at home for that purpose." If this news, they wrote, had

> ... reached your honour's knoledge, you are already armed against their efforts, and excuse your humble servant, if that you are not, I hope that these few lines will put you on your Guard although I write with a trembling hand for I know not how to conduct myself at present and if that my name should come to their ears and denies your protection [*sic*] my situation is bad—the Preeston People have no hand in the affair at all but they mean to stand fast by your honour and abide by the consequences so that we subscribe ourselves Your Excellency's humble servants and faithful friends.
>
> PS We rely on your Honour that our names may be a secret as we know not but our lives are depending.[24]

Any thought of post-prandial quiet fled. Electrified by the letter, convinced that some sort of rebellion, if not outright revolution, was at hand and must be nipped in the bud, Clarkson summoned a boat and had himself rowed ashore at speed. Having confided in Richard Pepys, the surveyor, he then strode, like a man possessed, all weakness forgotten, up the hill behind the Canvas Room to a wooden, open-frame tower where a great bell hung, the tocsin of the colony. The peals rang out over the shore to the fishing boats, to the men labouring in the forest, and up into the hills. Startled, the population rushed from whatever they were doing to the huge cotton-silk tree that had become the outdoor place for serious palaver. Peters was there, impenitent and impassive. From beneath the shade of the tree's branches Clarkson addressed himself, in the first instance, to Peters, but loudly and clearly enough for all to hear. He did not mince words.

> I said it was probable either one or other of us would be hanged upon that Tree before the Palaver was settled, and holding up the letter I stated the purport of it at the same time observing that I should always consider those who had sent it to me as the best men in the place and I hoped to be able, before I had done, to satisfy the whole Colony that they ought to feel the greatest Obligation to them for having put me on my guard that I might face the Business manfully and recue them and their posterity from the inevitable ruin which must take place if they suffered themselves to be inflamed by such pernicious Councils.[25]

Cries went up from the crowd to name the informers. Having flourished the letter (probably to the terror of those who had written it), Clarkson rapidly replaced it in his coat pocket and declared, as if he were playing some hero on the Drury Lane stage, that while there was still life in his body, he would not betray those names, nor would he ever forget their exemplary conduct. "I then called to their remembrance the many sacrifices I had made and was daily making to promote their happiness" and, as if he were on trial himself, "referred them to the whole of my Conduct toward them since I had known them." There were issues of practical ruin here, he insisted, but also of outrage to law and right behaviour. If they were cantankerous towards the company, should they not recollect how much the company had already spent on them "although they were perfect strangers to them"? And he "endeavoured to press upon their Minds the Criminality of their conduct if, after all that had been done for them, they could, for a moment doubt the sincerity of the Sierra Leone Company's views." Should they permit the "Demon of Discord" to establish itself, they could expect nothing but misery.

Understandably taken aback—relieved, perhaps, that Clarkson seemed to have concluded this astonishing performance—a few of the braver settlers attempted to set things right. With the deepest of respect, they said, and whatever he might have been told, he had quite misunderstood the nature of their representation. It was just because Mr

Clarkson was seen to be so daily inundated with matters trivial as well as serious that they meant nothing more than to relieve him of some of this burden. For that reason alone "they had chosen Thomas Peters their Chief Speaker or chairman as it was by his interference and interest that they were removed from Nova Scotia and 132 of them had signed a paper of this purport dated the 23rd of March which Paper Peters had intended last night to have put into the Governor's hands." Truly they had no other view than to "relieve the Governor of the fatigue of so many applications and expressed their sorrow that he should have taken it up so warmly, but that they hoped he would see it in a different light for that they assured him they had been most grossly misrepresented."[26]

Clarkson spoke again. "The alarm and agitation being so great I found it no easy matter to persuade them they were in the wrong, however after arguing with them for a long time, they at last gave way and with the liveliest feelings of Gratitude and respect they expressed themselves extremely hurt at what had passed and promised everything I desired begging of me with all the tenderness imaginable, some of them with tears, not to expose myself any longer to the Evening air as they observed I was much fatigued with talking to them and they feared it would materially injure me."

Thus ended the Easter rising at Freetown, which was, as Clarkson discovered when he perused the list of a 132 and found that it included some of his closest and most trusted friends, such as David George, surely no rebellion at all. Many of the names were New Brunswickers and people from Brindley Town and Digby—the same people whose trust Peters had won before going to London. But a good number were also Birchtowners. Peters, whom Clarkson now warily respected as "a man of great penetration and cunning," he decided probably had no design "to assume the Government," despite the warning letter that had described an imminent coup. Still, Clarkson resolved, "not only to keep an eye upon him myself but also to have his Actions watched and reported to me in Private."

Even if Clarkson's hair-trigger nervousness had exaggerated the crisis, there is no doubt that something serious had happened. Embedded in the proposal to "relieve" Clarkson of some of the pettier problems of the colony, however deferentially expressed, was, of course, the germ of Granville Sharp's ideas of free black self-government, beginning with local matters—the kind of things that were appropriate for duly elected tithingmen and hundredors. By following the lead of his informers and assuming that the situation was tantamount to a usurpation of his own hard-earned authority, Clarkson had put *amour-propre* before political reflection. How could the assumption of some public duties by the blacks possibly be any worse than the carnival of incompetence and corruption perpetrated every day by the whites under the eyes of an increasingly alienated population of blacks?

David George and his friends did what they could to calm Clarkson down. Remember, they said, all the betrayals in Nova Scotia? Here too there is *talk* of our receiving land, but only talk! You did say we should not be taxed with a quit rent, yet it is said that the company means to lay the tax on us in such a way that may yet make us slaves again. We are a people deceived many, many times. No wonder, then, that we may be suspicious, whether with cause or no.

Days later the colony still trembled, either in anger or in trepidation, from the effect of the palaver under the cotton-silk tree. Clarkson learned that someone had died of the shock of it. "A Young Woman seeing me land and walk at unusual pace up the Hill and hearing the Great Bell ring, immediately afterwards was so frightened, knowing her husband had signed the paper for Peters's appointment that she was taken with strong convulsions and soon after expired."[27]

Although he thought he had mastered the worst of the situation, Clarkson was told there were still ugly things happening; men suspected of being the informers were intimidated, others interrogated. Henry Beverhout, one of the Methodist captains, came to see him to insist that his flock had nothing to do with the agitation. Three days after the palaver Clarkson called another general assembly, this time in the Canvas Room, with all the free blacks lined up in their shipboard companies and under their black captains. The settlers were asked to sign a document stating that while they were in Freetown they would live obedient to its laws, which "as far as circumstances will permit" would be "made comfortable with the laws of England."[28] There was a general sound of assent.

A tornado was gusting up. The silvery floss from the cotton-silk trees was blowing now, high in the sky, coming in from as far away as the northern Bullom shore. Then it descended, covering everything with its delicate, drooping filaments. Out in the bay, sailors on the *Harpy* could still be seen picking strands out of the sheets and shrouds.[29]

F OR ALL THE SEVERITY of his demeanour, in the days and weeks after Easter Sunday 1792 Clarkson behaved carefully towards the blacks. But the key to re-establishing his authority with those among whom it had been shaken, he knew, was asserting himself over the whites—councillors, soldiers and sailors—whose conduct towards the blacks was the source of much of the anger. Whenever he had an opportunity to demonstrate his even-handedness, Clarkson seized it with theatrical eagerness. Grass and thatch for the repair of huts damaged by the storms was desperately needed, but as the line of forest and scrub was gradually being pushed back, the distance the blacks had to walk with bundles of grass on their backs made the task much harder. So Clarkson ordered a cutter from the *Lapwing* to go upstream, gather the grass and sail it back down to the colony. With the storms becoming more frequent, there was, he thought, no time to lose, so the order was given for a Sunday, a day when all kinds of work was being done around the settlement. But the *Lapwing*'s sailors, hating the idea that they were to have their rest interrupted to make life easier for the blacks, decided they would instead observe the Lord's Day, even though none of the seamen had hitherto been conspicuous for their piety.

Clarkson's decision to make an example of these recalcitrants was also based on the seamen's habit of referring to the settlers as "Black Rascals" and using "other insulting and degrading expressions highly injurious to the harmony of the Colony and extremely offensive to the Nova Scotians."[30] At issue, too, was the superintendent's authority over the squadron of ships. The master of the *Harpy*, Captain Wilson, whose behaviour was increasingly cantankerous, was prepared to countermand almost anything Clarkson said. A show of power was called for. Accordingly, Captain Robinson of the *Lapwing* was ordered to be present at the trial of four men said to be "ringleaders," each of whom was sentenced to three dozen lashes. This was the world of the slave plantation turned upside down. The white governor had ordered white sailors to be publicly flogged before all the assembled blacks for refusing to do something that could ease their toil and for habitually subjecting the blacks to abuse! Moreover, the man who would administer the flogging was himself a black, Simon Proof, who had sometimes performed this service in the British army. But Proof was not especially eager to be the instrument of the superintendent's exercise in salutory racial justice, and had to be talked into it. Clarkson told him that no matter how distasteful he might find it, the welfare of the colony depended on the public punishment.[31]

Under lowering clouds, the entire colony and the crews of the ships were summoned by the great bell on the hill and Clarkson made another speech.

> I now shortly addressed the Nova Scotians upon the necessity to protect their families and told them unless we could ensure a proper subordination in every department of the Colony it would be impossible for us to succeed. I declared that it was far from my desire to make any distinction between Black and White, on the contrary I wished them to consider each other as Brethren requiring mutual kindness from each other in their present arduous situation and no part of their Conduct would be more gratifying to me than to see them endeavour to lighten each other's hardships by a conciliatory and Christian-like conduct.[32]

The first of the guilty seamen, hands tied, was brought forward and leaned against the whipping post. Clarkson declared that he "punished only with a view to reformation," then told Proof to proceed. The sailor had a bullet clenched between his teeth the better to stand the pain, and worked his jaws on the metal as the stripes were laid on him. Through the first thirteen lashes the prisoner grimaced silently, but at the fourteenth, when his flesh opened, the bullet dropped from his mouth and released a scream. Clarkson ordered Proof to stop, then approached the sailor and asked him if he felt sorry for the offence and if he was willing to amend his conduct. When he grunted yes, he was untied and taken to the guardhouse. Not surprisingly, after a few lashes the second prisoner made his own gesture of contrition, likewise the third. "I dismissed the people," Clarkson wrote, "being satisfied a sufficient impression had been made."[33]

Gestures alone were not enough. A few days after the flogging Clarkson sent Nathaniel Gilbert back to London on the fastest of his ships, the *Felicity*, with letters for Thornton and the directors. To the Board of Directors, he detailed some of the worst abuses inflicted on the colony, especially the corruption at the storehouse, where, he told the directors, the company was being robbed every day by unscrupulous whites while honest blacks suffered. Until and unless they gave him proper power to over-ride the council, this state of unholy chaos would continue and he could not possibly be expected to be responsible for such a state of affairs. He ended, therefore, with an ultimatum: "Give me authority and if it does not come too late I will pledge myself to remedy the whole. If you do not my resolution is fixed. I must return home."[34] The private letters he sent were still more passionate and angry. He accused his brother Thomas of concocting the kind of government precisely calculated to make the settlers as miserable as possible; and to Thornton he thundered, "I call God to witness, who knows the secrets of the heart that I should rejoice to lay down my life to accomplish the great wishes of the Sierra Leone Company," but if they would not grant him what was needed, they had better consider a replacement.[35]

To get some sea breezes inside his clammy lungs Clarkson sailed a short distance with the *Felicity* out to the Banana Islands. When he got back, on the 26th of April, a thunderbolt hit in the shape of a grievance against Thomas Peters brought by a settler who claimed that Peters had purloined the property of a recently deceased man. Conscious of Peters's following, Clarkson did not leap at the opportunity to discredit his rival. Until hearing the grievance in person, he was inclined to dismiss is as a personal grudge. But it soon became apparent that *not* to act on what seemed to be indisputable evidence risked alienating at least as many blacks as would be offended by proceeding against Peters. On the 29th the worst storm yet struck Freetown, lightning bolts coming so close together that they flashed continuously for ten minutes, "appearing like Cataracts of fire, rushing down from the sky."[36] Clarkson made up his mind. Peters would have to be tried.

On the 1st of May Peters admitted having taken the goods, but insisted that the man had incurred a debt to him in Nova Scotia that had never been repaid, and that he had therefore merely been claiming property to which he was rightfully entitled. A black jury, however, disagreed, ruling that he had no right to the goods and ordering their return to the widow. No other form of punishment was handed down: Clarkson evidently felt the humiliation had been enough to do permanent damage to Peters's leadership. A sign of that was a letter from Peters himself, informing Clarkson that he had given up the property but asking him to appeal the jury's verdict. "Of course," Clarkson wrote, "I did not choose to interfere further in the Business."[37]

Despite Peters's fall from grace, Clarkson still felt insecure and took to summoning assemblies of the settlers for speeches that turned into rambling confessionals punctuated by veiled threats. On the 3rd of May he told them that he was "nearly worn out, that I came to this Colony to expect difficulties and [when] they could not be avoided I met them Cheerfully," but he had been grieved by the neglect of public works, with settlers "sneaking away before the hour of labour was over." Petulantly, half schoolmaster and half affronted Old Testament prophet, he declared that, were it not for his love of Africa, he would instantly retire to his friends in England, who were anxious to see him again, and that "unless I saw a great difference in their behaviour I should certainly leave them; that I did not wish to leave them in anger but on the contrary would shake hands with them all, wishing them from my heart as much happiness as they wished themselves. If they thought they could do better without me than with me . . . it was much better and more honourable for them to say so at once than suffer me to sacrifice my life in their Service without doing them any good."[38] This shamelessly self-pitying appeal, with its vision of imminent farewells, had precisely the effect Clarkson wanted: "An instantaneous expression of gratitude burst from the whole."

There were only so many times, however, when Clarkson could turn on these nakedly emotional appeals to loyalty and self-sacrifice. Besieged with complaints at all hours of the day and night, he took to sleeping sometimes aboard the *Amy.* But even there he would lie awake and the sounds of Sierra Leone would assail him from every direction: the drumming and singing from King Jimmy's town; the wailing hallelujahs from the night services that the Methodists and Baptists were holding; the roaring of drunken soldiers from their tents; the unstoppable, immense thrumming of the insects, millions of jointed legs rubbing, and then, deep within the serpentine chambers of his afflicted head, yet other throbbing sounds drilling away and not leaving him in peace. What would become of his memory, already so tattered and torn? He kept the worst of it from those over whom he must summon a semblance of authority. He must not seem perplexed.

He waited impatiently for an answer from the directors to his demands, but although ships came and went in the steely waters of Kru Bay, answer came there none. But at least some of those ships supplied him with new faces; men whom he thought, right away, might be sympathetic to his mission. Fresh blood was needed, since his old Nova Scotia comrade, the surgeon Charles Taylor, was himself sick, moody and (he blushed to acknowledge it) sometimes showed signs of indulgence in liquor, which was when he made no secret of his ardent wish to go back to England. Alexander Falconbridge, whom Clarkson thought one of the best of the bad bunch of councillors, at heart a good and even sensible soul (though with no sign of any aptitude in the way of commerce), was now also deep in his cups, often sick and vomiting, pitifully incoherent, subject to violent fits of evil temper, which were sometimes directed against his blameless wife. For some reason—perhaps because his little book on the slave trade had opened so many hitherto closed or indifferent minds—Clarkson felt for him, but at the same time knew (and wrote to tell the directors, who after all must be concerned with the investment) that Falconbridge was utterly unfit to be the "commercial agent" of the colony.

So Clarkson was cordial towards the new arrivals, among them an affable young American loyalist, Isaac DuBois from Wilmington, North Carolina (the country Peters had fled), who, although once a wealthy cotton planter, was deeply sympathetic to the blacks. Doubtless influenced by Carl Wadstrom, there were two Swedes: Adam Afzelius, a naturalist and student of Linnaeus, and Augustus Nordenskjold, a mineralogist, eager (over-eager, Clarkson thought) to explore inland for the veins of gold he had heard of and that lay in the territories of the old Naimbana's chief queen. But he could scarcely go there yet. The rains were relentless, and temperatures, especially at night, began to dive, adding cold to the misery of the continuous drenchings. The surveying and laying out of town and country lots went at snail's pace, engendering more fears among the settlers that, as in Nova Scotia, without their own plots, they were doomed to labouring for others.

Supplies were so limited that everyone was on short allowance. When a packet ship, the *Trusty*, arrived with desperately needed supplies, Clarkson discovered that they had been so carelessly packed into cheap barrels without iron bands that the casks had often split en route, exposing food, textiles and tools to ruin and rot. Barrels of spoiled pickled tripe lay about, adding to the appalling smells coming from the refuse area around the storehouse and inviting colonies of enormous rats to roam the grass-lined streets of Freetown. Drunkenness was becoming a serious problem, habitual among the sailors and councillors who, when they needed restocking, would send upstream to the slave factories on Bance and Gambier islands for it. But, to his dismay, Clarkson also noticed that liquor was starting to make inroads among "his" blacks. To his amazement the Methodist preacher Henry Beverhout had actually complained that Clarkson withheld grog from the blacks working on the experimental garden attached to his house. To Clarkson this could only mean that Beverhout had somehow fallen under the influence of Peters, who had evidently recovered from his temporary disgrace and was seen attending the night services of both Methodists and Baptists. Clarkson believed that Peters still wanted to be elected "Speaker-General" for the blacks and thought of him increasingly as a kind of black Cromwell, inciting them to voice their grievances and always parading his own authority as the person responsible for their coming out of Nova Scotia. On the 31st of May he got a letter from Peters, effectively acting in this capacity, requesting that Clarkson meet with the blacks "according to your promise; if not please give me the liberty to speak a few words to them today for I do not mean to live in such confusion."[39]

What was John Clarkson to do? Without ever quite acknowledging it, or merely discounting it as the effects of "ignorance" or gullibility, he was witnessing, along with many other kinds of transformations of African-American slaves, the birth pangs of their politics. Avoiding yet another grand palaver, for his physical condition was deteriorating again, Clarkson took a short sail along the coast to try to clear his head.

But he returned feeling only more uncertain about the path to follow in what were turning, in effect, into constitutional arguments with the blacks. Constantly wrong-footed by the irrepressibility of the arguments (and acknowledging the substance of many grievances), he was amazed that Abraham Elliott Griffith, the secretary-interpreter of the Naimbana, one of Sharp's protégés and someone on whom he thought he could depend, seemed to have lined up with Peters's "party." For on the 15th of June a letter signed by both of them made concrete proposals for a twelve-man panel that would include the two of them, to be appointed to settle internal disputes among the settlers. This was, in fact, a modest and perfectly reasonable request, but it made the defensive Clarkson jittery.

Active involvement, he decided, was the only way to blunt the edge of these demands for self-government. In the absence of Gilbert, the minister, Clarkson himself, despite his frailties, took over the work of preaching at the Anglican services, and when he could, inserted some sort of homily that would help the state of the colony. But he also felt he had to attend the night meetings and religious services of the Baptists and Methodists, so that when Peters "harangued" the people he would in his turn ask for their ear and get it. In the end, he ran out of reasons why Peters's jury panels of twelve ought not to be instituted. Indeed, he met with the twelve who had agreed, in the first instance, to serve, and found himself wholeheartedly agreeing with many of their complaints about the continuing obstructiveness of the surveying team, especially the engineer Cocks. Clarkson in fact went one better than Peters by suggesting that perhaps the captains of the black companies who had served so well on the voyage might be best for the jury, or that black males over twenty-one in each of twelve streets (presently named after the twelve directors of the company) should elect one of their number.

When he got back from another trip up-river to Bance Island to buy medicines from the slaving factory for the sick, including himself, on the 25th of June he was handed an extraordinary letter. It was signed by Henry Beverhout on behalf of his own company, but evidently spoke for many more.[40] There were immediate, material, concrete issues to which Beverhout addressed himself: "the pepel of our Companey Consesents to the wagers that your honer proposul that is to work for two Shillens a day as long as we drowr our provisions." They were happy to have a constable for each street "for to kepen pece." And they took it hard to be told they should have to pay for provisions from the stores when, after all this time, they expected to have their own lands and be able to support themselves from its produce.

But the document of the 25th of June was not just a list of grievances, more a social and political contract. It was an assertion, the first of its kind, of the civil and political rights to which the blacks knew they were entitled. It was, in fact, the first African-American demand for representation—a proper share in British freedom. "We are all willing to be govern by the laws of england in full but we donot Consent to gave it in to your hands with out haven aney of our own Culler in it." After listening to Clarkson threaten so many times to leave them should they not submit to everything he said, the blacks had clearly had enough of his emotional and political blackmail. They reminded him of what he had promised them in Wilkinson's church at Birchtown, and even called his bluff over his often threatened departure: "ther is non of us wold wish your honer to go way and leave us hear but your will be pleased to rember what your honer told the piepel in a maraca [America] at Shelburn that is whoever Came to Saraleon wold be free and should have a law and when theur war aney trial thear should by a jurey of both white and black and all should be equel so we Consideren all this think that we have a wright to Chuse men that we think proper for to act for us in a reasonable manner." It was their turn, gently, to make a threat: "we wish for pece if posable we can but to gave all out of our hands we cannot your honer know that we have laws and ragerlations among our self and be Consirent with the laws of England because we have seen it in all the parts whear eaver we have being Sir we do not mene to take the law in our hands by no meanes but to have your honer approbation for we own you to be our had and govener."[41]

To think of Beverhout's remonstrance as clumsy in its expression is to mistake patois for incoherence. It is, in fact, eloquent, both of deeply held grievances and of a budding understanding of political rights and remedies. More than that, it is impossible to read its conditional acceptance of Clarkson's executive power and the repeated allegiance to the laws of England without seeing the document as a chapter in the long transatlantic history of liberty. It had been the animus of American Patriots in the 1770s that somehow the rights of self-representation, implicit in their allegiance to the king, had been set aside by his minions. The whole, tortured history of the black loyalists had turned that charge back on America, which had, in its Declaration of Independence, promised equality but protected slavery. Now, once again, they saw the promise of making their own free society betrayed, and were summoning Clarkson back to honour his Birchtown speech and what they still, loyally, took to be the promise of truly British freedom. The king, one of the blacks told Clarkson when he responded to the petitions at a palaver the next day, "we know he is our friend, neither do we blame those who took us to Nova Scotia and New Brunswick [such as Guy Carleton and James Paterson] for they behaved well to us but we blame those who told lies to the King about us [the white loyalists and the white councillors] so that we now not having got our lands . . . makes us very uneasy fearing we shall be liable to the same cruel treatment."[42] Whatever else would happen, they would not be slaves again.

It is impossible to read the little manifesto of the 26th of June, notwithstanding Clarkson's paranoia about his rival, without seeing the hand of Thomas Peters in it. But Clarkson does not say this, and for the good reason that for a week now Peters had been ill, seriously enough for him not to make his usual appearances at the night services. When Clarkson gathered the blacks to talk about the petitions they had sent him, he was addressing a community in shock. For Thomas Peters, the "Speaker-General" of the blacks in all but official title, had died the previous night.

Astoundingly, Clarkson says nothing about this event other than to acknowledge that it had happened and that it had made for "agitation and confusion in the Colony." Peters's widow, Sarah, sent a poignant letter, not to Clarkson, whom she must have assumed would be unsympathetic, but to Alexander Falconbridge. Slightly ashamed that he must have become, to the Peterses, so much an enemy that the widow could not bring herself to address him directly, Clarkson copied that letter into his journal. Sarah begged Mr Falconbridge's favour to have some wine, porter, rum, candles and a length of white linen (doubtless to bury Thomas in): "my husband is dead and I am in great distress . . . my children is all sick. My distress is not to be equalled. I remain aflicted."[43]

Clarkson gave immediate orders to send Sarah Peters everything that she had requested. And when a small delegation, also nervous of what he might say, came to ask whether, contrary to regulations, he would allow a wooden coffin to be made for Thomas (normally coffins were allowed only if the wood could be supplied by friends of the deceased from their own supply of planking), he assented, if only so as not to be seen as vindictive. As for himself, recalling the absurdly extravagant obsequies for the drunken Dr Bell, Clarkson remained ostentatiously virtuous. Should he die in Sierra Leone (as seemed very likely), the council and settlers were under strict orders not to waste wood on his body. Let him sink, uncoffined, into the sodden soil. But Thomas Peters was buried in Freetown, as requested, in a solid wooden box—not solid enough, however, to imprison his ghost, which a month later was said to be walking the village. Told about this, Clarkson wrote, unconvincingly, "I never listen to anything that may be said respecting him."

A ND THEN, magically, harmony appeared in Freetown. Or at least Harmony Hall, which is the name John Clarkson gave to a new, single-storey frame building completed in mid-August 1792, and which was intended in the first instance to be a congenial mess for the officers and staff of the company and their wives, but expanded to include quarters for the bachelor men. Clarkson saw it as the symbol of a new beginning, a place where people, black and white, could gather—whether dining, talking or listening to yet another of Clarkson's inspirational homilies—and "draw together for the public good." But the hall became multi-purpose, a place to receive African chiefs such as King Jimmy, who, having conquered his aversion to Freetown, made appearances flanked by boys with horse pistols; black captains whom Clarkson wanted to consult; and officers and men from the Sierra Leone packets. It housed a throng "from morning till . . . sometimes midnight, of black and white, known and unknown, busy and idle persons."[44]

But harmony did not break out overnight. Even with the addition of the more pleasant and competent newcomers—the botanizing Swede Adam Afzelius, Isaac DuBois, and the new physician, Thomas Winterbottom—the white councillors and officials were not conspicuously more reconciled to each other or to their work. The surveyor Richard

Pepys and his wife complained bitterly and endlessly to Clarkson about their neighbours, "those vile people" the Whites, in charge of the storehouse. Alexander Falconbridge, the sad sack of a "commercial agent," had not only transacted no commerce whatsoever to date, but was now so drowned in alcohol that he was dismissed from his post. The dyspeptic Captain Wilson of the *Harpy* went from mad to madder. Reproached by Clarkson for not giving the visiting Naimbana the courtesy of a boarding and a salute, Wilson responded by banning Clarkson and anyone who agreed with him from the ship. Removed from command, Wilson then took control of the *Harpy* on his own authority, threatened bloodshed to anyone attempting a boarding and finally sailed off out of the bay before he could be stopped, taking with him some captive white passengers, many of them sick.

And yet, by the end of August, the chronically hag-ridden, frantic, melancholic Clarkson was feeling, if not exactly well, then somewhat better, and if not exactly happy, then modestly satisfied with the way things were now proceeding in Freetown. The rains were at last winding down. The occasional tornado came ripping and gusting along, but they were much fewer and less violent. The ants were still on the march, especially, and terrifyingly, in the dead of night, accompanied by swarming infestations of spiders and cockroaches. Clarkson and Anna Maria both noticed how the red ants would make war on the black ants, and were capable of carrying off live chicks, or even devouring doves while they were still perched in their dovecots. Leopards would occasionally stalk about the village at night seeing what they could pick up, one of them biting off more than it could certainly chew in the shape of David George's pet Newfoundland dog, brought from Nova Scotia and which, though mauled, put up a good fight.

Notwithstanding these continuing trials, those who had survived the first six months were noticeably healthier. The wave of mortality was ebbing, especially amongst the blacks, although Clarkson admitted later in the year that he dreaded what the census would tell him. When the counting was done it was seen that 14 percent of the immigrants from Nova Scotia had perished. With the whites it was closer to 70 percent.

For the sick, there was now a hospital in Freetown: a substantial building, one hundred feet long, built from prefabricated parts and shipped over in one of the supply vessels that were now making more frequent stops in Sierra Leone. They also brought fresh provisions and tools, but of greater importance for Clarkson were the letters he received from his brother, Wilberforce and the other directors, giving him the power he had demanded to run the colony as he saw fit. Beside the official good news, and supplies of hair powder, chocolate, wine and pickles, there were affectionate letters, not least because Thomas Clarkson had heard, to his horror, that his brother had been murdered and the colony again wiped out. Flooded with relief when they got his letters from Nathaniel Gilbert and realized he was still alive, they had capitulated to John's demands. "Take courage, my dear John," Wilberforce had written, "I give you Health and Spirits to undergo all your trials—we shall here do all we can to render your Situation comfortable & you will constantly be remembered by me in those Moments when the Mind runs to those for whom it is most interested."

So the lieutenant got what he wanted. The old council of eight in which he had been no better than a frustrated *primus inter pares* was abolished, replaced by a governor and just two subordinate councillors. Clarkson was so overjoyed by the change that he magnanimously commended the directors for their expression of Whiggish nervousness about seeming to deliver "arbitrary" power into the hands of a supreme chief. In his journal he decided that this August reformation should be thought of as the true foundation of the colony. Besides being governor, John Clarkson was now also Sunday pastor (for Gilbert's replacement, the Reverend Horne, took some time arriving), military commander, omniscient supervisor of surveying and town planning, and chief magistrate, empowered to adjudicate and legislate as he saw fit for the best interests of Freetown.

Instead of alienating the blacks, Clarkson, with his new authority did what he could to co-opt them. Cases concerning settlers were now heard only by all-black juries. One of the earliest and most upsetting was the trial of John Cambridge, a survivor of Granville Town and one of the captains of the London blacks, who, shockingly to Clarkson, had been caught selling a slave to a Dutch slave ship. When Cambridge was tried and found guilty, Clarkson, noting how much "violent feeling" there was among the settlers towards the man, confessed that "this business has plagued me greatly for the crime was so novel and so unexpected that I did not know how to meet it."[45] He delivered a long, impassioned speech, half sermon, half harangue, on the effect that stories of the free blacks turning slave traders would have on the reputation of the colony among both blacks and whites, and the damage it would do to the British goodwill necessary if it was to survive and flourish. In the end Cambridge was clapped in irons aboard the *Harpy* (before the mad Captain Wilson piratically sailed it away), to be taken back to England.

Protective about the moral calibre of the colony, Clarkson had originally banned the "old settlers" of Granville Town from coming to Freetown in case what he took to be their indolent ways and partiality to rum should corrupt the Nova Scotians. But when he had heard, from Abraham Elliott Griffith among others, about the depths of their privations he relented and readmitted them as full citizens of Freetown. Like the rest of the settlers, on the 13th of August they voted for their constabulary and peace officers, who were sworn in on the same day by Clarkson. In a gesture to Granville Sharp's original scheme, tithingmen had been elected from each unit of ten families, and hundredors from each group of ten tithingmen. It was hardly the system of devolved democracy that Sharp had envisaged; but it was nonetheless the first occasion on which African-Americans voted in any election, and the devolution of authority to the community's own people worked much as Clarkson hoped. When a white sailor was caught robbing the general store, only the posting of the constables around town prevented bad feeling from deteriorating into a riot.

Clarkson himself now had the authority to defuse trouble before it got seriously out of control, often by ignoring or countermanding instructions he had received from the company when they contradicted prior guaranteees he had given to the settlers in Nova Scotia. Unbeknownst to Clarkson, the company had decided to levy a quit rent. Discovering this bad news from their letters, he simply decided not to pass it on. The company had commandeered the waterfront for its own wharves and warehouses, cutting off settlers' lots from direct access to the water. This was precisely the obstruction that had aggrieved settlers at Digby and other places in Nova Scotia, and when they found they were to be blocked again their representatives, such as Isaac Anderson, reproached Clarkson with such fierce language that he walked out of the meeting. Privately, however, he conceded the justice of the settlers' complaints and decided, again unilaterally, to abandon company monopoly of the waterfront sites, allowing anyone lucky enough to draw a water-lot to take possession and, if they wanted, build their own docks and warehouses. To the directors in London he simply wrote that if they wanted the colony to succeed, "the Company must abide by my instruction."[46]

By October 1792 Freetown was no longer just an idea (and a far-fetched one at that). It was a place—a place quite unlike any other in the Atlantic world; it was a community of free black British African-Americans. Nine of the twelve streets ran at right-angles to the shore and were lined with neat little timber-frame houses, where the settlers and their families lived. They had survived the worst of the storms, even if they did constantly need rethatching and were vulnerable to being over run by columns of voracious ants, small packs of rats and the occasional foraging anteater. Intersecting the streets were what Clarkson called the three "beautiful avenues," one running along the shore, where the public buildings were sited. There were two open spaces for gatherings and palavers, one of them overlooked by the tower with the great bell that rang each day at sunrise to call the settlers to work. Besides Harmony Hall, Freetown had a school where Joseph Leonard from Brindley Town taught the children. It had, at last, a proper church, packed on Sundays and full enough of worshippers every night that the sermons, hymns and cries of devotional enthusiasm kept Anna Maria Falconbridge awake. It had a retail store where blacks actually sold goods to whites from visiting ships, as well as to each other, and a lively little fishing port from which twelve boats sailed out into the bay, coming back loaded with an abundant catch.

And at long last, with the rains receding, Pepys and his thirty survey workers were running lines delineating the cultivable lots for the black settlers. Not all were yet cleared, but in the little gardens in September herbs and vegetables began to poke above the surface. "The gardens of the settlers," Clarkson wrote on the 21st of September, "begin to look very pleasing, the Nova Scotians brought out with them a quantity of *good seeds* and have been able to furnish the officers with many vegetables, especially cabbages, besides satisfying their own wants."[47] The horticulture wrote the blacks' own extraordinary history in the soil:

melons, beans and corn from their American past; pumpkins, squashes and cabbages from Nova Scotia; papaya, mangoes, cassava, yams, groundnuts and rice from their new old country. Joshua Montefiore, who had come to Sierra Leone on the *Calypso,* one of the bedraggled survivors of a failed expedition to Bullom Island sent in competition with the company, looked at Freetown and gushed with admiration: "It is impossible to conceive the chearfulness with which they go to their daily labour [on public works] at five o'clock in the morning and continue till the afternoon, when each attends his domestic concerns and cultivates his garden. In the evening they adjourn to some meeting, of which they have many and sing Psalms with the greatest devotion until late at night. It is a pleasing sight on Sunday to see them go to church, attired in their gayest apparel with content and happiness imprinted on their countenances."[48] Even allowing for poetic licence, the place could be, then, as pretty as a picture, and Clarkson's secretary, John Beckett, evidently a dab hand with watercolours, did one for him in early November.

It was meant as a souvenir. For in late October Clarkson had told the settlers and the company people that he would be leaving Freetown at the end of the year. Everyone was thrown into consternation by this announcement, especially the blacks, who implored him to reconsider, and even the local chiefs—Jimmy, Queen Yamacouba, Signor Domingo and the Naimbana—whom he had gathered at a big palaver in late September to settle issues over the boundaries of the colony, and who made no secret of their trust and even admiration for the nervy, slender young man who now could speak their pidgin and who had grown to appreciate the drums. He was even able to act as a local chief himself when a settler took liberties with one of Signor Domingo's wives, provoking the outraged husband to threaten to shoot the transgressor. Loftily, Clarkson condemned the wickedness and the malefactor, while telling Signor Domingo (who liked to sport his pendant cross) that his conduct was un-Christian and that he ought instead to come to him with any complaint. "I said Signor Domingo you no like war but suppose you shoot my man you make war upon me and I could not keep my people from making war upon you and you know that would be wicked palaver."[49] This was the way Clarkson spoke now, when he had to, and he rather enjoyed it, much as he liked, to his amazement, the rhythm of the drums in Jimmy's village—the same sounds that had once bored holes in his temples.

Faced with, and complimented by, all these glum faces, Clarkson reassured everyone that his departure would certainly not be permanent. He had been gone from England more than a year and had never thought he would have to be governor of the colony; all he intended to do by returning was to spend a few months' leave in England to repair his health, see his brother, his friends and his patient fiancée, Susannah (after whom he had named a bay), and take the opportunity of speaking personally to the directors about the future of the colony rather than rely on intermittent dispatches. That was the way, he reassured the blacks, he could best represent their interests.

All the same, Clarkson's coming departure made the 13th of November an especially emotional event. He had decided to devote the whole day to "rejoicing" and led the entire population, men, women and children, up the slope of a hill at the back of the town. Although the land had been partly cleared to make way for the small farms, the "craggy steepness" slowed the climb. Clarkson took the opportunity to chat with the blacks as they walked, impressing on them how far they had already come—from slavery to redemption—but how much farther they still had to go if Africa was to be benignly affected by their achievement. Halfway up, the party paused for lunch at a brook that "spilled over the rocks in the most romantic manner" and filled Clarkson's already emotionally overloaded breast with a further shot of sublimity. Finally, they reached the top and looked down, hot and exhilarated, at the trim rows of their houses, at the church, the bell tower and Harmony Hall; then out to the turquoise sea, the rivers and woods and inlets, a prospect "too beautiful for me to describe." Then came the reward for the effort as Clarkson handed to forty settlers—eleven women and twenty-nine men—the certificates of the land grants they had drawn by lot, each about five acres—redeeming, if on a smaller scale than anticipated, at least one of the promises he had made to them in Moses Wilkinson's chapel on that rainy day in Birchtown just over a year before. Stirred, Clarkson spoke again to the people who had come with him, still like the Israelites of old following Moses to the mount (but so much better behaved!), telling them that the happiness of their children and, for that matter, the whole country around Sierra Leone would depend on them and their conduct.

A tent was set up with tables: harmony reigned on what he now called Directors' Hill. After dinner, Clarkson lifted his glass to the first toast: "The Sierra Leone Company and success to their virtuous exertions." Three volleys of musket fire from the sixty men who had cleared the hill rang out, followed by three cheers. From the fort down below, right on cue, came an answering salute of cannon, booming over the river mouth and then taken up by the guns of the ships moored at the mouth of the river, the smoke curling up into the air, where their masts were festooned with the colours. And so it went on into the gathering twilight, with drinking, huzzahs and cannonades. At last there was a brief moment of grace. Bumpers were hoisted; flares lit the hillside; music sounded and toast after toast resounded in the bat-swept darkness. To the Nova Scotians! To Miss Susannah Lee! To *all* wives and sweethearts! And among the succession of toasts, Clarkson recorded coyly, there was particularly "*one* attended with rapturous cheering, firing, etc."[50]

But with late November came the cool "smokes," the sea fogs drifting in from the harbour, and with them an unpredictable alternation of chills and warmth. And so it was with the lieutenant; more confident than he had ever been that, for a while at least—perhaps six months—he could afford to leave the colony, settled and with the seeds of its prospering deep-sown. Yet come the curling smokes, he worried. His temporary replacement was to be William Dawes, a military man whose most recent post had been governing and guarding the convicts at Botany Bay. To impress on Dawes that his work in Sierra Leone could hardly be *less* a matter of police and punishment, Clarkson gave him tutorials in the long history of the blacks, their escape from American slavery and everything since. If they seemed difficult to manage, over-hasty to take offence or suspicious of whites, there was very good reason for this mistrust, since until very recently all they had ever known was deceit, cruelty and betrayal. Dawes may well have felt he needed no instruction from Clarkson about equity. He had, after all, been dismissed from Botany Bay for refusing to launch a punitive raid on aborigines. Nonetheless, Clarkson took Dawes about the colony with him, trying to make the young man unbend, to become less rigidly formal in his address and demeanour. Clarkson worried too that some members of the old council, especially the surveyor, Pepys, who made no secret of his opinion that the governor had over-indulged the settlers, had told Dawes as much, hoping he would introduce a regime of greater severity.

If that was so, Pepys might have pointed to what he thought was Clarkson's most recent capitulation to the importunings of the blacks. With supplies dwindling, it had been decided that the two-shilling wage paid for a day's work would now only purchase half the rations the settlers had previously been getting. Consternation, fury and petitions greeted this arbitrary decision. Luke Jordan, one of the captains, wrote, "Consider your eccellent promise is to mak all man hapy sir we wont to know wither we is to pay as much for the half rassion as for the full." The next day another petition signed by twenty-eight heads of households, including Boston King, the preacher Cato Perkins, and the fiery Isaac Anderson, made the case that

> . . . we labours very hard with very small wages—which is very loo for the Expence of tools runs hard as we are Oblidge to have a good many therefore we are Come to a Rasalition to lay it before you in hopes yr honour will take in Consideration towards us we don't wish to offend, we Could wish as we only works for three shillings pr day to have our provisions free or else have our wages raisd and pay for it by free grace we wish to have our full provision as work men ought to have and our wages to be half in hard Cash and the other part in the Coloney mony by which there will be no grumbling.[51]

To all the other Freetown firsts, then, needs to be added the first free black labour negotiation—and one, moreover, that was successful. Clarkson conceded the case and, perhaps to Pepys's annoyance and Dawes's bemusement, restored the original ration.

Yet it was precisely Clarkson's willingness to listen, his openness to change his mind and his good faith and transparent affection towards them that won the blacks' respect as no other white Briton, with the exception of Granville Sharp, ever did. And although Clarkson was at pains to smooth Dawes's way by deliberately making him the bearer of whatever good news there was to bring, while taking on himself the role of admonisher, and although the settlers heard him out when he praised Dawes to the sky, many of them remained nervous, reconciled to Clarkson's going only if they could feel certain he would return.

On the 16th of December he spoke to them once more from a pulpit, as he had done the first time when he had seen them gathered in Birchtown. His text, of course, was from the Book of Exodus: and he spoke, feelingly, as patriarch, prophet, father and friend, even though he was still only just twenty-eight years old. In this colony I do not, he said, consider myself "as Governors in general do . . . but as the servant of God, the guardian of your morals and your instructor in religious and temporal duties." He was their Moses, their Aaron, their Joshua, their David. Then he spoke to them from his organ of truth, his heart: "I have professed an affection for many of you. I now declare . . . that I would willingly lay down my life to promote your general happiness; because if I could make you happy and get you once well settled, I should not despair but that your humble, industrious, temperate, peaceable and forgiving conduct would have such an influence on the un-enlightened Pagans of this continent that they would be anxious to embrace Christianity."

Then Clarkson turned, as was his wont, admonisher, lecturing the settlers that they were not to confuse liberty, their right, with licence; he spoke of his disappointment at their contentiousness over wages, and at their increasing indulgence in strong liquor, which he deeply deplored. He was sorry that not everyone had yet received their land, and might not before Christmas as he had hoped, but he had the strictest promises that those still without would shortly come into their possession. Without him, as with him, they must endeavour for right behaviour since "the happiness of every Black man throughout the world" turned on the outcome of the great venture at Sierra Leone. Then, causing a sudden, sinking feeling in the congregation that had packed the church and spilled outside under an awning, Clarkson said frankly that, as they knew, he never liked to make promises unless he could guarantee they would be kept. "I therefore cannot promise you to come back, but I will go so far as to say that I think the chances are ten to one that I shall; for I do not know any employment in this world that would be more pleasing to myself and I hope to my Creator than my best attempt to establish this Colony."[52]

When the time came for valedictions John did what he could, what his heart bade him. Perhaps remembering those who had sat with him on the *Lucretia* as he had sweated and shivered and rambled and raved until the shaking took him to the outer verge of life, he now sat with those on the same dark brink and held their damp hands. Augustus Nordenskjold, the seeker after minerals, whose journey up-country Clarkson knew, with a terrible certainty, would be the end of him, had sent word that he was in distress and sought help. It had been given, and Nordenskjold had come back ragged, skeletal, convulsed with sickness, altogether "more like a spectre than a man." He did not see out the year.

Nor did Alexander Falconbridge. Although he too was very ill, he finally "crawled from his sick bed," as his wife put it, to try to give at least some impression of activity as a commercial agent. He had been in the last stages of planning a trading mission when Clarkson had to give him the news of his dismissal. Clarkson was struck by the relatively impassive way Falconbridge took the blow. But this was a mask, and Anna Maria was not deceived. Long given to drinking his way out of depression and impotence, Falconbridge now took to the bottle with a vengeance. "By way of meliorating his harrowed feelings," Anna Maria wrote, "he kept himself constantly intoxicated; a poor forlorn remedy you will say; however it answered his wish, which I am convinced was to operate as poison and thereby finish his existence." John Clarkson agreed that Falconbridge initially drank more to muffle the pain of his humiliation, but then in such excess as to be unmistakably suicidal. "He has been killing himself by slow degrees for the last three months and for some days past his Bones have been through his skin in several parts of his Body."[53] When the issue of which ship he might sail home on was raised, Falconbridge retorted, half fatalistic, half in defiance, that he would never return to England. He imagined he might still live outside the colony in a vacant house. But on the 19th of December, to no one's surprise, he had a fit and died. Anna Maria did not pretend to grieve. She had borne the brunt of his self-pity, his rum-soaked ravings and his many physically violent outbursts. And she had begun a romance with the young Isaac DuBois, who must have been a source of consolation as well as protection. "I will not be guilty of such meanness as to tell a falsehood on this occasion by saying I regret his death, no! I really do not, his life had become burthensome to himself and all around him and his conduct to me for more than two years past was so unkind (not to give a harsher term) as long since to wean every spark of affection or regard I ever had for him."[54] Wasting no time (for no one knew their allotted ration of happiness in Sierra Leone), Anna Maria asked Clarkson for a licence to marry DuBois. Clarkson gave them his furniture and his blessing but—ever the uncle—asked them to wait a month before marrying.

There were many more emotional farewells. At Robana, the old Naimbana presented Clarkson with a bullock, the fattest anyone had ever seen in Africa, and to keep him safe, a talismanic charm on which was written a passage from the Koran. He wanted Clarkson to see his son John Frederic, over whose portrait, given the chief by Falconbridge earlier that year, the Naimbana expended many sighs and tears. Faced with Clarkson's departure, even some of the white officers said things he could not have expected. Richard Pepys, with whom he had been at constant loggerheads, claimed he would never "forget or Cease to love him."[55]

He waited for Christmas, the first the blacks had spent in their own Freetown. Whatever they had endured and would still endure, this was a time for celebration. On the Eve, they gave themselves over to music, sweet and sad, deep and wild, the sounds of America, of Nova Scotia, of Africa. A crocodile of Joseph Leonard's schoolchildren carolled to the houses. Then a file of fifes and drums snaked and skirled around the streets, right to the officers' houses, to wish them the season's greetings and a measure of their own rejoicing.

Clarkson—never entirely the master of his sentiment—was unashamed to expose the fullness of his heart. Before boarding the *Felicity* he had gone around the settlers' houses pumping hands, receiving embraces, trying to calm their anxieties. But his composure had collapsed when he received a procession of Freetown women who brought him, for the voyage, offerings from their little farms: yams, papaya, onions, six dozen chickens and six hundred eggs, often just a few from each woman. Clarkson doubtless thought back to Preston, a year and an age ago, where British Freedom and the struggling farmers had also promised (and delivered) him chickens and eggs for the sea voyage from

Halifax. There was something sacerdotal about the moment, and intense feeling welled up and inevitably broke through the thin wall of Clarkson's self-control. "When many of the poor Widows expressed the gratification they had felt in being allowed to add their little mite to my sea stock by giving me an Egg each, I could not refrain from tears."[56]

None of Clarkson's big moments, of course, were ever complete without mishap. After the *Felicity* had weighed anchor in the afternoon of the 29th of December and had sailed through the harbour, as salutes from both the shore batteries and the ships rang out, he saw a sailor blown overboard from the *Amy* after looking carelessly down a loaded gun. But when Clarkson gazed back at the quayside he saw the entire colony gathered, waving handkerchiefs and hats and shouting farewells, and this sight he would take with him across the ocean along with all those eggs.

And there were other important cargoes: the first seeds grown from Sierra Leone produce, destined for Sir Joseph Banks; one of Signor Domingo's daughters, destined for an English, Christian education; and the one man John Clarkson could not bear to part with: David George. David, who had in his time lived with slaves, Indians and British soldiers, and who had tramped, run and slogged through swamps and creeks, snowdrifts and river ice, was now to be faced with the high hats, white bonnets and rosy cheeks of Home Counties Baptists.

And David George was carrying back to England something precious: a petition addressed to Henry Thornton, Thomas Clarkson and the rest of the directors, asking them to return their governor to them and setting out in their own words just what he had meant, what he had done and what he had given. Forty-nine of the settlers had signed it, including David George himself; Boston King; Hector Peters, who had been Baptist preacher at Preston; Richard Corankapone and Sampson Heywood, who had made the epic winter journey by land and water from New Brunswick to Halifax; John Kizell, the Sherbro Bullom who had been brought home; Joseph Leonard, the schoolmaster; and eight of the black women and widows (there had been so many who had lost their men)—Charity McGregor, Phyllis Halsted, Catrin Bartley and Lucy Whiteford among them. And this is what they said:

. . . we the humble pittioners we the Black pepol that Came from novascotia to this place under our agent John Clarkson and from the time he met with us in nova-scotia he ever did behave to us as a gentilmon in everey rescpt [sic] he provided every thing for our parshidge [passage] as wors in his pour to make us comfortable till we arrived at Sierrleon and his behaveor heath benge with such a regard to us his advice his Concil his patience his love in general to us all both men and women and Children and thearfour to the gentilmon of the Sierleon Companey in England we thy humbel pittioners wold desier to render thanks to the honorabel gentilmon of the Sierraleon Companey that it heth pleased allmighty god to put it into the hearts to think of them when we war in distress and we wold wish that it might please the gentilmon of the Companey as our governer is a going to take his leave of us and a goin to England thearfour we wold Bee under stud by the gentilmon that our ardent desier is that the same John Clarkeson Shold returen Back to bee our goverener our had Comander in Chef for the time to com and we will obay him as our governer and will hold to the laws of England as far as lys in our pour and as for his promis to us in giting our lands it is the people agree to take parte of thear land now at present and the remander as soon as posable and we pray that his Excelency John Clarkson might Be preserved safe over the sea to his frinds and return to us again and we thy humbel pittioners is in duty Bound and will ever pray witness our hands to the sine . . .

   David George . . . et al[57]

XII

NEW YEAR'S DAY 1793. In the French Republic Citizen Louis Capet was on trial for his crimes as former king. But in Sierra Leone Isaac DuBois, the easy-going Carolinan cottton planter and vocal friend of the blacks was, all things considered, content. He was fashioning his wedding ring and had nuptials with the strong-minded Anna Maria, the widow Falconbridge, to look forward to. So he took up quill and ink and began his diary, "a fair and ingenuous statement of every thing as it happens."[1] Before departing, John Clarkson had asked his friend to keep a journal so that, in the interval before the governor's expected return later in the year, there would be no break in the record of the colony's history. DuBois was happy to oblige. Hit hard by the leave-taking ("spirits much more oppressed than usual"), he had sailed out into the ocean a few leagues with Clarkson before saying a final farewell in the watery darkness. The diary was an obligation as much to himself as to the governor, a bond between them.

Dejection cleared with the vanishing of the winter "smokes" over Sierra Leone. Although an unseasonable squall had blown through the colony on New Year's Eve, rain coming right through Anna Maria's thatched roof, afterwards the January sun shone from a clear equatorial sky. DuBois's natural ebullience returned. King Naimbana—said to be grievously sick—had just presented the colony with a bullock and, like everyone else, DuBois looked forward to the slaughter. He spent his days directing the work of clearing the hillside for the new company storehouse or out at Thompson's Bay setting out a cotton plantation. The evenings were for sharing a glass of wine with his handsome "neighbour" Anna Maria. Their relationship was never insipid, for Anna Maria had a vigorous mind and a tempestuous nature. Sometimes, so Isaac thought, she was apt to mistake his preoccupations with business as indifference towards her. Then she would get into a "pet," one of the stormiest being on the eve of their intended wedding. But this one, like the others, passed and on the 7th of January the two lovebirds were married by the sonorous Reverend Melville Horne. Although Anna Maria was not in the least embarrassed by violating the convention of a twelve-month period of mourning, the bride and groom had asked the clergyman to keep the event secret for two weeks. But the "poor parson was not born to keep secrets, he carried it piping hot to the ears of every one he met but desired every one he told it to not to mention it to any one—however in less than two hours if was known over the whole Colony."[2]

There was no honeymoon. As he busied himself with work on the stone storehouse, intended to replace the thatched, vermin-infested building that was forever falling down in heavy winds and rain, DuBois began to realize that the acting governor, William Dawes, was going out of his way to be unhelpful. Stonemasons whom DuBois could ill afford to lose were ordered to abandon work for him in favour of the fort that Dawes had decided was needed. A solemn young man, he had been, like Clarkson, a naval lieutenant, but prided himself especially on his expertise in artillery and engineering. In the event of a war with regicide France, Dawes had concluded, a proper fort would be indispensable. There was no time to lose. DuBois, however, thought otherwise. Surely the French republic, which advertised itself as the friend of liberty and whose Convention had abolished slavery, could be persuaded to treat Sierra Leone as neutral? DuBois was convinced that a solid warehouse and shop would be of infinitely more benefit to the colony than any fort. The "two engineers"—Dawes and the surveyor, Richard Pepys—he thought were "fort mad." But the more he voiced this view, the cooler he noticed Dawes becoming. Before long DuBois understood that the very worst thing he could do was to mention to the acting governor that this or that project had been the special concern of John Clarkson. For Dawes seemed not to want to hear anything about his predecessor, even though Clarkson was expected to return after a leave of a few months. No more did Pepys, who, although embattled with the governor, had made an unctuous personal profession of admiration to him before he had sailed back to England. And from mid-January there was another figure to complete this severe trio: Zachary Macaulay.

Four years later, in 1797, when Macaulay, as governor, found himself in yet another knock-down battle with the black settlers, someone must have tactfully pointed out to him how many difficulties might have been avoided had he only been able to unbend just a little and offer the Nova Scotians something other than the countenance of the pious evangelical. All too conscious of the dour demeanour he presented to the world, he wrote on his twenty-ninth birthday to his fiancée Selina Mills that "I have laboured much to correct the unkindness of my look and manner, but I find this difficult."[3] Impossible might have been more accurate.With one congenitally blind eye, darkly beetling brows and a right arm made useless from an accident, Zachary Macaulay found it easy to despise vanity. Ingratiation at the cost of compromising principle was likewise to be abhorred as a corrupt emollient. He was chipped flint and saw no reason to disguise the fact. Macaulay had indeed come from a stony place—Inverary in the western highlands of Argyll; he was a descendant of clan chiefs, and one of thirteen children of an impoverished Presbyterian preacher. All his life he would remain stern, calloused by the demands he laid on himself and those that he knew an exacting God expected to be fulfilled.

Since his father, the pastor, had no money for a university education, the one-eyed boy taught himself Latin and Greek. In Glasgow, a hotbed of the new Scottish learning, he became, for a brief moment, dizzy with dangerous knowledge. He fell in with Advanced Thinkers who flaunted David Hume's scepticism in the face of the kirk and, as often as they could, got tipsy on profane wit and strong liquor. Worse still, his guard down, Zachary allowed himself to be seduced by fiction: "When I was not draining the midnight bowl, I was employed in wasting the midnight oil by poring over such abominable but fascinating works as are to be found under the head of novels in the circulating library."[4] At sixteen, the sinner was packed off to Jamaica as the overseer of a sugar plantation. There, "in a field of canes amidst perhaps a hundred of the sable race, cursing and bawling while the noise of the whip resounding on their shoulders and the cries of the wretches, would make you imagine that some unlucky accident had carried you to the doleful shade,"[5] Macaulay continued to thumb his Voltaire.

But then came the Awakening. He was twenty-one. In 1789, on board the ship returning him to England, the long-stifled Presbyterian in him came out for an airing on deck. Under the oceanic sky Macaulay swore to leave off the bottle and, in fair weather and foul, was true to his word. Then, he rusticated a little for God. His sister Jean had married a Leicestershire country gentleman called Thomas Babington, who himself had seen the Light and turned Evangelical, becoming one of the group centred on Clapham. When Zachary went to stay with his brother-in-law, he contracted his religion in the most irreversible way. Babington (whose name became preserved in the annals of English history when Zachary and Selina made it the middle name of their son Thomas) gave Macaulay more than a spiritual rebirth; he also got him a job. For one of Babington's closest friends and a fellow "Saint" was Henry Thornton, the Evangelical banker and chairman of the directors of the Sierra Leone Company.

Although, as Evangelicals, they were committed to the abolition of the slave trade, neither Zachary Macaulay nor Henry Thornton was much interested in freedom. Looking askance at the monsters brought forth in revolutionary France by the abuse of liberty, their tepid enthusiasm became icy hostility. What stirred the Clapham Saints was commerce and Christianity, sustained in mutual nourishment, until they had converted the pagan continent into godly civility and prosperity. Granville Sharp's Sierra Leone had been, they thought, the naive fantasy of a well-meaning but indulgent patriarch. If the venture was ever to thrive, it would require altogether less liberality and more government. Their own minds were attuned to obedience—unconditional surrender to the will of God. The sentimental passions of the black Methodists and the frantic, noisy paroxysms of the Baptists they thought repulsively childish. When Macaulay heard a black preacher in Sierra Leone cry out that God is love, he shrank from the exclamation with incredulous revulsion. God was not love. God was Truth and the Law and He was owed submission. This respect for authority, Macaulay believed—and evidently William Dawes shared the conviction—John Clarkson had signally failed to provide for the deluded blacks of Freetown. With the mawkish, histrionic lieutenant out of the way, it was time to begin a reformation.

It was announced by the Great Bell calling settlers to morning and evening prayer, as if at school—an innovation that Anna Maria thought ludicrous, instituted as it was in the most fervently Christian community she had ever encountered. Along with her husband, Isaac, and their amiable, learned friend the Swedish botanist Adam Afzelius, she conspicuously failed to attend the daily services—conduct that branded all three as shocking atheists. But Anna Maria was indifferent to what the "parcel of hypocritical puritans" thought of her and Isaac. She had already written them off as most un-Christian for charging the settlers four pence a pound for meat from the Naimbana's slaughtered ox, which, after all, had been intended as a gift to the colony. Worse, acting governor Dawes had hardly waited for poor Falconbridge's body to cool before demanding "his uniform, coat, sword, gun, pistols."[6] This kind of pettiness was the least of it. To his deepening dismay, DuBois became convinced that Dawes, Pepys and Macaulay were together bent on uprooting the delusions (as they saw them) with which Clarkson had won the settlers' confidence. They set about this exercise in disenchantment in the most confrontational manner. Just before leaving, Clarkson had expressed his sincere regret to the settlers that not all their country lots had been laid out, but had faithfully promised them that the work would be swiftly completed so that the land could be occupied before the onset of the rainy season. To the settlers Clarkson's word was gold. But hardly had he gone than the surveyor, Pepys, ordered an immediate and indefinite halt to the work, making it impossible for the blacks to provide for themselves on their own land. Survival depended on buying provisions from the company store, which, since it had a monopoly, could set prices much higher than the 10 percent mark-up over capital and shipping costs that Clarkson had held to be reasonable. As a result, the only way to afford necessities was to labour for the company—on the fort, for example—and at rates inflexibly determined by its officials. The Nova Scotian experience of debt peonage seemed to be repeating itself. For were they not, as many of the settlers bitterly complained, now the slaves of the all-powerful company?

DuBois was beside himself with exasperation, very much the worldly American loyalist embattled with the cold-blooded British

Evangelicals. He came from Wilmington in North Carolina, and may well have known Thomas Peters. Although he had been one of the master class and the blacks had been slaves, DuBois mixed with them more easily, and listened to them more attentively, than the starchy Englishmen. John Clarkson, he thought, was cut from a different cloth: humane, generous and informal. He had grown to like him enormously, and now he took the systematic effort to undercut the man's authority and reputation as a slight to himself. The governor should know just what had happened in his absence. In a memorandum for Clarkson's eyes inserted into the journal he wrote, "If I am not to have the credit of finishing the works I have begun I shall quit the colony . . . Why does he [Pepys] not finish laying out the lotts of land that has already cost the Company upwards of two thousand pounds and which must cost as much more, besides the injustice done to the Nova Scotians in keeping them out of their lotts—should the compleating of them be postponed to next year?"[7]

The same night, the 6th of February 1793, that DuBois was penning his memorandum a "great palaver" took place in Freetown. The settlers were rowdy and angry, and no wonder. All Clarkson's promises seemed to have been set aside. The ship *York,* which had brought fresh supplies and which Clarkson had directed should be a floating hospital, had been appropriated by the company officials for their own accommodation and entertainment. The last straw had come when black settlers who had occupied waterfront lots and built houses there had been summarily informed by Pepys that those holdings had been merely temporary and that they were now to be moved out to make way for company buildings. Fury burst from the gathered blacks. Anna Maria reported them as saying, "Mr Clarkson promised in Nova Scotia that no distinction should be made here between us and white men; we now claim this promise, we are free British subjects and expect to be treated as such; we will not tamely submit to be trampled on any longer."[8] Why had the allotment of country plots been stopped? Mr Clarkson would never have suffered such a thing!

Far from feeling defensive at the accusations, Richard Pepys went on the offensive, aiming a shocking broadside against Clarkson's standing with the blacks. "Whatever promises Mr Clarkson had made them

in Nova Scotia," DuBois reports him as saying, "were all from himself . . . he had no authority whatever for what he said and that he believed Mr Clarkson was drunk at the time he made them." This slander,
DuBois went on, was repeated several times, Pepys adding "that Mr
Clarkson seldom knew or thought of what he said—so it was not to be
wondered why he should make extraordinary promises . . . besides
many disrespectfull things."[9] He completed his tirade by attacking Du-
Bois himself for allowing settlers to imagine they could ever occupy
prime waterfront property.

A bellicose sound—of chagrin, rage and consternation—went
around the assembly. When it disbanded, nothing else but the outrage
done to Clarkson and to themselves was talked of—nor anything else
the next day, nor for days afterwards. Conferring among themselves,
the settlers decided that, since they could not trust any record of what
had transpired to be safely communicated to the directors, they had better draft a petition and have two of their own number take it to England
to Mr Thornton and his colleagues, and let their benefactor Clarkson
know personally just how his solemn promises were being violated. The
object himself of an *ad hominem* attack, DuBois took their cause as his
own. In a "Memorandum" to Clarkson, DuBois described Pepys as being as "black Hearted a Villain as this day exists."[10] And he resolved that
if there should be a petition, he would show the blacks exactly what to
say and how, in no uncertain terms, to say it. Then we should see.

WHAT HAD HAPPENED to John? Eighteen months earlier Henry
Thornton and William Wilberforce had taken their leave of an
amiable young fellow, high-spirited, but full of open-hearted modesty;
a malleable man, receptive to counsel from his patrons. But the John
Clarkson who now presented himself to the directors of the Sierra Leone Company, or rather who burst in upon them, was altogether
changed: affability had turned to agitation, his pleasantly ingenuous
enthusiasm to peevish storms of hectoring. To be sure, they owed him
much—and took every opportunity, in private, to express their sincere
gratitude for all that he had done in Nova Scotia and Sierra Leone: for
saving the West African colony, they doubted it not, from untimely ex-

tinction. Had they not shown their appreciation by promptly renewing—after a three-month leave—his governorship, and indeed by agreeing to ship to Freetown the makings of a substantial frame house for his residence? But whether this wholehearted endorsement gave Clarkson licence to be quite so free with advice on how to run the company—indeed, to berate the directors on their "strict adherence to nonsensical forms," to castigate them for "their want of Method, want of Exertion" and the "oppressive" (as he supposed) economic demands imposed on the settlers, and then to register, with such vehemence, his displeasure with the quality of men they had sent for their administration—well this was quite another matter.[11] They thanked him for his concerns and for the frankness with which he had set them before the directors. Mr Clarkson could be assured that they would be properly considered and that in due course they would be pleased to attend on him once more.

That was all. And that, John Clarkson felt as he waited in London on the directors' pleasure one month, then two, hardly met the case. Nor did it escape his attention that although Thornton and the others expressed their appreciation to him in private, they scrupulously refrained from any words of public recognition of the debt he was owed: a debt of honour and gratitude, no more—he would never seek more—but surely no less?

There were other ominous signs that unforced warmth had been replaced by calculated chill. Asked by Thomas Clarkson if he would be so kind as to use his personal closeness with the Pitt brothers (the elder of whom, the Earl of Chatham, was First Lord of the Admiralty) to advance John to the captaincy he had indisputably earned, William Wilberforce made no more than a tepid gesture of support. Thomas, who was under much strain in the spring and summer of 1793, his funds drained for the Cause, his health broken from incessant travelling for the same Cause, snapped at the implied snub and wrote his old friend and comrade-in-arms a letter of strong reprimand: "My opinion is that my Lord Chatham has behaved to my brother in a very scandalous manner, and that your own timidity has been the occasion of his miscarrying in his promotion . . . Letters will not do, and unless personal applications be made you will not serve him."[12] Stung, Wilberforce wrote that he attributed this intemperateness to Thomas's commendable concern for his brother, but nonetheless had never expected to hear from his good friend the language of "disappointed suitors." He ventured to hope nothing would "interrupt the cordiality of our connexion."[13]

But something had, and would continue to interrupt it; and that something was the French Revolution. In recognition of their abolitionist labours, the National Convention of the Republic—the same body that had tried and condemned the king—had awarded honorary citizenship to both Wilberforce and Clarkson. Wilberforce, the close friend of William Pitt and Edmund Burke, recoiled from the honour in embarrassed horror; Thomas Clarkson, on the other hand, revelled in it. He had never forgotten his time in Paris after the fall of the Bastille and had (so his more circumspect friends believed, imprudently) joined the English celebrations of its second anniversary in 1791. As the revolution had become more militant and violent, Thomas had conspicuously refused to join the chorus of condemnation. Just a few days before John Clarkson's arrival in February, republican France had declared war on Britain. In broadsides and caricatures, the French were now portrayed as inhuman regicidal monsters who made no secret of their wish to spread their godless mobocracy from one end of Europe to the other. Accordingly, Britons who, in spite of the manifest evidence of the inhumanity, anarchy and atheism of the French "*banditti*," continued to wish them well (or who failed to express patriotic abhorrence at their crimes) were no Britons at all, but accomplices in a monstrous conspiracy to bring down Throne, Church, and Parliament, the entire ancient constitution of freeborn Englishmen.

Their closest friends never thought the Clarkson brothers Jacobins, but they were suspected of flirting with republicanism. At the end of 1792 Thomas had injudiciously expressed his view that republican government in France might be less onerous than the weight of monarchy. When the Manchester abolitionist Thomas Walker, the leading figure of the Manchester Constitutional Society, was besieged in his house by a patriotic mob demonizing him as a Jacobin and was then arrested for sedition, Clarkson, so far from repudiating his friend, made a point of going to see Walker at home before his trial. In the light of this unfortunate dalliance with wicked revolutionism, John's behaviour to Thornton and the directors, and his impassioned advocacy of the rights of the blacks against the established order of the company, began to seem not just naive but actually dangerous. A bloody rebellion was raging in St

Domingue and the last thing the directors wanted was to countenance anything that might encourage the blacks of Sierra Leone in their grievances. As they were mulling over their doubts about the wisdom of renewing Clarkson's governorship, letters arrived from Macaulay and Dawes confirming their doubts. While heaping praise on Dawes as a paragon of Christian energy and efficiency, "one of the excellent of the earth," Macaulay poured scorn on Clarkson and DuBois, accusing them of wilfully inciting expectations among the blacks that were inconsistent with anything promised by the company and thus sowing the seeds of contention and slovenly disorder. Henry Thornton was in no doubt whom to believe. Zachary Maculay was his protégé, his neighbour, his fellow Clapham "Saint," a man of unimpeachable rectitude and judgement. To leave Clarkson in no doubt about what would happen next, he actually showed him Macaulay's letter. Astounded that, without any of the experience or knowledge that he himself had earned through the trials of Nova Scotia, the ocean crossing and the first year in Africa, Macaulay would pass damning judgement on his competence, Clarkson allowed himself an observation on his critic's "illiberality."

On the very day that John Clarkson was leaving London for Norfolk to be married to Susannah Lee he was informed by the directors that, on further consideration, and with all due thanks for past services, he need not trouble himself with returning to Africa. They wished him well and anticipated his prompt resignation. William Dawes would be confirmed as governor in his stead. In a passion, Clarkson refused point blank to oblige. He would not, he wrote to his brother Thomas, "be the *first* to relinquish an employ wherein my Heart is and has been, so deeply interested in its success."[14] He was then summarily dismissed. But whatever the directors had stopped, they could not stop him caring for the infant colony nor keeping the personal promises he had made. It was typical of John Clarkson that at the moment when he discovered he had been traduced as an incompetent drunk, he continued to go about doing personal errands for the settlers he was most fond of. He had a long shopping list. He would get spectacles for Mary Perth, a loom for Joseph Brown, hooks for Luke Jordan and bolts of linen for Miles Dixon, as well as trying to find the British army officers who had helped John Cuthbert and Richard Corankapone during the war.[15] He, at least, would keep his word.

ISAAC AND ANNA MARIA DUBOIS had had more than enough. Estranged from the company men, distressed at the high-handed way the complaints of the black settlers had been dismissed, aghast at the slandering of Clarkson, they decided to return to England to try to recoup some of Isaac's considerable Carolina fortune that had been lost through his loyalism. That motives could be startlingly mixed, principles inconsistent with practice, is born out by the couple sailing aboard the Jamaica-bound slave ship captained by Anna Maria's brother-in-law. All the same, Isaac wrote ardently to Clarkson:

> You will not be pleased to hear of my leaving the Colony but I hope it is for the best, believe me unless the Directors will listen to truth their Colony is lost—such conduct, such every thing you little dream of—two of the Black Settlers, deputed by the whole, go home in the *Amy* to represent their grievances, they have been shamefully trampled on since you went away. All the ill-treatment I have received since you left this I am convinced has been due to my not taking a diabolical part which I shudder at—in poisoning the minds of the people against you—but all their efforts have been in vain—the people cry out loudly for your return—Adieu.[16]

Indeed they did. One of the settlers Clarkson most cared about, Richard Corankapone, one of the little band who had trudged through the snows of New Brunswick to reach the fleet at Halifax, had written to tell him that "the Body of the Colleny is Bent for your honer to Com and Be our governer."[17] In June 1793 Clarkson wrote back expressing his distaste that Pepys "has been making free with my name in an ungrateful and I may say wicked manner," adding that the people should be told in no uncertain terms that when he had made promises to them in Nova Scotia he had done so with the full authority of both the Sierra Leone Company and the British government. At the same time as telling Corankapone to look out for Pepys and to make sure that settlers safeguarded the certificates of land entitlement he had issued in Nova Scotia, Clarkson went to some lengths not to make his own standing a cause of further dissension in Freetown: "I assure you I will always support your rights as Men and I will recommend you for not suffering any people to take them from you but you must be obedient to the Laws or the Colony will be at an end."[18]

Deference, however, was not on the cards in Sierra Leone. Politics had come to the colony and would not, of its own accord, go away. Not everything from Granville Sharp's original sketch for a black "Frank-pledge" micro-democracy had become redundant. Towards the end of 1792 elections had been held, exactly as Sharp had specified, for "tith-ingmen" (one per ten households) and "hundredors" (originally one per ten tithingmen, but increased to one per five). Each head of house-hold voted for tithingmen, which meant, as women constituted no less than a third of all heads of household, that they too were enfranchised. Female voting was something that even the French Revolution in its most radical phase had not been able to contemplate. Indeed, the Jaco-bins were hostile to the idea. It was momentous, then, that the first women to cast their votes for any kind of public office anywhere in the world were black, liberated slaves who had chosen British freedom; women such as Mary Perth from Norfolk, Virginia, and Martha Hazeley from Charleston, South Carolina.

As Sierra Leone evolved into an Anglo-African city state, it was to his credit that, far from discouraging the annual elections, Macaulay actually thought the assembly of tithingmen and hundredors might function as a model of collective responsibility. In 1796 he even wrote a constitution, featuring a "House of Commons" and a "Senate," a third of which would be elected each year. But Macaulay also took it for granted that this body would contain, not aggravate, local arguments, and that it would be for the most part an agency of innocuous parochial government, empowered to round up stray pigs or legislate a tariff of fines for public drunkenness. But elections, wherever they are held, carry with them their own kind of potent political elixir. The act of vot-ing gives hope of representation, and legitimate authority to the elected. Carried out in a community of four hundred households, among a soci-ety of neighbours, the emotive force of an election was, if anything, sharpened. Everything we associate with political campaigns happened in miniature in Freetown. Impassioned speeches were made before im-provised meetings, some in public places, some in private houses. Post-ers and placards were nailed up outside shops and houses, and, since this moment marks the beginning of authentic black politics, congregations in churches and chapels heard campaign rhetoric as well as psalms: the Baptists less militant, the Methodists rather more.

It was not surprising, then, that a Methodist preacher called Cato Perkins, formerly a Charleston slave, was chosen by the assembled body of tithingmen and hundredors to take a petition of grievances that thirty-one of them had signed to Thornton and the company directors in England. With him went a carpenter, Isaac Anderson, also from Charleston, but born a freeman, who had already vented his grievance at the company's taking waterfront lots. The petition, drafted with help from DuBois, was a list of specific complaints: that the promised laying out of lots had been stopped; that the fort would probably never be built "and we think it is a great pity your Money should be thrown away but Mr Dawes says he would not mind to lose One Thousand Pound of your Honours money rather than not do what he wishes"; that they were overcharged by the company store; that the company bartered provisions against manual labour and paid them poorly "so that we have nothing to lay out for a Rainy Day or for our Children after us."[19] (The fate of their children, in fact, is a repeated, moving refrain in the lament.) But beyond these material grievances, the settlers' petition was coloured by a sense of affront at the authoritarian paternalism of the new regime. On the one hand, the document was careful to praise the company, and especially Clarkson: "The Promises made us by your Agents in Nova Scotia were very good and far better than we ever had before from White People and no man can help saying Mr Clarkson behaved as kind and tender to us as if he was our Father and he did so many humane acts of tender goodness that we can never forget them." But on the other hand, there was now a new stiff-necked Pharaoh and he had laid a rod across their backs (and watered down the rum!). "Mr Dawes seems to wish to rule us just as bad as if we were all Slaves which we cannot bear."

The petitioners were at pains to say they were not about to cause trouble in the colony—but nor should they be thought of as mere supplicants. Cato Perkins and Isaac Anderson were, after all, the delegates of an elected assembly, and every so often their words were laced with a telling thread of steel. "We do not wish to make any disturbance in the Colony but would chuse that every thing should go on quetly till we hear from you as we are sure we will then have justice." What they were after was self-determination. Had they been allowed to lay out lots themselves, the work would already have been finished. If they could choose their own governor "we would chuse Mr Clarkson for he knows us better than any Gentleman . . . We are sorry to tell your Honours that we feel ourselves so distressed because we are not treated as Freemen that we do not know what to do and nothing but the fear of God makes us support it until we know from your Honrs what footing we are upon."[20]

Even had the petition been a document of docile grovelling, it would still have been unacceptable to Thornton and the directors since it came from an unexpected and unauthorized initiative. But the undertone of menace, the likelihood that DuBois (also dismissed from company service for "disrespect" to Dawes) had had a hand in its composition, and the fact that it sought to reverse their decision about Clarkson evidently incensed the gentlemen of the company. Anna Maria, who, once she had got to England in October 1793, made a point of seeing Anderson and Perkins, reported that after they had landed penniless in Portsmouth, the company agent graciously loaned them £2 to get to London to see Thornton. Initially he seemed receptive to their petition; but shortly afterwards he sharply changed his tune, informing them that letters from Sierra Leone (Anderson and Perkins knew from whom) had dismissed the complaints as unfounded and frivolous. The two men would be lent further money only if they mortgaged their land to the company, and would be put out to work as servants pending their speedy return whence they came. John Clarkson was no longer their concern, so the directors would not, regrettably, be able to pass on to them his present address.

But Anna Maria and Isaac DuBois were only too happy to oblige. John and Susannah Clarkson were then living back in John's home town of Wisbech in Cambridgeshire, and as soon as he had read their petition in early November he wrote back saying that he entirely saw the justice in what they had to say and very much hoped the directors would pay it the attention it certainly deserved. To that end he, Clarkson, would write to Henry Thornton suggesting a meeting of the two delegates, himself, Thornton and whichever other directors were of a mind to attend. "We suppose the Directors did not like to see Mr Clarkson and us face to face," Cato Perkins told Anna Maria, "for Mr Thornton never answered that letter which obliged Mr Clarkson to write another; this he sent unsealed under cover to us that we might be convinced of his good intentions and integrity towards us."[21]

In his fenland fastness John Clarkson was indeed very angry over the discourtesy shown to himself—bordering, he thought, on vindictive hostility—and he was also irate at the shabby way the directors had treated Perkins and Anderson. Ever since he had set foot in Halifax a year and a half earlier Clarkson had tried to live up to the exalted expectations that the blacks had of their "Mosis," and every time they wrote him that "we look upon you so much our Friend that we think you will us done Justice by"[22] his impotence cut him to the quick. It was also evident to him that if the brusque fashion in which the directors were treating Perkins (sent to a theological college) and Anderson was meant to browbeat them into submission, it was having the reverse effect. "They will not give us any Answer," they wrote to Clarkson, "but send us back [to Sierra Leone] like Fools and we are certain, Sir that if they serve us so, that the Company will lose their Colony as nothing kept the People quiet but the thoughts that when the Company heard their Grievances they would see Justice done them."[23]

When Thornton did finally agree to see the two delegates again (without Clarkson, of course), it was only to inform them that complaints must be made in writing. This in turn produced the sharpest retort yet from Perkins and Anderson—the first shot, in fact, of what was about to become a long revolt against company rule. In the last, stunning irony of their epic history the black loyalists, even as they continued to profess their love for the king ("God bless him") and their hope that he would himself appoint their governor, were about to turn rebel. They were breathtakingly free of deference. It would be tempting to say that they sounded American, did not the taproots of their righteous indignation, their instinctive sense of betrayal, run much deeper—all the way back to the godly apostles of liberty in Oliver Cromwell's armies and parliaments. Perhaps they did not know it at the time (though London was brimming with such language in 1793), but Cato Perkins and Isaac Anderson were speaking with the voices of seventeenth-century commonwealthmen, made over into modern, radical, rights-driven politics. As much as any Manchester weaver or London tailor, Isaac Anderson the Charleston carpenter had become a British revolutionary.

"We did not think, Gentlemen, any thing more was necessary than the petition we brought and delivered to you from the people we represent but as you do not seem to treat that petition with the attention we expected, you oblige us to say something more on the subject . . ." They had always believed what Clarkson had told them in Nova Scotia, notwithstanding more recent assertions that he had had no authority to do so, and now his letter made his own honesty in the matter unequivocally clear.

We certainly hope your Honours intend to make good those promises and we beg to know whether you do or not? . . . If we are not of importance enough to this Country to deserve a Governor authorized by the King, we, with due respect to your Honours think we have a right to a voice in naming the man who shall govern us . . . we *will not* be governed by your present Agents in Africa, nor can we think of submitting our grievances to them which we understand is the intention of your Honours, for it is inconsistent to suppose that justice will be shown us by the men who have injured us and we cannot help express our surprise that you should even hint at such a thing . . . We hope your Honours will not think we have said anything here but what is respectful and proper; we thought it our duty to tell you the truth; we want nothing but justice, which surely cannot be refused us. We have so often been deceived by white people, that we are jealous when they make promises and uneasily wait till we see what they will come to.

We shall conclude, gentlemen by observing that since we arrived here we have avoided giving you trouble as much as possible, we did not come upon a childish errand but to represent the grievances and suffering of a thousand souls.

We expected to have had some more attention paid to our complaints but the manner you have treated us has been just the same as if we were *Slaves,* come to tell our masters of the cruelties and severe behavior of an Overseer . . .[24]

Perkins and Anderson added, for the benefit of Isaac and Anna Maria Dubois, "When they had read this over they seemed very much out of humour."[25] This was hardly a surprise, for the directors were unused to being dressed down. They asked again for complaints to be properly and civilly set down. In return they received another letter of admonition from the blacks, pointing out that, contrary to promises made in Nova Scotia that they would be "provided with all tools wanted for cultivation and likewise the comforts and necessaries of life" would be made available from the company store at a reasonable rate, they had been fleeced and worse still, "we are certainly not protected by the laws of Great Britain."[26] With that reply "the Directors were no better pleased than the first."

Nothing was resolved. In February 1794 Perkins and Anderson returned to Sierra Leone on the *Amy,* the ship that had brought them. Perhaps the directors imagined they had been sent away with a flea in their ear, chastened for their temerity. Perhaps again, they were not quite so sure, since there was some indecision about which would be the more prudent course—to pack them off back to Africa or *prevent* them from rejoining the colony. Back they went, though, bitterly disenchanted and more resolved on resistance. The effect of his stay in England was decisive in particular for Isaac Anderson. The man whom the directors had returned to Sierra Leone had become, thanks to them, militant.

ZACHARY MACAULAY watched seven square-rigged ships sail into Freetown harbour with some satisfaction. In spite of adversity and contention, Sierra Leone was prospering. It was a rare thing now for a settler to die of sudden disease. Cattle, timber and indigo arrived from upstream; a little fishing fleet brought back a catch every day from the open sea. Cassava, yams, melons and beans were being harvested. It was September 1794; he was governor of the colony now, and he ran it the way he thought it should always have been run: unsentimentally and economically.[27] Certainly there had been discord, fomented, as he thought, by a faction of perenially disgruntled agitators, among whom Isaac Anderson was regrettably conspicuous. Better he should not have returned from that embarrassing sojourn in England where he doubtless picked up all kinds of seditious notions from the English Jacobins! Now he had made confederates—many of them, alas, Methodists, and all too prone to excitement; men such as Nathaniel Snowball, Ansel

Zizer, and Nathaniel Wansey, who were much too quick to shout their pretended indignities before the credulous. Macaulay would much rather the assembly of thirty-six hundredors and tithingmen had not turned into a swarm of gadflies to irritate him in his administration with their buzzing and biting; but he still had hopes for it as a nursery of responsible government. Besides, doing away with it as a political nuisance would only fan the flames.

Macaulay put his faith in the sound and solid element among the settlers: David George and Richard Corankapone, men he could safely appoint as marshals in case of trouble. They had rallied to him in the summer when the colony had turned riotous. As so often, the matter had been escaped slaves. They materialized from forts and from ships as if Freetown were a safe haven. And inevitably it fell to him to appease the incensed captains who came in search of their property, hidden by the settlers, who appeared to believe that Lord Mansfield's ruling applied to the colony; that the air of *Sierra Leone* was "too pure for slaves to breathe." There were shouting matches, scuffles, abuse traded, hands raised, even threats with axes and knives. One such trader, a Scot, had told settlers harbouring his runaways just what he would do with them if ever they were got to the West Indies. In short order he had been set upon, and had come close to having his brains dashed out with a hammer. When Macaulay attempted to deal with those responsible the arresting marshal was in his turn attacked, and before long the whole town was in violent commotion. In the end order and authority had prevailed and the ringleaders of the riot sent to England for trial. But the muttering had gone on. It would never end. But what of it? Hardy realism was the only way for the colony to endure. Perhaps a future without African slaves might one day materialize; but for now they must needs accommodate themselves to what was; they lived among such men, tribes and captains both. Ships would sail up and downstream and some of them would have, perforce, live cargo. Those seven ships, for example, one of which appeared to be a warship, a frigate. Odd that he had had no notice of their coming. What might be their business?

All too soon Macaulay had his answer. Through the glass he saw the frigate's guns methodically raised, levelled and aimed—at him. The governor threw himself down on his terrace as a shot cracked past his head. Then there was a tremendous roar of sound as twelve-pound cannonballs and shot rained on the harbour from the ships. Tongues of flame and clouds of dirty smoke rose from the houses closest to the waterfront. The shouting, screaming and running began. Another look through the glass and Macaulay saw their false British colours run down, the tricolor of the *banditti* run up. What could he call on to defend Freetown? Dawes's fort had never been completed. Against the French ships' hundred cannon he had just twenty-four guns, some of them rusted in the tropical humidity, mounted on rotten carriages. There was no choice. After an hour and a half of bombardment came a pause followed by a demand from the French commander, Citizen-Captain Arnaud, that they hoist the tricolor. Zachary Macaulay had none. Instead, he ordered a white linen tablecloth to be flown as the colony's signal of surrender.

In retrospect some of the settlers murmured that the capitulation had been too hasty. But with the odds of battle so unequal, Macaulay undoubtedly believed he was sparing Freetown a massacre. There were fifteen hundred French sailors and marines armed to the teeth, and they could do with the colony what they wanted. Miraculously, the only fatal casualty in the cannonading had been a seven-year-old child, cut in two while being held in the arms of her mother, though many other settlers had been wounded, losing arms and legs.

But for the two weeks of their occupation, short of a general slaughter, the French did the worst they could anyway—and not just to the property of the British administration, but also to the blacks whom the National Convention had grandly emancipated. Amidst the burning houses and exhaustive plunder, Citizen Arnaud made it clear he saw little distinction between Britons and ex-slaves—they were all "Anglais." Shops, including Mary Perth's and Sophia Small's, were comprehensively looted; the Freetown public library torched; the colony's printing press dismantled and shot up; the dispensary and apothecary sacked, churches vandalized (for the Cults of Reason and the Supreme Being seemed not to have caught on in Freetown); Bibles trampled on; Adam Afzelius's manuscript on tropical botany destroyed; more than a thousand pigs killed; wounded and mutilated dogs and cats left to bleed to death on the grass streets. Farm allotments were dug up and, when what could be eaten had been devoured, the rest of the crops burned. When they felt like amusing themselves the French sailors turned to assaulting the settlers, stripping them of their clothes and beating them.

Those who could fled into the forested mountains, where they knew the terrain, and led the frightened whites to shelter in native villages. Not all of them were prepared to be helped. The surveyor, Richard Pepys, Clarkson's old enemy, was at least as terrified of the black settlers—who indeed had many scores to settle with him—as of the French, and took his wife and children into the rainforest where he died a week later. Others, though, discovered some sort of common cause in adversity. Macaulay remembered the night services they held together; and Mary Perth, the matriarch whose shop had been plundered by the French, led the black children who were being schooled in the governor's house into safety in a neighbouring Temne village. Macaulay could not but be impressed by her resourcefulness and courage. When he went out to Pa Demba's to see the children, Mary made him tea and gave him a bed for the night.[28] This, the Evangelical never forgot. After it was all over he put the children in her domestic charge, and when the time came for his own leave in the spring of 1795 he took some of the children with him for schooling in Clapham and kept Mary on as their nurse, matron and housekeeper. There she treated the bonneted ladies of the Common to her jams and her salty vernacular wisdom.

But it was too much to expect that when the French departed two weeks later Macaulay would emerge from the ashes a chastened man. If anything, the contrary was true; he had become an even more resolute version of himself. In no time at all, as the settlers were struggling to rebuild their destroyed town, the governor joined battle with them. Many of them in flight had managed to salvage things from the wreckage and fire—sticks of furniture, some foodstuffs in the company store, barrels of molasses, rope, nails and timber—and had willingly shared whatever they had with the fugitive whites. Now Macaulay ordered the return of these items, which he regarded as having been pilfered from the company. The settlers, on the other hand, who had risked life and limb to save what they could so that Freetown would not be entirely bereft as it tried to recover, saw the goods as legitimately theirs. They were not about to hand them back. It did not help matters that Macaulay had appropriated the best, undamaged properties in town to house the white officials as well as the hundred-odd white prisoners the French ships had taken and dumped on the burnt-out colony.

A confrontation ensued. Macaulay threatened to withhold schooling, medical care and the vote to anyone who refused to return salvaged property or to take a formal oath of allegiance. Since many of the precious land grant certificates issued by Clarkson had been destroyed in the conflagration Macaulay issued new ones, but with conditions inserted that violated the original agreements. Most glaring was the obligation of settlers to pay a quit rent of a shilling an acre on their lots, the tax for which Clarkson had expressly assured the Nova Scotians they would never be liable. Henry Thornton, who insisted on a quit rent, had written to Clarkson that despite the contradiction he hoped the matter would not be seen by the settlers "as a grievance." But how could that be possible when it was set at fifty times the rate for white Nova Scotians and, for that matter, the ex-convicts of Australia? The assembly of hundredors and tithingmen warned the people not to take up any land grants bearing those illegitimate obligations, and for the most part they were heeded. Black arrows were daubed on the houses of noncompliers—three-quarters of the colony. Deprived of education, the settlers responded by opening their own private schools. The most alienated among them, led by Nathaniel Snowball (who had been a young boy when he had fled with his mother from a plantation in Queen Anne County, Virginia) and Luke Jordan (who had been one of Clarkson's captains on the crossing), now decided to leave the colony altogether and found their own settlement on Pirate's Bay, land they had leased from the Temne chief Jemmy George about halfway between Freetown and Cape Sierra Leone. It was at this juncture, in November 1794, that Jordan, Isaac Anderson and "Daddy" Moses Wilkinson—until now no radical—wrote to John Clarkson that "we wance did call it Freetown but since your absence—we have Reason to call it a Town of Slavery."[29]

Macaulay and Dawes were their Pharaohs, John Clarkson their "Mosis and Joshua," and the people he had led across the ocean to what they all hoped would be a Promised Land still looked to him, wrote to him as their true redeemer, hoping against hope that he would one day come back to them. "We Raly look to you with ever Longing Eyes—Our Only Friend," Jordan and the others had written. "The day you leaved it we was very much Oppress by Government," wrote James Liaster in March 1796. "We Believe that it was the handy work of Almighty God— that you should be our leader . . . kind Sir and honoured Sir be not Angry with us but Oh that God would once more Give you a Desire to come & visit us here." "We could say many things," wrote Snowball and Jordan in the summer of 1796 before their move to Pirate's Bay, "but after all it will amount to no more than this that we love you and remember your Labours of love & compassion towards us with Gratitude & pray that Heaven may always smile on you & yours."[30]

Clarkson must have felt a pang when he read these imploring letters, not least because he knew there was nothing he could do about their plight and no chance of being allowed to go back to Sierra Leone. There were occasions, though, when the history came to him. In 1796 Boston King called on him at Purfleet in Essex, where Clarkson was managing a limeworks. King had taken his calling as preacher and teacher, begun in Preston, Nova Scotia, to the northern shore of the Sierra Leone River at a place called Clarkson's Plantation, where he set up a chapel and school for twenty pupils. Conscious that he himself needed better training as a missionary, he went back to England with Dawes, who placed him at Kingswood School near Bristol. It was there that King set down his whole extraordinary story for the Methodists. At some point in his stay he managed to stop hating white people: "I had suffered greatly from the cruelty and injustice of the Whites which induced me to look upon them in general as our enemies: And even after the Lord had manifested his forgiving mercy to me, I still felt an uneasy distrust and shyness towards them, but on that day the Lord removed all my prejudices, for which I bless his holy Name."[31] He might have spoken too soon. Discovering that, though forbidden to do so, King had gone to see John Clarkson, the company reneged on its promise to provide free passage from Africa and back again when he returned to be a missionary-teacher there. He was now to be charged fifteen guineas for the privilege. But he had gone through a lot worse than this since his escape from bondage. King reported this latest act of meanness to Clarkson, writing, with an almost audible sigh, "but Sir I regardeth it not because I know I shall be able to pay them and I do ashoure it will only serve to Attach my love more to you because I knew it was only out of Spite."[32]

King's touching loyalty may have consoled Clarkson somewhat for what he had heard of David George, whom he had brought to England to be introduced to prominent Baptists there. He duly did the rounds, meeting John Newton the slaver-turned-preacher who composed "Amazing Grace"; and related for publication his own eventful biography, from the lashings of the overseer to up-river life with George Galphin and the Indians, his smallpox-scarred ordeal at the siege of Savannah, the Shelburne days of frostbite and visions, and finally the oceanic exodus to Africa. Clarkson, he said, "was a very kind man to me and everybody . . . very free and good natured" and had been delighted when George had named his last-born son after him. But in the six months of his stay in England George became the directors' pet Christian, and he returned their generosity by betraying his old friend. Clarkson noticed the change of temperature in their communications, so it was not altogether a surprise when one of his correspondents in Sierra Leone confirmed that David George had become a company man. "Mr George has spoke very much against you," the letter said. Hurt by the desertion, Clarkson wrote on the back of the letter: "David George's Ingratitude."[33] Although he was still getting letters pleading with him to come back, he hardly had the stomach for it any more.

SO IT WAS not Clarkson who returned to Sierra Leone in 1796, but Macaulay. In all essentials he had not changed, but the colony had, and Macaulay noticed. It was more self-sufficient, self-confident and (he bitterly regretted this) politically headstrong. Materially, it was unquestionably doing better. The old, improvised dwellings of mud and thatch had gone. The four-hundred-odd houses were solidly timber-framed and divided on the inside into small rooms, though still without chimneys. Cooking was done in the little yards beside the houses, where chickens scratched and strutted, sharing the space with a hog or two. Mango trees leafed out between the houses to give fruit and shade.

No one talked of famine any more. The "Nova Scotians," as they called themselves, had put down roots; they knew exactly who they were, where they had come from, and what their place in the story of Africans and British and Americans was. They were a new Chosen People, God's black "Ezraelites." They sorely missed their "Mosis," but like the first Israelites, they would make a place for themselves without him if that was God's will. They clung to their epic exodus story, and dressed and ate and spoke with its memory always in mind. High animal skin or straw hats sat on the crown of the men's heads; on the women, long checked and printed dresses of gingham or calico, with aprons, were worn over voluminous petticoats notwithstanding the African heat. Many of the women coiffed their hair into tight braids or wore them high in shapes "like some antique yew tree of a Dutch garden." The men were even less inclined to go tropical, and were faithful to trousers, waistcoats and jackets. Both sexes sported handkerchiefs and, rain or shine, Jonas Hanway's umbrellas were compulsory items in their get-up. They were partial to corn mush, and before long there was a new drink in their diet. For in February 1796, while burning some brush on the hillside, Andrew Moore, an escaped slave from Augusta, later a gardener at Preston, smelt the unmistakable aroma of coffee. The beans lay on the ground, inadvertently roasted. A little expedition with the botanist Adam Afzelius confirmed the existence of wild trees. By March there were enough beans for a tasting, which produced a cup not at all inferior, it was said, to the offerings of London coffee-houses. Two years later some three thousand trees were producing over three hundred pounds of beans a year, the first cash crop of the colony.

Their speech and song were a hybrid of African rhythms, American hymns and formal declaratory English—the kind they used in their petitions and letters. It flowered in the schools where their children were taught, so Sierra Leone was very quickly becoming a literate community, and of course in the seven churches where they gathered every day for hymns and prayers and storms of jubilant or lamentational piety. They were who they were, and increasingly resistant to taking orders. They would not hand over to the company the goods they had saved from the ruin of the French raid; they would not be forced to buy from its storehouse (in recognition of this, the monopoly was abandoned) and bought instead from Sophia Small's well-stocked shop. They had no intention of paying the punitive quit rent the company claimed it was owed—"a chain to bind us as slaves forever," one of them said. They challenged the white officials to try to coerce it out of them. As far as they could see, the company needed them more than vice versa, a judgement confirmed by the setting up of companies of armed militia (in case of a return of the French) in many of which whites served under black officers; this was a prudent innovation since it was the latter, after all, who had the military experience going back to the American campaigns.

And they were certainly not going to be told how to order their private lives. The latest target of Macaulay's zeal was the number of technically illegitimate children in Freetown, the product of what he considered iniquitous and unorthodox conjugal arrangements. But of course these children were not in any sense abandoned bastards like the pathetic foundlings deposited at Thomas Coram's Home in London's Lincoln's Inn Fields. They were cared for in one or more homes, but it was precisely the lack of stigma that so irked the righteous governor. So did the shifting unions in which men and women both often took long-term lovers, and had children with them, without necessarily abandoning their spouses. There was in Freetown a surplus, not a deficit, of affection. These contingent unions were, of course, the product of a desperate and unpredictable history, going back to the plantations where they had been forbidden; to the dire necessity, during the odysseys of the war, of parting from loved ones in order to keep the children safe; to the breaking up of some families when the ships were waiting in Halifax harbour and both slaves and indentured family members had to be left behind; and to the terrible ravages of disease in the first year at Sierra Leone. All of this was quite beside the point for Zachary Macaulay, who had experienced none of this but had instead discovered the laws of God in an English country house. And he was scandalized by the fact that these irregular unions and their offspring were countenanced by the non-Anglican clergy. Taking the trusty David George up to his hilltop farm retreat, Macaulay proceeded to berate the unfortunate Baptist preacher on this iniquity along with other wicked habits of the Freetowners, such as their fondness for drink. George, who ran an ale shop, burst into tears, stricken with a crushing weight of guilt.

But there were some things that even the compliant George would not tolerate. When Macaulay declared any marriages other than those licensed and performed by the regular Anglican clergy to be illegal, he set off a storm of denunciation from the nonconformist ministers who had no intention whatsoever of having one of their most important pastoral functions taken away. George warned Macaulay that if he persisted, he would bring the colony to insurrection. But Macaulay went ahead with an attempt (later abandoned) to give the Anglican Church the monopoly over baptisms as well as marriages, succeeding only in alienating virtually the entire black community and causing uproar in the assembly of tithingmen and hundredors. But then Macaulay also thought he could manage the increasingly vocal and belligerent body that was simultaneously an embryonic legislature, court of law and administration. Every so often he would summon the settlers to listen to a tremendous dressing-down. Sounding remarkably like a British colonial governor in America in the 1770s or India a century later, Macaulay berated the blacks for listening "to every prating malicious designing tale-bearer, to every selfish and base deceiver who . . . would abuse or revile your Governors . . . you have often been made to see the folly of acting thus and yet you still return, like the sow to flounder in the same dirty puddle."[34] It was not surprising that the audiences for this kind of verbal abuse sharply dwindled. Instead of becoming more accommodating, the settlers became less so. Attempts to influence elections backfired, producing instead a militant opposition group whose members included Isaac Anderson, decisively radicalized by his humiliation in England. Much of their fractiousness Macaulay ascribed to women having the vote, so he did away with that in 1797 and hoped for a more manageable assembly. The next year's election did indeed produce, for the first time, two white tithingmen—but no discernible accommodation from the black majority. Some, indeed, now ran on a platform of restricting tithingmen and hundredors to blacks. The notion that whites would actually be disqualified by virtue of *their* colour struck Macaulay as amusing.

In 1799 Macaulay left the colony for good to take up the job of secretary to the directors in London, from where he would assert his firm opinion from a distance. His governorship had been a marvellous paradox: both hectoring and liberating. For while Macaulay had taken every opportunity to ram unpopular policies down the throats of the Nova Scotians, he had also encouraged them in the practice of self-government, never threatening to shut down the assembly of tithingmen and hundredors nor to pull back any of their administrative or legal powers. They still appointed black juries and organized the "labour tax" by which settlers put in six days' work a year on roads, bridges and the like—a Granvillian imposition to which no one objected, in contrast to the still uncollected quit rent. Only when some of the hundredors asked for the appointment of black magistrates and judges did Macaulay baulk, objecting to its "impracticality" given their lack of knowledge of English Common Law.

He had a point. But, of course, in the folk memory of Freetown their long journey had *begun* in the courts, with the news somehow spreading through the Southern plantations of Lord Mansfield's ruling for "Uncle Somerset," confirming that there was such a thing as British freedom, that in England the "air was too pure for slaves to breathe." Ever since that time—in the lines of loyalist slaves herded on to the ships at the Charleston evacuation; in the deceits perpetrated in Nova Scotia; in the wickedness of the company store prices; in the dilatoriness that had kept them off their land; in the abominable quit rent that in effect would make that landholding untenable—the blacks had believed that precious legal freedom had been set aside by those who had usurped the benevolence of the king, of their great patriarch Granville Sharp, of their personal saviour John Clarkson and of the true English courts and Parliament. Now they were determined to have their own and, if necessary, to make their own laws.

Paradoxically, then, what Thornton, Dawes and Macaulay had managed to do was to create, out of one of the most passionately loyal and patriotic people ever to follow the Union Jack, a contentious little *America* in West Africa: contentious and articulate, indignant over what they held to be illegitimate taxes, interference in their Churches, high-handed arbitrary governance and incompetent military defence. It had been a recipe for rebellion before. Now it would be so again. No wonder, in the months before he departed from Sierra Leone, Macaulay kept a candle burning all night in his bedchamber and loaded guns by his side.

MACAULAY HAD BEEN A ROD. His successor as governor, Thomas Ludlam, seemed a reed. He was twenty-three years old, slight where Macaulay had been rugged, constitutionally queasy, his intestines in chronic revolt against the discomfort of his position. The reed began by bending. The bar against children of dissident settlers being educated in company schools was lifted. Attempts to collect the quit rent (which had been accompanied by threats of disenfranchise-ment) were abandoned. Ludlam did his best to be gracious. But it was too late. The most militant of the tithingmen and hundredors—Isaac Anderson, James Robinson, a shopkeeper, and an erstwhile moderate called John Cuthbert, an escapee from Savannah—had, in their own minds, already crossed a line in which they repudiated the authority of the company altogether. They continued to insist on elected magistrates and judges, and when Ludlam and the directors predictably rejected the demand the assembly went ahead anyway and appointed Robinson as a judge and Cuthbert as Justice of the Peace. This was just the begin-ning. The black leaders wanted to redefine who was properly a voting citizen of Sierra Leone and who was not. A declaration issued by the tithingmen and hundredors stated that henceforth only the Nova Sco-tians "who came with Mr Clarkston" [sic] and Granville Towners were to be considered the true "proprietors" of the colony, entitled to vote, hold office and make laws for the colony. The white officials of the com-pany were henceforth to be considered "forenners" and entitled only to concern themselves with trade. Overtures were already being made, at the end of 1799, to the Temne King Tom to re-negotiate a direct lease between the black settlers and the chief. In the summer of 1800 there was wild talk in the assembly that if the whites continued to deny their demands, they should be taken out into the ocean in boats and set adrift without sails, oars or compass. In London, Wilberforce was horrifed by the news. The Nova Scotians were, he hurrumphed, "as thorough Jaco-bins as if they had been trained and educated in Paris."[35]

The directors ordered rigour. They had had quite enough of the nonsense of Sharp's Frankpledge democracy. They would send a new charter to do away with such pretensions and make it abundantly clear that the company, and not the tithingmen and hundredors, governed Sierra Leone. They would also dispatch a frigate with enough guns and marines to make the counter-revolution in Sierra Leone a reality. And they decided to transport to Sierra Leone 550 Maroons—escaped Jamai-can slaves who had created their own forest societies in the interior of the island, and who, in 1796, had waged war against the colonial gov-ernment. The Maroon history (itself a strange, sad epic) was following, almost literally, in the footsteps of the black loyalists: escape from slavery; a testy relationship with the imperial power; removal to Nova Scotia where, for a while, they lived in villages such as Preston, which had been emptied by the departed Americans—though they made less pretence of ever being interested in farming. Now the Maroons were following their predecessors to Sierra Leone. They had developed a reputation for no-quarter ferocity as fighters, and the company evidently hoped they would arrive in Africa as auxiliaries. Ludlam was understandably nervous—uncertain whether, if called on, the Maroons would fight for the company or join forces with the rebel Nova Scotians.

But the reed had bent far enough and was not about to break. Governor Ludlam appointed new black constables, counted those settlers on whom he could rely (twenty-seven, including Corankapone) and prepared to arm them in defence of the company's government. Then he warned the black leaders that, should they persist in their folly, a naval force would soon arrive and with it the means by which the company would make its will felt. The bluster had the reverse effect of what Ludlam had intended. Isaac Anderson believed that the radicals needed to act before the appearance of His Majesty's ships carrying the Maroons. Most of the black settlers were sympathetic to their cause, but understandably apprehensive about moving to outright rebellion. Many of their most serious grievances—the quit rent and the interference in the chapels' right to perform marriages and baptisms —had been effectively set aside. They had black juries; their *men* had the vote; they had their schools and dispensary back; they had their country farms and the right to trade on the rivers and sell in their stores. The more prudent of them worried about losing all of this for some sort of black republic.

But Isaac Anderson, Ansel Zizer, Nathaniel Wansey, James Robinson and the rest had the wind in their sails and thunder in their voices. When they spoke from Cato Perkins's Methodist pulpit on the 3rd of September, they spoke like the founding fathers of a new black nation. It was their Philadelphia moment. They declared the authority of the governor to be overthrown. Henceforth government and the making and enforcing of laws was to be in the exclusive hands of their elected assembly of tithingmen and hundredors. With a speed that would have shocked the Founding Fathers in Philadelphia, the rebels announced that a new code of laws and a provisional constitution would be promulgated in a week, and then posted in public on the 25th of September. After that date the old administration no longer had their allegiance: "All that come from Nova Scotia shall be under this law or quit the place." Anyone else (the whites) who obeyed the old government would be fined £20 for each transgression.

When published, the "new laws" were conspicuously free of high-faluting expressions of political theory and more concerned with the way the people of Sierra Leone led their daily lives. So price ceilings were set for comestibles—for butter, salt pork and beef ninepence a pound, for palm oil a shilling a quart. The company was required to buy produce from the settlers and to sell it or to export it without duties. Fines were established for, *inter alia,* keeping a "bad house" (£1), trespassing, theft, cutting wattles or timber without permission, pulling weapons (£2.10s), adultery, violating the Sabbath, and causing a sheep or goat to slink (£5). Men who left their wives for a mistress and women who left their husbands for a lover were fined equally (another first for Sierra Leone) the hefty sum of £10. Most optimistic of all was the law concerning the misconduct of children: recidivists were to be "severely corrected" by their parents if they wanted to avoid a ten-shilling fine. More decisively for their assumption of sovereignty, the hundredors and tithingmen reserved for themselves the right to issue writs and summonses. No debts could be collected until their magistrates had approved their legality.

As fast as the coup was going, it was not fast enough, for HMS *Asia,* with 550 Maroons and Macaulay's brother Alexander as one of its officers, was under sail from Halifax. But Anderson evidently hoped that the boldness of their declaration would somehow persuade Ludlam to negotiate a peaceful transfer of power, and that he could rally the majority of the settlers to defend the new regime if called for. Neither of these things happened. On the 25th of September a broadsheet with the declaration and laws of the 3rd was posted on the shutters of the house of the cooper Abraham Smith, an ex-slave who, appropriately enough, had come from Philadelphia, where he had joined the British army in 1779. It was torn down, then put up again. The next morning crowds of settlers gathered on Smith's doorstep, debating the placard. Not all of them were happy with what it said.

But Ludlam had had enough of debate. Resolved on suppressing the rebellion, he summoned loyal settlers and the body of white company men to the Governor's House on Thornton Hill, declared the rebels to be guilty of sedition and proceeded to distribute weapons. A warrant for the arrest of the leaders was drawn up. Corankapone and another of the loyal black marshals were sent to get four of them, said to be meeting at the house of a settler named Ezekiel Campbell. Two of them, Wansey and Robinson, were taken; others escaped. When he was brought to Thornton Hill, Wansey was bleeding from stab wounds. Corankapone's story was that while attempting to arrest the leaders, he had been beaten by Robinson with the pelloon club used to thresh rice, and his companion marshal, Edmonds, had been knocked unconscious. At that point the loyalists had opened fire. Other witnesses told a different story; that fire had been directed from the start at unarmed rebels, who only then went outside and tore up fence railings with which they set about the arresting party.

For Isaac Anderson, who counted himself lucky not to have been at Ezekiel Campbell's, blood had been spilt and there was no going back. He gathered as many of the radicals as he could—between fifty and sixty—armed them, and marched them to a camp at Buckle's Bridge just outside Freetown on the road to Granville Town. From there Anderson, now the de facto leader of the revolt, rejected appeals from Thornton Hill to disarm and warned that his tiny army would itself attack the Governor's House unless the prisoners taken on the 26th were released. The odds at that point were not in Ludlam's favour. He had just forty whites and loyal blacks and another forty African sailors from the company fleet, loyalty uncertain. And he thought—with some reason—that Anderson could call on Temne warriors from King Tom to make his band into a serious force. But at this moment, as Ludlam later wrote, "a most unexpected intervention of providence completely changed the face of affairs."[36] On the 30th of September a square-rigged naval vessel sailed slowly into Freetown harbour. It was the *Asia*, with its transport of militarized Maroons and forty-five British regular troops, and Ludlam had never been so happy to see a ship in all his life.

The weather turned ominous, with saturated clouds massing high on the crests of the forested hills above the frail rebel camp. Down there at Buckle's Bridge, besides Anderson, the abrasive Frank Patrick and the black Justices of the Peace Mingo Jordan and John Cuthbert, were a handful of others who had come all the way from New Jersey and South Carolina, from Preston, Birchtown and Little Joggin to this last fight. Somewhere, among the rebel band were two men who had decided to make their names mean something once more: Henry Washington and British Freedom.

The storm broke with a shattering detonation of the heavens, the worst that Sierra Leone could unload crashing down on three separate defiles of Maroon and white soldiers creeping towards Buckle's Bridge with the aim of surrounding the rebels. With the trails turning into foaming slurry, the manoeuvre was halted as the soldiers tried to get some shelter and protect their weapons as best they could. On the bridge the rebels huddled under capes. Doubtless there was a Nova Scotian umbrella or two.

Afterwards, in the dawn sunlight, with the morning screeching of the parrots for accompaniment, the Maroons pounced. The surprise was complete, the rout total. A few shots were fired, for two of the rebels—names unknown—were killed. Many more, including Isaac Anderson, escaped into the forest, but two days later he was brought to Freetown by the local chief with whom he had hoped to shelter. The Maroons combed the forest and villages for fugitives and took thirty-one prisoners.

It was out of the question, Ludlam thought, to wait and send the rebels back to England for trial, or to take the chance of judging them before the colony's black juries, which would be unlikely to convict. The new royal charter was on its way with its commission for white judges, duly arriving on the 12th of October, but getting rid of the insurrectionists was too urgent to be delayed. So Ludlam did what the authorities in reactionary England and revolutionary France had done when they decided they were in a state of emergency—he had the rebels tried under a specially created military tribunal. Three lieutenants from the *Asia* presided over the court, which made short work of its duty. Of fifty-five settlers declared to have participated in the sedition, thirty-three were permanently banished from Sierra Leone; some, including James Robinson, were sent to the British colony of Goree. Most were exiled to the Bullom shore. Should they attempt to return and be caught, they would receive three hundred lashes, effectively a death sentence. Isaac Anderson and Frank Patrick, one of Macaulay's bitterest antagonists and long

a thorn in the side of the company rule, were bound over as capital felons for the first quarter-session of the newly chartered regime. Patrick
was charged with stealing a gun. Anderson was accused of sending an
anonymous letter, the one that had demanded the release of the prisoners taken at Ezekiel Campbell's house on the night of the 26th: "Mr
Ludlow Sir we de sire to now whether you will let our Mends out if not
turn out the womans and Chill Dren."[37] Both crimes warranted the
death penalty, and Patrick and Anderson were duly convicted and
hanged. In the usual way, their bodies remained on the gibbets for some
days. Just two years earlier, Isaac Anderson had been delighted to send
John Clarkson a barrel of rice from his first harvest. Now what was left
of his corpse was being cleaned by the hyenas.

On the 6th of November the new royal charter of the company was
formally inaugurated to the ceremonious booming of the *Asia*'s guns.
Ludlam would not preside over its introduction, for his queasy stomach and delicate nerves had got the better of him and he had prematurely tendered his resignation. Perhaps, too—for he was no Zachary
Macaulay, unaffected by twinges of doubt—Ludlam might have felt
troubled by the liquidation of the extraordinary experiment in black
self-government. No more tithingmen and hundredors; no more sententious speeches in the chapels. All that survived of Sharp's Frankpledge
democracy were black juries.

For some of the black settlers, the end of firebrand politics must
have come as a relief. No one was trying to move them off their lots or
collect quit rent (although the company still claimed the *right* to do so).
No one was meddling with their Churches. Boston King could get on
with his missionary teaching; John Kizell, who had been seized as a
slave so many years ago in the Sherbro country and who now, as a free
man, traded with his own people from his boat, the *Three Friends,* could
get on with making money. Andrew Moore saw his discovery of wild
coffee burgeon into Sierra Leone's most important trade and profited
from it. Sophia Small could open her shop again, turn it into the biggest
retail concern in Freetown, buy more properties and marry her daughter to an English carpenter called George Nicol. When David George
died in 1802, the preacher he had sent to Preston, Hector Peters, happily
took over his ministry.

The embers of revolt were not quite extinguished. Some of those who had escaped from the Maroons at Buckle's Bridge had found shelter with the Temne King Tom and in 1801, and again in 1802, marched on Freetown and Thornton Hill, this time with African warriors. But they faced the Maroons, who had been given the confiscated properties of the convicted rebels and were certainly not about to surrender them now. Most of the Nova Scotians stayed prudently neutral or, like the perenially dependable Corankapone, turned out for the government, in his case dying in a battle for the Governor's House. The rains and the "smokes" rolled around the colony. Old names returned—among them Dawes and Ludlam for a spell of vindication, while Zachary Macaulay stayed in his company office in London writing instructions. Although Henry Thornton MP was nominally still the chairman, no one in or out of Parliament was in much doubt about who was really running Sierra Leone. But it was reluctantly concluded by 1807 that perhaps the company was running the colony into the ground. Local trade and a modest export in camwood, coffee, rice and sugar were doing well, but they were mostly in private hands and the company—without its quit rent revenue—was incapable of recovering the costs of defence or administration. When the bill that finally abolished the slave trade passed through Parliament that year, it was foreseen that Liberated Africans (as they were designated) taken from the slave traders by the Royal Navy or escaped from the factories would be bound to come to Sierra Leone. Freetown would inevitably become the station and headquarters of this great emancipation and it was evident to everyone, Thornton and the directors especially, that it needed henceforth to be under the direct protection of the Crown. In 1808 the company was wound up, its flag was run down and the Union Jack run up.

Who was watching? Some of the exiled rebels of 1800, despite the draconian penalty laid on them, had been allowed to come back to Freetown in dribs and drabs. Others may have smuggled themselves in and, once again, given themselves new names. But not, I think, British Freedom. Together with Henry Washington and some others he was out on the northern Bullom shore amidst the half-abandoned remains of Isaac DuBois's cotton farms at Clarkson Plantation, at which point he disappears from our history. We can picture him surviving, perhaps as he had done at Preston, on a few acres, or more likely finding a way to do business with the local chiefs. And if he did indeed cling to that name, he could only do so by not crossing the river to Freetown. For he must have understood that he had had his day. Over there, no one had much use for British freedom any more. Over there was something different. Over there was the British Empire.

ENDINGS, BEGINNINGS

Histories never conclude: they just pause their prose.
Their stories—like the one just told—are, if they are truthful, untidy affairs,
resistant to windings-up and sortings-out. They beat raggedly on into the future,
into, in this case, an infuriated nineteenth century. But even as history
is overtaken by events, it leaves behind it a wake of recollection, a thin skein of
light on the murky ocean of time which jumps and dances like the fugitive flashes
we apprehend when, at last, we close our eyes.

[*FREDERICK DOUGLASS*, DAGUERREOTYPE, C. 1840–50]

1802

THE COUNCIL OF STATE of the Consular French Republic, led by Napoleon Bonaparte, reintroduced slavery, eight years after its abolition.

1806

AFTER HIS BILL to abolish the slave trade had met with yet another defeat in 1799, William Wilberforce all but gave up hope of Parliament. A French army was camped at Boulogne, and an invasion was in the offing. Few wished to hand the enemy any kind of economic advantage in the global struggle. After the battle of Trafalgar had ended that threat for good in 1805, the abolitionists became more optimistic. The union with Ireland in 1801 had brought into the House of Commons new members, many of whom made known their opposition to the infamous trade. In January 1806 William Pitt died and Charles James Fox, who had spoken for abolition in 1791, led the new government in the House of Commons. Sir Charles Middleton, the patron of James Ramsay and the mentor of Clarkson and Wilberforce, became First Lord of the Admiralty. After a bill stopping the import of slaves in conquered colonies, and forbidding British subjects from trading in neutral ships, passed in both houses of Parliament, Fox moved more boldly. On the 10th of June, a motion requiring Parliament "considering the Slave Trade to be contrary to the principles of justice, humanity and policy . . . [to] take effectual measures for its abolition" was passed, again in both Houses and by substantial majorities. Fox declared that if he should succeed in carrying through this measure, he should think his life "well spent." Four months later he was dead.

IN THE UNITED STATES moves to end the slave trade were helped by fears that the ferocious insurrectionary war still raging in St Domingue might have an American counterpart if the demographic imbalance between black and white were allowed to become even more lopsided. President Jefferson gave public endorsement for legislation to end the trade. But the slave population in Louisiana trebled in the two years since its purchase from the French in 1804. In that same year South Carolina had reintroduced the slave trade it had earlier abolished, in a last-minute effort to beat the coming prohibition on imports.

In Virginia planters shaken by the slave rebellion of Gabriel Prosser in 1800 took steps to rid the commonwealth of trouble-making free blacks. At the initiative of Governor Benjamin Harrison they were forbidden to own firearms. Schools for the children of free blacks were closed. Manumitted slaves were required to leave the commonwealth after a year.

In Sierra Leone Harrison's ex-slaves William and Anna Cheese and their descendants lived on peacefully in Freetown.

1807

IN MARCH 1807 Jefferson signed into law a bill outlawing the importation of slaves into the United States. After the 1st of January 1808 violators would be fined $20,000 and their ship and cargo forfeited.

Introducing a "Bill for the Abolition of the Slave Trade" in the House of Lords, Lord Grenville proclaimed that its enactment would be "one of the most glorious acts that had ever been undertaken by any assembly of any nation in the world."[1] In the Commons, with the bill's passage a certainty, the Solicitor-General contrasted the guilty conscience of Napoleon Bonaparte as he retired to bed, with Wilberforce "in the bosom of his happy and delighted family" sleeping with a perfect conscience in the knowledge that he had preserved the life of millions of his fellow creatures.[2] On the 10th of February, the bill was passed in the Commons by 283 votes to 16. On the 25th of March, George III gave the royal assent. After the 1st of January 1808, it would be unlawful for any British ship to carry slaves, nor could any be landed in other ships in the dominions of the British Empire.

IN MAY 1808, Thomas Clarkson's *History of the Rise, Progress and Accomplishment of the Abolition of the African Slave Trade by the British Parliament* was published. Four thousand copies were sold on subscription in advance of the publication date. After the "mild and genial dullness of the first three pages," Samuel Coleridge wrote to his fellow poet Robert Southey, the book was "deeply interesting, written with great purity as well as simplicity of Language . . . and nothing can surpass the moral beauty of the manner in which he introduces himself and relates his own maxima pars in that Immortal War—compared with which how mean all the conquests of Napoleon and Alexander."[3] An abridged edition of the book was printed expressly for use in American Sunday schools.

The Sierra Leone Company having been wound up, Zachary Macaulay and Henry Thornton turned their attention to the foundation of the African Institution, by means of which they hoped to diffuse the blessings of Christianity and civility throughout the pagan continent. Thomas Clarkson, whose Jacobinical errors had been forgiven if not forgotten, was brought within its fold of guiding lights. Granville Sharp, it need hardly be said, was acclaimed its patriarch.

The Royal Navy took up station in Sierra Leone to pursue and capture slave traders and to liberate their live cargo. Many of the ships taken in the first decade of patrols were, despite Congress's abolition, American and French.

1811

ONE OF THOSE who saw an American slaver, the *Rebecca* out of New York, apprehended by the Royal Navy at Freetown was Paul Cuffe, a fifty-two-year-old free black from Westport, Massachusetts, the son of a slave and a Martha's Vineyard Wampanoag Indian. Cuffe was an American success: the owner of land, gristmills, whaling boats. But he was also a Quaker, and a reading of Thomas Clarkson's *History* had made him an ardent abolitionist. He felt keenly the plight of slaves in the United States, but also the severe disabilities of his own free people in those states, including Massachusetts and Pennsylvania, which had abolished the institution. Through the transatlantic network of Friends he had heard of Sierra Leone and the African Institution, whose blessing he hoped to secure for a trading venture between the colony of free black Afro-Anglo-Americans and the United States. If all went well, he might even sponsor the settlement of American blacks in Sierra Leone. Cuffe was an American patriot who, forbidden by his Church from serving in the army or navy, spent the Revolutionary War running the blockade of the Royal Navy, a feat that still did not dispel suspicions that he was, at heart, a Tory. He would have been pleased if the Stars and Stripes and the Union Jack could be reconciled in the noble cause of Emancipation.

But his timing was terrible. Cuffe sailed in late December 1810 with a crew of nine, all black, including his nephew, Thomas Wainer, and John Marsterns, who was married to his niece Mary. Thirty-two days out, in early February, the *Traveller* was hit by a violent squall. It began to leak and take on water. At three o'clock in the morning, on the second day of the gale, the ship was "struck on our beem end," rolling so far over that its deck was perpendicular to the ocean. Before it could right itself, John Marsterns was washed clean overboard. Amidst the towering waves and screaming wind Marsterns found some rigging torn off the ship, and clung to it for dear life. Finally he managed to climb back aboard the ship. For three more days the *Traveller* was in grave danger of foundering, but somehow the little brig rode out the storm. Fifty-three days out, it was sailing under sunny skies and there was dolphin for dinner. On the fifty-eighth day Paul Cuffe saw the mountains of Sierra Leone rising from the sea.

In Sierra Leone the American dined with the British governor in his official residence on Thornton Hill. Cuffe prayed in the Methodist chapel and gave King Tom a Quaker Bible and an *Essay on Wars*, the substance of which, naturally, was their iniquity and futility—a message unlikely to make much of an impression on Tom, greybeard though he now was. On the Bullom shore, close to Clarkson Plantation, he met King George, who also got a Quaker Bible as well as an Epistle from the Yearly Meeting. Cuffe was impatient to begin trading with the likes of John Kizell, who shipped tons of camwood down-river in his fleet of big boats, but was obliged to await permission from the African Institution. The British government was gravely displeased—to the point of prohibiting American trade—with President Madison's truckling, as it believed, to the economic blockade of the despot Bonaparte. Cooling his heels, Cuffe continued to admire Freetown, especially its schools, which currently taught 230 children. Another school instructed black adults. Books and paper, he noted, were all free. "If Commerce Could be Interduced in the Colony," he noted in a letter sent to Quaker Friends in London, "it might have the good attendencey of keeping the young men at home and in Some future day Quallify them to become maneggers of themselves and when they become thus Quallified to Carry on Commerce I See no Reason why they may not become a Nation to be Numbered among the historians nations of the World."[4]

The trading licence finally arrived and Cuffe was about to set sail, taking Sierra Leone cargo back to America, when he received an invitation to go to England. This proved irresistible. Naturally he ran into dirty weather on the voyage north: "Very trying for Sales." Mid-voyage he spoke with a Captain Cates, sailing from Liverpool to Newfoundland, who gave Cuffe the "unhapey News" of an engagement between an American frigate and a British sloop off Sandy Hook, New York. This did not bode well for Cuffe's mission of transatlantic commerce and goodwill. But on the 12th of July 1811 a crowd lined the dockside at Liverpool—until three years earlier the joint capital, with Bristol, of the slave trade—to see the *Traveller*, with its black captain in his Quaker hat, and black crew. His pleasure at being made instantly welcome received a severe knock when three of his crew were pressed into the navy. Two were released, but it took Cuffe months to secure the freedom of the third.

Nonetheless, he was overwhelmed with kindness and instantaneous fame. In the United States he had not been able to keep much company with white Quakers, even less any other whites. In England he was made welcome everywhere. *The Times* and the *Edinburgh Review* enthused over him; he did the sights of London with William Allen and his son (the Royal Mint, the Zoo); toured a Manchester factory, marvelling at the gaslight; went to Parliament and met Wilberforce and Zachary Macaulay. To the king's nephew the Duke of Gloucester, who was also the patron of the African Institution, Cuffe presented an African robe, a dagger and a letter box, all from Sierra Leone. To his joy, through their friend and protégé Allen, Cuffe also made the acquaintance of

Thomas and John Clarkson. He wrote optimistically to his brother John: "I am endeavouring to have a . . . road opened from England to America and to Sierra Leone . . . in order that some good sober correctors [characters] may find their way to that counterey."[5]

In September 1811 Cuffe sailed back through yet more brutal storms to Sierra Leone, where he landed Manchester cotton manufactures and iron pots, tobacco and English pottery. In return he took on camwood and palm oil. William Allen had entrusted him with various seeds and even more precious silkworms for the colony, but was told by the governor that the people in Sierra Leone had better learn how to grow cotton before they tried their hand at silk.

1812

BY FEBRUARY 1812 Cuffe was ready to sail back to America with his cargo of Sierra Leone exports. It was, he hoped, the seed of something glorious. He had in mind, as he wrote to Thomas Clarkson, a commercial and settlement partnership between the United States and Great Britain to sustain the noble experiment in Sierra Leone and "assist the Africans in their civilization." He learned of several Afro-American families "that have made up thear minds to go to Sierra Leone."[6]

But the two countries were not minded to collaborate. Instead, they were at war. Once again, the British offered liberty to any escaped slaves able to reach the British lines or ships. Despite a much more difficult campaign in terms of geography, tens of thousands once again took them up on the offer. After the war a few thousand were once again shipped off, in freedom and extreme poverty, to Nova Scotia. The village of Preston, virtually empty since the exodus of the black loyalists, filled up with this second wave of African-Americans. Their descendants still live there today. Some of them have created a Black Loyalist Heritage Museum and Web site; the museum and history centre stand by the side of the road on which John Clarkson and Lawrence Hartshorne rode out to the hamlet in the brilliant autumn of 1791. In Preston the first thing you see are churches and schools from which black kids in sweats and trainers emerge every afternoon. Nova Scotia and the rest of Canada are still unsure about Preston. In Halifax they tell you it produces great boxers.

The inevitable gales blew Paul Cuffe into Westport rather than New Bedford. It was his home town, but that failed to prevent the United

States Customs Service from confiscating his ship and cargo for having done business with the enemy. To liberate his vessel, Paul Cuffe travelled to Washington and, remarkably, got to see both Albert Gallatin, the Secretary of State, and President Madison. According to *The Friend's Intelligencer*, Cuffe, the straightforward black Quaker, addressed Madison thus: "James, I have been put to much trouble and have been abused." Madison was sympathetic and ordered the property to be released.

On his way back to Massachusetts from the capital Cuffe was made brusquely aware he was not in Britain, much less Freetown. He was dealt with roughly in stagecoaches by white passengers who were incredulous that a black should presume to share carriage space with them. They attempted to evict him, but Cuffe, a dignified old gentleman in his flop-brimmed Quaker hat, stayed put.

Not long afterwards the British took Washington and burned the White House. More slaves escaped.

SUMMER 1814

GRANVILLE SHARP had become a bit of a wanderer. It was as though he was still looking for important matters but was no longer quite sure where to find them. He was almost eight years beyond his allotted three score and ten. A half-century had passed since he had been startled into zeal by the sight of Jonathan Strong's bloody face. The Satanic *business* had been cast down—he could go to his grave with that satisfaction; yet there were still slaves toiling in America and the West Indies. Well, others would have to see that infamy off. He was keenly conscious that whatever he had done had been the work of brothers, sisters, confederates in God's cause. They had been a concert. Now they were gone, like Mr Haydn's players at the close of the *Farewell* symphony, each putting out their light and vanishing into the shade. James's brass serpent had lain mute since his passing twenty years earlier. Four years ago the lid of the harpsichord closed along with the eyes of his sister Eliza, and scarcely a few months later his dear brother William had gone. The horns of paradise would surely greet *his* entrance. Granville himself no longer had the wind for his double-fluting; but every morning and most evenings he went to his harp, summoned the ghost of David and sang psalms and Hebrew melodies.[7]

He had suffered what each man must, the steady dwindling of powers—but no one could ever accuse him of idleness. Lately there had been the Bible Society and the Protestant Union and the African Institution; and he had done his best to put his memories and his correspondence in order, to make a history of the bundle. The Duke of Gloucester had assured him of his pleasure at receiving the manuscript.[8] Still, there was so much more to order before he could decently retire from his exertions. But every so often, sometimes in the middle of speaking urgently on some important topic, he was suddenly—and he knew not why—a little baffled; his famously sturdy power of recollection became unable to seize the matter it sought, so that his sentences sometimes trailed off without proper resolution.

As long as William had been alive Granville had shared the house at Fulham with his brother. Even after his death he liked to rattle around there, communing with memory, peering at the tide that had borne their harmonies. William's widow didn't seem to mind. But Granville had also taken a chamber in the Temple, where his books and papers were kept, and where he could keep his own company with not so much as a servant to disturb his meditations on the scriptures. In June 1813 he had offered some choice items documenting his long engagement in the law to the library of that Inn of Court. They had been gratefully accepted, but Granville insisted that he must go in person to the Temple to ensure their safe delivery. The Fulham nephews and nieces, looking at their frail and increasingly vague uncle, attempted to dissuade him but failed. Anxious lest he get lost, they then ordered the family coachman not to let Granville have the use of the carriage.

But Sharp had lost none of his tenacity. When the family assembled for breakfast the next morning there was no Granville. After a general enquiry among the servants, one of them revealed that Mr Sharp had got up early enough to take the stagecoach to London. Someone was dispatched right away to the chambers in the Temple, but found no Granville there either. He was on his way back, and later that afternoon appeared again at Fulham looking dishevelled and exhausted, and admitting to having eaten nothing since his dawn departure. On enquiry, it turned out that the coachman who had taken Sharp to London, worried by his appearance and behaviour, went in search of him at the Temple and found him at the door of his chambers "wandering about in a state of incertitude, being unable to guide himself to the part of town that he designed to reach. He was easily persuaded by the warm-hearted coachman to go back with him to Fulham and was thus happily preserved from more distressing accidents."[9]

From then on until his death, the gentlest imaginable, in July 1814, Granville Sharp stayed put, or was made to stay put, at Fulham. It was high summer, the season of the family's waterborne excursions long ago on the *Apollo* or the *Union*; of their concerts for the king and for the people on the riverbanks; of Miss Morgan the organ, Roma the musical hound, tea and Handel, the boats sailing along amidst clouds of gnats. Every so often, as if he had something to impart, Granville would come suddenly into a room where the nieces and nephews and their children were gathered. But he never opened his mouth. He would seat himself close by to enjoy their company and remain in the summer light for hours at a time. Now and again a trace of a smile stretched the gaunt jaw, so the family had no reason to suppose he was not content. But not a word came from him; not a word.[10]

1815

AT THE PARIS PEACE CONFERENCE after Napoleon's final defeat at Waterloo Thomas Clarkson, now turned pacifist, met the Tsar of All the Russias, Alexander I. It turned out that the emperor knew all about the Clarksons and Sierra Leone. "If I can at any time be useful to the Cause of the Poor Africans," Alexander told Thomas, "you may always have my Services by writing me a Letter." Three years later he supported Thomas's proposal to declare the slave trade a form of international piracy. Grateful, Thomas gave the tsar the usual African dagger.[11]

1816

IN LONDON the Society for the Promotion of Permanent and Universal Peace announced its foundation. It was pre-eminently the child of shared Anglo-American idealism. Quakers such as William Allen and (in Philadelphia) Benjamin Rush were its prominent advocates. Rush, ever the optimist, hoped to persuade the American government to cre-ate a Secretariat of Peace. The Clarkson brothers were, of course, num-bered among its founders. John Clarkson, who two decades earlier had declined to take the command finally offered to him by the navy on the grounds of its inconsistency with Christian principles, became the Peace Society's first treasurer. Nine years later, in 1825, an African Peace Society was formed in—appropriately enough—Philadelphia.[12]

In February 1816 Paul Cuffe returned to Sierra Leone with thirty-eight prospective black settlers. Even for the old sailor, this crossing had been a horror. "I Exspearenced 20 days of the most Trimindous weather that I ever remember exspearencing of. The Ship and Crew were Seemingly in Jepordy, but through mercy we were preserved."

When they had safely landed, the governor, Charles MacCarthy, received Cuffe and the settlers cordially. But a letter from Macaulay & Babington, the leading trader with Sierra Leone, refused permission for Cuffe to land his cargo of flour on the grounds of improper competition with his own exports.[13]

While in Sierra Leone, Cuffe observed the apprehension by the Royal Navy of slave ships, many of them from the republic that had outlawed the traffic. In two months, three American brigs and three schooners carrying slaves were captured by Royal Navy patrols and brought to Sierra Leone. Cuffe also knew that a substantial clandestine trade for the United States was carried on by Americans under other national flags, especially the Spanish. He was deeply depressed by this betrayal of Jefferson's Abolition Act, as he was by news of slave rebellions and brutal reprisals in South Carolina. On the other hand, Cuffe was happy that Governor MacCarthy provided both town and country lots for the nine American black families he had brought to Sierra Leone, most of them from Boston. He died in 1817, a little disconsolate that his Triangular Trade of freedom—between Sierra Leone, Britain and the United States—had not yet materialized.

The American Colonization Society began its work to transport free blacks to what would become Liberia. When the Anti-Slave Society of New York published a biography of Granville Sharp in 1846 the author, Charles Stuart, went out of his way to distinguish the foundation of Sierra Leone from the efforts of the American Colonization Society to transport free negroes to Liberia. In the British case, Stuart implied, settlement was the harbinger of abolition; in the American case it was a pernicious alternative to it:

Love, impartial brotherly christian love, was the source of Sierra Leone. Hatred and contempt for *color* . . . were the great source . . . of Liberia . . . The settlement of Sierra Leone cherished the best feelings of the English nation—sympathy for the oppressed, and benevolence towards desolate strangers, whom the proud world spurned and persecuted. The founding of Liberia cherished the worst feelings of the people of the United States; the idol-sin which distinguishes them from all other civilized people, *color-hatred* . . .[14]

Stuart exaggerated the virtues of the British and the vices of the Americans. But he was not alone in this invidious distinction.

1826

THE NEWLY APPOINTED Governor of Sierra Leone, Sir Neil Campbell, attempted to levy quit rents, but died within a few months, after which the contentious tax was finally laid to rest. The "Nova Scotians" now constituted no more than 10 percent of a population overwhelmingly made up of "Liberated Blacks" taken from the slave trade and the West Indian Maroons. But their presence was conspicuous in the churches and schools. At the Freetown Fair, the old "Negro Frolics" banned in Shelburne had been reborn as Sierra Leone's annual carnival. High hats, long printed skirts and bulky petticoats were still de rigueur at the horse and canoe races.

1828

ON THE 2ND of April John Clarkson lay down on his sofa to read the *Anti-Slavery Reporter.* Dislodged in 1820 from the management of the Purfleet limeworks by a new owner, Clarkson had been living in Woodbridge, Suffolk, as the senior partner of a country bank. The last he had heard from the Nova Scotians had been in 1817, when Hector Peters had written hoping "that we may behold each other face to face once more before we depart hence to be no more."[15] Through the *Sierra Leone Gazette,* edited by a second-generation Nova Scotian, Clarkson had managed to keep abreast of news from the colony. A version of the founding, based on his diary and notes, had been published in 1815, but the great drama of his life in 1791 and 1792 remained locked in the manuscript copies of his journal and in the memories of the now placidly amiable man; the Clarkson family's "fountain of innocent mirth."[16]

On this particular day he was feeling not especially mirthful. In his sixty-fourth year—John had made a will that January—he was feeling more than usually wintry about his future. A leg had been troubling him and he had found himself often short of breath. The discomfort was such that he asked for choice items from the *Reporter* to be read to him. Its matter filled him with melancholy. Both he and his brother Thomas had supposed that, with the slave trade choked off, the institution would itself atrophy; but it was plain that nothing of the sort had happened. Their work had been but half done. Stopping the reading, with its recitation of West Indian miseries still uncorrected, Clarkson said, exerting himself a little, "It is dreadful to think, after my brother and his friends have been labouring for forty years that such things should still be."[17]

And then without more ado John Clarkson died.

1829

IN BOSTON the black tailor David Walker published his *Appeal to the Colored Citizens of the World*, an incendiary attack on the hypocrisy of the United States for purporting to establish itself on the principles of liberty and equality while continuing to deny them to 3 million slaves. At the same time, he described the "English" as the "best friends" black people had in the world. Walker was aware of the persistence of slavery in the British West Indies, but evidently believed their days were numbered.

1831

DAVID WALKER was right. News of a slave insurrection in Jamaica and its brutal repression galvanized abolitionism in Britain. The Anti-Slavery Society, founded in 1830 in Freemasons' Hall in London with a commitment to end the institution, abandoned gradualism. Thomas Clarkson, William Wilberforce and Samuel Hoare were among its veteran campaigners. The cause was incalculably helped by the runaway success of *The History of Mary Prince, A West Indian Slave Related by Herself*, which went through five editions in its first year. "When we are quite done up," Mary wrote, "who cares for us, more than a lame horse? This is slavery. I tell it to let the English people know the truth; and I hope they will never leave off to pray to God and call loud to the great king of England, till all the poor blacks be given free and slavery done up for evermore."[18] But King William IV seemed as indifferent to the urgency as did his Tory ministers. However, there was another agitation in the country—for the reform of Parliament—and the two campaigns become ravelled up both in their moral passion and in their political and economic expediency. Parliamentary reform would save Britain from revolution; abolition would save the West Indies from carnage and the kingdom from perdition. Zachary Macaulay's son Thomas, a young MP, believed this to be the case, although he found the excessive fervour of the abolitionists slightly repellent.

1833

THREE HUNDRED and fifty thousand women signed one of the more than five thousand petitions sent to Parliament for the ending of slavery.[19] In May a bill was introduced by the Colonial Secretary of the Whig government and passed through the reformed House of Commons by a handsome margin. Its passage was eased by generous provisions of compensation for the owners and a two-year transition period (later abandoned) from slavery to outright freedom. In August the Emancipation Bill was signed by King William IV.

A month earlier, Wilberforce had died. But not before he had become reconciled with Thomas Clarkson, despite their deep, long-standing differences over the French Revolution and the war. "My dear old Friend," Wilberforce had written in his last letter, ". . . tho it is so long since there has been any intercourse between us, you and yours still occupy a constant place in my friendly remembrance."[20] After Clarkson had been told the sad news, his wife, Catherine, heard him lock the door of his study before abandoning himself to weeping.

1846

HE was the last of them all. Not just the patriarch of the Cause but, more improbably, the tenant of Playford Hall near Ipswich, let to him by an abolitionist admirer, the Earl of Bristol. There Thomas lived, deep into his eighties. When not making appearances at Anti-Slavery Conventions, he played the benevolent squire, making sure that none of his villagers and labourers went without sides of beef and flitches of bacon.

In the Hungry Forties his patch of Old England would, at least, be Merrie. And since there was still much to do by way of speeding American slavery to its end, he continued to write, looking up from his desk now and again to watch his wife potter about the flower gardens.

Old as he was, Thomas Clarkson was still a force to be reckoned with; his own voice was strong, his mind still surprisingly vigorous, and he seemed more than ever seer and sage. Abolitionist crusaders came from all over the world to Britain to concert their anti-slavery campaigns, and could not leave without paying their respects to the old man. Especially not the Americans, who importuned Clarkson so often and so insistently for his autograph and locks of his white hair that his wife, Catherine, feared there would soon be none left.

In the early afternoon of the 20th of August 1846 two of them, one black, one white, along with a British radical Member of Parliament, George Thompson, sat in the drawing room at Playford Hall. The white man was William Lloyd Garrison, the Massachusetts editor of the *Liberator*, who had witnessed first-hand the moment of emancipation in 1833. Thompson, too, had earned his spurs by riding the crest of that transatlantic enthusiasm to lecture for abolition in the United States during the following year. In Boston a gang of teamsters had threatened to horsewhip Thompson and send him to South Carolina, where, they said, people would know what to do with him—a cry continually raised against the abolitionists. Although Clarkson had only learned at nine o'clock that morning that these two and their black companion intended to visit him, he was, as always, simply hospitable.

Why not? America was his cause now. In 1840, at the first World Anti-Slavery Convention, he had been made president, and in his eightieth year had received a silent, standing tribute from the five thousand delegates. Thomas's peroration, in the form of a blessing on them and the Cause, triggered an outbreak of tears from the assembly. His greatest distress was to learn how Christianity was being perverted to defend the racial iniquity; that 70 percent (he was informed) of all American clergymen apparently believed that the Holy Scriptures justified slavery. In 1844 fifty thousand copies of his *On the Ill Treatment of the People of Colour in the United States, on Account of the Colour of Their Skin* were published in America in a fierce counter-attack on this blasphemy.[21]

So Thomas Clarkson was known to Frederick Douglass, the third visitor who sat in his drawing room that late summer afternoon. And by now Thomas Clarkson would certainly have heard of Frederick Douglass, the orator who had held the British and Foreign Anti-Slavery Convention spellbound in May and had lit a fire at the World Temperance Convention in Covent Garden just two weeks earlier. Douglass was a twenty-eight-year-old escaped slave from Maryland, whom Garrison had met in New Bedford in 1841. Under Garrison's encouragement, Douglass—articulate, handsome, witty and charismatic—quickly became the star turn of the abolitionist lecture circuit, unsurpassable for his dramatic account of cruelty in the plantations and deadly in his satirical skewering of pro-slavery clergymen. He was constantly threatened with recapture and physical assault, but the effect of having his hand broken by a gang in Pendleton, Indiana, had been only to add fuel to his fire. In May 1845 Garrison had published an edition of five thousand copies of the *Narrative of the Life of Frederick Douglass*, an immediate runaway best-seller. Clarkson was bound to have a copy, to have seen in Douglass a vision of a redeemed American future. That afternoon the old man reached out, took one of Douglass's hands, enfolded it in both of his and exclaimed like the prophet: "God bless you, Frederick Douglass! I have given sixty years of my life to the emancipation of your people, and if I had sixty years more, they should all be given to the same cause."[22]

The admiration was fervently mutual. For Douglass, Thomas Clarkson was the embodiment of everything that was best about British freedom, which for him was not mere declaratory piety of the kind that he had come to despise in the United States, but reality. Britain, he said, was the place that changed him from a thing to a human.

To Douglass's amazement, this transformation had occurred even before he had set foot in Britain: on the saloon deck of the Cunard steamship *Cambria*, taking him in August 1845 from Boston to Liverpool. His last few days on American soil had reminded Douglass forcefully of why he was leaving. Massachusetts might have abolished slavery but it had certainly not abolished race prejudice. "Just before leaving . . . I was . . . refused permission to ride in an omnibus . . . on account of the colour of my skin I was kicked from a public conveyance just a few days before leaving that 'cradle of liberty'. Only three months before leaving that 'home of freedom' I was driven from the lower floor of a church because I tried to enter as other men, forgetting my complexion."[23]

Nor did the humiliations end when he boarded the *Cambria* together with James Buffum, a white abolitionist who was to accompany Douglass on his lecture tour, and the Hutchinson Family Quartet of singers—Jesse, Abby, Judson and Asa—whom they had persuaded to come along, partly as an inspirational warm-up act for the talks.[24] Garrison had arranged that Douglass should have stateroom accommodation (eight by twelve, two oil lamps); but needless to say he had been obliged to travel steerage—where Buffum, too, bunked down in companionable solidarity. By way of compensation—and unexpectedly—Douglass found himself to be a shipboard celebrity, famous to some of the passengers as the author of the *Narrative*; notorious to many more for the same reason. He wrote to Garrison from Dublin:

> I know it will gladden your heart to hear that from the moment we first lost sight of the American shore till we landed at Liverpool, our gallant steamship was the theatre of an almost constant discussion of the subject of slavery—commencing cool but growing hotter every moment as it advanced . . . The discussion was general. If suppressed in the saloon, it broke out in the steerage; and if it ceased in the steerage it was renewed in the saloon; and if suppressed in both it broke out with redoubled energy upon the saloon deck, in the open refreshing, free ocean air. I was happy.[25]

So were the Hutchinsons—so impressed by their own reading of Douglass's *Narrative* that they exploited the two-week captivity of the crossing to distribute copies to the passengers. Those who hailed from Georgia, New Orleans and Cuba and who owned slaves were not at all pleased with this presumption. Others, however, wanted Frederick Douglass to give a lecture on his experiences and on the institution of slavery in the United States, an initiative that angered the slaveowners even more. Douglass himself was uncharacteristically (but understandably) shy about this overture. Almost certainly he had already heard the threats to throw the impertinent black overboard. It was for the captain to decide whether or not such a lecture would be right and proper, and in the normal way of things shipboard prudence would have counselled against hearing the orator.

But Captain Charles Judkins was not the standard Cunard master. He was, rather, a reformed ex-slaver with a strong moral spine and he issued a formal invitation himself. An awning was slung over the saloon deck to give Douglass some distance from a possibly threatening crowd, but the Hutchinsons had the fire of the Cause in their bellies and persuaded Douglass to come out into the open and deliver his speech by the mainmast. In the late afternoon Judkins had the ship's bell rung to "cry" the meeting. A large audience assembled, not all of them friendly. Douglass appeared wearing his best: tall, imposing, morally and culturally aristocratic. But even before he could read from the odious slave statutes of South Carolina, the barracking began, and it rose into a human seastorm of abuse. The Hutchinsons then countered with renderings of inspirational and abolitionist hymns and anthems, "which like the angels of old, closed the lions' mouths so that for a time, silence prevailed."[26] Seizing the moment, Judkins stepped forward and delivered an introduction, half fulsome, half stern, but as soon as Douglass had begun, so did the interruptions. Again Judkins intervened, his voice calm, saying that he tried to please all his passengers: some of them had plainly expressed their great desire to hear Mr Douglass speak, and those of a different view might take themselves somewhere else aboard the ship. Douglass made another effort and was met by shouts of, "Ah, I wish I had him in Savannah. We would use him up!" and another "I will be one of a number to throw him overboard."

'The clamor went on waxing hotter and hotter till it was quite impossible for me to proceed," wrote Douglass. "I was stopped but the cause went on. Anti-slavery was uppermost and the mob was never more of service to the cause against which it was directed." One of the "mobocrats," as Douglass contemptuously called them, then made the serious mistake of berating the captain for allowing the "nigger" to speak. Judkins responded by ordering the bosun to fetch the irons and warned that anyone continuing in this conduct, threatening Douglass or interfering with his remarks would be clapped in the brig until the ship docked in Liverpool. The riot abruptly stopped, and the black-baiters slunk away to the saloon, growling. Judkins then turned to the sympathetic remainder of the crowd and declared, "I once was the owner of two hundred slaves but the government of Great Britain liberated them and I am glad of it." Moved, the Hutchinsons, who hailed from New Hampshire, spontaneously burst into a chorus of "God Save the Queen," which they followed (to emphasize that this was a transatlantic show of goodwill) with "Yankee Doodle Dandy," "America" and "A Life on the Ocean Wave." Just a day out from Liverpool there was a farewell dinner; toasts to Queen Victoria and the United States were drunk and Jesse Hutchinson proposed: "Our country is the world, our countrymen all mankind." The slaveowners dared not interrupt the applause.[27]

Douglass never forgot the dramatic denouement of this crossing; not least because the episode got coverage in the British press and was, as he wrote, in effect the "visiting card" of his impending lecture tour. But Judkins's behaviour was the first revelation of the difference between "monarchical British justice" and "democratic slaveowning mobocracy."

That difference became only more glaring during the tour itself. It was not just the enormous, wildly enthusiastic audiences that greeted him almost everywhere from Manchester to Glasgow to Finsbury Chapel in London. It was also what Douglass was able to do; where he was able to go. He remembered being greeted at the Boston menagerie, at a revival meeting in New Bedford, at the philosophical Lyceum, always with the same refrain: "We don't allow niggers in here."[28] In Britain, though, things were done differently. In London he was let into the Zoological Gardens, the Cremorne Pleasure Gardens, the British Museum and the panoramas in the Egyptian Hall in Piccadilly, all without any demur or hesitation. At the country house of the Marquess of Westminster, Eaton Hall, Douglass ran into some of his white fellow passengers from the *Cambria*—and they were not the sympathizers; queuing for admission as tourists, they were appalled to find the black man granted admittance together with themselves. But, as he told an audience at his farewell speech at the London Tavern in 1847,

I have travelled in all parts of the country—in England, Ireland, Scotland and Wales. I have journeyed upon highways, byways, railways and steamboats. I have myself gone, you might say with electric speed. In none of these conveyances or in any class of society have I found any curled lip of scorn . . . being in London I of course felt desirous of seizing upon testing the custom at all places here by going and presenting myself for admission as a man. From none of them was I ever ejected. I passed through them all; your colosseums, museums, galleries of painting, even into your House of Commons, and still more a nobleman . . . permitted me to go into the House of Lords . . . In none of these places did I receive one word of opposition against my entrance . . .

However much Americans "affect to despise and scorn the Negroes," Douglass went on, "Englishmen—the most intelligent, the noblest and best of Englishmen—do not hesitate to give the right hand of manly fellowship to a Negro such as I am . . . Why sir, the Americans do not know that I am a man. They talk of me as a box of goods; they speak of me in connexion with sheep, horses and cattle." In Britain, he said, it was different. And when he insisted that even the dogs of "old England" took him for a man, Douglass got a guaranteed cheer. At Beckenham in Kent, he said, a "dog actually came up to the platform, put his paws on the front of it and gave me a smile of recognition as a man. [Laughter] The Americans would do well to learn wisdom upon this subject from the very dogs of old England."[29]

Making these invidious transatlantic distinctions in 1846 was even more provocative than it seemed, for Britain and the United States were in one of their periodic cycles of mutual suspicion and recrimination. At issue were the north and west frontiers of the United States, in particular the boundaries of Oregon; and, for the British, the territorial integrity of Canada. Discussions between Peel's government and Polk's became frosty, then testy, then bellicose. So when Douglass charged headlong at the hypocrisies of American patriotism he was, in effect, hoisting the Union Jack. "The fact is," he thundered at the London Tavern,

. . . the whole system, the entire network of American society is one great falsehood from beginning to end. . . . In their celebrated Declaration of Independence they [the founding fathers] made the loudest, the clearest assertions of the rights of man and yet at that very time the identical men who drew up the Declaration of Independence and framed the American democratic constitution, were trafficking in the blood and souls of their fellow men . . . From the period of their first adoption of the constitution of the United States downward everything good and great in the heart of the American people—everything patriotic within their breasts—has been summoned to defend this great lie before the world . . . The people of the United States are the boldest in their pretensions to freedom and the loudest in their profession of their love of liberty yet no nation upon the face of the globe can exhibit a statute book so full of all that is cruel, malicious and infernal as the American code of laws. Every page is red with the blood of the American slave.

Then Douglass turned to the saving grace of British America—Canada—"a land uncursed by slavery, a territory ruled by the British power."[30]

It was a warm-up for an even more frontal assault when Douglass got home in the spring of 1847 and had to defend his right to criticize the United States. "I have no love for America as such; I have no patriotism, I have no country. What country have I? The institutions of this country do not know me."[31] Contrasting his free entrance to Parliament with the imprisonment and sale into slavery awaiting him should he presume to go to Washington, Douglass said that "under these circumstances my republican friends must not think me strange when I say I would rather be in London than Washington. Liberty in Hyde Park is better than democracy in a slave prison."[32]

Of course, Douglass was being hopelessly starry-eyed, but he would not hear of the usual American retort: that the British had better look to ameliorate the condition of their wretched manufacturing poor before presuming to criticize the United States for slavery—the same tack that had been used by Benjamin Franklin three-quarters of a century earlier. For, as he told his audience back in America,

Say what you will of England—of the degradation—of the poverty—and there is much of it there—say what you will of the oppression and suffering . . . there is also Liberty there, not only for the white man but for the black man also. The instant I stepped ashore and looked into the faces of the crowd around me, I saw in every man a recognition of my manhood and an absence, a perfect absence of everything like that disgusting hate with which we are pursued in this country.[33]

Douglass continued to cling to this romantic passion for British freedom, notwithstanding the stinging slight of being forced on the return journey west in the *Cambria* (without Captain Judkins) to occupy steerage again, despite being assured he would have a stateroom. But after he had related this to *The Times*, he was gratified to have "The Thunderer" thunder in an editorial on his behalf at the iniquity of deferring to *American* race prejudice, so blotting the copybook of British fair play. Such was the scandal caused by Douglass's accommodation that Samuel Cunard was obliged to go public with an abject apology and a pledge that such a thing would never happen again.

But there was a particular, personal reason why Douglass clung to his passionate belief in British aversion to slavery. For when, at that farewell meeting at the London Tavern, he said that "I go back to the United States not as I landed here—I came a slave; I go back a free man; I came here as a thing, I go back as a human being," he was not speaking loosely or figuratively. It really had been England that had redeemed him. For it was a Newcastle woman, Ellen Richardson, who had started a fund to pay off Douglass's owner, Hugh Auld. Once the appeal was known about, it took no time at all to raise the £700 that was paid over to Auld in return for the signed manumission. Henceforth Douglass was free, not only in legal title but also from the constant, gnawing fear that some day he might be recaptured and that terrible retribution promised by the slaveholders on the *Cambria* might be taken for his insolent crusade.

So for him, at least, the promise of British freedom had been fulfilled. "I prefer things to names," he wrote to Garrison. And since he was much at Westminster, we can assume that in the Abbey one of the solid things he went to see were the monuments in Poets' Corner to those Britons who had, in good faith and against absurd odds, begun, seventy-five years before, the good fight. Perhaps he communed for a moment with the first and foremost of them, a memorial to Granville Sharp erected by the African Institution in 1816. Such were the encomia, hyperbolic even by the standards of memorials,

HIS LIFE PRESENTED ONE BEAUTIFUL COMMENT OF GLOWING PIETY
AND UNWEARIED BENEFICENCE . . . HE AIMED TO RESCUE HIS
NATIVE COUNTRY FROM THE GUILT AND INCONSISTENCY
OF EMPLOYING THE ARM OF FREEDOM TO RIVET THE
FETTERS OF BONDAGE . . .

that it was thought prudent to add, lest posterity raise a sceptical eye-brow, an unusual afterthought:

READER, IF ON PERUSING THIS TRIBUTE TO A PRIVATE INDIVIDUAL
THOU SHOULDST BE DISPOSED TO SUSPECT IT AS PARTIAL OR
CENSURE IT AS DIFFUSE KNOW THAT IT IS NOT PANEGYRIC
BUT HISTORY.

Notes and References

ABBREVIATED SOURCES

AO: Audit Office, London
BL: British Library, London
CO: Colonial Office files
FO: Foreign Office files
JCAF: John Clarkson, "Mission to Africa"
JCAM: John Clarkson, "Mission to America"
GRO: Gloucestershire Record Office
NMM: National Maritime Museum, Greenwich
NYHS: New-York Historical Society
NYPL: New York Public Library
PANB: Public Archive of New Brunswick
PANS: Public Archive of Nova Scotia
PRO: Public Record Office, London
SRO: Shropshire Record Office

BRITISH FREEDOM'S PROMISE

1 British Freedom is among the named inhabitants of Preston petitioning Lieutenant John Clarkson on 26th December 1791, as he was organizing a fleet to take the black loyalists to Sierra Leone, not to be split up from their neighbours but to be kept together in the new colony. See the MSS copy of Clarkson's journal, vol. I, "Mission to America" (JCAM) in the NYHS Library.

2 For British Freedom's land allotment see PANS, vol. 370, 1784. See also James W. St G. Walker, *The Black Loyalists: The Search for a Promised Land in Nova Scotia and Sierra Leone 1783–1870* (New York, 1976), p. 29.

3 For the look of Preston see Clarkson's account in his journal entry for 11th October 1791: "Their situation appeared extremely bad from the poorness of the soil and from their having nothing to subsist upon but the produce of it."

4 Graham Russell Hodges, *Root and Branch: African Americans in New York and East Jersey 1613–1863* (Chapel Hill, North Carolina, and London, 1999), p. 89

5 Benjamin Quarles, *The Negro in the American Revolution* (Chapel Hill, North Carolina, 1961), p. 173; Bell to Sir Guy Carleton, 7th June 1783, Carleton Papers, NYPL.

6 David Walker (ed. Herbert Aptheker), "One Continual Cry," *David Walker's Appeal to the Colored Citizens of the World 1829–1830* (New York, 1965), p. 106.

7 Frederick Douglass, 4th July 1852, in Sidney Kaplan and Emma Nogrady Kaplan, *The Black Presence in the Era of the American Revolution*, revised edition (Amherst, Mass., 1989), p. 277.

8 Quarles, op. cit., pp. 51–52 .

9 The classic account of slavery and the Revolution remains David Brion Davis, *The Problem of Slavery in the Age of Revolution 1770–1823* (Ithaca, New York, 1973). More recently see the transforming work of Ira Berlin, in particular *Generations of Captivity: A History of African-American Slaves* (Cambridge, Mass., 2003), especially chapter 3, pp. 129–57.

10 Ibid., p. 115; Theodore G. Tappert and John W. Doberstein (trans.), *The Journals of Henry Melchior Muhlenberg*, 3 vols. (Philadelphia, 1942–58), III, p. 106

11 Quoted in Elizabeth A. Fenn, *Pox Americana: The Great Smallpox Epidemic of 1775–1782* (New York, 2001), p. 55. See also W.W. Abbot and Dorothy Twohig (eds), *The Papers of George Washington*, 39 vols. (Charlottesville, Virginia, 1983–), Series 2, pp. 64, 66.

12 Walker, op. cit., pp. 3, 12.

13 See Gary Nash introduction to the new edition of Quarles, op. cit.; Sylvia R. Frey, *Water from the Rock: Black Resistance in a Revolutionary Age* (Princeton, New Jersey, 1991), p. 211.

14 The identity of Ralph Henry's master (as well as Henry Washington's), and the year of their escape are recorded in the Book of Negroes, drawn up in New York in 1783 (copy in the NYPL), edited by Graham Russell Hodges as *The Black Loyalist Directory: African Americans in Exile after the American Revolution* (New York and London, 1996), p. 196 (hereafter BLD). The names and dates of the escaped slaves of Harrison, Middleton, etc., are likewise to be found in it.

15 Ibid., p. 11. Abraham Marrian embarked on the ship *Lady's Adventure*, bound for St John, New Brunswick, in the spring of 1783.

16 A copy of the Muster Book is preserved in the Shelburne County Genealogical Society, Nova Scotia, where Henry Washington is also listed as owning a town lot and forty acres of land at Birchtown .

17 Gary Nash introduction to new edition of Quarles, op. cit., p. xix.

18 See Gary Nash's fine and indignant sketch, "Thomas Peters: Millwright,

Soldier and Deliverer" in David Sweet and Gary B. Nash (eds.), *Struggle and Survival in Colonial America* (Berkeley and Los Angeles, 1981), pp. 69–85.

19 PRO AO 12/99 86.

20 Benjamin Woods Labaree, *The Boston Tea Party* (Oxford, 1964), p. 10.

21 James Otis, *The Rights of the British Colonist Asserted and Proved* (Boston, New England, nd), pp. 43–44; see also T. K. Hunter, *Publishing Freedom, Winning Arguments: Somerset, Natural Rights and Massachusetts Freedom Cases, 1772–1836*, Ph.D. dissertation (Columbia University, 2003). I am grateful to Dr Hunter for allowing me to quote from her dissertation.

22 *Virginia Gazette*, 30th September 1773; ibid., 30th June 1774; Gerald W. Mullin, *Flight and Rebellion: Slave Resistance in Eighteenth Century Virginia* (New York, 1972) p. 131.

23 Hunter, op. cit., chapter 2, fn 6.

24 It is apparent from Anthony Benezet's correspondence with Granville Sharp in 1772 and 1773 that Benezet assumed Franklin to be a wholehearted and active enemy of the slave trade, if not an outright abolitionist, and with good reason, given Franklin's long record of vehement indignation against both the illegality and the immorality of the traffic. But Franklin would prove a lot less consistent than his fellow Philadelphian Benjamin Rush in this opposition, and far more cautious when it came to proposing immediate and far-reaching reform. See Sharp Papers, NYHS.

25 Benjamin Franklin, "A Conversation on Slavery" in J. A. Leo Lemay (ed.), *Writings* (The Library of America, 1987), pp. 646–53.

26 Ibid.; Hunter, op. cit., chapter 2, p. 25.

27 Patrick Henry's letter was copied and sent by Anthony Benezet to Granville Sharp in London. It is preserved in the Sharp manuscript collection at the NYHS.

28 Charles Francis Adams, *Familiar Letters of John Adams and His Wife Abigail Adams* (New York, 1876), pp. 41–42; Wilson, op. cit., *Loyal Blacks*, p. 5.

29 All these petitions and articles are reproduced in Kaplan and Kaplan, op. cit., pp. 11–13.

30 Gerald W. Mullin, op. cit., p. 131; *Virginia Gazette*, 30th September 1773.

31 Ibid.; *Virginia Gazette*, 30th June 1774.

32 *William Henry Drayton*, "Some Fugitive Thoughts on a letter signed Freeman Addressed to the Deputies assembled in the High Court of Congress in Philadelphia. By a Black Settler" (Philadelphia, 1774), cited in Hodges, op. cit., *Root and Branch*, p. 136.

CHAPTER I

1 Surprisingly, there is no modern biography of Granville Sharp. But Prince Hoare, *The Memoirs of Granville Sharp Esq. Composed from his own Manuscripts*, 2 vols. (London, 1828), is an exceptionally full account of both his beliefs and his engagement through the Strong and Somerset cases in the

abolitionist cause. It can be supplemented by E.C.P. Lascelles, *Granville Sharp and the Freedom of Slaves in England* (Oxford, 1928), and there is an acutely perceptive characterization in David Brion Davis's magisterial *The Problem of Slavery in the Age of the American Revolution* (Ithaca, New York, 1975) pp. 386–402. The detailed accounts of the Strong, Hylas, Lewis and Somerset cases are drawn from Sharp's own MSS, letterbook and journal, including his transcripts of some of the proceedings at the King's Bench in Sharp Papers, NYHS.

2   Hoare, op.cit., I, pp. 119 ff; II, Appendix VI, p. xix; for more on the concerts and the paintings of them by Johan Zoffany, see John Kerslake, "A Note on Zoffany's 'Sharp Family,' " *Burlington Magazine,* 20, no. 908 (November 1978), pp. 752–54; see also the catalogue of the National Portrait Gallery exhibition "John Zoffany" (London, 1976), nos. 87–88.

3   The precise numbers of blacks in London or, indeed, Britain remains disputed. At the time of the Somerset case, it was said that there were as many as fourteen or fifteen thousand blacks in Britain, but since this figure was invoked by those warning that should a favourable judgement to Somerset be given, there would be a mass exodus of blacks from service, thrown on the city poor rates, it remains suspicious. Norma Myers, *Reconstructing the Black Past: Blacks in Britain 1780–1830* (London and Portland, Oregon, 1996), especially pp. 18–37, gives a much more conservative estimate based on baptizmal records. But since by no means all London blacks were baptized, this may err somewhat at the other end.

4   Sharp Papers, NYHS.

5   Ibid.

6   Hoare, op. cit., I, pp. 49–50; p. 61; see also Gretchen Holbrook Gerzina, *Black London: Life Before Emancipation* (New Brunswick, New Jersey, 1985), p. 97; David Dabydeen, *Hogarth's Blacks* (Manchester, 1987).

7   Sharp Papers, NYHS.

8   Ibid.; Hoare, op. cit., I, pp. 49–50.

CHAPTER II

1   For the Sharps' musical itineraries see Prince Hoare, *The Memoirs of Granville Sharp Esq. Composed from his own Manuscripts,* 2 vols. (London, 1828), I, pp. 215–17; E.C.P. Lascelles, *Granville Sharp and the Freedom of Slaves in England* (Oxford, 1928), pp. 119–26; also Sharp Papers, NYHS. A second boat, the *Union,* built in 1775, was grander, seventy feet long and moored off Fulham Steps. Three more boats were named after the Sharp women: the *Jemma,* the *Mary* and the *Catherine* (a canoe!).

2   John Kerslake, "A Note on Zoffany's 'Sharp Family,' " *Burlington Magazine,* 20, no. 908 (November 1978), pp. 752–54; see also the catalogue of the National Portrait Gallery exhibition "John Zoffany" (London, 1976), nos. 87–88.

3   Sharp Papers, NYHS, MSS notebook on the case of Thomas Lewis.

4   Sharp Papers, NYHS, ibid.

5   Lascelles, op. cit., p. 16, n. 1.

6   Thomas Clarkson, *History of the Rise, Progress and Accomplishment of Abolition of the African Slave Trade by the British Parliament*, 2 vols. (London, 1808; published in the USA, 1836, as *The Cabinet of Freedom*), pp. 68–79.

7   Ibid., pp. 65–72.

8   Sharp Papers, NYHS, MSS notebook on the case of Thomas Lewis.

9   For the Somerset case, see Thomas Jones Howell, *A Complete Collection of State Trials*, vol. 20, 1771–72, "The Case of James Sommerset, a Negro . . . ," vol. 12, George III, 1771–72; and T. K. Hunter, *Publishing Freedom, Winning Arguments: Somerset, Natural Rights and Massachusetts Freedom Cases, 1772–1836*, Ph.D. dissertation (Columbia University, 2003), especially chapters 1 and 5. See also Edward Fiddes, "Lord Mansfield and the Somerset Case," *Law Quarterly Review*, 50 (1934), pp. 509–10; Jerome Nadelhaft, "The Somerset Case and Slavery: Myth, Reality and Repercussions," *Journal of Negro History*, LI (1966), pp. 193–208; and the important James Oldham, "New Light on Mansfield and Slavery," *Journal of British Studies*, 27 (January 1988), pp. 45–68; idem, *The Mansfield Manuscripts and the Growth of English Law in the Eighteenth Century*, 2 vols. (Chapel Hill, North Carolina, 1992).

10 Lascelles, op. cit., p. 30.

11 Hunter, op. cit., chapter 1, p. 32.

12 Hoare, op. cit., p. 119.

13 Ibid., p. 114.

14 Folarin Shyllon, *Black Slaves in Britain* (London, 1974).

15 I am grateful to Stella Tillyard for this description of the interior of Westminster Hall.

16 Exactly what Mansfield said in this summation has long been in dispute. The version that has entered historical literature gives Mansfield the credit for arguing that if the rights of a slaveowner over his slave were to be recognized, a *positive* sanctioning law would have to have been expressly introduced by Parliament, since there was nothing in custom or immemorial usage that recognized property in humans. This is the version that appeared in Capel Loft's *Reports*, published in 1776. But as Jerome Nadelhaft first pointed out in op. cit., pp. 193–208, an alternative report in *The Gentleman's Magazine*, published closer to the judgement in 1772 (and supported by Mansfield himself in 1785) gives a far more restricted version of the statement, in which the judge confined himself to the power of a master to force a slave out of the country. The version given above is from Sharp's own amanuensis-transcribed notes of the trial in the Sharp Papers, and it seems to confirm the more conservative view of Mansfield's judgement. That view also disposes of what would otherwise have been an uncharacteristically contradictory about-face within the same speech from his initial, obstinate endorsement of Yorke-Talbot to something like the very opposite view.

17   Gretchen Holbrook Gerzina, "Black Loyalists in London after the American Revolution," in John W. Pulis (ed.), *Moving On: Black Loyalists in the Afro-Atlantic World* (New York and London, 1999), p. 130; *Morning Chronicle and London Advertiser,* 24th June 1772.

18   Sharp Papers, NYHS; Hoare, op. cit., I, p. 137.

19   Gregory D. Massey, *John Laurens and the American Revolution* (Columbia, South Carolina, 2000), pp. 47, 62–63; see also Henry Laurens to John Laurens, 20th January 1775, in *The Papers of Henry Laurens* (eds. Philip H. Hamer, David R. Chesnutt et al.), 15 vols. (Columbia, South Carolina, 1968–), vol. 10, p. 34.

20   Nadelhaft, op. cit., p. 195.

21   Quoted in James Oldham, op. cit., pp. 65–66; see also Gretchen Holbrook Gerzina, *Black London: Life Before Emancipation* (New Brunswick, New Jersey, 1985), p. 132.

Chapter III

1   Henry Laurens, the President of the Provincial Congress and of the Council of Safety, wrote to his son John on 20th August 1775 that "we have had the wettest Season from July to this day that I remember—it has rained every day." *The Papers of Henry Laurens* (eds. Philip H. Hamer, David R. Chesnutt et al.), 15 vols. (Columbia, South Carolina, 1968–; Model Editions Partnership, 1999), p. 326.

2   PRO CO 5/396.

3   Ibid.

4   Ibid.

5   Henry Laurens to John Laurens, 18th and 23rd June 1775, Hamer et al., op. cit., vol. 10, pp. 184–85, p. 320 n.4, p. 323.

6   Ibid., Charles Matthews Coslett to Lord William Campbell, 19th August 1775.

7   Campbell to Laurens, 17th August 1775, Hamer et al., op. cit., p. 328.

8   PRO CO 5/396.

9   Sidney Kaplan and Emma Nogrady Kaplan, *The Black Presence in the Era of the American Revolution* (Amherst, Mass., 1989), p. 25.

10   Sylvia R. Frey, "Between Slavery and Freedom: Virginia Blacks in the American Revolution," *Journal of Southern History,* 49, no. 3 (August 1983), p. 376; William T. Hutchinson, William M. Rachal et al. (eds.), *The Papers of James Madison,* 13 vols. (Chicago, 1962–), I, pp. 129–30.

11   Sylvia R. Frey, *Water from the Rock: Black Resistance in a Revolutionary Age* (Princeton, New Jersey, 1991), p. 56. Much of what follows is indebted to the account given by Frey, as well as the pioneering narrative surveyed in Benjamin Quarles, *The Negro in the American Revolution* (Chapel Hill, North Carolina, 1961).

12   Ibid., p. 55. See also *Virginia Gazette,* 4th May 1775.

13 Frey, op. cit., *Water,* p. 56.

14 Edward Rutledge to Ralph Izard, 8th December 1775, *Correspondence of Mr Ralph Izard* (New York, 1844), vol. I, p. 165; Benjamin Quarles, "Lord Dunmore as Liberator," *William and Mary Quarterly History Magazine,* 15 (1958), p. 495, n. 3.

15 Gary Nash, "Thomas Peters: Millwright, Soldier and Deliverer" in David Sweet and Gary B. Nash (eds.), *Struggle and Survival in Colonial America* (Berkeley and Los Angeles, 1981, pp. 72–73.

16 Ibid., p. 59.

17 Ibid., p. 62.

18 Kaplan and Kaplan, op. cit., p. 25.

19 Washington to Richard Henry Lee, 26th December 1775, in R.H. Lee, *Memoir of the Life of Richard Henry Lee* (Philadelphia, 1825) II, p. 9; Quarles, op. cit., *Negro,* p. 20.

20 Graham Russell Hodges (ed.), *The Black Loyalist Directory: African Americans in Exile After the American Revolution* (New York and London, 1996), p. 212 (hereafter *BLD*). Winslow's entry appears in the list of blacks embarking on HMS *L'Abondance* on one of the last loyalist sailings out of New York on 30th November 1783.

21 Frey, op. cit., "Between Slavery and Freedom," p. 378.

22 "Diary of Colonel Landon Carter," *William and Mary Quarterly History Magazine,* 20 (1912), pp. 178–79; Quarles, op. cit., *Negro,* p. 27.

23 All the cases mentioned are taken from the Book of Negroes, drawn up in New York in 1783. Copy in NYPL. See Hodges, *BLD*.

24 Allan Kulikoff, *Tobacco and Slaves: The Development of Southern Cultures in the Chesapeake 1680–1800* (Chapel Hill, North Carolina, and London, 1986), pp. 418–19.

25 PRO CO 5/1353/321. Although written in early December 1775, Dunmore was unable to find a ship to take his dispatches to the Secretary of State until the following February, by which time his position had deteriorated. Rather than supply Dartmouth and Lord George Germain with a revised summary of events, Dunmore preferred to send his letters as written, doubtless in archival self-justification.

26 PRO CO 5/1353/335; see also Francis Berkeley, *Dunmore's Proclamation of Emancipation* (Charlottesville, Virginia, 1941).

27 Quarles, op. cit., "Lord Dunmore," p. 501.

28 *Pennsylvania Gazette,* 17th July 1776.

29 Louis Morton, *Robert Carter of Nomini Hall: A Virginia Tobacco Planter of the Eighteenth Century* (Williamsburg, Virginia, 1945), pp. 55–56; Kulikoff, p. 419.

30 The most detailed account is Dunmore's own, in his letter of 6th December to Dartmouth, PRO CO 5/1353/321.

31 William J. Schreeven and Robert L. Scribner (eds.), *Revolutionary Virginia, the Road to Independence,* 7 vols. (Charlottesville, Virginia, 1973–83), vol. V, p. 9.

32 Dunmore to Dartmouth, 18th February 1776; PRO CO 5/1353/321.

33 Gerald W. Mullin, *Flight and Rebellion: Slave Resistance in Eighteenth Century Virginia* (New York, 1972) p. 134.

34 Ibid.

35 Ibid., p. 133.

36 On the Black Pioneers, see Todd W. Braisted, "The Black Pioneers and Others: The Military Role of Black Loyalists in the American War of Independence" in John W. Pulis (ed.), *Moving On: Black Loyalists in the Afro-Atlantic World* (New York and London, 1999), pp. 3–38.

37 Ibid., p. 13; Clinton Papers (William L. Clements Library, University of Michigan), vol. 263.

38 Ibid., pp. 11–12; Clinton to Martin, 12th May 1776, Clinton Papers, vol. 263.

39 Frey, op. cit., *Water*, p. 67.

40 Ibid., pp. 64–65; Peter H. Wood, " 'Taking Care of Business'—Revolutionary South Carolina: Republicanism and Slave Society" in Jeffery J. Crow and Larry E. Tise (eds.), *The Southern Experience in the American Revolution* (Chapel Hill, North Carolina, 1978), pp. 284–85, gives a much higher figure (disputed by Frey) of fifty fugitive blacks killed in the raid.

41 Pauline Maier, *American Scripture: Making the Declaration of Independence* (New York, 1997), p. 37.

42 For the history of the epidemic, see the excellent account in Elizabeth Fenn, *Pox Americana: The Great Smallpox Epidemic of 1775–1782* (New York, 2001), especially pp. 57–61.

43 "Particular Account of the Attack and Rout of Lord Dunmore," Peter Force (ed.), *American Archives,* 6 vols. (Washington, D.C., 1837–53), I, p. 151; see also Fenn, op. cit., p. 60.

44 John Thornton Posey, *General Thomas Posey: Son of the American Revolution* (East Lansing, Michigan, 1992), p. 32.

CHAPTER IV

1 Prince Hoare, *The Memoirs of Granville Sharp Esq. Composed from his own Manuscripts,* 2 vols. (London, 1828), I, p. 184.

2 Ibid., pp. 185–86; E.C.P. Lascelles, *Granville Sharp and the Freedom of Slaves in England* (Oxford, 1928), pp. 39–40.

3 Hoare, op. cit., I, pp. 189–90.

4 Hansard, *The Parliamentary History of England* (London, 1813), XVIII, pp. 695 ff.

5 Hoare, op. cit., I, pp. 211–12.

6 Charles Stuart, *A Memoir of Granville Sharp* (New York, 1836) p. 21.

7 Sylvia R. Frey, *Water from the Rock: Black Resistance in a Revolutionary Age* (Princeton, New Jersey, 1991), p. 147.

8 Hansard, op. cit., XVIII, p. 733.

9 Ibid., p. 747.

10 Hoare, op. cit., I, pp. 216–17.

11 The most detailed description of the action is found in Campbell to Lord George Germain, 16th January 1779, PRO CO/5/182/31. Benjamin Quarles, *The Negro in the American Revolution* (Chapel Hill, North Carolina, 1961) describes Quamino Dolly as an "aged slave," although the letter from Campbell says nothing about the black guide's age.

12 PRO CO 5/182/31.

13 David George's narrative on this page and elsewhere in the book is taken directly from "An Account of the life of Mr David George, from Sierra Leone in Africa, given by himself in a Conversation with Brother Rippon in London and Brother Pearce of Birmingham," *Annual Baptist Register* (1793), pp. 473–84; it is one of the earliest slave narratives and African-American autobiographies.

14 Quarles, op. cit., *Negro*, p. 145.

15 Prevost to Clinton, 2nd November 1779, PRO CO 30/55/20, 2042.

16 Todd W. Braisted, "The Black Pioneers and Others: The Military Role of Black Loyalists in the American War of Independence" in John W. Pulis (ed.) *Moving On: Black Loyalists in the Afro-Atlantic World* (New York and London, 1999), p. 21; *Royal Georgia Gazette*, 18th November 1779.

17 Allan Kulikoff, *Tobacco and Slaves: The Development of Southern Cultures in the Chesapeake 1680–1800* (Chapel Hill, North Carolina, and London, 1986), p. 419.

18 Gregory D. Massey, *John Laurens and the American Revolution* (Columbia, South Carolina, 2000), p. 155.

19 Sidney Kaplan and Emma Nogrady Kaplan, *The Black Presence in the Era of the American Revolution* (Amherst, Mass., 1989), pp. 64–65; Quarles, *Negro*, p. 80.

20 Massey, op. cit., p. 93.

21 Henry Laurens to John Laurens, 26th January 1778, *The Papers of Henry Laurens* (eds. Philip H. Hamer, David R. Chesnutt et al.), 15 vols. (Columbia, South Carolina, 1968–), 12, pp. 367–68. In September Henry Laurens warned his son "it is certainly a great task effectually to persuade Rich Men to part willingly with the very source of their wealth and, as they suppose, their tranquility," ibid., vol. 15, p. 169.

22 Massey, op. cit., p. 131; John Laurens to Henry Laurens, 17th February 1779; Hamer et al., op. cit., vol. 19, p. 60.

23 Quarles, op. cit., *Negro*, p. 63; Massey, op. cit., p. 141.

24 Massey, op. cit., p. 143.

25 Ibid., p. 162.

26 Quarles, op. cit., *Negro*, pp. 108–10.

27 John Marrant, *A Narrative of the Lord's wonderful dealing with John Marrant, a black (Now gone to preach the gospel in Nova Scotia)* (London, 1788).

28 Sylvia R. Frey, op. cit., *Water*, p. 142.

29 Ibid., p. 120.

30 "Memorandum for the Commandant of Charlestown and Lieutenant General Earl Cornwallis," 3rd June 1780, PRO 30/55/23, 2800.

31 "Memoirs of the life of Boston King, a Black Preacher, written by himself during his residence at Kingswood-School," *Methodist Magazine*, XXI (1798), p. 106; see also Phyllis R. Blakeley, "Boston King: A Negro Loyalist Who Sought Refuge in Nova Scotia," *Dalhousie Review*, 48, no. 3 (August 1968), pp. 347–56.

32 Boston King, "Memoirs . . . ," op. cit., p. 107.

33 11th December 1779; PANS RG1, vol. 170, pp. 332–33.

34 George, op. cit., p. 477.

35 For this incident and those following it, see King, op. cit., pp. 107–11.

36 Ibid.

37 Graham Russell Hodges, "Black Revolt in New York City and the Neutral Zone 1775–1783," in Paul A. Gilje and William Pencak (eds.), *New York in the Age of the Constitution 1775–1800* (Cranbury, New Jersey, 1992), p. 43, n. 26; see also Leslie M. Harris, *In the Shadow of Slavery: African-Americans in New York City 1626–1963* (Chicago and London, 2003), pp. 54–55.

38 Graham Russell Hodges (ed.), *The Black Loyalist Directory: African Americans in Exile After the American Revolution* (New York and London, 1996), p. 16 (hereafter *BLD*).

39 Ibid., pp. 34–35.

40 Graham Russell Hodges, *Root and Branch: African Americans in New York and East Jersey, 1613–1863* (Chapel Hill, North Carolina, 1999), p. 143.

41 Hodges, op. cit., *BLD*, p. 16.

42 Ibid., p. 146.

43 Ibid., p. 151.

44 Although Tye's "Colonel" was an honorific title given to him by the British army rather than a formal rank, there was no question that his exploits and his ruthlessness commanded a good deal of admiration from the regular officer corps.

45 For Tye's exploits, see Hodges, op. cit., "Black Revolt," pp. 36–38.

46 All these case histories are from the Book of Negroes in Hodges, op. cit., *BLD*.

47 Frey, op. cit., *Water*, p. 165.

48 Ibid., p. 169; the description is based on the diary of a Hessian officer who encountered such a train in the later stages of the war: Johann Ewald (trans. and ed. Joseph P. Tustin), *Diary of the American War* (New Haven, Conn., 1979), p. 305.

49 A Moravian diarist in Bethania, North Carolina, recorded in February 1781 Cornwallis's army leaving two wagons of meat behind while in pursuit of Nathanael Greene. See Elizabeth Fenn, *Pox Americana: The Great Smallpox Epidemic of 1775–1782* (New York, 2001), p. 124.

50 Fenn, op. cit., p. 132.

51 Frey, op. cit., *Water*, pp. 147–48.

52 The evidence sometimes cited, that slaves from Patriot plantations formed part of the spoils and traffic of the British army, was made a lot of by Patriot propaganda (as it had been ever since the Dunmore proclamation), but is

overwhelmingly circumstantial and not altogether credible. The "market" referred to in a letter to Cornwallis from General Alexander Leslie, that the smallpox epidemic at Portsmouth would ruin "our market," ought not to be taken to mean a market in humans. Had there been a clandestine slave trade in the army, expressly violating Clinton's orders in the Philipsburgh Proclamation, it would hardly be likely that one general would have alluded to it in formal dispatches to another.

53 Governor John Rutledge to General Francis Marion, 2nd September 1781, in Robert Wilson Gibbes, *Documentary History of the American Revolution* (New York, 1855–57), vol. 3, p. 131.

54 PRO 30/11/110.

55 Frey, op. cit., *Water,* p. 167; Fenn, op. cit., p. 129.

56 This extraordinary, haunting document was discovered by Todd Braisted in the Clinton Papers, vol. 170, p. 27, and is reproduced in his invaluable essay "The Black Pioneers," op. cit., p. 17.

57 Fenn, op. cit., p. 130.

58 Daniel Stevens to John Wendell, 20th February 1782, in *Proceedings of the Massachusetts Historical Society,* XLVIII, October 1914–June 1915, pp. 342–43.

59 Cruden to Dunmore, 5th January 1782, PRO CO 5/175/267.

60 Dunmore to Clinton, 2nd February 1782, PRO CO 5/175/264.

61 *Proceedings of the Massachusetts Historical Society,* XLVIII, March 1915, p. 342.

62 Leslie to Clinton, 30th March 1782, PRO 30/55/9957; for the abstract of "Pay for the Black Dragoons," PRO, Treasury Office, Class 50/2/372; for Wadboo, see Frey, op. cit., pp. 138–39.

63 Moncrief to Clinton, 13th March 1782, PRO 30/55/90/9955.

64 For details of the raid on Bear Creek, see Charles C. Jones, *The Life and Services of the Honourable Major General Samuel Elbert of Georgia* (Cambridge, Mass., 1887), p. 47; Kaplan and Kaplan, op. cit., p. 85.

CHAPTER V

1 In his journal, one of the primary sources for the meeting at Tappan, Chief Justice William Smith describes the *Greyhound* as a "yacht," but elsewhere in his memoirs, as Isabelle K. Savelle points out in *Wine and Bitters: An account of the meetings in 1783 at Tappan NY and aboard* HMS *Perseverance* (Rockland County Historical Society, 1975), p. 20, the vessel is identified as a frigate. The two ships took an unusual (not to say extraordinary) thirty hours to sail from lower New York to Dobb's Ferry, a distance of hardly more than twenty miles, so, as Savelle rightly concludes, they must necessarily have been beating against adverse tides and winds of the kind that regularly give a rough edge to the Hudson Valley spring.

2 On Carleton, see Paul David Nelson, *General Sir Guy Carleton, Lord Dorchester, Soldier-Statesman of Early Canada* (Cranbury, New Jersey, 2000); Paul R. Reynolds, *Guy Carleton: A Biography* (New York, 1980); Paul H. Smith, "Sir Guy Carleton, Peace Negotiations and the Evacuation of New York," *Canadian Historical Review*, 1969, pp. 245–64.

3 Smith, op. cit., pp. 251 ff.

4 Marion Robertson, *King's Bounty: A History of Early Shelburne, Nova Scotia* (Halifax, 1983), p. 69.

5 Ellen Gibson Wilson, *The Loyal Blacks* (New York, 1976), p. 42.

6 Sylvia R. Frey, *Water from the Rock: Black Resistance in a Revolutionary Age* (Princeton, New Jersey, 1991), p. 176.

7 Ibid.; also George Smith McCowen Jr., *The British Occupation of Charleston 1780–82* (Columbia, South Carolina, 1972), pp. 106–7.

8 Cruden to Nibbs, 16th March 1783, PRO CO 5/109/379.

9 See also PRO CO 5/109/375 and 377.

10 Frey, op. cit., *Water*, p. 178. Cruden, as Frey makes clear, was equally eager to help Southern loyalists recover their escaped slaves where he could.

11 Gregory D. Massey, *John Laurens and the American Revolution* (Columbia, South Carolina, 2000), p. 228.

12 Laurens's "Journal and Narrative of Capture and Confinement in the Tower of London" is in *Papers of Henry Laurens*, vol. 15, pp. 330 ff. The original is in the Rare Books and Manuscripts Division of the NYPL.

13 In his powerful *The Negro President: Jefferson and the Slave Power* (New York, 2003) Gary Wills argues that the entire early constitutional apparatus was constructed with an eye to maintaining the dominance of the South and its indispensable social and economic system.

14 Carleton was evidently so nervous about the consequences of the verdict that he waited some weeks to inform Washington, and then another five weeks before transmitting a full account of the court martial proceedings. See Smith, op. cit., p. 200.

15 An engraving by Jordan and Halpin, after a nineteenth-century painting said to describe faithfully the appearance of the de Wint House in 1783, apparently exists in the collection of the NYHS. Savelle, op. cit., p. 13.

16 Graham Russell Hodges (ed.), *The Black Loyalist Directory, African Americans in Exile After the American Revolution* (New York and London, 1996), introduction, p. xl, n.1 (hereafter *BLD*); for the 20th October 1782 sailing, see PRO CO 30/55/5938.

17 W.H.W. Sabine (ed.), *The Historical Memoirs of William Smith* (New York, 1971), p. 586.

18 Ibid., p. 587.

19 Sir Guy Carleton to General Washington, 12th May 1783, PRO CO 5/109/313.

20 Wilson, op. cit., p. 52; Washington to Harrison, 6th May 1783, *The Writings of George Washington from the Original Manuscript Sources, 1745–1799* (ed. John C. Fitzpatrick), 39 vols. (Washington, D.C., 1931–44), vol. 26.

21 Wilson, op. cit., p. 51.

22 Hodges, op. cit., *BLD* introduction, p. xvii.

23 "Memoirs of the life of Boston King, a Black Preacher, written by himself during his residence at Kingswood-School," *Methodist Magazine,* XXI (1798), p. 157; Phyllis R. Blakeley, "Boston King: A Negro Loyalist Who Sought Refuge in Nova Scotia," *Dalhousie Review,* 48, no. 3 (August 1968), p. 350.

24 There are, in fact, two Cato Ramseys inscribed in the Book of Negroes, the other being a fifty-year-old from Maryland, the former slave of a Benjamin Ramsey of Cecil County. This Cato had served as an orderly in the General Hospital Department of the army since 1778 and now had a wife, Sukey, and a five-year-old son, also called Cato. But it was Cato Ramsey of Virginia who is marked "GBC" (General Birch Certificate). Hodges, op. cit., *BLD,* pp. 39, 204.

25 "Precis relative to Negroes in No. America," PRO CO 5/8/112–114.

26 Hodges, op. cit., *BLD* introduction, p. xviii.

27 These and all the micro-biographies described subsequently are taken directly from the Book of Negroes in the *BLD* (see Hodges, op. cit.). The lists for *L'Abondance,* sailing for Port Roseway, Nova Scotia, on 31st July 1783, are on pp. 81–88 and 103–17. *L'Abondance,* which also made one of the later autumn sailings, carried more blacks to Nova Scotia than any other single vessel leaving New York. See also Esther Clark Wright, "The Evacuation of Loyalists from New York in 1783," *Nova Scotia Historical Review,* 5 (1984), p. 25.

CHAPTER VI

1 Details taken from contemporary accounts, in particular that of Alexander Falconbridge, who served as surgeon on four slaving voyages between 1783 and 1787; *An Account of the Slave Trade on the Coast of Africa* (London, 1788).

2 He is so described in the manuscript transcript of the hearing for a retrial preserved in the National Maritime Museum archive, Greenwich (hereafter NMM/*Zong*).

3 Falconbridge, op. cit., p. 25, makes clear that this was the normal condition of the slave decks, the floor "so covered in blood and mucus that it resembled a slaughterhouse. It is not in the power of the human imagination to picture to itself a situation more dreadful or more disgusting."

4 NMM/*Zong*.

5 According to Davenport, one of the lawyers appearing for the insurers, in NMM/*Zong*.

6 Ibid. The phrase comes directly from Kensal's deposition (now lost) to the court and quoted by counsel for the insurers.

7 "Swivels" were guns mounted on a platform allowing for 180-degree rotation, and were used on slave ships to police slaves when they were

brought on deck. See Jay Coughtry, *The Notorious Triangle: Rhode Island and the African Slave Trade 1700–1807* (Philadelphia, 1981), p. 73. The *Sandown*, for which a log survives for a voyage in 1793–94, had just such swivels. See Bruce L. Mousser, *A Slaving Voyage to Africa and Jamaica: The Log of the Sandown 1793–94* (Bloomington, Indiana, 2002), p. 7, n. 31.

8   NMM/*Zong*.

9   *The Life of Olaudah Equiano, or Gustavus Vassa, the African* (London, 1789); facsimile reprint (London, 1969). The discovery of baptismal and naval documents recording Equiano's birthplace at South Carolina was made by Vincent Carretta, whose *Equiano the African, Biography of a Self-Made Man* (Athens, Georgia) is the most recent and critically sophisticated of the biographies.

10 Charles Stuart, *A Memoir of Granville Sharp* (New York, 1836), p. 30.

11 Prince Hoare, *The Memoirs of Granville Sharp Esq. Composed from his own Manuscripts*, 2 vols. (London, 1828), I, appendix, p. xxxiii.

12 For details of Ramsay's career, see Folarin Shyllon, *James Ramsay: The Unknown Abolitionist* (Edinburgh, 1977).

13 Ibid., p. 33.

14 For the early Quaker abolitionists see Judith Jennings, *The Business of Abolishing Slavery 1783–1807* (London, 1997), especially pp. 22–32.

15 Ibid., p. 27. For the gathering momentum of the campaign against the slave trade following the *Zong* case, see Robin Blackburn, *The Overthrow of Colonial Slavery 1776–1988* (London, 1988), pp. 136 ff.

16 Ellen Gibson Wilson, *Thomas Clarkson: A Biography* (York, 1980), pp. 25 ff.

17 Thomas Clarkson, *History of the Rise, Progress and Accomplishment of Abolition of the African Slave Trade by the British Parliament*, 2 vols. (London, 1808; published in the USA, 1836, as *The Cabinet of Freedom*), I, p. 203.

18 J.R. Oldfield, *Popular Politics and British Anti-Slavery: The Mobilization of Public Opinion Against the Slave Trade 1787–1807* (Manchester and New York, 1995), p. 71.

19 Thomas Clarkson, *An Essay on the Commerce and Slavery of the Human Species particularly the African* . . . (Philadelphia, 1786), p. 90.

20 Norma Myers, *Reconstructing the Black Past: Blacks in Britain, 1780–1830*, p. 72.

21 PRO AO 12/19.

22 Ellen Gibson Wilson, *The Loyal Blacks* (New York, 1976), p. 138.

23 PRO AO 13/29.

24 PRO AO 12/102; PRO AO 13/119; Gretchen Holbrook Gerzina, "Black Loyalists in London after the American Revolution," in John W. Pulis (ed.), *Moving On: Black Loyalists in the Afro-Atlantic World* (New York and London, 1999), p. 92.

25 Mary Beth Norton, "The Fate of Some Black Loyalists of the American Revolution," *Journal of Negro History*, LXVIII, 4 (October 1973), p. 404. For comparative treatment of white loyalists, see the same author's *The British Americans: The Loyalist Exiles in England 1774–1789* (Boston, 1972).

26 PRO AO 12/99.

27 Ibid.
28 PRO AO 12/19.
29 AO 12/99; PRO AO 13/27; Norton, op. cit., p. 406; Wilson, op. cit., *Loyal Blacks*, p. 139.
30 Steven J. Braidwood, *Black Poor and White Philanthropists: London's Blacks and the Foundation of the Sierra Leone Settlement 1786–1791* (Liverpool, 1994), p. 25.
31 James S. Taylor, *Jonas Hanway, Founder of the Marine Society: Charity and Policy in Eighteenth Century Britain* (Berkeley, California, 1985).
32 It is possible, as Steven Braidwood suggests, that slaveowners could participate in the work of the committee, precisely to demonstrate that they were not as devoid of humane feeling as the abolitionists claimed. But Angerstein, a personal friend of Hanway's, was part of a network of active philanthropy that was ready to mobilize sentiment and money for almost any worthy cause.
33 Braidwood, op. cit., p. 67.
34 Ibid., p. 68.
35 Henry Smeathman, *Some account of the Termites which are found in Africa and other hot climates* (London, 1781), p. 33; idem, *Plan of a settlement to be made near Sierra Leone on the Grain Coast of Africa* (London, 1786).
36 In particular, Folarin Shyllon, *Black People in Britain 1555–1833* (London and New York, 1977), p. 128, who writes that "It was now only a question of time until the Government and the liberal and reactionary Establishment would coalesce in patriotic enthusiasm to preserve the purity of the English bloodstream by expelling from England the 'lesser breeds without the law.' " Mary Beth Norton (op. cit.) takes a similar view, although less adamantly stated. For a more balanced assessment of the evidence, see Braidwood, op. cit., pp. 72–107.
37 Copy of letter from Hopkins to Sharp, Rufus King Papers, NYHS.
38 Hoare, op. cit., II, pp. 3–17.
39 Ibid., I, p. 370; see also the MSS version in Sharp's commonplace book, GRO, Hardwicke Court Muniments, MSS, H:36.
40 Braidwood, op. cit., pp. 88–89.
41 Wilson, op. cit., *Loyal Blacks*, p. 144.
42 Ibid., p. 98.
43 *The Interesting Narrative of the Life of Olaudah Equiano or Gustavus Vassa: The African Written by Himself* (Leeds, 1874) in Henry Louis Gates (ed.), *The Classic Slave Narratives* (New York, 1987).
44 PRO T1/643–487. See the helpful commentary by Christopher Fyfe (ed.), Anna Maria Falconbridge, *Narrative of Two Voyages to the River Sierra Leone During the Years 1791–1792–1793* (Liverpool, 2000), p. 40, n. 38.
45 Much the most thorough investigation of the evidence surrounding the white women is Braidwood, op. cit., pp. 281–86.
46 Wilson, op. cit., *Loyal Blacks*, p. 149.
47 Ibid., p. 151.

CHAPTER VII

1   Anna Maria Falconbridge (ed. Christopher Fyfe), *Narrative of Two Voyages to the River Sierra Leone During the Years 1791–1792–1793* (Liverpool, 2000), p. 24 reports the Naimbana repeatedly calling the Europeans "rogues," but smiling as he did so and adding that he thought the English the "honestest" among them.

2   A *View of the "Province of Freedom,"* done in 1791, shows the flag still flying from its tree-pole on St George's Hill immediately above the huts of settlers (which in fact had been burned by King Jimmy the year before). Thompson also sketched a fine map of the immediate area of the settlement at the mouth of the Sierra Leone River. See Ellen Gibson Wilson, *The Loyal Blacks* (New York, 1976), between pp. 226 and 227.

3   Granville Sharp to James Sharp, 31st October 1787, Sharp Papers, NYHS; see also Prince Hoare, *The Memoirs of Granville Sharp Esq. Composed from his own Manuscripts*, 2 vols. (London, 1828), II, p. 83.

4   John Matthews, *A Voyage to the River Sierra-Leone* (London, 1788), reprinted in *The British Transatlantic Slave Trade* (ed. Robin Law), 4 vols. (London, 2003), 1, p. 79. Matthews's account was based on three years' experience in Sierra Leone between 1785 and 1787. He was a staunch defender of the slave trade, but his account of the topography, natural history, social economy and customs of the region (from descriptions of clitoral circumcision to the all-important palaver) is still rich and invaluably detailed, and my own account draws extensively from it.

5   The description of the Naimbana's style of dress is from Falconbridge, op. cit., pp. 24–25.

6   Steven J. Braidwood, *Black Poor and White Philanthropists: London's Blacks and the Foundation of the Sierra Leone Settlement 1786–1791* (Liverpool, 1994), p. 183.

7   On the fauna and the local Temne, Bullom and Mende names, see Matthews, op. cit., pp. 82–93.

8   Hoare, op. cit., II, p. 108.

9   Ibid., pp. 132–33.

10 J.R. Oldfield, *Popular Politics and British Anti-Slavery: The Mobilization of Public Opinion against the Slave Trade 1787–1807* (Manchester, 1995), pp. 155 ff; for the active involvement of women in the campaign see Linda Colley, *Britons: Forging the Nation 1707–1837* (New Haven, Conn., 1992), pp. 254, 260.

11 Judith Jennings, *The Business of Abolishing Slavery 1783–1807* (London, 1997), p. 54. For the importance of the print, see Oldfield, op. cit., pp. 164–65.

12 On this vexed issue see, most recently, Gary Wills, *The Negro President: Jefferson and the Slave Power* (New York, 2003), especially pp. 1–15.

13 See his long letters to Franklin and Rufus King (Rufus King Papers, NYHS), intended for copying and wider circulation.

14 Hoare, op. cit., II, p. 83.

15 Ibid., pp. 95–96.

16 Weaver to Sharp, 23rd April 1788, in Hoare, op. cit., II, p. 96.

17 Ibid., p. 98.
18 Ibid., p. 99.
19 Ibid., appendix xi, pp. xxviii–xxix; Braidwood, op. cit., pp. 195, 192–291.
20 Hoare, op. cit., II, p. 112.
21 Ibid., pp. 114–15.
22 Braidwood, op. cit., pp. 196–97.
23 PRO, Adm 1/2488, Savage's report, 27th May 1790.
24 Hoare, op. cit., II, p. 98.
25 For Falconbridge and the account of their 1791 stay in Sierra Leone, see Falconbridge, op. cit.; Alexander Falconbridge's *An Account of the Slave Trade on the Coast of Africa* is collected in the same volume.

CHAPTER VIII

1 Peters's second petition is in PRO FO 4/1 f 419; see also Ellen Gibson Wilson, *The Loyal Blacks* (New York, 1976), pp. 180–81.
2 Passenger list from Graham Russell Hodges (ed.), *The Black Loyalist Directory, African Americans in Exile After the American Revolution* (New York and London, 1996), pp. 177–80.
3 James W. St G. Walker, "Myth, History and Revisionism: The Black Loyalists Revisited," *Acadiensis*, XXIX, no. 1 (Autumn 1999), p. 89. Walker argues forcefully against Barry Cahill, "The Black Loyalist Myth in Atlantic Canada," *Acadiensis*, XXIX (Autumn 1999), pp. 76–87, that men like Peters were both conscious of their loyalism and their right to freedom.
4 This is, for example, how Boston King survives the worst years: see "Memoirs of the life of Boston King, a Black Preacher, written by himself during his residence at Kingswood-School," *Methodist Magazine*, XXI (1798), pp. 209–12.
5 Walker, op. cit.
6 Wilson, op. cit., p. 72.
7 Ibid., p. 21.
8 PANS.
9 Millidge to Parr, PANS MG, 15, vol. 19.
10 Ibid.
11 On Wallace, see Caroline Troxler, "The Migration of Carolina and Georgia Loyalists to Nova Scotia and New Brunswick," Ph.D. dissertation (UMI edns, Michigan, 1974), p. 134.
12 Parr to Carleton, 5th October 1782, PRO FO 3/ Provisions . . . for Loyalists; Mary Louise Clifford, *From Slavery to Freedom: Black Loyalists after the American Revolution* (Jefferson, North Carolina), pp. 43–44.
13 Wilson, op. cit., *Loyal Blacks*, p. 82.
14 See Marion Robertson, *King's Bounty: A History of Early Shelburne, Nova Scotia* (Halifax, 1983), pp. 64–66.
15 Of the 4,700 inhabitants of Shelburne in January 1784, 1,191 were white soldiers, 1,488 free blacks and 1,269 the euphemistically designated black

"servants." Robin W. Winks, *The Blacks in Canada: A History* (Montreal, and New Haven, Conn., 1971), p. 38.

16 Robertson, op. cit., pp. 182–85.

17 See Benjamin Marston, *Journal,* 26th May 1783.

18 Ibid., 4th June 1783.

19 Shelburne County, Court of General Sessions, 1784–86.

20 Diary of Captain William Booth, Shelburne Historical Society, Shelburne, Nova Scotia, transcript, p. 52.

21 This according to Millidge; see PANS MG, 15, vol. 19.

22 The Blucke house never got beyond a fairly rudimentary stage, according to a later witness who saw it some time before Blucke's death in 1795.

23 Sarah Acker and Lewis Jackson, *Historic Shelburne, 1870–1950* (Halifax, 2001), pp. vi–vii.

24 Marston, op. cit., 28th August 1783.

25 Ibid., 4th August 1784.

26 D.C. Harvey (ed.), *The Diary of Simeon Perkins, 1780–1789* (Toronto, 1958), p. 238; Winks, op. cit., p. 38.

27 "An Account of the life of Mr David George, from Sierra Leone in Africa, given by himself in a Conversation with Brother Rippon in London and Brother Pearce of Birmingham," *Annual Baptist Register* (1793), pp. 478 ff, for the verbatim text that follows.

28 Ibid., p. 478.

29 Ibid.

30 Ibid., p. 479.

31 Ibid., pp. 480–82.

32 Walker, op. cit., p. 77.

33 Recent excavations at Birchtown, the results of which can be seen on the excellent Black Loyalist Heritage Society Web site, part of the Canadian Digital Collections, or *in situ* at Birchtown itself, have convincingly shown just how desperately rudimentary the shelters were. See also Laird Niven and Stephen A. Davis, "Birchtown: The History and Material Culture of an Expatriate African American Community," in John W. Pulis (ed.), *Moving On: Black Loyalists in the Afro-Atlantic World* (New York and London, 1999), pp. 60–83. Boston King mentions in his "Memoirs" going into the woods in winter "when the snow lay on the ground three or four feet deep."

34 Wilson, op. cit., p. 104.

35 Caroline Watterson Troxler, "Hidden from History: Black Loyalists at Country Harbour, Nova Scotia," in John W. Pulis (ed.), op. cit., p. 43. For the Guysborough County loyalists, see G.A. Rawlik, "The Guysborough Negroes: a study in isolation," *Dalhousie Review,* 48 (Spring 1968), pp. 24–36.

36 Shelburne County Court of General Sessions, August 1786; see also Troxler, op. cit., "Hidden from History," pp. 46–48.

37 Shelburne County Court of General Sessions, 5th August 1786; Walker, op. cit., p. 51.

38 Shelburne County Court of General Sessions, 5th August 1786.

39 Ibid., July 1791.

40 Wilson, op. cit., p. 96.

41 Ibid., p. 94.

42 Some of these artifacts, together with a speculative reconstruction of the settlers' cabins, are on display in the modest Birchtown Museum run by the Black Loyalist Heritage Association. See Niven and Davis, op. cit.

43 A petition from Stephen Blucke to the Shelburne magistrates on 6th July 1791 asks for improvements on the Birchtown-Shelburne road to make travelling to market easier, especially in winter, when wares had to be carried either on backs or on sleighs. Shelburne County Court of General Sessions, PANS.

44 Wilson, op. cit., pp. 95–96.

45 Boston King, op. cit., pp. 208–12.

46 Winks, op. cit., p. 44.

47 See, for example, the petition on 18th April 1790 for relief from the Poor Tax, PANB, Land Petitions, 1790, RS 108, F1037.

48 Ibid.

49 This is Thomas Clarkson's account of how Peters first heard of the Sierra Leone project, but, as Wilson, op. cit., p. 178, rightly points out, Peters is known to have had long conversations with both Clarkson brothers, and since the story was published soon afterwards by the impeccable Thomas Clarkson in *The American Museum or Universal Magazine*, 11 (1792), it is certain to have been true, or at least taken from Peters himself.

Chapter IX

1 This is according to Thomas Clarkson, who was watching from the gallery, as recounted by him to Katherine Plymley of Longnor House, Staffordshire, the sister of an ardent abolitionist. Her diary, preserved in the Shropshire Record Office, is a superlatively vivid source for the progress and endurance of the campaign from October 1791. See the entry for 20–21st October (Book One).

2 Judith Jennings, *The Business of Abolishing Slavery 1783–1807* (London, 1997), p. 65.

3 Ibid., p. 55.

4 Plymley, op. cit., 24th October 1791.

5 Folarin Shyllon, *James Ramsay: The Unknown Abolitionist* (Edinburgh, 1977) p. 111.

6 Ibid.

7 For the demolition site as a place of festivity, see Simon Schama, *Citizens: A Chronicle of the French Revolution* (London, 2004), pp. 347–48.

8 Thomas Clarkson, *History of the Rise, Progress and Accomplishment of Abolition of the African Slave Trade by the British Parliament*, 2 vols. (London, 1808; published in the USA, 1836, as *The Cabinet of Freedom*); Ellen Gibson Wilson, *Thomas Clarkson: A Biography* (York, 1989), p. 56.

9 Clarkson, op. cit., II, p. 252 (in US 1836 edition).

10 Ibid., p. 251.

11 Ibid., p. 58.

12 Linda Colley, *Britons: Forging the Nation 1707–1837* (New Haven, Conn., 1992), p. 278.

13 Anna Maria Falconbridge (ed. Christopher Fyfe), *Narrative of Two Voyages to the River Sierra Leone During the Years 1791–1792–1793* (Liverpool, 2000), pp. 24–40.

14 Ibid., pp. 24–40.

15 He did this, for example, for the Plymleys at Longnor, where Katherine declared that the coffee "smelt quite well."

16 PRO CO 217/63; Ellen Gibson Wilson, *The Loyal Blacks* (New York, 1976), p. 186.

17 Ellen Gibson Wilson, *John Clarkson and the African Adventure* (London, 1980), pp. 15–42 contains a rich chronicle of the naval engagements John Clarkson would have witnessed and fought in.

18 Ibid., p. 30. This action took place while John Clarkson was serving on the *Proserpine* near Montserrat in November 1779.

19 Ibid., p. 53; Plymley, op. cit., SRO 567.

20 Wilson, op. cit., *Loyal Blacks*, pp. 186–87.

21 Thomas Clarkson's instruction to his brother resulted in one of the great confessional documents of the late eighteenth century, John's three-volume journal of his "Mission to America" (JCAM) and "Mission to Africa" (JCAF). A complete copy is in the hands of his descendants, the Maynard family, and was used by Ellen Gibson Wilson in her excellent history (op. cit., *Loyal Blacks*). Two further manuscript copies of the first two volumes were subsequently made for and by his daughters; one of these copies, in a fine hand, is preserved in NYHS and is my principal source for the following chapters. An additional copy is in the library of the University of Illinois at Chicago Circle. A substantial part of vol. 3 was published in *Sierra Leone Studies*, 8 (1927).

22 Thomas Clarkson to John Clarkson, 28th August 1791, Clarkson Papers, BL Add. MS 1262A, vol. 1, 41262–41267.

23 Wilson, op. cit., *Loyal Blacks*, p. 198; Wilberforce to Clarkson, 8th August 1791, Clarkson Papers, BL Add. MSS 41, 262A.

24 John Clarkson, "Mission to America" (hereafter JCAM), MS, NYHS, 6th October 1791.

25 A copy of this instruction is included in JCAM.

26 Ibid., pp. 47–48.

27 Ibid., pp. 51 ff.

28 Ibid.

29 Ibid.

30 James W. St G. Walker, *The Black Loyalists: The Search for a Promised Land in Nova Scotia and Sierra Leone 1783–1870* (Halifax, 1976), p 84.

31 "Memoirs of the life of Boston King, a Black Preacher, written by himself

during his residence at Kingswood-School," *Methodist Magazine,* XXI (1798), p. 213.

32 JCAM, p. 41.

33 Ibid., p. 57.

34 Ibid., p. 65.

35 Ibid., pp. 65–82.

36 Ibid., p. 82.

37 Wilson, op. cit., *Loyal Blacks,* p. 217.

38 Ibid., pp. 95–96.

39 Ibid., pp. 86–87.

40 Ibid., p. 93.

41 Ibid., p. 204.

42 JCAM, p. 113.

43 Ibid., p. 186.

44 Ibid., pp. 136–37; Clarkson's romanticism was confirmed by his taking time to endorse in his journal the commonplace that the "irregular scenes of Nature" he saw from the Windsor road were incomparably superior to "the laboured and methodical beauties of Art."

45 Ibid., p. 198.

46 Ibid., p. 131.

47 Wilson, op. cit., p. 217.

48 Wilson, op. cit., pp. 191–92.

49 Falconbridge, op. cit., pp. 54 ff.

50 Falconbridge, pp. 53–68, 69.

51 Sharp Papers, NYHS.

52 Falconbridge, op. cit., p. 69.

53 Prince Hoare, *The Memoirs of Granville Sharp Esq. Composed from his own Manuscripts,* 2 vols. (London, 1828), II, p. 167.

54 Clarkson to Wilberforce, 27th November 1791, Clarkson Papers, BL Add. MSS.

55 JCAM, pp. 188–89.

56 Ibid., p. 247.

57 Ibid.

58 Ibid., p. 262.

59 Ibid., p. 250.

60 Ibid., p. 290.

61 Ibid., p. 341.

62 Ibid., pp. 387 ff.

63 Ibid.

64 Ibid., p. 203.

65 Wilson, op. cit., *Loyal Blacks,* p. 224.

66 Wilson, op. cit., *Loyal Blacks,* p. 226.

67 Wilson, op. cit., *Loyal Blacks,* p. 228.

CHAPTER X

1 Details of both the physical conditions of the sailing, and of Clarkson's own condition are taken from the continuation of his Journal "Mission to America" (JCAM), which, after he fell seriously ill, became a more summary nautical log, but with vivid reports of the meteorological and marine conditions. After he recovered somewhat, Clarkson himself had to reconstruct what had happened to him from the account of others aboard the *Lucretia*, including his doctor Samuel Wickham, Charles Taylor and, until his own death, the master of the *Lucretia*, Captain Jonathan Coffin.

2 "Memoirs of the life of Boston King, a Black Preacher, written by himself during his residence at Kingswood-School," *Methodist Magazine*, XXI (1798), pp. 262–63.

3 Ellen Gibson Wilson, *John Clarkson and the African Adventure* (London, 1980), p. 76.

4 JCAM, p. 417. The account of what happened on 29th January was reconstructed by Clarkson from Coffin's tale before his own death.

5 Ibid., p. 422.

6 Ibid.

7 Ibid., p. 430.

8 Ibid., p. 433.

9 Ibid., p. 436.

10 "An Account of the life of Mr David George, from Sierra Leone in Africa, given by himself in a Conversation with Brother Rippon in London and Brother Pearce of Birmingham," *Annual Baptist Register* (1793), pp. 483–84.

CHAPTER XI

1 The identification of the hymn and description is from J.B. Elliott, *Lady Huntingdon's Connexion in Sierra Leone: A Narrative of its History and Present State* (London, 1851), pp. 14–15; Elliott's account was received from his father Anthony Elliott, who was a boy of fifteen in March 1792. See also Christopher Fyfe, *Sierra Leone Inheritance* (Oxford, 1964), p. 120; Ellen Gibson Wilson, *The Loyal Blacks* (New York, 1976), p. 233.

2 Mary Louise Clifford, *From Slavery to Freedom: Black Loyalists after the American Revolution* (Jefferson, North Carolina), p. 25.

3 John Clarkson's Journal, vol. I, "Mission to America" (JCAM), 24th March 1792; Frank Peters went back to his ancestral village with his wife, Nancy, and his mother, but after being accused of witchcraft, returned to live in Freetown.

4 Ibid., p. 452.

5 Ibid., p. 446.

6 Ibid., p. 447.

7 Ellen Gibson Wilson, *John Clarkson and the African Adventure* (London, 1980), pp. 79–80.

8   Ibid., p. 80.

9   JCAM, p. 455.

10 Ibid., p. 458.

11 Ibid., p. 461.

12 Ibid., p. 477.

13 Ibid., p. 165.

14 "Memoirs of the life of Boston King, a Black Preacher, written by himself during his residence at Kingswood-School," *Methodist Magazine*, XXI (1798), pp. 262–63.

15 Anna Maria Falconbridge (ed. Christopher Fyfe), *Narrative of Two Voyages to the River Sierra Leone During the Years 1791–1792–1793* (Liverpool, 2000), p. 82.

16 Wilson, op. cit., *Loyal Blacks*, p. 247.

17 John Clarkson's Journal, vol. II, "Mission to Africa" (JCAF), p. 37.

18 Ibid., p. 48.

19 Ibid., p. 7.

20 Christopher Fyfe (ed.), *Our Children Free and Happy: Letters from Black Settlers in Africa in the 1790s,* with contribution by Charles Jones (Edinburgh, 1991), p. 24.

21 JCAF, p. 20.

22 Ibid., p. 21.

23 Peters to Dundas, April 1792, PRO CO 267/9; Wilson, op. cit., *Loyal Blacks,* p. 232.

24 JCAF, p. 81.

25 Ibid., p. 82.

26 Ibid., p. 84.

27 Ibid., p. 89.

28 Ibid., p. 91.

29 Ibid., p. 95.

30 Ibid., p. 108.

31 Ibid., p. 110.

32 Ibid., pp. 112–13.

33 Ibid., p. 114.

34 Ibid., p. 138.

35 Ibid., p. 145.

36 Ibid., p. 154.

37 Ibid., p. 157.

38 Ibid., p. 163.

39 Ibid., p. 165.

40 Fyfe, op. cit., *Our Children,* pp. 25–26 for a text with the original pidgin spelling. In the same book Charles Jones's essay is an invaluable guide to the character of the black language and diction.

41 Ibid., p. 26. The original is in the Clarkson Papers, University of Illinois at Chicago Circle.

42 JCAF, p. 324.

43 Ibid., p. 325.

44 Wilson, op. cit., *John Clarkson*, p. 105.

45 From the entry of 5th August 1792, JCAF II, p. 17, refers to the transcript published in *Sierra Leone Studies*, 8 (1927), pp. 1–114.

46 Ellen Gibson Wilson, *Loyal Blacks* (New York, 1976), p. 264.

47 JCAF II, p. 51 (21st September 1792).

48 Quoted in Wilson, op. cit., *Loyal Blacks*, p. 275.

49 JCAF II, p. 100 (12th November 1792).

50 Ibid., p. 102.

51 Both petitions in Fyfe, op. cit., *Our Children*, pp. 28–29.

52 Wilson, op. cit., *Loyal Blacks*, p. 277.

53 Wilson, op. cit., *John Clarkson*, p. 117.

54 Falconbridge, op. cit., p. 95.

55 Wilson, op. cit., *John Clarkson*, p. 124.

56 Ibid., p. 126.

57 The original is in the Clarkson/Sierra Leone Papers at the University of Illinois at Chicago Circle; see also Fyfe, op. cit., *Our Children*, pp. 30–32.

Chapter XII

1 Clarkson Papers, BL, Add. MS 41263, ff 1–17; also reproduced in Anna Maria Falconbridge (ed. Christopher Fyfe), *Narrative of Two Voyages to the River Sierra Leone During the Years 1791–1792–1793* (Liverpool, 2000), pp. 134–35.

2 Falconbridge, op. cit., p. 172.

3 Ellen Gibson Wilson, *The Loyal Blacks* (New York, 1976), p. 354.

4 John Clive, *Macaulay: The Shaping of the Historian* (New York, 1974), p. 4.

5 Ibid.

6 Falconbridge, op. cit., p. 105.

7 Journal of DuBois, 6th February 1793; Falconbridge, op. cit., p. 182.

8 Falconbridge, op. cit., p. 113.

9 Ibid.

10 Journal of DuBois, 7th February 1793, p. 183.

11 Clarkson to DuBois, 1st July 1793, BL, Add. MS 41263; Falconbridge, op. cit., "Editor's Comment," p. 126.

12 Ellen Gibson Wilson, *Thomas Clarkson: A Biography* (York, 1989), p. 81.

13 Ibid., p. 82.

14 See "Editor's Comment" in Falconbridge, op. cit., p. 126.

15 Wilson, op. cit., *Loyal Blacks*, p. 288.

16 Falconbridge, op. cit., p. 129, n. 110.

17 Corankapone to Clarkson, 13th June 1793, in Christopher Fyfe (ed.), *Our Children Free and Happy: Letters from Black Settlers in Africa in the 1790s*, with contribution by Charles Jones (Edinburgh, 1991), p. 33.

18 Wilson, op. cit., *Loyal Blacks*, p. 289.

19 Fyfe, op. cit., *Our Children*, p. 37.

20 Ibid., pp. 38–39.
21 Falconbridge, op. cit., p. 144.
22 Perkins and Anderson to Clarkson, 30th October 1793, in Fyfe, op. cit., *Our Children*, p. 40.
23 Perkins and Anderson to Clarkson, 9th November 1793, in Fyfe, op. cit., *Our Children*, p. 41.
24 Falconbridge, op. cit., pp. 146–48.
25 Ibid., p. 148.
26 Ibid., p. 150.
27 William Dawes had returned to England earlier that year. He would return for another stint when Macaulay took a period of leave in 1795–96, but thereafter, until he left in 1799, it was Macaulay who most decisively, and for better or worse, stamped his authority on Sierra Leone.
28 Wilson, op. cit., *Loyal Blacks*, p. 319.
29 Fyfe, op. cit., *Our Children*, p. 43.
30 Ibid., pp. 49–50, 53.
31 "Memoirs of the life of Boston King, a Black Preacher, written by himself during his residence at Kingswood-School," *Methodist Magazine*, XXI (1798), p. 264.
32 Wilson, op. cit., *Loyal Blacks*, pp. 340–41.
33 Ibid., p. 340.
34 Ibid., pp. 329–30.
35 James W. St G. Walker, "Myth, History and Revisionism: The Black Loyalists Revisited," *Acadiensis*, XXIX, no. 1 (Autumn 1999), p. 232.
36 Wilson, op. cit., *Loyal Blacks*, p. 393; for a full account of the rebellion see PRO CO 270/5.
37 Fyfe, op. cit., *Our Children*, p. 65.

Endings, Beginnings

1 Robin Blackburn, *The Overthrow of Colonial Slavery* (London, 1988), p. 313.
2 Ibid., p. 314.
3 Ellen Gibson Wilson, *Thomas Clarkson: A Biography* (York, 1989), p. 118.
4 Rosalind Cobb Wiggins (ed.), *Captain Paul Cuffe's Logs and Letters 1808–1817*, (Washington, D.C., 1996), p. 119. See also Sheldon H. Harris, *Paul Cuffe, Black America and the African Return* (New York, 1972); Lamont D. Thomas, *Rise to Be a People: A Biography of Paul Cuffe* (Urbana, Illinois, 1986); Henry Noble Sherwood, "Paul Cuffe," *Journal of Negro History*, VIII (1923), pp. 153–229.
5 Wiggins, op. cit., p. 145.
6 Ibid., p. 225.
7 For the last years and death of Sharp, see Hoare, op. cit., pp. 311–21; for his American reputation, see the first American biography, Charles Stuart, *A Memoir of Granville Sharp* (New York, 1836). Stuart, pp. 71 ff, makes a strong

contrast between the Sierra Leone enterprise on the one hand, and the work of the American Colonization Society and the Liberian venture on the other, which he characterizes as a wicked exercise in the deportation of free blacks from their own country.

8   Hoare, op. cit., pp. 275–76.

9   Ibid., p. 313.

10   Ibid., p. 315.

11   Thomas Clarkson, *Interviews with the Emperor Alexander I at Paris and Aix-la-Chapelle in 1815 and 1818* (London, nd); Ellen Gibson Wilson, *John Clarkson and the African Adventure* (London, 1980), pp. 169–70.

12   Wilson, op. cit., *John Clarkson,* pp. 159–70.

13   MacCarthy to Cuffe, 6th February 1816, Wiggins, op. cit., p. 40.

14   Stuart, op. cit., p. 75.

15   Wilson, op. cit., *John Clarkson,* p. 178.

16   The phrase is Thomas's.

17   Wilson, op. cit., *John Clarkson,* p. 183.

18   *The History of Mary Prince, Related by Herself* (London, 1987), pp. 83–84.

19   Blackburn, op. cit., p. 455.

20   Wilson, op. cit., *Thomas Clarkson,* p. 165.

21   Ibid., p. 178, p. 255, n. 77.

22   Ibid., p. 189.

23   Philip Foner (ed.), *The Life and Writings of Frederick Douglass,* vol. 1, *The Early Years, 1817–1849* (New York, 1950), p. 230.

24   The wonderful story of the Hutchinsons' singing tour and their part in Douglass's adventure on the *Cambria* and in Britain is narrated in J.W. Hutchinson (ed. Charles E. Mann), *Story of the Hutchinsons (Tribe of Jesse)* (Boston, 1896), pp. 142 ff.

25   Douglass to Garrison, 1st September 1845, Foner, op. cit., p. 115.

26   Ibid., p. 117.

27   Hutchinson, op. cit., pp. 146–47.

28   Foner, op. cit., p. 12.

29   Ibid., pp. 231–32.

30   Ibid., p. 207.

31   Ibid., p. 23.

32   Ibid., p. 171.

33   Ibid., p. 235.

Further Reading

THE BLACK LOYALISTS, SLAVERY AND THE REVOLUTION

Rough Crossings builds on, and is deeply indebted to, the pioneering work of a number of historians who over the past half century have transformed what was once a marginal curiosity in the history of the American Revolution and Great Britain into something approaching a paradigm shift. The fundamental works are: Sylvia R. Frey, *Water From the Rock: Black Resistance in a Revolutionary Age* (Princeton, 1991); Graham Russell Hodges (ed.), *The Black Loyalist Directory* (New York and London, 1996); and idem, *Root and Branch: African Americans in New York and East Jersey 1613–1683* (Chapel Hill, North Carolina, and London, 1999); John W. Pulis (ed.), *Moving On: Black Loyalists in the Afro-Atlantic World* (New York and London, 1999); the classic Benjamin Quarles, *The Negro in the American Revolution* (Chapel Hill, North Carolina, 1996) with a new (and important) introduction by Gary B. Nash; James St G. Walker, *The Black Loyalists: The Search for a Promised Land in Nova Scotia and Sierra Leone 1783–1870* (New York, 1976) and the prolific and immensely readable work of Ellen Gibson Wilson, above all the exhaustively detailed *The Loyal Blacks* (New York, 1976).

THE SLAVERY QUESTION AND THE REVOLUTION

The starting point for any consideration of the painful paradoxes of slavery and the revolution is still David Brion Davis, *The Problem of Slavery in the Age of the American Revolution* (Ithaca, New York, 1973). But equally essential to see how the intellectual and moral issues played out in lived history is Ira Berlin, *Gen-*

erations of Captivity: A History of African-American Slaves (Cambridge, Massachusetts, 2003); Sidney Kaplan and Emma Nogrady Kaplan, *The Black Presence in the Era of the American Revolution*, revised edition (Amherst, Massachusetts, 1989); see also Henry Wiencek, *An Imperfect God: George Washington, His Slaves and the Creation of America* (London, 2005). Elizabeth A. Fenn's *Pox Americana: The Great Smallpox Epidemic of 1775–1782* (New York, 2001), about the epidemiology of the war, is a much larger book than its ostensible subject suggests, a tour de force of narrative and critical analysis.

THE BRITISH CAMPAIGN AGAINST THE SLAVE TRADE: SHARP AND THE CLARKSONS

There is now an abundant and constantly growing literature on this subject. For an overview of the global campaign see Robin Blackburn, *The Overthrow of Colonial Slavery, 1776–1848* (London and New York, 1988) and Hugh Thomas, *The Slave Trade: The Story of the Atlantic Slave Trade 1440–1870* (New York and London, 1997). An important collection of essays is David Eltis and James Walvin (eds), *Abolition of the Atlantic Slave Trade: Origins and Effects in Europe, Africa and the Americas* (Madison, Wisconsin, 1981). See also Walvin's *England, Slaves and Freedom 1776–1838* (Jackson, Mississippi, 1986); idem, *Black Ivory: A History of British Slavery* (London, 1992); Adam Hochschild's *Bury the Chains: Prophets and Rebels in the Fight to Free an Empire's Slaves* (New York, 2004) appeared after the present book was completed and elegantly narrates some of the same events and lives, though with more emphasis on the campaign in Britain itself. Deidre Coleman's *Romantic Colonization and British Anti-Slavery* (Cambridge, 2005), covering some of the same ground, also appeared too late for me to take full account of it. Among relatively recent and very important contributions are David Eltis, *Economic Growth and the Ending of the Transatlantic Slave Trade* (Oxford, 1987); Judith Jennings, *The Business of Abolishing the British Slave Trade 1783–1807* (London and Portland, Oregon, 1997); J.R. Oldfield, *Popular Politics and British Anti-Slavery: The Mobilization of Public Opinion against the Slave Trade* (Manchester and New York, 1995); David Turley, *The Culture of English Anti-Slavery 1780–1860* (London and New York, 1991). Studies of individuals include Kevin Belmonte, *Hero for Humanity: A Biography of William Wilberforce* (Colorado, 2002), which does not quite replace John Pollock, *William Wilberforce* (London and New York, 1977); Folarin Shyllon, *James Ramsay, the Unknown Abolitionist* (Edinburgh, 1977); Ellen Gibson Wilson, *Thomas Clarkson: A Biography* (York, 1980).

BLACKS IN BRITAIN AT THE TIME OF THE REVOLUTION AND AFTER

The crucial work is Stephen J. Braidwood's *Black Poor and White Philanthropists: London's Blacks and the Foundation of the Sierra Leone Settlement 1786–1791* (Liverpool, 1994). There are now a number of excellent survey histories of the black experience in Britain, especially Peter Fryer, *Staying Power: The History of Black People in Britain* (London, 1984) and James Walvin, *Black and White: The Negro and English Society 1555–1945* (London, 1973); see also Gretchen Holbrook Gerzina, *Black London: Life Before Emancipation* (London and New Brunswick, New Jersey, 1985). Norma Myers, *Reconstructing the Black Past: Blacks in Britain 1780–1830* (London and Portland, Oregon, 1996) is an important critical look at the sources for black history, especially its stereotypes. Cultural and literary issues are treated by David Dabydeen in *Hogarth's Blacks: Images of Blacks in Eighteenth Century Art* (Kingston-upon-Thames, 1985), and his anthologies of black writing, *Black Writers in Britain, 1760–1890* (Edinburgh, 1991).The most recent and by far the best critical account of Olaudah Equiano's life and writing is Vincent Carretta, *Equiano the African: Biography of a Self-Made Man* (Athens, Georgia, 2005).

NOVA SCOTIA AND THE BLACKS

Apart from James St G. Walker's crucial study, Robin Winks, *The Blacks in Canada: A History* (Montreal, New Haven and London, 1971) devotes two richly detailed chapters to the impact of the war and the loyalist settlement, both black and white. It should be noted that there is now a lively debate about the "mythology" of black loyalism in Nova Scotia, provoked by Barry Cahill in an article in the Nova Scotian history journal *Acadiensis* (Autumn 1999), with an equally lively and to my mind convincing response by James Walker. For Shelburne, see Marion Robertson, *King's Bounty: A History of Early Shelburne* (Halifax, Nova Scotia, 1983).

SIERRA LEONE AND THE BLACK LOYALISTS

The authority is Christopher Fyfe, in particular *History of Sierra Leone* (Oxford, 1962), and *Sierra Leone Inheritance* (Oxford, 1964). His editions of both *Narrative of Two Voyages to the River Sierra Leone During the Years 1791–1792–1793* by Anna Maria Falconbridge (Liverpool, 2000) and *Our Children Free and Happy: Letters from Black Settlers in Africa in the 1790s* (Edinburgh, 1991) have a wealth of scholarly information and critical commentary. Ellen Wilson Gibson's *John Clarkson and the African Adventure* (London, 1980) is yet another of this author's fine narratives to which this writer is indebted.

Acknowledgements

IT WAS MY OLD FRIEND (and one of the cleverest historians I've known), Sir Tom Harris, then Consul-General in New York, who provoked this book by saying, over lunch in Columbia University's Charter Room (the charter in question having been for King's College and signed and sealed by George II), that, of course, I'd know all about the thousands of free blacks in New York at the end of the Revolutionary War and what became of them. In fact, I had no clue what he was talking about. Soon, I did. But if he's responsible for instigating this enterprise, he certainly bears no share of the blame for its shortcomings.

The book could not have been written without the help of my superlative research assistant, Kate Edwards who was my second pair of eyes in the libraries and archives. Rebecca Grunwald helped with research into the *Zong* case and its impact on the abolitionist movement, and Samantha Earl helped with checking the references. I am deeply grateful to T. K. Hunter for allowing me the use of material from her Columbia Ph.D. dissertation on the Somerset case and its impact in America. Librarians and archivists in three countries could not have been friendlier or more helpful: in the Public Record Office in London, the Allan Library of the Royal Maritime Museum in Greenwich; the New York Public Library; the Public Archives of Nova Scotia in Halifax (where Barry Cahill was especially helpful, notwithstanding his scepticism about the entire Black Loyalist phenomenon); the Shelburne Historical Society Library and Archives; but, above all, I am grateful to the hospitable and immensely helpful librarians of the manuscript and rare book division of the New-York Historical Society, where two volumes of the John Clarkson journal are preserved, especially for allowing me the precious gift of reading them in the original rather than on microfilm.

Two provosts of Columbia University, Jonathan Cole and Alan Brinkley have been exceptionally generous in granting me leave to research and write the book. In my Columbia office Alicia Hall Moran has been a tower of strength in innumerable ways, not least in the hunting down of obscure and out of print secondary sources.

In the midst of my Nova Scotian pilgrimage, following the black loyalist trail, Calvin Trillin was kind enough to interrupt scholarly labours with hatfuls of chanterelles, generous hospitality and really good jokes.

Thanks and apologies are due to Michael Carlisle, James Gill, Michael Sissons and Alice Sherwood for having been generous enough to read the manuscript at various stages and offer invariably helpful and encouraging comments as it staggered along its wayward progress. As ever, Rosemary Scoular, Sophie Laurimore, Jo Forshaw and Sara Starbuck at pfd made sure the author didn't go completely off his trolley on days when he was supposed to be simultaneously filming, scriptwriting and reading proofs. My thanks also to Tom Stoppard for generously allowing me to steal his title.

Particular thanks are due to Christopher Fyfe who was kind enough to read the book for errors and saved me from many of the most egregious. Sean Wilentz, Eric Foner and James Basker have been generous enough to cast a discerning eye over the American portion of the book. Any remaining errors are, of course, entirely my own.

My editor at Ecco, Dan Halpern, has been a model of forbearance, generosity, enthusiasm, and critical smarts—especially since Rough Crossings turned out to be not quite the book he commissioned. I am also grateful to E.J. Van Laren for seeing the book through to publication in the United States and to Jill Bernstein and Jane Beirn in helping it get to the public.

My long-suffering family—Ginny, Chloe and Gabriel—have had to endure the roughest of crossings—namely surviving the more than usually stormy behaviour of the author during this particular literary voyage to which they have responded with the usual pouring of oil on troubled waters. I can't thank them enough for helping me get the thing to harbour. Gus has been a brick.

Friends at two institutions—Harvard University's Committee on History and Literature, and Queen Mary College, London, were kind enough to invite me to lecture about the arguments and stories rehearsed in this book. Their response—especially the comments of Homi Bhabha and Stephen Greenblatt at Harvard helped me clarify the history. And a number of other good friends and colleagues—Alan Brinkley, Eric Foner, Deborah Garrison and Stella Tillyard, all thought the history was worth a book to itself rather than the quarter of a book originally assigned it. Most adamant on that subject, as well as frankly open-hearted, wise and loyal on almost all my peculiar adventures in the history trade, was the scholar and good friend, Lisa Jardine, who invited me to lecture at Queen Mary College; whose infectious enthusiasm for the project made it absolutely impossible for me to have pusillanimous second thoughts, and to whom the book is lovingly dedicated with a measure of awestruck admiration for her bravery, brilliance and all round *menschlichkeit*.

Index

(Page references in *italic* refer to illustrations.)

Abernathy, Adam, 282
Abernathy, Catherine, 11, 282
Abolitionists, abolition:
 in America, 8, 16, 86, 11112, 163, 189,
  209–10, 402, 403–4, 410, 414–22
 Anglo–French rivalry and, 261–62, 264,
  265, 401
 boycott of West Indian sugar and, 265,
  275, 296
 in England, 6, 169–76, 188, 200, 208–10,
  215, 218, 259–66, 269, 273, 366, 371,
  396, 401–3, 412–22. *See also* Sharp,
  Granville
 in France, 262–64, 265, 364, 371, 401, 403
 persistence of race prejudice and, 403–4,
  415–16
 "revolutionism" argument against,
  264–65
Actaeon, 88
Adams, Abigail, 14–15, 17
Adams, John, 12, 14–15, 17, 66, 69–70, 85,
  166, 210
 treaty negotiations and, 136–38
Adams, Sam, 52
Adventure, 246
African Institution, 403, 404, 405, 408
African Peace Society, 410
Afzelius, Adam, 344, 349, 367, 381, 386
Alert, 123
Alexander I, Tsar, 409

Alfred, 176
Allen, William, 405, 406, 409
Alleyne, John, 47, 51–52, 168
"Amazing Grace," 174, 385
American Colonization Society, 410–11
"Am I Not a Man and a Brother?"
 medallions, 208–9, 260
Amy, 322, 327, 336, 343, 361, 378
Anderson, Daniel, 238
Anderson, Isaac, 352–53, 357, 383–84, 388
 in Freetown revolt, 390–95
 petition of grievances taken to London
  by, 375–79
Anderson, Messrs (slavers), 202, 204, 216,
  331
Anderson, Peter, 182
André, John, 145
Angerstein, John Julius, 184, 188, 437n.32
Anglican Church, 26, 112, 387–88
Anglicania, 165–66
Ann and Mary, 44, 45
Annapolis, Nova Scotia, 223, 225, 226, 227,
  231, 278, 287, 294, 303
Annis, John, 165–66
Anti–Saccharine Campaign, 265, 275, 296
Anti–Slavery Society (London), 412–13
Anti–Slave Society for New York, 410
Apollo, 35–36, 92
Appeal to the Colored Citizens of the World
 (Walker), 6, 412

Ark, 275–77
Armed Boat Company, 116
Armstrong, Aaron, 41, 43
Arnaud, Citizen–Captain, 381
Arnold, Benedict, 113, 118, 128, 145
Arundel, HMS, 170
Asgill, Charles, 140–44, 145
Asgill, Theresa, 142–44
Ashmore, Abraham, 215–16, 217
Ashton, Justice, 53, 54
Ashurst, Justice, 53, 54
Asia, HMS, 392, 393, 394, 395
Associated Loyalists, 116, 140–42
Atlantic, 194, 196, 198, 266
Attucks, Crispus, 10
Auld, Hugh, 421
Australia, 192, 195, 383
Ayscough, Sir William, 177

Babington, Thomas, 366
Bahamas, 132, 181, 185, 192, 244, 246
Banbury, John, 86
Banbury, Lucy, 86, 321
Banks, Sir Joseph, 186, 361
Banks, Mrs William, 36–37, 39, 41–43, 45,
    46
Baptist, John, 180–81
Barbados, 49, 50
Barber, Francis, 23, 25
Barrington, Admiral, 171
Bartley, Catrin, 361
Bear Creek settlement, 125–26
Beckett, John, 354
Beckford, William, 38–39
Beckwith, Major, 139
Beech, Thomas, 27–28
Belisarius, 194, 196, 198, 200, 267
Bell, Dr (company surgeon), 323, 326–27,
    328, 349
Bell, Towers, 5
Benezet, Anthony, 12, 14, 16, 57, 89, 91,
    166, 425n.24
Benson, Egbert, 145
Berlin, Anders, 187
Bestes, Peter, 15
Betsey, 323, 327
Bever, Dr (Oxford law don), 167–68
Beverhout, Henry, 308, 339, 345, 346–47

Bicknell, Charles, 56
Bicknell, John, 55–56, 100, 101
Birch, Samuel, 139, 150, 303
Birchtown, Nova Scotia, 9, 11, 223, 236–38,
    242, 243, 246, 249–53, 287, 311, 328,
    338
  Clarkson's recruitment mission in, 284,
    287–90, 292, 293, 303, 347, 348, 355
Bird, Mark, 76–77
Black, William, 242
"Blackbird March, The," 83
Black Brigade, 114, 115–16, 155
Black Dragoons, 4, 9, 124, 238
Black Pioneers and Guides, 4, 10, 84, 98,
    106, 116, 118, 122, 149, 155, 179, 197,
    219, 220, 222–23, 248, 268, 270
Blackstone, William, 31–32, 33, 37
Blair, Hannah, 73
Bland, Theodore, 149
Blowers, Sampson, 245, 280, 301
Blucke, Margaret, 155, 236, 250, 311
Blucke, Stephen, 11, 116, 155, 236, 237, 250,
    284, 287, 290, 311
Blue Salt, 95
Board of Inquiry, 151–52, 179
Boddington, Mr (Sharp's superior at
    Ordnance Office), 89, 90
Boddington, Thomas, 188
Bolman, John, 301–2
Book of Negroes, 5, 150, 152, 154
Boscawen, Admiral, 162
Boston, 5
  outbreak of hostilities and, 59, 66
  Patriot rhetoric in, 11–12
  punishment meted to, in wake of Tea
    Party, 70–71
Boston Massacre (1770), 10
Boswell, James, 22, 33
Boudinot, Elias, 143
Bowie, James, 202, 204, 207, 212, 214–15,
    216
Braidwood, Stephen, 188
Brindley Town, Nova Scotia, 224, 227,
    311, 338
Brissot, Jacques-Pierre, 262
Bristol, 88
Bristol, Earl of, 413
Brookes, 260, 263, 295, 307

Brown, Abby, 72, 155
Brown, Captain, 98
Brown, Dinah, 155
Brown, Joseph, 372
Brown, Mr (London apothecary), and family, 24–25, 26
Brown, Thomas, 123
Browne, Henry, 180–81
Browne, Mountford, 181
Browne, Thomas, 116
Brudenell, Reverend, 225, 227
Buffum, James, 416
Bulkeley, Richard, 294, 304, 311
Bull, Stephen, 85
Bullom people, 202, 204, 331
Bunker Hill, battle of (1775), 7, 66
Burgoyne, John, 93, 128
Burke, Edmund, 92, 259, 264, 371
Burke, Samuel, 181
Bute, Marquis of, 33

Cade, Elizabeth, 45, 49–50
Caesar (escaped slave), 149
Cambria, 415, 416–18, 421
Cambridge, John, 192, 196, 351–52
Cambridge, Sarah, 196, 206
Camden, Charles Pratt, 1st Earl of, 39
Campbell, Archie, 93, 94, 126
Campbell, Ezekiel, 393, 395
Campbell, Sir Neil, 411
Campbell, Sarah (née Izard), 61–62, 64
Campbill, Lord William (South Carolina governor), 60–65, 66, 88, 105
Campbill, William (Wilmington Patriot), 68
Canada, 66, 128, 132, 419, 420
see also New Brunswick; Nova Scotia
Cape Fear, slave insurrection anticipated in, 68
Caribbean, 129
see also West Indies; *specific islands*
Carleton, Sir Guy, 127–32, 136, 231, 250, 348
Asgill affair and, 140–44, 145
concession of American independence and, 128–31
fate of escaped slaves and, 134, 135, 138–39, 145–49, 150, 151, 153, 155, 225

Washington's dealings with, 127, 130, 138–41, 144–49
Carleton, Thomas, 228, 242, 253, 254, 270, 288
Carlisle, Thomas, 213
Carretta, Vincent, 161
Carter, Landon, 73
Carter, Robert, 77
Cartwright, Captain, 31
Catawba Indians, 126
Certificates of service, 4, 132, 139, 150, 151, 152, 155
Cevils, Hannah, 72
Cevils, Zilpah, 72
Chapel, Mr (George's owner), and his son, 94, 95–96
Charles II, King of England, 31
Charleston, 66, 85, 86, 88, 103, 106, 108, 112, 123, 138
battle of (1780), 100–101, 103–4, 105, 109, 122
evaluation of claims to freedom in, 134–35
Jeremiah case in, 59–65
loyalists in, after end of war, 5, 132–33, 134–35, 136, 151, 239
Charleston Council, 85
Chatham, William Pitt, 1st Earl of, 65
Cheese, Anna and William, 9, 402
Cherokee, 104, 105
Cherokee, 85
Civil War, American, 6, 103
Clara, Princess (daughter of Temne chief), 211
Clarkson, Catherine, 413, 414
Clarkson, John, 176, 257, 262, 266, 270–379, 383–87, 389, 395, 406, 411–12, 423n.1
appointed superintendent of Sierra Leone, 323–25, 327
authority over white councillors, soldiers and sailors asserted by, 340–42
black settlers' grievances and, 333–39, 345–48, 352–53, 357, 375–79, 383–84
changes in company's instructions for, 296–97
conversion experience of, 309, 326

Clarkson, John (cont.)
  Dawes's replacement of, 356–58, 364–65,
    366–69, 372
  death of, 412
  departure of, from Sierra Leone, 354–63
  disagreements between Sierra Leone
    Company and, 324–27, 342, 344, 351,
    352–53, 369–70, 371–72
  dismissed from governorship, 372
  emotional appeals made to settlers by,
    343, 347, 355–56, 358
  in England after return from Africa,
    369–72, 376–77, 384–85
  governance of Sierra Leone and,
    323, 325–26, 333–39, 342, 345–48,
    351–53
  illness of, 312, 313, 314, 315, 317, 322
  King's visit in England with, 384–85
  Macaulay's and Dawes's criticisms of,
    366–69, 372
  made governor of Sierra Leone, 351,
    370, 372
  naval career of, 271–74, 309, 370–71, 410
  as peace activist, 409–10
  Peters's challenges to, 306, 334–38, 345,
    346, 348
  Peters's death and, 348–49
  preparations of, for voyage to Africa,
    293, 295–96, 303–10
  recruitment mission of, 270, 274–96,
    300–303, 347, 348, 355, 378, 379
  rules of conduct established by, 306–9,
    322–23
  Temne and Bullom chiefs' relations
    with, 330–32, 333, 354–55, 360
  in voyage to Africa, 313–20, 322–23
  white councillors and employees
    disdained by, 325–27, 333
Clarkson, Susannah (née Lee), 274, 275,
  324, 355, 356, 372, 376
Clarkson, Thomas, 271, 274, 307, 355, 406,
  412, 413–15
  abolitionist campaign and, 173–74,
    175–76, 189, 208, 209, 259, 260, 261,
    403, 412, 413–15
  epiphany of, 173–74
  French abolitionists and, 262–64, 265,
    371

  honorary French citizenship awarded
    to, 371
  at Paris peace conference (1815), 409
  Sierra Leone settlement and, 218, 266,
    268, 269, 270, 274, 275–76, 296, 298,
    299, 324–25, 327, 332, 342, 351, 361,
    403
  Wilberforce's falling out with, 370–71,
    413
Clarkson's Plantation, Sierra Leone, 384,
  396
Clinton, George, 145, 146–47
Clinton, Sir Henry, 7, 10, 82–84, 86, 102,
  104–6, 108, 118, 120–21, 122–23, 124,
  125, 129, 133, 141, 220, 255
  Black Pioneers and, 84, 106
  complicated record of, toward black
    charges, 105–6
  Philipsburgh Proclamation of, 100, 104,
    105, 133, 134–35, 139, 150, 151, 177,
    226, 245, 433n.52
  proclamation of. See Phillipsburg
    Proclamation
Cocks, James, 323, 346
Coffee, 386, 395
Coffin, Jonathan, 315, 316, 317–18, 323
Coleman, Richard, 41
Coleridge, Samuel, 403
Collett, Violet, 155
Collingwood, Luke, 158–61
Commentaries (Blackstone), 31–32, 33
Committee for Effecting the Abolition of
  the Slave Trade, 259–62, 274
Committee for the Abolition of the Slave
  Trade, 208–9
Committee for the Relief of the Black
  Poor, 184–85, 437n.32
  Sierra Leone plan and, 186, 188, 190–93,
    194–95, 200
Common Law, English, 28, 31–32, 33, 38,
  42, 43, 46, 51, 52, 53, 55, 167, 190, 220,
  389
Concord, skirmish at, 7, 62, 65, 67
Condorcet, Marquis de, 262
Congress of the Confederation, 129, 130,
  132, 140, 143, 147, 148, 149, 152
Connecticut, black loyalist soldiers and
  partisans in, 101, 111

Connor, Susannah, 247
Constitution, British, 129, 151, 220
Constitution, U.S., 209–10
Continental army, 65–66, 106
    blacks' service in, 7, 76, 83, 101-4, 122, 177
Continental Congress, 7, 8, 65, 70, 83, 85,
    102–3
"Conversation" (Franklin), 13–14
Conway, General, 129
Coram, John, 60
Corankapone, Richard, 303, 361, 372,
    373–74, 380, 391, 393, 396
Cornwallis, Lord Charles, 105, 106, 116,
    118, 119–20, 121, 122, 125, 137, 179,
    433n.52
Cornwallis, Frederick, Archbishop of
    Canterbury, 37, 38
Country Harbour, Nova Scotia, 245, 246
Cowper, William, 175
Cox, James, 247
Creek Indians, 85, 95, 255
Croft, Peter, 60
Cromwell, Oliver, 377
Cruden, John, 119, 123–24, 133–34
Cruizer, 83
Cuffe, Colonel (loyalist partisan), 149
Cuffe, Paul, 403–7, 410
Cugoano, Ottobah (later John Stewart),
    176, 190, 199, 255, 268, 309
Cunard, Abraham, 231
Cunard, Samuel, 421
Cuthbert, John, 236, 372, 390, 393–94

Dalrymple, Henry Hew, 297, 298, 323
Dance, George, 19
Dartmouth, William Legge, 2nd Earl of,
    61, 64, 67, 74–75, 82
Davenport (lawyer), 168
Davis, Jameson, 246
Davy, William "Bull," 46, 47, 49, 50, 52
Dawes, William, 356–58, 364–65, 375, 376,
    381, 384, 389, 396
    Clarkson's policies set aside by, 366–69
    made governor of Sierra Leone, 372
Day, Thomas, 55–56, 100, 101
Dean, John, 176
Declaration of Independence, 5, 8, 9, 11,
    12, 59, 85–86, 92, 130, 348, 419

Declaration of the People's Natural Right to
    Share in Legislature (Sharp), 91
De Lancey, James, 138, 146
De Mane, Harry, 190, 196, 207–8
Destouches, Admiral, 118
De Wint, Amos, house, 144–45, 147
Diary or Woodfall's Register, 214
Digby, Nova Scotia, 223, 225, 226, 227, 235,
    287, 294, 338, 352
Digby, Robert, 129
Dix, Cuffe, 77
Dixon, Charles, 238
Dixon, Miles, 372
Dolben Bill, 200, 209, 215
Dolly, Quamino, 93, 104, 126
Dolphin, 283–84, 285, 286
Domingo, Signor, 331, 354, 361
Douglass, Frederick, 6, 399, 415–21
Drayton, William Henry, 62, 64, 66
DuBois, Anna Maria. See Falconbridge,
    Anna Maria
Dubois, Isaac, 344, 349, 359, 360, 363–64,
    367–69, 372, 373, 375, 376, 396
Duke of Buccleuch, 219
Duncombe, Richard, 195
Dundas, Henry, 266, 275, 278, 288, 335–36
Dunk, William, 116
Dunmore, John Murray, 4th Earl of, 7, 8,
    17, 61, 65, 70–83, 104, 118, 133, 228,
    429n.25
    black army of (Ethiopian Regiment), 67,
        72–83, 86–87, 111, 113, 117, 152, 182
    defeated at Great Bridge, 79–82
    epidemic striking troops of, 86–87
    flight of escaped slaves to serve with,
        72–74, 76–78, 83
    flotilla of, 83, 86–87, 150
    Kemp's Landing attacked by, 78–79
    munitions seized by, 66–67, 71
    Norfolk's destruction and, 82
    plantocracy's attacks on, 77
    proclamation of, 7, 17, 75–76, 105, 111,
        151, 245
    resistance of, after Yorktown
        capitulation, 123–24
    Scottish background of, 70
Dunning, John, 42, 47–48, 52, 168
Duryea, Jacob, 149

"Dying Negro, The" (Day and Bicknell), 55–56
Dyott, Captain, 250

Edmonds, Mr (marshal), 393
Edward VI, King of England, 31, 38
Edwards, Steven, 140
Egan, Pierce, 233
Eilbeck, Mr (slaveholder), 152
Elbert, Samuel, 126
Eleanor, 305, 310, 315, 316, 318–19, 327
Elizabeth I, Queen of England, 31, 38, 50
Elliot, Andrew, 144
Emancipation Bill (1833), 413
Emmons, Lucretia, 115
Equiano, Olaudah (aka Gustevus Vassa), 176, 190, 255, 309
  Annis case and, 165–66
  life story of, 161–65, 167
  Sierra Leone plan and, 193–94, 198–200, 206, 207, 268
  Zong drownings and, 161, 166, 167
Essay (Phillips), 175, 176
Essay (Ramsay), 171–72, 173
Essex Journal and Merrimac Packet, 15
Estaing, Admiral Comte d', 99, 100
Ethiopian Balls, 112–13, 123
Ethiopian Regiment, 79
  see also Dunmore, John Murray, 4th
  Earl of
Evangelicals, 269, 366, 368
Ewald, Johann, 122
Eyre, Sir James, 28

Falconbridge, Alexander, 196, 209, 297–99, 323, 326, 348
  death of, 359–60, 367
  as Freetown's commercial agent, 298, 344, 350, 359
  Sierra Leone settlement re–established by, 219, 266–67, 278, 298
Falconbridge, Anna Maria (later Mrs. Isaac DuBois), 196, 219, 267, 298–99, 329, 350, 353, 363, 364, 367, 368
  husband's death and, 359–60, 367
  petition of grievances and, 376, 377
  Sierra Leone left by, 373
Falconbridge, William, 219

Fanning, Colonel David, 181
Felicity, 310, 312, 314, 315, 316, 327, 342, 360, 361
1st Rhode Island Regiment, 101, 122
Ford, Keziah, 155
Fordyce, Charles, 80–81
Fort Johnston, 64, 68
Fort Murray, 79–82
Fort Sullivan, 86
Fortune, William, 111
Fowey, HMS, 67, 71–72
Fox, Charles James, 259, 401–2
France, 131
  abolition in, 262–64, 364
  as American ally, 129, 130, 136
  British rivalry with, 30, 162, 266, 272, 273, 364, 371, 401, 409
  Revolution in, 261, 262–64, 366, 371, 374, 413
  Sierra Leone attacked by, 380–83, 386
  slavery reintroduced in, 401, 403
  slave trade of, 261–62
Franklin, Benjamin, 52, 89, 91, 210, 420
  abolition and, 166–67, 189, 209, 425n.24
  responses of, to charges of American hypocrisy, 12–14, 57
  treaty negotiations and, 136, 137–38
Frankpledge, 30–31, 189–90, 210, 211, 219, 268, 352, 390, 395
Fraser, Mary, 123
Fraser, Patrick, 199, 200, 207
Fraunces, Samuel, 147, 151–52
Freedom, British, 3–5, 9, 235, 242–43, 281, 360, 394, 396–97, 423n.1
Freeman, Sambo, 15, 18
Freetown, Sierra Leone, 281
  see also Sierra Leone–second settlement in
Freetown Fair, 411
French Revolution, 261, 262–64, 366, 371, 374, 413
Frey, Sylvia, 8, 135
Furman, Shadrack, 179

Gage, Thomas, 15, 59, 65, 66, 71
Gallatin, Albert, 407
Galphin, George, 96, 97, 385
Gambia, 187

Garrick, David, 22, 46
Garrison, William Lloyd, 414, 415, 416, 421
Gates, Horatio, 118
Gemmel, Robert, 247
George, David, 11, 94–98, 99, 350, 380
   British forces joined by, 97–98
   Clarkson accompanied back to England
      by, 361–62, 385
   Macaulay's attempts at social control
      and, 387–88
   in Nova Scotia, 239–43, 249, 254, 282,
      286–87, 291, 293, 295, 305
   planning for Sierra Leone settlement
      and, 286–87, 291, 293, 295, 308, 310
   as preacher, 96–97, 239–43, 249, 282, 305,
      336, 385
   in Sierra Leone, 320, 321, 336, 338, 395
   slave life of, 94–96
   smallpox suffered by, 107–8
George, King (Bullom chief), 404
George, Phyllis, 94, 96, 99, 107–8, 239, 240,
      241, 293, 321
George, Prince of Wales (later George IV,
      King of England), 36
George II, King of England, 63
George III, King of England, 33, 36, 61, 69,
      70, 93, 121, 128, 131, 220, 402
   Africans' allegiance to, 205, 267, 331
   crimes of, in Declaration of
      Independence, 5, 59, 86
   free blacks' regard for, 4, 79, 114, 155,
      234, 254, 335–36, 348, 377
   Parliament addressed on colonies'
      rebellion by, 90–91
   Patriots' loyalty to, 348
Georgia, 7–8, 93–100, 163
   black loyalist soldiers and partisans
      in, 69–70, 84, 85, 93–94, 97–100, 123,
      125–26, 179
   black soldiers proposed for Patriot side
      in, 102–3
   embrace of Patriot cause in, 67–68
   slave bounties as recruitment incentive
      in, 11, 104
   slaves' flight from plantations in, 76, 94,
      97–98, 105
   see also Savannah
Germain, Lord George, 82, 86, 94, 124

Gesau, Mr (engineer), 195
Gilbert, Messrs, and Others, 167
Gilbert, Nathaniel, 322, 342, 351
Gilbert, Reverend, 323, 326, 346
Gloucester, Duke of, 405, 408
Glynn, John, 46, 47, 50
Gordon, Lord George, 195
Goree, 394
Granville Town, Sierra Leone, 202, 281
   see also Sierra Leone–first settlement in
Grasse, Admiral de, 121, 129
Gray, Sir Charles, 139
Gray, Jesse, 247–49
Gray, Mr (slave trader), 133–34
Gray, Samuel, 247, 248
Great Bridge, battles at, 79–82, 118, 182
Green, Jacob, 112
Green, Peter, 176
Greene, Christopher, 101
Greene, Nathanael, 126, 132–33, 136
Grenada, 297
Grenville, William Wyndham, Lord, 220,
      254, 255, 402
Grey, Captain, 108–9
Greyhound, 127, 433n.1
Griffin, John, 182
Griffith, Abraham Elliott, 196, 200, 210–11,
      267, 299, 346, 352
Griffith, Rebecca, 196, 206
Guysborough County, Nova Scotia, 235
Gwynn's Island, 87

Hackney, Dr, 195
Halifax, Nova Scotia, 229–31, 234–35,
      239–40, 244, 245
   Clarkson's recruitment mission in,
      277–81, 283, 284, 292–96, 320
   departure of fleet from, 310–12
   gathering for journey to Africa in, 295,
      303–10
Halsted, Phyllis, 361
Hamilton, Alexander, 102, 136
Hamilton, John, 246
Hamilton, Thomas, 246–47
Hammond, Charlotte, 154
Hammond, Mr (diplomat), 278
Hamond, Andrew Snape, 87
Handley, Scipio, 179

Hanway, Jonas, 183–84, 185, 188, 190–91, 193, 205, 207, 273, 386
Hardcastle, Joseph, 324, 332
Hargrave, Francis, 46–47, 51, 52–53
Harpy, 322, 326, 340, 350, 352
Harris, John, 247
Harris, Joseph, 78
Harrison, Benjamin, 9, 123, 149, 402
Hartshorne, Lawrence, 277, 280, 281, 300, 304, 306, 312, 334, 406
Hawkins, John, 31
Hawksmoor, Nicholas, 23
Hedley, Henry, 301
Henley, Lord Robert, 31
Henry, Patrick, 8–9, 14, 68, 71–72
Henry, Ralph, 8–9, 68
Herring, Simsa, 116
Hessians, 66, 93, 94, 97, 113, 129, 149, 226, 300
Heywood, Mr (lawyer), 168–69
Heywood, Sampson, 303, 361
Hill, Richard, 225
Historical Collections (Rushworth), 31
History (Clarkson), 403
History of Mary Prince, The, 412–13
Hoare, Samuel, 173, 184, 208, 209, 412
Holbrook, Felix, 15
Holmes, William and Deborah, 241
Holt, Lord Chief Justice, 31, 38
Hopkins, Rev Samuel, 189, 209, 219
Horne, Rev Melville, 351, 364
Howe, Robert, 7, 10, 89, 94, 105, 111, 113
Howe, William, 128
Huddy, Joshua, 115–16, 140–41
Hughes, Mr and Mrs, 302
Hume, David, 172, 186, 365
Humes, Tobias, 336
Humphreys, Major, 139
Hutchinson, Thomas, 15, 34
Hutchinson Family Quartet, 416, 417, 418

Indenturing, 8, 70
    of blacks in Nova Scotia, 221, 225, 244–45, 281, 283, 292, 300–302
Indians:
    British incitement of, 59, 60–61, 62
    see also specific peoples

Inglis, Bishop, 310278
Innes, Alexander, 105, 113
Instruments of Liberty, 192, 193
Intolerable Acts, 71
Irving, Charles, 164–65
Irwin, Joseph, 193, 194, 198–99, 206
Izard, Ralph, 105

Jack, King (Natchez leader), 95–96
Jackson, Bob, 73
Jackson, Hannah, 73
Jackson, James, 73
Jackson, Judith, 152
Jackson, Lydia, 301–2
Jacobins, 371, 374, 390
Jamaica, 25, 132, 365–66
    Maroons in, 17, 390–91
    slave insurrections in, 16, 17, 92, 390–91, 412
James I, King of England, 121
Jay, John, 136, 189, 209, 210
Jefferson, Thomas, 16, 61, 71, 74, 76, 118, 172
    abolition and, 8, 86, 402, 410
    Declaration of Independence and, 5, 8, 12, 59, 86
    slaves lost by, 8, 119
Jemmy George (Temne chief), 383
Jeremiah, Thomas, 59–65
Jimmy, King (Temne chief), 213, 214–15, 216–17, 219, 266, 268, 278, 299, 321, 330–32, 343, 349, 354–55
John Frederic ("Black Prince"), 299–300, 331, 360
Johnson, Gabriel, 116
Johnson, Samuel, 23, 25, 33, 46, 57
Joie, Chester, 15
Jordan, Luke, 329, 372, 383–84
Jordan, Mingo, 393–94
Joseph, 222–23
Judkins, Charles, 417–18, 421

Kemp's Landing, skirmishes at, 78–79, 118
Kensal, James, 159, 160
Keppel, Augustus, 137, 180
Kerr, James, 25–26, 27, 37–38
King, Boston, 106–7, 108–10, 112, 150, 151, 154, 321, 395
    Clarkson visited in England by, 384–85

in Nova Scotia, 236, 251–53, 254, 282
Sierra Leone settlement and, 308,
314–15, 328, 357, 361, 384
King, Robert, 163–64
King, Violet, 150, 154, 236, 251–52, 253,
314–15, 321, 328
Kingston, March, 124
Kirkpatrick (Annis's master), 165–66
Kite, Sir Robert, 27, 40
Kizell, John, 303, 321–22, 361, 395, 404
Knowles, Captain, 45, 47, 54
Kulikoff, Allan, 73–74

L'Abondance, 153, 154–56, 236, 435n.27
Ladd, Nathaniel, 303
Lafayette, Marquis de, 118, 262–63, 264,
265
Lagree, Liberty (formerly James), 5
Lagree, Venus, 154
Laird, Captain, 27–28
Lapwing, 217, 218, 265–66, 267, 298, 299,
331, 340
Laurens, Henry, 56, 60, 62, 64, 65, 85, 101,
102, 103, 136–38, 228
Laurens, John, 56, 62, 99, 100–102, 103,
104, 111, 122–23, 136, 137, 138
Lavendar family (Port l'Hébert), 285,
286
Lawrence, Betsey, 155
Lee, Arthur, 60–61
Lee, Sir John, 168, 169
Lee, Richard Henry, 83, 85, 119
Lee, Susannah. See Clarkson, Susannah
Lee, William, 119
Leile, George, 96, 98
Lemmon, John, 192, 196
"Leo Africanus," 214
Leonard, Joseph, 353, 360, 361
Leslie, Alexander, 117–18, 124, 132–33,
134, 179, 433n.52
Leslie, Mingo, 124, 238
Leslie, Samuel, 80
Lewis, Thomas, 37, 39–43, 45, 46, 47, 165,
168
Lexington, skirmish at, 62, 65, 67
Liaster, James, 384
Liberator, 414
Liberia, 410–11

"Liberty," rhetoric of, 6, 8, 11–16, 17, 67,
412
Lincoln, Benjamin, 100, 103
Lindsay, Dido Elizabeth Belle, 33–34, 169
Lindsay, John, 33–34
Lippincott (Huddy's killer), 141, 143
Lisle, David, 24, 25–26, 28, 37–38
Little Joggin, Nova Scotia, 223–24, 227
Livingston, William, 111–12, 115, 141
Lloyd, John, 173
London:
abolitionists in. See Abolitionists,
abolition–in England; Sharp,
Granville
blacks living in, 23–24, 25, 176–87,
190–200, 426n.3; indigence among,
182–85, 194–95; petitions for
compensation of, 178–82; resettled in
Africa, 185–200 (see also Sierra Leone)
London, Black, 10
Long, Edward, 172, 188
Long Island, battle of (1776), 113
Louis XVI, King of France, 143, 264, 363
Louisiana Territory, 402
Loyal, Anthony and Hagar, 116
Loyal Refugee Volunteers, 115
Luce, William, 116
Lucretia, 310, 312–20, 323, 359
Ludlam, Thomas, 389–95, 396
Lutwyche, Captain, 127, 144, 147
Lyttelton, William, 92

Macaulay, Alexander, 392
Macaulay, Selina (née Mills), 365, 366
Macaulay, Thomas, 366, 413
Macaulay, Zachary, 365–67, 374, 379–81,
385, 387–89, 394, 395, 396, 403, 405
Clarkson criticized by, 366–67, 372
French attack and, 380–81, 382–83
Macaulay & Babington, 410
Macbean, Mr (lawyer), 27
MacCarthy, Charles, 410
Macnamara, Matthias, 167
MacNeill, Daniel, 246–47, 249
Madison, James, 9, 66, 71, 119, 148, 405,
407
Maitland, James, 98
Malaria, 187, 206, 328

Malony, John, 41, 43

Manchester Constitutional Society, 371

Mansfield, James, 47, 50–51

Mansfield, William Murray, 1st Earl of, 18, 28, 32–34, 47, 70, 137, 165
  Lewis case and, 42–44
  Somerset case and, 44–46, 48, 49–50, 52–55, 57, 151, 169, 222, 245, 380, 389, 427n.16
  Zong case and, 167, 168, 169

Marian, Abraham, 9

Marie Antoinette, Queen of France, 143, 264, 265

Marion, Francis, 9, 124

Maroons, 17, 390–91, 392, 393, 394, 396, 411

Marrant, John, 104–5, 282

Marsh, George, 193

Marsterns, John, 404

Marston, Benjamin, 231–32, 233–36, 237, 238–39

Martin, George, 10, 84, 220

Martin, Josiah, 65, 66

Martin, Phoebe, 246

Martin family (Port l'Hébert), 286

Mary, 310, 314

Mason, George, 71, 119

Massachusetts, 219
  blacks' petitions to colonial governors of, 15–16
  persistence of race prejudice in, 403–4, 415–16
  slavery abolished in, 189, 222

Mathews, John, 126, 132–33, 135

Matthews, John, 273

May, Captain, 323

Mayo, Rev Herbert, 183, 184

McGillivray's Plantation, 100

McGregor, Charity, 361

McKenzie, John, 100

McNutt, Alexander, 236–37

Meade, Captain, 81

Mercantilism, 261–62

Mercury, 75, 78

Merselis, Ahasuerus, 116

Middleton, Arthur, 86, 136, 321

Middleton, Sir Charles, 169–70, 171, 172, 174, 175–76, 189, 199, 200, 261, 401

Middleton, Lady, 170, 172, 174, 175–76

Miles, Thomas, 309

Miller, George, 180–81

Miller, John, 95–96

Millidge, Thomas, 227

Milligan, Jane and Maria, 155

Mirabeau, Vicomte de, 262, 263, 265

Moncrief, James, 98, 106, 125, 248

Monmouth County Patriots, 115

Montagu, Lord, 25

Montefiore, Joshua, 354

Moody, Nancy, 154

Moore, Andrew, 386, 395

Moore, Daniel, Tina, and Elizabeth, 155

More, Hannah, 261

Morgan, John, 111

Morgann, Maurice, 144

Morning Chronicle and London Advertiser, 54, 167

Morning Star, 310, 322, 327

Morris, Charles, 227

Morris, Jacob, 149

Mosely, Patty, 73

Muhlenberg, Henry Melchior, 8

Murphy, Decimus, 4

Murray, John. *See* Dunmore, John Murray, 4th Earl of

Murray, Lady Elizabeth, 34

Myro, 212–13, 217

Naimbana (Temne chief), 202, 203–4, 211, 216–17, 267, 299, 331, 333, 344, 346, 350, 354, 360, 363, 367, 438n.1

Napier, Lieutenant, 81

Napoleon Bonaparte, Emperor of the French, 401, 402, 403, 405, 409

Narrative (Douglass), 415, 416

Narrative (Equiano), 161

Nash, Gary, 8, 9

Natchez people, 95–96

Nautilus, 195, 198, 203–4, 212

Negro Act, 63

Nelson, Horatio, 165

Nelson, Thomas, 119

Nepean, Evan, 275, 278

New Brunswick, 10, 185, 192, 193, 228, 235, 242, 253–54
  emigration to Sierra Leone from, 280–81, 294, 303, 338

Newcastle, Duke of, 32
New Hampshire, 7
New Jersey:
   abolitionist sentiments in, 111–12
   black loyalist soldiers and partisans in, 7, 111, 113–16, 177
   plans for slave uprising in, 5
Newport, Rhode Island, 101, 113
Newton, John, 174–75, 209, 385
Newton, Lydia, 154
New York, 76, 118, 177–78
   black loyalist soldiers and partisans in, 111, 113, 114–16, 177
   efforts to recapture escaped slaves in, 149–50
   embarkation of blacks from, 152–56, 222–23
   evacuation of British troops and white loyalists from, 145, 146, 222–23
   evaluation of blacks' claims to freedom in, 139, 151–52
   as haven for escaped slaves, 17, 109–11, 112–13, 149–50
   resistance to loyalist defeat in, 124, 138
   response to British capitulation in, 129, 131, 132
Nibbs, George, 133–34
Nicol, George, 395
Nordenskjold, Augustus, 344–45
Norfolk, skirmishes at, 78–82
North, Lord Frederick, 17, 48–49, 56, 65, 92, 93, 123, 125, 129, 227, 228
North Carolina, 7–8, 67–68, 76, 78, 79, 82–84, 118, 119, 120, 124, 150
Nova Scotia, 3–5, 9, 10, 11, 179, 180, 181, 185, 188, 191, 221–53, 352
   apportioning of land in, 221, 225–26, 227, 228, 234–35, 237, 239, 250, 270, 281, 288
   black churches in, 11, 249–50, 282, 304–5
   blacks' lawsuits against whites in, 246–49, 301–2
   blacks reduced to servitude in, 4, 221, 225, 226, 243–48, 281, 283, 286, 292, 300–302
   blacks serving in War of 1812 sent to, 406

   chosen as asylum for displaced loyalists, 228–29
   emigration to Sierra Leone from, 219–20, 255, 265, 268, 269–70, 274–327; Clarkson's recruitment mission and, 270, 274–96, 300–303, 347, 348, 355; departure of fleet, 310–12; preparations for voyage, 293, 295–96, 303–10; seeds brought along in, 353–54
   evacuation of black loyalists to, 5, 146, 152–61, 222–23, 435n.27
   free provisions for settlers in, 224–25, 227, 238, 243
   George's ministry in, 239–43, 282
   King's experiences in, 236, 251–53
   Maroons in, 391
   Peters's experiences in, 221–28, 235, 244, 278
   schools expressly for free black children in, 11, 282
   slavery in, 6, 244–49, 250, 280, 291–92
   white loyalists in, 225–26, 230–35, 237, 238–39, 240, 244–49, 277, 278–81, 283, 286–87, 327
   see also specific towns

Ogé, Vincent, 263
O'Hara, General Charles, 122
On the Ill Treatment of the People of Colour in the United States, 414
Ordington, Captain, 55
Oswald, Richard, 137–38
Otis, James, 12
Otter, 75, 78

Pa Bongee (Temne chief), 204–5
Pa Boson (Temne chief), 217, 267
Pa Demba, 382
Page, John, 76
Palmer, Brother, 96, 97
Paris peace conference (1815), 409
Parker, Peter, 88
Parliament, 44, 47, 129, 218, 389, 405, 420
   George III's address on colonies' rebellion to, 90–91
   reform of, 413
   Sierra Leone and, 268–69, 396

Parliament *(cont.)*
    slavery issue and, 6, 200, 209, 216,
        259–62, 265, 269, 396, 401–3, 413
Parr, Sir John, 226–27, 228, 231, 232, 235,
    239, 240, 244, 253, 270
    Sierra Leone plan and, 278–79, 288, 290,
        293–94, 320
Pascal, Michael, 161–62
Paterson, James, 108, 240, 348
Patrick, Frank, 393–95
Patrick, William, 72
Patriot, The, 9
Peckard, Peter, 173
Pennsylvania, 403–4
    slavery abolished in, 222
Pennsylvania Society for Promoting the
    Abolition of Slavery, 189
Pepys, Richard, 323, 336, 349–50, 353, 357,
    360, 364, 365, 367–68, 373
Perkins, Cato, 287, 357, 391
    petition of grievances taken to London
        by, 375–79
Perkins, Simeon, 239
Perseverance, 127, 139, 147, 433n.1
Perth, Caesar, 236, 287
Perth, Mary, 72, 287, 372, 374, 381, 382
Peters, Clairy, 68, 155
Peters, Frank, 322
Peters, George, 184
Peters, Hector, 282, 361, 395, 411
Peters, Peter, 317, 323
Peters, Sally, 68, 155, 222
Peters, Sarah, 348–49
Peters, Thomas, 10, 68–69, 83–84, 155, 368
    Clarkson's difficulties with, 306, 334–38,
        345, 346, 348
    death of, 348–49
    as emigrant in Nova Scotia, 221–28, 235,
        244, 278
    in New Brunswick, 228, 253–54
    planning for Sierra Leone settlement
        and, 219–20, 255, 265, 269–70, 274,
        276, 277–78, 294–95, 306, 308, 335
    in Sierra Leone, 334–38, 342–48
    trial of, 342–43
    turned politician, 254–55
Philadelphia Society, 91
"Philanthropos," 293

Philips, Lieutenant, 154
Philipsburgh Proclamation, 100, 104, 105,
    133, 134–35, 139, 150, 151, 177, 226,
    245, 433n.52
Phillips, James, 175
Phillips, William, 118
Pigot (lawyer), 168
Pinckney, Izabella, 123
Pioneers. *See* Black Pioneers and Guides
Pirate's Bay, Sierra Leone, 383
Pitt, John, 2nd Earl of, 370
Pitt, William, the Younger, 176, 184, 209,
    213, 218, 259, 260–61, 274, 370, 371, 401
Plantation Laws, 38
Plymley, Reverend and Katherine, 275
Plymouth Committee for Abolition, 209
Pomona, 215–17
Poor Law, 182–83
Porteus, Beilby, Bishop of Chester and
    London, 175
Portland, Duke of, 169
Port l'Hébert, Nova Scotia, 284–86
Port Roseway, Nova Scotia, 231–32, 237
Posey, Thomas, 87
Postell, Elisha, 247
Postell, Mary, 247–49
Press gangs, 273–74
Preston, Nova Scotia, 3–5, 11, 235, 242,
    311, 391, 406, 423n.1
    Clarkson's recruitment mission in, 279,
        281–83, 284, 293, 294
Prevost, Augustine, 98, 100
Prince, Mary, 412–13
Prince, Newton, 10
Privy Council, 260, 262, 297
Proof, Simon, 11, 341
Prosser, Gabriel, 402
Provey, Anne, 197
Province of Freedom. *See* Sierra Leone
Public Advertiser, 13, 39, 199, 200
Pulaski, Casimir, 99
Purple Heart, 144
Putnam, James, 281

Quakers, 89, 111, 163, 184, 208, 269, 280,
    409
    Cuffe story and, 403–4, 405, 407
    London Committee of, 173, 176

Quarles, Benjamin, 8
Quebec, battle of (1759), 128
Quit rents, 250, 287, 288, 297, 383, 386, 389, 390, 396, 411

Race prejudice, 403–4, 415–21
Ramsay, Rev James, 170–72, 173, 174, 175–76, 189, 200, 209, 261
Ramsay, Rebecca (née Akers), 170, 171
Ramsey, Cato, 150–51, 435n.24
Ramsey, David, 8, 103
Ramsey, John, 150
Raritan County, plans for slave uprising in, 5
Rawdon, Lord Francis, 246
Rebecca, 403
Redman, Captain, 318
Reed, Moses, 246
Refugee Cowboys, 114, 138, 146
Reid, James, 211–12, 217–18
Representation (Sharp), 37–38, 39, 42, 45, 49
Revolutionary War, 59–156, 177–78, 272, 273, 404
    black loyalist soldiers and partisans in, 3–11, 72–87 (*see also* Black Pioneers and Guides; Dunmore, John Murray, 4th Earl of); certificates issued to, 4, 132, 139, 150, 151, 152, 155; in Georgia, 69–70, 84, 85, 93–94, 97–100, 123, 125–26, 179; hearings on claims to freedom of, in New York, 139, 151–52; hearings on compensation of, in London, 178–82; music of, 113; names changed by, 4–5; in New York and New Jersey, 7, 111, 113–16, 177; promises made to, 4, 7, 8, 75–76 (*see also* Phillipsburg Proclamation); in Rhode Island, 101, 113, 122; smallpox among, 86–87, 105, 107–8, 112, 117–18, 119, 122; in South Carolina, 69–70, 85, 123–26; in Virginia, 67, 72–83, 86–87, 111, 117–20, 122–23, 152, 179, 182
    blacks fighting with Patriots in, 6–7, 11, 76, 83, 100–104, 122, 177
    British incitement of slave and Indian insurrections in, 17–18, 59–70, 84–85
    end of, 120–56; concession of American independence and, 127–32;

continuation of hostilities after, 123–26, 129, 131, 138, 140; embarkation of blacks after, 152–56; evacuation of British troops and loyalists after, 130, 133–35, 145, 146, 147, 153, 232–33; fate of escaped slaves after, 132–35, 136–39, 145–52; prisoner exchange after, 130, 132, 140–44; restitution of confiscated property after, 127, 130, 131, 132, 133, 134, 136, 233; treaty negotiations and, 130, 135–38; Yorktown defeat and, 7, 121–23, 125
    slaves' flight from plantations in, 8–9, 76–77; in Georgia, 76, 94, 97–98, 105; in South Carolina, 8, 76, 105, 110, 119, 120, 135; in Virginia, 8, 70, 72–74, 119–20
    southerners' embrace of Patriot cause in, 17, 67–68
Reynolds, Sir Joshua, 22, 33, 46
Rhode Island, 189, 219
    battle of (1778), 7, 101
    black loyalist soldiers and partisans in, 101, 111, 113, 122
    slavery abolished in, 222
Richardson, Ellen, 421
Richmond, Bill, 112
Ricketts, William, 195
Rights of the British Colonists, The (Otis), 12
Robbins, Joseph, 247
Roberts, Simon, 155
Robinson, Captain, 341
Robinson, James, 390, 391, 393, 394
Rockingham, Marquis of, 125, 129, 137, 140
Rodney, Admiral, 129, 171
Rose, George, 189, 198
Roussell, Hagar, 123
Rowley family, 271, 273
Royal African Company, 12, 218, 266
Royal Navy, 129, 148, 170, 171, 178, 189, 193, 250, 404
    Clarkson's career in, 271–74, 309, 370–71, 410
    slave trade and, 6, 169, 176, 187, 396, 403, 410

Runaways, 8–9, 11, 17, 66, 69, 91
  encamped on islands off southern coast,
    84–85
  flight of, to serve with Dunmore, 72–74,
    76–78
  Freetown as haven for, 380
  Howe's armada and, 91
  in London, 25, 37, 38, 45, 55
  New York as haven for, 17, 109–11,
    112–13, 149–50
  of Patriots vs. loyalists, 70, 77
  see also Revolutionary War–slaves' flight
    from plantations in
Rush, Benjamin, 16, 89, 409, 425n.24
Rushworth, John, 31
Russell, John, 115
Rutledge, Edward, 7, 9, 67–68, 85, 86, 103,
  104
Rutledge, John, 9
Rutledge, Pompey and Flora, 86

St Bartholomew's parish, slave rebellion
  in, 69
St Domingue, 99, 122
  slave insurrection in, 263, 264–65,
    371–72, 402
St George's Bay Company, 217–19, 265,
  268
St Kitts, Ramsay's ministry on, 170–71
St Phillips Castle, 178
St Vincent, slave insurrection in, 16, 17
Samson (black pilot), 93
Sancho, Ignatius, 25
Sandwich, HMS, 273–74
Sarter, Caesar, 15
Savage, Henry, 215–16, 217, 331
Savage's Plantation, 97
Savannah, 108, 123, 134
  British capture of (1778), 93–94
  loyalists in, after war, 132, 133
  siege of (1779), 98–100, 102, 103, 105,
    109, 179
Scarborough, 84
Schenkel, Mr (baker), 195, 197, 206
Scorpion, 60–61, 85, 104
Scott, John Morin, 145, 146
Sea Sermons, 171
Seven Years' War (1756–63), 61

Shakespeare, William, 112
Shanley versus Harvey, 31
Sharp, Archdeacon Thomas, 29
Sharp, Eliza (later Mrs Prowse), 22–23,
  36, 407
Sharp, Granville, 12, 13, 19, 22–57, 101,
  175–76, 184, 207–15, 273, 357, 403,
  407–9, 410, 425n.24
  abolitionist campaign and, 208–10, 215,
    260
  Annis case and, 166
  "Black Prince" and, 299
  education and early career of, 29–30
  Equiano and, 161, 164, 165, 166
  family background of, 22, 44
  family musical entertainments and,
    22–23, 35–36, 48, 92–93, 409
  Frankpledge democracy and, 30–31,
    189–90, 210, 211, 219, 268, 352, 374,
    390, 395
  free blacks turned slavers and, 207–8
  legal status of slaves in England
    researched by, 30–34, 37–38
  Lewis case and, 37, 39–43
  memorial to, 421–22
  Ordnance Office left by, 89–90, 92
  plight of blacks sent to Nova Scotia and,
    221–22, 244, 255
  Representation by, 37–38, 39, 42, 45, 49
  Revolutionary War and, 57, 89–91,
    92–93, 166
  Sierra Leone settlement and, 189–90,
    194, 195, 196–97, 200, 203, 207–8,
    210–15, 217–20, 255, 266, 268–69, 270,
    277, 296, 297, 299, 309, 324–25, 335,
    352, 374, 389, 390
  Somerset case and, 44–49, 54–55, 57, 166
  Strong case and, 24–29, 37–38
  Zong drownings and, 161, 166, 167–69,
    189
Sharp, James, 22, 27, 28, 30, 36, 49, 90, 203,
  218, 219, 407
Sharp, John (escaped slave), 154
Sharp, John (Granville's brother), 35, 90
Sharp, William, 22, 23, 24, 36, 90, 92, 212,
  407, 408
Shaw, William, 245
Shawnee, 71

Shelburne, Lord, 129, 130, 137, 140, 232–33
Shelburne, Nova Scotia, 11, 223, 232–39, 243–44, 249, 411
  blacks' lawsuits against whites in, 246–49
  Clarkson's recruitment mission in, 284, 286–87, 290–92, 293–94, 300–303, 304
  complaints about first wave of black emigrants in, 235–36
  creation of separate township near, 236–38 (See also Birchtown, Nova Scotia)
  economic downturn in, 244, 250
  George's experiences in, 240–42, 243
  riot against blacks in, 238–39
Shepherd, Elisha, 111
Shepherd, Mr and Mrs Thomas, 286
Sherbro people, 204, 268, 303, 321–22
Shrewsbury, HMS, 180
Sierra Leone, 11, 72, 185–220, 265–70, 273, 274–397, 411–12, 423n.1
  abolitionists' views on idea for, 188–90
  agreements with local chiefs for land in, 201–2, 203–5, 213, 214–15, 219, 267, 332, 390
  annual carnival in, 411
  T. Clarkson's vision for, 266, 268, 269, 296, 324–25
  Cuffe's trading venture in, 403–7, 410
  under direct protection of Crown, 396
  emigration from America to, 219, 404, 406, 410
  emigration from Nova Scotia and New Brunswick to, 219–20, 255, 265, 268, 269–70, 274–327, 280–81
  expansion plans for colony of, 332
  first settlement in (Granville Town), 185–208, 210–20; demise of, 206–7, 210–12, 214–17, 278–79; embarkation for, 194–98; Instruments of Liberty for migrants to, 192, 193; *Pomona* mission and, 215–16; recruitment of emigrants for, 190–93; relief supplies and new settlers sent to, 212–14, 217, 218–19; ships delayed at Plymouth en route to, 198–200; survivors of, 266–68, 298, 351–52; white artisans and professionals sent to, 195, 199,

206–7; white women aboard ship to, 195–98, 199, 267
  free blacks turned slavers in, 207–8, 351–52
  geography of, 203
  governance of, 11, 190, 211, 268, 296, 297, 298, 323, 325–26, 333–39, 342, 345–48, 351–53, 374–75, 376, 378, 380, 388–89, 390, 391–92, 395
  government support for settlement scheme in, 188, 437n.36
  health hazards and medical care in, 187, 206, 328–30, 350–51, 368
  Liberated Africans in, 396, 411
  Liberia compared to, 410–11
  London blacks' views on plan for, 190–93
  Pirates' Bay settlement in, 383
  plight of indigent blacks in London and, 182–85
  proposed as site for black colony, 185–88
  rainy season in, 194, 205–6, 304, 329, 332–33, 340, 342, 344–45, 350
  return of abductees from, 318–19, 321–22
  St George's Bay Company and, 217–19, 265, 268
  second settlement in (Freetown), 265–70, 274–397; accommodations in, 325, 329, 340, 345, 353; armed militia in, 386–87; blacks reduced to debt peonage in, 367, 375; Canvas Room in, 321, 334; certificates of approbation for migrants to, 281; J. Clarkson appointed "superintendent" of, 323–25, 327; J. Clarkson's departure from, 354–62, 363, 367; J. Clarkson's governorship of, 351, 370, 372; company store in, 367, 375, 382–83, 386; conjugal arrangements in, 387–88; culture and sensibility of "Nova Scotians" in, 385–87; Dawes's governorship of, 356–58, 364–65, 366–69, 372; DuBoises' departure from, 373; elections in, 374–75, 388, 390; escaped slaves in, 380; flogging of recalcitrant sailors in, 340–42;

Sierra Leone *(cont.)*
   fort construction in, 364, 375, 381;
      French attack on, 380–83, 386;
      Granville Town survivors in, 351–52;
      grievances among blacks in, 333–39,
      345–48, 352–53, 357, 367–69, 372,
      373, 375–80, 383–84, 391; Harmony
      Hall in, 349; land allotments in, 277,
      311, 333, 352–53, 353, 355, 358, 367,
      368, 373, 375, 376, 383; legal system
      and trials in, 342–43, 351–52, 388–89,
      390, 394, 395; local chiefs' relations
      with, 330–32, 333, 349, 354–55, 363;
      Ludlam's governorship of, 389–95;
      Macaulay's governorship of, 365,
      374, 379–83, 385, 387–89; militancy
      among settlers in, 377–80, 386–97;
      naming of, 281; new arrivals in, 344,
      349; Nova Scotians' arrival in, 321–22;
      passage from Nova Scotia to, 313–20,
      322–23; preparations for voyage from
      Nova Scotia to, 293, 295–96, 303–10;
      produce grown in, 353–54, 360–61,
      386, 395; recruitment of emigrants
      for, 270, 274–96, 300–303, 347, 348,
      355, 378, 379; revolt in (1800), 390–97;
      setting aside of J. Clarkson's promises
      for, 366–69, 372, 373; taxation in, 287,
      288, 297, 334, 339, 352, 383, 386, 389,
      390, 396, 411; white population of,
      322, 325–27, 329, 333, 335, 339, 340–42,
      344, 349–50, 388, 390
   Sharp's Frankpledge ideal and, 189–90,
      210, 211, 219, 268, 352, 374, 390, 395
   slave trade in, 187–88, 191, 193, 194, 202,
      204, 206, 207–8, 212, 213, 214–16, 277,
      287, 331, 351–52, 380
   West Indian Maroons in, 390–91, 392,
      393, 394, 411396
Sierra Leone, 310, 314, 327
Sierra Leone Company, 218, 283, 293, 294,
      296–99, 320, 323, 332, 336, 355, 356,
      373, 384
   changes in Clarkson's instructions from,
      296–97
   Clarkson's disagreements with, 324–27,
      342, 344, 351, 352–53, 369–70, 371–72
   demise of, 396, 403

   ending of slave trade and, 266, 268, 396
   new royal charter of (1800), 390, 394,
      395
   original guarantees of, 277
   petition of grievances sent to, 375–79
   setting aside of Clarkson's promises
      and, 367, 368, 369
   settlers' petition to, requesting
      Clarkson's return, 361–62
   settlers' revolts against, 377–79, 390–96
   Sharp's reservations about, 268–69
   storehouse of, 367, 375, 382–83, 386
   supply ships sent by, 320, 322, 325, 351
   waterfront lots commandeered by,
      352–53, 369, 375
Sierra Leone Gazette, 411
Sinclair, Molly, 246
Skinner, Stephen, 236, 286, 290–92, 311
Slave bounties, 11, 104
Slave insurrections, 5, 16–18, 102, 105
   British incitement of, 17–18, 59–70,
      84–85
   Jeremiah case and, 59–65
   in St Bartholomew's parish, 69
   southerners' embrace of Patriot cause
      and, 17, 67–68
   in Surinam, 16–17, 77
   trials for, under Negro Act, 63
   in West Indies, 16, 17, 92, 263, 264–65,
      371–72, 390–91, 402, 412
   in Wilmington, 68–69
Slave trade, 101, 120, 133–34, 138, 246,
      344, 412
   American, after passage of Abolition
      Act, 403, 410
   deaths during Atlantic crossing in,
      157–58, 176, 307, 435n.3. See also Zong
      drownings
   Dolben Bill and, 200, 209, 215
   of France, 261–62, 264, 265, 401, 403
   Liberated Africans taken from, settled
      in Sierra Leone, 396, 411
   opposition to. See Abolitionists, abolition
   print showing interior views of ship in,
      209, 263, 295
   in Sierra Leone, 187–88, 191, 193, 194,
      202, 204, 206, 207–8, 212, 213, 214–16,
      277, 331, 351–52, 380

Small, Sophia, 381, 386, 395
Smallpox, 86–87, 105, 107–8, 112, 117–18, 119, 122, 250, 304
Smeathman, Henry, 185–88, 190, 192–93, 203, 211, 266
Smith, Abraham, 392
Smith, Adam, 173, 186, 218
Smith, Caesar, 4, 302
Smith, Francis, 69
Smith, George, 69
Smith, Hugh, 195
Smith, Reverend, 63
Smith, Sukey, 73
Smith, Thomas, 116
Smith, William, 127, 130–31, 144, 145, 154, 259
Smithers, Anthony, 180–81
Smock, Barnes, 115
Snow, 39–40
Snowball, Mary, 155
Snowball, Nathaniel, 236, 379–80, 383
Société des Amis des Noirs, 262
Society for the Promotion of Permanent and Universal Peace, 409–10
Society for the Propagation of the Gospel, 227, 236
Society of the Bill of Rights, 47
Society of West India Planters and Merchants, 172
Somerset, 310, 314, 318
Somerset, James, 18, 44–55, 166, 168, 169
  arguments on behalf of, 49–52
  counsel in trial of, 46–48
  facts of case and, 44–45
  judgement in case of, 53–55, 57, 151, 222, 245, 380, 389, 427n.16
South Carolina, 7–8, 100–109, 118, 122–23, 138, 163, 402
  black loyalist soldiers and partisans in, 69–70, 85, 123–26
  black soldiers proposed for Patriot side in, 102–4
  embrace of Patriot cause in, 67–68
  Provincial Congress of, 60, 62, 63
  resistance to loyalist defeat in, 123–26
  slave bounties as recruitment incentive in, 11, 104
  slave rebellions in (1810s), 410

  slaves' flight from plantations in, 8, 76, 105, 110, 119, 120, 135
  see also Charleston
South Carolina Rangers, 85
Spain, 18, 273
Sperling, Mr (surveyor), 237
Squire, Matthew, 78
Stamp Tax (1766), 11, 163
Stapylton, Robert, 40–43
Steele, Mary, 222
Steele, Murphy, 120–21, 155, 222, 226–27
Steele, Thomas, 188–89, 198
Stephens, Moses, 180–81
Stevens, Daniel, 123, 124
Stewart, Allen, 223, 254
Stewart, Charles, 44–45, 47, 48, 54, 57
Stewart, John. *See* Cugoano, Ottobah
Stiff, Thomas, 178
Strange, Thomas, 245, 280, 311301
Strong, Jonathan, 24–29, 37–38, 45, 165, 407
Stuart, Charles, 410–11
Stubbs, Robert, 160
Sullivan's Island, 85, 88
Sumter, Thomas, 104
Surinam, slave insurrection in, 16–17, 77
Swedenborgians, 277

Talbot, Charles Talbot, 1st Baron, 28, 31, 32, 38, 54
Tamar, 62, 63, 65
Tarleton, Banastre, 114, 120, 261
Taxation, 65, 128, 288
  in Sierra Leone, 190, 287, 288, 297, 334, 339, 352, 383, 386, 389, 390, 396, 411
  see also Quit rents
Taylor, Captain, 212–13
Taylor, Charles, 283–86, 287, 303–4, 314, 315, 316, 318, 344
Taylor, Mr and Mrs (Baptist missionaries), 241
Taylor, William, 303
Tea duty, 11–12, 52
Temne people, 138, 187, 190, 267, 268, 330–32, 333, 354, 355, 382
  agreements with, for land for Sierra Leone settlements, 201–2, 203–5, 213, 214–15, 219, 267, 332, 383, 390

Temne people *(cont.)*
    "Black Prince" and, 299–300
    Freetown rebels and, 393, 396
    Pomona mission and, 216–17
Thomas, John, 41
Thomas, Juno, 154
Thomas, Phillis, 132
Thomas, Thomas, 327
Thompson, George, 414
Thompson, Jane, 154
Thompson, Thomas Boulden, 195, 198,
    199, 201–2, 204–5, 206, 212, 267
Thomson, Elizabeth and Betty, 154
Thomson, Grace, 155
Thornton, Henry, 218, 269, 295, 296, 299,
    312, 324, 332, 335, 342, 361, 366, 389,
    396, 403
    petition of grievances and, 369, 375–77
    quit rents and, 297, 383
    termination of Clarkson's governorship
        and, 370, 371, 372
Thornton, Samuel, 218
Tilley, John, 202, 214–15, 216
Titus. *See* Tye, Colonel
Tom, King (Temne chief), 201–2, 204–5,
    212, 213, 390, 393, 396, 404
Tomkin, Samuel and Mary, 73
Tomkins, Lydia, 116
Tom's River, skirmishes at, 115–16
Traveller, 404–6
Treasury, British, 186, 188–89, 193, 198,
    199, 200
Treaty of Paris (1786), 125, 130, 131,
    135–38, 146, 148, 151
Trespass Act, 146
Trinity Church, New York, 112
Trumbull, Jonathan, 145
Trusty, 345
Tybee Island, 85, 93
Tye, Colonel, 111, 114, 115–16, 140, 155,
    236, 432n.44
Typhus, 86, 105, 112

Union, 92–93, 426n.1

Van Sayl, Cathern, 116, 154, 236
Van Sayl, Cornelius, 154
Vassa, Gustevus. *See* Equiano, Olaudah

Venus, 305, 310, 315, 316
Vergennes, Charles Gravier, Count, 142–44
Vermont, 129, 146
    slavery abolished in, 101, 222
Vernon, 194, 196, 198
Vestal, HMS, 137
Villeinage, 31, 51
Virginia, 9, 13, 66–67, 70–83, 116–23, 124,
    129
    black loyalist soldiers and partisans in,
        67, 72–83, 86–87, 111, 117–20, 122–23,
        152, 179, 182. *See also* Dunmore, John
        Murray, 4th Earl of
    Cornwallis's defeat in, 121–23
    embrace of Patriot cause in, 67–68,
        70–71
    restoration of escaped slaves to owners
        in, 123, 149, 150
    restrictions on free blacks in, 402
    shirtmen militia in, 75, 78–79, 87
    slave bounties as recruitment incentive
        in, 104
    slave rebellion in (1800), 402
    slaves' flight from plantations in, 8, 70,
        72–74, 119–20
Virginia Convention, 77
Virginia Gazette, 18, 66, 72
Volunteers of Ireland, 246

Wadstrom, Carl Bernhard, 266, 344
Wainer, Thomas, 404
Wakerell, Mr (accountant), 323
Walker, Chloe, Samuel, and Lydia, 73
Walker, David, 6, 412
Walker, Henry, 154
Walker, James, 8
Walker, Thomas, 371
Wallace, Michael, 230, 235, 246, 278, 304,
    305, 311
Wallis, Margaret and Judith, 154
Wansey, Nathaniel, 380, 391, 393
War of 1812, 148, 406–7
Washington, George, 8, 65–66, 67, 83, 101,
    104, 113, 120–21, 122, 129, 136, 137,
    177, 394
    Asgill affair and, 140–44, 145
    Carleton's dealings with, 127, 130,
        138–41, 144–49

fate of escaped slaves and, 138, 145–49, 152

flight of slaves from property of, 9, 68, 70, 76

service of blacks in Continental army and, 7, 101, 102

Washington, Henry, 9, 68, 76, 236, 287, 396

Washington, Lund, 8

Watkins, Thomas, 180–81

Wayne, Anthony, 116

Wearing, Scipio and Diana, 248–49

Weaver, Richard, 192, 211–12

Wedgwood, Josiah, 209

Weedon, George, 123

Weedon, Judy, 154

Welsh, Justice, 39–40

Wesley, John, 249

West, Benjamin, 181–82

Westcoat, Mary, 247

West India Association, 188

West Indies, 231, 244, 255

    boycott of sugar from, 265, 275, 296

    free blacks' emigration to, 191, 211, 270, 288

    Maroons from, in Sierra Leone, 390–91, 392, 393, 394, 396, 411

    slave insurrections in, 16, 17, 92, 263, 264–65, 371–72, 390–91, 402, 412

    slavery in, 6, 16, 25, 221, 249, 272–73, 407, 412

    slaves taken to, at end of Revolutionary War, 132, 133–34

    see also specific islands

Whipple, William, 103

Whitbread, Samuel, 213, 218

Whitecuffe, Benjamin, 176–79, 196

Whitecuffe, Sarah, 178, 196, 206

Whitefield, George, 104

Whiteford, Lucy, 361

Whitten, Hannah, 154, 155

Wickham, Samuel, 306, 312, 314, 316, 317

Wilberforce, William, 189, 220, 269, 273, 274–75, 370–71, 405

    in abolitionist campaign, 174–76, 208, 259, 260, 261, 265, 273, 401, 402, 412

    Clarkson's falling out with, 370–71, 413

    death of, 413

honorary French citizenship awarded to, 371

Sierra Leone settlement and, 218, 274–75, 276, 277, 295–96, 324, 335, 351, 369, 390

Wilkes, John, 44, 47, 92

Wilkinson, Charles and Sarah, 309

Wilkinson, Miles, 73

Wilkinson, Moses, 73, 155–56, 242, 287, 289, 304–5, 321, 328, 347, 355, 383–84

Willes, Justice, 53, 54

William IV, King of England (formerly Prince William Henry), 250, 413

William, HMS, 7, 17, 75

William, Prince (black petitioner), 180–81

Williams, Jonathan, 180–81

Willis, Thomas, 149

Willoughby, John, 72

Wilmington, aborted slave rising in, 68–69

Wilmot, Sir John Eardley, 180, 181

Wilson, Captain, 340, 350, 352

Wilson, Ellen Gibson, 8

Windsor, Nova Scotia, 294

Winslow, Cato, 72

Winterbottom, Thomas, 328, 349

Wolfe, James, 128, 228

Woman suffrage, 374, 388

Wood, Lieutenant, 216

Woodford, Colonel, 80

Woods, Joseph, 173, 208

World Anti–Slavery Convention (1840), 414

Wright, Sir James, 66, 84

Wright, Joseph, 108

Wyvill, Christopher, 44

Yamacouba (Bullom queen), 204–5, 331, 354

York, 368

York, Duskey, Betsey, and Sally, 155

Yorke, Lord Chancellor, 28, 31, 32, 38, 54

Yorktown, battle of, 7, 121–23, 125, 182

Young, Dr, 195

Young, Sir George, 202

Zizer, Ansel, 379–80, 391

Zoffany, Johan, 34, 35–36

Zong drownings, 158–61, 166, 167–69, 171, 175, 189, 273

Grateful acknowledgement is made for permission to reproduce the illustrations:

Page
iv–v   Courtesy of the New-York Historical Socierty #77567T
1   Hulton Archive/Getty Images
19   National Portrait Gallery, London
257   Private Collection/Photograph by John Parker
399   © Bettmann/Corbis

PHOTO INSERT
1   National Portrait Gallery, London
2–3   By courtesy of the National Portrait Gallery, London and the Lloyd-
               Baker Trustees
4 (TOP)   By kind permission of the Earl of Mansfield, Scone Palace
4 (BOTTOM)   © Library and Archives Canada. Reproduced with the permission of
               the Minister of Public Works and Government Services Canada (2005)
               Source: Library and Archives Canada/Accession No. 1997–8–I/
               C–002833
5   Scottish National Portrait Galley, Edinburgh
6 (TOP LEFT)   National Portrait Gallery, London
6 (TOP RIGHT) National Portrait Gallery, London
6 (BOTTOM)   National Portrait Gallery, London
7 (TOP)   Wilberforce House, Hull City Museums and Art Galleries, UK/The
               Bridgeman Art Library
7 (BOTTOM)   Yale Center for British Art, Paul Mellon Collection, USA/The
               Bridgeman Art Library
8   Library of Congress, Washington DC, USA/The Bridgeman Art Library
9 (TOP)   Library and Archives Canada/W. H. Coverdale Collection of
               Canadiana/C–040162
9 (BOTTOM)   Nova Scotia Archives and Records Management